CONTEMPORARY JAPANESE LITERATURE

Edited by HOWARD HIBBETT

CONTEMPORARY JAPANESE LITERATURE

An Anthology of Fiction, Film,
and Other Writing Since 1945

c. 1

ALFRED A. KNOPF   NEW YORK   1977

895.608
CONTEMPORARY JAPANESE LITERATURE

THIS IS A BORZOI BOOK
PUBLISHED BY ALFRED A. KNOPF, INC.

Copyright © 1977 by Alfred A. Knopf, Inc.

All rights reserved under International and Pan-American Copyright Conventions.
Published in the United States by Alfred A. Knopf, Inc., New York,
and simultaneously in Canada by Random House of Canada Limited, Toronto.
Distributed by Random House, Inc., New York.

Library of Congress Cataloging in Publication Data

Main entry under title:
Contemporary Japanese literature.
    CONTENTS: Furui, Y. Wedlock.—Kōno, T. Bone meat.—Abe, K. Friends. [etc.]
    1. Japanese literature—20th century—Translations into English.
2. English literature—Translations from Japanese. I. Hibbett, Howard.
PL782.E1C6   895.6'08'005   77–74982
ISBN 0–394–49141–6

Grateful acknowledgment is made to the following for permission to reprint previously published material:
Grove Press, Inc.: *Friends* by Abe Kōbō, translated by Donald Keene. Copyright © 1969 by Grove Press, Inc.
Lorrimer Publishing Limited: Donald Richie's translation of the script for Kurosawa Akira's film *Ikiru.* Copyright © 1968 by Kurosawa Productions: published in the Modern and Classic Film Scripts series by Lorrimer Publishing Limited, London, and in the United States by Simon & Schuster.
Chicago Review Press, Inc.: "Still Life" (Nos. 1 & 2), "Nude Woman," and "Paul Klee's Dining Table" from *Lilac Garden: Poems of Minoru Yoshioka,* translated by Hiroaki Sato.
Alfred A. Knopf, Inc.: "The Bridge of Dreams" by Tanizaki Junichirō, translated by Howard Hibbett from *Seven Japanese Tales.* Copyright © 1963 by Alfred A. Knopf, Inc.
Japan Quarterly, Nagai Tatsuo, and Edward Seidensticker: "Brief Encounter" by Nagai Tatsuo, translated by Edward Seidensticker, from *Japan Quarterly,* VII, 2 (1960), pp. 200–211.
Grove Press, Inc.: "Aghwee the Sky Monster" by Oe Kenzaburō, translated by John Nathan, from *Evergreen Review,* No. 54 (May 1968). Copyright © 1968 by Grove Press, Inc.

Manufactured in the United States of America
First Edition

This book is the first to be published under a continuing program designed to encourage the translation and publication of major Japanese writings not previously available in English. Conceived by the Japan Society of New York, the program is supported by the Society and the *Asahi Shimbun* of Tokyo.

For Mariko, Reiko, and David

CONTENTS

INTRODUCTION

Japanese literature flourishes today in many forms. Far from withering in the electronic glare of a postliterate society, it has grown vigorously both as part of a luxuriant popular culture and as a protean art which deserves to be better known throughout the world. Some of the novels of Tanizaki and Mishima have been widely translated; the rich poetry and drama of Japan is at least familiar abroad through haiku, No, and Kabuki; the films of Kurosawa, if not Ozu, have won large international audiences. Yet the fact remains that only a very small fraction of the literary art of Japan is available outside of its formidably difficult language. It was not until 1968, the centennial year of the Meiji Restoration, that the Nobel Prize for Literature was awarded to a Japanese author, Kawabata Yasunari. Among critics in Japan, the surge of national pride over this belated cultural recognition was somewhat restrained by the suspicion that Kawabata's few translated novels—subtle tales set against the background of the tea ceremony, a geisha-attended hot-spring resort, or Kyoto, the ancient capital—were admired abroad chiefly for the exotic surface attractions so colorfully illustrated in tourist brochures.

The not-unjustified Japanese fear of being misunderstood by foreigners, in spite of the intense scrutiny that began after World War II, leads naturally to the view that only cultural products exhibiting the beauties of the "old Japan" can be profitably exported: traditional arts of all kinds; historical films with sword-fighting in picturesque locations; among contemporary writings, the nostalgic lyricism of Kawabata and Tanizaki or the flamboyant imagery of Mishima Yukio, whose tragic, anachronistic suicide baffled foreigners and Japanese alike. To be sure, there are writers such as Nagai Tatsuo whose delicate stories, like the archetypal Ozu film *The Flavor of Green Tea Over Rice* (*Ochazuke no aji*), are considered "too Japanese"—too colorless and pure—for jaded foreign tastes. Then there are the younger novelists who are thought to be too international, perhaps indistinguishable from Camus, Sartre, Moravia, Mailer, Salinger, and the many other modern authors enshrined in their imposing Japanese collected editions.

The Japanese continue translating Western literature as energetically as if they had not long since caught up with what they missed in the dark years of the War. Occupation censorship was mild by comparison with that of their own military rulers, and the heady atmosphere of freedom of thought encouraged writers and publishers of all persuasions to make a fresh beginning in the burnt-out ruins of Tokyo, as they had after the great earthquake of 1923. Though entirely dependent on domestic consumption, the publishing industry has grown as rapidly as the expanding Japanese economy, giving an ironic ring to the old hyperbole of a literary success that "drove up the price of paper in the Capital." In 1975 almost 30,000 books were published, on a par with the number published in the United States; and the proportion that could be generously classified as "literature" was about twice as large. While Japanese industry as a whole was shrinking in that recession year, book publishing increased its earnings by 16 percent, to $1.4-billion; the 2,700 magazines published by the same companies earned even more. The sheer volume of books and magazines would seem to require a nation of compulsive speed readers, indiscriminately devouring comic books and classics, immune to literary art. Actually, there is a huge, diversified audience crowding bookstores even in the age of television. Among the hundreds of periodicals devoted to literature of one kind or another, from popular weeklies to slender coterie journals, there are half a dozen first-rate literary magazines— each published monthly, in issues of about 300 closely packed pages of solid print. It is no wonder that editors are as hospitable to the short novel as they are to the short story, both forms in which Japanese writers have done much of their finest work. Serialized novels, too, are not only standard magazine fare but appear (morning and evening) in all the great daily newspapers, with their immense circulation.

The roster of best sellers reveals no very startling tastes: the major novelists —most recently Abe Kōbō—have appeared only infrequently; such spellbinding storytellers as Matsumoto Seichō and Shiba Ryōtarō (among the highest-paid individuals in Japan) are regularly represented by detective thrillers or daydreams of samurai conflict in simpler times; there are the usual practical how-to-do-it books (a 1971–72 best seller, issued by the enterprising firm Besuto Serāzu, Inc., was discreetly given an English title: *How to Sex*). More curiously, writers often find a mass market for essays, humorous or otherwise, published in volume after volume. The "nonfiction novel," whether fictionally garnished biography, memoir, or journalistic report, has a long history in Japan, and has become a favorite mode for exploring contemporary issues: the best-selling woman author Ariyoshi Sawako, after a novel on the problems of old age, has produced the daunting *Compound Pollution* (*Fukugō osen*, 1975), a minimally fictional work complete with statistical tables and charts. Inspirational writing, a field nearly monopolized by Ikeda Daisaku, the leader of the Sōka Gakkai movement, has been balanced in recent years by a doomsday trend vividly seen in *Japan Sinks!* (*Nippon chimbotsu*, 1973) and its obligatory film version.

Few Japanese novelists have disdained to turn out potboilers, since their reputations remain secure on the strength of their best work. Thus, at least half of Mishima's thirty-five novels were so obviously dashed off to earn money that one might have expected him to use another pseudonym, if not to deny their authorship altogether. Kawabata seems to have enjoyed writing novels that would appeal to the readers of conservative women's magazines. Gifted writers like Yoshiyuki Junnosuke and Nosaka Akiyuki often indulge in writing pornographic fiction for the more scandalous weeklies. Journalism, whether newspaper and magazine assignments or the innumerable symposia equally popular on television, occupies much of the time of all successful writers. Opinion-mongering on subjects ranging from the little decisions (Should hemlines be lower?) to the big ones (Shall we sign the Nuclear Nonproliferation Treaty?) is a lucrative sideline for all but the most seclusive purists, although social and political commentary tends to follow the standard homogeneous antiestablishment view of the proper Japanese intellectual. Within this prevailing harmony, however, there is a complex, ever-shifting dissonance of attitudes and emotions among the many small groups that together make up the *bundan*—the "literary world."

The compulsions of a lively commerce, and of the elaborate Japanese system of personal obligations, keep the *bundan* globe spinning too rapidly to allow a working author to step off into splendid isolation. Yet the expression of subjective feelings is such a dominant urge that Japanese critics have often complained that confessional writing refuses to give way to the long-desired panoramic social novel. The narrowly personal "I-novel" (*shi-shōsetsu*), developed from an imported Naturalism early in the twentieth century, is still the most tenacious form of contemporary Japanese fiction. Even such an imaginative writer as Abe Akira or Yasuoka Shōtarō seems reluctant to leave the spotlight, or to share it with anyone but members of the little stock company drawn from his immediate family.

The role of art as memory is conceived in highly personal terms, especially in attempts to master the appalling experiences of the War, the bad dream from which Japan awakened in August of 1945 to an unprecedented awareness of defeat and loss of its proudest values. The atomic devastation of Hiroshima and Nagasaki remains an obsessive theme for fiction. In general, the shadow of the War hangs over most of the stories, novels, and poetry of writers who were growing up during those traumatic years. The swift resurgence of proletarian literature, in theory optimistic, was somewhat checked by the "Red purge" of 1950, and then all but overwhelmed by the massive forces of an increasingly affluent society. Meanwhile, the American Occupation itself, once it could be treated critically in literature, provided chiefly a source of ironic amusement at its spectacle of cultural confusion. Hardships and humiliations were often seen in a humorous light. But the accompanying sense of emptiness and purposelessness seems to be a pervasive malaise even in the hardworking, prosperous Japan of today.

A few writers of the generations born after Tanizaki and Kawabata continue to cultivate the traditional beauties of Japanese literature, often nostalgically evoking the past. Others envision some of the nightmarish possibilities of the future—Abe Kōbō, for example, in his meticulously scientific allegories, or Ōe Kenzaburō, whose apocalyptic imagination seeks to cope with terrors yet to come. But they too, like Furui Yoshikichi and other significant contemporary writers, are concerned with the complex realities of present-day urban life: the way people actually live, and how they feel about it, about themselves and each other, within the vast, overcrowded, orderly but vulnerable megalopolis. The mythic element discernible in these works is part of the poetic truth of their vision. That truth, combining the deep insights and pleasures of art, belongs to the world as well as to the Japanese themselves and their ancient, now dangerously and exhilaratingly enriched island culture.

EDITOR'S NOTE

Japanese names are given in the normal Japanese order—that is, the family name preceding the personal name.

In the introductory commentaries preceding each selection, references to Japanese works will be in the following form, whether the given work has appeared in English translation or not: English title, followed in parentheses by the Japanese title and the original date of publication. Thus: *Fiery Comb* (*Kushi no hi*, 1974). Where a published translation does exist, the English publication date will be added, as in the following example: *The Temple of the Golden Pavilion* (*Kinkakuji*, 1956, tr. 1958).

For a comprehensive bibliography of translations, see *Modern Japanese Literature in Western Translations: A Bibliography*, International House of Japan Library, Tokyo, 1972.

CONTEMPORARY JAPANESE LITERATURE

⊞ FURUI YOSHIKICHI

Furui Yoshikichi was born in Tokyo in 1937. He graduated from Tokyo University in 1960 with a degree in German literature and went on to advanced study, translating (Broch and Musil), and teaching. In 1970 he resigned from Rikkyo University to devote himself to the writing of fiction. The next year he won the Akutagawa Prize—the major Japanese literary award to identify gifted new writers—for his short novel *Yōko* about a psychotic young girl found huddled in a ravine, cringing with fear of the enormous weight of the surrounding boulders. Furui is recognized as the leading figure of the "introverted generation" of the 1970s, the most promising novelist to appear since Ōe Kenzaburō. Critics have compared the texture of his beautiful, fine-grained prose to the density of an oil painting, as in his recent long novel *Fiery Comb* (*Kushi no hi*, 1974), a complex, mythic tale of a modern Izanagi / Orpheus in Hades. Like many Japanese writers, however, Furui is at his best in medium-length fiction. His short novels admirably fulfil Cyril Connolly's criterion of excellence in the genre: "an imaginary experience which enriches our understanding of existence and which involves two or three people, not a whole society," but which is heightened by means of "pressure and elimination—in fact intensity."

Such a work, one so constructed that "the reader who begins the book on the surface is led inward by a subterranean passage," is *Wedlock*. The Japanese title *Tsumagomi* is an archaic word—"wife-keeping," "secluding oneself with a wife"—found in a poem said to be the very first of the classic thirty-one-syllable *waka:*

Yakumo tatsu	Where eight clouds rise
Izumo yaegaki	In Izumo an eightfold fence—
Tsumagomi ni	To keep a wife
Yaegaki tsukuru	I'll build an eightfold fence.
Sono yaegaki wo	Ah, that eightfold fence!

This understandably primitive verse is attributed to the Storm God Susanoo, who, according to the *Kojiki*, the most ancient Japanese chronicle, was about to retire into seclusion with his bride after having slain an eight-headed dragon. Heroism on this order is hardly to be sought in the proliferating wooden- and concrete-box apartments that dot the fringes of Tokyo like so many ant colonies. Still, Furui's setting for the intimate confrontation of modern married life reveals elements of the past as well: the vanishing remnants of field and forest and traditional rural life, the rather savage crudity of the workers next door, the sexual rites presided over by the old woman who goes about her hobby of matchmaking with the air of a shamanistic sorceress. But even nature seems powerless to relieve the anxieties of present-day life, least of all in the apparently secure cocoons within which male and female share their fragile existence. Everyday routine has its own mysteries, whether the compulsive behavior of the insectlike commuter, the incantatory murmur of innumerable television sets, or the faint stirring of other lives beyond all-too-thin walls.

❖ Wedlock

(*Tsumagomi,* 1970)

Picking her way through dense summer undergrowth, a woman came out of the grove of trees behind the small apartment house. A dozen or so oaks had been left standing there on a vacant lot of about two hundred square yards. In autumn after the leaves were down, you could see through to a narrow unpaved street a stone's throw away where shoddy little two-storied houses huddled together, each as cramped and boxlike as its neighbor but straining to display a dignified privacy. The vacant lot seemed hemmed in, awaiting its doom, as if any day now it would be filled up by more of these jerry-built houses. But in the heat of summer, beleaguered nature once again asserted itself: the undergrowth thickened with a rank vigor, an almost obscene luxuriance, soon screening off completely the view of that new development so near at hand. From the apartments it looked like a grove with a decent depth.

The pale figure of the woman had emerged from these pathless summer thickets. Perhaps because the tall grass caught the skirt of her kimono, she paused and glanced down: as she twisted slightly to look at the back hem there was a glimpse of delicate flesh at the nape of her neck. She bent forward a little, gathering the skirt up with one hand and parting the grass with the other, and came out. Now he could see that she was an old woman—not wizened and decrepit, but plump, fair-skinned, extremely healthy-looking. Nevertheless her faltering steps indicated her age.

Hisao was standing beside his apartment building near the communal pump in an open space where a swirl of dust glittered in the noon sunlight. He had been peering deep into the grove with eyes dimmed and swollen by a week's illness. His first shock at seeing the woman in kimono appear out of the summer undergrowth was not so much from mistaking her age as from sheer giddiness —the feeling of a man who has just left his sickbed and is standing alone under the burning sun harboring a kind of fantasy, an illusion partly his own creation. Frowning, he watched the old woman as if something precious had been spoiled, possibly by himself. She was walking toward him with intoed steps; a certain womanliness still detectable around her hips stirred a faintly unpleasant feeling in him.

When she saw Hisao looking at her she halted, somewhat alarmed. Suddenly stooping, now seemingly bowed with age, she smiled a fawning, coquettish smile at him as he stood there blocking her way. He moved a step to the right to let her pass. He was still frowning. Then she gazed up into his face intently and came straight toward him as if to envelop an obstinate young man with her benevolence. Still facing him, this time very close, she beamed once again and asked in a startlingly youthful voice: "Say, is Hiroshi around the house today?"

Old as she was, she had somehow picked up the familiar ways of young people.

"Well, you know, I don't live there myself, so . . ."

Hisao meant to be brusque, but his tone had taken on the same familiarity. He could have said politely: "Sorry, I'm from the apartment next door."

"Oh, is that so? Really." For some reason the old woman seemed to be pretending not to understand. Nodding vigorously, she kept stealing sidelong glances at the one-story house next to his apartment.

She was inquiring about one of the half-dozen young laborers who lived there. They were working for a small construction firm that subcontracted on building projects; evidently they all came from the country, and their boss, who had trouble finding employees, was paying a high rent to provide this little house as their dormitory. Staying at home in bed this week, Hisao had for the first time begun to listen to the way the young men next door lived. Every morning before the couples in the apartment house got up there would be a commotion outside —noisy gargling at the communal pump at the edge of the field, loud voices talking a northern dialect, cheerful snatches of popular songs, and so on, followed at last by the clang of tools tossed into the back of a light truck, then the sound of the engine starting and, without fail, an odd, shrill whistle as the truck carrying the laborers drove away. After that, the day began for the office workers in the apartments. In the evening the morning's noisiness came home by the same truck: water was splashed at the outdoor basin, loud abusive voices shattered the smug silence of the neighborhood, the voice of the woman who cooked for them joined in, and an hour later the sounds of their voracious appetites penetrated even the second-floor apartments. Hisao winced when they turned the television on full blast after dinner, but fortunately it was not for long. Perhaps to young bodies tired and coarsened by heavy outdoor labor even TV entertainment seemed talky and slow-moving; in half an hour they were bored with it and rushed outside. As their rough voices receded along the fields to fade into the evening silence of a newly developed area, you began to hear all the other TV sets that had been drowned out by the boisterousness next door. Like good apartment residents, everyone kept the volume turned down discreetly, but that low, persistent sound would go on without a break far into the night, irritating Hisao's hypersensitive nerves. Meanwhile in about two hours the drunken voices of the men would come back along the fields. From a distance you couldn't tell if their voices were good-humored or not, but as they neared home you could begin to make out whether the shouting was friendly or angry. Sometimes they would stand outside roaring at each other in the darkness for a long time; sometimes they would no sooner go into the house humming a song together than they would begin slamming each other around; sometimes a noisy free-for-all would give way to bawdy singing. But after about fifteen minutes all that would abruptly end. Once they had their fill of roistering they dropped off to sleep as if a fuse had blown.

"You boys are off today, aren't you? Or do you go to work even on Sunday?"

The old woman peered searchingly into Hisao's face as he stood there trying to look the other way. She seemed to want to draw him out.

"I told you I don't live there," he objected. But instead of shedding his familiar tone he had made it worse.

"Oh yes, I guess you did." Again she nodded repeatedly, as if to soothe his feelings.

Still, it was no wonder she took him for one of the men next door. He was certainly dressed like one of those fellows going out on a summer day—tight pants, a pair of sandals, an aloha shirt pulled on over his bare skin, open in front and with the ends knotted together casually at his stomach. But what on earth would she make of his pale, slack-muscled arms and chest, his utter listlessness, after neglecting his health all these years and then having to spend a full week in bed? A woman her age could probably see that he was nearly thirty, and already married. Even among the men next door you could occasionally find a seasonal laborer or a migrant worker who was getting on in years and had a correspondingly gloomy air. He would look as if he had gone through all sorts of experiences. Though the old woman spoke of "you boys," she had asked him, as he was standing there before her eyes, if they worked on Sunday. Maybe she didn't really consider him one of them. He must look like a stranger, a newcomer who had turned up from somewhere or other . . . He began to feel a curious pleasure at having been mistaken for someone else. He imagined all kinds of other possible selves splitting off from him and wandering here and there through the world. Perhaps that was why he also began to feel uneasy, as if he wanted to cling to anyone who would call out to him. His sullen expression relaxed a little.

"Hiroshi's in, isn't he? Go on, get him for me."

She stared deep into Hisao's eyes. Apparently the men were avoiding her. Of course there was no reason why young fellows like that would want an old woman to visit them. Casting a wary glance on their deathly silent house, she smiled secretively at Hisao as much as to say, I'll look after you the same way I look after Hiroshi.

"But they all went out a while ago."

Hisao was conscious of regretting that he had to give a vague answer. The fact was that a little earlier the men had gone swaggering out together, all wearing gaudy shirts and dark sunglasses.

"Is that right?" There was a trace of severity in the old woman's eyes.

"Certainly it's right! If you think I'm lying, look into the house for yourself." He was surprised to find himself sounding so indignant. But it seemed to have convinced her.

"Is that so? They're out for a good time again. And Hiroshi went along."

Instinctively Hisao nodded assent. The old woman stared down the road past the fields, as if wondering where Hiroshi could have gone. Why should an unwanted old woman pay so much attention to a young man? At the same time he felt oddly envious of a man who was the object of such concern.

Hisao had soon begun to recognize the boy that all the older laborers in the gang called Hiroshi. It was in the spring of last year that he first appeared among them. You could tell from his speech that he came from the north; probably he had been hired and brought here immediately after getting out of middle school. Last summer he was still so shy that when he was out in just his shorts washing up at the communal pump, and happened to see Hisao and his wife Reiko coming along the road by the fields, he would hastily wrap the towel around his chest and flee into the house. Mornings and evenings, whenever the men gathered together, rough voices yelling for Hiroshi would fly back and forth. One after another, restless voices bawled at him, jeered him, called him like a dog; always the boy would give a low grunt from the back of his throat, something between an answer and a protest, and let himself be ordered around as they pleased. Obviously he was no match for the teasing of older men who had already spent several years in the city. Often when Hisao came home late at night all the lights would be blazing in the house next door and an uproarious drunken party would be going on. And in the darkness at the edge of the field the boy would be curled up like a shrimp, suffering from too much to drink. One night at the beginning of winter, when as usual the boy had been forced to drink heavily and was crouched over at the edge of the field, a window in the house clattered open and a brawny naked man stood there, arms folded majestically. He waited haughtily for Hisao to go by and then burst out in falsetto:

"Hiroshi, dear. Listen, Hiroshi, I'm *calling* you! What are you doing over there? Now please come here to me."

Only a moment ago Hiroshi had been vomiting, shoulders trembling, but out of the darkness came his faithful low grunt of reply feebly repeated over and over again. Still, he didn't seem to have the energy to stand up. Enjoying Hiroshi's embarrassment, the man at the window called out to him in a more and more feminine voice. But soon the voice turned hoarse and menacing, shouting: "So this bastard won't listen to me!" Then a grim shadow leapt out of the lighted window, landing heavily on the ground, and bounded off with fearful vigor into the darkness of the field.

Hisao stood in front of the apartment watching and finally saw two tangled shadows straggle back toward the house. In the light flooding from the window he could see the slender figure of the boy squatting there, his bottom touching the ground, as he clutched the sill with both hands to keep from being dragged in. By the time Hisao had climbed the stairs to his own apartment, everyone in the building seemed to be straining to hear the sounds that came from the house next door, sounds of grappling and scuffling, of panels splintering. Soon the free-for-all quieted down, to be followed by a heavy, inarticulate, animal-like gasping. There was something lonely about it, against the hush of those who were listening so intently. Before long, the gasping began turning into speech, gradually rising to a scream: "Kill me! If I'm so disgusting, kill me!" That brought a roar of raucous laughter from the men. But that half-theatrical screaming voice silenced the men's laughter and launched into a long, growling tirade, now defiant, now lamenting, in a fierce northern accent. Hisao found it completely unintelligible. "Listen! Can you understand that?" he asked Reiko, who had also been brought up in the north. Reiko was lying on the floor reading the evening paper, indifferent to all the noise outside. Lifting her head, she cocked an ear toward the window and listened attentively for a while with a look in her eyes as if she were staring off into the distance. Finally she smiled a restrained, vaguely uncomfortable smile and murmured: "Hiroshi's really giving it to them, isn't he?" Then she looked down at the newspaper again, but the corners of her eyes still crinkled with a smile.

After that Hisao seemed to recall that whenever the boy had too much to drink he would rant at the older men. It was only childish bluster, after all, hardly likely to frighten the others; and yet on the slightest provocation he would roar out in his fierce northern accent, and for their part, though they seemed to find his bluster hilarious, the men no longer ridiculed him as persistently as before. From about that time the boy's everyday dress and manner began to change. Now he always had a pair of sunglasses in his pocket. He would strut along with shoulders squared, chin down, forehead jutting out low. But even when he cut that sort of figure there was something childish about his whole bearing, and the stern look in his eye always showed a trace of embarrassment. So the older men winked at his airs and, if somewhat less freely than before, continued to order him around. Whenever Hisao passed him on the road along the field, the boy would lower his forehead, scowl up at him, puff out his chest, and, shoulders thrust back as if to assert his masculinity, give a truculent nod. Hisao was merely a college-educated office worker, but he was at least ten years older and not inclined to give in to such insolence. He would stare Hiroshi straight in the eye as they neared each other, and then suddenly beam at him. Instantly the boy's coarse manner would vanish and he would revert to childishness: awkward and crestfallen, he would begin to tremble all over helplessly.

The old woman sighed.

"So Hiroshi went along, did he? He's in with a bad bunch. They're all good-for-nothings. They were out drinking late last night, too."

How could she know that? Maybe she ran a shabby little drinking place around here, in which case she had her nerve grumbling about it. Still, there were some women in that business who would tell a young customer to stop drinking and go home. Anyway, the front door of the men's house had been left standing carelessly open, and you could see directly into a room where the floor was littered with sweat-stained underwear. The sliding panels were battered, and nude photos were pinned up everywhere. From a calendar or poster on the wall of the entryway came the neat smile of a rather vulgar-looking actress. The kind of face that often smiled down at you from the wall of a variety store at a country bus stop.

"Looks like there's nobody home."

The old woman peered in again to make sure. Then she turned to Hisao and began lecturing him.

"I know you work hard, all right, but I don't like the way you waste your spare time. No matter how hard it may be, you're better off working. It's when you're not that worries me. You're all young so you can't just stay cooped up in the house watching TV. At first you go in for pinball and drinking—well, that's not so terrible, but it gets to seem pretty tame so you try going out to horse races and bicycle races, and the first thing you know you're mixed up with bad women. And bad women make you all the more keen on drinking and going to the races. That's dangerous! These witches are after you! Your old mother back home is worrying. Don't go wandering around when you're off work. You've got to do something that's really satisfying."

The old woman was talking to him, of all people, a married man nearly thirty years old. Hisao looked down, so that she wouldn't notice his ironic expression. To a bystander, he would have seemed the very picture of an embarrassed young man hanging his head before an old person who was lecturing him.

"When I say satisfying, I don't mean it's enough just to please yourself. That's not real pleasure. You have to please others too, so the Buddha himself rejoices, and you go to bed truly satisfied, thinking, Ah, I've done some good things today. That's what I'm talking about. And then the next day you're back hard at work again, doing your best. That's the thing. Anybody can do it, once they make up their mind. If you have that kind of pleasure, young man, you won't leave any opening for an evil witch to get you!"

Anyway, the posture you held your body in had a strange effect, Hisao thought. At first it only gave an outward appearance; then little by little it brought about the appropriate kind of feeling. Or maybe for a young man to hang his head before an old person was something that had been handed down generation after generation since ancient times, until it had the power to sweep away minor differences in age and circumstances and attitudes. Could it be a kind of slow conditioned reflex? The way the old woman talked seemed to be making him feel a bit dejected.

"You know, even you boys won't go on running around like that forever. You'll soon get tired of it. You are already. That's why you get so drunk! Look into your own heart—you know you're longing for somebody to cling to. But you get restless and go chasing after bad women. Just make up your mind to change and I'll find you a good wife. Lots of girls with pure hearts come to our meetings. Old and young mingle together freely, you'll love it. We meet once every three days after supper, and get into a circle, and—"

Just then the old woman's eyes took on a wary look, and she studied him from head to toe. The moment her words broke off he had a feeling of emptiness. His faint urge to make up to her had been rebuffed. The old woman was looking at him as much as to ask what kind of person this might be. There in front of his own apartment house Hisao was being stared at like an intruder; yet he stiffened nervously and felt that he only wanted to avoid angering her, or letting her think she had been deceived. That tenseness stifled his ironic thoughts, and for an instant he was completely submissive. She smiled with an air of satisfaction.

"Straighten yourself out! You mustn't go on frittering away your life."

There was a certain caution about it, but her slightly distant smile enveloped him in an all-embracing benevolence.

"Yes, you're a little older, aren't you? But it's the same thing. Well, now . . . Today I have some other errands, but I'll be back to talk to you again."

With that, the old woman started walking away. Then she turned and added: "When Hiroshi gets home, ask him to come to tonight's meeting. I have some good news for him."

Then, still looking as if she had more to say, she turned her back to Hisao and with jaunty steps headed on down the road along the field under the broiling sun.

Feeling belatedly annoyed with himself, Hisao climbed the outside stairway to the apartment. Reiko was lying there on the matted floor of the inner room, too exhausted to move. She glanced up at him with a sigh and muttered: "You were being pressured pretty hard by that old woman, whoever she was."

The door in the entryway had been left open, and a warm breeze came wafting through from the kitchen-dining area, billowing the light green curtains out the window. Reiko was lying with her knees slightly propped up, her pale, sweltering body stretched out across the path of the breeze that was teasing the hem of her light dress. He could see that if she lifted her head to the window she would be able to look right down below the billowing curtain at the place where he and the old woman were talking. Although he had been standing with his back turned, he had a strange impression that as he listened to the old woman he noticed out of the corner of his eye, like something disagreeable, that curtains of various colors were billowing simultaneously out of all the apartment windows, the four windows downstairs as well as the four on their floor. The word "pressured" grated on his ears.

"Pressured? You know, after that row about the union split at work I'm getting allergic to words like 'pressure' and 'solicit' and 'win over.' When you talk like that you don't think of people as people."

"Yes, but around here when anybody comes to talk to you with a smile on his face you know very well he's after something. We get all kinds—salesmen, petitioners, missionaries. We really must look gullible."

This seemed to be aimed at him, and had a ring of impatience at a man who was such an easy mark. And he found himself agreeing with her. "Yes, even if you just stay at home you're bothered by solicitors."

"Hurry up and eat so I can get things put away."

Reiko lifted herself up slowly and sat with her legs curled to one side. She seemed ready at any moment to stand up and go to the kitchen. But instead she sat staring blankly at the opposite corner of the room, still showing in the lines on her forehead the irritation of a wife who has been forced to interrupt the flow of her household duties.

Hisao lay down on the floor a little way from her. After a while Reiko asked: "What did you talk about?"

"Oh, she said she'd find me a wife. Provided I change my attitude and stop running around."

Reiko's eyes crinkled like a young girl's, as if she had heard a delicious joke. "What can you do with a man like that? I thought you might be wanting a new job, and here you are wanting a new wife."

"I didn't ask her. She just took it into her head."

"That's no excuse. You shouldn't stand there and listen to that kind of talk."

Still, Reiko didn't seem particularly offended. She glanced out the window with a grimace, and stared hard at the place where he had stood drooping his head before the old woman. She was smiling to herself as if to say "She's really going at him!" It was the look of a woman watching a woman's behavior. Suddenly he felt that Reiko already knew the old woman very well.

"What kind of person is she, that old lady?" he inquired.

"How should I know?" Reiko rebuffed his question indignantly. Her fastidious glance darted irritatedly all around the room, as if to shake off something unpleasant. But then she abruptly calmed down again and brought her face quickly over toward her husband, who lay sprawled on his back. Smiling with a rather sexy gleam in her eyes, she asked: "What did that mean—'changing your attitude'?"

"Oh, she said I'd better spend my spare time doing something that's really satisfying."

"And what would that be?" Her question sounded as if she had been taken by surprise.

"Anyway, it seems she's telling me to come out to these meetings. The idea is, if I do there'll be lots of young girls around, and I can get to know them. Come to think of it, it's pretty brazen soliciting."

"Men are the brazen ones."

Unexpectedly she had drawn up a woman's line-of-battle. He looked at her, and again Reiko glanced out the window, grimacing. Compared to the eyes of the old woman, which benevolently enveloped all men's desires, these were irascible and rejecting eyes. Nevertheless, the two women seemed to have something in common. Didn't all women come to look at men with a similar expression? Even so, when did Reiko pick it up? Pondering these questions, he followed his wife's gaze and was reminded of the figure of the old woman walking away along the field.

"But she *is* a stranger, isn't she?"

The words came spilling thoughtlessly out of his mouth, but that was in fact his impression of the old woman. Still looking out the window, Reiko said almost resentfully:

"Stranger or not, how would you know? You just leave in the morning and come back in the evening. You hardly even recognize the people who live in your own apartment house."

Now that she had given him a piece of her mind, Reiko seemed content. Drawing in her legs, she sat up straight on the tatami. Then, with the determined sigh of a hard-to-please housewife, she stood up. Lately her hips had become noticeably fuller.

Hisao lay on his back, testing his readiness to go to work the next day. It was really more a matter of will than of physical strength. Strictly speaking, his illness had not warranted staying home a week. He had left work early on Monday and ended up taking off five straight days, right through Saturday. By Tuesday morning, however, his 104° fever had disappeared without a trace. Yet for three days after that sudden fever—Tuesday, Wednesday, and Thursday—he had spent all his time dozing in bed, mind and body completely slack. That was understandable. But by Thursday evening he knew he could have gone to work the next day. Nevertheless, he did not hesitate to have his wife call his office from the landlord's house to tell them he had not yet fully recovered. He decided to take off Saturday, too.

And so for a whole week, from Monday afternoon when he was still delirious with fever until the old woman began to talk to him a little while ago, he had spoken to no one besides his wife. How long had it been since they were together like that? Over five years, at least half a year before they came to live here. Still students, they had lived together in a one-room apartment near the heart of the city, spending an entire year in seclusion, seeing almost no one. An altogether intense year, a year, now that he thought about it, saturated with the smell of sweat. This was his first uninterrupted week of inactivity since then.

It had all started Monday morning. As he put on his shoes in the entryway at the usual time, his whole body was attacked by an indescribable feeling of lassitude. For a few minutes he stood there on the concrete floor waiting for further symptoms.

"Should I take the day off?" Hisao had asked himself. But nothing more definite seemed to develop, not even a headache or a stomachache. After a while the feeling lost its initial severity and became refined, diffusing itself into all the nooks and crannies of his body. Somehow his forehead was heavy and his knees weak. That was how he still felt when he left the house.

He walked as fast as he could to the nearest station, twenty minutes away, and boarded the crowded commuter train. By the time he had changed trains twice and reached his destination, he must have had a fever. But it was hard to tell. Already worn out by the worst heat of the summer and now struggling for breath in the crammed train, he could not detect the onset of the fever. Only when he arrived at the office and felt the cool air from the air conditioner did he realize that he was no longer steady on his feet.

As he sat at his desk wondering whether or not to go to the infirmary, he found himself slipping off his chair. All at once there he was, sitting down on the floor.

His fellow workers crowded around in a circle. No one immediately tried to help him, but they all nodded earnestly, full of sympathy for a casualty in their ranks.

"You've been overdoing it. There's a limit, you know. Better get some rest . . ."

People on both sides who had badgered him during the union fight, glaring and snarling at each other, now gathered quite harmoniously and watched over him as he sat there on the floor, unable to stand up. Presently they bore him off noisily on their shoulders to the infirmary. He had become their charge.

When he awoke some time later he found a young man in a white coat standing by the bed, peering into his face and talking to him in the tone one might use to a child who has fallen asleep in someone else's home.

"You're feeling a lot better now, aren't you? Why don't you try to get up? You just had a touch of heat exhaustion—nothing to worry about. I gave you a shot to reduce the fever. There's a company car waiting, so why not go home and get lots of rest? Best thing for you. I've already told your section chief."

Before he could recall why he was sleeping in such a place, he instinctively sat up straight in bed and politely thanked the doctor, who seemed younger than himself.

In the car he again fell into a feverish sleep. The stifling blend of exhaust fumes and fever was penetrated from time to time by the shadowy trucks that rumbled by, making the car shake. As he sat deep in his seat the shining black flow of asphalt slid silently backwards under him, now speeding up and now slowing down, each shift of speed provoking a mild nausea in the pit of his stomach. Only his fitful sleep made the ride endurable. He felt as if his half-dead body were being carried along on a conveyor belt.

When he got home he knocked at the door, waited a moment, and then let himself in with his key. Dragging the bedding from the closet, he spread it out almost in the center of the tatami room. Then he took off his suit and dropped it on the floor; as he stood there in his underwear he looked once around the empty room. It was a strangely cold, unfamiliar open space. But he lacked the strength to stay on his feet any longer, and he plopped down on the bedding like a man falling at the side of a road. Without knowing why, he turned his head toward the door in a last effort of concentration.

Some time later his wife Reiko had come tiptoeing gingerly toward him. After gazing at his face from a slight distance she reached out to put her hand on his forehead and whispered: "What a fever!" By that time he thought he had been sleeping in a strange room, not in his own apartment. Reiko must have taken a taxi to hurry to his side. She was carrying a market basket, so she must have been out shopping when she learned of her husband's sudden illness. With such thoughts he dropped off to sleep again.

After one of his deep slumbers he had awakened with his sense of location even more confused. A whitish figure was busily working by his bedside. He was still in the company infirmary; the smell of medicine drifted uneasily in the air. Through the concrete walls he could hear telephones ringing incessantly far and near. Outside in the corridor some girls were gossiping as they walked by, chattering happily about the former troubles . . . He had felt guilty about lying in bed while his companions were hard at work, but when he tried to get up his body wouldn't respond. As he squirmed and tossed he began to lose consciousness once more. That white figure was fidgeting restlessly around him, but following it with his eyes he gradually began to think that he was sleeping in the car again. Like a stream of oil, the asphalt ribbon slipped endlessly away, mirages flickering before him. And endlessly he had to combat the nausea. It was a moment that refused to pass . . .

Then he found himself resting in another unfamiliar room, to which someone happening upon him by the roadside had been kind enough to bring him. The white figure was still working busily, standing or sitting. Just as he was thinking he ought to thank him and go home, he heard a car rumble into the garage directly below his bed. That would be for him—his illness must have been reported to the right place already. Again he was carried along over the stream of asphalt.

These sensations were repeated all night long. Sometimes he seemed to be in different places at the same time. The security of a solid sense of location was swept away, and his body was hurled into oceanic space; his only solace was listening forlornly to the throbbing of his temples. Echoing that throbbing, the space kept expanding in all directions to a fearful depth. Every part of that space was void, and yet it seemed eternal, like a hollow enclosed within an immense rock. But there was also something obscene about it.

The next morning, as dawn whitened the window by his pillow, he began to recover his sense of place. Against the growing light in the window a swollen but familiar face floated up out of the dark beside him. As the posts and ceiling boards drank in the scanty light, their grain stood out vividly in relief. The tatami mats, sun-scorched and badly frayed, exuded a smell of sweat and weariness that they had absorbed for many years, a smell noticeably stronger than that of the two people lying here. He felt he was with Reiko in the run-down apartment house where they had lived years ago. Or, perhaps, that he had arrived at a hotel late in the night, and was greeting the morning after having been stuffed into a kind of maid's room. Still, it was the feeling of a single, definite place. Half dreaming, he felt as relieved as if he were safely home at last.

Then, suddenly, he realized that he was in his own apartment. The six-mat room with a dining-kitchen: a square living-space in which the wet parts and the dry were crammed together without an inch to spare. There was the tall wardrobe, and the clean stainless sink that he could see from his bed. The grain of the smooth ceiling boards never caught the light; the tatami mats, reversed by the landlord only last spring, still looked brand-new. It seemed as abrupt as a cut from one scene to another in a movie—there was no nuance to the shift. For a moment that made him anxious. But the expression on the face of the woman sleeping at his side, her face turned toward him, was the same.

After lunch, while he was still lying sprawled in the breeze, Reiko brought in a tray holding three peaches, a plate and knife, and an aluminum bowl, and sat down by his pillow. Peaches had been his first nourishment after the fever abated. Their ripe, pungent sweetness seemed to soothe the tender membranes of his mouth and throat. Now, almost a week later, his body apparently still depended on those gentle, refreshing peaches; other food seemed heavy to him —he could never manage more than half a meal. He always left the table early and sprawled out to await the peaches.

Reiko placed the bowl of peaches on her lap and leaned forward as she peeled them. With a very ripe peach, she made an x-shaped cut in the thin skin and then stripped it off with her fingers. With a firm one, she put the knife in just under the skin and began paring vigorously. When he tried it, the more cautiously he peeled, the more stubbornly the flesh of the peach would cling to the skin. Next she would thrust the knife slantwise into the dripping peach, avoiding the pit, and, not so much cutting the flesh as shaving it off, pile up slices on the plate. Two of the three peaches were meant for him, but Hisao would lie there taking one slice after another from the heaping plate until there were hardly any left. But she seemed rather indifferent to them, and merely popped a slice into her mouth now and then while peeling, as if to see how they tasted.

A box of the peaches had arrived half a month earlier from Reiko's family in the country. Perhaps for that reason Reiko peeled them with an air of authority befitting the mistress of the house. No doubt her mother had peeled peaches for her that same way. Sometimes he had the notion that his life was being sustained by Reiko's peaches. Of course he was still getting his salary, and in that sense even now he was the one who sustained the household. However, his body was inclined to refuse other food, so that as he devoured the peaches his wife peeled for him, the word "sustained" began to take on a more direct meaning.

It occurred to him that there was nothing strange about a woman behaving like the mistress of the house: after all, whether they were married or only living together, the man went out to work and the woman stayed at home taking care of household affairs. Still, it always gave him an odd feeling to think of his wife in that role—here in a little two-room apartment with no extra space inside or out, no children, nothing to manage but a monthly salary, no ancestral rites to perform. Especially during this week of dozing in bed he had noticed that when he happened to awaken and let his eyes rove around the room he would often find himself staring fixedly at his wife, as familiar as she was to him.

It must have been Tuesday afternoon that he woke from a pleasant nap after the fever had subsided and saw Reiko squatting down plumply before the cupboard in the dining-kitchen scrutinizing the bottom compartment. The fever seemed to have sharpened his sense of smell, and he could detect various odors wafted in on the breeze that passed from the front door to the window of the inner room: the aroma of fermented bean paste and soy sauce and sake, and also a sourish odor. Was it getting moldy in the back of the cupboard, or had it become infested with cockroaches? Reiko was frowning squeamishly, with an occasional sigh, as she slid the things in the cupboard aside one by one and peered in. Shifting the angle of her gaze slightly now and then as if not to overlook even a particle of dust, she kept on squatting there in front of that shallow cupboard. For a long time he could not look away from her.

After that—was it the same day or the next?—Reiko was standing at the kitchen counter when he heard a man's voice at the door. There was only a short, swaying curtain between the tiny entryway and the kitchen, and the front door had been left open to let in the breeze; from his bed Hisao caught a glimpse of the young man from the grocery standing outside in the afternoon sun. Reiko could have given him her order from where she stood, and yet she had quietly asked him to wait a minute, dried her hands carefully on her apron, lifted the lid of a pot and checked the flame, and then walked on around the table toward the entryway. As she stood in the shadow of the curtain for a moment she smoothed her hair with one hand. Then she drew the curtain aside and went out, closing it immediately behind her. To the man waiting in the sunshine even the mistress of this cramped dwelling emerged from secluded depths within. Lying there half asleep, Hisao vaguely imagined what the young man thought about the hushed scene he had glimpsed for an instant beyond the curtain.

Toward evening on Thursday he was again awakening drowsily from his lazy convalescent slumber. Just then Reiko came in with an armload of laundry, pushing through the entry curtain that was brightened by the last rays of the sun. Paying no attention as his gaze hovered around her breasts, she strode over toward him, sat down beside the bed, and began folding the laundry. Piece by piece, she smoothed the wrinkles neatly out of each of the white undergarments, still smelling of the sun, then folded it and put it into a bottom drawer of the wardrobe beside her. Drawn in by her purposeful movements, he followed his wife's eyes as they shifted with no waste motion from laundry to drawer, from drawer to laundry. Every time she put away a piece of underwear she leaned forward from her hips, thrusting her body out diagonally from the floor mat, and peered into the drawer to make sure that everything was in order. Apparently she always checked over with her sharp eyes, and not merely from force of habit, these actions that she repeated daily. When Reiko had at last finished putting away the underwear she inched a little closer to the wardrobe, examined the drawer once more from side to side, and then pushed it smartly shut. Hisao felt a sharp twinge of lust. Until a little while ago that underwear had been dancing in the wind on the clotheslines outside, mingled with the laundry of other families; and an intensely vivid image of underwear twisting wantonly, fluttering in the wind, rose up before him. Yet what came into his mind as the most wanton image of all was not that of the undershirts or slips dancing outside, but of the housewives sitting quietly within.

At that moment, as he was lying there beside his wife, he felt like a bachelor furtively spying on someone else's household from outside the window. Within every window a woman was secluded, staring just as seriously at all the things of daily life, boiling down to an even richer density an existence that had always been denser than a man's. She was boiling it down endlessly. For a time the thought oppressed him.

Once again Reiko was directing a serious look at one of the peaches and the knife. Once again he felt a slight shiver as he watched her eyes from the side. If that steadfast gaze were to sweep toward him with undiminished strength and meet his own gaze, his furtive, undercover, voyeur's gaze . . . It was hard to understand how husbands and wives could look at each other, could exchange glances day after day.

"What are you staring at like that?" said Reiko irritatedly, without looking up.

"I was just noticing how voluptuous you're getting around the hips," Hisao answered hastily, surprised at his own reply.

"And you're supposed to be an invalid!" Curiously enough, Reiko was blushing.

And you're supposed to be an invalid, Reiko had said. Eating nothing but peaches, letting himself be treated like a ne'er-do-well by that old woman, indulging in irresponsible thoughts with his wife there beside him—to judge from all that, he was indeed still an invalid. Both physically and mentally, Hisao wanted this condition to last a while longer. It was not such a busy time that he couldn't take two or three more days off. Yet to go on dragging out his convalescence was dangerous. Exactly because he felt this way he ought to avoid it. Glancing at the few peaches left on the plate, he asked his wife:

"Aren't the peaches from your family about running out?"

"They ran out long ago."

Although he had expected that, her brief reply made him feel all the more disappointed.

"Oh . . . So you bought these at the store?"

Keeping her serious look fixed on the knife, Reiko again replied briefly:

"No, they're the same kind. Hiroshi brought them over."

He felt the taste of the peach in his mouth go sour. Never had he dreamed that he was letting himself be nourished back to health by peaches received from that boy. In the shadow of dark sunglasses, embarrassed eyes seemed to be observing his lewd bachelor's fantasies as he gobbled down a peach that his wife had peeled.

"So he really is from the same village, is he?"

"You can tell by listening to him talk."

"Does he know you come from there?"

"I wonder."

Reiko turned to look out of the window and smiled. It was a smile implying that something deep had been touched on by a person who didn't really understand it. In his primary-school days whenever he tried out a new dirty word in front of the girls in his class, they would suddenly look very grown-up and exchange that kind of smile. Being from the same place seemed to yield a similar secret understanding.

"But that must be why he brought them."

"Certainly not. He brought them to you. Because you're sick, he said."

"Did you tell that boy all about it?"

"I didn't have to. He saw for himself—saw you come staggering home."

Instinctively Hisao shut his eyes. When he had got out of the air-conditioned car at the edge of the field, his vision had suddenly narrowed. Heat poured from the sky, the earth seemed in flames all around him, he was being broiled inside and out. At the left fringe of his vision—what he saw was painfully bright but cut off sharply at each side by a dark blur—stood a slender figure that seemed to bear the field on his shoulders. Now that he had been told about Hiroshi, he felt sure it was someone who was looking hard at him. He had to clench his teeth at every step. Although the apartment was there before him, he was separated from it by a limitless expanse of white shining dust—no matter how far he walked he could never reach it. It must have been then, tortured by having to drag his feverish body home under the blazing sun, that he wanted to veer off his path and stand in the sweep of wind gazing as idly as he pleased . . .

When he opened his eyes, Reiko was staring at him almost cruelly.

"You really looked awful!"

"Can I help it if I'm tottering around in the broiling sun with a 104-degree fever?"

But Reiko would not be deflected.

"When I came past the field with my market basket, that boy was standing by the side of the road looking at me with the strangest expression. I glared back at him, and he seemed confused, but still he kept his eyes on me. To tell the truth, I thought: What a fresh kid! I passed him and went up the stairs, but when I turned to look back before I opened our door he was still there, his chin stuck out, staring up at me like an idiot."

Reiko frowned and wrenched her shoulders around, as if to shake that stare from the back of her neck. Then her voice darkened.

"Where I come from, whenever somebody died the neighborhood children would stand in front of the house like that, staring at the people who went in and out—"

"Stop treating me like a dead man!"

"But I thought you were at your office."

"Then why were you so worried?"

"I couldn't help thinking of my parents . . ."

"And your husband was lying senseless inside."

"It really gave me a shock."

The words came out in a low, forced mutter, and Reiko, apparently forgetting all about Hiroshi, once more began the story of finding her husband lying there in the room. How many times had she told him? Always her eyes misted with excitement and, oddly, her voice seemed to take on an accusing tone. Her old northern accent would revive; she would begin to sound like the young fellows next door.

Brushing aside her premonitions, Reiko had taken out her key and tried to unlock the door. The lock turned, all right, but the door refused to budge. Wondering what could be wrong, she tried the key the other way and pulled the knob again. This time the door swung open. Her first reaction was the disturbing thought that for once she had gone out without locking up. A pair of men's shoes had been kicked off on the concrete floor at the entrance. They were repulsively large, heavy shoes. One of them was upside-down, lying near the threshold; the other was resting toe up against the step, as if its strength had been exhausted just as it was about to crawl into the room.

Reiko said it didn't occur to her immediately that her husband had come home. She was startled, remembering that the boy had looked as if he wanted to tell her something but was afraid to. Perhaps he had seen something happen. Perhaps someone had boldly unlocked the door and gone in. Yes, come to think of it, not long ago her husband had got drunk and lost his key, and had had the landlord make a duplicate for him . . .

With an effort, she had calmed her trembling body and peered in around the edge of the doorway curtain. The curtains of the inner room were drawn, and the bedding was spread out with the pillow toward her, just the opposite of the way they slept. Someone was curled up under a mound of terrycloth blanket. The face was hard to see, half-buried by a sheet, but it appeared to be a strange man, dead drunk.

"If that's what you thought, why didn't you run and call the police?"

It was a story he had heard over and over again, and yet he always found himself interrupting, worried over his wife's safety. "Well . . ." Reiko's face took on a vacant look. "I don't know. Finding a strange man in our bed with his face buried in our white sheets—somehow I felt I couldn't tell anybody about it."

Hisao was left tongue-tied.

Anyway, Reiko stared in for a long time from behind the curtain, unable to take her eyes off the man. Then the thought slowly dawned on her that it might be her husband. It began to look like him. Gradually her trembling subsided. Still, she was not quite sure. She couldn't simply run up to him. Finally, since staring would get her nowhere, Reiko made up her mind to it and went on in. She gingerly approached the bed. But as she kept her eyes fixed on the profile of the man sleeping with his cheek buried in the sheets she began to tremble again. Vaguely fearing that she could not tell the difference between this face before her and her husband's, she halted. She was just at the dividing line between the kitchen and the inner room. At that moment the man in bed suddenly turned over, sprawling out his arms and legs, and thrust his large head back over the edge of the thin mattress onto the tatami floor, rolling his eyes up at her as she stood there by his pillow. It seems that Reiko bent forward tensely, rooted to the spot.

"Don't ever look at me that way again." She was rebuking him as if that face still haunted her.

"Was it so awful?"

"Oh, I suppose it wasn't much different from your usual look—just kind of owl-eyed from the fever."

"If that's my usual look, how can I help it?"

"Don't loll your head out that way."

"Maybe it was like finding your husband at the morgue."

"Stop it. You're giving me the creeps."

Reiko glared at him. Avoiding her eyes, he smiled faintly up at the ceiling. It must have been unnerving. If only for a little while, Reiko had found a strange man curled up under a blanket in this apartment, in their very own bed. Yes, once the reality of a husband and wife was ever so slightly disturbed, it was surprisingly fragile. And now that she had had the experience of staring at her husband that way, perhaps there would be other occasions when she would see a strange man in him.

"You have no feelings," she suddenly declared.

"No feelings?"

"Hiroshi ran to the doctor for your sake."

That was the first he had heard of it. He remembered seeing a doctor, but could that have been in his own home?

"You had him go on my account?"

"That's right. You couldn't even talk, so I got scared and ran outside—Hiroshi was still there at the edge of the field, looking straight at me. He seemed to be waiting for me to send him on an errand. As I hurried down the stairs he came running over. The first thing I knew, I was blurting it all out in dialect. Then he went rushing off."

Hisao began to feel uncomfortable. At the time, whether because of his illness or because of his surge of relief at seeing her, he had only panted speechlessly; Reiko, frightened, had run out without really knowing anything about his condition. And so Hiroshi went racing off to the clinic utterly unable to describe his illness. He must have had to report exactly what he had seen: the man next door staggering along under the broiling sun. There was no telling what the doctor had imagined.

"I can see I've put people to a lot of trouble," Hisao sighed.

"Yes, you have," Reiko chimed in coolly. "Making them rush around for you."

"Don't be ridiculous. A man flat on his back can't go to the doctor."

"That isn't the point."

"Then what is?"

Reiko threw her paring knife into the bowl and turned toward him.

"And what was *that* all about? You sat bolt upright when the doctor came, as if you were perfectly fine—apologizing for bothering him, telling him you just fell asleep and really needn't have troubled him."

"Did I say that?"

"You certainly did. What was that supposed to mean? Saying your wife could take care of things?"

"Oh, that." Recalling what had happened he burst out laughing. Even delirious with a 104° fever he was still glossing it over, wanting to avoid dragging in any outsider, wanting to be as free as possible from any involvement. He thought he had succeeded. But in the meantime Hiroshi had been watching, had run to the clinic for him, had brought him peaches. There were no secrets. A hollow laugh welled up within him and floated lightly to the ceiling. Reiko began to look grim. Hastily, like a child who has been scowled at, he explained.

"The fact is, I thought I'd been taken to a hospital. Look, after all, I collapsed. And the hospital saw to it that you came hurrying to my side—that's what I thought."

Reiko looked down at him irritatedly.

"So that's why you said 'I'm going home now.' You sounded ready to go off alone, and when I asked where you thought you were going you just repeated it and then fell asleep. Making a fool of me."

Reiko lapsed into silence, sitting there in front of the billowing curtains with her arms around her legs and her slender chin pillowed on her knees. Sometimes she rubbed her chin against her knees, or pressed it down hard, as she stared at the tatami. She seemed to have tired of being the mistress of the house; now she looked like a peevish little girl crouched in a corner of the nursery, squashing a daddy-longlegs against the floor mat with her thumb and wishing that the house would catch fire and blaze up, reddening the whole sky, killing everybody, or else perhaps wondering if she should go far, far away, all by herself. Now the fullness in her breasts and hips that had come while she was living with Hisao was only a weight that made her gloomy. Still lying sprawled out on his back, Hisao looked up at Reiko. He realized with a start that he had bent his head backward on a slant, his eyes wide open, goggling up at her. No doubt it was a habitual pose of his, since he seemed to fall into it unconsciously. Aware of its ugliness, he stealthily moved his head back to its former position, trying not to let his wife notice. As if she had been waiting for this, Reiko looked up, her chin still thrust against her knees, and muttered in a low, meaningful voice:

"Go ahead and have that old woman find a nice bride for you."

He decided to take the safe way out.

"Don't forget, I'm not Hiroshi. I'm getting on in years!"

Reiko herself seemed ready to drop the subject. She lifted her head, smoothed her hair with her fingertips, and, knees still together, started to get up. But then she hesitated, holding one hand lightly against the hollow at the pit of her stomach, and glanced into his face.

"She knew it when she was talking to you, that old woman. She knew you were my husband."

"But she doesn't know who you are, does she?"

"I think she remembers me."

Reiko looked rather equivocal, as if she wanted to say something and yet wanted to conceal it. He began to feel a kind of jealousy, and his tone became demanding.

"So she *has* talked to you."

Reiko did not deny it.

"And you pretended you didn't know anything about her."

"It's true she came slipping up behind me the other day when I was on my way back from shopping. She gave me quite an earful as we walked along."

"What did she have to say?"

"Well—that was three days ago, the first time you went outside and stood in front of the apartment house. You know, to see how you felt before deciding to go back to work. The old woman saw you from somewhere. Your husband was standing by the field a little while ago looking sick, she said. She asked if anything was wrong—you ought to take care of yourself!"

"I suppose I did look sick. After all, I was just out of bed."

"Yes, but then she started off on a long-winded story about how her own husband dropped dead years ago, and what a hard time she had. She pulled out all the stops. That's what I call shameless."

It was his turn to be shocked. He was beginning to feel persecuted. Didn't it seem as if the old woman and Hiroshi and Reiko had all joined hands around him as he lay dozing in this room? But why on earth had the old woman, today, treated him as if he were single? Somehow that line of questioning seemed dangerous; instead, he lashed out like a man angered by being told he looked as if he didn't have long to live.

"So the old bitch wanted to make you an unhappy widow. She seems to be working hand in glove with the undertaker."

"Wha-a-t?" Now Reiko had changed her tone, as innocent as could be. Again there was a sexy gleam in her eyes as she looked at him.

"That kind will say anything, if you look like an easy mark to them."

"You and I were both dupes?"

"She's sniffed out something. She has a keen nose."

"I suppose so. After you got sick you began to seem like Hiroshi, young and willful, and flighty. I had a notion of what she was telling you, when I saw you out there with her just now."

"So she talked to you about remarrying too!"

He had said that to stop her, but Reiko only looked down uncomfortably and smiled.

"She didn't say I ought to. Just that somebody whose husband died started coming to their meetings, and it helped her get back her will to live. Before long she found happiness with one of the other members."

"To hell with that old windbag."

"Don't get so upset. She's only an old woman."

"What the devil did she think she sniffed out about you?"

"That's what I mean. She thought you might go off somewhere."

"But that's about me."

"Well, who else would I be concerned about?"

They looked at each other. If either of them pressed for an answer they would soon be attacking the slight unfaithfulness—the slight but unexpectedly deep unfaithfulness—which they had committed toward each other in their hearts. And so they paused, with the delicate sense of balance of a man and woman who had been together for ten years, from the time they were hardly more than children until now on the verge of taking their leave of youth. The image of the old woman came into both their minds.

"As soon as the old bag corners the wife and tells her her husband's going to die, she corners the husband and tells him if he makes up his mind to change she'll find him a good wife."

"She must think we're just living together."

Hisao lifted himself up from the bed and sat gazing out of the window beside his wife. The hot, dusty road along the vegetable fields that the old woman had taken stretched out toward the expanse of already yellowing rice plants. Beyond that was the high paved road over rice fields that cut through to the main highway. From time to time, when no cars were in sight, that road looked like the embankment of a river basking in the brilliant summer sunlight—you could almost see water flowing and thickets flourishing beyond it. In the calm as they gazed out of the window together Reiko started talking again.

"Maybe she didn't realize you were my husband. We can't even be sure who the man was that she saw standing in the breeze at the edge of the field three days ago. When you listen to her you begin to wonder who you are yourself."

"You do begin to feel that way."

"When I was a little girl, I knew an old woman like that. She was always walking around the neighborhood, and if she happened to run into you when no one else was there she'd stop you, no matter who you were, and start lecturing you. She really didn't seem to know who she was talking to. They say she'd buttonhole a man one day and tell him how to get along with his wife, and the next day tell the very same man to get married and settle down."

"I suppose one person was like another to her."

"And yet they say the people she lectured couldn't help being affected by it."

"That's because we have all kinds of people inside us. When we get a serious talking-to, something always stirs in our hearts."

He had an odd sense of freedom.

"Anyway, it's rude," said Reiko, frowning hard.

With their heads side by side, they gazed out at the road along the fields.

Evidently Reiko had lost the impulse to get up and work. Before they realized it, both of them were lying flat on their backs again. The heat seemed more oppressive, and they no longer had the energy to talk. Heads together, they stretched out in opposite directions to share as much as possible of the slight breeze. Drowsiness had narrowed their vision, and now they were completely out of each other's sight. Reiko was lying a little more in the breeze, and occasionally, when it bellied out the curtain, the ends of her fine hair would come streaming across the tatami and tickle his ear. It gave him a disagreeably warm, unclean feeling, as if her hair needed washing, or dirt had caked at the base of his ear.

What on earth had the old woman sniffed out?

The unanswered question invaded his drowsiness. Hisao lifted his head, craning to see Reiko. It was the very posture he took whenever he wanted to tell her something as she was sitting at his bedside. Could *that* have been it? he wondered, feeling depressed. Fortunately Reiko seemed to be asleep; she was lying there with her arms flung out on the tatami, breathing evenly. Knowing that he was not being seen, he purposely strained his head back and gazed intently at his wife's sleeping figure. From this vantage point he could look down the undulating line of her childish forehead and nose, her breasts that rose and fell with her breathing, her knees that she held propped up. The skirt of her dress had slipped back, and its gently rumpled folds disclosed the pale whiteness of her inner thighs. Just then, as if to avoid his gaze, Reiko pressed her cheek down against the tatami, shifted onto her side, and let her bent knees slump gradually to the floor. With her arms drawn up together close to her chest, her whole body formed a softly angular S.

In the passing breeze he thought he had detected a long-forgotten smell: the smell of routine kisses, of all-pervading sweat and fatigue. The curtains seemed to bulge painfully out of the window, full of the odor of a closely secluded couple. Stretched out on the floor in just this atmosphere, this hint of a breeze, they had talked solemnly about beginning married life, exactly as if they were talking about parting. They were living like amoebae that had layered together and were trying to blend their cell fluids into a single circulating liquid. After a whole year of this kind of life they were so exhausted they had come to the point of putting an end to it.

They had talked of making a new life together as husband and wife. Not from attachment to the past—that subtle charm had been squeezed out long ago. There remained only the haunting shame of a couple who had become too intimate, the fear that, if they were to leave each other now, a part of both of them, the shameful part, would split off and go its way alone, and they would be tortured by the nightmare of pursuing it in their imagination forever.

Finally it was agreed that after half a year, if he had found a job, they would begin a new life together as an ordinary couple. Both of them doubted that things would actually turn out that way. But once they began living apart and came to the college from their separate homes, trying to look like strangers and yet, perhaps in the crowd at the bulletin board in front of the placement office, greeting each other casually with their eyes—every time they met they were increasingly aware that the shame each felt was mirrored in the other. Meanwhile, as he neared his decision on a job, they would stop together in a quiet place to talk over their situation, exchanging secretive, intimate glances, joyful or sorrowful as matters developed.

Now, five years later, after living together without either the usual honeymoon or that first wave of marital boredom, they had become a typical married couple. Seasonal products arrived regularly from Reiko's family in the country.

From time to time, though, when they visited other couples, as soon as the door opened an unfamiliar odor would come drifting out. Hisao felt that it was somehow obscene. And when they went home again after two or three hours and opened their own door, he would have the same sensation. Once, a little drunk, he had blurted out in front of his wife: "This isn't the smell of a family, it's the smell of a man and woman living together!" Reiko had responded gaily: "If you talk like that, I just might walk out on you tomorrow!" But for a moment she had frowned.

Had the old bag sniffed them out?

When you thought of it, the way the old woman talked to the two of them was not inconsistent. To a sensitive bystander that smell might suggest a couple ready to break up. An addled old woman with failing sight but a keen nose would catch a whiff of this lingering scent and tell the wife her husband might not be around long, and then tell the man to mend his ways and she would see that he got a fine young bride. Unable to look people over carefully or talk logically to them, she would no sooner sniff out something than she would foist off one of her ready-made pieces of advice.

Yes, the apartments around here were about right for a young couple living together these days. Even a laborer in his early twenties, for example, if he saw any point to supporting a household, could make enough money to afford these cheap rents. He would have come from the country. As he got used to the city he would begin to go from job to job. Somewhere they would meet, and decide they couldn't live alone any longer. They would run out on all their debts. Even if they wanted to make things legal there would be no one to stand security for them . . .

To a young man in these circumstances, setting up a household meant changing all his relations with society. When he came home his own woman was there, he had his own nest. At worst, that nest and society might be linked only by his earning a living. Perhaps he just took a regular job, and yet compared with the days when he was still adrift in the city, his life was now incredibly brighter and more stable. Before, he had been confused, and had looked for everything out in society . . .

However, a man and woman who have come together with only each other to depend on are not children, nor do they have anyone to keep them from separating. Everything is up to the two of them. If a couple who just happened to fall in love begin thinking along those lines, it's all over.

The old woman was obviously going around sniffing out all kinds of cases.

If a man went and stood in front of his home a certain way, the situation couldn't last much longer. If a woman looked a certain way from the rear when she was walking home after having been out shopping . . .

Probably any "close" couple would seem to her to be going down the wrong path, so long as they weren't attending her meetings, weren't being baptized by her benevolence. In short, the old woman would feel she had to save them. Or perhaps she was the descendant of a local priestess who used to take charge of bringing young people together in the days when this was still a remote countryside—someone of that kind. As she got older and was mistreated by her own daughter-in-law she would begin to feel the blood of her ancestors racing through her veins and would busy herself arranging marriages, or possibly spying on the lives of ordinary-looking couples, whether married or not, who had their little nest out here. She would be keeping a sharp lookout for couples who seemed uncertain about their relationship.

Still, how exactly *had* Reiko looked from the rear as she walked along?

Clearly she hadn't rebuffed the old woman. A college-educated girl need only glare at her and make some clever reply, to have her scurry off, thinking: That smart-aleck can suffer, for all I care—she deserves whatever monster she gets.

Reiko had listened to her without a word. And not necessarily because she was struck speechless.

He was bothered by that bland expression his wife must have had as she fell into step with the old woman and listened attentively to her lecturing. Two silhouettes passed his window, going down that blazing white road on the embankment. Now and then the two nodded to each other. Each time they nodded, he felt like a distant stranger. A transient, for all the world like Hiroshi. And yet every action of hers awakened a secret response in him, troubling him with a deep emotion that was at once shame and love.

Again he drew his head back and looked at his wife. Reiko was sleeping just as she had been: her body bent loosely at the waist, her cheek pressed against the tatami. Still looking at her, for a time he saw in his mind's eye the two silhouettes moving along at the same pace. Reiko's head was turned toward the old woman and she was making some reply. He felt he had to hear from her own lips what Reiko had said. Turning over to lie on his stomach, he poked her moist shoulder with his fingertip. "What is it?" Reiko lifted her head and looked toward him with unfocused eyes.

But then, as if he had awakened from a dream, he forgot what he wanted to ask. Instead, he found himself blurting out unexpected words.

"Listen, she told me if a man keeps on running around, he'll get caught by some bad woman."

"That's how boys like Hiroshi get into trouble."

"She wasn't talking about him, she meant me!"

"So who's the bad woman?" Reiko murmured. "I suppose it's me."

She tittered and closed her eyes, curling herself up a little more tightly. Again her breathing became low and even. The heat seemed even worse, and the motion of the curtains was heavy with their breath as they lay there perspiring. Feeling pleasantly languid, he began drifting off to sleep with the image of the old woman still before him.

Right now she would be buttonholing some man or woman, giving them an earful.

Hisao woke up covered with sweat. He could tell that it was near sunset. The room was dim and muggy. Perhaps the wind had shifted; the window curtains hung still. The kitchen appeared deeper than usual in the faint light; beyond it, the entrance curtain, dyed rose by the evening glow, made the doorway look distant. He had a dragging fatigue as if reawakening after having made love in the middle of the day in the stuffy room.

Reiko was sleeping beside him, still curled up. Hisao sighed: he had to go back to work the next morning. For the moment he felt too exhausted to sit up. If he wakened Reiko his daily life would start to slide toward supper. After that he would spend a few hours doing nothing in particular, then it would be bedtime. And when he woke up he would have half an hour till he left home for work. Lying sprawled out flat on the tatami, Hisao felt as if he was damming the flow of time with his own body.

Actually, the room was getting darker every minute. In contrast, it seemed to be lighter and clearer outside. At this time of day nobody could see in even if the window was left open. This was the hour when a couple who led a cocooned married life in ancient times would open the door that had been closed all day long, come out to a veranda, and watch the darkening sky together; refreshed, they would stroll about the field in the evening breeze waiting for the arrival of another night. But Reiko was fast asleep, all unaware that it was time for supper: perhaps she was tired after this week, perhaps it had exhausted her. As he watched her sleeping innocently he noticed that her everyday expression had faded away; for a moment an unknown woman seemed to have slipped into the room and taken her place. Desire flickered up in him, but he became gloomy again as he remembered that he was going back to his office tomorrow.

After a while he stood up. Without waking his wife he went through the kitchen to the entrance. He put his shoes on and called out toward the inner room: "I'm going for a walk." There was no answer, but he could hear her slowly turn over in the depth of the darkness.

All the windows of the apartment house were lighted except for the one on the second floor where that dark, quiet room was hidden behind the folds of its drawn curtains. He followed the street along the field for the first time in a week. As he walked farther he recalled how he used to feel in the old days on his way back from Reiko's apartment. Reiko would be too glum to see him off; she would sit there moping in her dark room. He would be troubled by various notions of what was going on in her mind, but still feel a quiet relief at breathing the outdoor air.

A late breeze ruffled the yellowing ears of rice plants in an upland field. The sun had already set; autumn clouds were clustered high in the pale clear sky; below, the wind drove a scattering of clouds that seemed leaden within, perhaps fragments of a towering mass. The evening glow had faded until it dimly reddened only the ends of the clouds, which were stretched thin like silk floss; as he lowered his eyes from the pale sky to the rice field he could see a faint rosy light in the ears of the rice plants. His own arms had the sallow skin of a convalescent, but in the rosy light they almost seemed bronzed and muscular. Hisao walked on along the field.

Farther down the road on the right was another disorganized new development, more houses crowded together overwhelming the rural scenery. Immediately after a neat row of two-storied houses came a flock of lately built matchbox-sized ones, already looking weatherbeaten. An apartment house like their own stood in discreet silence: its residents had all the window curtains drawn as if ashamed of being able to peep down inside the wall of their neighbor's big garden. The houses around this area had been popping up like mushrooms. Instead of spreading gradually out into the field from the main road they were dotted in groups here and there according to the order in which farmers had sold their land. All these groups differed from one another in the floor level and the distance between houses, no doubt reflecting changes in the regulations. Only because newer ones had been built around them, some houses that were fashionable a few years ago and were still occupied by the same people seemed degraded and shabby-looking, as if embittered by the fickleness of the present day.

Along the road there were a few splendid residences with wide, jutting terraces, the new homes of farmers who had sold their land. Most of the imposing nameplates carried the same family name. Flashy architects must have had entire control over their clients; the houses displayed their ostentatious designs as if decked out in unaccustomed formal dress. Still, unlike the houses of rich city people, they had none of the snobbish air of being shielded from view by high walls. Over a hedge or a low Western-style picket fence Hisao could look into a spacious garden where farm produce was spread out on straw mats, and chickens were pecking their feed beside a sports car.

Above all, the flowers planted in every garden, large or small, suggested to him that these were people with a vigorous desire for life. Flowerpots even lined the windows of the apartment house. He was surprised to realize that he and Reiko had been indifferent to nature. No flowers had ever appeared in their window. Perhaps they lacked the energy to support lush growth. That might have been one of the things the old woman sensed about them.

However, once he turned his back to the residential area on the right side of the street, there was a wholly different view. Fields lay spread out in the dusky light just as in the old days. Here and there stood a dark grove around an old farmhouse, its great thatched roof buried under long, wild branches rustling in the west wind, branches reaching out toward the darkening sky. In contrast to the open farmers' residences on the other side of the street, these houses were surrounded with tall, dense hedges; from any direction you could see only the massive rooftops. Year by year, they would sink deeper into luxuriant nature. Someday the people who lived in them would come to miss the sunshine and casually chop down trees and build new houses.

Between one grove about a hundred yards away and another farther to the left, the fields narrowed and gently descended to a hollow, then crept out and gradually widened again, merging into woods veiled in mist. The rural scenery seemed to stretch endlessly beyond the woods; this sense of depth always allured Hisao's gaze, though he had learned a long time ago that immediately beyond the woods were other small houses crowded together. He turned and began walking back along the straight road, his gaze absorbed in the gentle flow of the fields. The rice plant ears were still drinking in the rosy light, all swaying in the direction he was walking. The weariness of a convalescent suddenly descended on him. He was feeling almost intoxicated.

By the time a group of five or six young men came barging up, Hisao was already within sight of his apartment house. He looked at them blankly: they seemed familiar. All of the men glared back at him as much as to say "Who's this bastard?" and then turned in toward the apartment house. The last one nodded, jerked a shoulder at him as they passed, and grunted hello. It was Hiroshi.

"Oh, Hiroshi!" Hisao called out from behind. He realized that his voice sounded too familiar, almost as bad as the old woman's. The men stopped and turned around. They looked at him silently but seemed to quiver with pent-up power, ready to explode in taunts or abuse. Whether from sunburn or drink, they were red all the way down their necks. The gaudy shirts they wore when they went out were unbuttoned, showing a glimpse of undershirt and bellyband. They had the cuffs of their trousers rolled up and their socks off, stuck in their pockets. Two of the men were carrying half-gallon sake bottles, each holding one by the neck. Evidently they meant to finish off their evening at home.

Hiroshi left the group, squaring his shoulders menacingly, and came toward Hisao. As he stood before him he seemed to remember that he was not wearing dark glasses; his slantwise questioning glare wavered, and turned into the gaze of an innocent adolescent. Hisao gave him the message politely: "Around noon an old woman came to see you. She wants you to attend tonight's meeting." Then he added: "You went after the doctor for me the other day . . ." But he faltered, unable to keep the right degree of intimacy in his tone.

Hiroshi scratched his crewcut head and rocked nervously on his heels, looking desperately embarrassed. As if asking Hisao's advice he said abruptly: "That old woman—what am I going to do with her?" Without waiting for an answer he went back to his group. Then he looked over toward Hisao, bowed his head, and said: "Sorry to bother you." When the men asked him what was going on, he snapped: "None of your business." Hiroshi was cross all by himself.

The apartment window was still dark. Hisao went inside and peered through the gloom but Reiko was no longer lying on the tatami; instead, he saw a pale rounded form in the corner of the room. She was sitting holding her knees in her arms, leaning back rather drunkenly against the chest of drawers, her rich thighs exposed from her puffed-out skirt. As he went closer he could see that she was staring into the darkness with wide-open eyes. She didn't seem to notice him.

"What's the matter?" he asked, as he stood in front of her. "Why are you sitting here in the dark?"

"Oh, I felt so good, I was sort of melting away," she murmured. Her voice seemed muffled by sleepiness.

The men next door were being noisy again. From the window they were shouting after Hiroshi to buy this or that, or not to forget something else, or to try the corner butcher . . . Hiroshi's unusually cheerful, obedient voice answered from farther and farther along the fields: "OK, leave it to me. Would a thousand yen's worth do?" . . . Apparently a drinking party would soon begin. Pressing her lips against her knees, Reiko listened attentively.

As he watched her, Hisao remembered something she had told him a long time ago.

It was when she was ten years old, at the end of the summer—in fact, just about this time of day. Reiko had been sitting for a long time leaning against the chest of drawers in the corner of her room. Carpenters had come to work at their house; from the garden you could hear the steady hammering and planing, and men shouting at each other. Perhaps the garden cottage was being rebuilt; anyway, her parents were too busy with it to pay attention to her. Her older sisters had hurried off somewhere to see their friends. And one of the carpenters had a huge tattoo on his back. It was the first time she had ever seen such a thing; she was so frightened of it that she kept the sliding doors to the veranda tightly closed. Soon it was getting toward dusk, and the room was becoming dark. The work in the garden showed no sign of ending. Her sisters had not yet come back. Having nothing to do, she sat in the corner with her hands clasped around her knees and began to doze. Half asleep, half awake, she listened to the sounds outside. Before long an indescribable sensation began to steal over her. It was as if her spirit, or rather her physical awareness, would expand out of her body and fill the garden, becoming quite painful, and then shrink down quickly and come back within her body. That awareness would envelop the sounds outside, become dense, and then return. Whenever the hammering or the men's hoarse voices started up again in the garden they would immediately sink deep within her and begin to vibrate resonantly. Her whole body would tingle. She would have to clasp her knees hard. Then the sensation of expanding would begin all over again . . .

When she told him, he had drawn on his smattering of knowledge to suggest that it might have been the first sign of sexual feeling. "I wonder," Reiko had said, smiling a vague, childish smile.

Even now, when her breasts and hips were ripening into those of a mature woman, her face hovered there in the darkness with the vague expression of a child who had just been awakened.

After a little while Hisao said: "Isn't it about time you got dinner?"

"I suppose so," Reiko sighed, staring at her knees. Then she slowly rose up on her haunches like a docile animal.

Dinner was already part of the office worker's life that would resume tomorrow. Realizing he would have to hurry off in the morning without eating properly, he refused himself any further indulgence. If he tried, he could eat. After all, it was no different from a child's preferences in food. About an hour later than usual the two had their quiet dinner together sitting opposite each other in the kitchen. By the time they finished, the drinking party next door was already in full swing.

It was past nine o'clock, long after washing the dishes, that Reiko began bustling around in the kitchen. Hisao had settled down in front of the TV set. Reiko herself came in once, as if the day's work were over, and sat beside him watching it for a while. Then her eyes took on a faraway look—something seemed to have occurred to her—and she went out to the kitchen. He wondered if she intended to peel a few more peaches, but for some reason she started working busily and didn't come out again.

The evening hours flowed by even more easily than the daytime hours that he had drowsed away. Over the sound of the television came the drunken voices of the men next door, mimicking the dialogue of a solemn TV drama. How differently the very same hours passed for those men and for himself. But as such thoughts ran through his mind he kept on watching the TV.

"Why don't you take your bath now?" Reiko said. Hisao turned, looking away from the TV for the first time, and saw that a full-scale housecleaning seemed to be under way in the kitchen. The table had been moved to one side, and the floor was so crowded—with bottles of sake and beer and soy sauce, canned goods of all sizes, plastic containers, a rice bin—that it made you wonder how a small kitchen could hold them all. The bottom doors of the cupboard were standing wide open, exposing the empty interior to the brightness of the fluorescent light.

Reiko stood in the middle of her chaotic kitchen looking down, her face grimy, with a damp rag in one hand.

"What are you doing? At this time of night."

"Well, there's a kind of musty smell in the cupboard."

Frowning as if the smell still lingered, Reiko slowly crouched down before the cupboard. Then she rubbed the inside of the cupboard vigorously with her rag, stopped, and peered hard into it. He felt a little intimidated by the ferocity of that gaze, and suddenly recalled having seen it before.

"Weren't you looking into the cupboard two or three days ago?" he asked innocently.

"It's been bothering me for quite a while. But you see how much trouble it is to take everything out . . ."

"So why tonight?"

"I wanted to move the rest of the peaches to the refrigerator but when I opened that cupboard I just couldn't stand it any longer."

She sounded like a stubborn child. Hisao got up from the TV set and went into the kitchen beside her. Reiko was squatting on her rich thighs and leaning forward almost to the floor, squeamishly inspecting the freshly wiped cupboard. Then she straightened up again, almost regretfully, and began picking up the cans and bottles one by one, wiping the dust from them, and putting them neatly back in the cupboard. The work seemed infinitely lonely. Hisao bent over her to watch what she was doing. Suddenly Reiko stared up at him with a suspicious look in her eye and said icily:

"Instead of standing there, go and take your bath. There's never any end to these things."

The bathroom was next to the toilet, off to the right of the entryway beyond the kitchen. On the third day after his fever subsided, Reiko had told him to take a bath, and he had been startled by the thought that such a nook existed in their little apartment. Perhaps the fever had erased a part of his memory, but it was the same reaction he had had when they first came to look over the apartment five years ago. That day they had spent almost an hour examining every inch of the tatami room and dining-kitchen, never suspecting that there was a separate bath. Just as they were about to leave after having checked the toilet at the side of the entryway they casually glanced at another door of about the same width. When they opened it, expecting to find a closet, they were confronted by a bright, snug little pink cubicle. Both of them were astonished. There within the narrow space of a single-mat room, laid out as compactly as a miniaturized hotel bathroom, were a pink enameled tub barely large enough to get into, a pink-tiled drain floor, and a mirrored washstand. Everything fitted together so neatly that you could not imagine the faucets or the gas water heater in a different place. Instead of a window there were narrow vents at the top and bottom of the outside wall, both carefully inset with metal screens. Compared with the crude construction of the rest of the apartment, the scrupulous attention to detail of this room seemed somehow obscene.

Yes, he had certainly had the impression of something "obscene." Naturally the apartment they had lived in before did not have its own bath. At first Reiko had disliked going to the public bathhouse. She complained about feeling as if others could see the change in her body, but when he pointed out that none of the women around here had known her, she only disliked it all the more. Still, as the days went by she got used to going to the bathhouse and would set out with her little washbasin looking exactly like all the other women who lived in the building. Sometimes he would make love to her as soon as she came back. Whenever he did, he felt as if he caught a faint whiff of the bathhouse—the scent of perspiration with a tinge of chlorine—rising from her bare skin. And yet that did not in the least disturb the intimacy of their intercourse. There was nothing obscene about it.

By contrast, it had seemed to him, there was a kind of lewdness in the very cleanliness and rationality of their own little cubicle, so like the "bath" of a cheap hotel room "with bath and toilet." And the fact that it was part of their daily lives gave it a special zest. Of course the feeling disappeared once they were settled in. He had always liked to take a long soak. After he began working he became even fonder of it. Sitting there in the cramped little tub with his arms around his knees he would let the day's worries slowly unravel. Not that he consciously tried to solve his problems; all he did was soak until they no longer bothered him. It never even occurred to him to think about his wife.

Now, though, as he tried to let himself enjoy the self-indulgent pleasure of the bath, Hisao could not shake off the thought of Reiko's earnest gaze as she peered into the cupboard. He smiled sardonically. Sitting at home in his bathtub worrying about his wife! Yet he could not easily recapture the serenity that had been put to flight by that gaze. A thing like that stays on her mind for days, and then late one night she starts working as if she can't put up with it another minute. Once she finished cleaning the cupboard, that earnestness, that solitary tension would again disappear into the depths of her everyday behavior and flow along submerged, under pressure. Hunching over in the tub he strained to listen to the sounds from the kitchen. Along with bottles clinking and slippers shuffling across the kitchen floor, and almost as clearly, came sounds from the neighboring apartments upstairs and down. Low voices would occasionally utter a few distinct words; someone would stand up on the tatami, walk around sluggishly, and then sit down again with a thump; here and there the bath water would be running . . . Fearful of losing track of Reiko among all these other sounds, Hisao sat hugging his knees and listening for her, as if anxiously imagining what was happening to someone far away. Then he began to feel that there was something lewd about his own posture. Before he realized it he was stealthily keeping guard whenever he made the least movement, trying not to let even his wife hear a splash.

When he finally got out of the tub after a long soak, he found the kitchen tidied up and Reiko sitting on a chair staring at the closed cupboard doors. She looked tired. The sliding door to the inner room was shut, making the dining-kitchen seem even smaller; now it was really boxlike. When he asked if she had finished cleaning, Reiko sighed and gave a noncommittal nod. Then she muttered: "There's no use doing any more . . ." She let herself slump in the chair as if weary of the struggle, but under heavy eyelids the severity of her stare at the cupboard was exactly as before.

Hisao put his hand on her shoulder. "Call it a day and go have your bath. The next raise I get, we'll find a three-room place." As he tugged gently Reiko's head swayed back and forth but she kept her gaze fastened on the cupboard. Perhaps he was taking the wrong tack. "It's all right, go have your bath," he urged again. At last Reiko got up, put away a few little things she had overlooked, and went reluctantly toward the bathroom.

When he heard water running into the tub, Hisao felt a kind of relief. He sat down on the kitchen chair his wife had just left and began smoking a leisurely cigarette. Then he got up, intending to watch TV until bedtime, opened the door to the inner room—and gasped.

The light was out, and their two sets of bedding were already spread out neatly on the floor. But the darkness was throbbing with the bawdy songs of the construction gang. It was hard to tell where the voices were coming from, perhaps because talking to Reiko in that tiny kitchen had somehow constricted his senses. He only knew that rough voices had filled that empty bedroom.

The men were out in the darkness of the field. As he listened, the bawdy singing stopped and the voices launched into a solemn, drunken exchange. Two of the men were having a long argument, and the others, though they sounded angry, were trying to calm them down. Then in the midst of all the confusion somebody burst out screeching as if he were being strangled. It was another dirty song. Instantly all the other gruff out-of-tune voices joined in. For a while each of the men seemed to be howling his own lewd thoughts to the sky. But no sooner had their full-throated, painful-sounding roar dwindled to a single soft, muffled melody than the whole performance took on an even more indecent tone; they seemed to be dancing around with little hand gestures, swinging their hips rhythmically. However, that didn't last long. A man who had forgotten the words began bellowing out nonsense, disrupting the song and turning it into a medley of frustrated cries. One was simply shouting, paying no attention to anyone else. Another began to plead sentimentally. Now and then a man would dash out over the soft earth of the vegetable field with heavy footfalls, all the while uttering a long-drawn-out shriek; after that unbroken shrill cry receded into the distance it would circle around in a whistling arc and begin coming back. One of those who ran out into the field was making a growling noise, his voice caught in the back of his throat, apparently trying to howl as vulgarly as the rest. That must have been Hiroshi.

Hisao lay flat on his bed, listening to the uproar. Sometimes the voices would fade into the distance, as if the shouting came from across a river, but then they would swell up and fill the bedroom, and that rhythmic, hip-swinging dance would begin again. Now the voices were not so much lewd as they were gloomy, or comical, or nakedly and poignantly obscene. During the pauses in the bawdy singing he could hear the stealthy sound of running water beyond the closed door of the bathroom, as if Reiko was afraid of being overheard by the men.

Finally the singing stopped and for a time angry voices flew back and forth confusedly. Soon a hoarse, smothered voice rose up out of the depths of the darkness. One by one the other voices quieted. Hisao found himself straining to listen, trying to catch what was being said in that peculiar, sermonlike intonation. Occasionally someone would chime in, or urge the speaker on; after such interruptions or little bursts of cackling laughter the voices would fall still again under the spell of the story. Solemnly that hoarse, older voice went on, as if painstakingly delivering some essential truth about spiritual enlightenment. Then an emotion-charged young voice burst out: "That's rape, ain't it?"

"Don't be stupid," the hoarse voice admonished gravely.

"Didn't you knock her down?" another voice asked in an agitated tone.

"Yeah," the hoarse voice replied imperturbably, "I gave her a whack and flattened her."

"Ain't that rape?" came the awed response.

"No," said the hoarse one brusquely. He paused, letting it sink in. "You're wrong. The next thing, I got down on my knees right where she was laying. I bowed my head in the dirt and begged her: 'For god's sake, please let me do it!' "

"Putting on a lousy act! At a time like that."

"Who the hell was acting? I didn't even know why, but I kept saying it over and over, the goddamned tears pouring out."

"What did the woman do?"

"She lifted her head and looked at me."

"But what did she say?"

"She said, 'Go ahead and do it.' "

The men fell silent. It was a simple, honest silence, as if they were absorbed by the words that had just been uttered. The silence conveyed all the more vividly how the men were squatting in a circle there in the darkness. Then it was shattered by someone screaming "I can't take it!" All at once there was a jumble of voices—"It's a lie!" "The hell it is!"—and a frantic surge of echoing laughter. Voices shrilled out in falsetto—"Do it!" "Go ahead!"—as bodies thumped together. Groans of "You bastard!" mingled with shrieks of laughter as the men launched into a free-for-all. Soon a deep masculine voice called out: "Hey, Hiroshi honey, are you still here?" Hiroshi answered with an inarticulate growl. At that, all the men began teasing him, vying with one another in imitating high-pitched women's voices.

"What should we do? Ooh, I feel so guilty!"

"Our Hiroshi's still a little young for *that!*"

"Of course he is! Hiroshi's a virgin!"

"Go right in the house, have a pee, and go to bed, now."

After a pause, somebody shrieked out hysterically: "Later that old bag will come and get into bed with you!"

"You son of a bitch!" Hiroshi yelled, flying at him. The man gave a shriek, but obviously Hiroshi was no match. The shriek was followed by a mocking laugh.

"Hiroshi, dear, I *told* you to stop!"

"Shame on you, Hiroshi!"

"If you get hurt I'll feel so sad!"

The men seemed to be clustering around him, uttering seductive little feminine remarks. For a while they tussled together playfully, but then a voice like a rusty knife said: "Let's give it to him!" There was a repeated thudding like a sandbag being punched. Hiroshi went down, yelling: "What the hell do you think you're doing?" Some of the men seemed to be grappling with him on the ground as he resisted fiercely. He began to sound childishly shrill like a boy whose voice had not yet changed: "Stop it! Hey, don't get funny . . . Drink my piss!" A constant chuckle was audible along with the heavy breathing of the men who were pinning him down.

Then a single piercing cry scattered the men in all directions. Hiroshi was left alone within a wide circle of embarrassed laughter. "I'll kill all of you!" he shouted furiously and dashed into the house. A man hurried in after him: "Hiroshi! Listen, Hiroshi." Hisao could hear snatches of their exchange. "Don't go for that knife!" "I can't take it any longer." "Think of your poor mother!" "Tell her I loved her, will you?" The low, gruff voice went on earnestly trying to soothe Hiroshi, who seemed carried away by his own ranting. At last the two of them came back out of the house.

After that it was all Hiroshi's show. Apparently the other men felt intimidated by his theatrical raging, familiar as it was, and instead of contradicting him, gravely echoed his words. And yet were they really afraid of him? Half-taunting, half-servile, their voices followed after him as he strutted back and forth shouting at them. After a while Hiroshi's long outpouring of emotion was all that could be heard as it receded into the distance along the fields. It degenerated to a faraway whine, and then was swallowed up in the silence. At that moment, beyond the sliding door, Reiko muttered plaintively: "Oh, damn it!" She sounded as if she had just noticed some fatal error.

"What's the matter?" Hisao called. There was no answer. He got up and opened the door, and saw Reiko standing beside the table, wearing a pale nightgown she had put on after her bath.

"I forgot to take out the garbage pail."

"Can't you do it tomorrow morning?"

"Things have to be done right."

Reiko cast an annoyed glance at the already locked front door. Her whole body seemed to quiver with impotent anger. Kitchen refuse had to be left in a communal plastic container at the edge of the vegetable field, to be picked up by the garbage truck.

"I wonder if the men next door are still carousing," she asked a little anxiously. For a moment they listened in silence. It seemed the men were off somewhere drinking again.

"Anyway, I'll go," said Hisao, coming into the kitchen. But Reiko wouldn't hear of it.

"Never mind. It's just taking it out. And then I've got to rinse the pail at the pump."

With that, she wriggled out of her nightgown and let it drop to the floor, ignoring him as she pulled on her rather soiled summer dress directly over her freshly bathed skin, and stepped down into the entryway.

"Hey, I said I'd do it," he called to her.

"Never mind. You wouldn't know how. Go on to bed, I'll be back soon." Reiko had a dogged expression on her face as she went out holding the heavy pail with both hands.

Hisao returned to bed. He could hear the familiar clip-clop of her wooden sandals as she came around under the window and walked quickly on along the field. Then there was the dull, distant sound of the kitchen pail thumping against the rim of the can as she emptied it. After that there seemed to be only darkness and silence again. He lay in bed listening, waiting to hear the clatter of her sandals.

But the sound of footsteps didn't come. After a time the horizon of silence was broken by the hum of deep masculine voices. Out of the half-quarreling, half-friendly babble he could occasionally hear a woman's voice rise up sweetly. All the men were talking amiably together as they came back along the field. They stopped near the pump, and began laughing rather self-consciously at one another. Then he heard Hiroshi say: "We'll clean your bucket. Hey, you, wash this out for the lady!"

Someone retorted: "The more you kowtow to this son of a bitch the worse he gets!" But the voice didn't sound angry.

"Oh no, you mustn't!" he heard Reiko say in a playful, intimate tone. "I can't let a bachelor do that for me. What if his girlfriend saw?"

"I don't have a girlfriend," a melancholy voice said over the sound of running water. Another voice put in: "Just sit down, lady."

After the water stopped running he heard Hiroshi's guttural, half-swallowed voice once more.

"Say, how about a drink? You drink, don't you? Weren't you and your husband at that rooftop beer garden by the station the other day? Come on, just a little one! I'm feeling good tonight. You, there, bring her a teacup!"

"Stop showing off in front of the lady, Hiroshi."

"Idiot! We're from the same place. Watch it, or I'll knock you down!"

"Come off it, now. You've got a lot of nerve tonight!"

"I sure have!"

Still muttering, someone went bounding off into the house, and came out again at once, clinking a sake bottle and teacups together rhythmically. Voices called out "Hand it over!" and "Let me pour!" as they struggled for the bottle, but then Hiroshi's knifelike cry cut through: "Leave this to me!" Evidently he had snatched the bottle away.

"Only a tiny bit!" Reiko implored him. "Just leave it to me," Hiroshi answered. "Come on, drink up!" The men fell into a fascinated silence. A low, grunting cheer rose like a sigh. Hisao sat up in bed and peered through the little gap between the curtains. There, where the old woman had harangued him earlier that day, he could see the pale figure of Reiko sitting on a stone surrounded by a ring of half-naked men. She seemed thoroughly at ease, taking little sips from a teacup which she held delicately between her fingertips as if she were at a tea ceremony. Hiroshi was kneeling down before her resting a big bottle of sake against one knee; he was stripped to the waist too and sat there imposingly waiting on her with elbows thrust out akimbo. The men encircling them had squatted like children, hunching their bronzed, sweaty backs. They looked up delightedly as Reiko sipped from the teacup.

With a gasp, Reiko drained the cup of sake. "Have another!" someone cried. "That's enough," Hiroshi commanded sternly.

Hisao left the window and lay down on his back in bed again. Outside Hiroshi was still in high spirits, dominating the party. The other men were chatting in subdued voices. Suddenly Hiroshi's tone changed to a plaintive appeal.

"You know, ma'am, tonight I really want you to hear my story. Can you imagine living with these savages day after day? I can't talk about anything serious with them."

At that moment somebody yelled "Come off it, you bastard!" and Reiko let out a scream like a young girl trying to escape. There was the thump of a body against the ground.

"Ouch! Who the hell shoved me? And you let me fall, ma'am, jumping back like that." Hiroshi's grumbling voice vividly suggested the hurt, clowning expression on his face.

"You poor guy! So she wouldn't catch you!" A roar of cheerful laughter went up. Reiko joined in, sounding embarrassed.

When the laughter died down he could hear her clear voice saying "Well, good-night. Thanks for everything." All the men called good-night to her. Their voices were strangely gentle. After Reiko's footsteps had come all the way up the stairs, the men began to leave. Yawning as they exchanged their now-familiar quips of "Do it!" "Go ahead and do it!" they clumped noisily into the house.

"I'm back," he heard her call from the entryway. Then her footsteps turned in to the bath. The sound of water splashing continued for some time. After that Reiko came out almost silently and busied herself at something just on the other side of the sliding door. Finally he heard her switch off the kitchen light. In the enveloping darkness the door quietly opened and her white body came gliding out and dropped on the bed beside him. She must have poured cold water over herself: her taut skin felt chilly to his touch. As he ran his hand down from her breast along the line of her flank she gave a deep, alcoholic sigh.

Just then a low voice that seemed to issue from a slack, trembling throat called from the depth of the darkness outside the window: "Hiroshi. Are you still awake, Hiroshi?" The men next door seemed to be fast asleep. Patiently the voice went on calling, moving from place to place along the edge of the field but not coming any nearer the house. Such a subdued voice seemed unlikely to awaken anyone, but its very stealthiness made it seem as if it might subtly invade the mind of a sleeper who had a secret wish to hear it.

"Do you suppose their meetings go on this late?" Hisao murmured into his wife's ear.

"Mmm. They're really dedicated." There was a touch of sarcasm in Reiko's answer as she snuggled up to him.

Gradually, calling Hiroshi's name over and over, that disagreeably trembling voice seemed to become younger and fuller, to take on a sweet, feminine quality. As Hisao lay there with one arm around her he felt himself yielding to the illusion that Reiko's voice was still echoing outside, floating in the darkness beyond the window. Some time later he heard soft footsteps in the street below.

Out of the depths of the darkness came a long, quiet exchange between the old woman, who had begun whispering earnestly, and Hiroshi, awkwardly grunting in agreement.

Reiko may have been listening too. Her eyes were half-closed as she lay there in her husband's arms.

TRANSLATED BY HOWARD HIBBETT

▚ KŌNO TAEKO

In 1962, when she won an award for "little magazine" authors, Kōno Taeko had already had over a decade of apprenticeship in one of Japan's innumerable literary groups. The following year she received the Akutagawa Prize, and she has continued to be a prolific, prizewinning writer of short stories and novels. Like Kurahashi Yumiko and the still younger Kanai Mieko, she is viewed as one of the distinguished but rather difficult women authors who have come to play an increasingly major role in modern Japanese literature.

Kōno Taeko was born in 1926, the daughter of an Osaka wholesaler of mushrooms, seaweed, dried sea slugs, and other delicacies. During the War her education was interrupted by compulsory work in a factory producing military uniforms; she has said that the War's end was the beginning of her youth. In spite of poverty and illness, she went on to pursue her literary goals with a Tanizaki-like devotion to sadomasochistic fantasy. But Kōno grounds these fantasies in the realistic world of everyday life, particularly the everyday life of couples, married or only living together, whose sexual affinity is somewhat pathological.

"Bone Meat" is the title work of her fifth collection of short stories, published in 1971. It should be mentioned that most Japanese regard raw oysters with the dubious attitude so often held by foreigners toward sashimi—"raw fish."

❖ Bone Meat

(*Hone no niku,* 1969)

It was last fall, but the woman could not seem to take it into her head to dispose of the belongings the man had left behind when he deserted her.

A day or two before, it had been raining. Four or five days later she noticed his umbrella and her own lying by the window. She had no recollection of putting the umbrellas there, so perhaps the man had done it. In her panic over being deserted, however, perhaps she had forgotten what she herself had done. She opened them, and found they had dried completely. The woman carefully adjusted the folds of each, wound around the strap, and hooked the metal ring over the button. But after standing her own umbrella in the umbrella rack inside the shoe cupboard, she wrapped the man's umbrella in paper, along with another of his she had found there, tied them up with a string, and put them away in the closet.

It was, perhaps, around the same time that she threw away the man's toothbrush. One morning, as she was about to pick up her own toothbrush, her eyes fell on his lying beside it. The bristles at the end of the transparent, light-blue handle were bent outward from hard use. Once, he had come home with an assortment of six toothbrushes for the two of them which he had bought on sale. She also recalled having bought them toothbrushes two or three times. Whether the toothbrush that remained was one of the six the man had bought, she didn't know. But as she picked it up she remembered his purchase and, seeking an excuse for discarding it in the painfully worn-out bristles, dropped it in the wastebasket. Next, she threw in three or four old blades from his safety razor. She also removed the blade still clamped in the razor, on which were hardened bits of soap mixed with the man's whiskers, and discarded it. But the razor she wrapped in his dry towel, together with several small boxes of unused blades, and put them away in his underwear drawer.

That drawer was the top one in the woman's wardrobe. Previously, the man's clothes had hung inside together with hers, but before leaving he had collected them quickly. However, the woman later noticed a faded gray lizard-skin belt which he no longer wore, and that too she put in his underwear drawer.

There were other things of his that ought to have been put away. Two or three of his shirts were probably at the laundry, and she intended to go pick them up and put them in the drawer too, though she hadn't done it yet. She couldn't imagine he had gone to get them . . . Atop the wardrobe lay his four clothing boxes, a couple of which seemed full; she put them in the closet in place of her own.

The man's pillow stayed where it was for quite some time. Each night when the woman laid out the quilts, she first took the man's pillow out of the bedding closet, holding it by the opening of its oversized pillowcase, and put it back when she had finished taking out the quilts. And in the morning when she put the quilts away, she took it out once again. This continued for several weeks before it occurred to her to pack it away. She washed the case and set the pillow in the winter sun, choosing as bright a day as possible; then, replacing it in its cover and putting it into a nylon bag, she laid it on top of the man's clothing boxes in the closet.

The woman knew perfectly well that the man would not be back. How many times had she been unable to refrain from saying things like "I'd be better off without you!" and meaning them. And one day when she had again been unable to restrain herself, the man had replied "So it seems, doesn't it?" and left. The remorse she felt afterward had been painful. She acutely regretted having become accustomed to speaking in that way, and having said those words once again the day the man took her up on them. But what made it so painful, in retrospect, was that she had no right to regret, considering the man's attitude for some time past as well as his adroitness in taking advantage of her words. And the pain bereft her of the energy to pursue him.

The woman no longer wanted even to ask the man to come pick up his things. His reply was certain to be: "Do whatever you like with them." And, in fact, perhaps what he had left there he cared nothing about. As their relationship had begun to deepen and he stayed at her place for long intervals, he had little by little brought over personal things he needed. But even after he was virtually living with her, he didn't move out of his own lodgings, where he must have still had a dresser and desk, several boxes of clothing, ski equipment, and bedding. He had taken away the everyday clothing he had kept for convenience in her wardrobe; furthermore, it seemed that he was rising to a higher position at work. Surely he felt no attachment to the worn-out things he had left behind.

The woman, however, was at a complete loss as to how to dispose of them. Aside from putting them away, she simply could not decide what to do with the objects the man had left lying about. If she called him to come for them, it would be equally disagreeable whether he told her to throw them out or said: "Are they still there? Well, just send them over." Even if someone else would see to it, getting in touch with the man like that was itself distasteful. Yet it was also disagreeable to take it upon oneself to throw away someone else's belongings— still quite useful things—or to have them carted off by a junk dealer. Besides, she couldn't give these things, which the man had abandoned along with herself, to someone else.

She regretted she had not had him take all of his belongings when he left. She regretted it with all her heart.

The first hints that the man was beginning to think of a life in which she had no part appeared even before his work took a turn for the better. His decision to abandon her had been reflected in both his private and public aspects; even the clothing he wore was all newly made. She felt the sympathy of a fellow-sufferer for the old clothes that he took no more notice of, and yet felt scorned by the very things she tried to pity. And thus the woman found even more unbearable these troublesome leftover belongings.

She had several times considered taking the man's underwear, which filled the top drawer of the wardrobe, and his woolen clothes that lay mixed with her own in the tea chest on the lower shelf in the closet, and making a single bundle of them, but the mere thought of it made her feel weary and feverish. If one were to open them and look, there might also be just enough room to put the man's underwear and woolen clothing in his suitcase which was on the tea chest, or in the four clothing boxes that she had put in place of her own on top of her suitcase on the upper shelf. The man's rucksack and canvas shoes, also on the upper shelf, might well fit into one of these too. But she didn't feel like opening any of them. She always felt that the things the man had left weighed upon her.

She was no longer envious when she thought of the man's delight as he abandoned her and his belongings with the single comment "So it seems." She had decided that the best method of dealing with the perplexing problem of the man's belongings was herself to abandon them entirely, along with her own, and move to a new place. But she didn't have the money to move to a new place or to buy all the necessary things for it. Although the woman would have liked to abandon it all, she could not, and even her own belongings and the place itself became repugnant to her.

The woman could only trust that circumstances would arise in which her lack of money presented no obstacle. She felt she would like to burn it all—the man's things, and her own, and the place. If she too were to burn up with them, she thought, so much the better. But she merely hoped for it, and made no plans. Strangely, for a woman who wanted even herself to be destroyed in the conflagration, she was inclined to be wary of fire. She always recalled one late winter night in her childhood, when there was a fire close by and she saw an old man from the burning building, with a padded jacket slipped on over his flannel nightshirt, being swept along in the crowd, barefoot on the asphalt where water streamed from the fire hoses.

Now she was even more careful. She was tortured by the fear that if she were to start a fire accidentally it would seem like arson. When she went out, especially, she felt she had to check for fire hazards two or three times, all the more so if she was in a hurry. Once, after she had locked the door and taken a few steps, she suddenly became uneasy. Unlocking the door and reentering, she checked the outlets and gas jets. She held an already wetted ashtray under the faucet in the kitchen and ran more water in it until the ashes floated. Reassured, she went out, but she hesitated as she was about to drop the key into her handbag. She couldn't help recalling an impression she had had just now. When she picked up the ashtray she had been reminded of how she had smoked half a pack of cigarettes the man had left behind. Ordinarily, the woman smoked only her own brand. When she ran out, even if the man had some, she found it unsatisfying to make do with a brand not her own, and she would take the trouble to go and buy some. However, the day the man left, or perhaps the next day, when her cigarettes ran out, she was so distressed that she did not want to go. Her eyes fell on the half-empty pack the man had left, and in her agitation she thought, Oh good— any brand, as long as there are cigarettes. All that the woman had disposed of among the things the man had left behind was the discarded toothbrush, the old razor blades, and the cigarettes. A moment before, when she had held the ashtray in her hands, she had the dreamlike feeling that everything would, happily, burn to ashes like the cigarettes. She felt then, suddenly, that when she had first locked the door she had already taken care of all possible fire hazards. Having gone out a second time, she found herself worrying that she might now have unthinkingly contributed to an outbreak of fire. And again she had to use her key.

Winter was almost over, and from time to time a springlike sun shone. The woman recalled how, last year about the same time on just such an afternoon, she and the man had gone out together. Where they had gone and with what purpose, she had forgotten, but she retained a vivid impression of the window of a shop where they had stopped to buy bread on the way home, and of various sorts of bread in steam-clouded cellophane wrappers.

As she waited for her bread, the woman looked again at the loaves heaped in the window and noticed a glass case next to them. In it were a number of whole chickens glowing in an electric rotisserie, roasting as they revolved. She took the bread and, glancing around at the man, moved toward them.

"Are you going to buy some?" the man said.

"I thought I might," she replied.

"Are the ones here good?"

"Hmm, I've never bought any from here before . . ."

Inside the glass case each row of four chickens, richly glazed, rose, turned, and sank back down. As they rose again, with hardly a trace of the severed necks, they seemed to be lifting their wings high. The row of plump breasts rose, then began dropping out of sight, and the bones that peeped out from the fat legs as they rose made the chickens appear to be falling prostrate, palms up, withdrawing in shame.

The woman stood waiting for the man to speak and watched the movement of the chickens. The man, too, seemed to be watching them and said, finally: "Would you mind not buying any? Lately they're fattening chickens with female hormones. It seems a man shouldn't eat too much of it."

The woman wondered if he weren't thinking of American chickens. She had been present when one of his friends, home from the United States, had spoken about cooking for himself there. He said that he had often bought small fried shrimp that were sold cheaply at the market, and salted and ate them. He had often bought halves of roast chicken cheaply too. "They weren't so tasty, though. They're fattened with hormone injections," he had said, pantomiming an injection. The woman didn't remember for certain whether he had said simply "hormones" or "female hormones," nor did she know whether Japanese chickens were so treated or not, but she wondered if the man weren't misremembering that comment. She didn't say anything, though. She realized she could hardly claim they didn't often have roast chicken.

"I see. Well, shall we have oysters? On the half-shell?" Although that too they certainly had often enough.

"Yeah, that would be better," the man agreed this time.

They went into a department store. What with the heat from the steam that clouded the inside of the bread's cellophane wrapper, and the store's intemperate heating system, the woman breathed a sigh of relief when she stood before the cool abalone-filled glass water tank of the shellfish stall in the basement. Pointing to the oysters in the glass case next to it, where frost had crystallized on the horizontal bars, she asked for ten of them. The clerk picked out ten of the larger ones and put them in a short, wide oilpaper sack, and then on a rear table wrapped it up in two sheets of paper. As she took the parcel, the woman could feel the same bulk and weight as always.

She had become skilled at opening the oyster shells. In the beginning the man had opened them, and she had enjoyed watching him do it. But he relied on strength alone to break open the shells, always leaving their contents in a sorry state, so the woman learned from someone else and undertook the task herself. With the rounded side down and the hinge toward her, she held one firmly on the cutting board, tilted at an angle away from her. The brownish color and rippled surface merged so that it was hard to tell the seam from the shell. Searching for the point near the middle of the edge where the inside of the shell peeked through, or, if she couldn't find it, somewhere in that area, she inserted the knife forcefully, blade turned outward, taking care not to damage the oyster, then turned the blade sideways, slipped another small knife between the shells, and with the tip of that blade scraped downward, cutting the hinge. Then the top shell would loosen abruptly and she would catch a whiff of the seashore. But if the top shell had not been cut loose completely she once again turned the blade in the opposite direction and sawed upward. That usually did the trick.

That evening, too, the woman opened the oyster shells in this way and laid them on a plate of ice cubes. She added lemon wedges and carried it to the table.

"Go ahead and have some," the man said, taking one from the center of the large plate, dropping it with a clatter on the small plate before him, and trickling lemon juice over it.

"Mm," she replied, but did not reach for one.

"No, really," the man continued, lifting the edge of the oyster he was about to eat with his fruit fork.

"Mm," she again replied, but took pleasure in not reaching for one.

She watched the man's hand, clenched so tightly around the fruit fork that it appeared even more delicate, as he maneuvered it right and left, trying to cut loose the hinge muscle. He seemed to have done it neatly. As he lifted the oyster to his mouth, seaweed still clinging to its shell, he worked it slightly with his fork and the sound carried the smell, taste, and freshness of the seashore.

"Is it good?" the woman asked. The man nodded, laid aside the shell, and with the same hand took another from atop the ice on the large plate. He placed it on his small plate and the woman squeezed lemon juice over it.

When he had progressed to his third and laid the shell on the table, the woman transferred one of the shells he had discarded to her own plate.

"Have some of these," said the man, indicating the large plate.

At this, she took even greater pleasure in not doing so, and instead scraped with her fork at the bit of muscle left by the man. At last she got a tiny piece of white meat on the tip of her fork, and rubbed it against her lips. She liked to hold the morsel of meat pressed firmly to her lips and feel her tongue become instantly aroused with the desire to have its turn. The hinge muscle lay in a slight hollow of the shell, and she had still not taken quite all of the meat the man had left there. She again moved her fork toward it, urged on by lips and tongue that had already finished off the first piece. As her hand holding the fork responded violently to the impatience of the urging, she found herself struggling with the bit of meat. This made it that much more difficult to get loose; once loosened, more difficult to get hold of; and when at last she lifted it to her lips, her hand trembled. Holding both her fork and the empty shell aloft in her hands, she savored the eager rivalry of her lips and tongue for the meat.

The woman did not yet lay aside the shell. All that was left of the oyster was a brownish arc in low relief, where some flesh was still attached. She sliced at it with her fork and, bringing the shell to her mouth, tipped it up. The woman felt that all the parts of her mouth were contending for the taste, the smell, the freshness of the seashore. So it seemed, from the intensity of the rivalry in there. But it also felt to her as if all of these many parts stirred simultaneously with the pleasure of gratification. Before her, she could see nothing but the glistening inside of the shell, with its matchless white, pale purple and blue, and yellow. All the parts of her mouth reverberated at once with pleasure when she put that last brownish ridge of meat to her lips, because it seemed that this fresh glistening flowed in, too, with a rush.

"Ah, that's good," the woman sighed, at last putting down the shell.

"That's because you're only eating the best part," the man said.

"True . . ." Nodding emphatically, she took the next shell that lay beside the man's plate.

"Shall I give you one?" the man suggested after a few minutes, speaking of the oysters on the bed of ice. "Or maybe I'd better not."

"Let me have just one," the woman said, holding her fork in one hand and a shell with a bit of meat attached in the other.

"For you, that'll be plenty." He pointed to the shell in her hand.

"Don't say that—please give me one," she said.

The man quickly picked one off the ice and laid it with a clack on the small plate in front of her.

"Try it and see," he said. The woman, with this departure from the usual order of things, felt somewhat at a loss. He went on: "They don't seem to be as good as usual. I was hungry, so at first I didn't realize it."

The woman put down the shell she was holding and, cutting loose the oyster the man had laid on her plate, she sucked it from its shell. In an instant the entire cold, slippery thing slid through her mouth that had leapt so at just the tiny morsel of meat.

"How is it?" the man asked.

"Well, I can't really tell," she replied. What she could tell was that it was not nearly so good as the taste of the hinge muscle scraped from the empty shell or the other bit of meat that had given her such ecstasy. And it seemed distinctly inferior to the flavor, the smell, the freshness of the seashore called up in her mind by the voluptuous sound the man made when he raised the shell to his lips and sucked out the oyster. Even the flavor evoked by that sound amounted to little more than imagining a long-past and much-faded sensation. For the woman, the whole raw oyster always tasted the same. She could by no means tell by tasting one whether tonight's oysters were as good as usual.

"They don't seem quite so good to me," the man said.

The woman noticed that it was unusually bright and sunny for a winter's day. "Are they diseased, I wonder?"

"No, you could tell right away. The taste is completely different."

The man took another from the large plate. He loosened the oyster, but did not squeeze lemon over it; picking it up in its shell, he raised it to his mouth with an air of examination.

"Maybe it's just me. They look all right, don't they?" he said. He laid one from the large plate onto the woman's plate and one on his own. There remained one more on the large plate. When she had finished hers, the woman ate that one too.

She gathered the empty shells on the large plate of melting ice and carried it to the drainboard. She washed the knife she had used in the preparation, put it in the dish drain, and picked up the cutting board from where she had left it. As she was rubbing it clean under running water at the faucet, something broad and sharp pricked her palm. She shut off the water and felt the board to see what it was, then took the board to the man.

"Look here." She took his wrist and placed the palm of his hand on the board. He withdrew it immediately.

"What happened? It's so rough," he said, touching it again lightly with his fingertips.

"This is where I opened the oysters. When I stick the knife in hard, the edges on the bottom are crushed and cut into it. It always happens." The woman spoke as though in a dream. It did happen every time, but for once, instead of smoothing it with pumice as usual, she couldn't resist bringing it to show him, because she felt dissatisfied that the scene they always played when they ate oysters on the half-shell had not been followed. The man took her hand and stroked it. She wished she might feel that on another part of her body.

"Do you think it's all right?" she asked.

"It's a cutting board. So it can't help getting bloody sometimes."

That evening, however, which ended without the usual fulfillment of the scene she associated with the taste, was the last time they ate oysters together. Before too many more days passed, spring was upon them and the raw-oyster season was over. The summer passed and autumn came, and by the time the air again began to turn cold, the man had already left.

This year as the days turned more and more springlike, the woman had grown very thin. The man's belongings, as always, remained with her. To him they were invisible, but they weighed upon her whenever she was at home. These troublesome belongings of his, and her own which for lack of money she could not abandon, and the place, became all the more unbearable to her, and she frequently saw herself being swept along the crowded late-night street flooded by the fire hoses, barefoot, with something thrown quickly over her nightgown.

It was about this time that the man's stored belongings, which weighed so on her conscious mind, gradually began to obtrude on her vision. It was as though the top drawer in the wardrobe had changed into some semitransparent material, so that the man's underwear within it shone white and what seemed to be his socks shone black. Little gauze-covered windows appeared here and there in the thick paper sliding doors of the closet, and the bulky shapes of his suitcase, the umbrella package, his clothing boxes, his rucksack, and his pillow showed through. From within one of the drawers he had used in the desk, too, a plastic box began to be visible.

The woman herself thought that she must be terribly weak. At meals, she must try to eat as much as possible. She must gain some weight. She must get stronger. If she didn't, perhaps the wardrobe drawer, the closet door, and the drawer in the desk would turn to glass. Perhaps too the man's suitcase and clothing boxes would become glass cases, and his rucksack and canvas shoes would become like the nylon pillow cover, or a cellophane bag. At this rate, she might very well find herself being swept along barefoot in the night in the crowded street flooded by water from the fire hoses, with only something slipped on over her nightgown. It might happen, she thought, if she didn't eat a lot at mealtimes and recover from this weakness.

But when she tried to carry out her resolution, the woman realized that she ate even less. It had always been a peculiarity of hers that when she was excited —pleasantly or unpleasantly—she would become strangely hungry. She seemed to give way to the excitement and gorge herself whenever she had been aggravated into saying "I'd be better off without you!" and meaning it, and especially during her agitation after the man left her. But she had by now lost the energy and the momentum of the excitement, and her appetite no longer asserted itself even in that form. No matter what was set before her, after one or two bites she could not proceed.

Since girlhood, the woman had hardly been what could be described as plump. However, from about the time the man began gradually bringing in his personal belongings, she had started to gain a little weight.

Their tastes concurred, and they both liked dishes with bones or with shells. The woman was poor, and the man's prospects, up until about the time he abandoned her, had not looked good, so in order to serve such dishes often, they had to economize on their other meals. Even so, it was mostly the bones or shells which went to the woman. But although she seldom ate richly, she began to gain weight.

The woman recalled this odd phenomenon as not odd in the least. The man would attack a boiled tuna tail avidly and set the plates rattling, and although the woman called what little was left a "bone-tail," the flavor that could be drawn from each hollow in it made her want to exclaim: "Are there such flavors in this world!" Likewise the sight of the scarlet-wrapped slender morsel of flesh bursting from the single lobster claw granted her made her want to sigh. All those varied bone and shell dishes began to give her the feeling that a sense of taste had been awakened throughout her body; that all her senses had become so concentrated in her sense of taste that it was difficult for her even to move. And when she awoke the next morning, she felt her body brimming with a new vitality. It would have been odd had she *not* gained weight.

Even after she had noticed a change in the man's behavior and had become critical of him (though not yet to the point of being unable to refrain from saying "I'd be better off without you!"), the two of them continued to enjoy these dishes with bones or shells. Whether because of that or because their relationship had not yet deteriorated too badly, she continued to gain weight.

The day the man had said that males probably shouldn't eat too much chicken, she had deferred to him, although afterward he still brought home roast chicken any number of times. In the intervals between roast chickens, the woman sometimes fixed boiled tuna tail as before, or bought the head of a coastal sea bream and boiled it. Because of the season, that night was the last time they had oysters on the half-shell, but during the summer they often ate abalone. The man liked the whole abalone, and seemed to enjoy begrudging the woman the least morsel. For her part, she took intense pleasure in savoring the meager flavors of the big shell itself.

The woman had never been critical of him when they had dishes with bones or shells, because at those times he never made her anxious or brought her troubles to mind. He coveted meat even more fiercely than before, and she even more wholeheartedly savored the tiny bits of bone meat. They were a single organism, a union of objectively different parts, immersed in a dream. Sometimes both would sigh simultaneously from the excess of flavor, and then laugh so much that they had to put down the food they were holding.

The woman, now grown thin, realized that she longed only for the taste of those dishes. It was not only herself and his belongings that the man had deserted, but that taste as well. However, her sense of taste did not yet seem to understand that it had been abandoned. When she ordered one of the old dishes with bones or shells and something else was brought out, she rejected it at once, saying "No, not that!" The woman began to wonder if this weren't how a mother, abandoned with a young child by her husband, must feel. And like the mother, she now took pity on the young child's unreasonableness, now scolded it, at times hugged the still uncomprehending child and cried; she even thought of killing the child and then committing suicide. Once, at her wits' end with the unreasonableness of her own sense of taste, she raptly imagined the man to be standing just beyond the grillwork partition devouring a chicken thigh, then tearing the stripped bones apart at the joint and throwing the pieces in to her, so that suddenly she felt she heard the sound as it hit the floor. If she could be sure that she would be able to share it, she thought, she wouldn't mind being swept along the crowded asphalt street barefoot where water streamed from the fire hoses, with only something slipped over her nightgown. Then, becoming aware of the semitransparent top drawer of the wardrobe, she stared at it, trembling. She lacked the courage to look around at the desk drawer, which of course must have become transparent, or at the little gauze-covered windows that must have appeared here and there in the thick paper doors.

"You going to burn this?" The voice seemed to belong to one of the children in front of the large cooperative trash incinerator.

"Yes, I am."

"Give it to me!"

"I can't do that, I have to burn it. Throw it in, please. I'll buy you an even fatter red pencil. That's right—that's the way."

"Are you going to burn the clothing box?"

"The box? Yes, I am."

"Shall we help you?"

"Well, thank you. But you mustn't open it. I don't want the contents to get scattered around. Just burn it that way."

"OK. Everything in here can burn, huh?"

"Yes. Can you burn these up for me? I have a lot to bring over here."

"Bring all you want."

"That's great."

"Shall we help you carry it over?"

"Would you mind?"

"Of course not."

The words echoed pleasantly in her ears. It was an exhilarating feeling. Tomorrow when she awoke, she would no longer be troubled by anxiety over the semitransparent drawer or all the little gauze-covered windows in the thick paper doors, or whether they might be getting even worse. It was months since the woman had felt calm, and so exhilarated; the thought put her completely at ease.

Just then, there was a knock at the door.

"Aren't you the one who used the incinerator today?"

The woman realized that she hadn't checked on how the schoolchildren who had helped her had left things, but she knew it was part of the dream, so it was all right. Trying to keep from awakening and interrupting her dream, she kept her eyes shut, the quilt pulled up around her head, as she rose and went to the door.

"Won't the people who use it later have a hard time? Leaving a mountain of bones that way. We're supposed to clear out what's left unburned. Why, there are oyster shells alone to fill a bucket."

To fill a bucket—what fraction of the oysters they had eaten together would that be? But there weren't very many from the last time, so when might these shells be from?

The siren of a fire engine wailed somewhere continuously. But what caused her dream to recede was less the siren than the words she had just heard in her dream. From the ashes of the man's belongings, that there should be so many bones and shells! "Is that so? Is that so?" she said nodding, and the siren, to which was added a furiously ringing bell, filled her ears. Was what she had been told in the dream perhaps prophetic? The bell stopped, and just then the siren arrived blaring under her window. But the woman, her eyes closed, nodding "Is that so? Is that so?" simply snuggled deeper into the quilt as it seemed to begin to smolder.

TRANSLATED BY LUCY LOWER

■■ABE KŌBŌ

Among living Japanese writers, Abe Kōbō has achieved the greatest worldwide reputation. His ironic, meticulously detailed avant-garde novels are as well known in Eastern Europe and the Soviet Union as in the West. In Japan, his work is thought of as deracinated and cosmopolitan—a condition in which Abe takes pride, seeing himself as "a man without a hometown," a survivor of modern urban life who refuses to indulge in sentimentally nostalgic yearnings for the past. Mishima Yukio once commented, with mingled envy and dismay, that it would be hard to find another writer in the thousand-year history of Japanese fiction who has so drastically reduced its traditional high "humidity."

Abe Kōbō (Kimifusa) was born in Tokyo in 1924 but grew up in Mukden —he was seven at the time of the "Manchurian incident"—until he returned to Tokyo to prepare to become a doctor, like his father. By 1948, when he graduated from the Medical School of Tokyo University, his father had died and he had already decided to pursue a career in literature rather than medicine. Before long he began to attract attention with stories of Kafkaesque metamorphoses into a vegetable, a cocoon, a stick, or that *sine qua non* of Japanese identity, a calling card. Although his works reveal deep social and philosophical concerns, he has remained an inventive literary experimentalist.

In Abe's most famous novel, *The Woman in the Dunes* (*Suna no onna*, 1962, tr. 1964), the laboratory for his dehumidification experiment is a sand pit; in others it is the lonely, labyrinthine city—Tokyo, any metropolis. Isolation is their common theme: in *The Face of Another* (*Tanin no kao*, 1964, tr. 1966) a horribly disfigured man wears a mask to seduce his estranged wife; the detective-hero of *The Ruined Map* (*Moetsukita chizu*, 1967, tr. 1969) loses his own familiar mask of personality as he searches through the sordid underworld of the city for a missing person; the world of *The Box Man* (*Hako otoko*, 1973, tr. 1974) is the limbo of the city's rubbish, where some try to protect themselves from the dangerous "other" by hiding under a shell of anonymity. "The city," Abe has said, "is the place where people first had to deal with the stranger who is not an enemy. I think they still have not succeeded completely."

Much of Abe Kōbō's formidable energy has been devoted to writing for stage and screen: notably, adapting *The Woman in the Dunes* and later novels for the brilliant films directed by Teshigahara Hiroshi. In recent years Abe has had his own acting company, and has himself produced and directed his daring, innovative plays. *Friends,* a tragicomic drama in thirteen scenes, is one of the most penetrating and original works of the modern Japanese theater. It was first presented in the Kinokuniya Hall, Tokyo, on March 15, 1967, in a performance directed by Naruse Masahiko.

❖ Friends

(*Tomodachi,* 1967)

MIDDLE DAUGHTER, *twenty-four years old; a trim-looking, sweet girl who gives the impression of being a crystallization of good will*

GRANDMOTHER, *eighty years old*

FATHER, *a gentleman who at first glance might be taken for a clergyman; he wears a worn but quite respectable suit and carries a briefcase*

MOTHER, *her old-fashioned hat and glasses become her*

YOUNGER SON, *he once won a prize as an amateur boxer; he carries a guitar under one arm and a suitcase in the other*

ELDER SON, *clever, but frail-looking and rather gloomy; formerly a private detective; he carries suitcases in both hands when he enters*

ELDEST DAUGHTER, *thirty years old; a prospective old maid who still preserves her dreams of being raped by some man*

MAN, *thirty-one years old; section head in a commercial firm*

YOUNGEST DAUGHTER, *a little devil, though she doesn't look it*

MIDDLE-AGED POLICEMAN

YOUNG POLICEMAN

BUILDING SUPERINTENDENT, *a woman*

FIANCÉE, *she works in the same office as* MAN; *looks like a city girl*

REPORTER, *formerly on the staff of a weekly magazine*

. . . Scene One

The curtain rises to the sweetly seductive melody of "The Broken Necklace" (music by Inomata Takeshi).

> *Night time in the big city—*
> *Now that the string is broken, the beads of the necklace*

Scatter here and scatter there
In every direction.
Poor broken necklace, where is the breast that warmed you once?
When did you leave it, where has it gone?
Little lost beads, little lost beads.

Two large, partitionlike walls meet in a "V" at the middle of the stage. Shadows of human figures, four each from left and right, appear on the walls and, to the rhythm of the music, gradually grow larger, until in the end they seem to loom like giants over the audience.

As the music comes to an end, the owners of the shadows reveal themselves from the wings on both sides. The composition of this family of eight could hardly be more average, but one senses something peculiar about its members. They move mechanically, nobody as yet showing any expression on his face.

MIDDLE DAUGHTER *steps forth from the group and advances to the center of the stage. The music should continue, but without words.*

MIDDLE DAUGHTER *(taking up the words of the song that has been heard, her voice pleading and romantic):* But we can't just leave them to their fate. We'll gather up those poor little beads. Yes, we'll gather them up and run a new string through them. *(She turns to* GRANDMOTHER.*)* We can do it, Grandma, can't we?

GRANDMOTHER *(in a completely matter-of-fact tone):* Of course we can. That's our job, isn't it?

MIDDLE DAUGHTER *(turning back to audience and continuing her previous remarks):* It's wrong for there to be lost children and lonely people. It's all wrong. But you can't make a necklace without running a string through the beads. *(She turns to* FATHER.*)* We'll be the string for the necklace. Won't we, Father?

FATHER *(with a look of having heard this before):* Don't you think I know it already, that being a string is our job?

MIDDLE DAUGHTER *(singing to the music):*

Where is the breast that warmed you once?
When did you leave it, where has it gone?
Little lost beads, little lost beads.

YOUNGEST DAUGHTER *suddenly gives a loud sneeze that stops the music.*

MOTHER: My poor darling. *(To the others, reproachfully.)* If we don't settle down somewhere soon, it'll be ten o'clock before we know it.

YOUNGER SON: That's right. *(He yawns ostentatiously.)* I for one have had enough of this gabbing.

ELDER SON *(sharply):* Don't talk like a fool. It's our job, isn't it?

ELDEST DAUGHTER *(without expression):* That's right. It's our job.

The music begins again.

MIDDLE DAUGHTER *(resuming her exalted tone):* And that's why we must go on. We must search out all the lonely people and offer them our love and friendship. We are the messengers of love who can heal their loneliness. We must sniff out the faint wisps of sadness that escape like drops of starlight from the windows of the city, and go there with our gift of joy. *(She spreads her arms open as if introducing the family to the audience.)* Yes, we are the angels of broken necklaces.

Each member of the family simultaneously shines a flashlight from below on his face and smiles timidly. The contrast with the mood of what has preceded should be as strong as possible.

Blackout.

. . . Scene Two

The partitions are drawn aside to reveal Man's room. The furniture and household accessories should all be of one color, either a reddish brown or gray.

A door leads to the kitchen at stage-right front. At stage-left rear a door leads to another room. The entrance door to the apartment is at stage-left front. Next to the door, in the hall, is a rather elaborate coat rack. (This rack will later be used as a cage; it must therefore have suitable vertical and horizontal supports.) All the furnishings, including the doors, should be simplified and abbreviated as much as possible.

MAN *sits at the desk. He wears a jacket and jiggles his leg as he telephones. The telephone is the only real object in the room.*

MAN: Well, that's about all for now. I'll call you later on to say good night . . . What? It has yellow spots? Sounds like an alley cat, doesn't it? . . . No, I'm sorry. I assure you, I have absolute confidence in your taste . . . Oh, just a second. *(He removes the receiver from his ear and listens.)* No, it wasn't anything. I can't imagine anyone coming to see me now, at this hour of the night . . . Yes, isn't that what I've been saying all along? Next payday I'd like you to move in here for good. You should have your things packed and ready by then.

The eight members of the family approach slowly and hesitantly, walking on tiptoe.

It sounds like rain? Yes, maybe it is raining. It couldn't be footsteps—it'd take too many people for that. You know, the insurance agent in the apartment below mine is a nut for poker . . . Of course the noise has nothing to do with me.

The footsteps suddenly grow louder. MAN *cocks his head and listens. The family enters from stage right and crosses stage front in a single line.* YOUNGER SON, *who has in the meantime passed his guitar to* ELDER SON, *goes past the entrance to Man's apartment, then turns back; at which all the others stop in their tracks.* FATHER *and* YOUNGER SON *stand on either side of the entrance.* FATHER *takes out a notebook and, after thumbing through the pages, compares what he finds with the name on the door. He nods and gives the signal to* MIDDLE DAUGHTER, *who is standing behind him. She comes forward and stands at the door, then knocks gently.*

MAN: Say, it's at my door! *(He glances hurriedly at his watch.)* Must be a telegram, at this hour of the night. *(*MIDDLE DAUGHTER *knocks again and he calls to other side of the door.)* I'll be with you in a minute! *(The family is visibly relieved. He speaks into the telephone.)* I'll go out and have a look. I'll call you later. Here's a kiss. *(He makes a noise with his lips and puts down the telephone.)*

. . . Scene Three

GRANDMOTHER, *having slipped around from behind* MIDDLE DAUGHTER, *peeps through the keyhole. She sees* MAN *coming to the door.*

GRANDMOTHER: My goodness—what a handsome man!

FATHER: Shhh! *(He takes* GRANDMOTHER *by her sleeve and pulls her back.)*

MAN: Who is it? Who's there?

MIDDLE DAUGHTER *(in a girlish voice):* Excuse me, please. I'm sorry to bother you so late.

MAN: Who is it, please? *(He is disarmed to discover the visitor is a young woman, but is all the more suspicious.)*

MIDDLE DAUGHTER: I'm so sorry. I intended to come earlier.

MAN *shakes his head doubtfully, but eventually yields to curiosity and opens the door a little. Instantly* YOUNGER SON *inserts his foot into the opening.* FATHER *takes the doorknob and pulls the door open. The family, moving into action, assembles before the door.* MAN, *dumfounded, stands rooted.*

MIDDLE DAUGHTER: Oh, that's a relief! You hadn't gone to bed yet, had you?

FATHER *(in the tone of an old friend):* Of course not! The young folks these days are night owls, all of them.

MOTHER *(pushing* GRANDMOTHER *from behind):* Shall we go inside, Grandma? The night air is bad for you.

MAN *(his voice choked):* Who are you, anyway?

GRANDMOTHER *(ignoring* MAN *and starting to go in):* Oh, dear, it's pretty bare, isn't it?

ELDEST DAUGHTER *(exhibiting strong curiosity):* What do you expect? It's a bachelor apartment, after all.

MIDDLE DAUGHTER: That's right. And that's why it's so important somebody come and help him.

MAN *(baffled):* Just a minute, please. I wonder if you haven't got the wrong party.

ELDER SON *(with a melancholy smile):* I used to work for a detective agency, you know.

MAN: But still—

YOUNGEST DAUGHTER: I'm cold.

MOTHER: Poor darling. You'll take an aspirin and get to bed early.

MOTHER, *her arms around* YOUNGEST DAUGHTER, *propels* GRANDMOTHER *into the apartment.* MAN *tries to prevent her, but* YOUNGER SON *sees an opening and darts inside.*

MAN: What do you mean, breaking in, without even taking off your shoes?

YOUNGER SON: Oh—sorry. *(He removes his shoes.)*

The family takes advantage of Man's distraction to surge into the apartment in one wave. FATHER, *the last in, shuts the door behind him and turns the key.* MAN, *in face of the concerted action of the eight of them, is powerless to resist. The members of the family scatter around the room with a kind of professional competence, neatly surrounding* MAN. *They flash at him their usual bashful smiles. They seem to have got the better of him.*

MAN: What's the big idea? It's enough to give a man the creeps.

FATHER *(unruffled):* Please, I beg you, don't get so upset.

MAN: If you've got some business with me, how about explaining exactly what it is?

FATHER: It puts us in an awkward position if you're going to turn on us that way . . . *(He looks around from one to another of the family as if enlisting their support.)*

MAN *(excitedly):* Puts you in an awkward position! You break in, without warning, on a total stranger, and you say it puts you in an awkward position! I'm the one who has something to complain about.

ELDER SON *(taps on the wall):* Pretty good! The walls have been soundproofed.

ELDEST DAUGHTER: It's freezing in here. Doesn't he have an electric heater, I wonder.

MAN *(unable to take any more):* Stop loitering around my apartment! All of you, get out of here! Now!

YOUNGER SON *(coolly):* Why, I feel as if we weren't wanted.

MAN: That's not surprising, is it? Of all the crassness!

YOUNGEST DAUGHTER *peeps into the back room.*

YOUNGEST DAUGHTER: Look, there's another room here.

GRANDMOTHER: It won't be easy dividing the space with only two rooms for nine people. *(She goes up beside* YOUNGEST DAUGHTER *and examines the other room with her.)*

MIDDLE DAUGHTER: We can't be fussy, you know. We didn't come here for our amusement.

MAN *stands at the door to the back room, blocking it. He is bewildered and uneasy.*

MAN: Out with all of you, and right now! If you refuse to go, I'll charge you with trespassing.

YOUNGEST DAUGHTER *(with an exaggerated show of terror):* Oh, he scares me!

MOTHER *(admonishingly):* There's nothing for you to be afraid of. He's really a very nice man. There, just look at his face. He's just pretending to frighten you, that's all.

GRANDMOTHER: That's right. He's what I'd call a handsome man. If I were only ten years younger . . .

MAN: I've had all I can stand! *(He starts to lift the telephone.)*

FATHER *(quietly restraining him):* Now calm yourself. You seem to be under some terrible misapprehension. You're making such a fuss anybody might think we intended to do you some harm.

MAN: What *do* you intend, if not to harm me?

FATHER: Why should you say such a thing?

MAN: You're in a stranger's home here.

FATHER *(with an expression of dismay):* A stranger's home?

ELDER SON *(contemptuously):* A stranger's home! He certainly takes a very narrow view of things.

MAN: But, as a matter of fact, we are strangers, aren't we?

FATHER *(soothing him):* You mustn't get so worked up over each little thing. Have you never heard the saying that being brothers marks the first step on the way to being strangers? That means, if you trace strangers back far enough you'll find they were once brothers. What difference does it make if we're strangers? A little thing like that shouldn't upset you.

MOTHER: Yes, when you get to know us better you'll see we're just so relaxed and easygoing it's positively funny. *(She laughs.)*

MAN: Don't act silly. Whatever you may think, the fact is, this is my apartment.

ELDEST DAUGHTER: That's obvious, isn't it? If it weren't your apartment, you wouldn't be here.

YOUNGER SON: And if it weren't your apartment do you suppose we'd have listened in silence all this time to your bellyaching?

MIDDLE DAUGHTER: I thought I told you to lay off him.

YOUNGER SON: I apologize. The fact is, I have a wee bit of a hangover. Damn it!

YOUNGER SON *shadowboxes briefly to cover his confusion.* MIDDLE DAUGHTER, *acting as if she has suddenly noticed it, puts out her hand to remove a bit of wool fluff from Man's jacket.* ELDEST DAUGHTER *tries to beat her to it. But* MAN *shrinks back from both of them, and neither is successful.* YOUNGEST DAUGHTER *chooses this moment to disappear into the kitchen.*

ELDEST DAUGHTER: I'm going to take off my coat, if you don't mind.

FATHER: Yes, we can't go on standing around this way indefinitely. Why don't we sit down and discuss things in a more relaxed mood?

They all remove their coats and hats. YOUNGER SON *also removes his jacket. Eldest Daughter's dress rather emphasizes her physique.*

MAN *steps forward resolutely, pushes* FATHER *aside, and picks up the telephone and dials with an air of determination.*

MAN: One, one, zero. *(He pauses, his finger inserted in the zero.)* Leave at once! Otherwise, I have only to release my finger and I'll be connected.

YOUNGER SON: To the police?

ELDEST DAUGHTER: Aren't you carrying things a bit too far?

FATHER *(perplexed)*: It's a misunderstanding . . . a complete misunderstanding.

MAN: I have no time to bandy words with you. I'll give you until I count ten, that's all. I advise you to start getting ready. *(He starts to count slowly.)*

YOUNGER SON *stands menacingly before* MAN. *He looks at the family to see whether they want him to go ahead.*

FATHER *(sharply)*: Stop! I forbid you to use violence.

MOTHER: Yes, we don't want people saying bad things about us. Stop it!

ELDER SON: How about, as a last resort, abiding by the will of the majority?

Man's attention is caught by the words "will of the majority." He slows down the speed of his counting.

ELDEST DAUGHTER: Even if we win a majority decision, it'd still be picking on someone weaker than us, wouldn't it?

ELDER SON: Don't be an idiot. The will of the majority means . . .

FATHER: Let's drop the whole matter. We know which side is going to win anyway. There aren't any thrills in this game.

GRANDMOTHER: Where might is master, justice is servant.

MIDDLE DAUGHTER *(somewhat uneasy)*: What do you intend to do, anyway?

MAN: That's what I'd like to know. When I count one more, that'll make ten.

FATHER: It can't be helped. If you think it's absolutely necessary, do whatever you think best. It won't be very pleasant, but who knows?—it may prove more effective in bringing you to your senses than repeating the same old arguments.

MAN: Don't try to intimidate me! You're prepared, I take it? I'm really phoning the police.

FATHER: Go right ahead.

MAN *(releasing his finger from the dial emphatically):* Don't say I didn't warn you!

MOTHER *(sighs):* It's true, just as they say, a child never knows its parent's love.

MIDDLE DAUGHTER *(sighs):* This is the test run.

. . . Scene Four

The telephone rings at the other end, then stops as the call is put through. The members of the family betray their tension in their expressions as they stand around the telephone. YOUNGER SON *puts a cigarette in his mouth.* GRANDMOTHER, *with an obsequious smile, tries to snatch away the cigarette, but* YOUNGER SON *brusquely pushes her hand aside and lights the cigarette.* MAN *is worked up, but he keeps himself on guard against the family.*

MAN: I'm sorry to bother you, but I've been intruded on by a crazy outfit . . . No, it's not exactly a burglary . . . But there are eight of them. I've tried in every way I know to persuade them to leave, but they absolutely refuse to listen . . . No, it's not a vendetta or anything like that. They're total strangers . . . Yes, forced entry would be about right. I suppose you could call it a kind of burglary in that sense . . . That's right, eight of them . . . I? I'm all alone . . . Will you? Sorry to bother you. The place—it's a little hard to explain. Would you mind telephoning 467–0436 and asking the superintendent for directions. That's her number. My name is Homma and I'm in Apartment 1 2 . . . No, I don't think there's any immediate danger of violence, but there's no telling under the circumstances . . . Yes, I'd appreciate that. I'll be waiting for you . . . *(He heaves a sigh and puts down the telephone.)*

ELDER SON, YOUNGER SON, *and* ELDEST DAUGHTER *smile to themselves, each with obvious satisfaction.*

FATHER *(admonishingly):* There's nothing to smile about! I'm sure he was quite in earnest in doing what he did.

ELDER SON: But how can I help smiling? Burglary, he called it! Burglary! If a cat denounced a mouse as a burglar you couldn't keep the mouse from smiling just by telling him he shouldn't.

ELDEST DAUGHTER: I realize of course he doesn't mean any harm.

YOUNGER SON *(imitating Man's voice):* Yes, sir. There are eight of them, but I am all alone.

The members of the family start giggling again.

MAN *(challenging them):* Don't be so stubborn. You still have a few minutes left before the patrol car comes. I advise you not to waste your last chance.

YOUNGEST DAUGHTER *sticks her head out from the kitchen. Her face is smeared around the mouth with something she has been eating.* GRANDMOTHER *quickly surmises what has happened.*

GRANDMOTHER: Look at that! She's been nibbling something in the kitchen.

YOUNGEST DAUGHTER *(wiping her mouth and singing out):* The menu for tonight is two bottles of milk, six eggs, a loaf of bread, one bag of popcorn, one slice of mackerel, a pickle and some relish, two slices of frozen whalemeat, salad oil, and the usual spices.

YOUNGER SON: Quite a sweet tooth, hasn't he? Is there nothing in the way of liquor?

YOUNGEST DAUGHTER: Now that you mention it, there were two bottles of beer. That's all, I think.

YOUNGER SON: That's fine. I wanted a hair of the dog that bit me. *(He claps his hands in anticipation.)*

MOTHER: You can't drink it alone. We've got to save it to drink a toast to our new friendship.

ELDER SON: It's certainly not much of a menu in any case. You could find a better selection at a roadside diner.

MIDDLE DAUGHTER: Leave worrying about dinner to me. Those ingredients are more than enough for me to make quite a decent soup. *(She goes to the kitchen.)*

MAN: At last you've shown yourselves in your true colors. Out-and-out robbery is what I'd call it. The police will be here any minute. How do you plan to explain yourselves?

FATHER *(calmly):* You'll find out soon enough, when the time comes.

MAN: What will I find out?

ELDEST DAUGHTER: There's nothing for us to explain, is there? We're not doing anything we feel especially ashamed of.

MAN: Well, can you beat that? You talk as if you have the right to install yourselves in here. On what grounds can you justify—

MOTHER *pauses in her unpacking of her suitcase.*

MOTHER: But you're all alone here, aren't you?

MIDDLE DAUGHTER *(through the kitchen door):* It's terrible being alone. It's the worst thing that can happen to anybody.

ELDEST DAUGHTER: Yes, loneliness is bad for a person. In the first place, it makes you lose all resilience.

MAN: Supposing that's true, what business is it of yours?

FATHER: We're your friends. We can't abandon you, can we?

MAN: My friends?

FATHER: Of course we are. There are millions, even tens of millions of people in this city. And all of them are total strangers . . . Everywhere you look you see nothing but strangers . . . Don't you think that's frightening? There's no getting around it, we all need friends. Friends to help us, friends to encourage us.

GRANDMOTHER: In traveling, a companion; in life, sympathy. A wonderful thing, isn't it?

YOUNGER SON *(to* FATHER*):* Can't I have just one bottle of beer?

MAN *(nearly screaming):* I've had enough! I'm quite happy being alone. I'll thank you to stop your uncalled-for meddling. I don't want your sympathy. I'm enjoying my life just the way it is.

FATHER *(hesitantly):* But in general it's true, isn't it, that lunatics claim that they alone are sane?

MAN: Lunatics?

FATHER: Forgive me. I was using the word entirely by way of a simile.

MAN: As long as you're on the subject of lunatics, the description suits you all very well.

FATHER: Of course, it's difficult to define what we mean by a lunatic.

MOTHER *sits before the mirror and begins to apply vanishing cream.*

MOTHER: Nobody actually knows himself as well as he *thinks* he does.

ELDEST DAUGHTER *(suddenly clapping her hands):* That's right! I just remembered, I know a shop where they sell neckties that would look marvelous on you. I'll take you there the next time I go.

MOTHER *(reproving):* Instead of talking about such things you'd do better if you started helping in the kitchen. My stomach is beginning to tell me I need something to eat.

ELDEST DAUGHTER *(sulking):* Lend me your nail-polish remover, will you?

GRANDMOTHER: I'm in charge of dividing up the jam!

MAN: Who the hell *are* you all anyway?

YOUNGER SON *(with an air of arrogant assurance):* I'll tell you this once and for all—the most important thing for anybody to learn is how to get along with other people. A man who can get along with other people will stay out of trouble.

ELDER SON: It has been proven statistically that most criminals are antisocial.

FATHER: Be that as it may, please trust in us, and feel secure in your trust as a passenger on a great ocean liner. I'm certain that one day you'll need us and be grateful to us.

MAN: I've had all I can stand of your high-pressure salesmanship. Of all the colossal nerve!

FATHER: But we have no choice. You consider yourself to be a human being, don't you? It stands to reason, then, that it is your privilege, and also your duty, to live in a manner worthy of a human being.

YOUNGER SON *begins to strum the melody of "The Broken Necklace" on his guitar.*

MIDDLE DAUGHTER *emerges from the kitchen and begins to sing the song, still peeling a carrot. The peel hangs down to the floor in a long, unbroken coil.*

MIDDLE DAUGHTER:

> Night time in the big city—
> Now that the string is broken, the beads of the necklace
> Scatter here and scatter there
> In every direction.
> Poor broken necklace, where is the breast that warmed you once?
> When did you leave it, where has it gone?
> Little lost beads, little lost beads.

. . . Scene Five

Two policemen are led to the door of the apartment by the SUPERINTENDENT, *who is a woman. The policemen have apparently been dropped some sort of hint by the* SUPERINTENDENT; *at any rate, they seem uncommonly lax in their demeanor.*

It may be that the SUPERINTENDENT *has been on bad terms with the* MAN, *or that she may already have been bought over by the family; or it simply may be that she is pretending to be neutral for fear of getting involved—this is not clear.*

The SUPERINTENDENT *points out the door of the Man's apartment and starts to make a hurried exit, but the* MIDDLE-AGED POLICEMAN, *with a wry smile, plucks her back by the sleeve, his gesture suggesting a man catching a bug. The* YOUNG POLICEMAN *puts his ear to the door and listens to the sounds emanating from within, consulting his wristwatch as he does so. Then, with great deliberation, he presses the bell next to the door.*

MAN *rushes to the door in response to the bell, all but knocking down the members of the family nearest to him (probably* GRANDMOTHER *and* MIDDLE DAUGHTER), *and pushes the door open. This action barely misses causing the* YOUNG POLICE-MAN *to fall on his ear.*

MAN *(flurried, but with great eagerness):* Oh, I'm sorry. Well, this will give you an idea of the situation. Come in, please, and have a look for yourself. The culprits are still holding out. I'm glad you got here in time. Oh, there are two of you? *(He notices* SUPERINTENDENT.) It's good to have you along too, to back me up. Please step right in. Don't mind about me.

The policemen and SUPERINTENDENT, *at his urging, go inside. The* MIDDLE-AGED POLICEMAN, *standing at center, runs his eyes professionally over the family. They betray no noticeable agitation. With absolute self-possession, they all stop what-ever they were doing and return the policeman's suspicious stare with smiles and nods that all but overflow with a sincerity that could only come from the heart.*

MAN *(excitedly):* They're eight of them altogether. The other one's in the kitchen.

YOUNGEST DAUGHTER *enters from the kitchen, wiping her mouth. She obviously has been nibbling again.* GRANDMOTHER *gives the girl a severe look and starts to scold, but* FATHER *and* ELDER SON *restrain her casually.*

YOUNGEST DAUGHTER: Here I am.

MOTHER: Say hello to the gentlemen.

YOUNGEST DAUGHTER *(in a childish, bashful manner):* Good evening.

MIDDLE-AGED POLICEMAN *(confused):* Hmmm. Well then, what's the offense?

MAN *(failing to catch the words):* Excuse me?

YOUNG POLICEMAN: Their offense—what specific injury have you suffered?

MAN *(indignant):* I don't have to specify, do I? You've caught them red-handed in the act.

The members of the family continue to smile, quite unperturbed. Their smiles are confident and beyond all suspicion. MAN, *however, has become so upset by the passive attitude of the policemen that he is flustered and does not seem to have become aware of the performance the family is putting on.* MIDDLE-AGED POLICE-MAN *looks as if the smile tactics of the family have got the better of him. He lowers his eyes to his notebook and reads as he speaks.*

MIDDLE-AGED POLICEMAN: According to the complaint, illegal entry has occurred on these premises.

MAN: That's it precisely!

MIDDLE-AGED POLICEMAN: In other words, even though you, the injured party, have plainly indicated to the parties responsible for the injury your wish that they not intrude into your apartment . . .

MAN: Naturally I've indicated it.

MIDDLE-AGED POLICEMAN: . . . the offenders have brutally ignored or resisted the wishes of the injured party . . .

MAN: Ignored is a mild word for it.

MIDDLE-AGED POLICEMAN: Have you got any proof?

MAN: Proof?

YOUNG POLICEMAN: Have you any evidence of violence a doctor might be able to put in a medical certificate—broken bones or bruises?

MAN *(losing his temper):* I don't need any such evidence. All you have to do is look. They're eight against one.

MIDDLE-AGED POLICEMAN *(considers this seriously):* Eight against one and not a single bone broken? That makes it a little harder to prove violence, doesn't it?

MAN *does not speak and the* YOUNG POLICEMAN *lets his glance run over the smiling faces of the members of the family.*

YOUNG POLICEMAN *(to* MIDDLE-AGED POLICEMAN*):* The question would seem to arise, rather, why the complainant should have conceived such hostility toward these people—his motives, I mean.

MAN *(dumfounded)*: Do you suspect *me?*

MIDDLE-AGED POLICEMAN: It's not that we *suspect* you. But complaints lodged over private, family matters often create a lot of trouble for us.

MAN *(in earnest)*: This is preposterous. These people are complete strangers!

The members of the family, exchanging glances, smile sadly; one or two rub their chins as much as to say, "There he goes again!" and others wink at the policemen, enlisting their support. All remain silent as before.

MIDDLE-AGED POLICEMAN *(to* YOUNG POLICEMAN*)*: What are we to do about this, anyway?

YOUNG POLICEMAN *(to* MAN*)*: I'd be glad to offer my services in helping to patch up the difficulties amicably.

MAN *(almost writhing with impatience)*: Why can't you accept what I say? I tell you I have absolutely no connection with these people. It doesn't make sense to talk of patching up our difficulties amicably.

YOUNG POLICEMAN: That's a little hard to believe.

MIDDLE-AGED POLICEMAN: Have you any positive evidence that these people are strangers, as you claim?

MAN: Why don't you ask them?

The members of the family maintain their smiles intact. They even contrive to mingle a subtle suggestion of embarrassment in their smiles, exactly as if they were sympathizing with the policemen's predicament, or feeling embarrassment themselves over the deranged behavior of one of their own family.

MIDDLE-AGED POLICEMAN: That won't be necessary. I think I've got a pretty good idea of the essential points. It's my conclusion that there has been no injury to speak of.

MAN *(so enraged he stammers)*: I'm disgusted. What more can I say to convince you? . . . And if you go on insisting that there has been no injury, even after what's happened, well, there's nothing left for me to say.

MIDDLE-AGED POLICEMAN: Excuse me for mentioning it, but you wouldn't be suffering from a persecution complex, would you?

MAN *(to* SUPERINTENDENT*)*: You can tell them, ma'am, can't you? You know I'm the one who's always paid the rent. And the name—the apartment is registered in my name, and letters are delivered regularly here to me, under my name. That's right, isn't it? This is my apartment. There's no doubt about it. I'm the only one with any rights here. That's correct, isn't it? You can surely vouch for me, can't you?

SUPERINTENDENT *(irritated)*: Well, I can't say for sure.

MAN: You can't say for sure?

SUPERINTENDENT: I've always made it my practice, as long as a tenant pays the rent promptly each month, never to butt into his private life.

MAN: But at least I can ask you to vouch for the fact that I am the tenant.

SUPERINTENDENT: I'd rather not go into such things, but you know, in a place like this the person living in an apartment isn't always the same as the person who pays the rent.

MIDDLE-AGED POLICEMAN: I can imagine.

SUPERINTENDENT: Take the case of a young, unmarried woman, living alone . . .

At once FATHER *and* YOUNGER SON *react, but they restrain each other and instantly revert to the virtuous smiles they have displayed up to now.* GRANDMOTHER *begins to search the desk drawer.*

MIDDLE-AGED POLICEMAN: Hmmm. I see.

SUPERINTENDENT: In extreme cases we may be sent money orders without even the sender's name.

MAN *(furious):* But I . . . I signed and sealed the contract, didn't I?

MIDDLE-AGED POLICEMAN: Come, now. You mustn't get so excited. Of course I understand your problem, but if there's no injury worth reporting at this stage . . .

MAN: But it's illegal entry, isn't it? It's trespassing, isn't it?

YOUNG POLICEMAN: We always ask the concerned parties in such private disputes to try to settle them among themselves. The police have their hands full as it is, what with the shortage of men.

MAN: I've told you, haven't I, these people are total strangers.

MIDDLE-AGED POLICEMAN: Well, in the event you suffer any specific injuries, please don't hesitate to get in touch with us again. *(He winks to the family, as much as to say that he has sized up the situation perfectly.)* It doesn't look as if I can write a charge—it won't make a case. I'm sorry to have bothered you all.

MOTHER *(as if the thought has suddenly struck her):* Oh, are you leaving so soon? And to think I haven't even offered you so much as a cup of tea.

MIDDLE-AGED POLICEMAN: Please don't bother.

MAN *(utterly bewildered):* But . . . just a second . . . what do you mean by . . . I've never heard of such a damned stupid . . . What am I going to . . . It's crazy. No matter how you look at it.

The SUPERINTENDENT *and the policemen ignore* MAN, *who runs after them as if to implore their help. They go out very quickly and shut the door behind them. Once outside, they exchange sarcastic grimaces and exit at once.*

. . . Scene Six

YOUNGER SON *strikes a chord on his guitar, as if by way of a signal. The smiles that seemed to have been imprinted on the eight faces of the family are instantly replaced by their normal expressions.*

FATHER *(consolingly):* That, my friend, is what people mean when they talk of good, common sense.

ELDER SON: Good, common sense, and at the same time, accomplished fact.

GRANDMOTHER: The proof of the pudding is in the eating.

ELDEST DAUGHTER: It seems to come as quite a shock to him. He's still standing there in a daze.

MOTHER: It'll do him good to have such an experience once.

YOUNGEST DAUGHTER: I don't understand him. Why, even a child knows how lonely it is to be without friends.

YOUNGER SON: His whole outlook's warped. He's bluffing, that's all.

MIDDLE DAUGHTER: I wish it wouldn't take him so long to understand what a miserable thing loneliness is, and how lucky he is to have us . . . *(She seems to be addressing herself to* MAN *only. She wraps the long peel from the carrot around her neck.)*

MAN *(suddenly turning on her):* I've had all I can stand of your meddling.

FATHER *(as if reasoning with himself):* It's certainly irritating, but this is no time to lose my temper. Patient care is the only way to treat the sick.

MIDDLE DAUGHTER: Would you like a glass of water?

MAN *(unmoved):* Stop bothering me! I swear, I'll get rid of you, if it's the last thing I do. You can make up your minds to that! I tell you I won't stand being humiliated this way!

MIDDLE DAUGHTER *(unwrapping the carrot peel around her neck):* If we don't do something about it, the broken necklace will never be the same again. Isn't there anything we can do to convince him of our sincerity?

ELDEST DAUGHTER: Humpf. Such exquisite sensitivity!

MIDDLE DAUGHTER *(with an abrupt shift of mood):* Don't act so sour!

FATHER: Now, now—don't forget, anybody who creates dissension or starts a quarrel must pay a fine.

GRANDMOTHER *(still rummaging through the desk, but her tone is magnanimous):* It's a long lane that has no turning . . . There's nothing worth making a fuss over.

MIDDLE DAUGHTER *(to* YOUNGEST DAUGHTER*):* Come on, help me in the kitchen.

GRANDMOTHER *(sharply):* This time don't do any nibbling on the sly. It's disgraceful.

YOUNGEST DAUGHTER *sticks out her tongue, then exits with* MIDDLE DAUGHTER.

MAN (*suddenly becoming aware of Grandmother's suspicious activities*): It's all very well for you to talk, but what are you doing there, anyway?

GRANDMOTHER: I was just looking for a cigarette.

MAN: Cut it out! Stop acting like a sneak thief!

GRANDMOTHER (*with exaggerated dismay*): Oh—I'm a sneak thief, am I?

FATHER: Of course you're not a sneak thief. I ask you all to refrain from making remarks that might cast aspersions on anyone else's character.

ELDER SON: How about setting a fine of a hundred yen on any remark which is decided by majority vote to be offensive?

FATHER: An excellent suggestion. Yes, that appeals to me. There's no such thing as being too discreet when it concerns a person's character, is there?

GRANDMOTHER (*more engrossed than ever in her search for cigarettes*): Imagine calling me a sneak thief! A cigarette only turns to smoke, no matter who smokes it.

MAN: Stop rummaging that way through my desk!

MAN, *thinking he will stop* GRANDMOTHER, *steps forward automatically, only for* ELDER SON *to stick out his foot and trip him.* MAN *flops down magnificently.*

ELDER SON: Oops—excuse me!

The family at once rushes over to MAN *in a body and surrounds him, lifting him to his feet, massaging his back, brushing the dust from his suit, and otherwise showering him with extreme attentions.*

ELDEST DAUGHTER: Are you sure you're all right?

MOTHER: You haven't hurt yourself?

YOUNGER SON: Can you stand okay?

GRANDMOTHER: No pain anywhere?

FATHER: No broken bones?

MAN (*freeing himself*): Lay off, for God's sake!

ELDER SON (*apologetically*): I'm sorry. I was just worried you might get so carried away by your feelings you would resort to violence.

MAN: Wouldn't you describe what you did as violence?

ELDER SON: Not in the least. It was a precaution against violence.

YOUNGER SON (*cheerfully*): We won't let you get away with that! Allowing yourself to get involved in a quarrel is just the same as starting one. You'll have to pay a fine. Or would you rather make amends in kind?

ELDER SON (*dejectedly*): I don't have to tell you how hard up I am for money.

ELDEST DAUGHTER: But even if he prefers to make amends in kind, it won't be easy. How can anybody trip himself?

YOUNGER SON: Can't you think of anything better to do than butt into other people's business? Do you plan to go on removing nail polish forever? It's just a matter of time before you dissolve your fingertips. (*To* MAN.) I wonder if you'd mind tripping my brother back?

MAN *(angrily):* Don't be an idiot!

YOUNGER SON: It can't be helped, then. I'll take over as your substitute.

As soon as YOUNGER SON *finishes speaking he gets up and deftly trips* ELDER SON, *who tumbles over with a loud groan.* YOUNGER SON *at once drags* ELDER SON *to his feet, only to trip him again, without allowing him an instant's respite. He repeats this a third time, and is about to trip him a fourth time when* MAN, *unable to endure any more, cries out.*

MAN: That's enough, for God's sake!

MOTHER *(relieved):* At last, he's forgiven you.

ELDER SON *(grimacing with pain and rubbing the small of his back):* Thanks.

YOUNGER SON: Well, what do you know? Perspiring seems to have relieved my hangover a little.

GRANDMOTHER *(suddenly):* I've found them! *(She clutches a package of cigarettes.)*

MAN *takes a step in her direction only to remember immediately what happened to him the last time. He stops in his tracks.* FATHER *can't quite allow* GRANDMOTHER *to get away with it and takes away the cigarettes.*

FATHER: That's going too far, Mother.

MAN: Sneaking around my desk like a cat. She's a regular cat burglar! *(He puts out his hand, expecting to get back his cigarettes as a matter of course.)*

FATHER *(withdrawing his hand, sounding surprised):* What did you just say?

MAN *does not speak.*

GRANDMOTHER: He called me a cat burglar!

FATHER: A cat burglar!

ELDER SON *(calmly):* That calls for a fine. Number one, right?

FATHER *(his voice is strained):* I see . . . Without warning, it's come to this . . . I may seem a little too much of a stickler for the rules, but if we hope to live together amicably . . .

ELDER SON: Yes, a rule's a rule . . .

ELDEST DAUGHTER *(massaging her face):* Just a minute. There's nothing to get so upset about.

GRANDMOTHER *(getting angry):* You're always trying to be different from everyone else.

ELDEST DAUGHTER *(ignoring her):* I think cats are sweet. I adore them. They're the most aristocratic of all animals.

ELDER SON: But there's a big difference between cats and cat burglars, isn't there?

ELDEST DAUGHTER: And there's also a big difference between burglars and cat burglars.

GRANDMOTHER *(excited):* Then you say I'm a cat?

ELDEST DAUGHTER: Don't be so conceited, Grandmother!

GRANDMOTHER: But that's what he said . . . He plainly called me a cat burglar.

ELDEST DAUGHTER: I'm sure he meant it as a compliment.

FATHER: Now wait, please. The meaning is quite different, depending on whether the emphasis was on burglar or on cat. In other words, did he mean a cat that resembled a burglar, or a burglar that resembled a cat?

GRANDMOTHER: I don't care what he said, I'm not a cat.

YOUNGER SON: That's so, I guess. If you were a cat, Grandma, that'd make us all half-breed cats.

FATHER: Therefore the logical meaning must be a catlike burglar.

ELDER SON: That rates a fine, doesn't it?

ELDEST DAUGHTER *(persisting):* Why should it? He didn't say she was a burglar plain and simple, but a catlike burglar.

ELDER SON: But a burglar's a burglar. The only difference is whether or not the word has an adjective before it.

GRANDMOTHER *(moaning):* I'm not a burglar!

ELDEST DAUGHTER: Do you mean to say that applying a different adjective doesn't change the meaning of a word? Well, that's the first I've ever heard of *that* argument! If a big fish and a little fish, a sunny day and a cloudy day, a decrepit old man and a snotty-faced kid, a brand-new car and an old buggy, a smiling face and a crying face all amount to the same thing, then there's no distinction either between a burglar man and a burglarized man. I've never heard such a funny story.

YOUNGER SON: It looks as if you've lost the first round, Brother. Eh?

ELDER SON: A woman's superficial cleverness, that's all it is.

ELDEST DAUGHTER *(assertively):* A cat is a superb animal.

MOTHER *(indifferently):* I don't like cats.

ELDEST DAUGHTER *(her tone is extremely objective):* They say that a dislike of cats is the mark of an egoist.

YOUNGEST DAUGHTER *(sticking her head in from the kitchen):* But people who don't like cats often act like them.

YOUNGER SON: You don't say! That's not bad, you know.

MOTHER *(to* YOUNGEST DAUGHTER*):* Children should be seen and not heard.

YOUNGEST DAUGHTER: Hurry up and help us in the kitchen.

ELDEST DAUGHTER: I have more important things to do. We're having a serious discussion.

GRANDMOTHER: Anyway, I'm not a cat.

ELDEST DAUGHTER *(her tone becoming hysterical):* Stop it, won't you? I can't stand you speaking so sneeringly about cats.

MAN *(finally having had all he can take):* Won't you drop the whole thing, for pity's sake? I can settle this by paying a hundred yen—right? It's too ridiculous. *(He starts to look in his pockets for his wallet.)*

ELDEST DAUGHTER *(coquettishly):* Oh? But that's cheating . . . After I went to all the trouble of taking your side . . .

FATHER *(recovering himself):* That's right. You don't leave us much to say if you're going to talk in such extremes . . . We still haven't reached any conclusion, after all . . . The situation has become unexpectedly complicated.

MAN: What's so complicated? *(He continues to search his pockets.)*

FATHER: I meant merely that our opinions continue to be opposed.

ELDEST DAUGHTER: Yes. You must remember you aren't alone any more. There's someone on your side. Anyway, cats are absolutely marvelous animals.

MOTHER: But I don't like them.

GRANDMOTHER: I told you I wasn't a cat!

FATHER: There you have the problem.

MAN: What difference does it make? The long and short of it is that I have to pay a fine. Right?

FATHER: But the basic principle of communal living is respect for the opinions of each person.

MAN *(his voice dropping sarcastically):* Is that so? I'm delighted to hear it. I'll be sure to remember that. *(He is still unable to find his wallet, and begins to look rather worried. He takes his coat from its hook on the wall and starts to search the pockets.)*

FATHER *(to the others):* What do you say, all of you? Wouldn't this be a good point to try to put some order into the discussion? Now, if you'll permit me to express my opinion, the question, it seems to me, is whether the animal known as the cat—when, for example, it is compared with the dog . . .

ELDEST DAUGHTER: There's no comparison!

YOUNGER SON: Still, nobody ever talks of a dog burglar.

ELDEST DAUGHTER: That's because dogs are stupid.

ELDER SON: That's a lie.

ELDEST DAUGHTER: What do you know about it?

ELDER SON: There are police dogs, but I've never heard of police cats.

ELDEST DAUGHTER: Of course not. Cats have a higher social status.

MOTHER: But, it seems to me, cats are lazy.

YOUNGER SON: Wait a second. Hard workers don't necessarily get very far.

ELDEST DAUGHTER: That's precisely it.

YOUNGER SON: But if you'll permit me to express my own preferences, I like dogs better.

ELDEST DAUGHTER: They certainly suit you. Let sleeping dogs lie. Go to the dogs. Lead a dog's life . . .

YOUNGER SON: Don't be too sure of yourself with cats, you caterwauling, cat-calling, caterpillar . . .

ELDEST DAUGHTER: Every dog has his day.

YOUNGER SON: Catnip is to a cat as cash to a whore in a cathouse.

ELDEST DAUGHTER: Dog eat dog. Die like a dog. Dog in the manger.

ELDER SON: You see—friends and foes are all confused. A majority decision is the only way, Father.

MAN: I wish you'd drop the whole thing. A majority decision! *(He is still searching frantically.)*

ELDER SON: At this rate we'll never get to eat dinner.

MIDDLE DAUGHTER *(emerging from the kitchen with a frying pan in her hand):* Sorry to keep you waiting. Dinner will be ready in just a few minutes. Sis, please help me dish out the food.

MAN *(pauses in his search, with vehemence):* Dinner—of all the crazy nonsense! What crass nerve, here, in my house! Listen, I warn you, I intend to use every means at my disposal to obstruct anything you do. *(To* MIDDLE DAUGH-TER.*)* Get rid of that mess. Throw it in the garbage can, now!

MIDDLE DAUGHTER *(recoiling):* But that would be a terrible waste!

FATHER *(looks into the frying pan):* Mmm. It certainly smells good.

ELDER SON: I'm convinced that food is meant to be eaten with lots of company. Nothing is drearier than shoveling in a quick meal. I can tell you that from my own personal experience.

MAN: Unfortunately, there are some people whose temperament is such that they prefer to live alone.

ELDER SON: Well, I can see that once you've argued yourself into a point of view you'd want to stick to it.

While they are talking MIDDLE DAUGHTER *exits.*

ELDEST DAUGHTER: My sister used to take a course in cooking. *(At last she gets up and starts toward the kitchen.)*

GRANDMOTHER *(to* ELDEST DAUGHTER*):* I'm in charge of dividing up the jam.

ELDEST DAUGHTER: It's quite something to have been able to make a curry with the ingredients she had. *(She exits.)*

YOUNGER SON *(stifling a yawn):* I feel more like sleeping than eating now . . . My hangover is beginning to take its toll.

GRANDMOTHER: I'm no good without my food. I can't get to sleep without first putting my tapeworm to bed.

MAN *(strangely self-possessed):* In that case, you should stay awake all the time. Stay awake for years, or maybe dozens of years, as long as you like. I warned you, didn't I, that I intend to do everything in my power to obstruct you? That wasn't an empty threat. I assure you I intend to carry it out. I'll make sure you don't get to eat even a slice of bread.

GRANDMOTHER: Why won't we?

ELDER SON *(with a faint smile):* He talks exactly as if he's turned into a magician or something, doesn't he?

MAN *(walking toward the kitchen):* You're going to laugh on the wrong side of your faces!

MOTHER *(to the people in the kitchen, in a casual voice):* You've put away everything harmful, haven't you?

MIDDLE DAUGHTER *(from the kitchen):* Of course we have. I've hidden everything —the tile cleanser, the rat poison, the cockroach spray. They're in a safe place.

YOUNGER SON *(in a loud voice):* It might be a good idea, while you're at it, to stow away the detergents and soap powder too.

MIDDLE DAUGHTER: Right.

MAN *stops in his tracks in dumb confusion at the kitchen door.*

ELDER SON: You see! He intended to use one of them.

YOUNGER SON *(to MAN):* You planned to use a spray to squirt foam over the dinner, didn't you?

FATHER *(a consoling expression on his face):* For good or for evil, everybody tends to think, more or less, along the same lines.

YOUNGER SON: Foam—that reminds me—beer! *(As if appealing for sympathy he looks up at ceiling.)*

While the preceding conversation has been going on, MOTHER *has at last finished removing her makeup. She puts away her beauty aids and, rising to her feet, turns to face the others. All of a sudden she takes hold of her hair and pulls up, to reveal she is wearing a wig. She blows into the wig, fans it with her hand, and after shaking it out thoroughly, puts it back on her head.*

MOTHER *(to MAN, with an artificial laugh):* You don't mind, do you? You're not a stranger any more, after all. *(Abruptly changing her tone.)* By the way, what ever happened to the fine we were talking about?

FATHER *(perplexed):* We didn't seem to be able to reach any conclusion in our discussion of cats, and the person in question doesn't seem very enthusiastic about a majority decision.

MAN *(searching frantically through all his pockets, and even in the cuffs of his trousers, with an intense display of determination):* I'll pay, I tell you. You don't suppose I want to be in your debt for a mere hundred yen! I'm paying, not because I recognize I was at fault, but simply because I don't feel like arguing over anything so extremely stupid.

The attention of the entire family is at last attracted by his distraught actions, and they observe him carefully. MAN *suddenly stops searching, as if he found what he was looking for.*

MAN: Damn it! That's funny . . .

MOTHER: Was it your wallet? Or do you carry your money loose?

MAN: I carried it in a wallet with my monthly pass . . . I can't imagine . . .

The glances of the others converge at the same moment in accord on ELDER SON. *He returns their gaze. There is a moment of silence.*

ELDER SON: What's the matter with you all? Have I done something wrong?

YOUNGER SON *(crooking his index finger to suggest a robber with a gun)*: Did you
do it, Brother?

ELDER SON *(with feigned innocence)*: What are you talking about, anyway?

FATHER *(uneasily)*: It's not true, is it? I'm sure you wouldn't stoop to that sort
of thing . . . At a critical moment like this we must, above all, show the
greatest respect for the integrity of the individual.

YOUNGER SON: But he's got a criminal record, you know.

ELDER SON: Stop it! You're ruining my reputation!

*At this juncture the people in the kitchen begin to stick out their heads and observe
what is going on.*

YOUNGER SON: Everybody of course has committed youthful indiscretions.

ELDER SON: Haven't I told you I've completely given up all that?

MOTHER: Please. Look into Mother's eyes. Yes, look straight into my eyes.

ELDER SON: I've come back to you, haven't I? You can see that I have . . . I learned,
so well it hurt me, how wonderful it is when people can trust one another
and what a blessing it is when people who trust one another can live
together. So I came back to you, from that horrible world where every man
is a stranger . . . Do you think I'd betray you all? No, stop it, please . . . As
far as I'm concerned, the one thing that makes life worth living is being
together, hand in hand.

GRANDMOTHER *(apparently unimpressed)*: You aren't trying to make us cry, are
you?

ELDER SON: I'm serious, I assure you.

YOUNGER SON: I'll bet if ever I tried to lie seriously I could really warm up to it.

ELDER SON *(uncertain how he should react to this comment, betraying his confusion momentarily)*: I understand the situation perfectly . . . And I'm glad
. . . I don't feel in the least offended. I'm flattered you should retain such
a high opinion of my former skill.

MOTHER *(brooding)*: Then, you mean . . .

ELDER SON: I leave it to your imagination.

FATHER *(embarrassed)*: That won't do . . . You, better than anyone else, are in
the position to put the matter straight. How can you speak of leaving it to
our imagination? I thought we had promised not to recognize private
prerogatives when it came to money.

ELDEST DAUGHTER: Yes, he himself was the first to propose that.

YOUNGER SON *(as if reading aloud)*: As previously agreed, in cases where suspicions
have been aroused with respect to monetary matters, no one, whosoever he
may be, for whatever reason, may refuse a request for a body search.

GRANDMOTHER: Love flies out the window when poverty comes in at the door.

FATHER: I can't understand it. You have the best brains of the lot of us, there's
no getting around it. And you're amenable to reason. We all depend on you.
It's intolerable that we should have to treat you like a defendant in court.

ELDER SON *(laughs):* You have nothing to worry about.

FATHER *(relieved):* Then you're innocent?

MOTHER: You should have set our minds at rest sooner.

ELDER SON: I mean, I haven't done anything that warrants a physical examination.

ELDER SON *suddenly raises his hand and reveals that he is holding Man's wallet. The following dialogue by members of the family occurs almost simultaneously.*

MOTHER: You took it, then!

ELDEST DAUGHTER: You've got to keep your eye on him every minute.

YOUNGEST DAUGHTER: Take me on as your apprentice, won't you?

YOUNGER SON: Now I know why you're never short of cigarette money.

MOTHER *(firmly):* Hand it over, here!

As MOTHER *steps forward,* MAN *springs to his feet with an incomprehensible cry and makes a grab for Elder Son's hand. The wallet instantly disappears.*

MAN *(carried away, searching Elder Son's pockets):* What've you done with it? Give it back!

ELDER SON: Oh, you're tickling me! *(He holds up his hands, as before a gunman, and twists himself free.)*

MOTHER *(severely):* You know the rules, don't you? I take charge of the safe.

ELDER SON *(to* MAN*):* I surrender! If you would kindly look in the right-hand pocket of your pants . . .

MAN *doubtfully puts his hand into his pocket and with an incredulous expression he produces the wallet.*

MAN: This is it, all right.

YOUNGEST DAUGHTER *(clapping her hands):* He's a regular wizard!

MIDDLE DAUGHTER *(reproving):* You mustn't say that! You're not to admire him.

MOTHER *(to* ELDER SON, *angrily):* Haven't you done quite enough? Surely you can't have forgotten all about your own family.

MAN *(turning wallet upside down and shaking it):* Not a thing. There's not a penny in it . . . *(He stands there glaring at* ELDER SON, *grinding his teeth, for the moment unable to find even words of protest.)*

ELDER SON *(apparently enjoying it):* A pro who couldn't do that much wouldn't be worthy of the name.

MOTHER: I won't allow it—sneaking off with other people's money.

GRANDMOTHER: Like a cat burglar?

MOTHER *(to* MAN*):* How much was in it?

MAN: How should I know?

MOTHER *(to* FATHER*):* Don't just stand there, without saying anything. Don't you think it'll set a bad example if we shut our eyes to this sort of thing?

FATHER: That's right, a very bad example . . . Still, I don't understand it . . . I thought we'd thrashed the whole thing out, only to find you're still keeping secrets from us. Why do you do it? It's not like you.

MOTHER: I beg you, don't make your mother any unhappier than she already is.

ELDER SON *(blandly):* That's what you say, Mother, but were you really so confident you could fleece this guy out of his money entirely by persuasive tactics?

MOTHER: Fleece him out of his money? I was going to take custody of it!

ELDER SON *(to* MAN*):* Are you willing to let my mother take custody of your property?

MAN: Take custody of my property? She could ask till she was blue in the face and I'd still refuse!

FATHER: There's no getting around it. Money troubles are the worst cause of disharmony among friends.

MAN *(his anger returning):* Can it! You've got no reason to call me one of your friends . . . And as for taking custody of my property . . . I'm getting nauseous. You give me cold chills.

ELDER SON *(to the others):* Now you have a pretty good idea of the situation. You couldn't call him exceptionally cooperative. And he's just as attached to his money as the next man. He wants to have his cake and eat it. You'll find he's a hard customer to deal with. Supposing I hadn't used my special talents . . . I can't help being rather skeptical about whether that money would've ended up, as we hoped, in Mother's safe.

FATHER: That doesn't mean you have the right to grab it for yourself.

ELDEST DAUGHTER: That's right. Stealing a march on the rest of us is unfair.

MOTHER: I wonder if a person who always tries to get the lion's share for himself hasn't got something twisted inside him? It makes me unhappy.

YOUNGER SON *(whispering into his brother's ear):* I'll go to your defense, if you like, for a service charge of twenty percent.

ELDER SON: Don't underestimate me.

MIDDLE DAUGHTER *(hesitantly):* What do you intend to do about dinner?

GRANDMOTHER: I'm in charge of dividing up the jam.

MAN *(suddenly bursting into a rage):* Are you still yattering on about such things? To talk about dinner, in the midst of this crazy farce! Listen to me. I'm the original victim. Nobody else has a claim on my money, and I want it back. What possible difference does it make whether he takes sole possession of the money or two of you take it? It's illegal either way. The fact is, it's mine, and I'm the only one qualified to investigate what's happened to it. *(Suddenly he has an idea.)* That's right! The situation has assumed a completely new aspect. My friend, you've pulled a real blunder. You have enabled me to file a formal complaint. A flagrant act of pickpocketing has occurred. This time there's no doubt about it. Even the members of your family will testify. Well, are you going to give back my money? Or will I have to bother the police again?

FATHER: There's something in what he says . . . As things stand, your old tricks have boiled down to nothing more than theft, plain and simple.

MOTHER (sighs): You've really done a dreadful thing.

FATHER: You've ruined everything. In order to carry out our mission of spreading love for our neighbors, we ourselves must be models of neighborly love.

MIDDLE DAUGHTER steps forward, seemingly unable to bear what is happening.

MIDDLE DAUGHTER (to ELDER SON): Why don't you say something? You must've had some reason, surely? Say something. Don't just grin that way.

YOUNGER SON: There are some things about which all you can do is grin. Wouldn't you agree, Brother?

MAN: It looks as if the wolves have finally shed their sheep's clothing. The salesmen for Neighborly Love, Incorporated!

ELDEST DAUGHTER (fiercely): I'm sick of it. After all we've gone through, I don't want the bother of moving again. (To ELDER BROTHER.) I suppose you think you're the only one with the privilege of doing exactly what you please?

YOUNGEST DAUGHTER (in a low voice): There's a cold wind blowing outside.

GRANDMOTHER: I don't understand it. What devil got into him that he should have done such a thing?

ELDER SON (his expression becomes severe): Your own shortcomings don't seem to bother you.

FATHER (soothing him): Believe me, I understand what you've been going through . . . I understand perfectly . . . I'm sure you need more pocket money . . . You'd like to lead a more cheerful life . . . But you must recognize the eternal law that happiness which is for yourself alone is certainly not true happiness . . .

ELDER SON: I am gradually losing my amiability.

MOTHER: The brazen nerve of the thief!

ELDER SON: But, Mother, haven't I been following the ideal of neighborly love? Anything I have is yours, and anything you have is mine . . . Aren't you overdoing it a bit when you treat me like a pickpocket or a thief?

FATHER: I understand . . . I understand perfectly.

ELDEST DAUGHTER: It doesn't help much, no matter how well you understand him. We're the ones who suffer in the end.

ELDER SON: You wouldn't be jaundiced because you can't do as much yourself?

ELDEST DAUGHTER flares up; FATHER quiets her with a gesture.

FATHER: Depending on the end, a certain leeway is permitted in the means. But the fundamental thing, of course, is the end. Neighborly love is a splendid ideal, but if it is only an ideal, it's a little too abstract, isn't it? Why don't we think it through together? What is the common end we all share?

ELDER SON: I wonder if any of you know how many times altogether I have been insulted in the course of this argument?

FATHER: "Insulted" is an exaggeration. It distresses me to have you take it that way. My only hope was that I might rouse you somehow from your errors.

ELDER SON: Would you like to know? Don't be too surprised—fifty-three times!

YOUNGER SON: Fifty-three times? That's a little too precise!

ELDER SON: I assure you, there's been no padding. I made a careful count.

ELDEST DÁUGHTER: Isn't that silly? He has nothing better to do with his time, it would seem.

ELDER SON: There! That makes fifty-four times.

MOTHER: When someone of your age tramples the peace of the family underfoot, it's not surprising that he should be insulted a hundred times, or even a thousand times.

ELDER SON: Fifty-five times.

YOUNGER SON *apparently has a glimmering of what his brother has in mind.*

YOUNGER SON: Ah-hah. I'm beginning to see . . .

ELDER SON: Now it's my turn to ask you a question. What are these ends you keep talking about that seem to justify everything?

MOTHER: The family safe is one of them. *(She holds up an unusually large purse that she takes from her suitcase.)*

ELDER SON: What's this? *(He pretends to peep inside.)* Mother . . . there's quite a bulge in the pocket of that purse.

MOTHER *(surprised, looking inside the purse):* Dear me, why it's . . . *(Bewildered, she takes out a handful of bills and change.)* Oh . . . how shocking! *(She gives a forced laugh.)*

The next instant the faces of everybody present except MAN *change completely in expression. Now they are all smiling.*

YOUNGER SON: I was completely taken in, I must say.

ELDEST DAUGHTER: You certainly more than live up to your reputation.

FATHER: I have to apologize . . .

MIDDLE DAUGHTER: Oh, I'm so glad. *(She looks around the family.)* We're all good people, aren't we?

YOUNGEST DAUGHTER: I wonder if I should start practicing too. *(She flexes her fingers.)*

MOTHER: Really, it's enough to take a person aback. He was always a mischievous child, but I never expected . . . *(She removes her glasses and starts to count the money with an air of efficiency.)*

MAN: Hey! Stop it! That's my money! You can deduct the hundred yen for the fine.

ELDER SON *blocks* MAN, *who starts to make a rush for the money.*

ELDER SON: You're wasting your time. I don't suppose you noted down the numbers of the bills or marked them?

At the same time FATHER, YOUNGER SON, ELDEST DAUGHTER, YOUNGEST DAUGH-
TER, *and even* GRANDMOTHER *form a kind of defensive setup around* MOTHER.
It might be effective for YOUNGEST DAUGHTER *to brandish a cleaver.*

YOUNGER SON: You see how easy it is for trouble to arise over money.

YOUNGEST DAUGHTER: A clever burglar absolutely refuses to touch anything except cash.

MAN *(to* ELDER SON*):* Your own words prove that you yourself admit that you've
picked my pocket.

ELDER SON *(playing the innocent):* I picked your pocket? *(He turns to family.)* Did
I say anything like that?

MAN: You weren't the only one. The whole lot of you, without exception, all
admitted it.

ELDEST DAUGHTER: I don't know anything about it.

GRANDMOTHER: Do you think any grandchild of mine would ever do such a
wicked thing? I wouldn't let him, even if he tried to.

MAN: You're all in cahoots to cover up for him, aren't you? And just a minute
ago you were denouncing him so!

MOTHER *(paying no attention to the arguments around her; to* MAN*):* Tell me, how
much did you have?

MAN: I have no idea.

ELDEST DAUGHTER: Pretty careless of him not to know how much he has in his
own wallet.

MIDDLE DAUGHTER: A little carelessness makes a man more attractive.

ELDEST DAUGHTER *(darting a sidelong glance at her):* Doing your best to make
a hit with him, aren't you?

FATHER *(looking into Mother's hands):* Well, how much is there, anyway?

MOTHER *(complaining):* Not much. 5,600 yen. That's all.

FATHER *(frowns):* 5,600 yen . . .

ELDER SON: I suppose it's just before his payday.

MOTHER *(sarcastically):* I see. I'm sure that explanation suits your convenience.

ELDER SON: There's something disturbing about your tone.

MAN *(not missing the chance):* You see! You're admitting to one another that you
swiped the money from me.

FATHER: Young man, if you're going to jump to such conclusions, you'll make it
hard for all of us. People often conduct discussions on a purely hypothetical
basis.

MAN: Stop quibbling!

FATHER: Well then, shall I concede a point and admit that the money was yours?
But you don't even seem to know the amount of this valuable commodity.
Don't you realize that the world is swarming with sinister people who have
their eye on other people's wallets? The thought of it makes me shudder.

MAN: Wouldn't you yourselves qualify without any trouble for membership in that gang of sinister people?

FATHER: Don't be absurd! We've acted entirely out of good will. We felt it our duty to protect your money by taking custody of it.

MAN *(excitedly)*: What right have you anyway . . . without even asking me . . .

FATHER *(emphatically)*: It's a duty, a *duty*. I have no intention of insisting on any rights.

MIDDLE DAUGHTER *(heatedly)*: Yes. It's true even of companies—they're all making mergers and amalgamations, aren't they? And the same thing applies to human beings too, I'm sure. Two is better than one, three is better than two. The more people put their strength together, the more . . .

GRANDMOTHER: Little drops of water, little grains of sand, make the mighty ocean . . .

MOTHER *(still looking suspiciously at* ELDER SON*)*: But there's only 5,600 yen altogether. That won't last for two days, feeding nine people.

ELDER SON *(angrily)*: You talk just as if it were my fault.

MOTHER: I didn't mean it that way.

ELDER SON: After I tried to be smart, and save you some trouble . . . *(In a self-mocking tone.)* This is what they mean when they talk of a man who's fallen so low in the world his artistic accomplishments learned in happier days are his only support.

FATHER *(trying to save the situation)*: What do you mean? Haven't we all been praising your skill, without uttering so much as a word of complaint?

ELDER SON *(going up to* MOTHER*)*: If that's the case, I wish you'd stop giving me that look.

MOTHER *(turning aside and wiping her glasses)*: It's a lot harder than you suppose, trying to make ends meet for a family of nine . . .

ELDER SON *(sits beside* MOTHER*)*: I *do* understand, Ma. But I wanted you, if nobody else, to believe in me. In the course of less than ten minutes I was insulted fifty-five times . . . and that by the people I trusted most in the whole world, my own family . . . It was painful, I tell you.

MOTHER *(hesitantly)*: Talking that way won't do any good . . .

ELDER SON *(ignoring her; to* MAN*)*: Payday in your company must come the day after tomorrow or the next day, doesn't it?

MAN *is taken by surprise. He is unable either to affirm or deny this.*

ELDER SON *(standing abruptly; speaking as he goes away from* MOTHER*)*: So you see, Ma, there's no need for you to worry over such a paltry sum of money, is there? If people can't live a little more expansively . . .

MOTHER *(with an expression that suggests she hasn't grasped the situation very well)*: I know, but no matter how much money you have, it always seems to sprout wings and fly away. *(Suddenly noticing something.)* Ohh . . . it's gone!

FATHER: What's gone?

MOTHER *(to* ELDER SON*)*: You've done it again, haven't you? *(As she stands a 100 yen coin drops from her lap.)*

ELDER SON, *flashing the bills ostentatiously, folds them and puts them in his pocket.*

ELDER SON: Received with thanks the sum of 5,500 yen, representing fines collected from all of you for those fifty-five insults. Look, Ma, the missing hundred yen coin dropped on the floor. That's his share of the fine *(points at* MAN*)*. It's wonderful how exactly the accounts have balanced.

They all stand motionless, too dumfounded to say a word. A fairly long pause.

MOTHER *(her voice is like a moan)*: Dreadful, dreadful . . .

ELDER SON *(perfectly self-possessed)*: Words, like chickens, come home to roost. *(Turns back to* MAN*.)* I hope it's been a good lesson for you too. Now you know how severe the penalty is for betraying another person's trust . . . But of course, I owe this extra income all to you. It's too late today, but I'll treat you to a drink, tomorrow if you like. There's nothing to feel squeamish about. I got the money completely legally . . . You see, nobody can say a word against it . . . Yes, it really serves as an object lesson.

MAN *(suddenly shouting)*: Get out of here! I'll give you the money, only get out of here, now! If it's not money you want, I'll give you anything else, only go!

YOUNGEST DAUGHTER *(playfully)*: Do you really mean it?

GRANDMOTHER *(hurrying to the kitchen)*: The jam is for me. You promised from the start.

MAN: Go ahead. Take anything you like. Only go.

They begin to take their pick of the things in the room excitedly. But nobody as yet does anything positive.

YOUNGER SON: He's certainly become a lot more generous, hasn't he?

ELDEST DAUGHTER: Do you mind if I look in the other room?

MAN: Go right ahead. Don't mind me. If you'd like the rats in the ceiling, you can have them too. But all this is on one condition—you leave at once. I'll give you five—no, ten minutes, that's the limit. I won't make allowances for even one minute beyond the deadline.

FATHER *(timidly)*: I appreciate your kind intentions, but I wonder if two different questions aren't involved?

MAN: Two different questions?

FATHER: Your offer to turn over all your possessions to us, without holding anything back, is more than we dared hope for. That is precisely the way that true communal living is to be brought about . . . But when you tell us that in return we must leave you, aren't you guilty of something like a logical contradiction?

MIDDLE DAUGHTER: That's right. Living together is what gives meaning to the act of sharing.

YOUNGER SON: What's yours is mine, what's mine is yours.

ELDEST DAUGHTER: You smell of liquor!

YOUNGER SON: That's why I've been pleading with you to let me have a quick pick-me-up.

MAN *(turning on* FATHER*):* You can't have forgotten it was you yourself who claimed you respect the wishes of the individual.

FATHER: Of course I respect them. But you're not the only individual, are you?

MOTHER *(to nobody in particular):* If you ask me, there's nothing here anybody'd want. The place lacks the bare necessities. It'd take a bit of doing even to make it habitable.

MAN: This is *my* apartment!

ELDER SON *(coldly):* This is the apartment *we've* chosen.

YOUNGER SON *(trying on Man's shoes, which have been left at the entrance):* Well, what do you know? These shoes fit me perfectly!

MAN *suddenly kneels on the floor. His voice, completely altered, sounds pathetic.*

MAN: Please, I beg you. Please don't torture me any more . . . Of course I understand it's all a joke—it is one, isn't it—but I'm exhausted . . . I just don't feel like joking . . . Maybe something I've said has offended you, but please, I beg you, leave me here alone.

MAN, *continuing to kneel, bows his head, like a victim awaiting his sentence.*

The members of the family, struck speechless, exchange glances. But their expressions are not merely of surprise—heartfelt sympathy and pity seem to have shaken them.

FATHER: Stand up please, young man. *(He places his hand on Man's elbow and helps him to his feet, then dusts his knees.)* It's embarrassing for us if you're going to act that way. Our only wish is to promote your happiness in whatever way we can, to serve you somehow . . . That's what first led us to come here.

ELDER SON: Or, it occurs to me, you may have subjectively interpreted our actions as being in some way opposed to your wishes—clearly, a misunderstanding . . . In other words, there may exist a difference of opinion concerning means.

MIDDLE DAUGHTER *(enthusiastically):* But hasn't it become warm in here, just because we're all together this way? It feels just like spring, even without having our soup.

ELDEST DAUGHTER: Spring? It feels more like summer. Oh, it's hot! *(She removes her jacket and exposes her bare throat and arms.)*

MAN *(weakly):* But I like being alone . . .

MIDDLE DAUGHTER: Why must you say such cruel things?

YOUNGER SON *(sounds at the end of his patience):* It can't be helped. Everybody's sick until his sickness gets better.

So saying, YOUNGER SON *begins to strum his guitar. The following dialogue is declaimed to the rhythm of the guitar.*

MIDDLE DAUGHTER:

>The streets are full of people,
>So full of people, they're ready to burst.

YOUNGER SON:

>But everywhere you go,
>There're nothing but strangers.

MIDDLE DAUGHTER:

>I'm still not discouraged,
>I go on searching—
>My friends, where are you now,
>My loved ones, where are you now?

ELDER SON:

>They've gone to the pinball parlor.

FATHER:

>They've gone to a bar.

MOTHER:

>To the beauty parlor or the department store.

GRANDMOTHER:

>They're eating eels and rice.

YOUNGEST DAUGHTER:

>They're riding escalators,
>They're going to an amusement park.

ELDEST DAUGHTER *(meditatively; if necessary, can be sung to music):* And I have dreams. I dream of a streetcar on tracks that stretch far, far away. A streetcar packed with people goes running away over the tracks. Under the weight of all those strangers packed inside, it shoots off sparks. And in the sparks thrown off by all those innumerable strangers, I am burnt to a crisp, like a little fish forgotten in the oven.

YOUNGER SON *(in a soft voice):* Like a dried sardine, with only little bones.

MIDDLE DAUGHTER:

>I'm still not discouraged,
>I go on searching.

> My shining sun, where have you gone?
> Come back and melt away my loneliness!

FATHER *(whispering confidentially to* MAN*):* That's why we've come all the way here. We heard your voice crying for help and we searched till we found you through the long dark tunnel they call other people. We wanted to bring you, if not the sun, at least the light from a glowing lump of coal.

MAN *(driven into a corner):* I never cried for help. I . . . It refreshes me to be alone.

ELDER SON: That's conceit, pure conceit! Why, in prison the thing that hits you hardest is solitary confinement. *(An expression of recollection crosses his face.)*

ELDEST DAUGHTER: I'm *completely* hopeless when I'm alone. Even when I'm left to look after the house, as soon as I'm by myself I feel as if I'll go out of my mind.

GRANDMOTHER: It's all written down in Mother Goose. Let me see, how did it go again? *(To* MOTHER.*)* You remember, don't you?

MAN: I don't interfere with other people and I don't want to be interfered with myself.

YOUNGER SON *begins to play with feeling "The Broken Necklace."* MIDDLE DAUGH-TER *sings to the tune. When they reach the second verse the telephone rings suddenly. For a moment they are all startled into attitudes of* tableaux vivants.

ELDEST DAUGHTER: Shall I answer?

MAN *(confused):* It's all right. I'll go. *(He runs to the telephone and grabs it, but he does not lift the receiver at once.)* Will you do me a favor? At least while I'm talking on the phone, will you please keep quiet?

YOUNGER SON: At least while you're talking on the phone? Have we been making so much noise?

FATHER: Shhh. *(He puts his hand to his lips and silences* YOUNGER SON.*)* Go right ahead. Don't worry about us. *(He looks to the side. At the same time the other members of the family strike poses of ostentatious indifference.)*

After another brief hesitation, MAN *resolutely lifts the receiver. But he is still worried about the family, and his voice is extremely tentative.*

MAN: Hello, yes, it's me. *(Pause.)* No, nothing special. No, I mean it, it's nothing . . . All right, then, good night . . . The day after tomorrow? It's not necessary, I tell you. There's nothing I need your help on at this stage . . . Well, good night. You're going to bed, aren't you? No, it's not that. We can talk when I see you again tomorrow.

Suddenly YOUNGEST DAUGHTER *emits a protracted strange noise in the process of stifling a great sneeze.* MAN, *alarmed, covers the mouthpiece and glares at* YOUNG-EST DAUGHTER.

FATHER: Shh!

MOTHER: Do be quiet!

YOUNGER SON: Stupid, isn't she? *(He picks up his guitar without thinking, and the guitar, bumping against something, resounds.)*

ELDER SON: You're the one that should be more careful.

YOUNGER SON: You're making more noise scolding me . . .

MAN: I beg you, stop it please!

GRANDMOTHER: I don't understand. Why do you have to act so secret? We're not hiding from the police, after all.

ELDER SON: It's from his girl.

ELDEST DAUGHTER *(reacting sharply):* His girl?

ELDER SON: I've surveyed the whole situation.

ELDEST DAUGHTER: But isn't that strange? It's a complete contradiction. After all his insisting that he prefers to be alone . . .

MAN *(desperately):* I beg you, keep quiet, please! *(Into the telephone.)* I'm terribly sorry. There was a funny noise in the kitchen . . . What? Of course I'm alone . . . A sneeze? A woman's sneeze? Don't be silly.

ELDER SON: I've never heard anything so disgraceful. Stumbling all over the place.

FATHER *(simultaneously):* Shhh!

MAN *(instantly covering the mouthpiece):* I thought I told you to please shut up.

ELDEST DAUGHTER: It may be your girlfriend, or I don't care who, but why must you keep our being here a secret? It's insulting.

MAN *(into the telephone):* Just a second, please. There's that funny noise again in the kitchen. *(He covers the mouthpiece.)* Think a minute and you'll see why. How can I possibly explain such a thing so that an outsider could understand? It's crazy . . . It'll only make things more complicated if I make a mess of explaining.

YOUNGER SON: Would you like us to explain for you?

FATHER: A good suggestion. We'll have to make it clear, sooner or later, whether we're to ask her to join us or to break with him.

ELDER SON: Making things clear is my specialty.

ELDEST DAUGHTER: It's easier for a woman to talk to another woman.

MAN *(protecting the telephone from* ELDER SON *and* ELDEST DAUGHTER, *both of whom come forward at the same time):* I give up. I surrender. But won't you please let me deal with her? In return, yes, I agree to let you stay here for tonight only. That's fair enough, isn't it? You can use any and all of my apartment, as you please . . . I promise not to interfere in any way with your meals . . . All I ask is that you keep quiet while I'm making this call.

FATHER *(looking around at the others):* He hasn't made any conditions that present special difficulties, has he?

ELDER SON *and* ELDEST DAUGHTER *(simultaneously moving back):* I suppose not.

MAN *(hastily returning to the telephone):* It wasn't anything. It must have been the wind . . . Hello . . . Hello . . . *(He realizes that the other party has hung up on him and dazedly puts down the telephone.)*

ELDEST DAUGHTER: Did she hang up on you?

MIDDLE DAUGHTER: That wasn't nice of her, was it?

MAN, *unable to say a word, crouches beside the telephone, his head in his hands.*

YOUNGEST DAUGHTER: He must really be in love with her.

MOTHER: Don't butt into grownups' affairs.

FATHER *(to* MAN*):* You know her phone number, don't you?

ELDER SON: I know it.

FATHER: Should we call and apologize?

MAN *(moaning):* I beg you, please leave things as they are.

MIDDLE DAUGHTER: Why don't you get to bed?

MOTHER: That's right. It must be about time.

MAN: I don't want you worrying about me. You don't suppose, in the first place, I could get to sleep with all the noise going on here.

FATHER: Of course we intend to retire to the other room. Come on, everybody, get ready!

Hardly has he spoken than the members of the family throw themselves into furious activity. ELDER SON *and* YOUNGER SON *take a hammock from their suitcase and suspend it.* MOTHER *and* YOUNGEST DAUGHTER *bring blankets in from the next room.* GRANDMOTHER *inflates an air pillow.* ELDEST DAUGHTER *and* MIDDLE DAUGHTER *swiftly remove Man's outer clothes. Then the whole family lifts* MAN *willy-nilly onto the hammock.* MAN *shows some resistance, but in the end proves no match for their organized activity. By the time* MAN *sits up in the hammock the family has already withdrawn to the next room. They peep in and throw* MAN *their radiant smiles.*

FAMILY *(whispering in unison):* Good night!

MIDDLE DAUGHTER *sticks out her hand and switches off the light in Man's room. The stage becomes dark with only a spotlight on* MAN. YOUNGER SON *enters on tiptoe and crosses the room on his way to the kitchen.*

YOUNGER SON *(in a low voice):* Beer!

Slow curtain.

. . . Scene Seven *(Intermission)*

The music of "The Broken Necklace" is played in the lobby during the intermission. Presently, the actress who has appeared as SUPERINTENDENT, *still dressed in the costume for the part, makes her way among the spectators, both in the lobby and in the auditorium, distributing the following leaflet.*

An Appeal . . .

Some people, it would seem, have been critical of my attitude toward the tenant in Apartment 12. Unpleasant rumors are being spread that I was bought over by the visitors or (what's worse) that I reached some sort of understanding with one or the other of the two brothers and gave him a passkey to the apartment.

I realize, having had the misfortune to lose my husband only a few years ago, there is nothing I can do about it if people, meaning to be sympathetic, say, "She must've needed money," or "She must've been lonely." But I will take an oath that I am speaking the absolute truth when I say that the first time I ever laid eyes on those people was when I saw them in Apartment 12. But in my business you get to be a pretty good judge of character, and I could see at once that there was nothing particularly suspicious about those people. The tenants in this building are all my valued guests, and the guests of my guests, you might say, are also my guests. That's why, as I'm sure you'll understand, I couldn't very well make uncalled-for remarks simply because there's been some sort of misunderstanding.

I wish also to take advantage of this occasion to confide a secret, in all candor. To tell the truth, situations of this kind are not in the least unusual. When you're in my business you see this kind of thing happening all the time. I wonder if all the commotion hasn't simply proved the gentleman doesn't know much about people? I beg you, ladies and gentlemen, not to be deceived by any false rumors or to let your confidence be shaken in our apartment house.

THE SUPERINTENDENT

. . . Scene Eight

The curtain rises to disclose the benches in a public park somewhere. Sounds of cars and people passing make it clear that the park is in the city. The sounds, however, are filtered and the buildings surrounding the park are concealed by trees (or something suggesting trees); the spot is somehow isolated from the outside world. The woman sitting on a bench who seems to be waiting for someone is the person with whom MAN *was talking on the telephone, his* FIANCÉE. *She glances at her wristwatch, then looks left and right. Her expression suggests she is immersed in thought.*

YOUNGEST DAUGHTER *enters from stage right, skipping along in a way that suggests she is kicking a stone. She strolls past* FIANCÉE. *When she reaches far stage left she gestures as if looking off to the other side of the trees. She strikes a peculiar pose and exits, still maintaining the pose.*

As she leaves, ELDER SON *enters from stage left. Evidently Youngest Daughter's pose was a signal to him.* ELDER SON *struts up to* FIANCÉE.

ELDER SON *(with a slight bow of the head):* Excuse me. *(He starts to seat himself beside* FIANCÉE, *indifferent to her reactions.)*

FIANCÉE: I'm sorry, but I'm waiting for somebody.

ELDER SON: Oh, I see. *(He decides not to sit, but shows no sign of going away. He continues to stare boldly at the woman.)* I was impressed even by your picture, but you're far more charming in the flesh. Oh, you've changed the way you do your hair, haven't you? A natural effect looks better on you than fancy styling. That only goes to show how good the foundations are.

FIANCÉE: I don't think we've met . . . *(Her expression reveals mingled caution and curiosity.)*

ELDER SON: But I know all about you . . . Of course, you make such an impression that nobody who ever saw you once could forget you the second time. It's only natural, I suppose.

FIANCÉE: I wonder where I've had the pleasure . . . ?

ELDER SON: Last night, in the drawer of your fiancé's desk.

FIANCÉE *(at last catching on):* Then it was you last night . . .

ELDER SON *(nods):* Yes, it was. Against my own inclinations I interrupted you in the midst of your telephone call.

FIANCÉE *(sharply):* Have you come as his stand-in?

ELDER SON: Heaven forbid! I wouldn't do such a thing even if he asked me. To tell the truth, he and I have had a slight difference of opinion concerning what happened last night.

FIANCÉE: And you've come to tell on him?

ELDER SON: How severe you are! I wonder what he could've told you about us? I gather from your tone he hasn't been too friendly. I suppose he's trying to clean up the mess he left behind by shifting the blame onto us for that telephone call.

FIANCÉE: What happened anyway?

ELDER SON: How can I answer unless I know the nature of his explanation?

FIANCÉE *(finally induced to discuss the matter on his terms):* I couldn't make the least sense out of him. He was so vague that I . . .

ELDER SON *(with a suppressed laugh that does not seem malicious):* I can well imagine . . . I wonder if the problem is that he's timid, or clumsy at expressing himself, or can never get to the point, or that he's too earnest or too good-natured or too inflexible, or that he's stubborn or an introvert or self-centered . . .

FIANCÉE *(mustering her courage):* Were there also women present?

ELDER SON: Yes, four—no, five.

FIANCÉE: Five!

ELDER SON: But there were men there, too—three of us, besides him.

FIANCÉE: What were you all doing, so many of you?

ELDER SON: It's a little hard to explain.

FIANCÉE *(rather irritated):* But generally speaking, when people have gathered together for a purpose there's some sort of name for their activity. Would you describe it as a meeting, or a card game, or a drinking party? Is there anything that can't be given a name?

ELDER SON: That's the crux of the problem. *(He takes out a comb and smooths his hair.)* I'd really be most interested to hear how *he* would answer that question. *(He puts away the comb.)* But I've been making a great nuisance of myself, when you've more important things on your mind. *(He bows and starts to leave.)*

FIANCÉE *(standing before she realizes):* Wait a moment! What is it you came to tell me, anyway? You and he make a good pair—one's just as vague as the other. I don't suppose you could have come for the express purpose of mystifying me.

ELDER SON *(sanctimoniously, his eyes lowered):* Of course not. But when I meet you face to face this way I suddenly lose my courage.

FIANCÉE: Go ahead. You're not bothering me.

ELDER SON *(lighting a cigarette; slowly):* To be perfectly honest, I don't really understand his feelings . . . Correct me if I'm wrong, but I gather he's engaged to you and has been planning to hold the wedding in the near future.

FIANCÉE: Yes, he only recently managed at last to rent that apartment. It's more than he could afford, but we needed it to get married.

ELDER SON: In other words, he and you are already as good as married. Right? Why, then, should he have had to keep things a secret from you, of all people, in such a furtive way? If I may cite a rather vulgar example, you often see in the advice to the lovelorn column how a man is extremely reluctant to introduce the girl he's interested in to his parents or his family . . . In such cases is it not fair to assume in general that the man's sincerity is to be doubted?

FIANCÉE: You mean you and your family are in that relationship with him?

ELDER SON: Of course, I don't know how he would answer you.

FIANCÉE *(reduced to supplication):* For heaven's sake, please tell me! Who are you all and what is your connection with him?

ELDER SON *(avoiding the issue):* Oh, yes. I've just remembered. It was something he let slip in the course of the conversation last night, but I wonder if it doesn't give us a clue to his intentions. He seems to hold extremely prejudiced views against any form of communal living, and even with respect to family life he seems to be feeling something close to dread.

FIANCÉE: I can't believe that.

ELDER SON: He went so far as to say that it actually refreshed him to be all alone in a crowd of total strangers.

FIANCEE: But he's even made arrangements with the movers to have my furniture taken to his place at the end of the month.

ELDER SON: I'd like to believe that he got carried away by his own words. Or maybe he was just bluffing . . . After all, with such a pretty girl as you . . .

FIANCÉE: You still haven't answered my question.

ELDER SON: Oh—you mean our relationship with him? I wonder if it wouldn't be better, though, for you to get him to verify it with his own mouth. I wouldn't want my words to have the effect of implanting any preconceptions . . . It's not that I'm trying to pretend to be more of a gentleman than I am, but I just wouldn't want to make a sneak attack, or anything like that . . . I realize that it must be hard for you to understand, but basically speaking, we're closer to him than blood relations.

FIANCÉE: You must have known him a long time, then?

ELDER SON (calmly): We don't set too much store by the past. The same holds true of a marriage, doesn't it? The real problems are always in the future.

FIANCÉE (again withdrawing into her shell): Then was it something like a political meeting?

ELDER SON (looking at his watch): I'm sure he has no intention of trying to strengthen his position by lying to you . . . He may in fact be planning to use this opportunity to reveal to you his true feelings. Anyway, I advise you to sound him out. Maybe we'll meet again, depending on how your interview turns out.

FIANCÉE (looking stage left): Oh, there he is now.

ELDER SON (showing no special embarrassment): I hope and pray that all goes well. But I suppose I'm also half-hoping that things don't go well. In that case I'll get to see you again. (Suddenly, as if he had remembered something urgent.) Excuse me, but would you mind sitting there again? Just the way you were before . . . Hurry!

FIANCÉE, overcome by his urgency, sits as requested.

ELDER SON (with a conspiratorial smile): That's right. Now I can see the dimples in your knees . . . Aren't they sweet? I could eat them up, those dimples.

FIANCÉE, flustered, brings together the hems of her coat. At the same moment MAN hurriedly enters from stage left. He catches sight of ELDER SON, and stops in his tracks with an expression of amazement.

. . . Scene Nine

FIANCÉE, *noticing* MAN *approach, stands and turns toward him as he speaks. In other words, her actions should be simultaneous with the beginning of Man's dialogue.*

MAN *(to* ELDER SON, *sharply):* What are *you* doing here?

ELDER SON *turns to* MAN *as if having become aware of his presence only then. Far from showing any embarrassment, he smiles broadly, as if greeting an old friend.*

ELDER SON: Late, aren't you? This will never do!

MAN *looks from* FIANCÉE *to* ELDER SON *and back, then steps forward aggressively.*

MAN: What's the meaning of this, anyway?

FIANCÉE *(unable to hide her guilty conscience):* It was a complete coincidence.

ELDER SON: But as far as I'm concerned, an accidental meeting that only a marvelous necessity could have brought about.

MAN *(angrily):* I don't know what mischief you've been up to, but you're to get the hell out of here, right now.

ELDER SON *(still smiling):* Don't be uncouth. Well, I'll be saying good-by. *(He winks secretly at* FIANCÉE.*)* Go to it now, the both of you. *(He makes a clownish gesture with his hand, then saunters off to stage left.)*

The couple stands for a time in silence, still looking off in the direction ELDER SON *has gone. They slowly turn and exchange glances, only to avert their eyes.* FIANCÉE *sits down on the bench, and* MAN *then also sits. Each occupies an end of the bench.*

MAN *(gloomily):* What was he filling your ear with?

FIANCÉE *(looking at* MAN *reproachfully):* Before we go into that, it seems to me you have a lot of explaining to do.

MAN: Explaining? There's nothing worth explaining. It's just as I told you on the phone this morning. I'm the victim. I'm sorry I worried you with that call last night. But even that was their fault, if you get right down to it.

FIANCÉE: So it would seem. It's pretty hard to keep someone from guessing, even over the phone, when you have eight people in the room with you. But tell me, why was it necessary for you to act so secretly, as if you were playing hide-and-seek with me?

MAN: I thought I'd told you. I couldn't think of any way of explaining in an intelligible manner who those people were or what they were doing.

FIANCÉE: And you're going to explain now, is that it?

MAN: Unfortunately, I still don't know what happened, even now.

FIANCÉE *(a little defiantly):* But I thought you asked me here in order to explain.

MAN *(bearing up under the confusion):* Yes, that's so . . . But my real purpose was not so much to explain as to get you to understand how difficult it is to make an explanation. Maybe I won't succeed in making you understand . . . How could you understand an outfit like that? I suppose that if it happened that I had been on the receiving end of this story, I wouldn't have been able to believe it either . . . I don't know where to start. The only way to describe what happened is to say it was plain crazy.

FIANCÉE *(losing her temper):* That certainly doesn't seem to be an explanation of anything.

MAN: But have you ever heard anything like it—a bunch of complete strangers suddenly march in on me without warning, and install themselves in my apartment, exactly as if it were their natural right?

FIANCÉE *(coldly):* It *is* a little unusual.

MAN: It certainly is. As a matter of fact, even the policemen who came after I called refused to take it seriously. *(His voice becomes more emphatic.)* But I assure you, it happened. This impossible thing has befallen me.

FIANCÉE: That man who was just here also thought it was strange. He couldn't figure out what your motive was in keeping their presence such a secret.

MAN: A secret? It's simply that I couldn't think how to explain, don't you see? So he encouraged you to act suspicious. But you're carrying your foolishness too far. Tell me, what possible advantage could there be in it for me to cover up for that bunch of parasites?

FIANCÉE: For a parasite, that man just now certainly acted like a gentleman. Unlike you, he didn't say one harsh thing. Why, he didn't even try to justify himself.

MAN: Yes, that's their technique.

FIANCÉE: I understand, by the way, that five of them are women.

MAN: Five of them? *(He bursts into derisive laughter. His voice takes on a triumphant note.)* Five women? That's a good one. Gradually I'm beginning to catch on to their tactics.

FIANCÉE: Was he lying, then?

MAN: No, it wasn't a lie. The five women include a seventy-year-old grandmother, a housewife of fifty, and a junior-high-school student.

FIANCÉE *(beginning to lose her confidence):* They certainly make an odd group of people.

MAN: No, there's nothing odd about them. Didn't I tell you? They're all one family—five children, the parents, and the grandmother, a family of eight. Five women . . . that's good. You couldn't call it a lie, and it was effective as a trick. You must've been imagining I was involved with some sort of secret society.

FIANCÉE: You were the one who first gave me that impression.

MAN *(with an expression of relief):* When you've seen what the facts really are, they don't amount to much, do they?

FIANCÉE: You can't blame me. You exaggerated so much.

MAN *(resuming his subdued tone):* It would've been easier to explain if they had actually been a secret society or a gang. But when they look so absurdly and indisputably like a family, it makes it impossible to complain to anybody.

FIANCÉE *(dubious again):* But are you sure these people have no relationship to you at all?

MAN: Absolutely none.

FIANCÉE: I can't understand it. Are you sure there wasn't some reason behind it, however slight? It's hard to imagine otherwise that they'd move in on you like that.

MAN: They say that I'm lonely and that they intend to envelop and warm me in their neighborly love.

FIANCÉE: They've ignored me completely, then?

MAN: No, I'm sure that, as long as you were willing, they'd be delighted to have you join them.

FIANCÉE *(with intensity):* This is no laughing matter.

MAN *(holding his head between his hands):* That's why I told you they were monstrous parasites.

FIANCÉE: Why don't you tell them to leave?

MAN: I have, of course.

FIANCÉE: Firmly? And clearly?

MAN: In a voice so loud it hurt my throat. *(Weakly.)* But it still didn't do any good. It made no impression on them. They have the nerve to say that occupying our apartment is not merely their privilege but their duty.

FIANCÉE *(after a pause, uncertainly):* Is that really all? Is that all there is to it?

MAN: As far as I know.

FIANCÉE: You've explained three of the five women, but what about the other two?

MAN: Stop it! If you'd only seen how I struggled with them.

FIANCÉE: It's funny . . . my engagement ring doesn't seem to fit my finger any more . . . I wonder if I should take it off.

MAN *(bewildered):* What do you mean?

FIANCÉE: I want you to be frank with me. If you've been putting on a show in order to get rid of me, you needn't go to all the trouble.

MAN: There you go again, tormenting me with your groundless accusations.

FIANCÉE: But what else can I do, as long as you're unable to take back our apartment from those people?

MAN: Insult added to injury! If I'm to be deserted even by you, I'll lose the will to fight altogether.

FIANCÉE *(suddenly sharp):* Then I can really trust what you say?

MAN: Of course! Haven't I been begging you over and over, till I'm hoarse, to do just that?

FIANCÉE: Then how would it be if I visited the apartment tomorrow with a friend?

MAN: A friend?

FIANCÉE: A man who used to be a feature writer for a weekly magazine. Exposés were always his strong suit, so I'm sure he's one person who'll be able to tell what's going on.

MAN: Are you trying to spite me?

FIANCÉE: Let the chips fall where they may. I'm only after the guilty party. If things are the way you've described them, I'm sure the family will be the ones to suffer. You understand, don't you? I desperately want to believe you.

MAN: In that case, I have no objections. There's nothing more I want than to have you believe me.

FIANCÉE: I do want to believe you.

MAN: And I want to be believed.

Suddenly YOUNGEST DAUGHTER *pops up from behind the bench and starts tiptoeing off to stage right.* MAN, *sensing somebody is there, turns around, and, with a shout, grabs her arm.*

MAN: Wait!

YOUNGEST DAUGHTER *(letting out a scream):* Murder!

MAN, *surprised, releases her arm.* YOUNGEST DAUGHTER *sticks out her tongue and runs off.*

FIANCÉE: Who was that?

MAN: One of the five women in the case.

The stage darkens.

. . . Scene Ten

A strangely shaped male head emerges from the darkness. The left and right sides of the face do not seem to match, giving an impression of madness. This is the REPORTER *who has come at Fiancée's request. (By changing the lighting, however, it is possible to make the expression change to one of extreme gentleness.)*

REPORTER *(abruptly, all but shouting):* Marvelous, isn't it? I mean it, it's really marvelous. This is what I've dreamt of for years, the model of what family life should be, solid and generous as the earth itself.

In another corner of the stage the faces of the members of the family are revealed, forming a group. They begin to sing a chorus of "The Broken Necklace" to the accompaniment of Younger Son's guitar. The chorus gives way to a solo by MIDDLE DAUGHTER *and the stage gradually becomes lighter.* FIANCÉE *stands in another part of the stage, looking utterly baffled.* REPORTER *goes up to* MIDDLE DAUGHTER, *applauding.*

REPORTER: I'm impressed. Yes, impressed. That one word "impressed" sums up my feelings. Tell me, young lady, what is your philosophy of life? *(He takes out a notebook and holds his pencil poised.)*

MIDDLE DAUGHTER: My philosophy?

REPORTER: I mean, what you believe in . . .

MIDDLE DAUGHTER: Let me see . . . Maybe it is to forget myself.

REPORTER: Marvelous! Not to believe in your own existence is infinitely more of a strain on rationalism than believing in something that doesn't exist. *(To* FIANCÉE.*)* Thank you. Thank you for having introduced me to such wonderful people. I'm grateful to you from the bottom of my heart.

REPORTER, *overcome by emotion, spreads open his arms and all but embraces* FIANCÉE. *She steps back in confusion.*

FIANCÉE: But it isn't as if we'd especially asked them to stay here.

REPORTER: Well, ask them now. They're not the kind of people to insist on formalities. *(To family.)* That's right, isn't it?

FATHER: Go right ahead.

FIANCÉE: But I don't think it's necessary any more.

ELDER SON *has been combing his hair and winking at* FIANCÉE. *Now, seeing his chance, he steps forward with a theatrical gesture.*

ELDER SON: Young lady, why do you disappoint us by saying such things? Your adorable lips were never meant to pronounce such uncouth words as "necessary" or "unnecessary."

YOUNGER SON *(singing to the accompaniment of his guitar):* Chase him, chase him, but still he trots after you, that pooch is really sweet . . . *(He suddenly gets down on all fours at Fiancée's feet.)* Lady, I'm your pooch!

FIANCÉE *is driven into a corner of the stage, but ends up by bursting into giggles.*

REPORTER *(suddenly cries out):* No! This'll never do! I mustn't go on procrastinating any more. *(To* FATHER.*)* I've definitely made up my mind. I'm going to join you. I'd like you to include me in your group. Where are the headquarters? Where should I apply for membership? What are the prerequisites? The entrance fees? The conditions?

The members of the family exchange meaningful glances.

FATHER: It's hard, after having been praised so enthusiastically, to know how to answer.

REPORTER: Please believe me! I'll keep it an absolute secret.

MOTHER: A secret? We haven't any secrets, have we?

GRANDMOTHER: We're honest people, we are.

REPORTER: I don't mean to suggest I suspect you of anything. But surely your family couldn't be the only people carrying on this great movement?

FATHER: Well, of course . . . The world is not such a hopeless place.

REPORTER *(greatly in earnest):* I understand. You're saying that it's presumptuous for anyone like myself to hope to be admitted to your ranks.

ELDER SON: Somehow I think you're overestimating us a little . . .

REPORTER: Such modesty!

FATHER: What we've been doing is just plain, ordinary . . . Let's put it this way. All we're doing is what anybody with the least grain of normal human decency couldn't help but do.

MOTHER: You might say we're knitting a fabric, not out of yarn but out of people.

REPORTER: Such humility! That fabric will spread as it is knitted, from village to village, from town to town, until soon it grows into an enormous jacket covering and warming the country and the entire people. This is magnificent! Such magnificence, and such humility! I will become your disciple. Yes, I will sit at your feet. But at least you can tell me where I can find the headquarters of your knitting club.

FATHER: If you'll forgive me for saying so, you should act more spontaneously, as the voices within you command.

REPORTER: Then it's all right if I go right ahead as I please, without any license or authorization?

FATHER: Why should you hesitate? When what you want to do is right, you should throw yourself into it, with full confidence.

REPORTER: Thank you!

FATHER: As long as you perform your services with sincerity and devotion, one of these days you're sure to receive word from headquarters recognizing your work.

REPORTER: Then there is a headquarters?

ELDEST DAUGHTER: I wonder.

FATHER: I'm sure there must be one. It stands to reason . . .

ELDEST DAUGHTER: But we've never once received word from headquarters, have we?

REPORTER *(surprised):* Not even you?

FATHER: Society is demanding. But that's no reason to doubt the existence of a headquarters—it doesn't get you anywhere. If you want to believe in a headquarters, why, there's no harm in that.

REPORTER: I see . . .

ELDEST DAUGHTER: I don't mean to deny it myself. Either way, it doesn't affect my beliefs.

REPORTER: Ah? Your beliefs? *(He gets his notebook ready.)* I wonder if I might ˙trouble you to tell me a little about them.

ELDEST DAUGHTER *(emphasizing the importance of her words):* Ask not, but give . . . That sums them up in a nutshell.

REPORTER: Ask not, but give . . . That's quite something . . . Ask not, but give . . . Isn't that splendid? How can any man be so obstinate, even after you've said *that* to him? It beats me. A feast is set before him and he refuses to eat! What a disgrace! Something must have happened to his head!

Suddenly MAN, *who has been lying in the hammock, sits up.*

MAN: Give? Don't make me laugh! What have they ever given me? The dirty swine!

REPORTER: Who's that?

FATHER: You might call him a kind of blotting paper, I suppose.

REPORTER: Blotting paper?

ELDEST DAUGHTER *(going up to* MAN*):* That's right. I've never seen anyone so unresponsive.

REPORTER: Repulsive, isn't he?

The stage becomes dark again, leaving light only on MAN *and* ELDEST DAUGHTER. *She produces a small bottle of whisky from the pocket of her dressing gown and takes a swig.*

ELDEST DAUGHTER: Come on down, Mr. Blotting Paper.

MAN: At your service, Miss Parasite.

ELDEST DAUGHTER: Do you know why I've never married?

MAN: Today I made the most terrible blunder. I absent-mindedly sent the car-pool manager some papers that were supposed to be delivered to the chief of the planning department.

ELDEST DAUGHTER: Speaking of your company, that reminds me—you took your time coming home from work today. Did you stop off somewhere?

MAN: Are you kidding? You and your family took away my pay check, envelope and all. There's no chance of my stopping off anywhere.

ELDEST DAUGHTER: Don't try to fool me. I know all about it. You stopped off to see—what was his name?—the lawyer, didn't you?

MAN *does not respond.*

ELDEST DAUGHTER: He telephoned us immediately afterwards. And we all had a good laugh. *(She giggles.)* Why, even the lawyer . . . *(She hurriedly changes her tone.)* But you mustn't be offended. We're . . . how shall I say it . . . we're considerate. That's why, even after we had our big laugh, we decided not to tell you.

MAN: Then, there's nothing more to say, is there?

ELDEST DAUGHTER: I suppose not. Of course, we should have said something, if only to induce you to reconsider your attitude, but we refrained.

MAN: You keep saying you haven't told me, but aren't you telling me now?

ELDEST DAUGHTER: I must be drunk!

MAN: You're running around like a broken-down neon sign.

ELDEST DAUGHTER: What a thing to say!

MAN: Damn him! And he calls himself a lawyer!

ELDEST DAUGHTER *(to herself):* I mustn't be over-eager.

MAN: Anyway, it isn't easy talking to you. There's no getting around it, you're one of the family.

ELDEST DAUGHTER *(in a syrupy voice):* Then, you have some feeling for me?

MAN: Heaven forbid!

ELDEST DAUGHTER: If you're still interested in that girl, I'm sorry for you, but you'd better forget her. My brother's talents as a thief aren't restricted to the contents of people's pockets.

MAN: I can't believe in anything any more.

ELDEST DAUGHTER: Doubt is the door to progress . . . Talking about doors, I can't help feeling all the time as if I'm a door that's been left permanently ajar . . . Please, come down from there. Hurry!

MAN: You know, the lawyer was in tears . . .

ELDEST DAUGHTER *(suddenly laughs):* I gather he was wearing a bandage on his head?

MAN: It's a wonder he can still stay in business!

ELDEST DAUGHTER: It's just a matter of getting used to it. Nowadays it's not all that unusual for a man to be visited by friends like us.

MAN: But the bandage clearly shows there's been violence.

ELDEST DAUGHTER: Even love has its whips, hasn't it?

MAN: The lawyer said eleven parasites had descended on him!

ELDEST DAUGHTER: He must be an even better quality of blotting paper than you.

MAN: What the devil's the matter with this hammock?

ELDEST DAUGHTER: Excuse me, but I'm taking off my clothes. I feel unbearably hot. I suppose it must be the whisky . . . *(She is wearing under her dressing gown only net tights and a short negligee.)*

MAN: If such a thing as hot ice existed—there may be, for all I know, in fact I'm sure there is—a snowstorm in midsummer, sunstroke in midwinter . . .

ELDEST DAUGHTER: The bottle will be empty if you don't hurry.

MAN *(writhing):* That's funny. What's happened to this hammock?

ELDEST DAUGHTER *(as if she has made a surprising discovery):* Just feel me . . . I really seem to be hot and cold at the same time. I wonder why.

MAN: But what the hell's wrong with this hammock?

. . . Scene Eleven

Lights are suddenly turned on in the room. ELDEST DAUGHTER *wheels around in astonishment.* MIDDLE DAUGHTER *stands in pajamas by the wall, near the door of the adjoining room. Her hand is still on the wall switch.*

ELDEST DAUGHTER *(angrily):* So you were listening!

MIDDLE DAUGHTER *(quietly and calmly):* Yes, I heard everything.

ELDEST DAUGHTER *(retrieving her gown and putting it back on):* What a way to talk! Not a scrap of respect for other people's feelings . . . I've never known anyone less lovable than you.

MIDDLE DAUGHTER: But it's something important.

ELDEST DAUGHTER: I don't care how important it is. Who ever heard of leaving the lights burning indefinitely? Why even he looks as if the light's too strong for him.

MAN (seems rather dazed): Yes, it'll soon be morning.

MIDDLE DAUGHTER (ignoring him; to ELDEST DAUGHTER): Are you drunk?

ELDEST DAUGHTER (losing her temper): I tell you, I'm going to give you a piece of my mind if you keep tormenting me with such stupid tricks. I don't care how important you think it is, eavesdropping is still eavesdropping. You didn't listen because it was important. You listened and then you found out something that happened to be important. Why don't you at least pretend to be a little embarrassed? (To MAN, still fiddling with the hammock, unable to get out.) I'm sorry, really I am . . .

MIDDLE DAUGHTER: Hmmm. Isn't what you really have to apologize for something quite different?

ELDEST DAUGHTER (worsted in the argument, she adjusts the front of her gown): I don't know what you're talking about, but there's something weird about you. (She goes toward the door.) Anyway, with your permission, I'd like to get a little sleep.

MIDDLE DAUGHTER (showing her first emotional reaction): No, you can't! Stay right where you are! You're an important witness. (She calls through the door to the next room.) Father, Brother . . . would you come here a minute?

ELDEST DAUGHTER (agitated): What are you up to, anyway?

YOUNGER SON (calling from offstage): Which brother do you want?

MIDDLE DAUGHTER: Both of you! Hurry! It's extremely important.

Noises from the next room—sleepy murmurs, fits of coughing, and the like—suggest people getting out of bed reluctantly.

MAN (becoming uneasy): Isn't there some sort of misunderstanding? Well, misunderstandings get cleared up sooner or later. There's nothing to be so excited about . . . But what the devil's happened to this hammock?

ELDEST DAUGHTER (glaring at MIDDLE DAUGHTER): After all this uproar I'm sure we'll discover that the mountain labored to bring forth a mouse. You're not going to get away with paying a hundred yen fine this time . . . I trust you've got a good stock of pin money.

MIDDLE DAUGHTER (quietly): It hurts me to tell you, but this is no mouse. You mean to say you haven't caught on yet?

ELDER SON, FATHER, and YOUNGER SON, in that order, appear from the next room. All look groggy, as if they just got out of bed. Each is muttering to himself.

YOUNGER SON: Damn it! I've got another corker of a hangover.

ELDEST DAUGHTER *starts to make a sneering remark, but* MIDDLE DAUGHTER *interrupts at once.*

MIDDLE DAUGHTER: He was planning an escape!
FATHER *(at once wide awake):* Escape?

They all show reactions of astonishment.

MIDDLE DAUGHTER *(slowly goes up to Man's hammock):* He was just about to try running away.
FATHER *(turning to the sons):* Running away! Things have taken a serious turn.
ELDER SON *(extremely confused):* I can see that everything has not been arranged exactly as he might have wished, but still.
MAN *(apprehensive):* That's an exaggeration. The fact is, I'm here now. Right? Run away? Fat chance I'd have, when I'm wrapped up in this crazy hammock like a tent caterpillar. *(With an unnatural, forced laugh.)* Run away . . . why I can't even get out to take a leak. I'm suffering, I tell you!

MIDDLE DAUGHTER *takes the cord at one end of the hammock and jerks it loose. The hammock at once opens out, and in the recoil* MAN *drops to the floor.* MAN *makes feeble sounds of laughter, but none of the others so much as smile.*

MIDDLE DAUGHTER *(helping* MAN *to his feet):* I'm sorry. Did you hurt yourself?
ELDEST DAUGHTER *(aggressively):* So, it was your handiwork, was it?
MIDDLE DAUGHTER: I didn't want to mention it, but you've been flirting with him for the past three days, haven't you?
ELDEST DAUGHTER: Don't say anything you'll regret! For the past three days? Go ahead, be as jealous as you like—that's your privilege—but if you get carried away to any such wild conclusions, the rest of us will be the ones to suffer.
MIDDLE DAUGHTER *(cool; to* FATHER *and the others):* I had a feeling tonight would be the crisis. So, just to be on the safe side, I tied up the hammock after he went to sleep.
ELDEST DAUGHTER: That's a lie! An out-and-out lie! Ask him to his face. He'll say which of us is telling the truth. *(To* MAN, *seeking his assent.)* That's right, isn't it?
MAN *(hesitates before answering):* It's true she's kindly come here every evening for the last three days to keep me company, but . . .
ELDEST DAUGHTER *(unabashed):* I've no intention of hiding anything. I've been trying my best to advertise myself, hoping he'd respond to my overtures. But to hear you talk, I was inducing him to run away! That's going too far, even for a false accusation.
MIDDLE DAUGHTER *(spitefully):* It's quite possible tonight was the first time you resorted to open inducement. But how about hints?
ELDEST DAUGHTER: Mystification doesn't become you.
MIDDLE DAUGHTER *(imitating Eldest Daughter's manner of speech):* "There's

nothing to be worried about. This place and time exist just for the two of us . . . If you pretend that nobody else is here, why it's just the same as if nobody were actually here. Think of the others as being insubstantial as the air . . ."

ELDEST DAUGHTER *(bursts into laughter):* How disgusting! Aren't those the usual clichés every woman uses when seducing a man? Didn't you even know that?

FATHER: What was this direct incitement she resorted to tonight?

MIDDLE DAUGHTER *(again imitating* ELDEST DAUGHTER; *with passion):* "You must give up all hope of getting rid of them. You'll just exhaust yourself with useless efforts. Yes, it'd be better to run away than try to chase them out. We'll run far, far away to some distant place where nobody knows us."

ELDEST DAUGHTER: That's enough!

FATHER: Mm. That was pretty direct.

YOUNGER SON: Even with my hangover I can't help being impressed.

ELDER SON: And what was his reaction to her incitement?

MIDDLE DAUGHTER *(severely):* I felt it was certainly a good thing I had tied the hammock so he couldn't get out.

ELDER SON: What a mess!

MAN *(in confused tone):* But don't you think it's unfair to base your judgments on such a one-sided . . .

FATHER *(reassuringly):* It's all right. It's all right. Please don't worry about it any more.

ELDER SON *(to* ELDEST DAUGHTER*):* But were you serious in trying to tempt him into such a thing?

ELDEST DAUGHTER *(sulkily):* What makes you think I was serious? Don't insult me. It doesn't take much common sense to see that there's absolutely no likelihood of his running away. This is the most disgusting thing I've ever heard of, making such a fuss, so early in the morning.

MIDDLE DAUGHTER: What makes you so sure he can't run away?

ELDEST DAUGHTER: You don't see?

MIDDLE DAUGHTER: I certainly don't.

ELDEST DAUGHTER: He's the acting department head. His fortune's assured—he's a rising star. He knows better than anyone else, I should think, how important his work is to him. He can talk all he wants about how he likes to be alone, or how he longs for freedom, but one thing he can never in the world do is to give up his job.

ELDER SON: That sounds logical, all right.

ELDEST DAUGHTER: Supposing he ran away from here without giving up his job. He'd have to find somewhere else to stay, and it'd be simple enough for us to find out where he went.

ELDER SON: Yes, that'd be no problem.

ELDEST DAUGHTER: And once we found him we surely wouldn't spare ourselves the trouble of moving in with him, would we? We'd go to help him again, as our natural duty, wouldn't we?

FATHER: Of course. We couldn't neglect our duty. That would be out of the question.

ELDEST DAUGHTER *(her self-confidence quite recovered):* And even he must be fully convinced, after living with us for almost two weeks, how strong our sense of duty is. *(To* MAN.*)* Am I wrong?

MAN: No, I am deeply aware of it.

ELDEST DAUGHTER *(triumphantly):* Well, there you have it, ladies and gentlemen.

They all strike various attitudes which suggest they are ruminating on the above.
ELDEST DAUGHTER *throws* MIDDLE DAUGHTER *an unconcealed smile of derision.*

FATHER: In that case, the incident is not as serious as we had imagined.

YOUNGER SON: Then, I hope you'll pardon me if I go back to bed before the rest of you. I may vomit at any minute.

MIDDLE DAUGHTER: I can't help being worried, all the same.

ELDEST DAUGHTER: The more you talk, the more shame you bring on yourself. Pretending to be an innocent little girl is all very well, but it's exhausting for the rest of us to play your game.

MIDDLE DAUGHTER: But when I heard him say, "All right, let's run away!" I was so frightened I shuddered with fear. I wonder if a man can talk in that tone of voice if he doesn't mean it.

ELDEST DAUGHTER: A mere impression, even from someone as bright as you, is not sufficient evidence.

ELDER SON: Yes, if it was nothing more than an impression

YOUNGER SON: O.K. That settles it. *(He exits, staggering, to the next room.)* It's probably my liver.

FATHER *(cautiously, observing* MAN*):* Finally, just as a formality, I'd like to ask the subject of our discussion his opinion. Then I'll adjourn the meeting.

MAN *(gradually regaining his self-confidence):* My opinion? After all we've gone through? *(He laughs.)* That's no longer of any importance, is it? How shall I put it? To tell the truth, it's as if some devil got into me tonight . . . Or rather, as if I'd been bewitched by a goddess . . . I felt when I was talking as if I were singing the words of a song . . . *(To* ELDEST DAUGHTER.*)* I'm not the kind to flatter people, but I really felt as if I were swimming in a pool of whisky . . . When I proposed that we run away I wonder if I wasn't expressing, in spite of myself, the reverse of what I actually felt—my desire to hold fast to you. *(To* FATHER.*)* People sometimes say precisely the opposite of what they're thinking.

In the course of the above dialogue GRANDMOTHER, MOTHER, *and* YOUNGEST DAUGHTER, *in that order, stick their heads in from the next room. They observe what is happening with expressions of intense curiosity.*

FATHER *(reflectively):* I see . . . Well, now we seem to have heard the opinions
of everyone. *(He looks from* MIDDLE DAUGHTER *to* ELDEST DAUGHTER.*)* How
about it—will you agree to leave the final judgment to me?

ELDEST DAUGHTER *(in good spirits, now that* MAN *has flattered her):* That's fine
with me.

MIDDLE DAUGHTER: I don't suppose I have much choice.

FATHER *(abruptly gives order to* ELDER SON*):* Prepare the cage!

They all look astonished. But ELDER SON *instantly moves into action. The other
members of the family follow him, displaying remarkable teamwork: one arranges
the coat rack in the hall, another produces a lock, another overpowers* MAN, *still
another throws a blanket over him. Finally,* MAN, *wrapped in the blanket, is shut
up inside the coat rack, which has been converted into a cage. A large lock is hung
on the outside.*

MAN *at length manages to stick his head out from inside the blanket.*

MAN: What're you doing? Didn't I promise you I wouldn't run away? This is
inhuman! There's no excuse for it. It's inhuman!

ELDEST DAUGHTER *(with an expression of inability to understand it herself):* Yes,
really, what's happened? After he assured us so positively he had no intention of running away . . .

MAN: That's right. You tell them . . . There must be some mistake!

FATHER: The thing is, you insisted a little too emphatically that you wouldn't run
away.

MAN: It's natural for a man to be emphatic when he's speaking from the heart.

FATHER: You yourself were just expressing the view that sometimes people say the
opposite of what they feel.

MAN: That's a false accusation!

GRANDMOTHER: The blind man envies the one-eyed man.

FATHER: In a matter of this gravity there's no such thing as taking too many
precautions.

YOUNGEST DAUGHTER *looks into the cage as if she were watching a monkey at the
zoo.* MAN *spits at* YOUNGEST DAUGHTER.

MAN: Get the hell away!

YOUNGEST DAUGHTER: Isn't he awful? Even a chimpanzee wouldn't be so rude.

MOTHER: Don't get too close to him. He's still overexcited.

MAN: Damn it! All your clever talk about neighborly love and the rest was a lot
of bunk . . . Not even a slave would endure such treatment.

MIDDLE DAUGHTER *(severely):* There's been a misunderstanding. A terrible misunderstanding. You've taken everything in the wrong spirit.

MAN: Shut up! I don't even want to see your face!

FATHER: Yes, the misunderstanding was definitely on your side. And you still don't seem to understand that these measures have been taken because we earnestly desire your safety and security.

MAN: Understand! You don't suppose there's any chance I would understand that!

MIDDLE DAUGHTER: But running away means disappearing. And that's a much more frightening thing than you seem to suppose. You don't think we could expose you to such a danger, knowing how frightening it is to disappear.

ELDEST DAUGHTER *(still not satisfied)*: I think you're overrating him.

ELDER SON: It seems to be our fate always to have our efforts rewarded by enmity.

MOTHER: In short, the world's fallen on evil days.

MAN *(gasping)*: But if I can't go to the office, you'll be the ones to suffer. I wonder if you've thought about that.

FATHER: We don't intend to keep you in there forever. Just as soon as your frame of mind improves, of course we'll let you out.

MAN: Isn't that nice? You expect my frame of mind to improve? You amaze me. Don't you think it's a lot more likely to boomerang on you? Don't you realize I'll get to hate this place more and more?

FATHER: Please, just leave things to me. While you're meditating over your solitude in there, the pleasures of your ordinary everyday life, how you used to go to the office each morning, will come back and the happy memories will gush forth inside you like a fountain.

MOTHER: That's right. Happy memories are generally of quite ordinary things. They leave the deepest impression.

FATHER: And then your desire to escape will drop from you like the scab from a wound that has healed.

MIDDLE DAUGHTER: And your peace of mind will come back again.

FATHER: Now for the blankets.

The instant after FATHER *speaks several blankets are draped over the cage. The stage darkens at once.*

. . . Scene Twelve

The stage blacks out completely for a moment, but almost immediately afterwards the inside of the cage is illuminated. MAN *sits, his knees cradled in his arms, and his face pressed against his knees.*

He suddenly raises his head and looks uneasily around him. He listens attentively. Then he lies down on his side in a fetal posture. The next moment he gets on all fours like a dog. He starts to imitate a dog's howling, at which the howling of a real dog is heard from a loudspeaker. MAN *again lies on his side in a fetal posture.*

. . . Scene Thirteen

Now light and dark are reversed: inside the cage is dark and outside is light. It is daytime. MIDDLE DAUGHTER *enters from the kitchen carrying a breakfast tray.*

MIDDLE DAUGHTER *(standing before cage):* Are you awake? I've brought your breakfast.

MAN *(dispiritedly):* Thanks.

She puts the tray on the floor for the moment, removes the blanket covering the cage, then slips the tray into the cage from the end.

MIDDLE DAUGHTER: How do you feel?

MAN: How do you expect? *(He stares at the food, then begins to eat little by little, but without enjoyment.)*

MIDDLE DAUGHTER: You don't seem to have much of an appetite . . . If you don't go out and get some exercise soon—

MAN: What's the weather like today?

MIDDLE DAUGHTER: It seems to be clearing gradually.

MAN: The place is strangely silent. Is nobody here?

MIDDLE DAUGHTER *(sitting down and staring at* MAN *through the bars of the cage):* Father has gone to the miniature golf links. My older sister's at the beauty parlor and the younger one at school. The rest are out shopping, I suppose.

MAN *(entreatingly):* Couldn't you let me have a look at the newspaper, even if it's only the headlines?

MIDDLE DAUGHTER: Nothing doing. We must keep you quiet while you're convalescing.

MAN: You're certainly a hard girl to figure out. Sometimes I think you're kind, only for you to act just as much of a stickler for the rules as the others. Sometimes you seem affectionate, but then you're just as stubborn as the others.

MIDDLE DAUGHTER *(smiling):* That's because you only think about yourself.

MAN *(laughing faintly):* I know, that's what you say. But surely not even you pretend that shutting me up this way is for my own good.

MIDDLE DAUGHTER: But it's the truth.

MAN: I don't believe it.

MIDDLE DAUGHTER: It's strange, isn't it? My head is so full of you that I've never even given a thought to anything else.

MAN *(taken aback):* If that's the case, how can you fail so completely to understand my feelings? I have you and your family to thank for the opportunity to study to my heart's content the blessings of neighborly love.

MIDDLE DAUGHTER *(suddenly dejected):* I do understand. I understand much better than you suppose.

MAN: What do you understand?

MIDDLE DAUGHTER (*speaking hesitantly*): Well, for example . . .

MAN: For example?

MIDDLE DAUGHTER: The fact that your sickness has not in the least improved.

MAN (*his interest aroused*): I see . . . You may be right.

MIDDLE DAUGHTER: If I listen very carefully I can hear it, the sound of your heart flying far, far away.

MAN: Just like a bird.

MIDDLE DAUGHTER: And the commuter's train, your time card, the desk with your nameplate on it, the street corner with your company's building—they're all gradually melting away like sculpture carved of ice.

MAN: You do understand.

MIDDLE DAUGHTER (*changing her tone*): Oh, that's right. I was forgetting something important. Here. (*She takes a little packet wrapped in paper from her pocket.*) My brother asked me to give this to you.

MAN (*unwrapping the packet*): From your brother, is it? I see.

MIDDLE DAUGHTER: That's an engagement ring, isn't it?

MAN: It's a kind of metal object. It used to be an engagement ring once.

MIDDLE DAUGHTER (*staring at* MAN *with great earnestness*): Oh, I'm so worried.

MAN: About what?

MIDDLE DAUGHTER: You seem already to have gone farther away than I had thought.

MAN (*laughing cynically*): How sentimental we've become!

MIDDLE DAUGHTER: Sentimental? That's not it at all. I meant to say you're a traitor!

MAN: A traitor!

MIDDLE DAUGHTER: How about a glass of milk?

MAN: Yes, I'd like one. The food today was a little too salty.

MIDDLE DAUGHTER *hurries into the kitchen and returns immediately with a glass of milk. She watches affectionately as* MAN, *with a word of thanks, drains the glass with one gulp.*

MIDDLE DAUGHTER (*holding out her fist; she has something in it*): If I give you the key to this lock, will you promise not to scold me even if I tell you I love you? (*She opens her hand. The key glitters in her palm.*)

MAN (*at a loss for words before this too-sudden realization of his wishes*): That's the easiest thing in the world. Why, if you hadn't been a member of your family, I'm sure I would have spoken first, and told you I was in love with you . . . I'm not saying this just to please you . . . I'm sure I would have. (*He starts to shake.*)

MIDDLE DAUGHTER: Are you cold?

MAN: It must be an excess of joy. And now, for the key . . .

MAN *tries to take the key, but his shaking has become so violent that he cannot manage to grasp it. Suddenly Man's face is shot with fear.*

MIDDLE DAUGHTER: If only you hadn't turned against us, we would have been no more than company for you . . .

Man's shaking suddenly stops. He lies motionless. MIDDLE DAUGHTER *tenderly drapes a blanket over the cage and, kneeling beside him, quietly sobs.*

MIDDLE DAUGHTER: There's no need any more to run away . . . Nobody will bother you now . . . It's quiet, isn't it? You look so well . . . Your sickness must be better.

YOUNGER SON *appears without warning from the next room.*

YOUNGER SON *(putting on his shirt):* Hey, what're you bawling about?
MIDDLE DAUGHTER: Oh, were you there all the time?
YOUNGER SON *(having sized up the situation from Middle Daughter's appearance):* So, you've done it again.
MIDDLE DAUGHTER: What else could I do?
YOUNGER SON: You're hopeless . . . But there's no use crying over spilt milk . . . Well, we're going to be busy again, what with one thing and another.
MIDDLE DAUGHTER: He was such a nice man. Really sweet. And so sensitive. At the slightest touch his heart would start to pound.
YOUNGER SON *(brushing the dandruff from his head):* We borrowed in advance on his retirement pay. We've got nothing to complain about as far as our balance sheet is concerned.
MIDDLE DAUGHTER: Show a little more tact in what you say. What I lost and what you lost are not the same things.
YOUNGER SON *(looking around the room; to no one in particular):* It's funny with belongings. I don't know why it is, but every time we move we seem to have more and more of them.
MIDDLE DAUGHTER *(throwing her arms around the cage and caressing it):* If only you hadn't turned against us, we would have been no more than company for you.

The melody of "The Broken Necklace" begins to sound, this time in a melancholy key. The members of the family return in full strength and arrange themselves in a line. They are already dressed for travel. They all take out handkerchiefs and press them to their eyes.

FATHER: The deceased was always a good friend to us. Friend, why were you destined for such a fate? Probably you yourself do not know. Naturally, we do not know either. *(He opens the newspaper.)* Here is the newspaper you were waiting for. Please listen as I read, without the least anxiety. *(He begins to read snatches from the main news items of that day's newspaper, ranging from international events to advertisements.)* Yes, the world is a big place. A big place and a complicated one. *(To* MIDDLE DAUGHTER.*)* Come, be more cheerful. *(He lifts her to her feet.)* They're all waiting for us. *(To* MAN.*)* Good-by.

They all wave their handkerchiefs and put them back into their pockets.

FATHER: Nobody's forgotten anything?

They begin to march off. The curtain falls slowly. Halfway off the lighting is extinguished, and all that can be recognized is the laughter of the family.

TRANSLATED BY DONALD KEENE

■ YASUOKA SHŌTARŌ

Yasuoka Shōtarō was born in 1920 in the city of Kōchi in Shikoku, where his ancestors had been rural landowners for many generations. The son of an army veterinary surgeon, he led a transient life as a boy, moving from one army post to another. By the time he went to live in Tokyo in 1931, he had been to a half-dozen different schools, and had understandably acquired a distaste for education. Despite his conspicuously undistinguished academic record, however, he managed to enter Keiō University in 1941. In 1944 he was called to active service and was immediately sent to Manchuria. The day before his unit was dispatched to the Philippines, he was hospitalized with what was later diagnosed as Pott's disease. He was sent back to Japan, but did not recover completely until 1954, the year of his marriage.

In 1951 Yasuoka's short story "The Glass Slipper" (*Garasu no kutsu*, tr. 1961) earned a nomination for the Akutagawa Prize, which he won two years later with his two stories "Pleasure Without Cheer" (*Inki na tanoshimi*) and "Bad Company" (*Warui nakama*). Since then his reputation in the Japanese literary world has been secure.

Yasuoka Shōtarō is best known as a writer of stories and essays, but his short novel *A View by the Sea* (*Umibe no kōkei*, 1959) ranks among the finest examples of the genre. It is a detached, almost cruel, yet moving account of his mother's death in an insane asylum. Yasuoka is also a literary critic of distinction. He has written perceptive essays—all intensely personal and idiosyncratic, and a little askew—on such major writers as Shiga Naoya, Ibuse Masuji, and Tanizaki Junichirō.

"Prized Possessions" (*Aigan*) is probably one of the best-remembered of Yasuoka's early short stories. It is certainly quite characteristic. No one else writing then about the degradation of living in the immediate postwar years had quite Yasuoka's way of covering indignities with a cloak of self-mockery and near-comedy. "I've always had a weakness for grotesquery," he says, truthfully enough, in the story. Sometimes this weakness becomes unattractive—perhaps too demeaning—in his writings; but often, in the sense of helplessness that it expresses, it touches the reader (especially the Japanese reader) with its peculiar kind of humanity.

❖ Prized Possessions

(*Aigan*, 1952)

"Cleaned out" is what they say, as if poverty were something that cleansed. We —Father, Mother, and I—have been virtually without income for some years now, and I know that it isn't quite like that—empty rooms, cold clean air blowing through, simple living, and that sort of thing. Rather, poverty to me is more suggestive of something warm, sticky, and messy that clings to you; it means disorder and sickly stuffiness. There is nothing at all bracing or simple about it.

Father used to be a professional soldier but, probably because he was a veterinary officer, managed to avoid being accused of war crimes. It is four years now since he returned home safely from the South Pacific. In all that time, he has hardly ever stepped out of the house. Apparently he had some pretty intimidating experiences during internment, for he is still fearful of being beaten up. Mother, by nature a more enterprising and outgoing person, would, it was thought, show her mettle in times like these; and she did indeed get into the business of peddling saccharine, but the venture quickly ended in disaster when our neighbors found out that she had been selling them very questionable stuff at an appallingly high price. Her reputation was ruined for good, it seems; for our neighbors have remained openly suspicious of her whenever they have any dealings with her, such as when it's her turn to help with the local food rationing. She suffers from a terrible inferiority complex now, and is unsure of herself no matter what she does. It's the way she handles money that worries us particularly, of course. She seems to have lost the ability to add and subtract, and when she goes out to do her day's shopping, she hands her purse over to the shopkeeper and asks him to take out the right amount. It's that bad. Then there's my own illness. I got Pott's disease while in the army, and I still haven't been cured. Much of the day I loll about in bed, recuperating, so to speak.

The kind of confusion that can take over a family which has lost all capacity to manage its affairs has to be seen to be believed. Open a drawer in our tea cupboard and you will find, no doubt to your surprise, a saw. That's there because Mother, in one of her weaker moments, imagined that it was a plane for shaving dried bonito. Father, for his part, hoards and jealously guards everything he deems potentially useful as though he were still at the front. Piled up in some strange order on the staggered shelves on the side of the alcove are such items as his veterinarian's saw, scalpel, glass fragments, seeds of unusual plants, his old rank badges, khaki-colored thread wound around a leather bobbin, and so on. Once swallowed up in this whirlpool of rubbish, his handkerchiefs and socks, even his shirts and underpants, are no easier to extract than salt from the sea. I need hardly say there are cobwebs all over the house—on the transom work, ceiling, electric light cords, anywhere you can think of. They are different from ordinary cobwebs, however, in that clinging to them are thin, fluffy bits of white stuff, resembling flowers growing out of mildew. They are in fact bits of angora rabbit fur. Let me say here that even cats I have never liked very much. I have always wondered at those people who seem to adore these impertinent beasts that come and rub their hairy bodies against your skin and stink up the house with their pee. But I have learned that compared to rabbits, they are immeasurably more tolerable.

It all started when one of Father's former subordinate officers—Mother and I didn't know him—dropped in one day to see "the general," as he still called him. We didn't know it then, but in the space of that short visit he managed to put a strange notion into Father's head. The next morning Father, dressed more respectably than usual, went out. Our response to this unexpected event was not without a slight sense of foreboding, but it was on the whole optimistic. Could it be that he had found himself a lucrative job? "He looks quite impressive when he dresses up like that, doesn't he?" Mother said. I nodded solemnly, remembering that in the old days, whenever something important was about to happen, like a promotion or an advantageous transfer, he went out exactly like that, dressed up and not saying a word. But alas, our optimism was without cause. Father returned late that evening hugging a huge box, minus the wristwatch he had bought in Singapore. Someone had taken it off his unprotected wrist as he was coming home. Anyway, that was when those disgusting creatures entered our lives. Just as a truly evil man has the face of an angel, so these rabbits, both the male and the female, seemed extraordinarily endearing as they crouched quietly and timidly on the floor, their red eyes shining in the light. Would you believe it, but I found myself saying, "How pretty!" Mother brought out some bread, and each time she held out a little piece, one would gingerly stick its neck out, then suddenly snap at it and hop off with its prize to a corner of the room. They amused and cheered us, these lively little creatures with their pure white bodies. Their presence seemed to brighten up the whole house. Father of course was very pleased with himself. "In half a year," he said, "they'll start bringing in eight thousand yen a month." Mother looked like a child who had suddenly been offered an enormous piece of candy. "My goodness!" she said with feeling, her toothless mouth wide open. And as Father proceeded to tell us about his scheme —a year's yield of fur would be so much, which would mean so many pounds of yarn, which in turn would produce so many yards of cloth, etc.—Mother became so ecstatic she laughed uncontrollably. Oh no, she cried out joyfully, Father was being much too modest in his estimate; why, that much cloth would fetch far more than eight thousand yen a month! It was as though she was already seeing piled up around her mountains of cloth and yarn.

I saw out of the corner of my eye a small black ball rolling on the floor. I looked, and found that there were many others just like it all around us. "Shameless" is the only word to describe it. Every time they jumped up in the air, another black ball would pop out from the crotch. There was not a trace of shyness in either face, no show of cringing, as the process continued. I looked at their utterly expressionless faces, at their cretinous red eyes with their vacant stares, and felt a nasty foreboding.

The next day Father began working like a maniac. He was at his most irritating, I had found, when he "worked." Indeed, nothing irritated me more. Normally, his "work" meant stripping off the turf in the garden and turning over the soil when the weather was fine, or, if it was wet, making boxes of various sizes and shapes for which there was no conceivable use. Neither activity brought any tangible benefits, obviously, and as a hobby, it made no sense. What particularly mystified me was the energy he put into it. Half hidden in a cloud of swirling dust—we live by the Kugenuma shore, noted for its strong winds and rough seas —he would wield his hoe, giving a crazed, high-pitched cry each time he brought it down. It was like looking at some madman doing an unending dance, and the sight filled me with despair at the loneliness and pointlessness of the effort. One rain, and all he had would be a waterlogged field of sand where nothing would grow. "You're wasting your time!" I would shout at him across the veranda from my bed. "I wish you would stop! Look at all the sand you're sending into the house!" "What did you say?" he would shout back, glaring at me, his hoe held still for the moment above his head. "So what! What if it is a waste of time!"

The coming of the rabbits provided him with a new obsession. He began to construct rabbit boxes. These were classified as nesting boxes, feeding boxes, exercise boxes, and so on, and each new model in a given category seemed more ingenious than its predecessor. The ideas he had picked up when he was making all those purposeless boxes before were now being put to good use. But they were so original that even when it came to a simple thing like lifting the lid off one of them, only he would know how. The sounds of sawing, planing, chiseling, and hammering now reverberated through the house without cease. MEANINGLESS ENERGY found its way through my skull into my brain, leaving no room for anything else.

What sort of a cry a rabbit made was something I hadn't thought about before, but I discovered that it was a squeak—*chū, chū.* It was, I found, a profoundly disappointing sound; and like the Emperor's voice when I first heard it on the radio, it made me feel quite hollow inside. This strange, futile cry I had to listen to all the time; for, fearing the invasion of burglars and stray dogs, Father had put their boxes in the closet at the end of the corridor, no more than three feet away from my pillow. Rabbits, it would appear, sleep during the day and become active at night. At irregular intervals, but never stopping, various sounds reached me as I lay in my bed in the darkness. One moment I would hear their teeth grinding away at the wood, next their feet stamping on the floor, then their droppings or pee going down the drainage system (this was a remarkable affair constructed of tin, designed to meet the rabbit's moving bottom whichever way it was turned).

A typical night for me after the coming of the rabbits went like this. In the middle of the night I awaken from a bad dream. In the dream always, a huge rat has crawled into my bed and is gnawing at either my feet or my head. Being awake is worse than the dream, for then I am assailed by real hobgoblins. From the tips of my toes, embedded in the ticklish wadding of the coverlet, a strange itchy sensation crawls up my legs and finally buries itself in the afflicted part of my spine. Everything I have on me begins to feel terribly constricting. I tear off the plaster cast, then my undershirt, and scratch my back hard, but to no avail. All that the scratching does is to drive the itch farther inside. In a desperate effort to force it out, I place my fingers on my chest between the ribs and push as hard as I can. As though in response to my anguish, the animals start making more of a din than ever. In the next room there is a duet of snores going on, interrupted by idiotic cries and mutters.

Father suddenly neighs like a horse—he is laughing. He cries out, "Woobik!" He has been saying the same thing in his sleep ever since he returned from the War, and I have come to realize that what he is really saying is, "Want milk!" He was the youngest of nine sons, and was given his mother's milk until the spring of his thirteenth year. At first I was inclined to suspect that he was not asleep at all and that it was a clever ruse on his part to persuade us of his unfitness for work. But I have since changed my mind, having observed the sincerity of his envy as he watches me drink my convalescent's ration of dried milk. His nightly dream, then, is quite authentic, brought on by both an immediate desire and unforgotten childhood pleasures. I'm not in the least shocked by Father's mother fixation, if that is indeed what he suffers from. I find it rather funny, as a matter of fact. True, the picture of Father sucking away at his mother's breast is grotesque, but then, I've always had a weakness for grotesquery. This is not to say that the cry "Woobik!" in the middle of the night does not startle me every time. That the word is nonsensical and I have had to guess at its meaning, albeit correctly, makes it all the more sinister in its suggestiveness.

Made a nervous wreck by this din in the dark, I begin to imagine that my body is about to disintegrate from both outside and inside. The noise becomes unbearable, and I try to pull the coverlet up over my head. But all I succeed in doing is to pull out handfuls of cotton wadding; most of the coverlet remains caught in my legs. The itch in my spine gets worse and worse. It is something, I feel, that rises bubbling like marsh gas out of the debris in my chaotic room —the dust, the rags, the mucus-soaked paper tissues—and seeps into my body. In an attempt to contain the itch that is beyond my reach, I hold my body absolutely taut. I hear again the rabbits crying in the closet, "chū, chū." What an incredibly feeble cry, I think to myself, for creatures that can bang about so.

The rabbits soon produced babies. These thrived under the skilled care of my veterinarian father. He never told us what he had paid for his two rabbits, but we could guess that they represented a considerable financial investment. Every day he would weigh each of the babies, take the mother's temperature, and fuss neurotically over the texture and mix of the food he gave them at regular, short intervals. This exacting routine left him no time for the boxes. The ingenious drainage system, now long neglected, was a shambles. But let alone find the time to fix it, he couldn't even get around to building a compartment for the babies. Inevitably, then, we found ourselves virtually sharing our own quarters with the entire rabbit family. Our house was turned into a veritable animal hut. That was bad enough, but what bothered me far more was that we, all three of us, began to resemble these creatures that cohabited with us. Even before the babies were born, there had been bits of rabbit fur all over the house. But now they literally filled the air, and our heads, covered with the stuff, looked like haloed apparitions emerging from a cloud of smoke. Because he was constantly brushing the rabbits, big and small, Father looked by far the strangest. There was rabbit fur in his nostrils always. As I watched him across the dinner table biting his food with his front teeth, the fur in his nostrils quivering with each breath, I would catch myself thinking of him as being one of them. Mother, too, seemed unable to leave the baby rabbits alone. They revived in her all her maternal instincts, I suppose. All day long she held them in her arms, and would even take them to bed with her, holding them close to her breast inside her kimono, not minding their scratching. In baby language and in hardly more than a whisper, she would repeatedly tell them—I presume it was they she was talking to—stories about me as a baby. Even Father would chide her then. "Hey, those are rabbits, not humans!"

Saucers, bowls, and pans with bits of gruel, fish skin, tea leaves, etc., stuck to the bottom lay on the floor everywhere. Father was to blame for this. Can't let all those good vitamins go down the drain, he said—he seemed to have committed to memory the exact nutritional content of every food he gave the rabbits—and refused to let Mother wash them. But what bothered me even more than the dirty dishes and pans was that while we ate, he would stare shamelessly at our plates to see how much he could hope to salvage for his rabbits. Mother, however, welcomed Father's hoarding of leftovers. Having become slovenly in her old age, she wanted to have as little to do with the kitchen as possible. It was a double blessing for her: she could now stay away from the kitchen sink, and better still, she could serve us any horrid concoction she liked, for the less we ate, the more the rabbits got, and therefore the greater was her husband's satisfaction.

Of course, our house became a haven for bugs and slugs of every description. They crawled about happily here and there in every room, coated with sauce or soybean paste. Mother, now a woman of leisure but with no one else to talk to (her neighbors would have nothing to do with her), became my constant bedside companion. She would lie flat on her back on the floor beside me and play with the baby rabbits or, when she got bored with that, daydream about sweetcakes. "My, that was good!" she would cry out desperately. Yet unlike Father and me, she got fatter by the day. Her belly and face got quite round, and her legs, peeping out of the open folds of her kimono, were as plump as a child's. Her kind of life must excite one's imagination, for she would without warning start describing my future bride. It was like opening some cheap novel in the middle. Anyway, what I found intolerable was that this imaginary bride she was describing invariably became none other than herself. As we lay thus side by side through most of the day, a whole army of flies, attracted to our house from the neighborhood, would eventually congregate around us. Used to the presence of all such creatures, I didn't mind them particularly. But even I was a trifle appalled when I happened once to pass my hand through my hair, and a pair of mating bluebottles flew out and away.

Father was now engaged in an ambitious project. By some mysterious means known only to those who have served long in the army, he had managed to acquire some glass tubes, wire netting, copper wire, and suchlike, and with surprising speed and efficiency had built himself a scientific apparatus. Its purpose was as follows: to extract from human hair a certain nutrient, feed it to the rabbits, and thus accelerate their development. Clearly, the apparatus was no sudden inspiration. I remembered that recently, whenever he clipped his hair, he would carefully wrap up the clippings in a newspaper and put it away among his "treasures" on the shelf. But it soon became apparent that his stock of his own hair clippings was by no means enough for his purpose. He would mutter, ostensibly to himself but quite audibly, "A barber would have lots of hair to spare." What he was trying to tell us, of course, was that he wanted Mother or me to go to a barbershop and ask for some. Having no desire to go on a fool errand like that, we would look away innocently, pretending not to have heard. He would then hang his head despondently. At such times he looked more like a rabbit than ever. Finally I deliberately told him a lie: "A barber told me today that the prefectural health department had prohibited the sale of hair. A barbershop runs the risk of being shut down if it's caught doing it." The lie was extraordinarily effective. He shook his head in silence several times (which was his way of summoning patience in the face of adversity) and stopped muttering about barbers.

I was mistaken, however, in thinking that he had given up all thought of getting other people's hair. He took to staring at me wistfully, then sighing like a bad actor—"Haaa . . ." And at night, as I lay in bed, he would watch me furtively, waiting perhaps for a chance to creep up to my bedside. And then one night, unable to restrain himself any longer, he blurted out, "What a lot of hair you have!" He scratched his own head wildly as he said this. Instinctively I covered my head with my hands. Oh God, I thought, he goes to sleep earlier than me and wakes up earlier; by four in the morning, he's usually awake; with that beloved chrome-plated scalpel of his, he could shave my entire head clean while

I was still asleep. My fear, though fanciful, was not entirely unjustified: I did have a thick head of hair, too thick indeed for comfort. As I put out the light that night and tried to go to sleep, I thought I could see Father bending over me in the manner of a slaughterhouse foreman about to start on a carcass with his skinning knife. From such fantasizing it was easy to fall into wondering whether I had not become one of *them*—one of those stupid, timid, yet shameless animals living with us.

But all my father's hope and hard work came to nought, even more helplessly than a prized potato field that is ruined by a mere two or three days of rain. As though *our* taking in the rabbits had been the immediate cause, angora wool ceased to be marketable. But this should not have surprised us. After all, rabbits were the easiest things to breed, and even without Father's as-yet-unproduced patent medicine they grew plenty of hair. All those plans for selling the fur and spare rabbit babies and making eight thousand yen a month, of winning first prizes at rabbit shows, turned out to have been just empty dreams. But the rabbits survived the crumbling of Father's hopes. They rushed about as wildly as before —no, they were even wilder, for the babies were now full-grown, and Father was too deflated to care what they did—distributing tufts of fur that floated about us like ashes of disillusionment. They invaded the alcove and knocked down the scientific apparatus that stood there in vain resplendence, scattering glass tubes and bits of wire all over the room. With these were mingled Father's hair clippings, mostly gray, which the rabbits had got at by biting through the newspaper wrapping.

Mother began to complain incessantly that she'd had to sell all her clothes in order to buy bean-curd remains for them. As she watched them eat, she seemed to see bits of her clothes being munched away. Not long ago, she had joyfully envisaged them as the provider of shawls, gloves, and other finery for herself. The feeble *"chū, chū"* of the rabbits now was constantly being drowned out by the hysterical cries of an aging woman: "How dare you pee there!"

One day Mother came home with a "visitor." This was the first we had had in thirteen months. He wore high boots, and came on a bicycle with a wicker basket attached to it. As he lugged the bicycle in through the front gate, Father and I watched and waited like soldiers in a fort: "Is he friend or foe?" Mother ran up to me and whispered in my ear, "He works for a sausage factory. Don't tell Father." I accepted the information with equanimity. The rabbits had become white elephants, and the sooner they were disposed of the better. Indeed, if the man had cooked a tasty rabbit dish then and there, I would have eaten it gladly.

The meat buyer was led to the veranda, where the rabbits had been brought together. He said ingratiatingly, "What magnificent specimens!" Father, still ignorant of the visitor's identity, acknowledged the compliment with a shy bow and a schoolgirl blush. Perhaps thrown into confusion by this, the meat buyer suddenly reached for the nearest rabbit and picked it up by the skin on its back.

He said in a voice so loud I thought I could see the doors shake, "All you laymen get taken in!" The rabbit hung in midair helplessly under the man's bare arm. Its limbs were all drawn in; the fur on its stomach fluttered softly in the breeze. "Laymen wanting to make money on the side always want horses or cows to begin with. But when they find they can't get them, they go for pigs. And when they find they can't get pigs either, they settle for rabbits. That's when the trouble starts. Ordinary domestic rabbits at first, then angoras, then chinchillas and rexes. There's no turning back then. You leave the rabbits, and go on to monsters like nutrias and guinea pigs. When you've reached the guinea-pig stage, you're finished."

We listened to his loud voice, our eardrums shaking, and understood nothing. It was like listening to a foreigner's gibberish. He continued: "Cows ending up as guinea pigs—that's very funny!" He paused, waiting for his own laughter to subside. "Anyway, you've got to be careful. Rabbits are edible, sure, but try eating a guinea pig. Mind you, these angoras aren't that great to eat either."

At that moment the captive rabbit, its taut gray skin showing through the fur, suddenly straightened its limbs out and bit the meat buyer's arm. I felt blood rushing to my head. For some reason all that my eyes saw then were the rabbit and the hand that held it by its back. "Bite him again!" I said to myself. "Son of a bitch!" the man cried out, and swung the rabbit at the pillar on the veranda. Its head made a sickening crunching sound as it hit the wood. But it was not dead as it lay at the foot of the pillar. Its red eyes, wide open but probably unseeing, looked at us. The meat buyer picked it up and threw it into the basket on his bicycle. He then grabbed the others by the ears one by one, and stuffed them all in. The lid was closed and secured by a cord. Through the mesh the rabbits' white fur appeared, moving, it seemed, with a life of its own. The meat buyer pulled some dirty bills out of his wallet. He turned toward my father, then looked away quickly—did he sense some rabbitlike quality there?—and handed the bills to Mother.

The man's bicycle was now near the gate, beyond the vegetable garden where mysteriously only those vines that Father planted for rabbit fodder flourished. We stood by the veranda and watched it go, not saying a word to one another.

TRANSLATED BY EDWIN MC CLELLAN

▟KOJIMA NOBUO

Kojima Nobuo was born in 1915 on the outskirts of the central Honshū city of Gifu, the son of a maker of Buddhist altars. After graduating in English literature from Tokyo University, he was drafted and sent to China; at the end of the War he was serving with an intelligence unit in Peking. On his return to Japan he began a career in teaching which he has continued along with his writing career.

Kojima made his rather late literary debut with the short story "Rifle" (*Shō-jū*, 1952), a vignette of a young soldier whose passion for his rifle gives rise to a bewildering sequence of associations, sexual and existential. But his first published work was "In a Train" (*Kisha no naka*, 1948), a memorable picture of postwar degradation, here compressed into a nightmarish ride on an overcrowded train, with the humor sometimes lapsing into farce as in his later, more widely read stories.

Beneath the broad satirical humor of such works as "The American School," Kojima expresses his sympathy for the everyday heroics of little people. He has said that what he found on the postwar scene was mainly a simple, purposeful, even heroic, if sometimes pathetic, struggle for survival. Since the 1960s he has written gloomy, reflective novels characterized by a finer, though equally relentless, irony. *A Close Family* (*Hōyō kazoku*, 1965), which won him the first Tanizaki Prize, is centered on a painfully insecure man—a university teacher and translator—who is the acutely self-conscious witness to the gradual disintegration of his family, and himself.

❖ The American School

(Amerikan sukūru, 1954)

It was past eight-thirty and still the official had not appeared. The teachers had been told to assemble by this hour for their excursion to the American school, and most of them had come twenty minutes or so early. Having made their way to the Prefectural Office through the morning throngs of commuters, all thirty of them were now left sitting here and there on the deserted stairs and around the gravel drive. There was one woman among them. She had apparently gone to some trouble to dress for the occasion; but her high heels, hat, and new plaid suit only made her look more sad and shabby.

As soon as they were all present, the teachers went en masse to the Office of Education on the second floor, only to be driven back down to this place which had not even been mentioned at the organization meeting a week ago. Right after the roll call the chairman of that meeting, an administrator from the Office of Education, had read off a list of instructions. The first was to assemble promptly at the appointed time. The second was to dress impeccably. The latter had created a stir which did not die down until the promulgation of the third point, that they must maintain a solemn silence at all times. Finally, they were to pack a lunch, for they would have to march to and from the school, a total distance of some eight miles; and even teachers had learned to feel proper hunger pangs in the three years since the War.

An American jeep ploughed through the gravel of the driveway, rounded the sharp curve, and came to a stop in front of the prefectural building. A teacher who had been sitting just inside the door jumped to his feet and moved away.

There was one man who had all the while been standing straight as a ramrod. The best-dressed and healthiest-looking of the group, he was conspicuous in an almost disconcerting way. At the previous week's meeting he had repeatedly raised his hand with questions for the chairman, a man by the name of Shibamoto. "Are we only supposed to observe?" he had inquired at one juncture. "What do you mean?" Shibamoto asked. "I was just wondering," he said, "if we might not give them a demonstration of our oral method." With a slight swagger that accentuated his heavy judo wrestler's build, the official reiterated loudly that the purpose of the excursion was to observe. He added that the Office of Education had gone to considerable lengths to secure permission for the visit. The man, whose name was Yamada, had at last given up this line of questioning.

He seized the floor once again in the commotion that followed the remarks on proper dress. "Quite right, sir," he said. "We must all present a neat appearance, whatever the cost. Any sloppiness would reflect on the profession. Worst of all, it would raise serious doubts about our competence to teach English. They despise us as a defeated people to begin with, and when they see the clothes we wear—I know, because I interpreted for the inspectors when they came to our school—they just look the other way. Not to mention the toilets . . ." His speech was interrupted at this point, and by now everyone was staring at him, with particular attention to his feet. There was scarcely another pair of leather shoes in sight. Undaunted, he resumed as soon as the mutters died down. They should avoid speaking Japanese in front of their hosts, he insisted, in order to display to the fullest extent their command of English. This was greeted by more general muttering, and a shrill outcry from the man sitting next to him: "What non-sense!" Yamada turned to face the heckler. But before he could launch into a longwinded defense of his proposal, Shibamoto called for order with the request that both Mr. Yamada and Mr. Isa refrain from intemperate language.

Isa had once been pressed into service at election time as interpreter for the Occupation inspection team (all elections were to be conducted impartially under the watchful eyes of the authorities). He was taken by jeep from one small village to the next, and was expected to keep his American counterpart informed of what was going on. Still only about thirty years old, he had never had a single conversa-tion in English; occasional attempts at practical application of the language in the classroom had left him tingling with embarrassment; and when word came that the Americans would soon be visiting his school he had feigned illness, lying in bed for several days with an icebag pressed against his forehead, where there was not the slightest trace of fever. Only fear of unknown reprisals at the hands of the Occupation officials had deterred him from a similar stratagem at the time of the elections.

The moment he was packed into the jeep with a Negro soldier, he had turned to the fellow and said, in English: "I am truly very sorry to have kept you waiting." This was met with silence, and when he repeated the words three times over, the soldier only stared at him coldly and uncomprehendingly. The phrase he had prepared several days ago and practiced constantly since was clearly too formal and correct. From then on he limited himself to two words, "stop" and "go." For those five hours he felt as if he were being boiled alive, though outwardly he appeared to be merely loafing on the job. And in either case, the result was that he was of no use to anyone.

As soon as they approached the first polling-place, he fled. He tried to reason with himself, before sneaking off to hide, that it would go still worse with him than if he had refused to come in the first place. But the prospect of being addressed in that unfamiliar language in front of a crowd made his knees quake. By the time the Negro noticed his absence and came back to find him, he was long gone.

Isa was not by nature so craven; indeed, as the jeep drove into the village he had felt a strong impulse to do violence to his keeper. But after they slowed down, it seemed easier to escape, and so he jumped off the rear and made for the wooded slope above the road. On discovering that his passenger had fled, the soldier went after him, partly out of fear at being left alone in these dark hills. Deep in the woods Isa saw the man coming. He called out to him in Japanese: "You'll have to speak our language. Speak Japanese or else! What would you do if someone really said that to you?" As the face of his adversary drew near, a neatly trimmed beard, features strained in an effort to make out the indistinct words, it gave a feeling of loneliness. The beard contributed an incongruously civilized air, and as the face moved still closer it seemed almost to show some understanding of the stream of Japanese that issued forth from behind the trees. Isa babbled on as fast as he could. When the Negro at last realized that the words were not in his language, he threw up his hands and shrugged his shoulders. Seated behind the wheel again, he looked even lonelier than before, as if unaccountably intimidated by this creature who spoke scarcely a word of normal English, and who would lapse without warning into Japanese gibberish. He ceased to pay any attention at all to Isa, and proceeded as though chauffeuring an honored guest around the countryside. A pointless errand on the whole; but at least, it occurred to him, the man might be of some service in helping him deal with hostile natives.

Each time an American jeep drove up, Isa drifted a little away from the prefectural building. Yamada's foolish suggestions at the organization meeting were still fresh in his mind, especially the proposal of a demonstration class, which had aroused in him an instant panic that persisted to this moment. Well, he would simply keep a close watch on Yamada and shut him up if necessary. He had, however, already yielded on one point: he was wearing a pair of black leather civilian shoes. They were an odd match with his khaki uniform, but he had wanted at least to spare himself the embarrassment of army boots. Likewise, having set out with his lunch box in an old army bag, along the way he had taken the box out, folded up the incriminating bag, and stuck it under his arm.

Yamada continued to stand alone surveying the scene expectantly. Whenever a jeep pulled up he would bustle over to explain the situation. "We represent the English teachers of this prefecture," he would begin stiffly. "We are very devoted to the English language. We work very hard to teach the English. We are now utilizing the latest methods of instruction, just like you have in your country."

"If you work so goddam hard, what are you hanging around for at this hour?" one driver replied, reaching down with a look of extreme boredom to hand him a cigarette.

"I do not smoke," said Yamada.

"Are you the chief?"

"Our leader is an official of this prefecture. He is very late for our appointment. Government officials are lazy people. But you must not think that all Japanese are like that."

The soldier, who was black, threw up his hands in disgust. "I am truly very sorry to have kept you waiting," he said, and drove off.

Yamada did not know what to make of this parting remark. The American had perhaps been mocking Japanese officials. He looked at his watch again and muttered to himself. What would their hosts think if they arrived late at the school? Something must be done. He called out to those of his colleagues who were sprawled within earshot, "Will some of you come up to the Education Office with me? If we don't do something we'll be late. They have our names on file at the school. We'll be disgraced. 'What can you expect from a defeated people?' they'll say."

Yamada noticed that Isa, who was sitting only a few feet away, kept his back turned as though preoccupied with some important business. He went over to investigate and found him with his lunch box open on his lap. Isa had been up since three, riding his bicycle to the nearest station, then taking a combination of streetcars and trains until he reached this distant city. He was hungry; rather, he thought he ought to be hungry by now.

Yamada stood for a moment in silent amazement. "This is no time to be eating," he said. "Come with me to the Education Office. If the officials there won't cooperate, we'll speak to the Occupation personnel."

The bare mention of the local Occupation force was enough to upset Isa. He had already noticed the bearded Negro in one of the jeeps, and had seen Yamada accost him. Indeed, it was one reason for beginning his lunch now. This was a high-risk area where he might be addressed in English at any moment. A mouthful of food would, he sensed, offer some defense against any demand that might be made of him. And so he did not answer Yamada, and regretted having challenged him at last week's meeting, thus attracting his attention. Isa had decided not to speak a word in any language today, for if he began by conversing in Japanese he would surely end by having to speak English. The best strategy was a tight-lipped silence that would lead people to believe he was indisposed. Then no one, neither official nor colleague, would think it strange if, when his turn came to talk at the school, he had nothing to say. Without looking up from his lunch he waved his chopsticks in the air by way of a reply.

"What kind of answer is that?" Yamada put his question in both languages and waited for an answer. Isa pretended not to hear. Yamada was given to venting his wrath in English. "Oh, for shame!" he exclaimed, stalking off towards the overdressed instructress, Michiko, who capitulated on the spot and followed him up the stairs.

On their way into the office they bumped into the tardy official. Shibamoto was wearing his Sunday best, which consisted of a long overcoat and a soft felt hat. As he led them out of the building, he blew a whistle to assemble the others.

Yamada protested that the whistle would sound a shrill note of unreconstructed militarism; furthermore, for the same reason, they should not march in a solid phalanx. Shibamoto granted his point and ordered the group to fall out. When the command was given to reassemble in loose ranks, Yamada placed himself like a staff adjutant at Shibamoto's side. The rest of the teachers straggled behind in a long procession, with Isa bringing up the rear.

Shibamoto made a brief announcement: "We received notification that the time for our visit had been changed. Sorry for the inconvenience. They were very pleased with the first group. Try to keep up the good record. Ready?"

It was about four miles to the American school down an asphalt road that ran straight as the crow flies from the outskirts of the city. Strung out like a chain gang, the teachers set out with Shibamoto and Yamada in the lead. Isa, at the other end, made no effort to move up. He found himself walking beside the woman, and this was somehow reassuring. Within ten minutes they had reached the asphalt road. There was an uninterrupted flow of traffic traveling to and fro among the various installations of the large base that stretched out for miles around the school. A sigh rippled through the group at the sight of this long black ribbon which was clearly not made for walking.

Isa watched with secret admiration as Michiko took a pair of sneakers from her cloth bundle and put them on. What foresight! The men around him were all wearing long overcoats, with a sprinkling of army issue such as he himself had on. The poverty revealed in their bulky clothing showed up starkly against the hard pavement. "I don't want you in rows, but do move closer together," Shibamoto cautioned. "You mustn't look so straggly—there are Occupation personnel all around you." Cars and jeeps were in fact flying by, thick and fast, though there was not another pedestrian to be seen anywhere on the forbidding road.

The presence of a single woman in their midst was enough to mitigate the ragged, faintly subversive spectacle created by the twenty-nine men. Before five minutes had gone by, a car coming from the opposite direction pulled up beside Michiko. A soldier stuck his head out the window and spoke to her. "What are you people doing here?" he asked, echoing the question put to them several times in front of the prefectural building. Michiko stated the purpose of their excursion in clear, correct English. "You're an English teacher, are you? Well, you're pretty damn good, I'd say." The soldier thrust some cans of cheese in her hands and drove off.

It was not until Michiko laughed out loud and tugged at his sleeve that Isa turned to face her. With eyes studiously averted from the exchange with the soldier, he had begun to reconsider his choice of companion. Walking beside the woman, he was easy prey for any number of foreign soldiers. He felt the weight of the can that Michiko had stuffed into his pocket while he was staring at the rice paddies below the road. Living in an era when true goodwill was translated into gifts of food, he was naturally pleased and flattered, and especially so for having failed to notice that she had received two cans from the soldier and had to give one away to keep the other. What if he was a little more vulnerable being next to her, he had only to look the other way when the enemy approached, and there were these unexpected benefits.

It had occurred to Michiko as they started down the asphalt road that she had forgotten something. In her rush this morning to change after sending off her son, her only child by the husband she had lost in the War (he too had been a teacher), it must have slipped her mind. She poked around in the cloth bundle and her suspicions were confirmed. Luckily the missing article was one that could be borrowed in a pinch; and at the moment the two cans of cheese plopped into her hands, she had picked Isa as her most likely benefactor.

Tranquilly and with unexpected warmth, the winter sun shone down upon the black surface until the glare began to affect one's eyes. Cars continued to pass by in both directions, and then a jeep drove up, this time from behind, and slowed down almost to the pace of the procession. Two soldiers, one white, one black, leaned out to look the group over. Yamada turned around and waited until the jeep drew up beside him. "Haro boys! What are you doing?" he hailed them.

With a look of mild surprise one of the soldiers asked in return: "Only one woman?" Having verified with their own eyes, without listening to Yamada's reply, that the woman they had passed was the only one, they stopped the jeep in the middle of the road and waited. As Michiko approached they called out to her: "Ojosan! Ojosan!" They asked where she was going and told her to get in. Her quick response was livelier than when she spoke in Japanese, her face more expressive, even distinctly feminine. "I'm on a group excursion," she said. "I really can't go ahead by myself."

The soldiers exchanged an approving glance as they inspected the proper Japanese lady from top to bottom. They tore the wrapper from two bars of chocolate and, with a parting nod full of regret, tossed them down to Michiko. She broke one of the bars into pieces and passed them out to a few people around her, this time omitting Isa. Afterward the teachers who had dropped back toward her at this point showed no disposition to move up again.

They had not been marching in close ranks from the outset, and by now the group had split into two separate platoons: Shibamoto, Yamada, and their followers in the lead, Michiko and her attendants in the rear, with a gap of over a hundred yards in between.

It came to Isa by slow degrees that his shoes hurt. Each step brought new pains. He began to regret having worn these ill-fitting genuine leather shoes; and when he reflected that he had put them on to please Yamada, to speak the foreign tongue in the right style—simply to hold down his job—his regrets gave way to anger. The pain grew more and more acute. He struggled to keep up with Michiko, but even this was too much for him. He now noticed with a twinge of envy how smooth and easy her stride had become since she abandoned her high heels for sneakers. No one else, either in his platoon or the group up front, showed signs of suffering from the same problem. He himself had never paid much attention to shoes until this moment. The offending pair, on loan from a colleague, had seemed just right when he first tried them on. A tiny discrepancy was enough, it appeared, to cause a great deal of pain. Isa became suspicious of the colleague who had lent him the shoes. For all he knew, the man could be in league with Yamada.

There was no telling how much farther they had to go, for the view ahead was blocked by a rise in the road. When Isa looked back to see how much ground they had covered he was distressed to find the prefectural building looming still quite large behind them.

About fifteen feet ahead, Michiko stood looking over her shoulder in his direction. "Is something wrong?" she asked when at last he caught up with her. At his mumbled reply apropos of shoes her face took on a look of utmost gravity. Having set out in new shoes herself, she had more than an inkling of what she would have endured but for the sneakers. "That will never do. We still have a long way to go. Maybe you should hitch a ride—why don't you stop one of these jeeps?"

Isa's pain yielded to astonishment and terror. What she suggested would not have occurred to him in his wildest dreams. "If it ever came to that!" he muttered as he stumbled forward in an effort to keep up, putting as much weight as possible on his toes to relieve the pinch on his insteps. He hoped to set her mind at ease and avoid further suggestions of drastic remedies, but he soon realized that his awkward gait only made matters worse.

Michiko slackened her pace and walked silently at Isa's side as if to subdue his pain by force of her own calm will. Until now she had found him a tedious companion, thoroughly wrapped up in himself for no apparent reason. But as soon as she began to share in his suffering, faint memories stirred within her of the love, long forgotten, that a woman can also share with a man. She did not, however, lose sight of her objective. She meant to have from him that homely article left behind in her haste. What love she felt for him was bound up with her hopes of getting it, and seemed to emanate like hunger pangs from somewhere near the pit of her empty stomach. While more cars whizzed by she spoke to him again in a soothing tone, as if to stroke his heaving back. "You really ought to get yourself a lift," she said. "Shall I ask for you?"

"No! No thank you! Never mind! I'd sooner go barefoot."

"Now really, I don't see why . . ."

Isa felt like biting his tongue for breaking his vow of silence. Yet had he kept quiet Michiko would no doubt have hailed a jeep immediately, and at her fluent English they would have picked him up without further ado. Then where would he be? No matter how dire his need, the very thought of riding next to a foreigner again made him sick. He remembered all too vividly his day of torture with the black soldier. He had felt as though at any moment he could murder the man, and if it had gone on for another day he surely would have done so, unless, of course, he had first found a way to escape.

The tender feelings which Michiko had summoned up from deep within her subsided in the face of Isa's stubborn refusal. The sweat now trickling down her body served as a nagging reminder of her impure motives. Very well, she thought, she would get what she was after anyway. And even that didn't really matter so much, she could if necessary do without. Resolved to not so much as look back at him, she forged ahead toward Yamada's platoon. The others followed in her wake, leaving Isa far behind.

Up front, Yamada and Shibamoto were trading boasts. Shibamoto, by his own account, had been one of a handful of judo experts in the prefecture before the War disrupted things—a fifth-degree black belt, no less. And contrary to malicious postwar propaganda, devotees of the martial arts were not all war criminals. One had only to consider himself, holder of a prominent post in the administrative section of the prefectural Education Office. Moreover, he taught judo not only to the local police, but to the Occupation personnel themselves, and had in fact got the job through his American supervisor.

Yamada's ears perked up at the mention of Occupation personnel. He was intensely interested in every kind of contact with the Americans, though so far his own had been restricted to interpreting. He had a consuming ambition to study abroad, to which end he schemed and fretted the livelong day.

Eager to establish his credentials with such a well-connected man, Yamada explained that he had conducted any number of demonstration classes at his school; that although they were supposedly professional teachers of English, few of his colleagues made a good showing . . . Yes, said Shibamoto, he had heard about all that. From a leather briefcase the likes of which were seldom seen in these times, Yamada removed a mimeographed schedule of a typical demonstration class, which he happened to have brought along.

"Rook heah, see for yourself," he said, breaking momentarily into English. "I hope sometime soon to hold a teaching seminar here in the city—with the backing of the administrative section, of course. And we would certainly welcome cooperation from the Americans." He handed Shibamoto his card. His name and titles appeared in Japanese script on one side, Roman on the other. "I might not look it now, but I hold a second-degree black belt in fencing," he volunteered.

"Is that so? I suppose you've had some experience in your day," said Shibamoto.

"You bet I have!" Yamada slashed the air with an imaginary sword. "This might not be the time to mention it, but when I was in OTS I got to whet my blade a bit, if you know what I mean."

"It must be hard, cutting off heads."

"Not really. It takes a good arm, a sharp sword, and practice, of course. That's all."

"How many did you polish off?"

"Let's see . . ." Yamada paused and looked around. "About twenty, I guess. Half of them must've been POWs."

"Any Yanks?"

"Naturally."

"How did they compare with the Chinese?"

"Well, there's quite a difference in how they take it. When you come right down to it, they show their lack of what you might call Oriental philosophy."

"You're lucky they never caught up with you."

". . . I was only following orders."

Yamada was suddenly aware of the dangerous turn in the conversation. What had he been saying? He fell silent. Noticing that Shibamoto had removed his overcoat, he hastily took off his own and stuck it under his arm. He looked over his shoulder at the disorderly procession and his taut, swarthy features collapsed into a disdainful grimace.

"What do you think of this mess?" he said to Shibamoto. "If the War were still on and this were a real march . . . ! But what can you expect from a bunch of high school teachers?"

Yamada fixed Isa hawklike in a distant gaze. In this perspective the laggard could not fail to arouse contempt and indignation. While Yamada stood at the side of the road the group straggled by in little clumps, their pace so listless that he wanted to ask with the Americans what business they had on this highway. He made up his mind to stay where he was and wait for Isa to come along. Over the past week he had not forgotten Isa's vague but unmistakable hostility. As he waited, the word "insubordinate" popped into his head. It seemed to furnish a key to understanding this queer fellow. With his own tales of martial valor still ringing in his ears, Yamada became again the company commander he had been until three years before. But for all the brutal self-assurance restored to him in this transformation, he did not bark out a reprimand to Isa, preferring to take him by surprise.

Michiko passed by first. "His shoes pinch," she explained, pointing back at Isa.

"His shoes pinch? Ridiculous!" This went beyond simple insubordination. To dawdle over such an infantile triviality was inexcusable. At this rate he was likely to start whining about his bladder or a sore throat and fall still farther behind. Well, what was the matter with his shoes? Yamada stared at the black blobs of Isa's feet scraping across the asphalt in the distance. He waited till the dusty shoes had shuffled up diffidently under his nose before he spoke. "Are those your shoes?" he snapped, in English.

Isa had not noticed Yamada at the side of the road. His eyes were wide open with the effort of bearing the pain, but he could not see a thing.

"It's your fault this group is in such a shambles. It only takes one straggler like you to throw everyone out of step."

Michiko came back and repeated to Yamada her suggestion that Isa ask for a ride.

"From the Americans?" Yamada's shoulders fell as he studied Isa's feet. Ignoring Michiko, he lashed out again at Isa: "That is out of the question. Mistah Isa, have you no pride? Maybe for ap-pen-di-ci-tis. But for *shoes?*"

Several other teachers had wandered back to see what was holding things up and stood looking over Yamada's shoulder. "He'd do better to go barefoot," one of them said. This solution had occurred to Isa any number of times since the pain began. But each time he had rejected it for fear of being spotted by the Americans, who were sure to question him about his bare feet and force him to ride in a jeep.

Yamada changed his tone. "Try to keep moving, at least. You've got everyone stopped in their tracks wondering what to do about you—Oh, Mr. Shibamoto. What do you think, sir?"

When Yamada failed to return to the front rank, Shibamoto had planted himself at the roadside like a stone Jizo. Once the leaders dropped out, the rest of the procession ground to a halt.

"If this keeps up we'll be late, sir. We'll be disgraced. The main thing is to make sure the Americans don't see him. Oh, for shame!"

"What seems to be the trouble here?" Shibamoto had not yet grasped the cause of Yamada's excitement. When the problem was put to him he proposed that Isa go ahead and remove his shoes. Yamada and a few others would walk along on either side and shield him from the passers-by.

Shibamoto's proposal was duly adopted and Isa was promptly relieved of his suffering. It even struck him that this pavement could have been made for bare feet, which were not, after all, without some resemblance to the rubber tires of a car.

Michiko brooded over the man who was once more walking beside her, though likely soon to lag behind again. Isa seemed as unresponsive as ever, and she made no attempt to speak to him. But his stubborn streak had begun to remind her of her late husband. Surrounded by Yamada and the others, he strode along unshod and full of purpose, a shy but spirited little man in the jaws of adversity. That is what her husband had been when he went off to war.

Her thoughts drifted back to that day when she had struggled to keep up with the column of soldiers bound for the front as they marched the five miles from their base to the station. They had not paused once along the way, pushing ahead at an unrelenting pace that did not allow for last-minute farewells. Her husband marched with clenched teeth and scarcely cast a glance in her direction. The only time he turned his head to face her, he made a curt gesture with his hand as if to drive her away. There had of course been others besides herself, among them aged mothers calling out their son's names as they stumbled after the swift procession.

Michiko had understood her husband's embarrassment then. The feelings of the barefoot man next to her now were no doubt of the same kind. Perhaps she would speak to him once they were at the school. She was suddenly aware again of the high heels pressing through the cloth against her hands like hard little buds about to flower. Yes, after she had changed her shoes at the school she would have a word with him.

Isa showed no sign of faltering, indeed he fairly loped along, with none of the strain that was beginning to tell on the others. He was, however, still shy of foreign eyes, though his fears were very different from Yamada's, and he walked somewhat stooped over. He hurried ahead driven by the desire to reach his destination at the earliest possible moment, and in the happy expectation of freedom from any further need to propel himself. He was too absorbed in the delicate task of simultaneously staying out of sight and rushing forward to reflect that he would still have to move about at the school, and then make the trek back to the city.

Taking but small comfort in Isa's return to the fold and the restoration of some semblance of order, Yamada dwelt on the disgust which the man's every action stirred up in him. He decided the time had come to broach to Shibamoto the subject that had been in the back of his mind all day. "You know, sir," he began, "we really ought to give a demonstration class while we're there. It's a rare opportunity to show them what we can do, and maybe we can get them to evaluate and rank us while we're at it."

Shibamoto was busy surveying the buildings of the American school, which had come into view as soon as they passed the crest in the road. He gave Yamada a doubtful look and did not reply. When Yamada pressed the point by suggesting that he himself could make the request, Shibamoto wearily repeated that their hosts might find the exercise troublesome.

"I don't see why it should be any trouble. It will be our show—a demonstration of what English teachers in this country are capable of. Afterwards we'll let them give us a few pointers, that's all. As a judo expert I'm sure you can see the wisdom of our taking the offensive, so to speak."

This was a thrust that Shibamoto could not parry. He would have to let the man have his way. He had never met such a cocky instructor, he thought, as Yamada announced once again that he would take the bull by the horns.

Isa did not miss a word of this exchange. When he saw Shibamoto weaken, his thoughts turned instinctively to escape. Slipping easily through the loose cordon they had strung around him, he sidled off to the edge of the road and unbuttoned his fly. Yamada was still preoccupied and failed to notice this dereliction; the others were too tired to bother with him.

Just then Michiko was accosted by another jeep. She broke into a cold sweat as she ascertained that the melancholy black face looking down at her wanted to know about Isa, who stood relieving himself up the road. But her fears were set to rest when she heard the soldier ask, "What's with the bare feet?" She explained, and the jeep rumbled off in Isa's direction.

Isa wheeled around in alarm, and at one glance recognized his old adversary. He backed away, stunned by the accuracy of his presentiment that he would see the man again today. When he reached the shoulder of the road he turned and leaped into the field below. Here he was far less protected than he had been on that wooded slope. The soldier was beckoning to him with a miniature package of cigarettes. The next moment Yamada was yelling at him. "He's only trying to do you a favor. What's the matter with you!" Joining forces, the soldier and Yamada clambered into the field. Together they dragged Isa back up to the road and bundled him into the jeep. The vehicle bearing the solitary captive soon vanished in a cloud of sand, and raucous laughter swept through the ranks.

Above the road ahead some crows flocked and veered off to one side as if to clear a path for the car passing far below. Or perhaps they were preparing to scavenge around the American school. Michiko watched this scene and savored a certain relief, accompanied by a quiet, private laugh, at the removal of the burden that Isa had become for her. She no longer imagined that she could understand his excessive timidity, unless, she speculated, he had done something awful during the War.

Isa sat hunched up in the back of the jeep. He quickly averted his eyes from the driver's seat and peered out at the dwindling faces of his colleagues. Although their features were already blurred, he could clearly see that they were laughing. Yet, for all their scorn, their company was far preferable to the predicament that now filled him with despair. The general laughter left little doubt that Yamada would succeed in squeezing out of him some sort of performance in English. As far as he was concerned, it was now all but inevitable; that is, it seemed quite within the realm of possibility, which was for Isa tantamount to inevitability.

On their first encounter the Negro had mistaken Isa's cowed silence for sullen contempt, with overtones of a personal animus against himself. Afterwards he had Isa's credentials checked through the Education Office, without bothering to state the cause of his curiosity; and when the record showed no reason for the man's refusal to speak English, he felt that his suspicions had been confirmed. This unlooked-for second meeting was a stroke of luck: he would have a little revenge for that business in the woods.

The jeep screeched to a halt and Isa found a pistol pointing into his face. Then came the command: "Speak English, man. Let's hear it again. 'I am truly very sorry to have kept you waiting.'"

Isa trembled all over and stammered out the phrase as dictated. Below the trim moustache the mouth of his captor opened in a loud guffaw. The pistol was only a toy, he said. Humming a jazz tune, he started up the engine and drove on.

At the American school the soldier bade Isa a friendly farewell as he climbed out of the jeep. "Maybe we'll meet again," he said, with some appreciation, it appeared, of the karma that had already brought them together twice. Isa felt weak inside at the mere suggestion.

As soon as the jeep was out of sight Isa, still barefoot, ran toward the fence enclosing the school playground. After a few moments' rest he put on his shoes and crouched down to look around. The children at recess on the playground, boys and girls mixed together, ranged from the early grades through junior high school. Even now, in midwinter, they were scampering about in a colorful assortment of light clothes, a sweater here, a blouse and jumper there. Isa retreated into the shadow of one of the buildings to continue his inspection from a less public vantage point.

Along with a sense of relative security, he experienced an overwhelming mental fatigue. He closed his eyes for fear of fainting and felt the tears well up behind his eyelids. At first he could not tell what had brought on his tears, but he knew it was a joy so intense as to be close to sorrow. With his eyes still closed he slowly discerned the source of his bliss in a murmuring of soft voices, sweet and clear as a mountain stream. They seemed to come from another world, perhaps in part because the words made little sense to him.

Isa opened his eyes and saw a cluster of young girls, twelve or thirteen years old, chatting with each other about fifty feet from where he was hiding. He concluded that he and his colleagues were members of a pathetic race which had no place here.

Listening to these mellifluous English voices, he could not account for the fear and horror which the language had always inspired in him. At the same time his own inner voice whispered: It is foolish for Japanese to speak this language like foreigners. If they do, it makes them foreigners, too. And that is a real disgrace.

He pictured clearly to himself the outlandish gestures that Yamada affected when he spoke English. There was no dignity in talking just like a foreigner. But it was equally demeaning to speak a foreign tongue like a Japanese. This was the fate that awaited him today, he knew, if he were called upon to talk at the school. The few times that he had begun his class with a halting goodo-moaning-eburybody he had afterward flushed crimson and felt himself at the bottom of some dark ravine. No! That was not for him. He would sooner make himself over into a whole new man.

Enrapt with the schoolgirls' merry fugue, Isa did not hear the jeep return. The soldier got out, whistling another tune. Some distance from where Isa remained hidden, he stood leaning over the fence and searched out his son. Having been on urgent business to the barracks that adjoined the school, only after it was finished did he remember Isa's feet. The boy, who looked to be of junior-high-school age, came running to his father, and a few moments later disappeared into the school.

Presently a beautiful tall lady of a type one often sees in American movies appeared before Isa's eyes. With the black boy in tow, she advanced swiftly and purposefully toward the fence. Isa stole off into the shade of a nearby grove, lest she find him crouching there and take him for a thief. He shut his eyes and mentally blocked his ears, to no avail; he could distinctly hear her footsteps and the sound of her voice calling out as she came closer and closer. Although he suspected that her call was meant for him, and had in any case resigned himself by now to being caught, he still did not respond. He kept his head down and his eyes closed until he felt a touch on his shoulders and heard the word ". . . shoes?" At this he stood up and bowed.

When he opened his eyes and saw the lady standing right beside him, he was all but blinded by the look of abundance on her face: features that spoke of an ample diet, material well-being, and pride of race. She was for all that only human, and a fellow schoolteacher as well. So he tried to tell himself, but he could not quite believe it. Next to her—she stood at least a head taller than he—Isa felt weak around the knees, and in reply to her questions he only nodded and bowed. In the end, like a timid servant with his mistress, he allowed himself to be led off toward the school.

Isa caught enough of the cascade of soothing words that poured from her lips like melting snow to realize that he had that meddlesome Negro to thank for his new predicament. "I only want to do something about those feet," the lady said. "I'm not going to poison you." He wanted to say thank you—that much he could manage. But once he had opened his mouth she would expect him to keep up a steady conversation. He had better just play dumb and follow her like a dog.

Isa sank back into despondency when he thought of the interrogation to which, as a solitary Japanese among a horde of foreigners, and an English teacher of sorts, he was sure to be subjected. He was too busy brooding to notice the gaggle of students that trailed behind him as he limped along, until a few sharp words from the lady sent them shouting and laughing back to the playground.

She kept smiling at him and making what sounded like friendly remarks, which required him to play deaf as well as dumb. But he had begun to receive contradictory signals from his conscience. To atone for the appearance of in-civility he had given so far, he was tempted to fall down and kiss the lady's feet, or at least the ground beneath them. Caught between these conflicting impulses, Isa took it into his head to carry her books for her. He moved abruptly to her side and, without a word, tried to wrest the heavy books from her arms. He had the appropriate phrase on the tip of his tongue but was too embarrassed to say it. Perplexed by this dumbshow, the lady clutched the books to her breast. When he continued to tug at the books, bowing and grinning abjectly, she eventually guessed his intention and thanked him; but she would not surrender her burden.

It was enough for Isa that she had recognized his gesture. Hereafter, how-ever incompetent he might appear at the school, he would not be considered a barbaric ingrate. As they approached the building, he felt something like the relief of a condemned criminal who had made one last plea for forgiveness from his fellow men.

Since the nurse was not to be found in the dispensary, the schoolmistress led Isa to her own office, where she shut the door firmly and turned the key. Once again Isa had a sinking feeling, such as the toy pistol had produced in him a while ago. "Sit down," said the lady, whose name, he gathered from the sign on the door, was Emily. "We lock the door so we can smoke," she explained. "Even the men do. It sets a bad example for the students, you see."

It took Isa some time to decipher this statement. From the moment he entered the room he kept his eyes glued to the floor and let his ears tune out her speech, which he dimly imagined to be a reproach for his earlier rudeness. In any case the words seemed to have nothing to do with his feet, and it was not until he raised his head, afraid of appearing very rude indeed, that he saw the smoke and half grasped their meaning. Still standing in silence, he traced the upward spiral of smoke with his eyes, the better to extricate himself from Miss Emily's gaze.

Out of the clear blue sky came the order: "Take off your shoes!" Or so he interpreted her sharp utterance. But no sooner was he down to his army socks than she burst out laughing and murmured something about coffee. Then he thought he heard her say, though it made little sense to him, that he should "help himself." When Isa, thoroughly confused, began to pull up his socks, in a single violent motion Miss Emily lunged at him and stripped them off. She gaped at his exposed feet, at first with simple curiosity, then with a look of distress on detecting the raw wound where the skin had been scraped away. "Dear me," she exclaimed, putting out her cigarette.

It was by no means easy for Isa to make such a spectacle of himself in front of a foreign lady, here in this secret room. But so long as he was not obliged to speak, he was resigned to suffering these minor indignities. Nevertheless, he was desperately eager to return to the group, to become again only one among many.

After drinking a cup of coffee by herself, Miss Emily went out into the corridor, locking the door behind her. As she left, Isa understood her to say that she was going to consult with the nurse, which was encouraging—but why had she locked the door? Only then did he finish puzzling out her remark upon entering the room, to the effect that they mustn't let the students see them smoke. Yet that was only part of it, he knew. She was also worried about his wandering around the school on the loose, or still worse, escaping again, like a wounded animal that runs away when one is only trying to help it. As soon as Isa reached this point in his train of thought he felt an irresistible impulse to flee that very moment. He immediately opened the window, jumped out, and started to run.

After a few steps he felt the ground against his bare feet and remembered his shoes. He could not just leave them there, they did not belong to him. As he was hoisting himself back up through the window, the door opened across the room and he found himself face to face with Miss Emily.

While Isa was still lurking behind the trim modern buildings of the American school, Yamada wasted no time in approaching Michiko. In the past he had seen her from a distance conversing with foreigners in a free and easy manner. Since the beginning of today's excursion, when he dragged her off to the Education Office, he had been scheming for a chance to examine her English at first hand. It was not uncommon for members of his profession to test each other's mettle on some trivial pretext, like samurai picking quarrels simply to show off their prowess. Yamada was a past master at this sort of thing. And when he came up against colleagues whose English was better than his own, especially if they were women, he would try to defeat them on other grounds, to browbeat them if need be with the brute strength of his manly will. But in the end he often lost anyway.

Yamada had bided his time while Isa was tagging along beside Michiko, with what seemed to be warm encouragement on her part. Now that that nuisance had been removed, he could proceed with his interrogation. He unleashed a barrage of questions in English that left her scarcely a moment to catch her breath. What schools had she gone to, where did she graduate, had she taken special lessons in conversation, how many American friends did she have????

At first, even Michiko, with her considerable abilities, could not bring herself to reply in kind to her countryman's tirade in a foreign language. She answered only haltingly, and half in Japanese. But when Yamada showed no sign of relenting, she saw what he was up to, and resented his contempt for her sex.

And what, if she might inquire, was the big attraction of English for him? Would he like to try a demonstration class with her sometime? Wasn't it curious that he pronounced certain words with a kind of Boston accent, others in a sort of Southern drawl, which was a little like mixing Kyushu speech with the slow country dialect of Aomori?

Yamada was staggered by the woman's counterattack, delivered in rapid-fire, thoroughly natural English. It was not so much her fluency as the substance of her remarks that defeated him. She was more than a match for him, he conceded; he would have to find some other weakness. In his experience, when dealing with women, food and clothing were the best bet.

"That's a fine outfit you're wearing," he said, lapsing back into Japanese. "Did you get it before the War?"

"Yes," she answered softly. "That is, the material comes from a robe that belonged to my husband. He was killed in the War."

"I'm sorry to hear that. It must be hard for you." Yamada peered shrewdly into Michiko's face as he added: "If you need rice, I can get it fairly cheap."

"That's very kind of you," she said. "May I have your card?"

"And if you'd like a little piecework to do at home, perhaps I could find you something."

"I would certainly appreciate it. Men really are much better at arranging these things, aren't they!"

The procession had at last come to a halt in front of the gate to the school compound. As soon as Yamada noticed the guard looking over their credentials, he burst in with the information that one of their number had preceded them by jeep. Turning back to Michiko, he then announced in English: "I imagine that he is still barefoot, and has concealed himself somewhere behind the school."

"What makes you think that?" asked Michiko.

"Elementary," said Yamada. "The man does not know the language." Lowering his voice, but still speaking English, he suggested that the time had come for her to change her shoes.

Michiko did not need prompting; it had been on her mind all day long. Yet Yamada's sharpness surprised her. He must have been watching her closely since the march began. From now on, she in turn would have to keep an eye on him. Maybe he had Isa pegged, too, she thought. But was it possible that the poor fellow was still slinking around behind some building? She searched the corners of the compound as their final destination came into full view.

At the center of a large tract of land traversed by neat rows of houses stood the long-awaited school, an almost solid wall of glass on the side facing south. The fields that once occupied the site had been leveled away without a trace. An American observer would not have found the compound remarkable, much less luxurious. But the solid houses planted sparsely over the landscape, the spacious bedrooms illuminated by lamps even in broad daylight, the young Japanese maids attending to the needs of American babies—all of this was clearly revealed at a glance, and impressed the weary visitors as a vignette of some heavenly dwelling place.

Michiko reflected that her command of a foreign language and her general level of education might set her far above most of the residents; nevertheless, it was she who had walked four miles for the privilege of visiting their school, she who had reveled secretly in the pathetic expectation of showing off her high-heeled shoes. Surrounded by this verdant park, she now saw herself as too small and destitute even to set foot in such a place.

"What's the point of our sitting in on their classes?" she overheard a colleague complain to Shibamoto. He was the one, she recalled, who had been so quick to urge Isa to go barefoot. "What can we hope to learn from classes held in a place like this? The only lesson we'll leave with is the one we've learned just getting here: we lost! These magnificent buildings that we're only allowed to peek at—they were built with our taxes. Doesn't it make you want to cry?"

Michiko turned away, ashamed that she had perhaps been noticed before with her hands pressed sorrowfully over her eyes. She felt equally awkward in her present pose, and so she moved a few steps apart from the group, bent over and, though it scarcely mattered anymore, put on her high heels. The first thing she saw as she raised her head again was Isa, shoes still dangling down from one hand, coming toward her across the playground—and standing motionless in the background, the beautiful figure of an American schoolmistress. Michiko wanted to change back into sneakers.

The long march on an empty stomach had reduced some of the group to sullen anger, others to a numb exhaustion. Their leader rose up to his full height, and with a few heaves of his broad shoulders began to harangue them. "You mustn't forget that you're here by special invitation. We in the administrative section worked hard to get it for you, and if anyone misbehaves we are the ones who'll be blamed—You there, what do you think you're doing?" As he spoke, Shibamoto's roving gaze was arrested by a man sitting on the ground with his back to the group. It was Isa. Shibamoto resumed in the same hectoring tone: "I must ask you not to sit down right in front of the school. You look like a beggar. When did you get back?"

"You see, sir, that's what I meant," Yamada interjected. "We have to put our best foot forward, bargain from strength. Otherwise we might as well not have come in the first place. Leave it to me."

Shibamoto cut him off with a vague "We'll see," and quickly moved on to the next item on the agenda. He took a sheaf of printed questionnaires from his briefcase and passed them out to the teachers. As they studied the form he explained that they were to use it to record in detail their impressions of the school; afterwards it would be collected and put on file for future reference.

"What can we possibly write down? What would it prove, anyway?" cried Michiko in a shrill voice. She was visibly overwrought.

"Never mind," Yamada interrupted again. "You can just put down what I have. I intend to comment very critically on the instructional objectives of this school, the aptitude of their teachers, and so forth. I'll show it around when I'm done, and everyone can use it as a model. You needn't worry about that. Instead you might give some thought to . . ."

"No, no, you've missed the point," said Michiko impatiently.

"Well, then, what is the problem?"

Michiko fell silent. There was no use trying to explain to the likes of Yamada. And Isa—what a timid little soul! But he did seem to have a way with women. She would have to get to the bottom of this business with the schoolmistress. For the moment Yamada and Isa were confused in her troubled thoughts.

Just then the iron gate in front of the school opened and a thirtyish, bespectacled man stood before them with a welcoming smile. He introduced himself to the group as Mr. Williams, the Principal. At his appearance the teachers ceased their idle chatter and prepared to begin their visit. Yamada barged through the gate ahead of the others, who hesitated and deferred to one another before following him in. Isa came last, dragging his feet, as the gate swung shut behind them.

Hardly any doubt remained in Isa's mind about Yamada's devious plan, which he had sniffed out from its inception, to face off with him in a demonstration class before the day was over. He was determined to silence Yamada on this subject and prevent the encounter at any cost. But so far no suitable defense had suggested itself, and he approached the potentially fateful classrooms with ever more halting steps.

The group advanced in double file so as not to interfere with the students passing to and fro. Yamada had already attached himself to Mr. Williams. After the Principal's every utterance he would raise his hand as if to call for attention, turn to the person behind him, and communicate his version of the remark. This would be relayed in some form or other from one teacher to the next until it reached the end of the line: a procedure arrived at spontaneously, whether as a throwback to the rigid military chain of command or by simple analogy with a bucket brigade. It took some time for the message to be transmitted to Michiko and Isa in the rear, and in the interval all but the most provocative implications were filtered out.

Mr. Williams's opening remarks, that is, Yamada's rendering of them, went as follows: "Since the school was to be built with Japanese funds, we had little choice but to go along with the specifications given to us by some Japanese architects. The results, as you can see for yourselves, were less than satisfactory. To begin with, the budget was barely twenty percent of what would be considered normal back in the States. In our country we place great emphasis on bright and cheerful surroundings, and this school certainly does not meet those standards. We have twenty students in a class here, which is three too many. The ideal is seven-*teen*. Now I understand that in your country there are seven-*ty* in a class. Imagine! Classes that size are really out of the question. They necessitate regimentation, and this inevitably leads to militarism."

Here Yamada's voice trailed off into silence as Mr. Williams's expression took on a sudden severity, accompanied by a pudgy finger pointed at Yamada's forehead. When Yamada resumed interpreting, he spoke at first in tremulous tones.

The subject had changed to salaries, which, Mr. Williams assured them, were paid by the American government. The lowest salary level at the school, the one for beginning instructresses, was still about ten times the average wage of Japanese teachers, according to the figures he had heard. This was, it was true, a bit more than they would receive in comparable jobs at home; but things were a good deal more expensive in such a remote country; and if the discrepancy seemed excessive, it should be borne in mind that the standard of living which American teachers had to maintain was, after all, extremely high, so it was only natural that the basic salary be of a different order.

The only part of this speech to reach Isa's ear was the startling information, passed down the line with a collective sigh, that the teachers at this school got ten times as much money as they did. This so amazed Michiko that as she repeated it to Isa she had to lean on him to keep her balance. "We should have listened to our colleague there," she commented. "We should have just turned around and gone home."

"Right. That's so," said Isa.

"Did that woman do something about your feet?"

"Right. She did."

"What did you talk about?"

"Nothing."

"Look at those two over there—how disgusting!" Michiko muttered censoriously.

Isa looked in the direction she had indicated and focused on two students who stood holding hands in a corner of the corridor, their eyes closed in mutual infatuation. Miss Emily came up behind the couple and tapped them both gently on the back, not so much to chastise them, it appeared, as to alert them to the presence of visitors. Afterward she turned toward Michiko and smiled.

"It looks like paradise from the outside," said Michiko, "but there's no telling what goes on between these walls."

"Right. That's so."

Michiko did not know what to make of Isa's laconic responses. She looked at his frightened, rabbitlike eyes and recalled what Yamada had said about him. Then he broke his silence.

"Why must I go through this humiliating ordeal?"

"What ordeal? You mean having to go barefoot before?"

"No. I mean having to look at all this beauty."

"Beauty? From a certain point of view, I suppose."

"I'll tell you why. Simply because I'm a so-called English teacher."

"Oh? You don't like speaking English?"

"I d-d-detest it!"

Michiko was not surprised. There were a lot of men like that, the opposite type from Yamada, and Isa must be one of them.

Although the teachers had been told that they should each choose a class to visit and go their separate ways, they preferred to stick together. In the end Shibamoto divided them arbitrarily into three subgroups and dispatched them to different classrooms, with the veiled threat of force that was always present in his judo master's bearing. These smaller units soon congealed so that each proceeded as one, like flocks of peasants being herded around the capital.

Michiko hovered next to Isa. She could hardly forget the small favor she had yet to beg of him, after dwelling on it the length of that asphalt road. Moreover, it was reassuring to have him by her side—here, where almost anything might happen, and now, while she felt so despicably drab in the shadow of the foreign lady. Isa seemed to her the perfect companion for the occasion.

Meanwhile, Isa stayed as close as possible to Yamada, watching his every move, and fervently wishing that he might fall down some stairs and break his neck. He was even prepared, should the opportunity arise, to give him a little nudge. Failing that, in his present position he could at least intervene without delay if Yamada broached the subject of a demonstration class. And as one of his entourage, Isa was spared the necessity of pronouncing a single word of English, for Yamada had appropriated the role of spokesman for their party.

Isa and Michiko followed hard on Yamada's heels as together they entered the designated room, where they found a drawing class in session. Yamada soon retired to the supply closet to note down his observations. When he had finished he faced Michiko and whispered slyly: "Take a good look. With all their money and their fancy buildings, the children can't draw worth a damn."

There was a meek chorus of agreement from several colleagues who stood nearby, hanging on Yamada's every word. Michiko herself shared his opinion of the drawings, but she did not wish to be associated in any way with these people. They were the mean and cunning sort of Japanese; she and Isa were different, Michiko told herself, looking to Isa for confirmation. She caught him stooping over his shoes again: a new pair of sneakers which, she quickly deduced, must have come from that schoolmistress. They were much too big for him and he was trying to compensate by lacing them up tight. The moment Isa's eyes met hers, he blushed and turned the other way.

Michiko proposed that they have a closer look at the work now in progress. As they moved into the classroom and studied the drawings, they found themselves submerged in a waterless sea teeming with fish of various colors, shapes, and sizes. They were all unique, each one the product of a collaborative effort by a small group. Over by the window a few junior-high-school students of both sexes were sketching the thatched-roof cottages which appeared in the distance, beyond the confines of the American compound. They began to steal glances at the visitors over their shoulders, then one of the boys pointed at Shibamoto with his right hand while with his left he indicated a drawing of a seadevil. On closer inspection of other drawings, it was discovered that Yamada had been turned into a shark, Isa into a flying fish, suggested, perhaps, by his emaciated figure, and Michiko a goldfish. In the same fashion the whole party emerged within the next few moments as a school of highly distinctive fish.

As soon as they were back in the corridor, Yamada said to Shibamoto: "What kind of school are they running here, allowing such insulting behavior—and even toward a lady! I think we should submit a written protest. How about the rest of you? And you, Mrs. . . . ?"

"I didn't really mind it so much," said Michiko. "In fact, we sort of asked for it, with our down-and-out attitude."

"Down-and-out? I'm talking about a serious failing in their instructional objectives, a complete lack of discipline. That art teacher ought to be severely reprimanded. But why should I waste my breath! If you don't mind being turned into a goldfish, that's your business."

Not a glint of amusement alleviated Yamada's peevish expression as he finished berating Michiko and began to make further notations in his little book. "What did they do with you?" he asked Isa, looking up from his book. "Oh yes. It was a flying fish, and quite a masterpiece, too. They must have got the idea from the way you were flitting around in your bare feet."

Isa was at the moment too intent on his malevolent wishes to hear.

Isa stood at the door of the classroom in his borrowed sneakers and listened to the lady whose initials they bore teach English. Michiko had gone inside with the others, this time without trying to coax him into coming along. After a while the group filed back into the corridor one by one and clustered together to exchange comments in a half-whisper.

"You might almost say that our English is better than theirs," Yamada observed to Michiko in Japanese. "Weren't you amazed at all the mistakes in their grammar?"

"But the teacher is pretty, isn't she?"

"Hmm. It's like hiring a movie star to teach at a ridiculous salary."

"You were right about *him*—he really does hate English," said Michiko, switching languages as she again changed the subject.

"I know all that. I am also aware that he harbors some marice toward me."

Michiko acknowledged to herself that in referring to Isa as "him" and making her remark in English she had stilled the pangs of guilt which she would normally have felt in this betrayal of trust. And that, she reflected, was no doubt one reason for Isa's hatred of the foreign language: when you spoke it you stopped being yourself. It was too easy to be carried away by the titillation of the words, words not exactly your own. She knew she ought to get away from Yamada, the sooner the better.

When Michiko was back at Isa's side again she startled herself by blurting out, "If you hate speaking English so much, you must hate me too."

"It's different with women," said Isa.

"Women make good mimics. Is that what you mean?"

Maybe that *was* what he had meant, Isa could not be sure.

Without warning Michiko leaned over and whispered something in his ear. She had reverted to Japanese, to Isa's relief, but he could still make out only the general drift.

"You mean even you . . . ?" Isa blushed a deeper hue than Michiko, though she had brought the matter up.

"Have I embarrassed you again?" she asked.

It was perhaps in part the extraordinary scene now unfolding before their eyes that had driven her to divulge such a delicate matter, and so impetuously. They were now in the gymnasium, where, in preparation for tomorrow's basketball game with a neighboring school, a rally was being conducted by a spirited cheering section. A trio of girls in uniform, sixteen or seventeen years old, stood in front of the others calling out the names of the players with mounting fervor. When the shouting had risen to a high pitch of frenzied excitement, like a line of chorus girls they all began to lift up their skirts while the cheerleaders launched into cartwheels and somersaults.

"It's all set for the demonstration class this afternoon—you and me," said Yamada, who had appeared out of nowhere and taken Isa by surprise.

"I-I-I don't know what you're talking about. I have nothing to do with it."

"Well, you know now. Shibamoto decided on the two of us. I'll meet you after lunch, as soon as the hour for visiting classes is over. And don't try to run away. Shibamoto would not be pleased." Thrusting his jaw out toward Michiko, he added in an insinuating tone: "I'm sure you can get some coaching from her."

Yamada had in fact not the slightest desire to stand in front of a class next to Isa. The man was sure to bring disgrace on the whole profession. But in the middle of the rally he had caught sight of Michiko whispering in Isa's ear, then watched as Isa blushed and nodded in agreement. At that moment he had declared war.

Yamada went directly to the Principal and made his proposal with the same lunatic zeal he had shown to Shibamoto. Shibamoto stood by, wondering anxiously how the Principal would react to this bizarre request, which sounded less like a bid for a classroom demonstration than a demand for satisfaction by a man whose honor had been challenged. Yet, whether because like Shibamoto he saw no way out, or because he was soon to return to America and hoped it might yield a piece of Japanese bravado to regale his friends with, the Principal had accepted the proposal on the spot.

Yamada took leave of Isa and Michiko with a few curt instructions as to where they were to eat their lunch: on some benches in the schoolyard, about three hundred feet outside the gate—and nowhere else.

With quivering lips Isa stared vacantly after Yamada as he retreated across the gymnasium.

"Isa-san. I'll take your place this afternoon," said Michiko.

"It's too late for that," Isa replied. "Either I knock him out, or I quit my job . . . or else I go ahead with the class and just stand there without saying a word."

Isa made as if to run after Yamada, but the sores on his feet seemed to be acting up again, and he had barely managed to limp forward a few steps when Michiko seized him by the hand and held him back.

"Wait a minute," she said. "Please don't forget the little favor I asked you a moment ago. If you'll let me have them now, I'll wash them right away."

Isa's immediate response was a blank look and an incessant blinking of his rabbit-eyes.

"You know, what we talked about before," Michiko prompted.

Isa finally understood what she wanted. All right, she could have them. But only after he had finished with them. Even at this juncture, on the brink of coming to blows with Yamada, he could not ignore his other concern, one from which he was never altogether free.

With sudden resolution Isa removed from his satchel a small bundle wrapped in newspaper and thrust it toward Michiko, all the while keeping his eyes on Yamada's vanishing figure. Michiko reached out in some confusion to take the coveted article from him—hardly ten seconds had passed since he had at last seemed to grasp her wish. But like an overeager relay runner, Isa had moved too soon, and he was off before the bundle was safely in her hands. Uneasy about the transaction to begin with, Michiko now blushed furiously, fumbled, and in the end lost her balance. Her high heels slid out from under her, and with a piercing shriek that filled the corridor she toppled over onto the floor. The bundle lay open where she had hurled it aside in her fall, revealing a pair of black chopsticks.

It remained a secret shared by Isa and Michiko alone that she had fallen while clutching at this homely artifact of their native land. As soon as Mr. Williams arrived on the scene, he loudly ordered the Japanese who had gathered around to disperse, whereupon up and down the corridor foreigners came rushing out of every other door. The Principal drove off this new crowd, leaving only a few women to help Michiko to the dispensary.

Afterward, as he questioned Shibamoto about the accident, Mr. Williams kept adjusting his glasses in an irritable gesture that suggested he found it all very regrettable. What had Michiko and Isa been up to? he wanted to know. Yamada, having rejoined them, interpreted stiffly for Shibamoto to the effect that the man with the limp had been struggling to catch up with yours truly to request that he be allowed to substitute for his colleague in today's demonstration class; meanwhile, the lady, who cherished similar aspirations, had been strenuously attempting to dissuade her colleague from his determined course when she slipped and fell. "It all proceeded from their pedagogical dedication," Yamada concluded on Shibamoto's behalf, "and their devotion to the English language."

"Ah yes. The old kamikaze spirit," said the Principal.

The heavy irony was lost on Yamada, who took the remark as a compliment, and presented it as such to his superior. Shibamoto fluttered his eyelashes in silent modesty.

Seeing that his sally had been deflected by misinterpretation, Mr. Williams pushed back his glasses again and turned on them with his sternest expression. "From now on, there are two things which I must strictly forbid," he announced. "The first is for any Japanese instructor to conduct a class here, to engage in any attempts to do so, or in any way to involve himself in the educational process at this school. Secondly, in the future high heels will not be permitted on these premises. If there are any violations, we will have to terminate all further visits."

After spitting out these injunctions with an air of finality, the Principal strode rapidly down the corridor to the door of the dispensary. He showed no inclination to enter, merely surveying the situation from outside.

A long pause ensued during which Yamada neglected to translate Mr. Williams's last pronouncement. When he was summoned back to reality by a poke in the ribs from Shibamoto, he spun around and fled toward the exit, without so much as a word of explanation. Then, with Shibamoto in the lead, the rest of the group hurried after, as though suddenly reminded of some vital errand. Only Isa was left behind, alone once again.

TRANSLATED BY WILLIAM F. SIBLEY

■ KUROSAWA AKIRA

with Hashimoto Shinobu and Oguni Hideo

The belated Western discovery of the rich art of the Japanese film occurred when Kurosawa Akira's *Rashōmon,* which in Japan had ranked a modest fifth among the best ten domestic films of 1950, won the Grand Prix at the 1951 Venice Festival. In his acceptance speech Kurosawa said that he wished the prize had gone to a film about contemporary Japan, one that illuminated present-day conditions of life. The following year he made *Ikiru* ("To Live"). Written in conjunction with Hashimoto Shinobu and Oguni Hideo, two of the scriptwriters with whom he often collaborated during this period, *Ikiru* remains his finest statement of the question explored in all of his best films from the 1943 *Sugata Sanshirō* through the 1975 *Dersu Uzala:* What should we do with our lives? In *Ikiru* the question is negatively asked, since the hero knows that he will die, but the answer is one shared by many of Kurosawa's pictures, including *Yōjimbō* (1961), *Tsubaki Sanjūrō* (1962), and the superb *Seven Samurai (Shichinin no samurai,* 1954). The solution to the problem lies in action, specifically in social action—something that leaves the world a slightly better place in which to live. Seen in this light, Kurosawa is one of Japan's major social critics. He himself has said that he makes films only for the young of Japan, hoping to reach them with his message. But he has also said: "Sometimes I think of my death. Then I become restless, wondering how I can bear to breathe my last, with so much yet to do, having lived so little . . . It is from such thoughts that *Ikiru* came."

Kurosawa Akira was born in Tokyo in 1910. He studied Western-style painting but turned to films in 1936 after answering a newspaper advertisement from the PCL Studios: anyone who would like to become an assistant director was advised to send in an essay pointing out the basic defects of Japanese films and how they could be remedied. Kurosawa was dubious ("I thought to myself, If the defect is basic, how do you remedy it?"), but passed all the examinations and got the job. In the early 1940s he also began to be recognized for his screenwriting, and was at last allowed to direct his script *Sugata Sanshirō.* He has continued to write for his own films, later always with collaborators, and has also written a number of scripts for films directed by friends and protégés.

A perfectionist in all aspects of cinematic art, Kurosawa spares no expense in production, shoots film at the generous ratio of ten to one, and edits the original footage himself. Always, as in *Ikiru*, his technical virtuosity, his brilliant use of camera angles and movement, of flashbacks and other devices, serves the larger purposes of his compassionate Dostoevskian humanism. He has paid homage to Dostoevski with an ambitious, overly literal adaptation of *The Idiot* (*Hakuchi*, 1951). But it is in *Ikiru* that Kurosawa expresses most powerfully his affinity with the spirit he admires in his favorite author: "Ordinary people turn their eyes away from tragedy; he looks straight into it and suffers with the victims."

Ikiru was a Tōhō Production, released October 9, 1952, with Shimura Takashi in the leading role.

❖ Ikiru

Titles white on black; slow, rather melancholy music; then, a close-up of an X-ray negative while a voice is heard explaining.

NARRATOR *off*: This is an X-ray picture of a stomach; it belongs to the man this story is about. Symptoms of cancer are there but he doesn't yet know anything about it.

Cut to the City Hall, the desk of WATANABE KANJI, *Chief of the Citizens' Section. He sits behind a desk piled high with papers and is busy putting his seal to various documents. Then he stops and looks at his watch.*
Cut to the front of the office, the information counter; a number of women are talking with SAKAI, *the Section Clerk. On the counter is the notice: "THIS WINDOW IS FOR YOU. IT IS YOUR LINK WITH THE CITY HALL. WE WELCOME BOTH REQUESTS AND COMPLAINTS."*

WOMEN: And my child got a rash from that water . . . It smells bad too . . . There are millions of mosquitoes . . . Why can't you do something with the land? It would make a good playground.

SAKAI *excuses himself and goes to* WATANABE'S *desk, telling him that some petitioners from Kuroe-cho are there.* WATANABE *tells him to send them to the Public Works Section, then looks at his watch again.*

NARRATOR *off:* This is the main character of our story, but he's not very interesting yet. He's just passing the time, wasting it, rather. It would be difficult to say that he is really alive.

WATANABE *suddenly looks up at the sound of laughter. Cut to the office where everyone is looking at the office girl* TOYO, *who has suddenly broken into laughter.* ONO, *the Assistant Chief, speaks sharply to her, telling her to please watch her behavior during working hours. Cut back to* WATANABE, *who takes off his glasses.*

TOYO: But it was funny.
ONO: What was?
TOYO: This joke that someone passed around.
ONO: Read it then.

Cut to TOYO *standing up. She hesitates, then begins to read from a newspaper clipping.*

TOYO *reading:* You've never had a day off, have you? No. Why? Are you indispensable? No, I just don't want them to find out they can do without me.

She laughs, but no one else does.
Cut to WATANABE, *who has been listening. Now he puts his glasses on again and goes back to stamping papers.*

NARRATOR *off:* This is pretty bad. He is like a corpse and actually he has been dead for the past twenty-five years. Before that he had some life in him. He even tried to work.

WATANABE *wants to clean his seal and is looking for some paper. He opens a desk drawer full of old documents. The top one reads A PLAN TO INCREASE OFFICE EFFICIENCY. He tears off the first page, cleans his seal, throws the paper into the basket, and goes on stamping, while the* NARRATOR *continues off.*

NARRATOR *off:* But now he neither tries nor even wants to. His ambitions have been well smothered by City Hall. But, he's busy—oh, very busy. Still, he is doing little. He has to keep busy simply to stay where he is. Is this as it should be?

WATANABE *seems to feel uncomfortable; he takes his tablets, and drinks some water.*

NARRATOR *off:* But before he begins to think seriously, his stomach must get worse and more useless hours must accumulate.

Cut to the WOMEN *from Kuroe-cho arriving at the office of the Public Works Section, where the* CLERK *in charge says that he is sorry, but this matter comes under the authority of the Parks Section. Wipe to the Parks Section, where the* CLERK *is telling them that the matter seems to be concerned with sanitation, hence they had better go to the Health Center. Dissolve into the Center, where they are told that the Sanitation Section will take care of them; a lively fugue is built under these scenes, based on a motif from the opening music. Wipe to the Sanitation Section, where they are told to go to the Environmental Health Section. Wipe to that Section, where they are told they must go to the Anti-Epidemics Office. Wipe to that Office, where a* CLERK, *hearing it is about mosquitoes, directs them to the Pest Control Section. Wipe to that Section, where a* CLERK *swats a fly before directing them to the Sewage Section. Wipe to the Sewage Section, where a* CLERK *says that theirs was indeed formerly a sewage area but that a road ran over it, so, unless the Road Section approves . . . Wipe to the Road Section, where they are told that since the City Planning Department's policy is not yet established, they had best go there first. Wipe to the Planning Department, where they learn that the Fire Department had wanted the section reclaimed because of such poor water facilities, so they had better go there. Wipe to the Fire Department, where the* CLERK *says that it is nonsense, they do not want dirty water, it would ruin their hoses. Now if they had a swimming pool or something there, then the Fire Department might be interested. Wipe to the Children's Welfare Officer at the Educational Section, who tells them that such a big problem as this should be taken up with the City Councillor. Wipe to the Councillor's office. He is saying that he will give his personal introduction to the Deputy Mayor. Wipe to the office of that official, who is saying that he is truly happy when citizens take it upon themselves to make such suggestions, and for that reason they have established a special Citizens' Section. Wipe back to the Citizens' Section.* SAKAI *is again at the counter and does not remember them; he tells them to go to the Public Works Section. The*  WOMEN *become angry.*

WOMEN: What do you think we are anyway? What does this sign here mean? Isn't it your section's responsibility? Don't worry, we won't bother you again . . .

They start to leave. After a moment's hesitation, he runs after them, and catches them at the door.

SAKAI: Just a moment, please. I'm sorry. You see, our Section Chief is out today. If you could possibly just submit a written petition.

All the staff stand up, to watch the women go.
Quick shot of WATANABE'S *empty desk.*
Dissolve to the office. Two of the staff are eating their lunch and drinking tea as they talk, back to camera.

SAITO: It is certainly unusual for him to be out.
ONO: Well, he hasn't been looking too well lately.
SAITO: Yes, but it wouldn't be good if he stays out too long.
ONO: Funny, though. Certainly he wouldn't take sick-leave just for a cold. Besides, I need his seal.

Cut to another part of the office. Two other members of the staff are eating their lunch, while they talk.

KIMURA: It's too bad though. Another month and he'd have had thirty years without one day off.
OHARA: Yes, but you notice that now he's away certain people seem a lot happier. Well, everyone wants to get on in the world.

Cut to another part of the office, where they are also having lunch.

SAKAI: Wonder what that medicine is he's always taking.
TOYO: Something for his stomach. And lately he hasn't been eating his noodles for lunch.
NOGUCHI: That's another record. I've never seen him eat anything else.
SAKAI: I wonder who the new Chief will be.
TOYO: What's the hurry? You have a long way to go.

Cut to a long shot of ONO *and* SAITO. *They have heard* TOYO'S *remark and look up, startled.* ONO *is Assistant Chief.* *Cut to* WATANABE'S *empty desk.*

Cut to WATANABE *walking down a hospital corridor.*
Dissolve to WATANABE *at the hospital drinking-fountain, in the waiting room.* WATANABE *is trying to get a drink of water, but a man gets there before him.* WATANABE *waits, then drinks, and then looks at himself in the mirror.*
Cut to WATANABE *sitting down. Another* MAN *a few chairs away comes and sits next to him.*

MAN: Stomach trouble, eh? Me, I've got something chronic. Lately it's got so that I just don't feel right unless my stomach hurts.

A NURSE *calls a name and the man, the same one that drank before* WATANABE *did, gets up and goes into the office.*

MAN: Now, that fellow there. They say it's ulcers but I think it's cancer. And having cancer is the same as having a death sentence. But the doctors here always tell you it's ulcers, that an operation's unnecessary. They tell you to go on and eat anything—and when you hear that, you know you've got a year left, at the most. Your stomach always feels heavy, and it hurts; you belch a lot and you're always thirsty; either you're constipated or else you have diarrhea, and in either case your stool is always black.

WATANABE *is feeling more and more uncomfortable. Quiet, sinister music. He changes seats but the* MAN *follows him. Shot of* WATANABE *becoming more and more uncomfortable.*

MAN: And you won't be able to eat meat, or anything you really like, then you'll vomit up something you ate a week ago; and when that happens, you have about three months left to live.

Cut to a long shot of WATANABE *alone in the waiting room. The slow and melancholy music of the opening is heard. He is small in the distance, almost lost in the large waiting room. A* NURSE *suddenly calls his name; she calls it several times because he does not hear. He finally hears, and rises. The music fades.*
Cut to the X-ray room, two DOCTORS *and a* NURSE *are waiting.*
Cut to WATANABE *entering, then a shot of their faces as they wait for him to sit down. Quick close-up of the* DOCTOR'S *face, then* WATANABE'S.

DOCTOR: Yes, please sit down. Well, it looks as though you have a light case of ulcers.

Cut to WATANABE's *hands. He drops the coat he is carrying. The music begins again. Cut to their faces.*

WATANABE: Be honest with me. Tell me the truth. Tell me it's cancer.

The DOCTORS' *faces; the* NURSE's *face; the back of the young* DOCTOR's *head—he is looking at the X-ray picture. She picks up* WATANABE's *coat.*

DOCTOR: Not at all. It's just a light case of ulcers, as I said.
WATANABE: Is an operation impossible?
DOCTOR: It's unnecessary. Medicine will fix you up.
WATANABE: But what shall I eat?
DOCTOR: Anything you like, so long as it's digestible.

Cut to WATANABE. *Hearing this he lowers his head so that it almost touches the desk.*
Wipe back to the DOCTORS.

YOUNGER DOCTOR: Will he last a year?
ELDER DOCTOR: No. Six months at the most. What would you do if you only had half a year to live? Miss Aihara, what would you do?
NURSE: Well, there's some poison there on the shelf.

The YOUNGER DOCTOR *turns back to look at the X-ray negative. Close-up of the negative, the sound of the buzzing of the X-ray machine is heard.*
Cut to the street: trucks, cars, WATANABE *walking, but all without sound. When he tries to cross the street, a truck races past, and there is a sudden burst of sound. The traffic streams in front of* WATANABE *and he, small, on the opposite side of the street, cannot cross.*
Wipe to the front of WATANABE's *house at night. The camera slowly moves toward the front door. The sound of walking and of someone humming the song "Too Young," then the voices of* WATANABE's *son,* MITSUO, *and his daughter-in-law,* KAZUE.

KAZUE: There's no lights on—power gone off again, I wonder?
MITSUO: No, the neighbor's lights are on.

KAZUE: That's funny. Is your father out, I wonder? Where's the key?

MITSUO: It's in your bag.

The camera has moved toward the door. Cut from an extreme close-up of part of the door to the hallway from the inside. The two of them open the door and come in.

KAZUE: It was open. Did that maid forget to lock up? Really, that woman forgets everything.

MITSUO: She lives so far away, that's why. It takes her so long to get home that she forgets about everything else.

KAZUE: It wouldn't cost that much more to have her live in.

MITSUO: You know Father. He'd never hear of it. Always the minor official.

Cut to the corner of the hallway. They are moving through the dark to the bottom of the stairs.

KAZUE: It's just as cold inside as it is outside—that's what's wrong with Japanese houses.

MITSUO: I always hate coming home. It would be nice to have a modern house.

Cut to the two of them on the stairs in the dark.

KAZUE: Well, we could build one for about five hundred thousand yen, couldn't we? Though we might have to use your father's retirement pay.

MITSUO: He'll get about seven hundred thousand, and a monthly pension too. And he's got about a hundred thousand saved up.

KAZUE: But do you think he'll agree?

Cut to the darkened upstairs rooms.

MITSUO: Well, he'll just have to live by himself if he doesn't. That will probably be the most effective way. After all, he can't take his money with him.

KAZUE *laughs.*

MITSUO *finds the light and turns it on.* WATANABE *is at his feet; he has been sitting there in the dark.*
Cut to WATANABE's *face, then cut to his son's.*

MITSUO: Father, what's the matter?

WATANABE *in despair:* Oh, nothing; nothing at all.

He stands up, confused, then goes downstairs to his own room.
Cut to MITSUO *and his wife looking at each other. She begins to turn on more lights.*

KAZUE: But he heard everything we said. Really, that was very rude of him. And he shouldn't have come up here, not while we were away. I call that very impolite.
MITSUO: Why didn't he say what he wanted to? Why did he run away like that?

Cut to WATANABE *in his darkened room downstairs. He turns on the light. Pan with him as he goes to a small shrine in the corner of the room and opens it.*
Cut to MITSUO *upstairs; he is lying on the bed, and* KAZUE *is making him move to take off the bedspread. He looks at her, and she comes and sits on the bed. She then lies down beside him.*

KAZUE: Don't look like that. Let's forget about your father and think a little more about us.

They have turned on the radio and from it comes "Too Young." She turns towards him, hugs him, and tells him to hold her.
Cut to WATANABE'S *room. He is sitting before the open shrine. Cut to the small shrine and to the photograph of his dead wife inside it. Close-up of the picture. Close-up of* WATANABE *looking at it. Big close-up of the picture.*
Dissolve to a motor-hearse, seen through the rain-flecked windshield of a following car. The sound of windshield wipers. Cut to the back seat: WATANABE, KIICHI, *his brother,* TATSU, *his sister-in-law (all much younger), and* MITSUO, *as a child, are going to a funeral.*

TATSU: And she was so young, too—oh, but it must have been hard for her to leave her little boy behind.
KIICHI: Stop crying.

Cut to the hearse ahead, turning a corner. Cut to the little boy, MITSUO. *Cut to the hearse again, then back to* MITSUO; *the melancholy music of the opening is heard. (The hearse is always seen through the windshield, its image cut by the wipers.)*

MITSUO: We have to hurry. Mother is leaving us behind.

Cut to the back seat. WATANABE *is holding his son, tears in his eyes.*
Cut back to WATANABE'S *room. From above comes the sound of the song as well as* MITSUO *and* KAZUE'S *muffled laughter. He looks up to where the sound is coming from. They seem to be making love.*
Cut to another room, where WATANABE *and* KIICHI, *his brother, are talking. Both men are much younger.*

KIICHI: You say you can't get married again because of Mitsuo, but just wait. When he grows up he's not going to be all that grateful; after he gets married himself you'll just be in the way. And that is why you ought to get married again now. My wife says that you're naturally sloppy and she says she can't stand the thought of you living all alone and getting more that way.

WATANABE *has been absently turning the pages of a book while his brother has been talking. Now, however, he hears his son calling him.*
Cut back to his room. Again he hears the voice, stands up, walks to the stairs, and starts going up them.
Cut from the top of the stairs. WATANABE *is halfway up when* MITSUO'S *voice continues off.*

MITSUO *off:* Good night. And lock up, will you?

WATANABE *stops, then rests his head against a step, then starts back down into the darkness whispering "Mitsuo."*
Cut to the hallway. He slowly crosses it and locks the front door. Then from a corner he takes a baseball bat and jams it tight, as is apparently his habit, against one of the sliding doors so that it cannot be opened from the outside.
Cut to a close-up of the baseball bat; at the same time, the sound of a ball being hit; the roar of a crowd; the opening music, soft under the sound of the crowd.
Cut to WATANABE *excitedly watching a baseball game. He turns to the* MAN *next to him.*

WATANABE: Mitsuo! Wasn't that a wonderful hit? See that? That batter is my—

Cut to the baseball game, flashpan of the young MITSUO *running to home plate. Cut to* WATANABE, *who again shouts his son's name. Flashpan to the ball game. Something has gone wrong. Cut to* WATANABE *and the* MAN.

MAN: What's that guy think he's doing anyway?

Cut to WATANABE *in his room, sitting down, the camera descending with him.*
Cut to WATANABE *at the ball game, sitting down, the camera descending with him.*
Cut to WATANABE *and* MITSUO, *the latter on a stretcher, in a hospital elevator going up, the camera ascending with them.*

WATANABE: You be brave now, Mitsuo; after all, a little appendix operation isn't anything at all.
MITSUO: But, aren't you going to stay?
WATANABE: I . . . I have some things to do.

The elevator door opens and the boy is wheeled out.
WATANABE'S *voice is heard repeating his son's name over and over again, as throughout the following scenes the music rises.*
Cut to the hallway. He is still standing there, repeating his son's name to himself.
Cut to a railway station. It is wartime; the students have been mobilized and are being sent off. Hundreds of people are there: fathers, mothers, brothers, sisters, all waving flags and throwing streamers.
Cut to MITSUO, *now older, in his uniform. He is looking at his father, he calls his name and is very near to tears; he steps down from the train. The train starts; his father pushes him back onto it; he turns towards his father, searching for his face as the train pulls away. All of this time the voice of* WATA-NABE *can be heard calling over,* "Mitsuo, Mitsuo, Mitsuo."
Long dissolve from the boy's face to WATANABE *in the hall. He starts to go up the stairs, but stops halfway.*
Dissolve to his room. He hangs up his kimono; puts his trousers under the pallet to press them, winds his pocket watch and puts it on the table, reaches for the alarm clock and begins to wind, then drops it. All of this is obviously done by force of habit. Then he suddenly stops. He does not move; the seconds pass; then, without warning, he turns and crawls under the covers. He seems afraid and pulls the covers over his head. He begins to weep.
A wide shot of the room. Over the huddled WATANABE *are two framed letters on the wall. Cut to a close-up of one of them which reads:*
"LETTER OF COMMENDATION. MR. WATANABE

*KANJI IS HEREBY GIVEN RECOGNITION FOR HIS
TWENTY-FIVE YEARS OF DEVOTED SERVICE."*
The sound of weeping continues.
Cut to the hallway of the house. It is daytime. SAKAI, *the clerk
in* WATANABE'S *office, is at the door talking to the maid.*

MAID: But he always leaves for work at the same time.

SAKAI: Huh? He hasn't been to the office for five days, hasn't
even sent in an absence report. I was told to come and
see what had happened.

She goes into the house to call KAZUE.
Wipe to a telephone booth. KAZUE *is inside talking.*
Cut to an office. MITSUO *is on the telephone and we hear their
conversation.*

MITSUO: I can't believe it.

KAZUE: But it must be true, that man from his office said so.

MITSUO: But what could he be doing?

Cut to WATANABE'S *office. The others are talking; long shot
of his empty desk.*

SAKAI: It's true, and his family was really surprised.

TOYO: But this is awful.

ONO: Well, I can make all the decisions, of course, so long
as he's not here.

TOYO: But you have to go and get his seal so that I can leave.

ONO: You mean you're resigning?

Cut to a close-up of TOYO.

TOYO: Yes—this work doesn't suit me.

Wipe to KIICHI'S *house.* MITSUO *is there. They are eating
dinner.*

MITSUO: And he's taken fifty thousand yen out of the bank,
too.

KIICHI: You don't say . . . Well, maybe he's found himself
a girl. Good for him if he has.

TATSU: Now, now . . .

MITSUO: But that's impossible.

KIICHI: Not at all. It's men like him who fall the hardest.
Look, he's been a widower for some twenty years now.
And he did it all for you, too. Now he can't stand it any
longer and so he goes out and finds someone for himself.

MITSUO: That's nonsense—why, he doesn't look at all well. He's so thin, and his skin's got so dry. Have you seen him recently?

TATSU: Yes, about four days ago. One morning he came over, seemed to want to talk about something. But you know how my husband is. He just looked at him and asked if he'd come for a loan.

KIICHI: I didn't think then that he'd come wanting to talk about some woman, not looking like that.

TATSU: Now, now. My husband, you see, thinks that all men are as bad as he is. Still, Mitsuo, are you certain that something didn't happen over at your house?

MITSUO: No, not that I know of.

But he is evasive and will not look at his aunt and uncle. Cut to a railway crossing. It is evening, almost dark. Cut to a black dog, hunting for food in the dark. Cut to a small drinking stall. Inside a man is at the counter writing. He finishes a page and turns to the STALL-KEEPER.

WRITER: Would you take this over to my house? A guy from a magazine is there waiting for it. And on the way back get me some sleeping tablets.

KEEPER: But the drugstore's closed.

WRITER: Is it that late?

KEEPER: The shops close early around here.

WRITER: If I don't have those pills with my whiskey, I just don't sleep.

He hands the page to the STALL-KEEPER, *crumpling the rest of the manuscript in his hand.*
Cut to WATANABE *over in a dark corner; he is hardly visible. He gets up and comes over toward the* WRITER.

WATANABE: Excuse me, but I can let you have some.

He puts the bottle of pills on the counter in front of the WRITER, *then goes back to his table. The* STALL-KEEPER *goes out and the black dog lopes in.*

WRITER: Thanks, may I have them at the official price?

WATANABE: Oh, I was planning to throw them away anyway.

WRITER: Then let me pay for your drinks. You're quite a drinker, aren't you? Here, let me give you a bit more.

WATANABE: No, I can't . . . I'd just throw it all up. I have gastric cancer.

WRITER *concerned:* Cancer?

WATANABE: Yes.

WRITER: Then you shouldn't drink like this.

He puts his hand on WATANABE'S *shoulder.*

WATANABE: I don't really want to talk about it . . .

WRITER: But to drink, knowing that you have cancer . . . it's like committing suicide.

Cut to the WRITER *looking at him; cut to* WATANABE.

WATANABE: No, it's not that easy. I'd thought of ending it all, but it's hard to die. And I can't die just yet. I don't know what I've been living for, all these years.

Cut to the WRITER.

WRITER: Do you have any children? *He receives no answer.* Well, does your stomach hurt?

Cut to WATANABE.

WATANABE: More than my stomach, it's . . . *He presses his chest.*

WRITER: But there must be some reason for all of this.

A shot of both of them.

WATANABE: No, I'm just a stupid fool, that's all. *He pours himself a cup of sake and drinks it.* I'm . . . well, I'm angry with myself. Up until a few days ago I'd never spent anything on drinking. It was only after I found that I didn't have much longer to live that I . . . *He pours himself another cup of sake.*

WRITER: I understand, but you still shouldn't drink. Does it taste good?

WATANABE: No, it doesn't. *He puts down his cup.* But it makes me forget. I'm drinking this expensive sake now because . . . well, because I never did before. It's like drinking poison. I mean, it seems like poison, yet it's so soothing. *He smiles.*

WRITER: I know what you mean.

There is some food on the table which WATANABE *has not eaten. He sees the dog, drops the food on the floor, and the dog bolts it down. Cut back to the two men.*

WATANABE: I have about fifty thousand yen with me. I'd like

to spend it having a really good time. But, and I'm
ashamed to admit it, I don't know how to. If you
would . . .

WRITER: Are you asking me how to spend it, to show you
how?

*A train passes very near, shaking the stall and making the
bottles rattle.*

WATANABE: Yes, that is what I wanted to ask you to do.
WRITER: But—
WATANABE: It took me a long time to save this money, but
what I mean is that now I can spend it.

*During the following speech, shots intercut between the two
men.*

WRITER: I understand. Look, keep your money. You'll be my
guest tonight. Leave it all to me. *He goes across to another
table to get his bottle of whiskey; he picks it up and comes
back to sit down. He looks at* WATANABE *very closely.* You
know, you're very interesting. I know I'm being rude, but
you're a very interesting person. I'm only a hack writer,
I write trashy novels, but you've really made me think
tonight. *He pours himself a glass of whiskey.* I see that
adversity has its virtues—man finds truth in misfortune;
having cancer has made you want to taste life. *He drinks
the whiskey.* Man is such a fool. It is always just when he
is going to leave it that he discovers how beautiful life can
be. And even then, people who realize this are rare. Some
die without ever once knowing what life is really like.
You're a fine man, you're fighting against death—that's
what impresses me. Up until now you've been life's slave
but now you're going to be its master. And it is man's duty
to enjoy life; it's against nature not to. Man must have a
greed for life. We're taught that that's immoral, but it
isn't. The greed to live is a virtue. *They have moved to the
doorway; the sound of a train passing.* Let's go. Let's find
that life you've thrown away. Tonight I'll be your Mephis-
topheles, but a good one, who won't ask to be paid. *He
looks down at his feet.* Look, we even have a black dog!

*He kicks at the dog and it yelps; over this is the sound of a
celeste.*

Cut to a close-up of a pinball machine, the ball bouncing to the sound of the celeste.
Cut to the two of them in the pinball parlor.

WRITER: See this little silver ball? That is you; that's your life. Oh, this is a marvelous machine, a marvelous machine that frees you from all of life's worries; it's an automatic vendor of dreams.

Medium shot of them playing the pinball machine. WATANABE *looks very excited.*

Wipe to the two of them in an enormous beer hall. They are sitting with enormous steins of beer in front of them. The writer is just about to speak when trombones, apparently part of a band, are suddenly extended over WATANABE'S *head as he stands up. Deafening music begins.*

Wipe to the streets; a number of fast pans follow the WRITER *and* WATANABE *through the crowds; shots from behind blinding neon signs and from behind the grillwork of fences; a girl races up and snatches away* WATANABE'S *hat; he turns and tries to chase her but the* WRITER *stops him.*

WRITER: No . . . girls are the most predatory of all existing mammals. To get that hat back would cost you more than it's worth. But, anyway, you could buy a dozen new hats if you wanted to. Now we're going to buy you a new hat to say good-by to your old life with.

Cut to them looking through an openwork screen into a small bar.
Cut to them at the entrance of the bar. Medium close-up of the WRITER *stopping to shape* WATANABE'S *new hat.*

Shot of them coming into the bar. From the record-player can be heard Josephine Baker's recording of "J'ai Deux Amours."
The PROPRIETRESS *and barmen stand smiling. She welcomes them, says it has been a long time, and they sit at the bar.*
WATANABE *has his new hat in front of him; when she tries to take it away from him, he, instantly suspicious, grabs it and holds onto it. The* WRITER *laughs; she smiles.*
Camera remains on the PROPRIETRESS *in medium close-up; the* WRITER *can be seen in the mirror behind her.*

WRITER: What's so funny? This man here has gastric cancer.
PROPRIETRESS: Then he shouldn't be drinking, should he?
WRITER: Stupid—no, take a good look at him. See, he's God and he's carrying this cross called cancer. Most people just

die the minute they learn this, but not him; he's different.
From that moment on he started to live.

She smiles again and the camera turns from them and pans
over their glasses to the mirror behind the bar. WATANABE
has put his hat back on, but his head is resting against the
bar.

WRITER: Isn't that right?

WATANABE *slowly raises his head, looks at himself in the*
mirror, and suddenly smiles.
Wipe to a big glass-and-neon cabaret. The camera pans down
the great stairwell, up which the WRITER *and* WATANABE *are*
coming, forcing their way through the crowd. A couple is
dancing on the landing, very close together. WATANABE *can-*
not tear himself away from the sight; the WRITER *pulls him*
on.

Cut to the top floor. Cut to a close-up of piano hammers
playing Boogie-Woogie music; a beer-drinking PIANO
PLAYER, *a dancing* GIRL; *she takes* WATANABE'S *hat, puts it*
on, dances around the room. Close-ups of the piano keys; of
the huge mirror which hangs above the piano; of the GIRL
dancing; of WATANABE *following her around the room; of the*
PIANO PLAYER, *smiling from behind the swinging bead-cur-*
tain. WATANABE *finally gets his hat back; the* GIRL *goes off*
dancing, falls against the keys of the piano, and the PIANO
PLAYER *turns.*

PIANO PLAYER: You folks got any requests?

The GIRL *comes over and sits on* WATANABE'S *lap.*

WATANABE: "Life Is So Short."
PIANO PLAYER: I beg your pardon . . . ?
WATANABE: "Life Is So Short." *He begins to sing.* "Fall in
   love, dear maiden . . ."
PIANO PLAYER: Oh, that one—it's an oldie, isn't it? Okay.

He rattles off an introduction, and then pours beer down his
throat; couples collect on the dance floor. Cut to the dance
floor as seen through the swinging bead-curtain. As it sways
back and forth, the couples one by one stop dancing, turning
to look. Cut to the GIRL, *she is moving slowly away from*
WATANABE'S *chair. The camera circles, in close-up, staying on*
WATANABE *as he sings.*

WATANABE:

> Life is so short,
> Fall in love, dear maiden,
> While your lips are still red;
> Before you can no longer love—
> For there will be no tomorrow.

> Life is so short,
> Fall in love, dear maiden,
> While your hair is still black;
> Before your heart stops—
> For there will be no tomorrow.

Tears stream down WATANABE'S *face. There is silence. Suddenly the* WRITER *stands up, springing into the frame.*

WRITER: That's the spirit!

He takes WATANABE'S *arm, pulling him out of the dance hall. Cut to a strip-show, a woman dancing on a lighted platform, slow, seductive music, the camera panning around her. Cut to her feet as a garment drops. The camera moves towards the* WRITER *and* WATANABE, *both looking at the girl above them. They are both drunk.*

WRITER: That's not art. A striptease isn't art. It's too direct. It's more direct than art. That woman's body up there. It's a big, juicy steak; it's a glass of gin, a shot of camphor; it's hormone extract, streptomycin, uranium . . . WATANABE *gulps.*

Wipe to the streets. Both are very drunk. WATANABE *starts across the road, and is almost run over, but the car stops in time.* WATANABE *takes off his coat as though he too were doing a striptease. He stops the traffic. The* WRITER *comes and pulls him out of the road.*
Wipe to an enormous dance hall: a great crush of people struggling on the dance floor, cigarette smoke rising from the pack. The band is playing a mambo. Cut as each section of the band strikes up: trumpeters, trombonists, percussionists, standing against the massed dancers.

Cut to WATANABE *in the crowd, dancing with a girl who is chewing gum. She is merely discomfited by the crush; he is nearly frantic. The* WRITER *is almost asleep on his feet; his girl pinches him; he opens his eyes and yawns.*

Cut to a speeding car, the camera traveling alongside it, reflections sliding over the surface. Inside are WATANABE, *the* WRITER, *and the two girls. The reflections slide over the window, past* WATANABE'S *face. He looks very ill. One of the girls is putting on lipstick; then she carefully removes her eyelashes. The other is counting a great roll of money.* WATANABE *looks at them, then out of the window.*

WATANABE: Stop the car!

GIRL: Stop the car! . . . Stop the car!

The car stops. WATANABE *opens the door and runs into the shadows. The girl looks irritated.*

WRITER *waking up:* What's the matter, have we got a flat?

GIRL: No, it's your friend; he's probably throwing up.

The WRITER *gets out of the car.* WATANABE *is slowly coming out of the shadows. In the distance over a loudspeaker comes the sound of a mambo. There is the noise of a train.* WATANABE *smiles—or tries to. He and the* WRITER *look at each other—perhaps* WATANABE *is remembering what he heard in the hospital, that when you begin to vomit you only have three more months to live. Both men are now completely sober. They get back into the car; the car starts.*

GIRL: What are you so gloomy about? I hate gloomy people. Come on, let's sing something nice and gay.

The girls start singing as loudly as they can; WATANABE *and the* WRITER *stare straight ahead.*

GIRLS:

> Come on'a my house, come on'a my house.
> I'm a'gonna give you everything.
> I'm a'gonna give you a Christmas tree.

Dissolve to a street near WATANABE'S *house. It is day, he is on his way home, still wearing his new hat. Cut to a close-up of the hat, the camera then panning down to his face.*

TOYO *off:* Mr. Watanabe!

Cut to the street. TOYO, *the office girl, is running up behind him. He turns and she catches up with him.*

TOYO: Your new hat almost fooled me. *He takes off his new hat.* I was just looking for your house. Are you going to work?

WATANABE: No.

TOYO: Do you have your seal?

WATANABE: No, it's at home.

TOYO: I want to leave—and I have this new job so I'm sort of in a hurry.

WATANABE: Come home with me, then.

Cut to them walking side by side.

WATANABE: Why are you leaving?

TOYO: The work is so boring. Nothing ever happens in that office. I've stood it for a year and a half now. The fact that you've been out for five days . . . *She looks at his hat* . . . and your new hat—that's all that's happened in a whole year and a half.

Cut to the upstairs room of WATANABE'S *house.* MITSUO *is tying his tie; his wife is standing next to him.*

MITSUO: Anyway, just don't say anything to him.

KAZUE: I've nothing to say to him.

MITSUO: Now, don't act like that. After all, it's your fault. If you hadn't started talking about his retirement pay . . .

KAZUE: Why blame everything on me? You were the one, if you remember, that started talking about money that night. He can't take his money with him, you said.

MITSUO: It's funny though. Just because of that . . . he wouldn't start acting like this, just because of that. And he's always come home before. Last night was the first time he's ever stayed out all night.

KAZUE: Well, let's not talk about it any more—we don't know what's wrong.

At that moment they hear something. KAZUE *runs toward the stairs.*

Cut to the hall. TOYO *and* WATANABE *are going into his room. The* MAID *takes his hat and stands looking at it. Cut to his room.* TOYO *takes his coat and puts it on a hanger. He is watching her, then turns to his desk. She walks toward him and puts her letter on his desk. As she walks around the room, she sees the framed letter of commendation on the wall.*

TOYO: Almost thirty years in that place, think of it. It gives me the willies. *She glances sideways at him.* I'm sorry.

WATANABE: That's all right. You know, lately, when I look
at that letter, well, I remember that joke you read out loud
in the office once. It was a very true joke. I've been there
almost thirty years and now I can't remember one day,
can't remember one thing I did. All I know is that I was
always busy and always bored.

He bows his head. She looks at him, then she begins to laugh.
Finally, he joins her.

TOYO: That's the first time I've ever heard you talk like that.
I didn't even know you could feel like that, I really didn't.

She laughs and impulsively stretches out her hands, takes his,
shakes them. The door behind them opens and the MAID
appears with the tea. She stops dead.
Cut back to the room upstairs.

MITSUO: Now don't be foolish. I know Uncle said the same
thing, but I just can't imagine him being in love with such
a young girl . . . *They sit on the bed.*

Cut to WATANABE'S *room. He is at his desk; the girl is*
kneeling politely some distance away. He looks up at her over
his glasses.

WATANABE: But this is the wrong form.

He looks at her; she looks away; then he takes up his seal and
stamps her letter of resignation anyway. He hands it to her;
she smiles.

WATANABE: Are you going to the office today?
TOYO: Oh, yes. I have to turn this in.
WATANABE: If you wait a minute I'll make my absence report
out. Would you take it in for me?
TOYO: Why don't you go to work yourself? Everyone in the
office is talking about it, they say it's "that time of life."
Are you really sick? You do look pale.
WATANABE: No, I . . .
TOYO: Where do you go every day when you pretend to be
going to work? And don't lie, either. Did you know that
Mr. Sakai came here yesterday to check on you? *She*
suddenly laughs. But, don't worry. After thirty years you
deserve some kind of rest. I'm not going to talk about you
the way Mr. Carp did.
WATANABE: Mr. Carp?

TOYO: That's just my name for him—but he is just like a carp, you know. Full of airs, but he doesn't have any backbone at all, and he always acts so superior, too—even with me. Just because he makes two hundred yen a month more than I do. WATANABE *laughs and she stands up, a bit embarrassed.* Well, I'll be going now. *She takes the letters and gets her coat. He looks at her.*

Cut to TOYO. *She has two large holes in her stockings.*

WATANABE: Wait, I'll go with you.

Cut to the upstairs window, from the outside. MITSUO *and his wife are looking out.*
Cut to the front gate, WATANABE *and* TOYO *are coming out, both smiling.*
Cut to the couple in the upstairs window, watching.
Cut to the couple below. She stops him, straightens his tie for him.
Cut to MITSUO *and his wife. She smirks; he looks down, worried.*
Cut to the staircase. The MAID *is on her way up to share the news.*
Cut to the street. WATANABE *and* TOYO *are walking and a waltz tune, played by strings and celeste, can be heard over.*

TOYO: But you're very lucky, living in a nice house like that. Why, at my place we have three families living in two rooms. You have a son, don't you?
WATANABE: Where can I buy some women's stockings?
TOYO: You want to buy some?—they ought to be selling them somewhere around here. They're for your son's wife, aren't they? Someone told me she was very pretty.

Wipe to a store. They are just coming out and she is holding a pair of new stockings all wrapped up, and is smiling.

TOYO: I'm so excited. Why, I'd have to go without lunch for three months to buy these. But why did you get them for me?
WATANABE: You had holes in your old ones.
TOYO: But that didn't make *your* feet cold.
WATANABE: I just . . .
TOYO: I didn't mean that. *She turns and smiles.* I appreciate it a lot—very much. I only said that because I felt embarrassed.

*Suddenly embarrassed, she walks behind him, then, laugh-
ingly, pushes him.*
*Wipe to a tearoom. He looks at her, passes her his piece of
cake. She smiles and helps herself to sugar, putting in lump
after lump.*

TOYO: Want me to tell you something? Well, I've given
    everyone in our office a nickname. It was something to do,
    so I wouldn't get so bored. Want to hear?
WATANABE: Yes.
TOYO: All right. Now, the first one is—Mr. Sea-Slug. Now,
    who is that? Someone that's hard to pin down, keeps
    squirming away. *He does not know. She giggles.* It's Mr.
    Ono!

WATANABE *smiles, nods.*

WATANABE: Of course.
TOYO: Next is Mr. Drain-Cover. Think, now. Someone
    who's damp all year round.
WATANABE: Mr. Ohara?
TOYO: That's right! And then there's Mr. Fly-Paper. A very
    sticky person. Come, you know. You don't? Mr. Noguchi.
    And do you want to know what I named Mr. Saito? He
    doesn't have anything special about him and yet he's the
    same all the time.
WATANABE: Saito? I don't know.
TOYO: Mr. Menu.
WATANABE: Menu?
TOYO: Yes, you know, like in cheap restaurants. The menu
    is always the same and it's never any good. *They both
    laugh.*
WATANABE: What about Kimura?
TOYO: I call him Mr. Jello because he's so weak and wobbly.
    I gave you a nickname too, but I won't say it. I won't
    because it wouldn't be nice to.
WATANABE: Please do. I wouldn't mind. Anyway, I'd like it
    if you made it up.
TOYO: All right. It's . . . it's Mr. Mummy. *She starts to laugh,
    then stops.* I'm sorry.
WATANABE: That's all right. *She begins laughing again, then
    he starts to laugh too.*

Wipe to outside the shop.

TOYO: Well, thanks for everything.

WATANABE: Do you have to resign today? Can't you put it off until tomorrow? Won't you stay with me today?

Wipe to a pinball parlor; he is teaching her how to play and she is enjoying herself. Wipe to an ice-skating rink; she is teaching him how to skate—they both fall down. Wipe to a fun-fair; they are eating noodles and laughing. Wipe to an ice-cream shop; she is eating; he smiles and gives her his portion. Wipe to a cinema; apparently a cartoon is on the screen, because she is laughing and leaning forward in her excitement; he is asleep beside her. Wipe to a Japanese-style restaurant; they are having dinner.

TOYO: But you don't eat at all—and you really do look exhausted.

WATANABE: No, I really enjoyed myself today.

TOYO: But, you fell asleep in the movie. You were snoring just when the best part came.

WATANABE: Well, last night . . . *He pauses and she laughs.* I can't tell this to anyone, I'm ashamed to admit it, but the reason why I've been like a mummy for the past thirty years . . . *She chokes on a glass of water* . . . Oh, don't misunderstand, I'm not angry you called me a mummy. It's true, and it couldn't be helped, it's just that . . . the reason I turned into a mummy was . . . well, it was all for my son's sake. But now he doesn't appreciate it. He . . .

TOYO: Well, you can't very well blame him for that. *She smooths her new stockings.* He didn't ask you to become a mummy. Parents are all alike—my mother says just the same thing. She says: I have suffered because of you. But, if you think about it, well, I appreciate being born, I really do; but I wasn't responsible for it. *She pauses.* But why are you talking about your son like that to me?

WATANABE: Well, it's just . . .

Close-up of TOYO *breaking into a smile.*

TOYO: I know you love him!

Close-up of WATANABE *smiling.*
Wipe to the street at night. WATANABE *is returning home alone. The sad music of the opening, now sounding even more desperate.*

Wipe to the interior of the house. WATANABE *is sitting, head bowed, at one side of the table; his son is reading the newspaper on the other side; the wife is nearby, knitting.*

MITSUO: It says here that the power shortage will last for a while.

WATANABE: Is that so?

Close-up of WATANABE, *his head lowered, although he seems to want to say something.*
Close-up of the son's newspaper; close-up of the wife, busy with her knitting; close-up of WATANABE *raising his head.*

MITSUO *off:* It says here that this is the warmest winter in thirty years.

WATANABE *does not hear, then realizing that something has been said, he looks up quickly.*

WATANABE: Is that so?

Cut to all three of them. WATANABE *leans forward. His hand shakes as he puts his cup down.*

WATANABE: If you don't mind, I'd like to talk to you for a few minutes. I wanted to tell you earlier, but it isn't a very pleasant story and . . .

MITSUO: I don't want to hear it. *Suddenly puts down the paper.* I've talked the whole problem over with Uncle today, and we both think it ought to be disposed of in a businesslike way. For example, I think that our rights to your property should be made clear.

WATANABE: Mitsuo!

KAZUE *gets up and leaves the room.* MITSUO *leans forward.*

MITSUO: You've already spent over fifty thousand yen on her —girls nowadays!

WATANABE: Mitsuo, what are you . . . ?

MITSUO: Father! We never meddle in your affairs. We've shut our eyes to your going out every night and doing I don't know what. I just made a practical suggestion. But you must consider Kazue and her family's position in this. The idea—bringing a girl here, and holding hands too. I was terribly embarrassed when the maid told me.

WATANABE *stands up. The camera pans with him as he hurries across the room and over to the stairs.*

Fade out. Then fade in to WATANABE'S *office—his chair is vacant. Cut to various scenes of the office workers talking to each other, whispering, smiling, smirking. Someone comes up to* ONO *and whispers.* ONO, *due to be promoted now that* WATANABE *is no longer there, laughs indulgently. Over all of this the voice of the* NARRATOR *is heard.*

NARRATOR *off:* The hero of our story has now been absent for about two weeks, and during this time, naturally, various rumors, various surmises have been repeated. All of these came to the single conclusion that Mr. Watanabe had been behaving very foolishly. Yet, to Watanabe, these same actions were the most meaningful of his entire life.

Cut to the window of a toy factory. The machinery hums; the window rattles; the building shakes—toy rabbits are stacked in boxes along the wall. Cut to outside. TOYO *and* WATANABE *are talking. She is wearing a turban on her head and has obviously been working—also, she is angry.*

TOYO: This isn't City Hall, you know. You can't take a whole day to do one hour's work here. Every second wasted means less money.

WATANABE: Meet me tonight—just tonight.

TOYO: I'm tired at night. I'd rather sleep. Besides, why do you want to go out with me every night? Let's just stop it. It's . . . it's unnatural.

WATANABE: Tonight—only tonight.

TOYO: No. This has to stop. Excuse me.

She turns and runs back into the factory. He walks away. Cut to WATANABE *alone among tables full of white mechanical rabbits. A door opens and she joins him.*

TOYO: All right, but tonight is absolutely the last time.

Wipe to the second floor of a large and fancy coffee shop. WATANABE *comes in and sits at* TOYO'S *table. In the rear, on the balcony, is a big group of boys and girls. A record-player is playing Poldini's "Waltzing Doll," and the boys and girls talk excitedly as a large birthday cake is brought up the stairs.* TOYO *looks at the couple next to them, then at the birthday party, then she yawns.* WATANABE *looks at her, leans forward.*

WATANABE: Let's take a walk.

TOYO: No, thank you. After the walk would be the noodle-shop; and after that would be the ice-cream parlor. What's the use? I know I'm being ungrateful, but I'm really bored. We don't have anything to talk about.

Cut to WATANABE, *looking at her. He lowers his head.*

TOYO: That look again . . .

Cut back to her, in close-up.

TOYO: You make me nervous. Why do you pay so much attention to me?

WATANABE: It's because . . .

TOYO: Because why?

WATANABE: Well, I just enjoy being with you.

TOYO: I hope it isn't love.

WATANABE: No, it's not . . .

TOYO: Why don't you speak more clearly—say what you mean!

Cut to WATANABE. *He lowers his eyes.*

TOYO *leaning forward:* Are you angry?

WATANABE: No. I don't know myself . . . *Close-up of him* . . . why I like being with you. All I know is that . . .

Cut to both of them at the table. The record-player begins "The March of the Wooden Soldiers."

WATANABE: . . . is that I'm going to die soon. I have gastric cancer.

Cut to a close-up of her. Cut to a close-up of him—he presses his hand against himself.

WATANABE: In here. You understand? I have less than a year to live. And when I found that out . . . then, somehow, I was drawn to you. Once when I was a little boy I nearly drowned. It is just that feeling. Darkness is everywhere and there is nothing for me to hold on to, no matter how I try. There is only you.

Close-up of her—she looks very uncomfortable.

TOYO: What about your son?

Cut to a shot of both of them; TOYO *with her back to camera.*

WATANABE: Don't even talk about him. I have no son; I'm
all alone.

TOYO: Don't talk like that.

WATANABE: You don't understand. My son is somewhere far
away, just as my parents were far away when I was drowning. I can't bear to think about it.

TOYO: But what help am I?

WATANABE: You . . . well, just to look at you makes me feel
better. It . . . it warms this . . . *He looks down* . . . this
mummy heart of mine. And you are kind to me. No,
that's not it. It's because you are so young and healthy.
No, it isn't that either. *He rises, comes to her side of the
table, sits down; she is repelled, and tries to move further
away.* You are so full of life and . . . and I'm envious of
that. If only I could be like you for one day before I die.
I won't be able to die unless I can be. Oh, I want to do
something. Only you can show me. I don't know what to
do. I don't know how to do it. Maybe you don't either,
but, please, if you can, show me how to be like you.

TOYO: I don't know.

WATANABE: How can I be like you?

TOYO: But all I do is work and eat—that's all.

WATANABE: Really?

TOYO: Really. That and make toys like this one.

*She has a toy rabbit in her pocket. She takes it out, winds it
up, puts it on the table in front of them; it hops toward him;
she picks it up, starts it over again.*

TOYO: That's all I do, but it's fun. I feel as if I were friends
with all the children in Japan now. Mr. Watanabe, why
don't you do something like that, too?

WATANABE: What can I do at the office?

TOYO: That's true. Well then, resign and find some other
work.

WATANABE: It's too late.

*Cut to her looking at him; then cut to both of them with the
mechanical rabbit between them.*

WATANABE: No, it's not. It isn't impossible.

*A shot of him, with tears in his eyes. She is afraid; she moves
back—"The March of the Wooden Soldiers" gets louder. He
suddenly turns to her, smiling; she shrinks back.*

WATANABE: I *can* do something if I really want to!

He picks up the rabbit. Cut to the boys and girls on the balcony, they are leaning over the rail.

BOYS AND GIRLS: Here she comes! Happy birthday to you, happy birthday to you!

WATANABE *hurries past them down the stairs, the rabbit in his hand. The girl, whose birthday it is, comes up the stairs, smiling, while the others continue to sing "Happy Birthday." Cut to* TOYO, *sitting alone. The birthday party is noisy and happy but she does not turn to look, she stares straight ahead. Fade out.*
Then fade in to the Citizens' Section. ONO *is coming into the office, followed by* SAITO, *the camera panning with them.*

ONO: Oh, he'll resign soon enough—his son was here asking about his retirement pay.
SAITO: Well, then you'll be our new chief, won't you?

ONO *smiles, satisfied, yet trying to appear modest.*

ONO: It's difficult to tell just yet.

He is about to hang up his coat, when they both see WATANABE'S *new hat hanging there; they look toward his desk. Cut to the desk.* WATANABE *is hunting for something, finds it and sits down.* ONO *and* SAITO *look amazed. They walk toward* WATANABE'S *desk. He looks up at them.*

WATANABE: Here, Ono, take care of this.

He hands him a document on which is written: "PETITION FOR RECLAIMING DRAINAGE AREA—KUROECHO WOMEN'S ASSOCIATION." There is a notice attached which says: "This Petition is to be forwarded to the Public Works Section." WATANABE *tears off the notice.*

ONO: But this petition should go—
WATANABE: No, unless we do something about it, nothing will ever be done. Everyone will have to cooperate, the Public Works Section, the Parks Section, the Sewage Section—all must cooperate. Now call me a car. I must make an inspection, and prepare a report today.
ONO: But this will be difficult.
WATANABE: No, it won't, not if you are determined.

The camera pans with WATANABE *as he hurries to put on his
coat. The noon siren is heard.* ONO *hurries to follow but*
WATANABE *is already out of the door.*
*Cut to outside where a light rain is falling. The door swings
to and* ONO *follows, worried. The sound of trumpets playing
the final cadence of "Happy Birthday" can be heard over.*

NARRATOR *off:* Five months later, the hero of this story died.

A picture of WATANABE *on the funeral altar. Cut to the entire
altar. It is in* WATANABE'S *room, which is now almost un-
recognizable in its funeral trappings. Everything is still and
there is very little movement. The entire office staff is there,
as well as the* DEPUTY MAYOR, *and all* WATANABE'S *family.
They are sitting on cushions laid out on either side of the
altar. Cut to outside the window, looking in. They are drinking sake. The sound of a car driving up and stopping. Cut
to the* DEPUTY MAYOR *listening.* MITSUO'S *wife gets up and
goes to the hallway. Cut to the hallway. A group of reporters
has gathered there.*

REPORTER: We'd like to see the Deputy Mayor, please, just
for a few minutes.

Cut to the room where the wake is being held. ONO *comes
in and whispers to the* MAYOR.

ONO: Sir, those reporters . . .

Cut to the MAYOR *politely leaving the room. Cut to the hall.*

MAYOR: Now just what's the idea—my conscience is clear.
REPORTER: Are you sure? We've been finding out a few
things.
2ND REPORTER: And though both you and the Parks Section
are claiming all the credit, wasn't it really this Watanabe
who made the park?
MAYOR: He was Chief of the Citizens' Section; parks fall
under the Parks Section.
2ND REPORTER: We know that, but what we want to know
is who did all the work? The people around there all think
it was this Watanabe, and they think it funny that he died
there.
MAYOR: What do you mean?
3RD REPORTER: They think something funny is going on.
For example, in your opening speech you didn't even

mention Watanabe. The people there say that this wasn't
right.

MAYOR: If it wasn't, what would have been then?

2ND REPORTER: Maybe it was a political speech.

The MAYOR *tries to laugh. Just then a flashbulb goes off. His
picture has been taken. He is disconcerted.*

3RD REPORTER: And Watanabe was given a seat 'way in the
back and was ignored. These people think that his dying
like that in the park means something.

MAYOR: Do they mean that he committed suicide in the
park? Deliberately sat there and froze to death?

3RD REPORTER: Yes.

MAYOR: Things like that happen in plays and novels. We
happen to know what killed Watanabe. It was gastric
cancer.

2ND REPORTER: Cancer?

MAYOR: Yes, an internal hemorrhage. He died quite suddenly and he didn't know that he was going to. If you
doubt me, Mr. Ono here will . . . *He indicates* ONO, *who
is now standing beside him* . . . Give them the name of
the hospital that made the autopsy.

Cut to the MAYOR *politely coming back into the room and
sitting down. The sound of an automobile going away, dying
in the distance.* ONO *returns and sits down. There is a silence;
everyone feels rather uncomfortable. The* DEPUTY MAYOR
takes a cup of sake.

MAYOR: The way that these reporters twist the facts. *He
drinks his sake, then turns to the others around him.* It's
not nice to say, but they truly fail to understand the
problems behind municipal projects. *They all bow, nod,
smiling, agreeing.* They simply don't understand organization. Now, that park, for example. They seem to think
that Mr. Watanabe built it all by himself. But that is just
silly. It is probably rude of me to say this in front of his
relatives, but I'm certain that Mr. Watanabe didn't have
this in mind—building a park all by himself. Of course,
he worked very hard toward helping and, I must admit,
I was impressed by his perseverance. But it was the work
of the section too. *All the section clerks nod in agreement.*
And, in any event, it is complete nonsense for anyone who
knows anything about the organization to say that the

Chief of the Citizens' Section could go and build a park
all by himself. *Everyone nods.* I'm sure that the deceased
himself would be amused. *Everyone laughs.* But, then,
none of us are exactly faultless, and in view of what I said
at that time, perhaps we should have given more recognition to those truly responsible, since the park has now
drawn so much attention. For example, the Chief of
Parks . . . *That gentleman bows* . . . and his superior, the
Chief of Public Works. *That gentleman also bows.*

PUBLIC WORKS CHIEF: It is good of you to say that, sir, but
it is my belief that the Chief of the Parks Section and
myself only pushed the plan, insofar as paper work was
concerned. When I think of his honor's painstaking
efforts to bring this plan to materialization, then I know
that it is the Deputy Mayor himself who should be rewarded. *Everyone smiles and nods at this.*

MAYOR: No, I've been criticized—criticized even for that
speech at the opening of the park. One of them called it
a political speech, didn't he, Ono?

He is about to say more when the MAID *comes in and tells*
MITSUO'S *wife that some women from Kuroe-cho have come
to pay their respects.*
*A group of women, many of the same who came to the
Citizens' Section before, now enter the room. They do not
wait to be invited, but walk directly to the altar. Many are
crying. They bow before the picture; they light incense. A
baby on the back of one of them starts to cry.*
Cut to MITSUO, *looking at them.*
*Cut to his wife. It is not proper for her to remain standing
in the middle of the room and so she kneels.*
*Cut to a view of the entire room. The officials are embarrassed
and frowning; only one of them,* KIMURA, *is affected; he puts
his hands to his eyes as though to hide tears. Then the women
get up to leave the room. As the women go, they bow to the
other guests and only one,* KIMURA, *bows in return. There is
a long silence.*
Cut to WATANABE'S *picture; cut to a closer shot; cut to one
even closer—the grain of the photograph is visible.*
*Cut to a view of the entire room. The wife, who has seen the
women out, returns and sits down. The silence continues
unbroken.*
Then the DEPUTY MAYOR *nods to the* CHIEF OF PUBLIC

WORKS *and the* CHIEF OF PARKS. *They kneel, bow to the shrine and altar, bow to the family, then politely and carefully take their leave.* ONO, *who has gone to see them out, returns.*

ONO: It's cold, isn't it?

KIICHI: Have a drink. *He holds out a sake bottle.* Oh, I'm sorry, this sake is cold. I'll go and get some warm. How about everyone getting together, sitting a little closer together?

There is a general movement, almost a scramble. ONO *successfully gets the seat just vacated by the* MAYOR. *Others must be content with lesser positions. Old* OHARA *stands up too late, looks for a seat on the other side; all are taken; he sits down, grumbling. Someone asks if they had gone off to a meeting.*

KIMURA: Yes, they couldn't bear it here any longer. Mr. Watanabe built that park, no matter what anyone says. And the Mayor knows it. That's why he . . .

ONO: Now, you're going too far. Mr. Watanabe just . . .

CLERK: It's not just because I'm in the Parks Section, but I know that our section planned and carried out the whole thing.

KIMURA: That's not what I mean.

SAITO: That's all right. We know how you feel, but why should the Chief of the Citizens' Section try to build a park anyway? It is outside his . . . his sphere of influence.

NOGUCHI: Anyway, no one built that park. It was just a coincidence. And no councillor would have done anything about it anyway, if it hadn't been that elections are coming up. KIMURA *is about to say something but* NOGUCHI *continues.* And, come to think of it, if it hadn't been for that gang that wanted to have a red-light district there, the project might not have gone so smoothly either.

OHARA: I just can't understand it. *He shakes his head, talking as though to himself.* Why should Mr. Watanabe change so? He changed so suddenly.

ONO: Yes, it was strange.

SAITO: That's it. Now that I think of it . . . Mr. Watanabe knew about his cancer. That's why.

Cut to ONO *as he turns to* MITSUO, *who has just returned with more sake.*

ONO: We were just speaking of your father—did he know he
had gastric cancer?

MITSUO: If he had, he would certainly have told me. I think
that Father was very fortunate in knowing nothing about
it. After all, to learn something like that is just like getting
a death sentence.

KIICHI *comes back into the room.*

ONO: Then Saito's theory is wrong.

KIICHI: What's that?

ONO: Mr. Watanabe changed so in the last five months, and
we can't understand why.

KIICHI: Oh, that. It was because of a woman. You know,
often an older man tries to hold onto his youth by keeping
a mistress. His complexion gets better, his eyes get
brighter ... *His wife is looking at him* ... Anyway, I think
he was keeping some woman.

ONO: Well, he did take to wearing a rather elegant hat.

There are smiles and nods at this. SAITO *turns and looks at
the picture of* WATANABE *on the altar.*

SAITO: That hat. It really surprised me.

Cut to the conclusion of the former scene where WATANABE
has handed the report to ONO. *The dialogue is as before.*

ONO: But this will be difficult.

WATANABE: No, it won't, not if you are determined.

The camera pans with WATANABE *as he hurries to put on his
coat. The noon siren is heard.*

ONO: But—

Cut to a vacant lot in Kuroe-cho; it is raining. WATANABE
*walks around in the rain, through mud, looking at where the
playground will be. One of the women runs up to him carrying an umbrella, holding it over him.
Cut back to the wake.*

SAITO: He seemed to be trying so hard. It just wasn't natural.

ONO: Well, that's true. Yet, you know, I can't believe that
the influence of a woman could have . . .

KIICHI: But . . .

TATSU: Don't.

OHARA: I just can't understand it.

PARKS CLERK: Well, there was a time when Mr. Watanabe's
 effort made things very difficult.

SEWAGE SECTION CLERK: You're right, but what I can't understand is why a man who had been an official for the
 last thirty years should—

KIMURA: That's because—

PARKS CLERK: And he really shouldn't have gone around
 trying to talk all the other sections into it like that. Naturally, they didn't like it—my chief in particular. He felt
 that the parks were all his own responsibility.

Cut to the Parks Section. WATANABE *is offering a petition.
The* CHIEF OF PARKS *turns wearily.*

CHIEF: Now, we have many park projects.

WATANABE: Please. The conditions there are terrible.

CHIEF: But it just isn't as easy as your plan here makes it
 seem.

Cut to the same location, some time has apparently passed.
WATANABE *is sitting to one side; the* CHIEF OF PARKS *is trying
to work, but cannot. He keeps glancing at* WATANABE *sitting
there, his head bowed. Finally, the* CHIEF *takes the petition
and, with deliberation, stamps it and puts it in the "outgoing" basket, then turns and looks at* WATANABE, *who does
not move. Cut back to the wake.*

SAITO: Mr. Watanabe just hung on until the Chief finally
 gave in.

PUBLIC WORKS CLERK: Now that you say so, it was just the
 same with my boss. That Watanabe, he just wouldn't give
 in. Why, my chief used to turn and run when he saw him
 coming.

Cut to a corridor in the City Hall. The CHIEF OF PUBLIC
WORKS *sees* WATANABE *coming, turns and hurries away, but
it is too late:* WATANABE *has seen him and starts after him.
Cut to the wake—most of the men are getting drunk.*

SANITATION CLERK: But what surprised me most was the way
 that he, a big chief like that, acted toward clerks like me.

Cut to the Sanitation Section. WATANABE *is going up to each
member of the office and bowing. Each must stand and return
his bow. With each bow* WATANABE *murmurs, "Please," as
the embarrassed clerks bow back.*

SANITATION CLERK *off:* And we finally gave in too.

Cut to the wake.

PUBLIC WORKS CLERK: We all felt sorry for him.

NOGUCHI: But it was you General Affairs Section people that gave him the most trouble.

GENERAL AFFAIRS CLERK: Oh, you think so?

ONO: It's true. I went around with him for almost two weeks. I'll never forget it.

GENERAL AFFAIRS CLERK: I'm sorry, sir.

SAITO: But what surprised me most was that incident when . . .

SAKAI: Oh, that. That was really surprising.

Cut to the stairway leading past the Citizens' Section. WATANABE *is walking at the head of a number of women, the wives from Kuroe-cho. He goes directly up the stairs, his own clerks staring at him. In the corridor at the top he takes off his coat, gives it to one of the women to hold, and goes into a door marked "DEPUTY MAYOR'S OFFICE."*
Cut to the wake.

ONO: And that wasn't all.

SAITO: What happened in the Mayor's office?

ONO: Well, I doubt that anyone ever stood up to the Mayor like he did.

Cut to the DEPUTY MAYOR'S *office.* WATANABE *is bowing;* ONO *stands behind him.*

MAYOR: I personally don't mind your pushing this park project like this, but some people might think that you were looking for publicity. The City Council has a lot of problems. It would be best if you'd just forget about it.

This taken care of, he turns back to his friends and continues an apparently interrupted conversation.

MAYOR: And so I attended that party last night, but, really, the geisha nowadays are no good at all. One of them didn't open her mouth all night, and later I heard that she's a geisha only at night, it's a kind of sideline.

FRIEND: How amusing!

WATANABE: Would you . . . please reconsider. WATANABE *has gone on bowing.* ONO *is trying to make him leave. The* MAYOR *turns, incredulous; his friends look up.*

MAYOR: What did you say?

Cut to WATANABE. *He is bowing, yet looking the* MAYOR *full in the face.*

WATANABE: About that park. Please . . . reconsider.

Cut to the MAYOR *staring at him.*
Cut back to WATANABE, *staring, and* ONO *trying to pull him away.*
Cut back to the wake. There is silence, then laughter. Most of the men are now really drunk.

SAITO: Yet, judging from the results, it wasn't such a bad plan.
SAKAI: No, it was dangerous. Just think of all the . . . the spheres of influence at City Hall.

Cut to KIMURA.

KIMURA: But the Mayor reconsidered, didn't he?
NOGUCHI: Oh, that. It was some councillor's idea. He made him do it. The whole thing was a sort of accident, you see, a kind of coincidence—you're just sentimental, that's all.

There is some laughter at the word "sentimental."

SAKAI: Yes, that's it, sentimental.
KIMURA: I don't think so. If you can't try to understand a man like Mr. Watanabe without being thought sentimental, then the world is a dark place indeed.
NOGUCHI: And so it is—very dark.
KIMURA: I don't know what it was that was keeping Mr. Watanabe alive, but sometimes I was almost afraid for him.

Cut to a corridor in the City Hall. KIMURA *has stopped at the top of the stairs and looks at* WATANABE *in the far distance. He is leaning against the wall, with apparently no strength left. Then, very slowly, he pushes himself along the wall in the direction of the* MAYOR'S *office. Cut to a close-up of* WATANABE.
Cut back to the wake.

PARK SECTION CLERK: And, come to think of it, there was that day at the park site.

Cut to the park site. Dust, gravel, a bulldozer. It almost runs

over WATANABE. *One of the women hurries up, pulls him back. She and several others take him to one of the houses, offer him a glass of water. He takes it and drinks some water. Cut to a close-up of* WATANABE *looking at the park site.*

PARK SECTION CLERK *off:* When he looked at that park
. . . *Cut back to the wake, the* CLERK *speaking* . . . his face
just glowed. It was . . . well, it was like a man looking at
his own grandchild.

KIMURA: Naturally, it was just that to him.

ONO: So, that's why . . .

KIMURA: That's why, no matter what anyone says, it was Mr.
Watanabe who built that park.

NOGUCHI: But if the Mayor and the councillors hadn't done
anything, there wouldn't have been any park. He just
didn't take into consideration all of those . . . those
spheres of influence up above.

ONO: Oh, I wouldn't say that.

NOGUCHI: No?

ONO: You remember what happened? With that gang that
wanted to have a red-light district where the park is?

Cut to a corridor. WATANABE *and* ONO *are walking along it.
Several men are lounging against the wall. One steps forward,
taking off his dark glasses.*

MAN: You chief of the Citizens' Section?

WATANABE: Yes, I am.

MAN: Wanted to see you. Look, mister, just don't poke your
nose in any more, okay?

He smiles, flicks WATANABE'S *lapel;* WATANABE *looks at him.*

WATANABE: Why? Who are you?

The MAN *grabs the lapels of* WATANABE'S *coat, tightens his
grip.*

MAN: Don't act stupid, I'm telling you, see? You just cut it
out and don't do anything dumb any more.

Cut to WATANABE. *He is smiling.
Cut to the group; the* MAN *releases him.* WATANABE *turns to
go into the* MAYOR'S *office. Just then another* MAN, *obviously
one of them, comes out and looks at* WATANABE.

MAN: This is Watanabe—remember him.

He stares hard at WATANABE, *who smiles back, and then goes into the office. The gang begins to move off.* ONO *stands looking after them. The second* MAN—*the threatening killer —turns and looks at* ONO, *who turns and hurries into the office.*

Cut to the wake. Everyone is now drunk. Old OHARA *is thinking, his head to one side.*

OHARA: But it's strange. I just can't understand why he changed like that—he must have known he had cancer.

ONO *suddenly sits up, drunk, makes a gesture.*

ONO: I just remembered!

Cut to a staircase in the City Hall. ONO *is obviously lecturing* WATANABE, *who leans, drawn and tired, against the railing.*

ONO: Now, this is too much. You've been doing this for two weeks now. The least they could do is tell you whether they have the money or not. And the way they treat you. At least they could do it nicely—it should make you angry to be insulted this way.

WATANABE: But it doesn't. I don't have time to be angry with anyone. *He goes on down the stairs.*

Cut to the wake. A general commotion, each person remembering something.

ONO: And then . . .

SAITO: Now that you mention it, I remember once when . . .

Cut to a bridge above the park site. It is sunset. WATANABE *and* SAITO *are walking across it.*

WATANABE: Oh, how beautiful . . . *He looks up* . . . For thirty years I have never watched a sunset. Now there's no more time.

Cut back to the wake.

SAKAI: It's all clear now . . .

NOGUCHI: He knew he didn't have long to live.

SAITO: That clears everything up, explains everything. Now I understand why he acted that way, it wasn't strange at all, it was normal.

ONO: We'd all do the same thing ourselves.

Cut to KIMURA.

KIMURA: We'll all die ourselves one day.

A general shot of the group. A pause, then OHARA *moves forward.*

OHARA: Look here, Ono. Now, I don't mean that . . . I mean Mr. New Chief of the Citizens' Section, that's what I mean. Look here, can't you hear me?

Cut to ONO, *drunk, pleased, and irritated, all at the same time.*

ONO: I haven't been appointed yet.

OHARA: All right then, Ono, what did you just say? That we'd have done the same thing ourselves? Don't make me laugh. *He drunkenly points to* ONO. You fellows couldn't do what Mr. Watanabe did. Don't make me laugh. Me, I only went to night school, and that's why I'll never be chief of any Citizens' Section. But you, Ono, someone like you! Well, just don't make me laugh.

SAITO *tries to stop* OHARA; *then pauses, struck with a sudden thought.*

SAITO: Compared with Mr. Watanabe, all of us are just . . .

OHARA: We're trash, that's what, trash. And you're trash too.

SAKAI: We're all trash. Oh, there are some fine men at City Hall, but after you've worked there for a long time, it changes you.

NOGUCHI: Yes, that's the place where you don't dare even think. If you do, you're dangerous. You must only act as though you're thinking and doing something.

PUBLIC WORKS CLERK: That's right.

GENERAL AFFAIRS CLERK: Yes, that's right.

SAITO: You can't do anything. Why, to get permission for a new trash-can you have to make out enough documents to fill up that trash-can.

SAKAI *moves forward excitedly, then suddenly begins to cry.*

SAKAI: And you have to put your seal on everything: stamp, stamp, stamp!

NOGUCHI: The way we live is by stealing time—people com-

plain about official corruption, but that's nothing compared with our criminal waste of time.

ONO *crawls on all fours into the middle of the room and waves
his arms.*

ONO: Listen, fellows! I know how you feel. I think about it
too, but what can you do with such a big organization—
anyway, there's no time to think.
OHARA: You fool! *They all look around at him.*
SAITO: But look, Ohara. In this organization where you can't
do anything, Mr. Watanabe did something, and he did
it because he had cancer.
SAKAI: That's just what I wanted to say. *He begins sobbing.*
NOGUCHI: Oh, it makes me mad.
SAKAI: Me, too!
NOGUCHI: And Mr. Watanabe never got any reward at all.

They are all crawling about on the floor.

SAITO: Oh, but when I think of what Mr. Watanabe must
have felt . . .
NOGUCHI: Whoever went and took the credit isn't even
human.
OHARA: Oh, come out and say it's the Mayor.
NOGUCHI: Now, you be careful what you say.

There is a pause. SAKAI *is crying softly.*

SAKAI: But I just wonder what Mr. Watanabe felt when he
was dying out there all alone in the park—just to think
of it makes me feel awful.

*Most of the men begin to cry now. Among those who do not
is* KIMURA.
Cut to WATANABE'S *picture on the altar.*
Cut to the doorway. The MAID *appears carrying* WATANABE'S
hat. It is now crushed and dirty.

MAID: Excuse me, but a policeman just brought this, he
found it in the park.

*Cut to a close-up of the hat in her hands. Everyone turns to
look at it.*

MAID: And he said he wanted to come in and pay his respects.

Cut. A young policeman comes in, bows, goes to the altar, prays, and then gets up to go.

KAZUE: Thank you for coming.

KIICHI: Won't you sit down and have a drink?

He indicates a cushion and pours the POLICEMAN *a cup of sake. The* POLICEMAN *is ill at ease, takes the sake, puts it down. He is apparently deciding whether to speak or not.*

POLICEMAN: I . . . I saw him in the park on that night. It was about ten. No . . . *Looks at his watch* . . . it was closer to eleven, I guess. He was sitting on one of the children's swings. I thought he was probably drunk, but I didn't do anything. If I had, then maybe all of this wouldn't have happened. I am truly sorry. *The* POLICEMAN *bows.*

Cut to MITSUO *looking at the hat that he now holds.*

POLICEMAN: But he looked so, well, so happy. How can I say it? And he was singing . . . and it was in a voice that, well, moved me.

Cut to the park. In the distance, behind a set of climbing bars, is WATANABE *sitting on a swing; snow is falling. He is singing. The camera pans along the bars, tracking in nearer.*

WATANABE:

> Life is so short,
> Fall in love, dear maiden,
> While your lips are still red;
> Before you can no longer love—
> For there will be no tomorrow.

Dissolve to WATANABE'S *picture over the altar. The song continues, there is a cut to the wake; shots of various faces; then of* MITSUO *standing up. Overcome, he goes into the corridor.* KAZUE, *followed by* MITSUO'S *uncle, goes out to him.*

MITSUO: And I found a box with my name on it, on the stairs that night, and in it were his bank book and his seal, and his retirement allowance papers.

KAZUE: He must have left them . . .

MITSUO: But that was bad of him! If he knew he had cancer, why didn't he tell us? *He begins to cry; his uncle comes forward.*

KIICHI: And his mistress, why didn't she come to the funeral?
  Maybe there wasn't any mistress.

*Cut to a close-up of a packing-case. In it are the framed letters
of commendation, an alarm clock, a white toy rabbit.*
*Cut back to the wake. The men are now sitting close together,
very drunk, very excited. During the scene* KIMURA *leaves
them and goes to kneel in front of the altar, looking up at*
WATANABE'S *picture.*

SAKAI: We must work hard.
NOGUCHI: Yes, with the spirit that Mr. Watanabe showed.
SAITO: We mustn't let his death be meaningless.
ONO: Me—I'm going to turn over a new leaf!
NOGUCHI: That's the spirit. Me, I'm going to work for the
  good of the public!

They are all shouting, waving their arms. Only KIMURA *at the
altar is still and silent.*
Fade out.
*Fade in to the Citizens' Section as it was at the beginning
of the film, only that* ONO *is now at* WATANABE'S *desk.* SAKAI
*deferentially, glancing back at the information counter,
comes to his side.*

SAKAI: Excuse me, but they say that the sewage water has
  overflowed in Kizaki-cho.
ONO: Well, send them to the Public Works Section.

Cut to KIMURA *looking up sharply at these words.*
Cut to ONO, *who stares back.*
Cut to KIMURA. *There is the noise of a chair being pushed
over as he stands up.*
ONO *can be seen, glaring at him.*
Cut to KIMURA. *He slowly picks up the chair and sits down.
As he sits the camera descends with him. His face is obscured
by the documents on his desk. It is as though he is being
buried alive in them.*
Cut to SAKAI, *apologetic at the counter.*

SAKAI: Would you please go to the Public Works Section
  with this?

Cut to the bridge above the park. It is sunset. KIMURA *comes
across the bridge on his way home. He stops to look.*

Cut to the park. Children are playing there and their mothers call them in for dinner.

Cut to KIMURA *watching them. He turns and starts off, the camera panning with him. The top of the swing comes into view. The tune "Life Is So Short," played on a solo flute, is heard over.* KIMURA *walks away.*

Fade out.

TRANSLATED BY DONALD RICHIE

■OZU YASUJIRŌ
with Noda Kōgō

The work of Ozu Yasujirō, perhaps Japan's greatest film director, abounds with qualities usually associated with traditional Japanese aesthetics: a pictorial use of asymmetry; emptiness, both spatial and temporal; a restricted view; a fixed subject matter. The seeming sparseness and economy of the Ozu film, its patterned surface and completely visible structure, are reminiscent of classical Japanese architecture and graphic art. Unlike Mizoguchi, however, whose scenes occasionally look like a real *suiboku* ink painting or a real Kōrin screen, Ozu internalizes this influence in his films. The story is often exquisitely and purposefully mundane (and always contemporary) and the characters are presented with a very selective realism. For this reason, his films—particularly *Tokyo Story*, his own favorite among them—seem, with their gentle humor, their extraordinary compassion, distant from the measured world of classical art. Yet traditional principles lie just beneath the surface. In all his major films, Ozu restricted himself to one elegiac theme: the Japanese family in dissolution. This too has led many critics to call him (usually in opposition to Kurosawa) the most "Japanese" of all film artists.

Ozu Yasujirō was born in Tokyo in 1903 and died there in 1963. His formal education ended with middle school, but he was able in 1923 to get a job as assistant cameraman—moving the camera from place to place—at the Tokyo studios of the Shōchiku Company. In a few years he became an assistant director and began writing for films; he made his own first picture from a script by Noda Kōgō, with whom he was to collaborate in writing original screenplays for his memorable postwar films: *Late Spring (Banshun,* 1949), *Early Summer (Bakushū,* 1951), and *Tokyo Story,* among others. "Mr. Ozu looked happiest when he was engaged in writing a script with Mr. Noda," one of his leading actors once said in an interview. "By the time he had finished writing it—about four months of work—he had already made up every image in every shot, so that he never changed the script after we went on the set. And the dialogue was so polished that he would not allow even a single mistake." If not literally true, this statement suggests why Ozu's careful workmanship resulted in such spare, effective dialogue. In his book *Ozu*, Donald Richie has observed that Ozu's mastery of characterization was predicated upon his mastery of dialogue:

> Even in Ozu's silent films the dialogue titles, and there are many of them, must be considered as important as the visuals. It is the dialogue, spoken or printed, that supports and creates the character and differentiates one character from another. Though there are many scenes without dialogue in Ozu's films, these occur only after a character has been established. We know him, initially, through what he says . . . In Japan Ozu's scripts are regarded as literature: the degree of verisimilitude and character delineation achieved is so great, yet the economy so extreme, that the scripts themselves qualify as works of art. Though the many nuances of the dialogue are only appreciable in the film itself, there is even in translation a feeling of rightness to the Ozu dialogue, of inevitability, that is uncommon in any medium and extremely rare in film.

A comparison of the published script of *Tokyo Story* with the film nevertheless reveals a number of slight differences. Scene 157 in the script, for example, does not include the elder sister once again chiding her father's drinking; the location of 166 has in the film been transferred from outside to inside; and the editing of the final sequence of the film is considerably different from the script.

Tokyo Story was a Shōchiku Production, released November 3, 1953, with Ryū Chishū, Higashiyama Chieko, Sugimura Haruko, and Hara Setsuko in the cast.

❖ Tokyo Story

(*Tōkyō monogatari,* 1953)

1. Onomichi, a morning in July. The town stretches from sea to mountains, the main street, the morning market visible.
2. The mountainside district. In the main street, at the end of a small alley, children are passing on their way to school.
3. The HIRAYAMA *house. In the room are* SHUKICHI, *seventy, and his wife,* TOMI, *sixty-seven. They are packing for their journey. She is putting things into their bag; he is looking at a railway timetable.*

SHUKICHI: According to this we'll pass through Osaka around six tonight.
TOMI: Keizo should be off work by then.

SHUKICHI: He'll probably be at Osaka Station. I sent him a
telegram.

*Their youngest child, KYOKO, a primary-school teacher, ap-
pears with two lunch boxes.*

KYOKO: Here is your lunch. I'm leaving now.

She puts her own lunch box in her bag.

TOMI: If you're busy at school you don't need to come and
see us off, you know.
KYOKO: I think I'll have time. It's the physical-education
period.
SHUKICHI: We'll see you later at the station then.
KYOKO: I've put the tea in the thermos, Mother.
TOMI: All right.
KYOKO: I'll be going then.

She leaves.
4. KYOKO in the entryway, leaving the house.
5. The lane. KYOKO is walking. Passing schoolchildren bow.
6. The HIRAYAMA house.

TOMI: Do you have the air cushion?
SHUKICHI: Didn't I give it to you?
TOMI: Well, it's not here.
SHUKICHI: I'm certain I gave it to you.
TOMI: Really?

*Outside the window appears the housewife from next door.
She is about 48.*

WOMAN NEXT DOOR: Good morning.
TOMI: Good morning.
WOMAN: So you're leaving today.
TOMI: Yes, on the early-afternoon train.
WOMAN: Really?
TOMI: Yes, we wanted to see our children while we still can.
WOMAN: That's nice. They must be looking forward to your
coming to Tokyo.
SHUKICHI: Well, I hope so. Would you keep an eye on the
house while we're away?
WOMAN: Of course. Your children have all turned out so
well. You're very lucky.
SHUKICHI: I suppose so . . .
WOMAN: And what beautiful weather.

TOMI: Yes, indeed.

WOMAN: So you both have a lovely trip and take care of yourselves.

TOMI: Thank you.

The WOMAN *bows, smiles, and leaves.*

TOMI: I still can't find it.

SHUKICHI: Oh, but it must be there.

He starts to look for it and then finds it among his own belongings. He holds up the air cushion.

Here it is.

7. Tokyo. The Koto district, a scene with many small factories.

8. An empty lot. In one corner is a signboard reading: "HIRAYAMA CLINIC. INTERNAL MEDICINE AND CHILDREN'S DISEASES."

9. The consulting room of the Clinic. From the looks of it, the Clinic is none too prosperous.

10. The stairway to the second floor.

11. The second floor, a room. A child's desk has been put out on the veranda. FUMIKO, *39, is just wiping it off. Then she goes back downstairs with a bucket.*

12. The stairs. FUMIKO *comes down them.*

13. The kitchen. FUMIKO *puts down the bucket, steps into geta, and looks into the door of the heater for the bath. Then she goes up again.*

14. A room. When FUMIKO *comes in, her second son,* ISAMU, *6, is playing by himself.*

FUMIKO: Now there is a good little boy.

She takes the washed bandages which have been drying on the sill and leaves.

15. The consulting room. FUMIKO *comes in and puts the bandages away. A child's voice saying "I'm back" is heard in the entryway.* MINORU, *the eldest son, 14, a middle-school student, has returned. He comes in.*

FUMIKO: Oh, you're back.

MINORU: I'm back. Have Grandpa and Grandma come yet?

FUMIKO: They'll be here soon.

16. The second-floor room. MINORU *comes up and sees that the room has been changed. He is very surprised.*

MINORU: Mama. Mama.

FUMIKO *comes up carrying two cushions.*

FUMIKO: What do you want?
MINORU: Why did you move my desk?
FUMIKO: To make room for your grandparents.
MINORU: But you didn't have to move my desk.
FUMIKO: It can't be helped. We had to have the space.
MINORU: But I need someplace to study.
FUMIKO *(crossly):* You study anyplace you like.

She turns and goes downstairs. MINORU *follows.*
17. The kitchen.

MINORU: All right, then. But where am I going to study?

FUMIKO *doesn't answer him.*

MINORU: Tell me, Mama. Where?
FUMIKO: Be quiet. You never study anyway!
MINORU: I do, I do.
FUMIKO: Now you say you study.
MINORU: All right, then, so I don't have to study. Right? No
   more study, right?
FUMIKO: Minoru!

The sound of an automobile horn is heard.

   They're here.

She goes to the entryway; MINORU *goes to the consulting
room.*
18. The entryway. FUMIKO *opens the door.*
19. Outside. KOICHI, *47, the eldest son and* FUMIKO*'s husband, gets out of the taxi. He takes the luggage. The old
couple get out, followed by* SHIGE, *44, the eldest daughter,*
KOICHI*'s younger sister.*

FUMIKO *(to* KOICHI*):* Oh, you're back.
KOICHI *(to his parents):* Well, Mother, Father, come on in.
FUMIKO: Please come in.
KOICHI: Yes, please come in.

20. The living room. ISAMU *stands watching as his mother
hurriedly arranges the cushions.* KOICHI *comes in first, followed by* SHUKICHI, TOMI, *and* SHIGE.

KOICHI: You must be tired. Did you sleep well on the train?
TOMI: Oh, very well.

She looks at ISAMU *and calls him over. He shyly runs away. They all look on smiling.* FUMIKO *greets the old couple with a formal bow.*

FUMIKO: You are most welcome. It is very good to see you again.
SHUKICHI: I just hope we're not inconveniencing you.
FUMIKO: Mother, it has been such a long time.
TOMI: It really has.
FUMIKO: It's wonderful to see you. How is our sister, Kyoko?
TOMI: Oh, just fine, thank you.
FUMIKO: She stayed on alone back there, looking after the house?
TOMI: Yes.

FUMIKO *gets up to go make tea.* SHIGE, *seeing this, follows after her.*
21. The kitchen.

SHIGE: I've brought a little something, nothing much. Some crackers. Got them in the neighborhood.
FUMIKO: Thank you.
SHIGE: Mama likes them. Have you anything to put them in? A dish.
FUMIKO: Yes.
SHIGE: Or a tray.

FUMIKO *selects a dish.*

FUMIKO: Here, how is this?
SHIGE: Just fine.

She begins putting the sembei crackers into it. FUMIKO *begins to make tea.*

FUMIKO: Did Noriko come to the station?
SHIGE: No, she didn't. And I phoned her too.
FUMIKO: I wonder what happened.

SHIGE *hands her the filled dish and goes back to the main room.*
22. The corridor. SHIGE *passes the consulting room and sees the children sitting there.*

SHIGE: What are you doing? Come on in here.

23. The living room. KOICHI *and his parents are on the veranda looking out over the garden.* SHIGE *and the children come in.*

SHIGE: These are your grandparents.

KOICHI *and his parents turn around.*

SHUKICHI: My, aren't they getting big.

He goes back into the room.

KOICHI: Minoru is in middle school now.
SHUKICHI: Really? *(He strokes* MINORU*'s head.)*
TOMI: And how old are you, Isamu?
KOICHI: Tell her how old you are.
SHIGE: How old are you?

ISAMU *shyly runs away and the others laugh.* FUMIKO *brings in the tea and sembei.*

FUMIKO *(to* KOICHI*):* The bath is ready.
KOICHI: How about a bath, Father?
SHUKICHI: Well . . .
SHIGE: Don't you want to change your clothes, Mama?
FUMIKO: Oh, the robes.
TOMI: That's all right. We brought our own.
SHUKICHI: Well, maybe I'll just go ahead.
KOICHI: Please do. I'll bring this.

He picks up his father's yukata robe and they leave. TOMI *follows them.* SHIGE *and* FUMIKO *go back to the kitchen.*
24. Upstairs. KOICHI *with his parents.*

KOICHI: Did Keizo meet you in Osaka?
SHUKICHI: Yes, we'd sent him a telegram and he was right
    there.
KOICHI *(to* TOMI*):* Was he all right?
TOMI: He sent you something.

She begins looking into her bag.

KOICHI: Oh, that's all right. Later. You have a towel, Father?
SHUKICHI: Yes.
KOICHI: Well, have a good soak.

He makes a small bow and goes out.
25. The kitchen. SHIGE *is just finishing a sentence when* KOICHI *passes and stops.*

SHIGE: What shall we feed them? What about some meat?
Sukiyaki maybe.
KOICHI: That sounds good.
FUMIKO: And some sashimi.
KOICHI: We don't need that too, do we? What do you think?
SHIGE: That's enough. We'll just give them meat.

The sound of someone in the entryway and a woman's voice calling, "Excuse me."

SHIGE: That's Noriko.

FUMIKO goes out.
26. The entryway. NORIKO, 28, widow of the second son, Shoji, dead in the War, is taking off her shoes. FUMIKO comes to welcome her.

FUMIKO: It's good to see you.
NORIKO: I got to the station too late.
FUMIKO: You went?
NORIKO: Yes, but they'd already gone. So I missed them.

She gives FUMIKO a wrapped package.

NORIKO: Here's a little something.
FUMIKO: Thank you.

SHIGE and KOICHI come to the door.

KOICHI: Nice of you to come.
NORIKO: I'm sorry I'm late.
KOICHI: They're upstairs.
NORIKO: I'll just go up and say hello.

27. The corridor downstairs. FUMIKO goes to the kitchen.
NORIKO goes upstairs.
28. Upstairs. The old couple, now in yukata, are unpacking.
NORIKO comes in and bows.

NORIKO: Welcome to Tokyo.
TOMI: Oh, what a long time it's been.
NORIKO: Yes, hasn't it.
SHUKICHI: You must have been very busy today.
NORIKO: Not really. But by the time I'd finished, it was too
late.
TOMI: You needn't have come today. We'll be here for some
time.

SHUKICHI: Still working for the same company? It must be hard for a person to be all alone.

NORIKO: Oh, no. Not really.

SHIGE *is heard telling her father the bath is waiting.*

SHUKICHI: I'll just go on ahead, then.

He goes downstairs. NORIKO *sees her mother-in-law folding an obi.*

NORIKO: Here, let me help you.

TOMI: Oh, no, that's all right . . . You know, it's just like a dream being here in Tokyo. And it didn't seem so far. Yesterday we were in Onomichi and today here we are with you.

NORIKO *nods and smiles.*

So—one should live long, after all.

NORIKO: You haven't changed at all.

TOMI: Of course we have. We're old folks now.

SHIGE *comes in.*

SHIGE: What are you two talking about?—Mama, I believe you've gotten bigger.

TOMI: Don't be silly. How could I have grown?

SHIGE: But you have. You've gotten even fatter maybe. *(To* NORIKO.*)* When we were children, she was so big I used to be ashamed of her in front of my friends. And then one day during a school festival she broke the chair she was sitting on.

TOMI: Oh, that chair was broken already.

SHIGE: She still thinks that.

TOMI: Well, it was.

SHIGE: Anyway, it doesn't matter.

The three laugh and go downstairs. In the corner sits MINORU*'s desk.*

29. The consulting room, later, that evening. MINORU *is studying.*

30. The kitchen. NORIKO *is helping* FUMIKO *clean up after the meal.* NORIKO *has finished a dish.*

NORIKO: Where shall I put this? Here?

FUMIKO: Thanks.

NORIKO: And where shall I put this?

FUMIKO: Oh, just leave it out.

31. The living room. SHUKICHI, TOMI, SHIGE, KOICHI *are relaxing.* ISAMU *is asleep;* TOMI's *lap is his pillow.*

SHIGE: Oh, Mother, how is Mrs. Ko?

TOMI: Mrs. Ko? Oh, she has had bad luck again. After her husband died—when was it, spring last year?—she went off to marry some man in Kurashiki. She took her child with her, and now I hear she's not very happy. Poor woman.

SHUKICHI: Really?

KOICHI: Papa, what was the name of that man, the one who worked for the city?

SHUKICHI: Mr. Mihashi? He died. *(To* TOMI.*)* Some time ago.

TOMI: Yes, that's true.

SHUKICHI: You remember Mr. Hattori?

KOICHI: Of the Military Affairs Section?

SHIGE: Oh, I remember him.

SHUKICHI: Well, he's living in Tokyo now.

KOICHI: Really?

SHUKICHI: I'm planning to visit him.

KOICHI: Where does he live?

SHUKICHI: Somewhere in the Daito district. Where is that now? His address is in my notebook.

NORIKO *comes in.*

SHUKICHI: All cleaned up?

NORIKO: Yes.

SHUKICHI: Well, thank you.

TOMI *offers some candy.*

TOMI: Here, have one. They're from Keizo.

NORIKO: Thank you.

FUMIKO *comes in, sees* ISAMU, *and apologizes for him.*

TOMI: Oh, he's sleeping very soundly.

SHIGE *(to* KOICHI*):* Going to take them around tomorrow?

KOICHI: Yes, it's Sunday, we'll show them something.

SHIGE: Good. Well, Noriko, shall we go?

NORIKO: I suppose so.

SHUKICHI: It was good of you to have come.
TOMI: And thank you for the very good dinner.

32. The hallway. FUMIKO *sees off* NORIKO *and* SHIGE.

SHIGE: We've stayed late.
FUMIKO: Not at all.
NORIKO: Thank you for dinner.
FUMIKO: No. Thank you.

33. The living room. TOMI *moves* ISAMU, *who is still asleep.*

KOICHI: You must be tired, Father. Mama, how about going
　　to bed?
SHUKICHI: Well, shall we go to bed?
TOMI: Yes.
SHUKICHI: Well, good night, then.

As he gets up, FUMIKO *comes in.*

KOICHI: Good night.
FUMIKO: I'll bring up the water soon.
TOMI: Good night.

They leave the room.
34. The staircase. SHUKICHI *and* TOMI *go upstairs.*
35. Upstairs. The two come in and sit down.

TOMI: Aren't you tired?
SHUKICHI: Not really.
TOMI: Well, I'm glad they are all well.
SHUKICHI: Yes. At last we're here.
TOMI: Yes. What part of Tokyo is this, I wonder?
SHUKICHI: A suburb, I think.
TOMI: It must be. It was a long ride from the station. I
　　somehow thought they'd live in some livelier part of the
　　city.
SHUKICHI: Here? Koichi wanted to move into a livelier place,
　　but I guess it wasn't all that easy.

The two sit, resting, thinking.
36. Next morning. One of the outlying suburbs, a bombed-
out section just now being built up.
37. A signboard: "URARA BEAUTY PARLOR."
38. Inside the shop. KIYO, *the assistant, is polishing a mirror.*
39. A room at the back. SHIGE *is having breakfast with her*
husband, KOZO, *49.*

KOZO: How long will they stay in Tokyo?

SHIGE: A few days more, I suppose. Hand me that, would you?

KOZO *hands her the pepper.*

KOZO: Shouldn't I go and see them?

SHIGE: Don't bother. They'll come here, anyway.

KOZO: I'll take them to the Kinsha-tei, or something.

SHIGE: You needn't bother.

KOZO: These beans are good. What are they doing today?

SHIGE: Stop eating all the beans up. *(Takes the dish away.)* Today my brother is taking them somewhere.

KOZO: Really? Then I'm free. It's all right not to go? Kiyo-chan, want your breakfast?

The voice of KIYO *is heard answering.*

40. KOICHI's *house. He is changing his clothes and* FUMIKO *is dressing* ISAMU.

FUMIKO *(to* ISAMU*):* And behave yourself. Grandpa and Grandma are going to be with us today. Do you understand?

ISAMU: I understand.

MINORU *comes in.*

MINORU: We're late. Aren't we going yet?

FUMIKO: We'll leave soon.

KOICHI: Go upstairs and see if they're ready. Say we are ready to go.

MINORU: All right. *(He runs off.)*

41. Upstairs. MINORU *comes in.* SHUKICHI *and* TOMI *are waiting.*

MINORU: Are you ready?

TOMI: We've kept you waiting.

MINORU: He says we can go now. *(Goes downstairs.)*

42. Downstairs. MINORU *comes in.*

MINORU: They're coming.

FUMIKO *smiles.* MINORU *hums a tune from a Western and goes into the consulting room.* ISAMU *is finished being dressed.* FUMIKO *pats him on the back and he runs off to join his brother.*

FUMIKO: Where will you eat?

KOICHI: At the department store. The children will like that.

FUMIKO: Good. Isamu likes the children's lunch there.

KOICHI: Really?

The front door is heard opening, followed by a man's voice.
KOICHI *answers and goes out.*
43. The hallway. A man is standing there in his shirt sleeves.
KOICHI *joins him.*

KOICHI: Well, how is he?

MAN: Well . . .

KOICHI: No appetite yet?

MAN: No. He'll only take a little something cold to drink.

KOICHI: Temperature still hasn't come down?

MAN: It's still around 102 degrees.

KOICHI: Really? Well, I'd better go see him.

MAN: Thank you. I'm very sorry to spoil your Sunday. *(He goes out.)*

44. The living room. KOICHI *comes back in.*

FUMIKO: Who was it?

KOICHI: Mr. Nakajima. The hypodermics are disinfected, aren't they?

She nods. SHUKICHI *and* TOMI *come in.*

KOICHI: Papa, I've got to go see a sick child. He's not doing at all well.

SHUKICHI: Is that so?

KOICHI: I'm sorry.

SHUKICHI: That's all right.

KOICHI: But it may take quite a while.

SHUKICHI: It doesn't matter.

KOICHI: I'll be going, then. I'm sorry, Mother.

He goes out, FUMIKO *seeing him to the door.*
45. The consulting room. The children are there. FUMIKO
comes in to get her husband's bag.

MINORU: Aren't we going yet?

FUMIKO *gives no clear reply, goes out.*
46. The entryway. KOICHI *is putting on his shoes when*
FUMIKO *appears.*

KOICHI: I may be late.

FUMIKO: But what will we do about them?
KOICHI: Well, we'll just have to go next Sunday.

He leaves. The children come out.

MINORU: Where's he going?
FUMIKO *(lightly):* To a patient's.

She leaves. MINORU *begins to pout.*
47. The living room. FUMIKO *comes back in.*

FUMIKO: I'm awfully sorry.
SHUKICHI: Not at all. A good doctor is a busy doctor.
TOMI: Yes, indeed.

MINORU *comes in;* ISAMU *follows him.*

MINORU *(pouting):* Mama, aren't we going? *(*FUMIKO *does not answer clearly.)* That's not fair.
FUMIKO: It can't be helped, can it? A patient needs him.
MINORU: It's not fair.
TOMI *(laughing):* There'll be another time.
MINORU: No!
FUMIKO: Minoru! You behave yourself. Just leave the room.
MINORU: You lied.
FUMIKO: You heard me.

MINORU *goes, stamping all the way.* TOMI *draws* ISAMU *to her.*

TOMI: Come here.
ISAMU: Don't want to. *(Runs away. Both* SHUKICHI *and* TOMI *laugh.)*
FUMIKO: What bad boys.
SHUKICHI: Well, boys should be lively.

At that moment there is a loud noise. MINORU *has thrown the heavy cushion of the consulting-room couch onto the floor.* FUMIKO *gets up and leaves at once.*
48. The consulting room. MINORU *and* ISAMU *are sitting on the couch,* MINORU *bouncing heavily.* FUMIKO *comes in.*

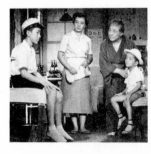

FUMIKO: You ought to be ashamed of yourselves. And you're supposed to be big boys.
MINORU: It's not fair.
FUMIKO: But we'll go next time.
MINORU: Always next time. We never go.

FUMIKO: But that man came suddenly, didn't he? It can't be helped, can it?

MINORU: You always say that.

She glares at him and goes back to the living room. MINORU *starts to shout;* ISAMU *imitates him.* FUMIKO *stops and turns back sharply.* MINORU *shouts.*

FUMIKO: This is too much. I'll tell your father.

MINORU: Go ahead.

FUMIKO: Very well. Just remember those words.

MINORU: I'm not afraid.

TOMI *looks in.*

TOMI *(mildly):* What's the matter?

FUMIKO *(smiling):* I wonder.

TOMI: Come on, Isamu. Let's take a walk. Why don't you come too, Minoru?

FUMIKO: Minoru.

TOMI: Come on, Isamu.

FUMIKO: Isn't that nice?—to go out with Grandma.

TOMI: Let's go, then. Come along, Minoru. Won't you come along?

FUMIKO: I'm sorry. *(*TOMI *goes out with* ISAMU.*)* You go too. Aren't you going?

MINORU: Don't want to.

FUMIKO: Very well, then. Do as you like.

She leaves angrily. MINORU, *alone, bounces some more, then gets up, sits in the revolving chair, and turns around and around unhappily.*

49. Upstairs. SHUKICHI *has taken off his suit and changed back into his yukata.* FUMIKO *brings in tea.*

FUMIKO: I'm very sorry.

SHUKICHI: Oh, that's all right. What's the matter with Minoru?

FUMIKO: I can't do anything with him.

SHUKICHI: Koichi was just like that too. Always had to have his own way. Never would listen to anyone.

FUMIKO: You must be disappointed, Father, not to be going.

SHUKICHI: No, not at all.

FUMIKO: Well, we'll go next Sunday.

SHUKICHI: That would be fine, thank you . . . After a few days here I think we'll probably go over to Shige's. *(Looks idly out of the window.)* Oh, look, there they are.

50. An empty plot, as seen by SHUKICHI. ISAMU *is playing and* TOMI *is kneeling beside him.*
51. The empty plot. TOMI *and* ISAMU.

TOMI: And what are you going to be when you grow up? *(*ISAMU *doesn't answer.)* A doctor like your father? *(*ISAMU *still doesn't answer.)* I wonder if I'll still be here.

52. Upstairs. SHUKICHI *is by himself looking vacantly out.*
53. Urara Beauty Parlor. There is only one customer, a woman, under a dryer. SHIGE *and* KIYO *are working.* KOZO *comes in.*

KIYO: Welcome back.

KOZO *greets the customer and goes to the back of the shop.*
54. The room at the back. The voice of SHIGE *is heard.*

SHIGE: There was a phone call.
KOZO: Who from?
SHIGE: Mr. Enomoto from Sugamo. How did the talks go?
KOZO: They're all done. Where are they?
SHIGE: Upstairs.
KOZO: I went to Asakusa and got some cakes for them.

He produces the bag. SHIGE *comes in.*

KOZO: Have one. They're good.

He begins to eat one.

SHIGE: They don't need such expensive cakes.

She takes and eats one.

KOZO: They're good, aren't they?
SHIGE: They're good, but they're too expensive. Sembei would have been good enough.
KOZO: But they had that yesterday.
SHIGE: They like sembei. Will you take them out someplace tomorrow?
KOZO: Tomorrow? I'm afraid I have to collect some bills.
SHIGE: Really? Koichi should do something then.
KOZO: I could take them to the Kinsha-tei, tonight.
SHIGE: What's on?
KOZO: Since last night—some *naniwabushi* reciting.
SHIGE: That's good. Take them, then. They haven't gone anyplace since they came to Tokyo.

KOZO: Yes, it's bad for them to stay in all the time.

SHIGE: Can't be helped though. There's no one to take them out.

KOZO *takes a memo book from his pocket, gets his soap and towel, and goes upstairs.*

55. TOMI *is alone upstairs. She is taking apart a kimono.* KOZO *comes in.*

KOZO: Well, she's got you working.

TOMI: Oh, hello.

KOZO: What a job we've put you to.

TOMI: No, not at all.

KOZO: Where is Father?

TOMI: He's out on the laundry platform.

KOZO: Don't you want to go to the bath? Father, Father.

56. The laundry platform. SHUKICHI *is sitting there staring vacantly. He turns upon hearing* KOZO's *voice.*

KOZO *(voice):* Let's go out to the public bath.

SHUKICHI *gets up and leaves.*

57. Upstairs. TOMI *puts the kimono away.* SHUKICHI *comes in and greets* KOZO.

KOZO: Let's go, and on the way back we can stop and get some ice cream.

TOMI: That would be nice.

KOZO: Let's go.

58. Downstairs. SHIGE *stands watching as* KIYO *clips the hair of a customer. The three come in.*

KOZO: We're just going off to the bath.

SHIGE: Those old wooden sandals of mine, Mama, you can use them.

TOMI: Really?

The three go out. SHIGE, *as though suddenly remembering something, picks up the telephone.*

SHIGE: Hello, is this the Yoneyama Company? May I speak to Mrs. Hirayama? Thank you . . . Noriko? It's me. Would you do something for me? Do you have any time tomorrow? You see, Mother and Father haven't been anywhere yet, and I wonder if you could take them out someplace tomorrow. I really ought to, but I'm just too busy here at the shop.

59. The Yoneyama Company. A small, crowded, untidy office; six or seven employees. NORIKO *is on the telephone.*

NORIKO: Will you wait just a moment?

She puts down the receiver and goes to her superior's desk.

Excuse me.

The man continues with his work.

MAN: What is it?
NORIKO: I know it's short notice, but could I have the day off tomorrow?
MAN: That would be all right.
NORIKO: Thank you.
MAN: How about the Asahi Aluminum?
NORIKO: I'll finish it today.

She bows and returns to the telephone.

I'll be at your place at nine tomorrow.

60. A sightseeing bus. SHUKICHI, TOMI, *and* NORIKO *are riding in it. The explanation of the girl* BUS GUIDE *is heard.*

GUIDE: Ladies and gentlemen, welcome to Tokyo. Let us trace the history of this great city of Tokyo.

61. Scenes of the Marunouchi district.
62. The palace seen from the bus window.

GUIDE: The Imperial Palace, formerly called Chiyoda Castle, was built originally by Lord Ota Dokan, some five hundred years ago. In its quiet setting with green pine trees and the moat—what a contrast to the bustle of Tokyo today.

63. The sightseeing bus going by. The Ginza.
64. A side street by a department store. The bus is stopped there.
65. The roof of the department store. The three look out over the city.

NORIKO: Koichi's house is . . . is this way.
SHUKICHI: Really?
TOMI: And Shige's?

NORIKO: Probably over there.

TOMI: And where is your house?

NORIKO: My place is *(looking in the opposite direction)* someplace over there, I think.

TOMI: I see.

NORIKO: It isn't very nice but I hope you'll drop in later.

GUIDE *(voice):* We'll all be leaving now.

66. The city seen from the roof of the department store.
67. Same day. View of NORIKO's *apartment house. It is an
old house, now lit by the evening sun.*
*68. A room on the second floor. A baby is sleeping under a
mosquito net. Next to it a young wife is folding up the
washing. The sound of knocking.*

WIFE: Who is it?

The door opens and NORIKO *comes in.*

WIFE: Oh, you're back early.

NORIKO: Is Miko-chan asleep?

WIFE: Finally. She just fell asleep.

NORIKO: Do you have any sake?

WIFE: Sake?

NORIKO *nods.*

NORIKO: My parents-in-law are visiting.

WIFE: I have a little.

*She gets up and brings a large sake bottle with some left in
it.*

WIFE: Will this be enough?

NORIKO: Yes. I'm sorry to have to ask you for the last of it.

69. Corridor. NORIKO *enters the room next door.*
70. NORIKO's *room.* SHUKICHI *and* TOMI *are looking at a
framed photograph of their second son, Shoji,* NORIKO's *dead
husband, who died in the war.* NORIKO *comes in.*

SHUKICHI: Where did he have this photo taken?

NORIKO: In Kamakura. A friend of his took it.

TOMI: When was it?

NORIKO: A year before he was drafted.

TOMI *(to* SHUKICHI*):* It is so like him.

SHUKICHI: With his head on one side like that.

TOMI: He always stood like that.

71. The hallway. NORIKO *comes out and again goes to the neighbor's room, knocks, and enters.*
72. Neighbor's room. The wife turns to her.

WIFE: What?
NORIKO *(smiles):* Do you have a serving bottle and a cup?
WIFE: Yes.

She goes to a shelf and brings back the cup and bottle and a small bowl.

Take these too. They're stewed green peppers. They're very good.

NORIKO *(receiving the cup, bottle, bowl):* Thank you very much.
WIFE: The sake things are clean.
NORIKO: I'm so sorry to keep bothering you.

73. NORIKO*'s room.* SHUKICHI *and* TOMI. NORIKO *comes back in.*

TOMI: Now don't go to all this trouble.
NORIKO: It's no trouble at all. *(She begins preparing the sake.)*
TOMI: Thank you so much for today.
NORIKO: You're very welcome. But I'm afraid you're tired.
SHUKICHI: Not at all. We saw so many places thanks to you.

NORIKO *brings a towel and wipes the table, then puts dishes and chopsticks into place.*

TOMI: I'm sorry you have to spend the whole day with us.
NORIKO: Not at all.
SHUKICHI: Was it really all right?
NORIKO: Certainly, Father. Please don't worry. When we are busy I even work on Sundays but it's quieter now, so I can take a day off.
SHUKICHI: Really? Well, then, it's all right.

NORIKO *gets up and brings the sake bottle. She gives the cup to* SHUKICHI, *fills it. He drains his cup and gives it to* TOMI.

NORIKO: I'm sorry I don't have anything much to give you.
SHUKICHI: It's very good.
NORIKO: Do you like to drink, Father?
TOMI: Indeed he does. In the old days he used to get very angry when we didn't have any sake in the house. Even when it was late he'd go out for it. *(*SHUKICHI *smiles*

ruefully.) Every time a boy was born I'd just pray he wouldn't become a drinker.

SHUKICHI: Did Shoji like to drink?

NORIKO: Yes, he did.

TOMI *(looking surprised):* Really?

NORIKO: He often brought his friends home here late, after the trains had stopped. After they'd been out drinking.

SHUKICHI: Really?

TOMI: Then you had as much trouble as I did.

NORIKO *(smiles):* Yes, but now I miss it.

TOMI: Poor Shoji. He lived so far from us. Maybe that's why I feel as if he's still alive somewhere. Father here often scolds me for my foolishness.

SHUKICHI: He died long ago. It's been eight years since . . .

NORIKO *(Nothing.)*

TOMI: I know, but . . .

SHUKICHI: He was such a stubborn boy. I'm afraid he gave you trouble.

NORIKO: Oh, no.

TOMI: Well, you've had your troubles too.

NORIKO *(Nothing.)*

The sound of knocking. NORIKO *opens the door. The delivery man stands there with bowls of food. She takes it and thanks him, then brings the food to the table.* TOMI *seats herself correctly in front of the table and takes the lid off her bowl.* NORIKO *puts a bowl in front of* SHUKICHI.

NORIKO: It's probably not very good, but please help yourself.

TOMI: Well, I'll just help myself then.

74. Same evening. The Urara Beauty Parlor. On a bench in the corner of the empty shop, KOICHI *and* SHIGE *are sitting. She is fanning herself.*

KOICHI: They're late.

SHIGE: They'll be back soon. How long do you think they'll stay in Tokyo?

KOICHI: Didn't they say anything?

SHIGE: Listen. Would you put up some money?

KOICHI: What for?

SHIGE: I'll put in some too. It'll take two thousand yen, maybe; no, three would be better.

KOICHI: What's all this about?

SHIGE: What do you think of sending them to the hot springs at Atami for a few days? You're busy, and I can't change my work schedule either. And we can't always ask Noriko. What do you think?

KOICHI: It might not be a bad idea.

SHIGE: I know a nice hotel—it has a good view and isn't expensive.

KOICHI: Sounds very good. Let's go ahead and do it.

SHIGE: I'm sure they'll like it.

KOICHI: Frankly I was worried. It costs money wherever you take them.

SHIGE: This is much less expensive. And there is the hot springs too.

She hears someone, calls out. KOZO *appears.*

KOZO: What are you talking about?

SHIGE: Koichi and I were just planning to send Mother and Father to Atami.

KOZO: Really?

KOICHI: It's a good idea.

KOZO: I've been worried about them myself, but too busy to do anything much about it.

SHIGE: Well, shall we?

KOZO: Let's. It's better that way.

KOICHI *(nodding):* Let's do it.

SHIGE *(nodding):* Even if they stay with us we just can't do anything for them.

KOZO: That's right. Atami's the place. *(Sits down. To* KOI-CHI.*)* They can enjoy the hot baths and they can rest. That's much better for an old couple than walking around Tokyo. Isn't that so? *(Looks at* SHIGE.*)*

SHIGE: Yes, that's right. *(Then, lowering her voice, as though whispering.)* My, but they're late, though.

KOICHI: Maybe they're still at Noriko's.

SHIGE: Probably.

She fans the mosquitoes away from her feet with her fan.
75. Atami. The mountains surrounding the city, the water-front wall.
76. An upstairs room in an inn near the sea. SHUKICHI *and* TOMI, *who have changed into hotel yukata, are drinking tea.*

TOMI: I didn't expect to be able to come to a hot springs.

SHUKICHI: We've cost them more money.

TOMI: Doesn't it feel nice here?

SHUKICHI: Let's get up early and go for a walk along the beach tomorrow.

TOMI: There must be many fine views. The maid here told me there were.

SHUKICHI: Really? *(He looks out of the window.)* The sea is so quiet.

77. *The quiet sea.*

78. *The same night. In the hall of the inn at the foot of the staircase. A large wall clock shows that it is 11:30. A maid comes in carrying a large plate of sushi. She goes upstairs.*

79. *The hallway upstairs. The maid takes the sushi into a room.*

80. *The room. Two rooms have been opened to make one. Two groups of guests have rolled back their bedding and are sitting playing mahjong. Including the women there are eleven or twelve people. It looks like a company outing. From the distance can be heard the song of a group of strolling singers, a Japanese pop love song.*

MAID: I've kept you waiting. *(She puts down the plate and goes out.)*

MAN A: Hey, here's the sushi—I'll take that tile!

MAN B: So *you* had them.

MAN C: Ouch! That hurts.

MAN D: No, no, it's good. *(Picks up a tile and throws it down.)* Damn it.

MAN C: Well, how's this one? *(Discards.)*

MAN B: *(Picks up one tile and discards another.)* Reach.

MAN A: Reach? You threw *that* away?

MAN B: I sure did.

MAN D: *(Discards.)* Goddamn it.

81. *Hallway. Sound of mahjong. The singers are getting closer. Two men who look as though they've been to a brothel go back into the room.*

82. *The room of the old couple.* SHUKICHI *and* TOMI *are lying on their pallets. The mahjong and the singing are loud. It appears they cannot sleep.*

TOMI: It's awfully lively.

SHUKICHI: Um . . .

TOMI: I wonder what time it is.

SHUKICHI: Um . . .

83. In the hallway. The noise is even louder.
84. In front of the inn. The singers are bawling out their song.
85. The room. SHUKICHI *has been patient, but now with an exclamation he sits up.* TOMI *also sits up and sighs as though disappointed. The singing is getting louder and louder.*
86. Atami. Morning. The mountains are very clear.
87. Upstairs hall. In a corner of the passage are last night's empty dishes and beer bottles. A servant humming a pop song sweeps the rooms.
88. On the breakwater. SHUKICHI *and* TOMI, *wearing yukata from the inn, are resting in the morning breeze.* TOMI *notices that* SHUKICHI *is pounding his neck with his fist.*

TOMI: What's the matter?
SHUKICHI: Um . . .
TOMI: It's because you didn't sleep last night.
SHUKICHI: No, but you did.
TOMI: I didn't sleep a wink.
SHUKICHI: You did. You snored.
TOMI: Really?
SHUKICHI: Anyway, this place seems to be meant for young people.
TOMI: That's true.

89. Upstairs, the inn. Two maids are sweeping out the room.

MAID A: Those newlyweds last night . . .
MAID B: You didn't think they were newlyweds, did you?
MAID A: She was smoking in bed this morning after he got up.
MAID B: He was sweet on her, though. He said: You belong to me—your eyes, ears, mouth, all of you is mine. He said that.
MAID A: Hmpf. Who's to know who belongs to who?

90. The sea wall.

TOMI: I wonder what Kyoko is doing at home now.
SHUKICHI: How about going on back home?
TOMI: You must be wanting to get back. *(Smiling.)*
SHUKICHI: No. You're the one who's homesick. *(Laughs.)*
    We've seen Tokyo. We've seen Atami. Let's go home.
TOMI: Yes. Shall we?
SHUKICHI: Umm.

They both get up, but she seems suddenly giddy and stumbles.

SHUKICHI: What's the matter?
TOMI: I felt a bit dizzy. I'm all right now, though.
SHUKICHI: It's because you didn't sleep well. That's why.

The two go in the direction of the inn.
91. Upstairs in the room. It has been cleaned, and tea and pickled plums are on the table.
92. The Urara Beauty Parlor. Same day, late afternoon. KIYO *is cleaning the machines.* SHIGE *is setting the hair of a woman who looks like a housewife. Another woman is under a dryer reading a magazine.*

SHIGE: Should we try the upsweep? I just know it would become you.
WOMAN: I wonder.
SHIGE: You have such a good neckline here at the back. We'd hold the hair down on the right and then accent the left with a wave.
WOMAN: Maybe next time.
OTHER WOMAN: Would you hand me another magazine?— and some matches too.
KIYO: Yes. *(Does so.)*
SHIGE: Going to work early today?
WOMAN: No, I'll go later.

The old couple appear.

KIYO: Welcome back.
SHUKICHI: Well, we're back.
SHIGE: Why have you come back so soon?
TOMI: We just got here.
SHIGE: You should have taken more time. What happened?

They go into the back room.

WOMAN: Who are they?
SHIGE: Oh, just someone we know. Friends from the country.
WOMAN: Oh.
SHIGE: Kiyo-chan. Here, you do the pin curls.

93. Upstairs. SHUKICHI *and* TOMI *are sitting.* SHIGE *comes up.*

SHIGE: Well, what happened? Why didn't you stay longer? How was Atami?

SHUKICHI: Very nice. We liked the baths.

TOMI: And we had a very nice view from the hotel window.

SHIGE: Of course. It's a really good modern hotel. Was it crowded?

SHUKICHI: A little bit crowded, I'd say.

SHIGE: How was the food?

TOMI: Very good. Sashimi and fish custard . . .

SHIGE: Of course. It's right on the sea.

TOMI: And they served big omelettes too.

SHIGE: Then why didn't you stay for a while longer? We wanted you to relax.

SHUKICHI: Well, we thought it was about time we went on home.

SHIGE: But it's too soon. You don't come up to Tokyo very often.

SHUKICHI: Still, we thought we'd better be going.

TOMI: Kyoko must be lonesome back home.

SHIGE: Mother. She isn't a baby anymore. And here I was planning to take you to the Kabuki.

SHUKICHI: We don't want to put you to any extra expense.

SHIGE: Never mind that—just take your time. However, tonight I do have this meeting here with the other beauticians.

TOMI: Are many coming?

SHIGE: Well, it's my turn to provide the place.

SHUKICHI: We came back at the wrong time.

SHIGE: That's why I wanted you to stay at Atami. I should have told you so.

KIYO *(looking in):* We've done the pin curls.

SHIGE: Oh? *(To her parents.)* Just a minute. *(Goes out.)*

SHUKICHI: What shall we do? *(As though downcast.)*

TOMI: I don't know.

SHUKICHI: We can't go back to Koichi's and trouble them any more.

TOMI: That's right. Shall we ask Noriko to put us up?

SHUKICHI: She can't have both of us. You go there alone.

TOMI: And what about you?

SHUKICHI: I'll go see the Hattoris. And I'll stay there if I can. Let's go out, anyway. We're really homeless now. *(Smiles.)*

TOMI *laughs, and they begin to take their towels from their luggage.*

94. A corner of Ueno Park. SHUKICHI *and* TOMI *are on a bench eating a bag of roasted beans.* SHUKICHI *looks at his watch.*

SHUKICHI: Noriko may be home by now.

TOMI: Really? It's still a bit early.

SHUKICHI: Umm.

TOMI: But if you want to visit the Hattoris, you'd better go now.

SHUKICHI: Yes, we'd better go now.

They stand up slowly and start walking, looking over the city from the bluff.

SHUKICHI: Look at how big Tokyo is.

TOMI: Yes, isn't it. If we got lost, we might never find each other again.

TOMI *suddenly remembers that she left her handbag behind; she returns quickly and gets it.*

SHUKICHI: Just look at you.

Again they walk side by side.

95. Evening. Outside the house of a professional scribe. The door is shut and the curtain is drawn.

96. Inside, room at the back. SHUKICHI *is talking fondly of old times with his old friend* HATTORI OSAMU, *68, and his wife,* YONE, *60.*

SHUKICHI: It's already been seventeen or eighteen years.

HATTORI: Really? And here you've been sending me a New Year's greeting card every year.

SHUKICHI: And so have you.

YONE: I suppose that Onomichi has changed a great deal.

SHUKICHI: Well, fortunately the city wasn't bombed during the war. Nishigosho, where you lived, is still just like it used to be.

YONE: Is that so? Well, it was a nice place. We used to like the view from the temple so much.

HATTORI: And after the cherry-blossom season the price of sea bream would always drop. All these years we've missed the taste of those delicious fish.

YONE: Yes. *(She suddenly seems to remember something, whispers to her husband; a single word of his reply, "later," is understood.)*

From upstairs a young man in a suit comes down, the lodger.

MAN: Tell my friends I'll be over there playing pinball, will you?

YONE *nods and goes into the kitchen.*

HATTORI: We rent the upstairs room to that man. He's really a playboy. Says he's a law student, but doesn't seem to know anything about it. Spends all his time at pinball or mahjong. I just feel sorry for his father back home.

YONE *calls something from the kitchen.*

HATTORI: Let's go out for a drink somewhere.

YONE *(coming in):* I just don't seem to have anything in the house.

SHUKICHI: Never mind. I came completely unexpected.

HATTORI: You remember our old police chief?

SHUKICHI: Numata?

HATTORI: Well, he lives nearby.

SHUKICHI: Is that so? What's he doing now?

HATTORI: He's retired and happy. His son is a big man at some printing plant.

SHUKICHI: Well, I'm glad to hear that.

HATTORI: Let's go see him.

SHUKICHI: By all means. That would be just fine.

97. *A column of neon signs somewhere around Ueno-Hirokoji.*

98. *Upstairs, a small restaurant, from where the neon signs can be seen.* SHUKICHI *and* HATTORI *and* NUMATA SAMPEI, *71, are sitting around a table, having a pleasant talk.*

NUMATA: Well, drink up.

SHUKICHI: No, I've had enough.

HATTORI: No. It's still early, and we don't get together like this every day.

SHUKICHI: I haven't drunk for a long time.

NUMATA: And you used to be such a drinker.

HATTORI: You remember when the Governor visited Onomi-chi?

NUMATA: You got drunk at the Takemuraya.

HATTORI: You too. And that young geisha who served . . .

NUMATA: Umeko?

HATTORI: You liked her, didn't you?

NUMATA: And the Governor happened to like her too. Remember?

HATTORI *(to* SHUKICHI*)*: And you liked her, too, didn't you?

SHUKICHI *(laughs ruefully):* Oh, the fool I've made of myself by drinking.

NUMATA: Not at all. Wine is good for the health. Come on now.

SHUKICHI *drinks.*

HATTORI: Well, you're lucky. Your children all settled.

SHUKICHI: I don't know about that.

HATTORI: I often wish at least one of my sons was alive. I often talk about it with my wife.

NUMATA: Both killed. That's hard. Both in the war. That's bad. And didn't you lose one?

SHUKICHI: Yes, my second son.

HATTORI: Well, I've had enough of war.

NUMATA: Losing your children is hard, but living with them isn't that easy either. It's a real dilemma. *(Drinks, offers the bottle to* HATTORI.*)*

HATTORI: Well, let's change the subject.

They all three sit for a moment in thought.

HATTORI: If I had an extra bedroom for you, we could drink till morning.

He gets up, goes into the corridor, claps his hands, calls for sake; he calls again and then goes downstairs.

NUMATA: I'm very glad you came.

SHUKICHI: I never dreamed I would see you here in Tokyo.

99. The blinking neon night sights.

100. The same night. A street on the outskirts of the district. It is late.

101. A late-night drinking place named the Okayo. NUMATA, HATTORI, *and* SHUKICHI *are all sitting at a bar, drunk, bottles and glasses around them. The proprietress,* OKAYO, *is middle-aged but still attractive.*

OKAYO: Here's a warm one. *(Puts a sake bottle in front of* NUMATA.*)*

NUMATA: Pour it for me, won't you?

OKAYO: You're so drunk today.

NUMATA: Just look, Hirayama. Doesn't she resemble someone you know?

OKAYO: Oh, you've started that again.

NUMATA: Who?

HATTORI: Yes she does. *(Holding his head, sleepily.)*

NUMATA: Who?

HATTORI: Why, that young geisha.

NUMATA: No, no. She was fatter. This one resembles my
wife.

SHUKICHI: Yes, you're absolutely right.

NUMATA: See—especially right here—

OKAYO: Why don't you go home? You've gotten drunk
again.

NUMATA: And both of them are bad-tempered too.

OKAYO: It's always this way. You're such a nuisance.

NUMATA: That's just what my wife says. Here, come pour me
a drink.

OKAYO *doesn't.* SHUKICHI *takes the bottle and tries to pour
for* HATTORI, *who has sunk down in his chair.*

HATTORI: No. I just can't.

NUMATA: Well, I think you are the luckiest of us all.

SHUKICHI: Why?

NUMATA: You've got sons and daughters to be proud of.

SHUKICHI: But you can be proud of yours too.

NUMATA: Not me. My son's no good. All he ever does is try
to please that wife of his. Never pays any attention to me.

SHUKICHI: But being a department head is a good position.

NUMATA: Department head, nothing. He's just an assistant
section chief. But I get to feeling so down that I lie about
it to people.

SHUKICHI: I'm sure it's not that bad.

NUMATA: No, he's a failure, a failure. My only son. And I
wasn't strong enough. I spoiled him. Now you. You
brought up your son proper. He has a degree.

SHUKICHI: Nowadays all doctors have to have degrees.

NUMATA: Maybe we expect too much of our children. But
they lack ambition, they lack real spirit. That is just what
I told my son. And then he said to me that there are too
many people in Tokyo and so it's hard to get ahead. What
do you think of that? Young people today just have no
backbone. Where is their spirit? *(SHUKICHI tries to protest.)* Well, I'm a disappointed man. But you—you

couldn't feel that way. You must be very satisfied.

SHUKICHI: Of course, I'm not, but—

NUMATA: You see? It's gotten so bad that even you can't be satisfied. Oh, I feel so sad. *(Rubs his eyes.)*

HATTORI: Oh, I just can't drink any more. *(Sinks back and closes his eyes again.)*

SHUKICHI: Well, when I came up to Tokyo, I was under the impression that my son was doing better than he is. Then I found he's only this little neighborhood doctor . . . so, I know how you feel. I'm just as dissatisfied as you are. But we can't expect too much from our children. Times have changed and we have to face it. That's what I think.

NUMATA: You do?

SHUKICHI: Yes.

NUMATA: There, you see? You too.

SHUKICHI: My son has really changed. But I can't help it. There really are too many people in Tokyo.

NUMATA: I wonder.

SHUKICHI: Well, maybe it's a good thing.

NUMATA: I suppose I should be happy. Nowadays some young men would kill their parents without a thought. Mine at least wouldn't do that. *(Laughs.)*

OKAYO: Look—it's twelve o'clock.

NUMATA: So what?

OKAYO: It's closing time.

NUMATA: You just get more and more like my wife. I like you a lot.

OKAYO *turns away, then sees* HATTORI, *sound asleep.*

OKAYO: And what are you going to do about him?

NUMATA: You leave it to me. Come on. Let's drink some more.

SHUKICHI: Wonderful, wonderful!

102. The same night. The hallway in NORIKO*'s apartment. A clock can be heard striking twelve.*

103. NORIKO*'s room. The bedding is spread out.* TOMI *is sitting up and* NORIKO *is massaging her shoulders.*

TOMI: There, thank you. That's quite enough.

NORIKO: Oh, not yet.

TOMI: Well, it's been a long day today. Back from Atami, then to Shige's house, then to Ueno Park . . .

NORIKO: You must be tired.

TOMI: No, not so much. And here I am making myself a nuisance to you. I'm very sorry.

NORIKO: Not at all. I really appreciate your coming. I am very happy you are here.

TOMI: I'm being a burden to just everyone. There now. That's really enough, thank you. You must go to sleep now.

NORIKO *finishes massaging her mother-in-law's shoulders, gets up, puts water and a cup by the pillow.*

TOMI: You have to get up and go to work tomorrow.

NORIKO: You need sleep too. We should both go to bed.

TOMI: Thank you. I think I will.

NORIKO *tucks* TOMI *into bed.*

TOMI: This is a real treat. To sleep in my own dead son's bed.

NORIKO *goes to shut the window.* TOMI *waits until she has returned.*

TOMI: Noriko. Forgive me if I'm rude, but it's been eight years now since Shoji's death, and yet you still have his picture up there like that. It, well, it makes me sad.

NORIKO: Why? *(Smiling.)*

TOMI: Because you're so young—

NORIKO: I'm not that young anymore.

TOMI: Yes, you are. And I feel we are somehow doing wrong by you. I've often talked with Father about this—anytime you have a chance, please get married again. If you don't, it would be just too hard on us.

NORIKO *smiles.*

TOMI: No, I mean it.

NORIKO: All right. If I have the chance.

TOMI: And you certainly will. Why wouldn't you?

NORIKO: Do you think so?

TOMI: You've had more trouble than happiness after marrying him. I know we should have done something for you.

NORIKO: Please. I'm quite happy as I am.

TOMI: But you should have had a better life.

NORIKO: But I'm happy. I like it this way.

TOMI: You may now, while you're still young. But as you get old you'll find it lonely.

NORIKO: Now I won't get to be that old, so don't worry.

TOMI *(near tears):* You're so nice.

NORIKO *(purposely lightly):* Good night, then.

She gets up and puts out the light, then lies down again. Tears rise to her eyes.

104. The Urara Beauty Parlor. The lights are out and the chairs are covered with white cloths.

105. The room at the back. SHIGE *and* KOZO *are asleep on their bedding. There is the sound of knocking, and then a man's voice calling out good evening. Both wake up. The sound of knocking, the voice calling their name.*

SHIGE: Who is it?

She gets up, pulls a robe around her, and goes out.

106. The shop. She turns on the light.

SHIGE: Who is it?

VOICE: This is Officer Takahashi. The policeman from the corner.

She unlocks and slides open the door. A policeman is there.

POLICEMAN: I've brought your friends. They're quite drunk.

SHUKICHI *appears, staggering.*

SHIGE: Papa! *(To the policeman.)* I'm so sorry about this.

NUMATA *also comes staggering in. The policeman says good night and salutes.* NUMATA *sees this and returns the salute. Both are close to being blind-drunk.*

SHIGE: Father. Who is this?

The two come in with their shoes on and throw themselves into the beauty-parlor chairs. SHIGE *returns from locking the door.*

SHIGE: Father. What is this all about? Father!

KOZO *comes out in his night robe.*

KOZO: What's happened?

SHIGE: He's not alone.

KOZO: Who is it?

SHIGE: Some stranger. Now, Father—what is this all about? Father! Answer me.

SHUKICHI *mumbles something, echoed by* NUMATA.

SHIGE: You've started up drinking again, haven't you? Just

started up, all over again. You, too. *(She shakes* NUMATA, *then sits down, dejected.)*

KOZO: What happened? Where did he drink so much?

SHIGE: How should I know? *(Then, in a loud whisper.)* He used to drink something awful. Used to come home dead drunk, upsetting Mama terribly. We all just hated it. But after Kyoko was born he stopped drinking. And now he's started all over again.

NUMATA *mumbles.*

KOZO: Well, what should we do? *(Wrinkles his brow.)*

SHIGE: I never dreamed he'd come back here tonight. *(Disgustedly.)* Even if he'd been alone.

She goes off into the other room.

107. The room at the back. SHIGE *comes in and sits down heavily on the bedding.* KOZO *comes in.*

KOZO: We can't leave them there all night.

SHIGE: It can't be helped, can it?

KOZO: Let's have Kiyo come downstairs and we'll put them up there.

SHIGE: You don't think they can make it, do you?

KOZO: Well, what will we do then?

SHIGE: Oh, what a mess. *(She gets up and gives him her blanket.)* You sleep upstairs. I'll put them in here.

KOZO *agrees, takes the blanket, folds it.* KOZO *goes.* SHIGE *continues folding up cushions to make pillows, pulling the sheets smooth. Dissatisfied, she talks to herself.*

SHIGE: Really, why didn't he tell me? It's so late and he's so drunk. I just hate drunkards. And dragging this stranger home.

108. In the shop. SHUKICHI *and* NUMATA *loll in the chairs, sound asleep, snoring loudly.*

109. Morning. NORIKO's *apartment house.*

110. The corridor outside NORIKO's *room. She returns with the washed breakfast dishes.*

111. In the room. TOMI *is preparing to go, putting on her tabi.* NORIKO *comes in.*

TOMI: Thank you so much. I had a good sleep.

NORIKO: That's good.

TOMI: But won't you be late for the office?

NORIKO: No, I have quite enough time.

She goes over to a shelf and brings something back.

NORIKO: I want you to take this. It isn't much.
TOMI: What is it?
NORIKO: It's nothing, just a little something for you to spend.
TOMI: Oh, no—
NORIKO: Please, Mother, do take it.
TOMI: But, you can't do this. No. It is I who should be giving
  you something.
NORIKO: Now, please, Mother. Just take it. *(She forces it into
  her hands.)*
TOMI *(protesting):* No, no.
NORIKO: Please.
TOMI: Must I? . . . Well, then. Thank you very, very much.
NORIKO: It is nothing. *(Laughs.)*
TOMI: You must need money yourself, and yet you do some-
  thing like this. I just don't know what to say, but *(takes
  her hand),* I do thank you, very much.
NORIKO *(lightly):* Well, we should be going.
TOMI *(wiping her eyes):* Yes.
NORIKO: And be sure to come here again, the next time
  you're in Tokyo.
TOMI: Thank you, but I'm afraid I won't be coming back.
  And you. I know you are busy, but do try to come to
  Onomichi.
NORIKO: I really want to. If only it were a bit nearer.
TOMI: You're right. It is far away.

She gets up to close the window. TOMI *also gets up, then
stops in front of Shoji's photo and looks closely at it.* NORIKO
notices that TOMI *has forgotten her toothbrush and tooth-
paste.*

NORIKO: Mother, are these yours?
TOMI: Oh, thank you. Really, I've gotten so forgetful.

She laughs and begins putting them into her bag.
*112. Night. Tokyo Station. The waiting room on the No. 10
platform. The passengers are lined up waiting. Among them
are* SHUKICHI *and* TOMI. KOICHI, SHIGE, *and* NORIKO *have
come to see them off.*

KOICHI: The train should be in Nagoya or Gifu early in the
  morning.

SHIGE: What time does it get to Onomichi?

KOICHI: One thirty-five in the afternoon tomorrow.

TOMI: Did you wire Kyoko?

KOICHI: Yes, I did. And Keizo will meet you in Osaka too.

NORIKO: I do hope that Mother will get some sleep on the train.

SHUKICHI: She always sleeps well anywhere.

TOMI: And even if I don't, I'll be home tomorrow afternoon.

SHIGE: Don't drink too much now, Father.

SHUKICHI: Last night was an exception. It was a reunion.

SHIGE: Is your headache all gone?

SHUKICHI: It's all right.

KOICHI: Yes, a person really shouldn't drink too much.

SHUKICHI: Well, you've been very good to us—all of you. We have really enjoyed our trip.

TOMI: And you were so nice to us, children. So, now that we have seen you, you needn't come down, you know, even if something should happen to either of us.

SHIGE: Don't talk like that. *(Laughing.)* This isn't a farewell.

TOMI: No, I mean it. We live too far away.

The voice of the loudspeaker is heard announcing the opening of the ticket gates. The passengers get up.

TOMI: It looks crowded.

KOICHI: Oh, you'll get seats all right.

The lines of passengers move forward. Clock above the gates. The voice of the announcer continues.

113. Osaka, cityscape, morning. Osaka Castle, the chimneys of the factory district.

114. Within the station precincts, from which the castle can be seen. KEIZO, 27, SHUKICHI's third son, hurries across the tracks.

115. An office in the railyard precinct. Four or five station officials are there. KEIZO enters and says good morning to them.

OFFICIAL: Good morning.

KEIZO: I'm very sorry about yesterday.

OFFICIAL: So your parents are here.

KEIZO: Yes, they weren't supposed to get off the train, actually, but Mother became ill.

OFFICIAL: What was the trouble?

KEIZO: She said she felt sick around here. *(Indicates.)*

OFFICIAL: Was it her heart?

KEIZO: Train-sickness, probably. She isn't used to long rides. It was a real bother. *(He sits at his desk and begins the day's work.)* Had to borrow blankets and send out for the doctor twice. What a mess.

OFFICIAL: How is she now?

KEIZO: She seemed to feel fine this morning.

OFFICIAL: How old is she?

KEIZO: Let me see. She's well over sixty. Maybe sixty-seven or sixty-eight, I guess.

OFFICIAL: Then she's quite old. You'll have to take care of her. "Be a good son while your parents are alive."

KEIZO: That's right. "None can serve his parents beyond the grave."

They both laugh.

116. KEIZO's *boardinghouse, cheaply built, in the outskirts of the city. Outside the window are many factory chimneys.* TOMI *is sitting up on her pallet and drinking powdered medicine.*

TOMI: I'll be able to leave tonight.

SHUKICHI: We could stay one more night here and then take a less-crowded train.

TOMI: But Kyoko must be worrying about us. Still, if we stay here we'll get to see more of Keizo. In just ten days we'll have seen all our children. And our grandchildren, too.

SHUKICHI. Some grandparents seem to like their grandchildren better than their own children. What about you?

TOMI: And you?

SHUKICHI: Well, I think I like my children better.

TOMI: Yes, that's true.

SHUKICHI: But I'm surprised at how children change. Shige, now—she used to be much nicer before. A married daughter is like a stranger.

TOMI: Koichi's changed too. He used to be such a nice boy.

SHUKICHI: No, children don't live up to their parents' expectations. *(They both smile.)* But, if you are greedy then there is no end to it. Let's think that they are better than most.

TOMI: They are certainly better than average. We are fortunate.

SHUKICHI: Yes, fortunate. We should consider ourselves lucky.

TOMI: Yes, we are very lucky.

117. Tokyo, morning. KOICHI's house. ISAMU is playing in the sand in the backyard.
118. The consulting room. FUMIKO is cleaning; KOICHI, reading a letter.

FUMIKO: Is she all right?
KOICHI: I think so. She sends thanks.
FUMIKO: She was tired, you know.
KOICHI: Yes, the trip was a bit long for her.
FUMIKO: Was she pleased with it, do you think?
KOICHI: Why wouldn't she be? She saw lots of places. Went to Atami too. She'll talk about Tokyo a long time.

He is about to go when the phone rings.
119. The hallway. KOICHI comes in and picks up the telephone.

KOICHI: Hello. It's me. A telegram? No, not yet.

120. The Urara Beauty Parlor. SHIGE is telephoning.

SHIGE: From Onomichi. It's so odd. Mama is critically ill, it says.

121. KOICHI's house, hallway.

KOICHI: That's strange. I just now got Father's letter. All it says is that they stopped off in Osaka because she didn't feel well. They got back home on the tenth.

FUMIKO has come to stand beside him and is listening with a worried expression. The front door is heard to open, and the voice of the telegraph messenger saying: "Mr. Hirayama— a telegram." FUMIKO goes out at once.

KOICHI: Just a minute.

122. The hallway. FUMIKO brings the family seal, stamps the receipt, and receives the telegram, thanking the man.
123. The hallway. FUMIKO brings the telegram.

FUMIKO: It's from Onomichi.
KOICHI: Read it.
FUMIKO: "Mother critically ill—Kyoko."
KOICHI: It came just now—the telegram.

124. The Beauty Parlor.

SHIGE: Really? All right. I'll come right over to your place.

125. KOICHI's house, the hallway.

KOICHI: We'll wait.

He hangs up.

FUMIKO: How did it happen? So suddenly! Is it serious?

KOICHI *starts to leave.*

FUMIKO: Shall I call Noriko?
KOICHI: Yes. Call her.

126. The company where NORIKO works. A young clerk takes the telephone call.

CLERK: Yes, this is the Yoneyama Trading Company. All right. Just a minute. It's for you, Mrs. Hirayama.
NORIKO: For me? Hello. Yes. Oh. I see. Yes . . . yes. Yes, I see.

She goes to her desk after having hung up and sits. Then she gets up and goes toward the emergency staircase.
127. The staircase. NORIKO stands on the landing deep in thought.
128. KOICHI's house, the consulting room. SHIGE is there with KOICHI.

SHIGE: But what can it all mean? If Father got sick I'd understand, but it's Mother. And she was so lively when she was here. Is she very bad?
KOICHI: I guess so. It says critically ill.
SHIGE: I suppose we'll have to go . . . You know, I felt something strange at the station. She said, "If anything should happen . . ." She must have had a feeling, somehow or other.
KOICHI: We'll have to go, in any event.
SHIGE: Yes, since she's critically ill. Well, since we have to go we'd better hurry. What about taking the same train?
KOICHI: We could, but I've got all sorts of things to do before I leave.
SHIGE: Me, too. This comes at such a busy time.

Patients come in—an old woman and a child with a bandage around its head.

KOICHI: Right over here, please.

SHIGE *goes into an inner room and* FUMIKO *comes out.* KOI-
CHI *tells her to take off the bandage. While she is doing so
he goes after* SHIGE.
129. Inner room.

KOICHI: Let's leave tonight.
SHIGE: Very well, so long as we have to. I'll see you later.

He is about to leave when she calls him back.

SHIGE: What about mourning clothes?
KOICHI: We might need them.
SHIGE: Yes. Well, let's take them and hope we don't have
to use them.
KOICHI: Yes, that's right.
SHIGE: I'll see you at the station, then.

130. Onomichi. The HIRAYAMA *alley.*
*131. The veranda of the house. On the drying pole are ice
bags, etc.*
132. The living room by TOMI*'s pallet,* SHUKICHI *and* KYOKO
are watching her. The clock strikes one. KYOKO *looks up.*

KYOKO: I'll be going to meet them.
SHUKICHI: That's very good of you.

133. KYOKO*'s room. She comes in, takes off her apron.*
134. The entryway. KYOKO *quietly leaves.*
135. The alley. KYOKO *is walking away from the house.*
136. The living room. SHUKICHI *watches* TOMI*'s sleeping
face. A light sigh escapes.* TOMI *moves slightly.*

SHUKICHI: What's the matter? Is it too hot?

TOMI *sleeps on.*

SHUKICHI: The children are coming to see you . . . Kyoko's
gone to meet them. They'll be here any minute . . . You'll
get well.

*She sleeps. He begins to fan her and continues to reassure
her. But with these words he is really reassuring himself.*
137. Flowers, shrubs, moving in the light breeze of July.
138. Evening, the kitchen. Under the dim electric light
KYOKO *is breaking ice.*
139. The living room. The DOCTOR *is there.* KOICHI *is also
examining* TOMI, *still in a coma.* SHUKICHI, SHIGE, *and*
NORIKO *look on, worried.*

DOCTOR: Well, I've bled her, but the blood pressure just doesn't seem to go down—and I can't get her out of this coma.

KOICHI: Really.

He examines her pupils using a flashlight.

KOICHI: The reaction is very weak, isn't it?

The DOCTOR *agrees. The examination now over,* KOICHI *thanks the* DOCTOR, *who says that he will come back later.* NORIKO *sees him out.* KYOKO *changes* TOMI*'s ice bag. Far away the whistle of a train.* SHIGE *whispers something to* KOICHI, *then turns to* KYOKO.

SHIGE: Where's Keizo? Has he answered the telegram?

KYOKO: Not yet.

SHIGE: But he lives closest of all.

NORIKO *comes in.* KOICHI *gets up and calls his father, indicates that* SHIGE *too should come with him.*

140. The next room. KOICHI, SHUKICHI, SHIGE.

KOICHI: Father, I don't like her condition at all.

SHUKICHI: What do you mean?

KOICHI: I mean it's dangerous. It is very serious when she sleeps for so long.

SHUKICHI: Did the trip to Tokyo cause this?

SHIGE: Oh, I don't think so at all. She was so lively in Tokyo. Wasn't she? *(She looks at* KOICHI.*)*

KOICHI: It might have been one of the causes.

SHUKICHI: What is it, then?

KOICHI: Just that we'll be lucky if she lives until tomorrow.

SHIGE: Until tomorrow?

KOICHI: It will probably happen around daybreak, I think.

SHUKICHI: So . . . *(Tonelessly.)* She's not going to live, then.

SHIGE*'s eyes suddenly fill with tears.*

KOICHI: Mother is around sixty-eight, isn't she?

SHUKICHI: So . . . she's not going to live.

KOICHI: I'm afraid that's right.

SHUKICHI: So . . . This is the end, then.

KOICHI *gets up and goes back into the living room.*

141. The living room. NORIKO *and* KYOKO *are looking anxiously at* KOICHI. *He sits silently by* TOMI*'s bed.*

142. The next room. SHUKICHI *and* SHIGE: *he sighs;* SHIGE *is sad.*

SHUKICHI: Then Keizo won't be in time, will he?

He gets up silently and goes to the other room.
143. The living room. SHUKICHI *comes in quietly and sits by* TOMI. *With pain in his face he looks down at her, blinking his eyes.*
144. Daybreak—the night at Onomichi has ended. The sky slowly brightens—it is near the time the sun will appear. The platform at the station, no one there; the streets, no one there. The sea wall, quiet waves washing on the stones.
145. The Hirayama house. SHIGE, KOICHI, KYOKO, NORIKO, *all sit sadly. Now and then, as though just remembering her sorrow,* KYOKO *wipes away her tears. There is now a white cloth over* TOMI'S *face.*

SHIGE: Isn't life short, though . . . *(She speaks sadly, and there is no answer.)* And she was so lively too. You know, she must have had a feeling that this would happen soon.

KYOKO *and* NORIKO *wipe away their tears;* KOICHI *grunts in assent. Then, as though remembering,* SHIGE *again speaks:*

Still, I'm glad she came to Tokyo. We were able to see her again. *(Turning to* NORIKO.*)* Did you bring any mourning clothes?
NORIKO: No, I didn't.
SHIGE: And do you have any, Kyoko?
KYOKO: No.
SHIGE: Then you'll have to borrow some. Get some for Noriko too.

Neither replies. The sound of a door sliding open.

SHIGE: Oh, that must be Keizo.

KYOKO *gets up and goes out.*
146. The entryway. KEIZO *is taking off his shoes.* KYOKO *enters.*

KEIZO: How is she?

KYOKO *cannot speak. She lowers her face.*

KEIZO: I see. I wasn't in time.

He sits down and listlessly finishes removing his shoes.
147. The room. KEIZO *comes in; all greet him.*

KEIZO: I was out of town on official business. *(To* KOICHI.*)*
   Had to go to Matsuzaka. I'm sorry I'm late. *(To* SHIGE.*)*
   The telegram came when I was away.
SHIGE: Oh.
KEIZO: This is a terrible thing. When was it?
SHIGE: This morning at three-fifteen.
KEIZO: If I'd taken the eight-forty to Kagoshima I'd have
   been in time.
KOICHI: Just look at her, Keizo. See how peaceful she is.

KEIZO *gets up, goes to the bed, takes off the cloth, and stares
down at the dead face. Tears well up. They all watch him,
wiping their eyes.*

KOICHI: Where's Father?
SHIGE: Where, I wonder.

NORIKO *gets up, looks into the garden, and goes to the entryway.*
148. In front of the house. NORIKO *comes out, looking.*
*149. An empty lot near a bluff overlooking the road and the
sea beyond.* SHUKICHI *stands there all by himself.* NORIKO
comes.

NORIKO: Keizo has just come, Father.
SHUKICHI: Has he? *(Then, with deep emotion.)* It was such
   a beautiful dawn.

NORIKO *looks down.* SHUKICHI *quietly turns back.*

SHUKICHI: I'm afraid we're going to have another hot day
   today.

She follows him, her head down.
*150. A temple compound under the hot light of the sun. No
one is there. The sound of a wooden temple drum being
struck.*
151. The main hall of the temple. TOMI's *funeral.* SHUKICHI,
KOICHI, SHIGE, NORIKO, KYOKO, KEIZO—*all facing the other
people who have come. Among them are the woman from
next door and a primary-school pupil representing* KYOKO's
*class. The reading of the sutra; the sound of the temple drum.
Then, for whatever reason,* KEIZO *gets up and goes out.* SHIGE
and NORIKO *look at him.*

152. A temple building. KEIZO *comes and stands there, then squats down and stares ahead of him.*
153. The cemetery, beyond it the sea. NORIKO *comes.*

NORIKO: What's the matter?
KEIZO: I can't stand that sound.
NORIKO: What do you mean?
KEIZO: With each beat it seems as though Mother is getting smaller and smaller.

He wipes his eyes. NORIKO *says nothing.*

KEIZO: I wasn't a very good son.
NORIKO: It's time for us to offer incense, now.
KEIZO: I can't lose her now. No one can serve his parents beyond the grave.

He gets up, starts back. NORIKO *wipes her eyes.*
155. The graveyard. In the distance the glittering sea. The voice of the priest reading the sutras.
156. The sea wall, waves washing over the stones.
157. Upstairs, an old-style restaurant on the sea road. SHUKI-CHI, KOICHI, SHIGE, NORIKO, KEIZO, KYOKO—*the six of them on their way back from the funeral, sitting around a table.* KOICHI *is pouring sake for* SHUKICHI.

KOICHI: It was here that we came to see fireworks, wasn't it?
SHUKICHI: Oh, was it?
SHIGE: Yes, it was the night of the Sumiyoshi Festival. Remember, Keizo?
KEIZO: No.
SHIGE: You were all excited and then fell asleep just after the sun went down. You lay there with your head in Mama's lap.
KEIZO: I don't remember it at all.
KOICHI *(to his father):* What were you doing in those days?
SHUKICHI: I was head of the Board of Education, I think.
KOICHI: It was a long time ago, wasn't it?
SHIGE: And once we went to Omishima during the spring holidays.
KEIZO: I remember that. And Mama got seasick.
SHUKICHI: Yes.
KOICHI: She was so full of life then. How old was she then?
    (To SHUKICHI.*)* Forty—
SHUKICHI: Two or three, I think.

SHIGE: You must take care of yourself, Father, and live for a long, long time.

SHUKICHI: Thank you.

He gets up and goes out. All the rest are silent for a while.

SHIGE: I may seem a bit heartless to say so, but I do rather wish he had died first. Look, if Kyoko marries, then he'll be left all alone.

KOICHI: Yes.

SHIGE: We could have looked after Mother in Tokyo. Kyoko, did Mother still have her gray summer sash?

KYOKO: Yes.

SHIGE: You know, I'd like it for a keepsake. All right?

KOICHI: I suppose so.

SHIGE: And that linen kimono she used to wear in the summer. Did she still have that too?

KYOKO: Yes.

SHIGE: Well, I want that too. You know where it is?

SHUKICHI *comes back and sits down.*

SHUKICHI: Well, thanks to all of you, we have gotten through this now. You have all been very kind to come and give your time so that we could mourn her. Thank you.

He bows. They all return his bow, formally.

SHUKICHI: And she would have been pleased to have been looked after so well by Koichi when she was sick.

KOICHI: I didn't do anything.

SHUKICHI: I remember when we went to Atami that she felt dizzy once.

KOICHI: It may have been a slight stroke.

SHIGE: Why didn't you tell us? Or, at least, Koichi.

SHUKICHI: I suppose I ought to have.

KOICHI: But that wasn't it. She was fat, you know. The stroke came suddenly.

SHIGE: It's just like a dream. *(Then, changing her tone, to* KOICHI.*)* When are you leaving?

KOICHI: Well, I can't stay too long.

SHIGE: I can't either. How about tonight's express?

KOICHI: What about you, Keizo?

KEIZO: I can stay.

KOICHI: Really? Then we'll leave tonight.

SHIGE: Yes. You'll stay with Father a bit longer, won't you, Noriko?

NORIKO: All right.

SHUKICHI *(to* NORIKO*):* If you're busy, you go with them.

KEIZO: Well, I guess I might as well go. I've still got to make out a report. And there's that baseball game too.

SHUKICHI: Really. Well, if you are all busy, you must go.

SHIGE: But now you'll be lonely.

SHUKICHI: I'll get used to it.

SHIGE: Kyoko, give me some more rice, will you? *(*KYOKO *silently fills her bowl.)* Keizo, you get us the train tickets, would you?

KEIZO: I'll have some more rice, too.

SHIGE: If only we can get seats.

The reflection of the sea shimmers on the walls and ceiling.

158. The seashore, waves washing on the stones.

159. The alley leading to the Hirayama house.

160. A patch of ground in the garden. SHUKICHI *is looking after the vegetables.*

161. The kitchen. NORIKO *is making a box lunch.*

162. A room. KYOKO *is getting ready to go to school.* NORIKO *comes in.*

NORIKO: Here's your lunch.

KYOKO: Thank you so much for everything.

NORIKO: I've only been a bother to you. You must come up to Tokyo now on your vacation.

KYOKO: Must you really go back today?

NORIKO *(arranging her dress):* Yes, I'm afraid I have to.

KYOKO: I'm sorry I can't see you off at the station.

NORIKO: That's all right. Now be sure and come to Tokyo.

KYOKO: I'm so glad you stayed. I think they might have stayed a little longer, too.

NORIKO: But they're busy.

KYOKO: They're selfish. Demanding things, then leaving right away.

NORIKO: But they have their own affairs.

KYOKO: But you had yours, too.

NORIKO: But, Kyoko—

KYOKO: They are selfish. Wanting her clothes right after her death. I felt so sorry for poor Mother. Even strangers

would have been more considerate. That's no way to treat
your parents.

NORIKO: But, look, Kyoko. At your age I thought as you do.
But children do drift away from their parents. A woman
has her own life, apart from her parents, when she is
Shige's age. She meant no harm, I'm sure. It's only that
everyone has to look after himself.

KYOKO: I wonder. Well, I won't ever be like that. That
would be just too cruel.

NORIKO: It is. But children get that way . . . gradually.

KYOKO: Then—you too . . .

NORIKO: I may become like that. In spite of myself.

KYOKO: Isn't life disappointing?

NORIKO: Yes, it is.

KYOKO *(smiling now):* You take care of yourself.

NORIKO: Thank you. Good-by.

KYOKO *goes to the veranda and looks toward the garden, then
calls out.*

KYOKO: I'm going now, Father.

Then she goes to the entryway. NORIKO *comes with her.*
163. The entryway.

KYOKO: Take care of yourself.

NORIKO: And remember to come to Tokyo on your vacation.

KYOKO: Good-by.

They smile and part.
164. The room. NORIKO *comes back in and tidies up.* SHUKI-
CHI *comes in, wiping his hands.*

SHUKICHI: Has she gone?

NORIKO: Father, I have to leave by the afternoon train today.

SHUKICHI: Do you? Well, I want to thank you for everything.

NORIKO: Please, I didn't do anything.

SHUKICHI: No, you have been a great help. *(Sits down.)* And
Mother told me how kind you were to her the night that
she stayed with you.

NORIKO: I couldn't do anything at all.

SHUKICHI: She meant it. She said that that was the happiest
night she had in Tokyo. I want to thank you too.

NORIKO: Oh, no—

SHUKICHI: But she was worried about you. She wondered

what would happen to you. *(NORIKO does not answer.)*
You can't go on like this, you know. I don't want you to
worry about me. I would like to see you married again as
soon as possible. And you must forget about Shoji. He's
dead. To see you going on like this hurts me. *(NORIKO
bows her head.)* I mean it . . . and she said she'd never
seen a nicer woman than you.

NORIKO: She overestimated me.

SHUKICHI: You're wrong, Noriko.

NORIKO: She did. I'm not the nice woman she thought I was.
If you see me like that—it embarrasses me.

SHUKICHI: No, it shouldn't.

NORIKO: No, really. I'm quite selfish. Whatever you may
imagine, I'm not always thinking of your son.

SHUKICHI: I'd be happy if you'd forget him.

NORIKO: There are days when I don't think of him at all
. . . Then sometimes I feel that I just cannot go on like
this. Sometimes at night I lie and wonder what will become of me if I stay this way. The days pass and nothing
happens. I feel a kind of impatience. My heart seems to
be waiting—for something. Oh, yes, I'm selfish.

SHUKICHI: You are not.

NORIKO: Yes, I am. But I couldn't tell Mother this.

SHUKICHI: That's all right. You are a truly good woman. An
honest woman.

NORIKO: Not at all.

SHUKICHI *gets up and from a drawer brings a woman's watch.*

SHUKICHI: This watch belonged to her. It's old-fashioned
now but she began to wear it when she was your age.
Please take this to remember her by.

NORIKO: But, I—

SHUKICHI: Please accept it. *(He gives it to her.)* She'll be
happy to know that you'll be wearing it. Take it for her
sake.

NORIKO: Thank you.

SHUKICHI: Please believe me. I want you to be happy. I really,
very sincerely, mean that. *(NORIKO covers her face.)* It's
strange. We have children of our own, but it has been you
who have done the most for us, and you are not even a
blood relative.

He lowers his head; NORIKO *weeps.*

165. The primary school. A children's chorus is heard.
166. A hill overlooking the sea. The sketching class is out,
children here and there. KYOKO *is moving from one group to*
another. Suddenly she looks at her watch and goes to the edge
of the hill.
167. The railroad below, the Tokyo train is coming.
168. The train.
170. Inside the train. NORIKO *is looking out of the window.*
171. The mountains of Onomichi as seen from the window.
172. Inside the train. NORIKO *looks at the watch. Holds it to*
her ear. The sound of a train whistle.
173. The Hirayama house. SHUKICHI *sits by the veranda and*
looks at the sea. Today again the WOMAN NEXT DOOR *speaks*
to him through the window.

WOMAN: Everyone's gone now? You'll be lonely, then.
SHUKICHI: Well.
WOMAN: It was really so sudden.
SHUKICHI: Oh, she was a headstrong woman . . . but if I knew
   things would come to this, I'd have been kinder to her.
   (The WOMAN *says nothing.)* Living alone like this, the
   days will get very long.
WOMAN: You will be lonely.

She leaves. By himself, SHUKICHI *looks out over the sea. A*
long silence.
174. The sea. A small island boat goes by.
175. SHUKICHI *by the veranda, looking vaguely out over the*
sea.
176. The ocean. The sound of the boat becomes as distant
as a dream. It is a July afternoon in the Inland Sea.

TRANSLATED BY DONALD RICHIE AND ERIC KLESTADT

■TAKEDA TAIJUN

Born in Tokyo in 1912, the son of a Buddhist priest, Takeda Taijun was trained to succeed his father as head of the prosperous family temple. In 1931 he entered the Chinese Literature Department of Tokyo Imperial University, but was soon arrested for distributing "anti-imperialist" leaflets; after spending a month in jail he withdrew from overt political involvement and also from the university. However, he continued his studies of Chinese history and literature, served as an army private in central China from 1937 to 1939, and began translating Chinese novels as well as writing essays and stories of his own.

His first important work was a passionate, subjective biography of the tragic Grand Historiographer of the Han Dynasty: Ssu-ma Ch'ien (*Shibasen*, 1943). In 1944 Takeda went to China again, this time to a post in the Sino-Japanese Cultural Association in Shanghai. Returning to Japan after the War, he established his reputation as a writer of fiction with *This Outcast Generation* (*Mamushi no sue*, 1947, tr. 1967), a somber short novel set in postwar Shanghai. Until his death in 1976 he was one of the most prolific of contemporary Japanese writers. He was perhaps the only one more profoundly influenced by China and its literature than by anything Western.

Unlike the Chinoiserie of Akutagawa, Tanizaki, and many others, the "China fiction" of Takeda Taijun reflects both his love of traditional Chinese narrative and his own deepest life experience. His works are by no means limited to exotic themes and settings, nor does this influence lure him into superficiality. Even "To Build a Bridge," one of Takeda's subtle evocations of the disarming simplicity of an old Chinese tale, has much in common with such a thoroughly Japanese story as "The Misshapen Ones" (*Igyō no mono*, 1950, tr. 1957), his powerful if somewhat rambling autobiographical account of the uncertain novitiate of a sex-obsessed young priest.

❖ To Build a Bridge
(*Hashi o kizuku,* 1951)

Though I no longer take my place before the Buddha and intone a sutra, I still wince when I hear the word "preacher." For I was born the son of a priest and reared in a temple. Even when it is not used in derision, the word somehow repels me. I choke, as if someone had suddenly brought a dank, moldy washcloth to my face. The heavy darkness of life in a temple and the strains and contradictions that set temple life apart have since my childhood held a certain horror for me.

I have escaped, or perhaps been expelled. In my small way, I am allowed to breathe what others have not used of profaned everyday air. I have a fair number of friends who are priests, however, and the fact that their ways of thinking are not those of the world is as clear to me as the light of day. Their pains, of a sort that few people would guess, come to me as if they were my own. Religious faith is the most spiritual of forces. Attaching themselves to this most spiritual of forces, they use it to balance their ledgers. They sell faith in return for offerings. There is an unavoidable awkwardness, a seaminess, in the transaction. The purer the priest and the deeper his faith, the more intolerable the shame of noting the distance between his life and the teachings of the Buddha Gautama.

Gautama was a prince who abandoned his court and chose the sage's way. He left his house and his family. It is the reverse with the priest of today: he must enter the house called temple. A temple is a place for public worship, a sacred hall for meditation; and at the same time it has a way of becoming the place where the priest takes a wife and begets children. Being of the intellectual classes —graduates of seminaries at the very least, and sometimes even doctors of letters —priests are most earnest in their efforts to clean their houses and cut away the lusts of the world. Alas, they are members of the human herd. It is not easy for them to become sticks and stones. Think of Gide's *Pastoral Symphony.* That minister was a stern man of conscience if there ever was one; and even he had to awaken to the fact that his holy love for the blind girl was not free of animal desire.

When I was a student, I once heard a lecture by a leader of the Buddhist reform movement. Hibiya Hall was packed to the top balconies. Daughters and wives of good families were there in all their finery. The speaker recounted memories of his youth. He was a fine gentleman in his dark suit, his hair a glowing black. In the bright lights and the smell of warm bodies, the strong-jawed face

—he was perhaps forty—glowed ever redder and brimmed with energy and vitality. He had the grand, senatorial manner.

"In this temple, someone is roasting fish for lunch. Unexpectedly, a member of the congregation comes to arrange for services. The priest is flustered, and tells his wife that the place must not smell of fish. He opens all the windows and fans at the smoke." The man aimed his darts expertly at the more ridiculous features of temple life. His smooth voice quite won the audience. There was a burst of laughter. The fair, double-chinned lady beside me nodded approvingly. But I could neither laugh nor nod. I was frowning darkly.

I had only the day before had to hear a friend recount his exploits in Tamanoi. Tamanoi is a dreary pleasure quarter; in its tangled back alleys painted ladies call insistently from little windows to potential customers.

" 'Hello, there, Baldy. Would you like to come play in my house?' That's what they said." He smiled wickedly, like a confirmed sinner. The women had noticed his shaven head and promptly named him Baldy. I was caught between my friend's twisted smile and the confident smile here on the stage. Somehow I could not follow the smile that beckoned to a brilliant future. I persisted in wanting to give myself up to the other, the twisted smile of the lust-ridden young priest. My sympathies were with Baldy, we had something in common. The surreptitiously roasted fish told of a desire. It was not to be dismissed, and what then of sexual desire? Even after I had left Hibiya Hall, it was there clinging to my skin and racing through my veins, as if sneering at me. Still less was sexual desire to be shrugged off. It would never let me go.

People have been harsh in their criticism of lustful priestly doings. The sheer number of evil priests, philandering priests, renegade priests on the Kabuki stage is evidence enough. In Japan, the light novelists of the Tokugawa Period, in China, the raconteurs of late Ming and early Ch'ing. In both countries, erotic novels, their tone violently satirical. Because plebeian writers could not strike directly at warriors and Confucians, they launched a flanking attack with amusing accounts of salacious priests.

"The Legend of the Priest's Bridge" survives in the Chinese countryside. It is told of the Bridge of the Pious Son, built during the Ch'ien Lung era.

The Pious Son early lost his father. He lived with his mother, who was having a secret affair with a priest. She was not a bad woman. Until the unfortunate affair, she had chastely served her dead husband, day and night she had thought of her children. As the wife and widow of a well-placed landowner, she wanted for nothing. She managed swarms of workers with the utmost skill; the household was sound and proper, and had the respect of the village.

Among the mud-walled, dirt-floored farmhouses that hugged the earth and seemed about to sink away into the endless fields of barley, a single mansion with brown brick walls, a black tiled roof, a stone watchtower with rope ladders hanging from it, and room after richly hung room. The lady of the mansion naturally attracted attention. Had she been the widow of a poor farmer, matters could have been arranged simply: she might have eloped, or adopted an attractive man into the family, or perhaps made herself a match in another village. Today, two centuries later, a widow in her thirties has considerable freedom to follow the promptings of her body—neither the world nor her own conscience is likely to condemn her. But, say the Confucians, "a woman does not have two husbands." She had been sternly trained by the family elders, and she had willingly made her own vows. She had been a woman of strict and unbending principle.

"I had hoped not to have to mention it." One day when the young willow shoots along the courtyard wall were swaying in the spring breeze, the Pious Son at length found it necessary to speak to his revered mother. His manner was hesitant, and his pale face was turned to the ground. "It is improper for a son to make unsolicited comments about his mother's behavior; and particularly when the matter is somewhat ugly, each word is like a festering sore. Respect for my mother and for my father's memory, however, compels me to speak."

His voice was choked. He was not a youth so forward as to mention the priest's name openly and make the frown on his mother's beautiful forehead yet darker.

The mother too was silent. Tears were streaming over her face. Shamed to the marrow, she had no answer. She vowed that she would not see the man again. The Pious Son was much relieved.

Yet the priest continued to read his sutras. When he came, the mother was lively and happy. Her face would soften, her eyes would shine. It was evident that she was unable to break with the man. The Pious Son was troubled less by anger at the clandestine doings of the priest than by forebodings about his mother. If the elders and the villagers were to make trouble, his mother would have no recourse but suicide. It would be the extreme of impiety to stand by when one's mother faced suicide. His responsibilities to the house as eldest son gave him the courage to rebuke his mother when the occasion demanded. If, however, his mother in her shame were to throw herself into the well, he would be virtually a matricide. Should he then rebuke the priest, and turn him out? But would not a man formidable enough to have made a conquest of so intelligent a woman spread scandal through all the villages and thus hasten her destruction?

Summoning his courage, the Pious Son spoke again: "It is impertinent of me, I know, but I think we would do well not to have that priest in the house. His visits can only bring ruin to my mother and our family."

"Do as you think best," said the unhappy mother, collapsing in tears.

The Pious Son forbade the visits. His father's dying injunctions and the warnings of soothsayers served as his pretext. His brother, who was very young and did not know the facts, protested.

"It would appear that my brother's feelings of piety have weakened, since he no longer has memorial services read for our father."

Gently, the Pious Son remonstrated with him.

But the mother, torn from the priest, fell into the deepest despondency. She was unable to sit still, she was unable to eat. She was like a dying person, a person utterly without spirit. One need not draw hasty conclusions about the priest's virtuosity in the bedchamber. There are reasons for supposing rather that the poor woman had already reached the breaking point. She was a lonely, foolish woman, overwhelmed by such feelings of utter isolation that the universe seemed to freeze around her.

Nonetheless, "the priest knew how to ingratiate himself." Our legend makes the point quite clear. "Ingratiate." I see the word before me, and I suddenly feel clammy and wonder if anyone is watching. I tell myself that I have fled the priesthood, but somehow, in subtly changed form, the ingratiating ways have crept back and are still with me. The diffident laugh and the ready bow are not the only ways of ingratiating oneself. There are more dexterous, more elegant and complicated ways.

As self-important men went in those feudal days, the priest was gentle with women, one may imagine. He brought cool water when she was thirsty and warm water to bathe her feet, and a lacquered chamberpot when necessary. Carefully, attentively, he helped her out of her undergarments or into her shoes. Late at night he eased her weariness, perhaps, with a sweet song. If he had had the boldness of a protestant like Shinran, he might have taken her for his wife, and roared out tidings of salvation for the unregenerate sinners of the world. And he could have put his ways of managing women to use in a new, moderately priced Buddhism. Did not Mohammed in the desert grow in power and influence when he took a widow for his wife?

The miserable woman grew weaker day by day. She no longer left her bed. Only the evil priest had power to save her. Deeply perplexed, the Pious Son debated the problem.

"In keeping the priest away, I have protected the honor of my ancestors; and by way of payment, I have brought my mother to the point of death. The priest is a rare medicine, one must admit it. A strong medicine, perhaps; but can a son be forgiven when he deprives a failing parent of the one effective medicine?" Coolly, coolly, he pressed to his conclusion. "There is something ugly about relations between my mother and the priest. But will I necessarily be ugly myself if, for the sake of filial piety, I bring them together? The venerable Confucius taught that it was a violation of filial piety for a son to turn his father over to the authorities as a sheep thief. What of my mother, then, who after all has not stolen a priest? She has had a priest forced upon her. To save her, there should be no objection to my using the most foul-smelling of medicines. And if I decide to do so, I must follow through to her full recovery. I must have her take dose after dose, until the effectiveness of the medicine is fully apparent. I must bring it to her parched mouth in a form easy for her to drink."

He summoned the priest, and showed him to her bedside. Son guiding lover to mother. Shameful, but he bore the shame like a man. His eyes shot with blood, his teeth gnashing, he stole out scarcely breathing, lest the servants hear, and let the man in at night and saw him out in the morning. Medicine, medicine. The philanderer was tonic and pill and ointment, a knife for surgery, a bandage for staying blood. "I am deeply impressed at your piety," said the ointment blandly, bowing twice and pushing open the bedroom door. How often, standing at his back, was the faithful elder son seized by an impulse to rip out the heart of this most effective medicine!

In spite of all precautions, the younger brother at length learned the secret. His face flamed like a winter sunset. "The foolishness of my brother!"

"My brother is being hasty."

"And if I were not? There! Do I not hear filthy laughter, the rustling of a priest's robes, the clicking of rosary beads? It is piety, is it, to pander to a rutting animal?"

"What my brother hears is the clicking of pills poured from a bag."

"Enough, enough. My brother is wholly shameless."

The brothers were clean in their anger and in their sorrow. But to the end the younger was unable to accept the cure his brother had chosen. True, he obeyed the latter's command as head of the family and promised to do nothing provocative; but from that day on, the poor youth seemed weary of the world. Was filial piety a matter of such twists? If his brother was following the teachings of the venerable Confucius, then was not Confucius in effect a pimp? The boy grew thin, and only the fire in his eyes was stronger, a sign of inauspicious things to come.

The tonic was wonderfully effective. The mother recovered. She was bright and frolicsome, a good four or five years younger. The Pious Son was insanely happy. The rippling of his mother's laughter was compensation enough for his pains. The younger brother, however, had had enough of them both. He tried to forget his own blood relatives, whom he could not forget.

He spent his days among the sheep in the hills. The vast, rolling pastures of that north country sent a strong wind down upon him. Be cold, it said. Swaying on the back of a water buffalo, he sometimes passed a night by the river. The muddy, yellow water made him feel the flow of days and months. Burned by the sun and wet by the dew, still he longed for the happy dinner table, a caress from his mother, a pleasant talk with his brother.

"What can be the matter with him?" The good woman was puzzled. "Have I done something wrong?"

"No," replied the elder son quietly. "He is only training himself in the hills."

The priest was too strong a medicine. The patient had acquired an addiction. The injections had to be continued. Even though it might drive his brother mad, the Pious Son had his duty: to follow his first intentions through.

The village was surrounded on three sides by a river. On the one road from the fourth side, guards were stationed to keep off bandits. In winter the priest could walk across the ice for his clandestine visits. When the water was low, he could make his way by small boat. But when the snow melted and the rains came, there were insurmountable difficulties in the way of stealing into the village. The injections so necessary to the patient had to be stopped.

"Why must we have fall and spring? If it could only be winter the whole year."

"How very true," said the priest. "Exactly what I pray to the Buddha every day."

These whispered laments reached the ear of the Pious Son. The journey across the ice in the howling winter wind was a trial beyond comparison with an ordinary pilgrimage. On stormy nights there was a danger of freezing or drowning. Had it been Greece or Rome, one would no doubt have heard praises sung of this healthy, unhappy love. The priest had to tuck up his skirts—the cold would have been unbearable if they had been wet—and when he came stumbling in, his calves and thighs would be stiff from the cold. Touched by his ardor, the woman would take the purple hands and feet in her own hands. "And all for me!" She would warm them against her belly.

As he lay there with teeth chattering, a wave of cold from his body assaulted her, and soon her teeth too were chattering.

Might not frozen injections lead to complications? And at this rate, one could not be sure when the hypodermic needle itself would break, or disappear. The future was so uncertain. The man and the woman might wish to die for love; but the Pious Son had his duty. He must guard the health of his mother.

He decided to build a bridge.

It was a formidable project, really beyond the resources of any one individual, but he was reconciled to throwing in everything. The villagers cooperated happily toward the improvement of communications. Time after time the stone base and the pillars were laid, time after time they were washed away. The whole village was mobilized. Young and old turned to the grand, sad task of bridge-building.

"Have they gone crazy?" Other villages looked on in astonishment at the mad project, noting that expense was no consideration.

Some among them may have felt that they had been outdone: "Bet they mean to sneak out at night and have fun in our village when they get it finished."

The villagers themselves joked about their bridge as they cut and carried stones.

"You've never seen the likes of the bridge we're going to have."

"And when it's finished, who'll get the most out of it?"

"That's easy. The priest, the lady's man."

They had not been long in smelling out the scandal in the landlord's household. They knew, too, that he was related to provincial officials. Reluctant to be put in chains, they kept it to themselves. But not even they had guessed that the bridge was being built to carry a hypodermic needle. That would be too foolish. The villagers were practical, and such impracticality was no less than miraculous.

"What difference does it make? The toll's paid, and the wife and old woman can get across with no trouble."

Several energetic young men promised that they would be the first to cross. They had no way of foreseeing who would in fact be first.

As the bridge neared completion, the first crosser stood on a hilltop, indifferent to the sweating and straining. "When it's finished, I'll leave town," said the young philosopher, breaking off his meditations. "I'll run away from this ugliness and never come back."

Only he knew his brother's real motives. All that money was going into the bridge for the sake of a debased filial piety. But whatever one might think of the motives, how beautiful the bridge was! A clean, unbroken curve, such as a fairy might trace in the sky with his staff. The fairy bridge was not for the priest. It was a bridge of hope, a bridge which the heavens had laid for the boy himself. He would leave. Then the advance, the ascent. Somewhat given to transcendental thoughts, the second son of the landowning family saw the bridge leap up as a symbol.

The end was in sight. But now the elder son had cause to lament to the heavens: his mother was near death. From another ailment, diarrhea. This time, only this time, the powers of the priest were ineffective. Indeed, they made matters worse.

The Pious Son, the mother, the lover had had the same prayer: "Make them hurry, make them finish it." The image of the bridge burned into the dimming eyes of the mother. "Bridge, bridge," she would moan. But the Pious Son no longer thought of the bridge and no longer thought of the river. The bridge would be finished, his much-loved mother would die. The bridge would then be but the skeleton of his filial piety. After his mother's death it would not be a holy crossing on the grand Way of Filial Piety. Quite the reverse: it would be a mockery, a monument to laugh derisively at the failure of filial piety. He had spent tens of thousands, and built a shame of solid stone.

"Stay with us at least until you can see the bridge." The priest was much upset.

"I am going to die," replied the woman in a low, hoarse voice.

"If you die, I shall die too. Die, die. You think I won't die?"

Thus the wasted, distraught hypodermic took his stand. He was not lying. He was resigned to dying for love, whatever flaming pits lay in wait for him.

And now the unfortunate elder son had only hatred. Revenge. Nothing more. For his mother, for his father, he must destroy the poison. As he looked down at the blanched face, even now being taken by death, and at the back of the priest who was pressing his own face against hers, a terrible look, compounded of murderous loathing and maddening grief, came into the eyes of the Pious Son. Had Confucius himself come up at that moment, the gaze would not have wavered in his direction.

The mother died on the day the bridge was finished. It was a fine, sunny day. The village was heavy with the scent of spring flowers. Swarming about the approach to their remarkable bridge, the villagers awaited the arrival of the young landlord. A donkey with a youth astride it wandered across, and the villagers took no more notice of the fact than to call out greetings to a member of a family to which they were greatly indebted.

Two men faced each other in the bedchamber where the dead woman lay. Each had loved her after his fashion. But the thought that the priest had loved his mother and, just as he himself, had been saddened by her death was enough to blow the Pious Son's rage into a sheet of flame. In his hand he held a dagger, a family heirloom. His handsome face was livid. Derangement gave his rage a special color—whether the true color of the Pious Son, or a discoloration, or something between, one cannot be sure.

"You know what you have coming." He flung the standard remark at his already defeated enemy.

"I shall die happily," said the priest.

He was already dead. An empty shell. The glittering dagger held no terrors for him. "Do it now. It will be easier than if I have to do it myself."

"That will be enough from you, bandit!"

He slashed and stabbed. There was a single cry of pain. The timid priest lost consciousness at the first thrust. It was what one might almost describe as euthanasia. The Pious Son had but lent a hand to one who wanted to die and could not. Still, no other revenge was possible. It was not only revenge. It was Filial Piety. His punishment was three years in exile.

Such is the story. If similarly pious sons have taken up residence in the reader's neighborhood and are commuting to some office or bureau, then the reader would do well, as also would near-by priests, to look to the ordering of his affairs. We need make no distinction between priest and layman. The matter concerns us all.

What a curious, intricate meaning, in any event, the bridge has at the center of the story. A sad, comical bridge, a bridge smelling of blood. Bridge of faith, bridge of tragedy, bridge of pale death—hardly a safe thoroughfare, whatever else it might be. Call it a bridge of passion, aflame like a red lotus. Man, who must have bridges, is a troublesome animal. In the mud under the bridge, rats male and female tumble over one another, and time is forgotten.

TRANSLATED BY EDWARD SEIDENSTICKER

■KURAHASHI YUMIKO

Kurahashi Yumiko was born in 1935 in a country town in Shikoku, the eldest daughter of a dentist. Her father wanted her to prepare for a career in dentistry, but by the time she had qualified she had also secretly gained admission to the Department of French Literature at Meiji University in Tokyo. In 1960, before graduating, she made a brilliant literary debut with her short story "Party" (*Parutai*, tr. 1961) about a cool young woman student who joins the Party at the urging of her lover, becomes pregnant by a "worker," and then decides to leave the Party.

Early in the sixties, Kurahashi Yumiko established herself as one of the most daring and prolific writers of avant-garde fiction, creating a bizarre antiworld peopled by such abstract characters as K and L (a twin brother and sister, of incestuous inclinations), S and M (a more conservative pair of lovers), and Q (an ambiguous "outcast" who emerges as a would-be revolutionary in one of her satirical novels). In her 1966 essay "Negativity and the Labyrinth of Fiction" (*Shōsetsu no meiro to hitaisei*) she declared firmly: "I abhor the intrusion of the disorder of 'facts' into the world of words I have constructed. The ironclad rule in reporting facts or events is the clarification of the Five W's—when, where, who, what, why—but my stories reject these restrictions entirely and instead build castles in the air. At an uncertain time, in a place that is nowhere, somebody who is no one, for no reason, is about to do something—and in the end does nothing: this is my ideal of the novel."

Returning to Japan in 1967 somewhat chastened by a year of study in the United States, Kurahashi began to turn from experimentalism to a more realistic manner, though enriched by a counterpoint of traditional or mythic themes. Her most recent novel, *The Bridge of Dreams* (*Yume no ukihashi*, 1971), combines an allusion to classical Japanese literature with the up-to-date subject of wife-swapping. Since then, she has preserved a bewildering silence.

To Die at the Estuary belongs to a group of five short novels published as *Anti-Tragedies* (*Hanhigeki*) in 1971. All five are based on themes from Greek tragedy, this one on Sophocles' *Oedipus at Colonus*. There is also a significant reference to the thirteenth-century meditative essay *Hōjōki*—"An Account of My Hut"—in which Kamo no Chōmei, living in Buddhist seclusion a few years before his death, reflects on the impermanence of life and on his doubtful progress toward enlightenment.

❖ To Die at the Estuary

(*Kakō ni shisu,* 1970)

The rains had ended, and as the couple came out of the station swallows were flying in a clear summer sky. The plaza in front of the station was much larger now, and the old man, Takayanagi, looked up at the high buildings that enclosed it and remarked that the town had certainly changed.

"But it must be thirty years since you were here, Father," Asako said.

As she opened a parasol to shield him from the fierce rays of the sun, she seemed too young to be his daughter. They were more like grandfather and granddaughter. Asako was too young in her white dress and white shoes, her face flushed and shining like a fruit that has drunk in the summer's sun. But in the air-conditioned coolness of the taxi her cheeks returned to their usual porcelain white. Her head poised on her slender neck hardly turned as her long eyes seemed to be carefully observing the rows of houses that passed by on both sides. Takayanagi looked at the profile of his young daughter, and for a moment had the feeling that he was looking at the face of someone quite unknown to him. He told himself that it was the face of a young woman who was both his daughter and his granddaughter.

Asako turned toward him and asked:

"Is it all right to go directly there?"

"Of course. Nagasawa seems to have taken care of everything. All we have to do is move in."

Takayanagi had been thinking for some years now of acquiring a house in his hometown and spending a few months of each year there. But since he disliked the bother of going down himself to look for a house or arrange to have one built, he had simply asked two or three people he knew to buy one for him if anything suitable turned up. His only specific requirement was that it be east of the town, on the northern bank of the river near the estuary. He intended to die there. This year such a house had been found. Formerly it was part of a restaurant, but the management had changed hands, the large annex with its own spacious garden had been converted into a hotel catering to short-time couples, and only the pleasantly small main building had been put up for sale. Takayanagi decided to buy it, and entrusted the whole business to an old classmate he had known since their primary-school days, a Doctor Nagasawa, who had retired and left his practice to his son.

The taxi turned toward a bridge and ascended a steep rise, then swung left and drove for some time down an embankment road that ran along the river. The river itself could not yet be seen. It was hidden from view by a great many buildings, mostly inns or restaurants.

When the driver found the house it turned out to be surrounded by a bamboo fence, and the gateway, though small, was in the old style with a roof over it. The name "Takayanagi" had already been put up. Nagasawa had arrived before them and was waiting. He came out onto the veranda and pointed out the various trees and shrubs in the garden.

"That's crape myrtle, that's paulownia, and that tall one's quite rare, aralia or something, and then there's loquat and rhododendron, all transplanted from the old garden. All but the pagoda tree."

Since a garden was not relevant to the purposes of the "hotel," that space was now wholly occupied by the so-called new building.

"But, I don't know, there doesn't seem to be any life in them. And it's not just because they were transplanted either. The air's pretty bad around here—you can blame it on the weird thing they've put up over there."

The embankment wall along the river blocked the view, but from the upstairs windows they saw an astounding sight extending along both sides of the river right down to the sea. Takayanagi gasped. It seemed unreal, as if his eyes had filmed over or he had gone blind and was suffering from a hallucination. This was a place he had grown up with, a place seen again and again in his dreams as he grew old. The river flowed through the town and here where it suddenly widened and emptied into the sea there should have been a wasteland, the remains of what was once a delta, tussocks of grass springing from sandy earth, and then, projecting from it into the sea, a long sandbar like a tongue with ripples washing gently over it. As a boy he would run among the summer grasses, or in spring dig into the soft sand bottom for shells. In summer the boys of the town would swim farther upstream, but when the tide was going out Takayanagi would often make his way down with the current, under one bridge after the other, swimming down almost to where it met the sea. Then when his body caught against the sand of this island he would lie there like a boat run aground, the sun burning down upon the deck of his back, and wait for the returning tide. At last the salt water would flow back from the sea and the current begin to turn. As he swam upstream again with the current the sharp spines of a flathead sometimes cut his legs.

Now most of the estuary had been filled in, and on this reclaimed land an oil refinery and chemical plant had been built, a glittering mass of silver storage tanks and pipes. To the old man it looked like a metal fortress, and yet he also thought that this was perhaps as it should be, perhaps it was even the kind of sight one ought to see at the end of a long journey. As an old man he had not intended to seek here what he had known as a boy. The sentimentality for such a quest, the addiction to seeking what might or might not be found, had all left him. But the sight that lay spread out before his eyes was so far beyond his experience that its very remoteness, the remoteness now of the whole estuary, made it seem an abode of the gods. Was this the setting he required for ending his days? If it was, Takayanagi accepted it.

His daughter looked at him with anxious, troubled eyes. Takayanagi did not like people to commiserate with him.

"Now that's really something. Unexpected, but most imposing."

"But it's so awful," Asako said plaintively, adding, "isn't it, Father?" in an almost accusing tone of voice. Takayanagi kept his face turned firmly away from her, looking fixedly at the black river and the silvery plant.

"That's what I wrote about in my letter the other day, and, well, there it is."

Takayanagi could not recall anything of the sort in Nagasawa's letter. Had he read it and just not been able to take it in? Or was his memory slipping? Whichever it was he felt irritated with himself.

"That's right, you did," he replied. "I must say I didn't expect a change on quite this scale, though. But it's not a bad thing. If the town can attract enterprises like that it must be prospering."

"This neighborhood's about the bleakest place in town now. Still, it's where you wanted to be, so here you are. About the only place old people can tolerate anymore is that residential section north of the castle."

Asako was silently looking at the sea beyond the plant. It was the height of summer, and the burning sun and the smoke belching out from the chimneys of the plant gave a cloudy whiteness to the sky. Perhaps it was only imagination, but the wind blowing in off the sea seemed to smell of hydrogen sulfide.

She smiled. "Anyway, we're near the sea. You can smell the sea breeze."

Could it come from the sea? Late that first night Takayanagi heard a kind of reverberation he found difficult to identify. Surely it was not the break and flow of the sea; it was more like a trembling within the earth itself. The sound came from the direction of the plant. Could it be the hum of machines working through the night, or the roar of something burning? The plant made relatively little noise, nothing disturbing. With all its tanks and pipes it was indeed plant-like, a vegetable growth. Perhaps there was some saplike fluid circulating ceaselessly throughout it. The old man decided it was that kind of sound.

He became aware that Asako too was lying with her eyes open as if straining to listen. He told her it was probably the noise from the plant.

"I don't hear anything like that," she replied. "Aren't you just imagining it, Father?"

"You're young, you see. There are strange sounds you don't hear when you're young. You start to hear them as you get older."

As death approaches, he had meant to say, but decided not to. Then he heard something like the cries of a woman coming from the hotel next door. That was what Asako must have been trying to catch.

She seemed unable to sleep because of the heat. Having kicked the light bedclothes off, she now lay rigidly on her back. The swelling outlines of her breasts showed, as if she were holding her breath.

"How old are you, Asako?"

"Nineteen," she answered, lying there looking up at the ceiling, her eyes open, unmoving.

"That's young. Too young. About the right age for my granddaughter," he said in a slightly odd tone of voice.

He was thinking that in fact Asako could be called his granddaughter although she did not know it. But this was something he could not tell her now. Asako had her life to live, and if one thread of that irrelevant past were loosened the whole thing would unravel in confusion, foulness, and blood. If she were covered by that filth and horror perhaps she would die of suffocation.

He thought how little she knew about her mother. When Asako was only five years old her mother had gone insane and hanged herself. She probably did not even recall the nature of her mother's death. Her mother's insanity had begun as no more than a form of neurosis. He had merely let it take its course, left his own wife to suffer and wind herself up within a cocoon of madness. Her suicide could be attributed to the birth of a child that was not his. That child was Asako, and the man who fathered her was Shuji, supposedly his own younger brother but in fact his son. Thus legally Asako was his daughter while in reality she was his granddaughter.

He felt he would tell her all this sometime, perhaps even in the near future. By "sometime" he meant just before he died, and Takayanagi had decided that his own death would occur when the gods called him, whether from heaven or earth or from the sea, or even from some such sacred ground, such an abode of the gods, as this metallic fortress in the estuary. That reverberation he had heard coming from somewhere deep in the night was perhaps a voice audible only to a man anticipating it. When the time came he too would enter the company of the gods. Then would not he himself be able to proclaim with the voice of a god the truth of those people who remained after him, the truth of what they were? He felt a small, nervous lift of excitement at the thought.

Asako must have got up before him.

The old man was aware of this while still half in his dream, a dream he had been drowning in since dawn, struggling as it came upon him like the rising tide. Perhaps it was fatigue from the journey, but the dream was as oppressive as if he were floundering in filthy sewage water. His hands felt inordinately heavy, their movements dull. He seemed to be trying to swim toward someone he wanted to meet.

It was someone out of his childhood, a blind beggar who lived beneath one of the bridges. Actually, the man did not beg; it was only because he lived in such a place that the children called him a beggar. His blindness too seemed appropriate to a beggar, someone crippled or disfigured; and so he became the undeserved object of their mockery and contempt. However he was not just a failure living out the rest of his days under the archway of a bridge. Takayanagi had learned from his father that the blind man was the descendant of feudal lords, the son of a former governor of this province, and even now, living in this makeshift hut with only the underside of a bridge for a ceiling, he was still being looked after by the present governor in some indirect way. His father had also told him that the man's condition was the result of a dreadful crime he had committed, but more than that he had not learned.

In his dream Takayanagi was a boy again, swimming at the rear of the blind beggar's hut. In the shadow of the bridge the water would be cold and dark, a place the boys of the town avoided, but in his dream the young Takayanagi swam as if paddling his way through the amniotic waters of the womb. Looking up at the rafters and crossbeams of the bridge, he saw that they were swarming with bats. He hid behind one of the slime-covered supports and peered into the old blind man's hovel. He had only seen the place from the front before, from the road that ran down below the bridge. Now, viewed from the back, it was unmistakably a beggar's hovel, filled with an almost obscene disorder. It was as if one were looking inside the belly of a wild animal. The blind man's daughter was at the rear of the hovel washing some indescribably filthy clothes. The boy strenuously raised his head from the surface of the river to avoid drinking its water muddied by menstrual blood and dissolving excrement, and as he did so the girl noticed him there and gave him a brilliant smile. Then the image changed to that of his smiling, young, beautiful stepmother.

There the dream broke off momentarily, and Takayanagi wondered if it was a repetition of something he had actually experienced in the past. He decided it was not.

At first he had not known that the blind beggar had a daughter. Then he heard from older boys that the old man made his daughter attract customers, whatever that meant, and his feelings of hatred and contempt for him became all the more violent. He thought it just that the old beggar be so scorned.

At the height of summer, either as they were on their way home from a swim or because that day they were bored with swimming, the boys would seek another kind of sport, and begin attacking this blind beggar. In their minds he was a hideous, evil monster which should be hunted out and destroyed. They would pass before his hovel shouting insults, sometimes even throwing stones. Once the old man was sitting crosslegged outside the door, like a wooden Buddha, and the boys found this even more provoking. Dreaming again, suddenly Takayanagi was in the lead and had hurled a stone. Although he took no proper aim his stone flew straight at that face, but at the last moment the blind old man made a slight movement of the head and dodged it. Then he stood up. Despite his thinness his size was astonishing. As he approached them with the stiff, faltering steps of some evil effigy come to life, the boys let out a cry of fear and scattered in all directions. Takayanagi fled too, but as hard as he ran, whenever he looked back there was this giant figure with its dark, mysterious, magnificent blind countenance, stumbling and coming after him, stumbling, and coming after him . . .

The cry seemed to have stuck in his throat, and as old Takayanagi tried to cough it out, he must have actually uttered a kind of cry. Asako heard it and was now at his bedside, anxiously calling him.

"Father!"

"What time is it?" he asked.

"It's past eight."

The upstairs room was exposed to full sun from the east and it was unpleasant to lie there in bed on a summer morning.

"We'd better have an air conditioner put in," he said.

"That place next door must have them in every room, and they seemed to be making quite a noise last night. Maybe that's what disturbed you."

Probably that was the sound he had thought was coming from the plant. Asako should have said so last night. He felt irritable.

"An air conditioner wouldn't bother me. It's not being able to sleep that I can't stand. Let's have one on each floor."

He felt the heat more than most and he intended to ignore Asako's complaint that air conditioning is bad for one's health.

Asako tied the apron strings at the back of her neck, and said:

"It seems easier to put up with the heat here than in Tokyo, even though we're farther south. There's the breeze off the sea, for one thing." Then she added: "But this morning there doesn't seem to be any breeze at all. Perhaps it's what they call the morning calm."

When she brought breakfast in from the kitchen she still seemed cheerful.

"Have you seen the kitchen? It's enormous, with all sorts of gadgets left behind; more like living in a restaurant than in a house. If we had a proper cook we could set ourselves up in business tomorrow."

There was vinegared cucumber, sliced very thin. Then, what he often ate here as a boy, long eggplants, fried. Apparently a greengrocer had turned up early that morning, making the rounds in a covered truck. Asako guessed it was because there were so many inns and restaurants in the area. Takayanagi had awakened with a good appetite.

"I seem to have had a bad dream last night," he said abruptly, and Asako stopped eating in surprise, her chopsticks poised in the air.

"In my dream I was a boy again. I threw a stone at a blind beggar and he got angry and came after me, on and on after me. He was an old man who'd built a sort of hut under the bridge down the river, and although we never really saw him beg, we boys used to torment him and call him a beggar. He lived alone with his daughter—a pretty girl, if you looked at her, probably a little older than you. Do you know that novel by George Sand, *La Petite Fadette*?"

"Yes. It's one of the village novels."

"Well, think of the girl in that and you'll get some idea what she was like. There was something very pure and graceful about her, and in the way she dressed and carried herself."

"How old were you at the time, Father?"

"Thirteen, maybe fourteen. Anyway it was after my voice changed, so I was certainly old enough to feel an attraction to her."

Saying nothing to Asako, he thought of how the girl had been taken by his father as his second wife. When Takayanagi grew into a young man he slept with this woman who had become his mother. He had been driven by the idea that it was something he had to do, in order to fulfill the prophecy made about him, and the remembrance of those days in hell was as vivid as ever.

"It would be nice if Grandmother could live with us in this house."

Asako's remark brought him back to the present. Why did she say that? What was she thinking? She could hardly know where his stepmother had come from or what she had done. Could it be that at some time she had suddenly understood everything? Perhaps it was merely because such a thought had crossed his mind, but as she lifted the teapot, her head turned a little away from him, there seemed to be a cloud shadowing her face, as if she knew some dark secret.

But that was impossible. Asako could only have heard it from his step-mother, and she was not the kind of woman who would talk about things like that.

"Why did you mention your grandmother?" he asked, as if expecting an answer.

"While you were talking about that old man and his daughter they seemed like you and me, Father, living here alone, and it made me sad. But then I remembered that we still had Grandmother."

"Are you lonely then, being alone with me?"

Asako shook her head firmly.

"You should have gone to college."

"I don't want to. Living with you has nothing to do with it."

"Then you should think about getting married. Nineteen's not too early."

"When I feel like it I will, and not give you a second thought."

There was a night of heavy rain and thunder as if the rains were back again. Then next morning came the burning heat of true summer. Takayanagi spent that morning in the now air-conditioned room reading the *Hojoki* and occasionally looking out at the garden whose plants had come back to life.

While he was still going to the office he had liked to read, regretting that he could not spend more time on books; sometimes he would even read the new foreign novels that Asako bought. Yet lately, now that he had the time for it, he found his interest in reading had waned. He had lost patience with the loquacious, effeminate meanderings of intellectually and spiritually empty prose. Certainly he found confessional writing particularly irritating. He had once told Asako he would be happy to give her his whole library, but perhaps because Asako herself was no great reader, or because she was not possessive about books, she had merely smiled and let the matter go.

However the *Hojoki* was among the few books he kept by his side, to take up whenever he felt so inclined. It said only what needed to be said, and said it in a man's voice, a voice free of weakness or ornamentation. Takayanagi valued it as an example of the way a man should speak at the end of his life. Nothing was known of how Kamo no Chomei had lived after writing this work, nor of how he had met his death. If, in the midst of writing, he had laid down his brush because he realized he understood nothing, Takayanagi accepted this silence as right. If he himself came to that realization, then it would be good to die in ignorance and silence. The struggle of youth to lay bare all the ugly realities of one's being was something he could do without.

Later that morning old Nagasawa came to see him. He brought his only grandson, Takashi, and wanted advice on how to get the young man into a certain private university in Tokyo, since Takayanagi was on its board of governors. Takayanagi listened agreeably, and made a note in his memo book. Then he asked Nagasawa about the young man's record in school. It was good.

"With grades like that there should be no problem about admission whether I try to clear the way or not. The size of any donation to the university has nothing to do with it. You could pay out as much as you liked, but if the grades were too low, even the chairman of the board couldn't help you."

The young man listened calmly to this conversation about himself, nodding from time to time, but showing no sign of embarrassment or of trying to make a good impression.

When Nagasawa's business was finished, Asako served them ceremonial tea. She was wearing a summer kimono and her face was lightly made up. As she set the tea bowl before Takashi, she permitted herself a cold, restrained smile.

Nagasawa mentioned that the young man was studying the No dance, the simpler kind that does not require costume.

"He's been under Mr. Miura since last year."

"That's the Komparu school, isn't it?" Takayanagi asked the young man. "What are you practicing at the moment?"

"*Tamura.*"

"You enjoy your lessons, do you?"

Takashi looked as if he was not sure how to reply.

"I admire your grandson," said Takayanagi. "He manages to avoid saying more than needs to be said. That's good. His grandfather tends to be garrulous, perhaps a sign of old age."

"I've never known what to say to these taunts of yours."

"No offense intended, believe me. Just speaking the truth."

"That's why I've never known what to say."

Asako served a light lunch neatly arranged on bamboo ware with leaves folded in half-moon shapes.

"To judge from this sparse elegance, the girl seems to be playing at tea ceremony," Takayanagi said, but Nagasawa paid the appropriate compliments.

Asako saw the guests off as far as the gate. When she came back she laughed and said:

"That boy Takashi certainly is odd."

"What's he done?"

"He was just getting in the car when he got all the way out again and asked me what character I used for my name."

"Don't say that didn't please you."

"I really wouldn't know."

Takayanagi felt a sudden chill. A boy had now invaded their lives as he had invaded the lives of the old blind man and his daughter, and the thought troubled him.

At night one could see the fire of waste gas burning at the top of a towerlike chimney of the refinery. It was like a giant blazing candle, but Asako said it looked like a devil's tongue, weird and repulsive.

"A very literary sentiment. But I suppose you could say that about the way I see it. In fact, to me it looks like a torch set on holy ground, a sacred flame offered to the gods."

"Do you really see that as a place for gods to be living?"

"Gods, or at least some kind of spirits, used to live there in the past. They were spirits of women's hatred."

Successive generations of inbred feudal lords will produce some abnormal individuals; and an ugly tale of one of them, of the wholesale abduction and torturing to death of the town's maidens, was still told in this castle town. The corpses had been buried in that wasteland, it was said; but some years later there was an earthquake, followed by a tidal wave that washed the skeletons away, the floodwaters carrying the bones off and finally depositing them on the banks of the castle moat, where they lay scattered like dead white flowers. After that the grove of pines on the shore facing the wasteland became notorious as a place where women went to hang themselves.

"They used to say that if a woman who had grown weary of her life went near the pine grove, ghosts would appear in every tree in the form of a human head larger than you could put your arms around, and they would dangle there giving off a sulphurous light, crying together, calling. That tale goes back two hundred years."

"I wonder if anything of the grove is left?"

"I shouldn't think so. They seem to have built a landing stage for oil tankers in that area."

"Then there's nowhere for the ghosts to live, is there?" she asked in all seriousness.

"I don't suppose there is. But when you consider that a refinery now stands where there was only wasteland, rank grass blown by the sea wind, perhaps those evil spirits have changed into benevolent ones ensuring the prosperity of the place. They must be pleased to be living in such up-to-date surroundings."

As a boy he had heard something of the kind from the blind man, although of course there had been no mention of oil refineries. The old man had said that the vengeful spirits of the murdered women or women suicides only awaited the ceremony of prayer to be joyfully apotheosized into guardian deities. Occasionally the old man would also speak of the future of certain individuals.

Probably that was why the people of the town came to think of him as a fortuneteller. When the boy heard some of the local wives talking about going to the old man to have their fortunes told, he suddenly felt well disposed toward him. He would explain to the other boys that this was no beggar but a practitioner of the ancient art of divination. Still, the old man had never been seen with a bundle of divination rods, nor, being blind, could he have read anyone's palm. Later when the boy became his friend, he had several opportunities to witness what happened. The old man simply remained silent and let his visitor speak. A woman who wanted her fortune told would talk on and on about herself, working up to a plea for some divine revelation. Then the old blind man would utter a dreadful rebuke, a kind of scolding—he might even spit out harsh, merciless words as if putting a curse on her—and he would angrily drive the visitor away from his door.

"All I tell people who come here is how worthless they are. Coming to a place like this and depending on a stranger only proves it. But to gain the power to know your own worthlessness can be a form of help. First I listen to what the person has to say, and in what he says all that he is appears to me, and I know that one so weak cannot decide his own fate. Then I utter certain words that seem not to come from a human mouth. In that way the fates of various people are determined."

"Then you must be a prophet," the boy Takayanagi said, but the old man shook his head severely.

"I am no prophet. There is no resemblance between me and the prophets of the Old Testament. You should think of the words that come from my mouth more as an oracle, the ambiguous words of the gods."

Later on it was to be the words the old man uttered to him just before he died that were to determine his life. Among them were words declaring that he would couple with his mother. When Takayanagi had done exactly as foretold, he had intended it all to be through the power of his own will. Now that very exercise of the will seemed predetermined by the words of the old man.

Old Takayanagi looked at the burning fire, at what Asako had called the devil's tongue, and sipped hot coffee she had just made for him from fresh-ground beans.

"Grandmother really loves coffee," she suddenly said.

"Yes, she does," Takayanagi replied, noticing that this was the second time Asako had mentioned his stepmother.

"She can't get proper coffee like this in that old people's home, but she still gulps down lots of instant coffee even though she complains how awful it tastes."

Last year he had had his stepmother, Aya, permanently placed in a home for the aged in the resort area of Izu, a hundred miles southwest of Tokyo. To Asako this was simply getting rid of her. Takayanagi had cut off his relatives like a doctor amputating useless limbs. He had done so with Asako's elder sister, Kyoko, when he married her off, and Kyoko herself, though she visited home once with her first-born child, had in recent years made no attempt to keep in touch except for an occasional telephone call to Asako. Takayanagi never mentioned her name. And long before that, when Asako was born, he got rid of Shuji by sending him abroad. Asako would not know about that.

"Do you often go to visit your grandmother?"

"Yes. Two or three times a month."

Since the unknown visits had been so frequent, she sounded as if she had boldly made up her mind to confess. In the way she spoke, and in the way she held her shoulders, he sensed a direct criticism of himself.

"Is she well?"

"Yes."

"She's well in her head too? After all, she's past seventy. She isn't getting senile and saying anything funny, is she?"

"She seems perfectly all right. She doesn't go on about the old days like most elderly people. She watches television a lot, and seems to remember things that happened recently, as if she had more interest in the present than in the past."

He was impressed by Asako's precise view of old age. For a person lapsing into second childhood, recent impressions were the first to disappear from memory, with only ancient recollections persisting oddly. Takayanagi had been afraid that it was of such ancient events that young Asako might have been told again and again on her visits.

"In that case she shouldn't be causing any trouble, so now is hardly the time to take her out of there. When she's finally going to die all we can do is to put her in the right hospital. There seems to be no question of her ever living with us again. Both Mother and I are people who have nothing left to do but die, and we separated so that we could die on our own, apart from each other. Mother's the sort of person with the strength to do that. You shouldn't bother your head so much with the affairs of old people. That goes for my affairs as well."

He felt his words were too harsh, but he had no intention of retracting them or softening them in any way. That was how he truly felt, and as he got older he found he had no wish to say anything more than was required to express his thoughts.

Asako looked straight back at him with tears in her eyes, but then lowered her long eyelashes. Her face was reflected in the glass windowpane, over the image of the burning fire, gold-colored flames tinged with red. It was as if Asako's hair were on fire.

"There's a fireworks display tonight."

Apparently Takashi had come to invite Asako out to see it. Takayanagi said he himself didn't care to go wandering about at night, but he urged Asako to let him take her. She hesitated, saying she had to get his dinner, but asked Takashi if he wouldn't mind waiting twenty or thirty minutes. Then she started setting the table and hastily preparing what was available. At last she went to put on a little makeup.

Meanwhile Takashi sat in one of the wicker chairs on the upstairs veranda, and Takayanagi in the other.

He had no idea what one talked about with a boy of seventeen or eighteen, but brought up the question of student revolt, which had recently spread from the universities to the high schools. At Takashi's own high school it seemed there were signs of trouble among the students, egged on by various "rebel" teachers.

"So you're a bit concerned about the All-Out Offensive, or whatever it's called, are you?" Takayanagi said, tempted to make fun of him.

"It gets on my nerves," the boy replied. "The Student Left bunch is no good, but the ones who really irritate me are the teachers. That's not the way to do things."

"You mean these 'rebel' teachers?"

"They're the worst, of course. They're making a first-class mess of things."

Asako had changed into a light summer kimono.

"We're ready to go then?" Takashi asked.

"Yes," Asako replied stiffly, not looking in his direction.

"Hurry up and go, you two. It seems to have started already."

The noise of rockets exploding one after the other rattled the glass windows. It was Asako, rather than Takashi, who seemed most eager to leave.

"Well then, with your permission, sir, I'll take her to see it."

Takashi looked slightly over-intense as he bowed to Takayanagi, and then turned his eyes urgently toward the girl.

"We can go down here if you like, and walk along the riverbank," Takashi suggested, as they descended the steps from the first bridge.

It was high tide, and the river, swollen with black water, had risen almost to the level of the path. There were pools of water in places where the asphalt had crumbled and caved in. Presumably it had once been a favorite promenade, now abandoned and allowed to fall into disrepair as the river grew dirtier and dirtier. Asako sometimes had to squeeze right up against the embankment wall to avoid the water, wondering to herself if this could be the same river in which her father used to swim.

"Some people have taken boats out," she said.

"We can go in a boat if you like. But the river smells especially bad at high tide."

"I'd rather just stroll along like this."

"The main display is farther up the river. An awful lot of people will be going to see it, so we probably can't get very close. Anyway we'll go as far as we can."

By the time they reached the third bridge, it was indeed crowded with sightseers both on the river path and on the bridge itself. The display was at its peak and the fireworks exploded continuously, unfolding and spraying out above their heads in chrysanthemumlike patterns. Sparks of flame fell like occasional drops of rain.

"We mustn't get separated in the crush," Asako said, and grasped Takashi's hand. From then on, jostled by the crowd, they only tried to get away to some place with fewer people. There was no hope of reaching the wooden grounds of the shrine across the river, where one would have the best view of the final set piece. The smell of acetylene lamps from the special night stalls mingled with the sweaty odor of the crowd.

They crossed the bridge and went down an incline into the main road, where streetcars were running. There was a smart little coffee shop with white walls, and as they went in Asako released his hand. Wiping her palm and fingers with the hot towel, she said:

"All the feeling seems to have gone out of the fingers of this hand."

"It was like gripping a practice sword with all one's might."

"You do *kendo* too?"

"Until last year. I was captain of the school team."

Asako looked intently at him. Unlike most present-day young men, he wore his hair cropped short, and the lines of his face were simple and clear-cut, with no surplus fat. It was like looking at a very large dog which had intelligently pricked up its ears. That is the kind of dog I rather like, she thought. But what she said was:

"I have the feeling we've known each other before, like brother and sister."

"Then I'd be your younger brother," he said seriously.

"And that would make me your respected elder sister, I suppose, though I can't say I feel much like one. Still, I could hardly be younger than you."

"I can't help feeling, well, as if you're a good deal older. For example, you might be my young stepmother, something like that. Maybe that's because I don't have a mother."

"I don't have a mother either. She went out of her mind and killed herself when I was five."

"Then let's not talk about our mothers."

"Sorry. Anyway it's not very nice when you start calling me your stepmother. What a thing to say!"

"But your father's the same age as my grandfather, isn't he? So while you're a daughter I'm a grandson, and that seems odd to me."

"I'm too young for his daughter, that's all."

"But he's only sixty, and you're nineteen, which means he was forty-one when you were born. There's nothing so unusual about that, is there?"

"That's true, but still . . ." She gave a feeble laugh. Then, looking out in space, she went on:

"I'm only thinking out loud, and if you don't like it you don't have to listen, but the truth is I have a feeling I'm not really my father's daughter. Father sometimes looks at me as if he's looking at an object, or a kind of mysterious moving thing, a strange animal, you might say. When there's a real blood connection between people it doesn't matter how hard you are to each other; even if you loathe one another the way close relatives sometimes do, there's still a kind of softness there, a feeling that deep down, essentially, one forgives the other. Father doesn't have that feeling for me. When he looks at me as he does, staring right into me, I get a really desperate feeling that I don't know who I am anymore. I suppose that makes me start imagining I'm not his child. And sometimes I think I must know who I am, even if it means cutting Father open to find out; I work myself up like that. I suppose I'm possessed by an evil spirit." She smiled at Takashi, though with unhappiness in her eyes.

"There are good spirits as well as evil ones—white magic, you know. But I can't help feeling there is something remote in you, as if you were living in a world of spirits."

"That's how I feel about my father and grandmother, as if they're not really human. I don't know quite what it is about them, but it's as if they've done things no normal person could do, and yet have gone on living as calmly as ever. After Mother died they brought me up like that."

"Is your grandmother still alive?"

"Yes, but Father's stuck her in an old people's home in Izu, and it doesn't look as if he'll even go to see her before she dies. I've been going there two or three times a month, trying to worm something out of her. It's not that I like her or feel sorry for her, I just think I might be able to learn a secret about myself."

Asako leaned over the table, propping her cheek with her bare arms, and looked up wickedly at Takashi.

"Do you know Racine's *Phèdre*? The heroine's the same Phaedra who turns up in Greek tragedies and legends. One of my fantasies is that Grandmother and Father are like Phaedra and Hippolytus."

"And what was there between them?"

"Phaedra was the young queen of Theseus, but she was cursed by Aphrodite so that she fell in love with her stepson Hippolytus. Grandmother was grandfather's second wife. There's only twelve or thirteen years difference between her and my father."

"Did she tell you anything about this?"

"No. It's just my intuition. But you only have to watch the two of them together. You can feel a link between them, they're still bound by a psychological connection ever since the physical one. You know that warning system where an infrared ray you can't see makes a bell ring when you cross it? Something like that."

"Then you could be the child of your father and grandmother?"

"I've suspected that, but thinking about it I had to laugh. Grandmother would have been seventy-three, less nineteen, that's fifty-four when I was born."

Asako asked Takashi the time. It was still before eight, but she began worrying about her father. Also, she was hungry.

"I'd like to see you again," she said quietly, almost submissively.

"Next time I'll bring the car, and we can go for a drive."

Takashi's voice was unfaltering but a little strained.

When Asako got home the front door was locked. Fortunately she had the spare key in her bag. At first she thought her father might already be in bed, but it seemed too early for that, since he was in the habit of staying up later than most people his age. The air conditioner had been left on, and that was the only sound in the house, like a human voice quietly intoning away. The house was chilly. Suddenly she had a premonition that her father had died, perhaps had taken his own life. Her blood ran cold.

Takayanagi was nowhere in the house. She could not believe he had merely gone for a walk, to see the fireworks or to stroll around town; possibly, it occurred to her, he had gone in search of a place to die. She went upstairs and glanced over his Japanese writing desk, but there was only his tobacco tray and his tea things, all tidily arranged. A few books were piled on the small shelf at the side of the *tokonoma*, and on top of them lay a clothbound notebook. It bulged slightly since he had left his fountain pen between its pages, and she found herself opening it. The first words she read were:

My property. Two-thirds Asako. Rest disposed as law requires.

And then:

Other things to write besides will.
What blind man said. Oracle. How fulfilled.
About Aya. Masayo, Shuji: my children, made brother and sister.
About Junko and Shuji. Asako: my grandchild, made child.
Dealing with Shuji.
Junko's illness, suicide.

For Asako these were words whose connections she could not grasp. Aya was her grandmother, and Masayo and Shuji her aunt and uncle. Junko was her own mother. A network of threads seemed to hold all these names together in a horrifying set of interrelations, but the panic of knowing she was reading what she should not read—apparently rough notes for her father's will—kept her from making any sense of it. Perhaps her father had heard voices calling him, a summons to death, had been drawn outside, and was now wandering along the estuary. If that was so, she could do nothing about it. The thought seemed to give her a mooring, like a ship's anchor finally touching the bottom of the sea. Regaining her wits at last, she telephoned Nagasawa.

A woman answered, a maid or nurse probably, then Nagasawa came on.

"I think my father . . ."

"That's right, he's here. Hold on and I'll call him."

She felt the strength drain from her, and began to cry.

"Father, couldn't you have—"

"Nagasawa invited me over to watch the fireworks, and we had a little something to drink. I'm fine, on top of the world. Stop sniveling. I'll get home all right, so don't worry. You needn't wait up. How did your date with Takashi go? Did you enjoy yourself? You're home early enough, anyway!"

He seemed fairly drunk, talking with rare exuberance. As she listened, the tears ran down her face.

"Come home as soon as you can, please," she said, sounding as if her nose was blocked up.

Asako went downstairs and saw that the dinner she had prepared earlier for her father lay untouched. She started to eat, but noticed that she was totally unaware of what she was eating; she had only a sense of her own empty nothingness. Even her body seemed unreal to her. She sat like a puppet awaiting the return of its master. She hoped that her father, her master, would come home soon. But if he never came home again, perhaps the puppet would develop the strength to move of its own will. When she understood that somewhere within her was a desire for her father's death she felt a truly physical chill. She got up and turned off the air conditioner.

She started to think about the notebook, but did not feel like touching it again.

Takayanagi was a good drinker, but out of practice; obviously he had overindulged. The next morning he remembered only patches of what had happened. It must have been Takashi that drove him home, but his telephone conversation with Asako was hard to recall. Again, he had no idea what he said to her as she was putting him to bed. Perhaps he had even told her some acid truth that would eat its way into her mind. Still if his drunkenness was enough to loosen his tongue, it could just as well have made him drop off immediately to sleep.

He had got up that morning at his usual hour, but of course with no appetite.

After drinking a little cold vegetable juice Asako made for him, he went upstairs again and stretched out in the wicker chair. When he moved his head the room seemed to sway. He thought he might be getting sick.

He rested the clothbound notebook on his stomach, opened it, and looked indifferently at the notes he had scribbled in it after Asako went out last night. Now they bored him; he did not feel like adding any details under the various headings. Hearing Asako come upstairs, he hurriedly closed it and slipped it between some magazines and the *Hojoki* on his desk. She brought him a glass dish of sliced white peaches. She sat in the rocking chair opposite him as he ate. Takayanagi usually sat in that chair himself, but this morning had prudently chosen the more stable wicker chair with the footrest.

"Don't you think it's a good idea to turn off this air conditioner and open the windows?" she said. "There's plenty of breeze up here. And in summer it's surely more pleasant to let your skin perspire a little."

"All right then," Takayanagi agreed.

From time to time Asako talked like a housewife running a family, and since he found it tiresome to argue with her he would usually do what she said. And this morning, what with his hangover, he did feel very, very weak. For Asako's benefit he was acting the part of an old man on the verge of his second childhood. At least he felt sure he was only acting, although Asako might not see it that way.

She opened the window and let in an extremely warm breeze, in place of the cool artificial one.

"Now that feels good, doesn't it?"

He closed his eyes. As he lay there limp in the chair, devoid of all strength, suddenly the sensation of floating on his back down river with the current came vividly to him. He could hear the sound of water beating behind his ears, and even feel the burning rays of the sun on his eyelids.

"This is how I used to float down the river."

"What *are* you talking about, Father?" Asako said sharply.

"That river has died. There's nothing alive in it now, nothing swimming, not even a dog. How about asking Takashi along and going for a swim in the sea?"

"Do you mean yourself as well, Father?"

"I certainly do. I swam off the west coast of Izu only two or three years ago. If the beach slopes out gently, I won't have to worry about being carried out of my depth."

"We'd better ask Dr. Nagasawa first."

"That old fraud! Anyway, he was a gynecologist. Spent most of his time giving illegal abortions, from before the war, apparently."

Takayanagi opened his eyes. Asako was rocking back and forth in the chair opposite him, her face hidden by the magazine she was holding, a woman's magazine with an actress on its cover. Her bare knees shone like two white peaches. As she sank deeper into the chair her short skirt revealed the insides of her thighs. She seemed absorbed in her magazine, unaware that he was looking at her. Finally she let one of her slippers drop and crossed her legs. As he watched her legs rising and falling with the movement of the chair he found that he was being aroused by the sight, and closed his eyes again.

He had lost his virility years ago and what he had come to desire in women was the same as when he was a virgin; his desire had again taken on an abstract form with no carnal purpose behind it. Even the powerful attraction he felt toward the thighs and calves of young girls was a kind of regression to his boyhood. Then he had been obsessed by the legs alone, as if cut off from the rest of the body, independent living things. The sight of attractive legs made him wish to possess only them, and because he knew that was impossible he would feel a deep, sorrowful pain. The blind man's daughter had legs that aroused that pain.

Toward the end of spring the boy would often go with Aya down to the estuary to search for clams and shells. Her legs would be bared to the thighs, and to look at them like that from behind would make him unhappy. He thought of them as the legs of a goddess, but he kept the thought to himself. As the goddess's legs became wet and sandy the boy would feel a strange, ambivalent lust for them.

He wondered if Asako's legs were those of a goddess, and he opened his eyes to see. Perhaps he was too close, but Asako's crossed legs looked unexpectedly strong and sensuous.

She abruptly laid her magazine aside and stood up.

"I'll make some tea."

As he watched her walking barefoot across the room he saw that she had indeed the slim legs of most girls nowadays. The legs of a goddess should be a little fuller, more rounded.

"Lead me by the hand," the old blind man said.

During his afternoon sleep Takayanagi had returned to his boyhood again, and his hand was in the inhumanly strong grip of the old man's huge hand.

They were not by the hut under the bridge but in the center of the wasteland in the estuary. The blind man lived in a new hut now among the rank grasses of the wasteland. The bridge had been rebuilt, and the old man and his daughter expelled from the town; Takayanagi's father, at the request of the governor, had given them this hut built for workmen on land which had previously been used by his company for storing timber. From then on, the boys saw little of the old man, who somehow was no longer called "the beggar." For Takayanagi he had the aura of a recluse possessed of a wisdom beyond the merely human. Now that the boy's voice had broken he had drifted away from his former friends, and he would often go to visit the old man in what he thought of as the "grass hut" in which wise men and poets of old had lived. It was on such a visit that the old man had taken the boy's hand and said he wanted to walk.

In that grip the boy felt a mysterious power. If fate assumes the heavy shape of powerful men, then it seemed to have become this blind old man and it was taking the boy by the hand. Although entrusting his hand to the boy, the old man walked quite freely and easily among the summer grasses, almost like an ordinary person. There was none of the stumbling, clumsy movement of the usual blind man being led; rather, the boy felt like a small boat being towed in the wake of a large ship.

They went down into a hollow which was enclosed by a crumbling L-shaped stone wall. Tall, wild yellow spirea was in flower, and pink convolvulus straggled over the stone wall.

"It is dark here. What place is this?" asked the old man.

"It's a place people always told us to stay away from. Long ago a mad lord in the castle used to torture women to death and then have their corpses thrown away here. They say if you come here your arms and legs will rot and fall off, or you'll fall asleep and your flesh will melt away till there's only a skeleton left. Lots of other horrible things, too."

"And do you believe all that?"

"No. Children often come here to explore. When I was little I came any number of times with my friends. But I was the only one who dared to climb over the wall and come right in."

The boy spoke with pride. "I'm not afraid of superstitions. Anyway, nothing happened to me afterward."

"You mean nothing's happened yet. You don't know what's going to happen now, do you? You don't even know that something is going to happen."

"Don't try to frighten me!" Takayanagi had meant to say it jokingly, but he was aware that a whine had crept into his voice. Perhaps the old man intended to strangle him. To conceal his terror he tried to apply his mind to other things. But even this attempt would be discernible to the old man, not with his blind eyes but with those other eyes he had. The boy turned to look at him, but silhouetted against the sun in the west, the old man was only a black shape, the incarnation of darkness. What was this man then? The boy realized that he knew nothing of him. All that he had been told—that he was a blind beggar, a tramp who practiced fortunetelling, the descendant of feudal lords—all of it was of no use in answering the question of what he really was.

"There is nothing to fear," the old man said. "We shall have a long talk. The sun is still high. But first, find me a place to sit."

The boy seated the old man at a shaded spot on the crumbling wall. He himself sat close by, on a stone about the size of a human head.

"This is a bad place, a place of terror. The earth here has drunk in blood. It is still haunted by evil spirits, although this could not be known to ordinary folk. But the spirits gathered here are like flabby entrails, the shapeless ghosts of inferior souls. They possess little power; enough, perhaps, to create miasmas to disturb the mind of some weak-spirited person from time to time, but no more than that. There is nothing to be anxious about."

"I don't believe in such things, but I wouldn't be afraid, anyway. I don't believe in any superhuman power. That's why I've brought you to a place other people won't come near."

"I wasn't brought by you. It was I who brought you here. You seem to trust too much in the power of your own free will."

"I refuse to believe in any gods or fates, in anything that surpasses the power of man!" Takayanagi shouted.

That shout must have broken his dream. As his head surfaced into the present, old Takayanagi realized he had been sweating in his sleep. The afternoon breeze was blowing in from the estuary, but it was the heat from the roof clogging the room like raw cotton that gave the real feeling of high summer. As a boy he had felt that same heat among the summer grasses on the wasteland.

He looked down into the garden full of burning sunlight. The trees and shrubs seemed dusty and shrunken, enduring the heat. On the opposite bank the oil refinery glittered, casting back the full rays of the sun, as if at close range one might hear the crackle of burning metal.

Takayanagi was wearing a lemon-colored polo shirt, rather bright for an old man, and its heavy terrycloth had made him sweat. But a little natural perspiration felt pleasant in the heat of the day.

"Yes, the sun is still high."

He spoke quietly to himself, looking up at the sky with its thin haze of smoke, and tried to reconstruct the dialogue with the blind man. He became the old blind man and asked his boyhood self:

"So you really don't believe that anything surpasses man?"

"Man is the measure of all things."

"But aren't there things you can't measure with your human yardstick? Like me, for example? Look at me."

The old man turned his head, exposing his face to the sun. The boy had never looked straight at those blind eyes. Perhaps he had always managed to avoid looking because he knew unconsciously that he could not bear to see them. He had not thought the old man was blinded by cataract or glaucoma or an infection, and he had not wanted to think there were more terrible ways in which a man could lose his sight.

The old man had no eyes. The boy could not tell if they had been gouged out or destroyed, or even if he had never had eyes. Now there were only two holes, and around them the skin was mysteriously wrinkled and scarred as if it had been burned. No eyelids moved. It was like looking at the remains of a volcano which had erupted once and was now silent.

"I burned out these eyes with red-hot iron rods," the old man had said in a low voice. "It was the rage within me. Not because I had looked upon what I should not have seen, my own evil deeds. Nor was it because I could no longer bear to look upon misfortune. I had believed that these eyes could see all things, and because they had not seen what they should have seen, I destroyed them in the wildness of my rage. But that, too, was mere foolishness. I had meant to gouge out my shame, and now my shame is only made visible. These scars are the signs of my defeat. What defeated me was a power that surpasses the power of man. These are words you dislike, but it was the power of the gods. Certainly what I call the gods is no more than a word men use. And yet it is also certain that they sway men in what they do. Men use the word 'god' for what sways them, guessing at the source of that power against which they themselves are so power-less. By good fortune most men live their lives without ever hearing the voices of the gods. They live like puppets unaware of what moves them. There are mechanical puppets who believe they move only by their own free will, all unaware of the clockwork mechanism inside them, and of the beings who placed it there. But I was different. At least I was aware of the mechanism set within me to make me move as I did. Call that mechanism fate, if you will. It is constructed from the words of the gods. Once a man took those words apart to show me their terrible meaning. Do you understand? That man was as I am now, an old beggar. Yet I am hardly as old as you think. I look older than my years because I grappled with the machine, used it harshly, and these are my scars. Be that as it may, this beggar who prophesied my fate was also blind. I think he had cast away his sight so as not to see what need not be seen, and see only what men do not see. What he said to me was: 'While you remain in the light of the sun you will murder your father and couple with the mother who gave you birth. Help will come to you only after you have lost the light of the sun.' "

The old man paused, his face turned as if in pursuit of the sun journeying westward. The sky darkened. The piled-up cumulus clouds seemed ready to descend. A moist wind presaging a thunderstorm began to rustle the summer grasses.

"Remember this well. This will happen to you."

The boy tensed, and gooseflesh stood out on his body. Could the old man be referring to him? Or was he only repeating the words of the other blind man? The old man perceived that the boy was going to stand up, and stretched out a hand to restrain him.

"Wait. There is more to be said. These things happened long, long ago. The same things may have happened countless times since then. Probably they will go on happening over and over. While men use language, links are made, one link of horror fitting into the next, and a chain is formed. Why was I caught in one link of that chain, in one round circle of it? Because the gods had chosen me. Because they had decided to set this mechanism, this hell, within me. What other explanation can there be? I went against the gods: I tried to smash the mechanism. I would outwit their machine: I would spit their words back in their faces. I had been told what I would do in the future. Very well, but my will was free, and so the ability to do otherwise was mine. I used all my power in order that the prophecy, the words the gods had let me hear, should never be realized. I ran away from my father and mother. I was the wisest of all men; about things human, about those things of which man is the measure, there was nothing I could not understand. I succeeded in many endeavors. But let me be brief; there is little time left. In one thing only I did not succeed: escaping the mechanism of the gods. Finally I did all as had been foretold. I killed a drunkard in self-defense, and so killed my father. I married his widow, my mother. Children were born to us, all cruelly deformed except my youngest daughter. A priest told me I was being punished for having committed evil, an obvious judgment; but because I wanted to know what evil, and why, I began studying the question of who I was and what I had done. To be truthful, it amounted to no more than an intensive gathering of testimonials about myself. Who was I? A man who had killed his father and taken his mother to wife, that was all. But that equation had already been worked out for me. I had only worked it out again for myself by an enormous and elaborate procedure I referred to as 'self-awareness'; I had shown that the solution of the equation was unmistakably correct. Now you may wonder if these things happened because I already knew the solution, and constructed the equation accordingly. In other words, although I claim I killed my father and coupled with my mother in all ignorance, surely the truth is that these acts had been foretold, and I committed them knowing that I had to. Or can we say that it was simply coincidental, all done in perfect ignorance? If that is so, I am no more than the victim of a calamity. I myself, this wretched man, was merely used by the gods for their diversion. But the gods had already pronounced my fate. Surely, the gods had chosen *me*, a man to whom they could reveal everything, a man who would oppose their plan but who would eventually surrender to them of his own free will, carrying out that plan to the letter. I *was* that kind of man, I knew all and was an accomplice of the gods, but my eyes, those eyes of which I had been so proud, were not able to discern it. Then in my rage I burned out my eyes and saw for the first time. Yet even that had already been prophesied. Do you remember? The blind beggar said that help would come when I had lost the light of the sun. Losing the light of the sun meant losing my eyes. And was it not said in the very first words of the prophecy that all this would happen while I remained in the light of the sun? The whole prophecy was true, and until I knew its meaning I had to perform one foul act after another until finally I destroyed my eyes. Can it be that the gods thought I was a man who would immediately grasp that meaning? If so, the gods overestimated me, since such perception is beyond human ability. Probably they were pleased that I was foolish enough to act the part of their accomplice to the very end. In that case there must be some recompense for me. And that time is now approaching . . ."

The sky grew darker and darker, and there was thunder in the distance.

Takayanagi got up from his wicker chair, opened his notebook, and wrote down the words that the blind man must then have said.

Losing the light of the sun meant that I should come to see what I had not seen until then. That did not mean myself. The question of who I am myself is not worthy of consideration. I am nothing but myself. What I first saw was the shape of those beings who had controlled all that I had done. Also I saw the intimate relation between those beings and myself. That was part of the help to come to me; but ultimate help lies somewhere far beyond knowledge and wisdom. Casting away my sight has meant losing the light of the sun, but, more than that, I am to go where the light of the sun cannot be seen. The ultimate help the gods will grant me as my final reward is no more, and no less, than death. This is what the prophecy had been telling me from the very beginning.

"You have some eccentric ideas."

Nagasawa repeated it as their car arrived at the beach inn. Takashi was driving with Asako at his side, and the two old men in the back seat.

"I don't insist on swimming. The main object is to have a few drinks at this inn, whatever it's called, and then take a little nap in the sea breeze."

"We'd both be well advised to avoid the cold water. No point reminding ourselves we're no longer young."

The shore was full of rocks, and from early August the sea became so rough that people stopped coming to swim. A few boys were ducking underwater in search of sea urchins and shells, and a woman in a flowery dress holding a parasol was walking along the rocky shore. She stepped gingerly from one rock to the next as if they felt burning hot to the soles of her bare feet.

"Was this beach always so deserted?" Takayanagi asked as they looked out from the inn.

Nagasawa shook his head. "I'm afraid I don't remember. I only came here once, and that was half a century ago."

"People tend to use the beach on the other side of that point," said Takashi, who had already stripped to his swimming trunks. "They've put up a hotel and a marina recently, and lots of people go. It's always been like this here, so I don't suppose it will change."

Asako put on her bathing suit in the next room, came in again briefly, and went down to the beach with Takashi to have a swim before lunch.

For some time the image of his daughter sliding open the door and appearing there almost naked in what was presumably a "bikini" remained with Takayanagi. Being indoors she had seemed particularly white and naked. Perhaps she had done it on purpose, wanting to show herself off. Takayanagi disliked senseless exhibitionism. Nor did he like those preposterous huge round sunglasses she was wearing.

"That gave me quite a shock. At first I thought some film star had turned up." Nagasawa also seemed taken aback by the girl's audacity, and he followed the two of them with his eyes as they made their way down to the beach.

"I didn't think she was that sort," Takayanagi said, looking rather shaken.

"But it's because she's young, I suppose. Young people will do things we can't understand."

"She's grown up into a fine girl. It's all very well for her to be properly dressed, keeping herself under control, and that suits her, too; but so does that bikini, doesn't it? Anyway, my grandson's old enough to be very interested in her."

"And she's old enough to be interested in him, I expect. But she's had nothing to do with men, and I doubt if she thinks of Takashi that way."

"I can't make out Takashi either. I don't know if he's peculiarly mature for his age or if he's still a complete child. Whichever it is, young people nowadays don't seem to go through adolescence the way we did, with pimples and all the rest. I suppose they stay children longer. Yet they can do things with a reckless nerve we grownups don't have."

"That's because they're children. Those two are probably playing with each other now like little children playing doctor."

Nagasawa gave an embarrassed grunt and started looking nervously out of the open window.

Takayanagi thought of the blind man's daughter and what they had done together in the shadow of the breakwater. Probably that too had been a kind of playing doctor. He must have been fourteen or fifteen, and she would have been twenty-six or -seven. He was already equipped for penetrating her, but he had somehow been unable to do it. In the sea nearby were many large crabs swimming about with their spatulate legs. Her body was wet with spray, and he felt like one of those crabs as he slowly clambered over her. But when he tried to kiss her lips she suddenly struck him in the face.

Then Takayanagi's father had taken her and made her his new mother. When he was twenty it was she who had tried to kiss him, and he had slapped her with his open hand. Aya reminded him that she had once fended him off.

"They're taking their time," Nagasawa said.

"Shall we start without them? The children can have lunch later." Takayanagi called the maid. "It won't be much more than ordinary fisherman's fare, but at least everything will be good and fresh."

It was indeed. Though not very attractively served, all the seafood, starting with lobster and sliced raw turbot, had a sweet fresh flavor with a strong scent of the ocean. The sake was drawn straight from the cask, and they drank it cold out of aromatic cedar cups.

The wind bells hanging above the veranda tinkled in the sea breeze, over the sound of the waves. Occasionally there was the rustle of pine branches brushing against the wooden eaves. As the sake went to their heads the colors of sky and sea became indistinguishable. The clouds crossing the sky were like ships with white sails.

"It's a good feeling, just on the verge of being drunk. Makes you forget you're going to die."

"With your constitution you needn't think about that for another ten years," replied Nagasawa, his face now red.

"It has nothing to do with my constitution. There are voices that only I shall hear, and when they call me it will be good-by to all this. I don't think it will be very long till I hear them, coming from where the river flows into the sea."

"You've had too much to drink; I can't imagine what you're talking about. If you don't mind I think I'll have a little . . ." Nagasawa lay back with his arm as a pillow and went to sleep.

Takayanagi peered beyond the narrow stretch of sandy beach to the shallow inshore sea with its many rocks, trying to make out the figures of Asako and Takashi. The one with the orange cap swimming between the rocks seemed to be Asako. As the waves broke they scattered a foam of white lace over that speck of orange.

Asako and Takashi ran with long, loping strides across the scorching sand. When they came under the shade of the pine trees the needles pricked the soles of their bare feet. At the bottom of stone steps leading up to a shrine on the hill there was a small wayside shop, sheltered by screens of marsh reeds, where an old woman was selling licorice water and old-style fizzy lemonade.

"Rustic, isn't it?" said Asako, sitting on the wide bench covered with straw matting provided for customers. "I suppose licorice water is different from arrow-root water."

"I suppose so," Takashi replied.

"When I was a child I used to drink something like this, dogtooth violet dissolved in hot sugar water, I think. That was mostly in summer, or when I was sick. I had a weak stomach."

"Sweet sake would taste good right now."

"I even drank it in winter, when I was in Kyoto and used to go up into the hills, to Takao and then down to Sagano. Can I have a bottle of fizz too?"

"You're going to have both?"

"Certainly. You don't often find these things anymore. Drinking fizz is really quite poetic: bubbles bubbling up and up, what bliss! This will be only my third bottle in my whole life."

"It's past twelve-thirty. We'd better be getting back. They're probably waiting for us, and ready for lunch."

"Waiting for us!" Asako exclaimed, stretching her white neck to drain the lemonade. "Those two will have started long ago, and they'll have had enough sake to forget all about us. Let's go for another swim."

Asako pulled the hood of her beach coat over her head, put on the huge sunglasses that seemed to project some distance from her face, and walked off, waving a cheerful good-by to the old woman squatting in her shop.

"Asako," Takashi called, and ran after her.

"My head feels a little strange," she said, almost singing the words.

"Has something happened between you and your father?"

"Only that I've had a good look at his notebook on the sly. I read all of it. *Losing the light of the sun meant that I should come to see what I had not seen until then . . . Casting away my sight has meant losing the light of the sun, but, more than that, I am to go where the light of the sun cannot be seen. The ultimate help the gods will grant me as my final reward is no more, and no less, than death.* Can you make anything of that, Takashi? I can't. All I understand is that Father is thinking about death, but this talk about gods is like talking about strangers from an unknown country. What sort of arrangement has he made with these gods, anyway? He'll be saved by them when he loses the light of the sun, which means going blind; then he'll be able to see what the gods see; and finally he'll die and go where there is no sun. That seems to be his salvation. But Father's not blind; he's got wonderful eyesight, doesn't even need reading glasses. Of course it must mean that this 'I' isn't Father at all, but that blind beggar he's talked about. Maybe he's writing a novel with the blind man as narrator."

Asako went on wondering aloud as they walked along the water's edge until they reached an old boat that had been washed halfway up on the shore. The hull seemed rotten, but the bare wood inside was bone dry. She put her foot on the edge of the boat and swarms of sea lice scurried under the hull.

Asako stretched herself out in the boat with her head at its bow.

"I want to get a tan."

"If you get too sunburned you may have a sunstroke. Especially with that fair skin of yours."

She covered her forehead and eyes with her straw hat. Takashi got into the boat too and, placing his hands on either side of her as if about to start doing push-ups, lowered his face toward hers.

"Asako!" he said.

She laid her finger across her mouth, motioning him to be silent. Then she raised her body slightly, slipped her hands behind her back, and untied the thin strip of cloth covering her breasts. The small, swelling breasts were even whiter than the surrounding skin, like the full orb of the moon at the height of day. The sun burned down on her flesh, and as it drank in the heat it seemed to be changing into some other, warmer substance.

Takashi gazed at her breasts like a well-trained dog sitting patiently looking at its dinner. Suddenly he knelt down reverently, as if performing some kind of ceremonious courtesy, and pressed his hands against the small, firm, rounded breasts. As he did so her flesh seemed to melt and flow, becoming as soft as ripe melon, and something like the butt of a pencil poked up under his hands. He put his mouth to it, a nipple that had pushed up its little towerlike head.

Asako lay dead still, looking up at the sun through her straw hat, letting the boy's lips and hands move at will. Only when the hat was brushed off and his mouth sought hers did she squirm violently and push him away.

As they walked back, trailing their shadows across the sand, Takashi said:

"I was going to tell you something in the boat, but I stopped."

"Tell me now."

"I heard from my grandfather recently that your grandmother—your father's stepmother, that is—was the daughter of that man who lived under the bridge."

"The blind beggar's daughter, you mean?" she replied in an even tone. "I knew that."

"Father, there's something I want to talk to you about," Asako said after breakfast.

These past few days Takayanagi had spent most of his time drinking with Nagasawa. Asako had never hesitated to warn him to restrain himself, but now she let him do exactly as he pleased. Takayanagi thought she might be watching a weak, senile old fool destroying himself.

"Sister telephoned."

"Ah, Masayo phoned, did she?" he said, then realized with a shock his mistake. Masayo was Takayanagi's child by his stepmother, and thus in fact Asako's elder sister; but she had been registered as the child of Takayanagi's father, which made her officially his own sister and Asako's aunt.

Asako seemed quite unconcerned.

"No; *my* sister," she corrected him, explaining that Kyoko wanted to come and stay with them for a week or so at the end of the month, bringing the children.

"So it's all arranged," he said with a forced smile.

"No, it's not. Naturally they'll only come if you don't object."

"Naturally. And naturally they all mean to stay in this house, I suppose."

"Yes." Asako shrugged. "I said myself I didn't really think that was possible."

"You needn't have bothered."

He spoke as if trying to hold down something rising within him.

"Don't bother saying what needn't be said. If people want to come, let them."

"Then it's all right?"

"I'll tell her myself. Tonight. And I'll tell her I probably won't be here."

"Are you going back to Tokyo?"

"I don't know," he said, and then, in a pleasanter tone: "There are other places."

He stood up and looked toward the oil refinery in the estuary.

"Aren't you going to switch off the air conditioner and open the windows?"

"The smoke from the factory chimneys smells too awful," she said.

Later Asako reappeared wearing cotton pants that were ragged around the ankles, as if the cuffs had been savagely ripped off.

"Just going for a drive with Takashi."

"That's a pretty funny get-up. Won't your legs be too hot in pants?"

"The car's air-conditioned. This way I won't catch cold."

He wondered if Asako and Takashi had become lovers since that trip to the beach. But surely they were too young to fall in love. He couldn't imagine what kind of emotional life two such children could have. None, probably; no passion, no soul: just two innocent little animals frisking about.

Takayanagi himself as a boy had had no soul, and hence no possibility of emotional rapport with Aya. Then when he reached young manhood he made this goddess his woman by virtually raping her. When he did that, his actions had been guided by the old blind man's words. Indeed, Takayanagi and Aya confided in each other only when Aya herself confessed that she had always intended to make her father's words come true.

Masayo and Shuji had been born; then his father had died of cancer. Takayanagi had meant to tell him the truth of his illness, but Aya stopped him, saying his father was too weak to bear such knowledge. When a man has one foot in the grave there is no point in flogging him to death.

"My father never prophesied that the two of us would kill him," she had said.

"I wonder."

"Then why didn't we?" Aya watched to see if his expression would change, and smiled.

"Don't expect us to act out the plot of a tragedy. We betrayed my father to the limit of our powers. Your own father was more than human, and so he could bring about atrocities on a grander scale. He seems like someone out of an ancient myth."

Takayanagi decided to record that in his notebook too, and went to the low cupboard and took out the small metal box in which he kept it. The box was unlocked. Ever since he had been going out so often he had been careful to keep the notebook locked in that box. If he had forgotten to lock it, Asako would certainly have read his notebook. He did not trust her.

Distracted, he forgot what he had intended to write. He sat down in the wicker chair, opened his notebook in front of him, and tried to concentrate on it. After a while he closed the notebook again.

"It's no good, I can't bring it to mind," he muttered to himself.

Perhaps all the things he had meant to bring to mind had vanished in the same way. When you no longer know anything, it is best to lay down your pen. No need to go on stringing one irrelevant word after another, only to end with Asako reading it on the sly.

He got up, wrapped the notebook in newspaper, tied the parcel firmly, and called a taxi. As he waited for it he looked at his reflection in the mirror and grinned. He had put on dark glasses and was wearing a brick-red polo shirt; except for the fact that his close-cropped hair was half gray, he looked absurdly young for his age, rather like a rich middle-aged American with thick, bronzed forearms, coming ashore from his yacht.

"Just take me down toward the refinery," he told the taxi driver. "You can go as slow as you like."

"It's pretty bleak around there, sir," the driver said, looking dubious. "Nothing much to see."

"That's all right. I used to play in the fields there when I was a boy, and before I go back to Tokyo I want to see how it's changed. When you get to the mouth of the river, turn off along the ocean and you'll come to a pine forest. About that far will do."

"The pine forest near the river? A lot of it's gone now, and it'll take a good ten minutes to get to where it starts."

"That's all right."

The taxi crossed a new bridge that had been built downstream, the estuary opening out in sweeping curves to their left, and ran along the fence of the refinery. The rough concrete embankment wall that kept the estuary from view seemed to go on forever, like the wall of an enormous prison.

"It does seem awfully desolate around here."

"Well, it's mostly tanks and pipes."

Under the burning midday sun there was no sign of workers in this landscape, and the plant seemed like a vast, barren metal graveyard. No buses or trucks were on the road, though occasionally they passed a bus stop. Takayanagi decided that this was truly an abode of the gods, but refrained from saying anything to the driver. He had the car stop at a place where the embankment wall was low, intending to climb up to look at the sea. And he had something to throw away.

The top of the embankment wall was almost over his head. Takayanagi placed the newspaper-wrapped notebook on the wall, stepped back a few paces to gather momentum, and then dashed forward and tried to scramble up it. His failure only made him determined to keep on trying. Just as he managed to get one leg on top the driver came bellowing after him, and leaped nimbly up on the wall, grabbing hold of his arm in an almost threatening way.

"Don't get any funny ideas, now!"

Apparently he had thought Takayanagi was going to do away with himself.

"No, no, I only want to throw this into the ocean, that's all." Takayanagi pointed to the paper parcel. The driver picked up the parcel, and seemed relieved. "You see? No human limbs or anything. I'm just throwing it away to keep it out of my child's hands."

"Ah. Some of those dirty pictures, is it? Or maybe a book?"

"Something like that."

The surface of the water seemed surprisingly far below. No waves broke against the wall as the dark, purplish water ebbed and flowed. The sandbar that had stretched out like a long tongue must have ended around here, but there was no sign of it anywhere.

"It must be pretty deep here."

"Pretty deep, I guess. There's a landing stage for tankers a bit farther on, and the whole sea bottom must have been dug out around here."

At that, Takayanagi hurled his parcel out into the sea. It sank into the turbid water and vanished.

Going back to the car, they set off again, and immediately arrived at the landing stage. No oil tankers were there, only a black dredging barge at work. The driver asked if he wanted to get out and take a look, but Takayanagi told him to go straight on. Finally they arrived at the pine forest.

"There's nothing but miles of pine trees from here. It's not much of a coast for scenery."

It was the same kind of pine forest you found throughout this region, the same uninhabited shore. No children swimming, no fishing boats out, a landscape unrelated to human life stretching on into the distance. But at a fork in the unpaved road they saw a car parked among the trees.

"Doing it in the car's all the rage lately," the driver said, turning to grin at Takayanagi. "There's a couple up to something in that car."

"I didn't notice," said Takayanagi, in a tired voice.

"Somebody saw us," Asako said.

"No one who'd recognize us, anyway."

"That was a taxi. Isn't it odd for a taxi to go by out here? Maybe Father has been following us to see what we're up to."

"You're imagining things. Are you really afraid of your father?"

"I'm afraid all right, anyone would be. The more you try to find out about him the less you can understand him."

"Shall we get out of the car?" Takashi asked. "In a place like this we could go for a swim naked."

"No thanks. It gives me the creeps, all that empty sea and pebbly beach, and no one anywhere along the shore. If there was someone else in the water I wouldn't mind going in."

"I'll go in, and be that someone."

"Stop it."

Asako put her arms around his neck and pulled him down, curling herself up in the awkwardly narrow space of the seat. Since she would not allow him to kiss her mouth, he fondled her breasts. She had slipped buckskin shoes on over her bare feet, and a white ankle revealed below the ragged fringe of her cotton pants attracted his attention. Grasping her foot, he pressed his lips to that ankle, then to her calf. When he pulled off her shoe and rested his cheek against the small, deeply arched sole of her foot he was aware of a faint odor of new leather and rubber.

At the same time Asako groped for his hard, tautly erect penis. When she took hold of it he closed his eyes and became quite still. Asako thought to herself he was behaving like a surgical patient under an anaesthetic. As she toyed with his penis, rubbing it between her palm and fingers, she felt as if she had a big dog on its back, with all four paws in the air.

An afternoon thunderstorm had been threatening, and as they crossed the bridge at the mouth of the estuary, large drops of rain began to beat on the roof of the car. Asako was driving them back. Near her house Takashi said:

"I don't think I want to stop in at your place today."

"We're not going to my place. We're going to finish what we just left off."

She was looking straight ahead, expressionless, and drove on past the house and turned in through the gateway of the hotel next door. She put on her big round sunglasses, then smiled quickly at Takashi as if making some sort of signal to him.

"Here?" said Takashi, putting on his own sunglasses. "You really have tremendous nerve, Asako. I don't know how you do it."

The strange darkness of the sky made Takayanagi uneasy, unable to settle down, and he wondered if perhaps he shouldn't take a quick bath. He got the bath ready, and as he was sitting soaking quietly in the wooden tub a sudden haze seemed to descend, inside the house as well as outside. He got out of the tub and hastily dried himself, peering into the garden, where a violent rain was beating down. He closed the shutters and went upstairs. The rain seemed to dash against the overhanging eaves, and he decided to have a drink as he watched it through the window. He went to get the little cask of sake and wooden cup he had received as a parting gift from the inn he had visited with Nagasawa.

The surface of the river looked as if it were being flailed by bundles of silver threads. From time to time misty clouds raced over it. The estuary and sea beyond had faded behind the rain, dissolving and mingling with the black clouds into such darkness that the landscape seemed not of this world. He wondered if there were an entrance to a sunless world over there, and as the lightning began to flash he knew it to be the same landscape he had seen that time as a boy.

The old blind man stood up.

"Now I must go."

As he spoke, large drops of rain began to strike his face and neck. The boy took his hand to lead him back to the hut, but the old man started walking in the opposite direction.

"Where are you going?"

"Come with me. I want you to bear witness."

Holding the boy's hand in his own, which felt like a hand carved out of hard wood, he walked toward the sea.

The rain began falling heavily, and thunder was approaching. He wanted to warn the old man that he might be struck by lightning, but the old man only walked faster and faster, so fast and sure that one could hardly imagine him to be blind, pushing his way through thick clusters of swamp lilies until they reached the sandy spur. Here a large tongue of soft, watery sand stretched out toward the sea. Eaten away at the edges by the incoming waves, porous with the myriad little holes drilled by the rain, the sand became softer the farther one went. Walking in bare feet felt like walking on something fleshy, something very like a tongue in fact. The boy stopped in fear. If they went any farther they might be sucked down into that mud. The old man let go his hand.

"You can watch from here. You must not come with me. And listen: If you don't watch right until the end, if you move before it's over, something terrible will happen to you. You understand? You don't need to worry about me. The voices are calling me. The voices are telling me that it is time to go with them, that I am not to keep them waiting any longer. Truly I have lived too long; I have kept them waiting a long time. The stupidity of what I have done . . ."

The boy understood where the old man was going. But what would the entrance to the country of death be like? Because he wanted to see it, the boy forgot his fear.

After two or three steps the old man turned.

"Don't come," he shouted. "It is not the time for you to come. When you go back, tell my daughter: 'You will couple with your own son and give birth to his child.' Tell her that. I have already told you what will happen to you, and that is what will happen. But you are not to go mad. Stay sane."

As the old man walked on, he seemed to grow larger and larger, ignoring the laws of perspective. The shoal of sand seemed endless, since the old man never sank beneath the waves. But the rain was heavy and the black clouds hung low, and at last he was about to be obliterated by that strange darkness. At that moment the old man was enveloped in a glow of purplish white light, and there was a bursting sound as of something being rent apart.

A great peal of thunder shook the house and made Takayanagi spill his drink. Lightning must have struck nearby, since the lamp had gone out. Already a little drunk, he wondered vaguely if the same kind of thunderbolt had fallen on the old man.

"What did happen then?" he asked himself.

The blind old man had been struck by lightning and had died. Man dies and returns to nothingness. But perhaps that old man had become more than man, had gone to some actual place. That thought still held Takayanagi in its grasp; and he found himself imagining that he might do the same. He laughed at his own stupidity and poured himself another drink.

His eyes seemed to have misted over, and he saw Asako emerge from the haze. She was soaked to the skin. Her disordered hair was dripping wet and clung to her face.

"What's happened to you? You're all drenched like some poor little beggar girl."

The blind man's daughter had looked like that as she came running through the rain that time. While he told her exactly what had happened she had said nothing but merely nodded her head. She had made no attempt to look for the body. Even after they were back in the hut and she was hanging his shirt and trousers up to dry she had still not wept.

"Are you crying?" he asked Asako, looking into her eyes. She shook her head, knelt down, and pressed her wet face against his lap. Barefoot, in those ragged pants, she was more like some little vagrant urchin clinging to him. He lifted the strands of wet hair from her neck. How she could go out in that sort of get-up with a boyfriend, and one younger than herself, he could not begin to understand. What was going on in her head? She must be emotionally empty, like a deserted wasteland, like an animal; and so she had gone off to romp like some little wild animal. The driver's words, "doing it in the car," came back to him.

Asako raised her head. Her eyes had become hard and glinting, uncanny-looking, like a wolf's eyes. Before Takayanagi could speak his mouth was stopped by the girl's lips. With a feeling of horror as if he were being savaged by an animal gone wild, he felt her lips on his. He thought he felt her hot tongue. Wondering what on earth was wrong with the girl, he put his arm around her slender shoulders, and noticed the frailty of her flesh.

Asako drew her face away from his and buried it in his chest.

"*Am* I your daughter?" she said. "I've read your notebook, you see."

Takayanagi gave a grunt of pain. The pressure on his chest was making it hard to breathe.

"If you've read it, you've read it. But such things have no meaning. All pure fantasy, something I ought to know better than to indulge in at my time of life."

"Who am I then?"

"You must decide that for yourself."

"But I can't. I must hear it from you."

"You are my daughter."

"So you are my true father, are you? As long as I can be sure of that."

"That's right. But what's happened to you today? I seem to be looking at some crazy girl. Was it Takashi?"

"No. He hasn't even kissed me. I don't think I'll see him anymore. I'll go away from here with you. We'll leave tomorrow."

"Will we?" he said, laughing at her now. "Even if you feel like playing the pathetic, grief-stricken heroine, I don't think I'll be leaving here, at least for the time being."

"But Sister's coming with the children."

"They can come. I said so this morning, didn't I? I've simply changed my own plans and will be here for the rest of the summer."

"I'm going to be awfully busy," Asako said, half sobbing and half laughing.

"You like Kyoko and the children, do you?"

"Not really. Only I'm not strong inside the way you are, Father, and I think it's nice to have relations, even if you don't particularly like them. Grandmother too."

"I can see you've been wanting to say that."

By the time Asako had taken her bath and put on her bathrobe the rain had stopped.

"There'll probably be a rainbow," she said, leaning out of the window. She could not see a rainbow.

The sun over the western hills lit up the rows of storage tanks glowing red above the black estuary.

TRANSLATED BY DENNIS KEENE

▝▘ MISHIMA YUKIO

To read any work by Mishima Yukio is now, inevitably, to see behind it the shocking images of November 25, 1970: Mishima in uniform on the balcony of the Self-Defense Force's Tokyo Headquarters haranguing the troops; Mishima committing *seppuku*, then being clumsily beheaded by his most loyal follower. In retrospect, the flamboyant burst of self-destructive energy seems, as Masao Miyoshi has observed, "called for by the shooting-star course of his life. This most talented and spirited of the postwar Japanese novelists produced over thirty novels, scores of plays, and numerous essays and pamphlets totaling well over a hundred volumes. Yet he also found time and vitality to practice *kendō* and *karate*, weight-lifting, and other body-building exercises, to sing, model, act in films, organize his own army and design its uniforms, get married, stay married, travel, run with the jet set, and entertain lavishly." Beneath the dizzying whirl of words and gestures was a volcanic pressure of feeling that this prolific writer diligently concealed.

Mishima Yukio, whose real name was Hiraoka Kimitake, was born in Tokyo in 1925, the son of a government official. He began his extraordinary literary career while still a student at the Peers' School, from which he graduated at the top of his class (he was awarded a silver watch by the Emperor). After studying law at Tokyo University he took a position in the Ministry of Finance, but resigned a year later, became a literary success with his scarifying autobiographical novel *Confessions of a Mask* (*Kamen no kokuhaku*, 1949, tr. 1958), and went on to produce in rapid succession the many brilliantly ornamented works that made him world-famous, a leading candidate for the Nobel Prize. His first novel was a highly ambiguous confession, by the austere standards of the I-novel, and for his later fiction Mishima turned to techniques as varied as the masks he assumed in order to dazzle the wider public of the mass media. His most ambitious novels—*The Temple of the Golden Pavilion* (*Kinkakuji*, 1956, tr. 1958) and the tetralogy *The Sea of Fertility* (*Hōjō no umi*, tr. 1972–74), which he began writing in 1965 and completed at the very end of his life—are works exploring his obsessive themes with the full powers of an imagination released by the freedom and security of fiction.

"The Boy Who Wrote Poetry" is a miniature portrait of the artist, an exception to his rule of keeping a strict separation between literature and life. As Mishima himself put it, he felt somehow compelled to write this story of a critical moment in his early development as a writer. In it John Nathan sees the passage in which two lines are quoted from Oscar Wilde's poem "The Grave of Keats" as a fully formulated equation already implicit in Mishima's earliest work: "*Destiny* (Genius) equals *Beauty* equals *Death*. The poet believes that his death has been ordained in the same preestablished harmony which has endowed him with genius. Genius and death are therefore consubstantially his destiny. Death is a *benefaction* because it is proof of the poet's genius and because, as his destiny, it is the aim and object of his life. The death the boy anticipates is a skyrocketing, incandescent death: Beauty itself." Nathan adds that the passage "assumes an even fuller significance when the phrase Mishima quotes from the Wilde poem is completed: 'Taken from life when life and love were new / The youngest of the martyrs here is lain, / *Fair as Sebastian, and as early slain.'* The figure of Saint Sebastian pierced by arrows was the central image in Mishima's sadomasochistic eroticism."

Behind the self-portrait of the cold, gifted schoolboy lies the ecstatically morbid image of Guido Reni's "Saint Sebastian" described in *Confessions of a Mask*—and of Mishima himself, photographed shortly before his death in an imitation of that pose, "arms roped above his head to a tree branch and arrows burning deliciously into his armpit and flank."

❖ The Boy Who Wrote Poetry

(*Shi o kaku shōnen,* 1954)

Poem after poem flowed with complete ease from his pen. In no time he would use up the thirty pages in one of his Peers' School notebooks. How was it possible, the boy wondered, that he could write two or three poems a day? When he was sick in bed for a week he put together *One Week: An Anthology*. He cut an oval out of the cover of his notebook to reveal the word "Poesies" on the title page. Below it, in English, he wrote "12th–18th May 1940."

His poems were attracting the notice of upperclassmen. It's all nonsense, he thought. They're making a fuss just because I'm fifteen.

But the boy was confident of his genius. He began to address his seniors with a decided impudence. He wanted to stop using phrases like "It seems to be." In all matters he would have to take care to say "It is."

Too much masturbating had made him anemic. But his own ugliness had hardly begun to bother him. Poetry was a thing apart from such physical feelings of revulsion. Poetry was apart from everything. From the subtle lies in a poem he learned the art of subtle lying. All that mattered was that the words be beautiful. Every day he pored over the dictionary.

Whenever the boy felt ecstatic, a world of metaphor materialized before his eyes. Caterpillars made lace of cherry leaves; a pebble flung past shimmering oaks soared off to the sea. Cranes ripped into the crumpled sheet of the overcast sea to search below for the drowned. Peaches surrounded by whirling gold bugs were lightly powdered with makeup; the air, like an arc of flames behind a statue, swirled and twisted around scampering people. Sunset was an omen of evil; it ran in deep tinctures of iodine. The winter trees thrust their wooden legs at the sky. And a girl lay nude by a stove, her body like a burning rose. He walked up to the window, only to find an artificial flower. Her skin, goose-pimpled in the cold, became one frayed petal of a velvet flower.

It was when the world was transformed in this way that he knew bliss. The boy wasn't surprised that the birth of a poem would bring him this kind of bliss. He knew, in his head, that a poem is brought forth from sadness, malediction, or despair, from the exact center of solitude. Yet for that to be the case with him, he would need a deeper interest in himself, some problem to tax himself with. Although he was convinced of his genius, he was curiously without interest in himself. He found the outside world more fascinating. It would be more precise to say that in those moments when, for no apparent reason, he himself was happy, the world unresistingly assumed the forms he would have it take.

Did poetry come to him to guarantee his moments of happiness, or was happiness made possible by the birth of his poems? He wasn't sure. All he knew was that this happiness was of a different order from the kind he felt when his parents bought him something he had wanted for a long time or took him on a trip, and that this was a happiness known to him alone.

The boy had no taste for sustained, intent scrutiny of either the outer world or his inner self. If the object catching his attention was not at once transformed into some image—if in May at noon the white glimmer of young leaves did not become the dark sheen of night cherry blossoms—he would quickly grow bored and stop looking. Substantial, uncongenial objects that could not be transformed he dismissed coldly: "There's no poetry in that."

One morning, having anticipated the questions on a test, he hurried through the answers, placed his answer sheet on the teacher's desk without bothering to look it over, and left the room before any of his classmates. As he was crossing the deserted grounds toward the school gate his eye caught the glimmer of the golden ball at the top of the flagpole. He was seized with an ineffable feeling of happiness. The flag was down. It wasn't a holiday. But he felt that the day was a holiday for his own spirit, and that the glimmer of that ball was celebrating it. The boy's mind slipped easily away, and turned to poetry. The ecstasy of this

moment. The fullness of this solitude. The extraordinary lightness. Lucid intoxication in every corner of his being. The harmony between the outer world and
his inner self . . .

When this state failed to come naturally, he would try to use something
around him to force the same intoxication. Holding a cigarette case of striped
tortoise shell to the light and peering through it at his room. Shaking his mother's
cosmetics bottle, and watching the tumultuous dance of powder leave the clear
surface of the liquid and quietly settle to the bottom.

Without the slightest emotion he used words like "supplication," "malediction," and "disdain."

The boy was in the Literature Club. One of the committee members had
lent him a key, enabling him to get into the clubhouse alone any time he wanted
to immerse himself in his favorite dictionaries. He liked the pages about the
romantic poets in the *Dictionary of World Literature:* in their portraits they
didn't have shaggy old beards, but were all young and beautiful.

He was interested in the brevity of the poets' lives. Poets must die young.
Even a premature death was far off for one only fifteen; from this arithmetical
security the boy was able to consider premature death without feeling troubled.

He liked Wilde's sonnet, "The Grave of Keats":

> Taken from life when life and love were new
> The youngest of the martyrs here is lain

The youngest of the martyrs here is lain. There was something astonishing about
how actual disasters befell these poets like benefactions. He believed in preordained harmony. The preordained harmony in a poet's biography. Believing this
was one and the same as believing in his own genius.

It gave him pleasure to imagine long elegies to him, posthumous fame. But
to imagine his own corpse made him feel a little awkward. Ardently he thought,
Let me live like a skyrocket. With my whole being let me paint the night sky
for a moment, then instantly burn out. He considered all sorts of ways to live,
and could think of no other for him. But suicide was repulsive. Preordained
harmony would find a more satisfactory way to kill him.

Poetry was beginning to make him lazy in spirit. If he had been more
diligent he would have thought more passionately of suicide.

At morning assembly the student monitor called his name. That meant a
more severe reprimand than being summoned to the teacher's office. "You *know*
what's the matter," his friends said intimidatingly. His face went white, and his
hands shook.

The monitor, as he waited for the boy, was writing something with a steel
tong in the dead ashes of the hibachi. When the boy went in, the monitor said
gently: "Sit down." There was no chiding. He said he had read the boy's poems

in the alumni magazine. He proceeded to ask him many questions about poetry and about his home life. Finally he said, "There are two types, Schilla and Goethe. You know Schilla, don't you?"

"You mean Schiller?"

"Yes. Don't ever try to become a Schilla. Become a Goethe."

The boy left the monitor's room and dragged himself back to class, dissatisfied and scowling. He had never read either Goethe or Schiller. But he knew their portraits. "I don't like Goethe. He's an old man. Schiller is young. I like him better."

The chairman of the Literature Club, a youth named R who was five years the boy's senior, looked after him. He took a liking to R too, because R clearly believed himself an unrecognized genius, and acknowledged the boy's genius without the least regard to the difference in their age. Geniuses should be friends.

R was the son of a peer. He affected the airs of a Villiers de l'Isle-Adam, was proud of his family's noble lineage, and infused his works with a decadent nostalgia for the tradition of aristocratic letters. R also had published a private edition of his own poems and essays. This made the boy envious.

Every day they exchanged long letters. They enjoyed this routine. Almost every morning a letter from R came to the boy's house in a Western-style envelope the color of apricots. No matter how long the letters were, they could only be so heavy; it was their curiously bulky lightness, the feeling that they were stuffed with buoyancy, that delighted the boy. At the end of the letter could be inscribed a recent poem, often written that very day, or if there wasn't time, an older poem.

The letters were trivial in content. They began with criticism of the poem each had sent in the letter before, and proceeded into an endless banter, in which each related the music he had heard, daily episodes in his family, impressions of girls he found beautiful, reports of books he had read, poetic experiences in which worlds would be revealed from single words, and so on. Neither the twenty-year-old youth nor the fifteen-year-old boy tired of this habit.

But the boy recognized in R's letters a faint melancholy, the shadow of some slight unease that he knew was never present in his own. An apprehension about reality, an anxiety about something that he would soon have to face gave R's letters a certain quality of loneliness and pain. The untroubled boy perceived this quality as an irrelevant shadow that would never fall on him.

Will I ever awaken to ugliness? The boy never considered such problems; he never even anticipated them. Old age, for example, which finally assailed Goethe and which he had to endure for many years. Such a thing as old age would never come to him. Even the prime of youth, which some call beautiful and others ugly, was still far away. Whatever ugliness he discovered in himself, he forgot.

The boy was captive to that illusion which confuses art and artist, the illusion which naïve and pampered girls all project on the artist. He had no interest in the analysis and study of the being that was himself, yet he always had dreams for himself. He belonged to the world of metaphor, the endless kaleidoscope in which that girl's nakedness became an artificial flower. One who makes beautiful things cannot be ugly. The thought was stubbornly embedded in the boy's mind, but somehow that most important question behind it never occurred to him: Was it necessary for one who is beautiful to make beautiful things?

Necessary? The boy would have laughed at the word. For his poems were not born from necessity. They came naturally; even if he tried to deny them, the poems themselves moved his hand and made him write. Necessity assumed some lack. There was nothing he could construe as a lack. First of all, he reduced all the sources of his poetry to the single word "genius," and he couldn't believe that there might be some deep lack inside himself that he was unconscious of. Even if he did believe it, rather than express it with the word "lack," he preferred to call it "genius."

Not that the boy was incapable of criticizing his own poems. For example, there was one four-line poem that his seniors praised lavishly; he thought it frivolous and was embarrassed by it. It was a poem to this effect: just as the cut edge of such transparent glass as this is tinted blue, so your limpid eyes may be hiding a measure of love.

Of course the praise of others delighted the boy, but his arrogance kept him from drowning in it. The truth was that he was not even very impressed with R's talent. R certainly had enough talent to stand out among the upperclassmen in the Literature Club, but that meant nothing. There was a frigid spot in the boy's heart. If R had not so exhausted his verbal treasury to praise the boy's poetic talent, the boy would probably have made no effort to recognize R's.

He was well aware that the price for his occasional taste of that quiet pleasure was the absence of any rough, boyish excitability. There was a baseball series called the "League Games" played twice a year, in the spring and fall, between the middle grades of the Peers' School and the middle schools affiliated with it. When the Peers' School suffered a defeat, the juniors who had cheered the players gathered around them after the game and joined in their sobbing. He never cried. He was never in the least sad.

"What's there to get so sad about, just because we lost a baseball game?" He wondered about these crying faces, so alien to him. The boy knew that he felt things easily, but his sensitivity lay in a direction different from everyone else's. Things that brought others to tears failed to echo at all in his heart.

The boy began to turn more and more to love as the material for his poetry. He had never been in love. But he was bored with basing his poetry only on the transformations within nature, and he turned to singing of metamorphoses occurring from moment to moment in the soul. He had no qualms about singing of things he had yet to experience himself. There was something in him that had always believed art to be exactly this. He did not at all lament his lack of experience. There was neither opposition nor tension between the world he had yet to experience and the world inside himself. Thus there was no need for him to go out of his way to believe in the superiority of his own inner world; a sort of unreasonable confidence even enabled him to believe that there was not one emotion in this world he had yet to feel. For the boy thought that to a spirit as keenly sensitive as his own, the archetypes of all emotion were already apprehended, though sometimes only as premonitions, and rehearsed, and that all experience could be constructed with the appropriate combinations of these basic elements of emotion. And what were the elements of emotion? He had his own arbitrary definition: "Words."

Not that the boy had attained a usage of words that was genuinely his own. But he thought that the very universality of many of those words he found in the dictionary made them varied in meaning and diverse in content, and therefore available for use in a personal, unique way by an individual. It didn't necessarily occur to him that only experience could bring words to creative fruition and lend them color.

The first encounter between our inner world and language brings something entirely individual into contact with something universal. It is also the occasion when the individual, refined by the universal, comes into its own for the first time. The fifteen-year-old boy was more than adequately familiar with this indescribable inner experience. For the disharmony he felt when he encountered a new word also led him to experience an emotion previously unknown to him. And it also helped him maintain an outward calmness incompatible with his youth. When assaulted by a certain emotion, the disharmony elicited in him would lead him to recall elements of the disharmony he had felt before a word. He would remember the word, and use it to fit a name to the emotion before him. The boy became practiced at taking care of emotion in this way. Thus he came to know all things: "humiliation," "agony," "despair," "execration," "the joy of love," "the sorrow of love's loss."

It would have been easy to call this imagination. But the boy hesitated to do so. Imagination requires the kind of empathy in which the self feels pain in imagining the pain of others. The boy in his coldness never felt the pain of others. Without feeling the slightest pain he would whisper to himself: "That's pain. That's something I know."

It was a sunny afternoon in May. Classes were out. The boy was walking toward the Literature Club room to see if there was someone he might have a talk with before going home. On the way he ran into R, who said: "I was hoping I'd find you. Let's talk."

They entered the barracklike structure where old classrooms had been divided up with plywood walls to house various clubs. The Literature Club was in a corner of the dark first floor. From the Sports Club they could hear noises and laughing voices and the school song, from the Music Club the distant echo of a piano. R slipped his key into the keyhole in the dirty wooden door. It was a door that, unlocked, still wouldn't open until he threw his body against it.

The room was empty. Inside was the familiar smell of dust. R went in and opened the window, slapped his dust-covered hands together, and sat down on a broken chair.

As soon as they had settled down the boy began to talk. "I saw a dream in color last night. I was going to write you about it as soon as I got home." (The boy fancied dreams in color to be the special prerogative of the poet.) "There's a hill of red earth. The red earth is very bright, and the sunset is shining a brilliant red, so the color of the earth is even more striking. And then from the right comes a man dragging a long chain. A peacock four or five times bigger than the man is tied to the end of the chain, and the peacock's feathers are all folded in as he's slowly dragged along, there in front of my eyes. The peacock is bright green. His whole body is green, and the green is glittering beautifully. I kept my eyes on that peacock as it was dragged into the distance, until it was dragged out of sight . . . It was a fantastic dream. My dreams are so vivid when they're in color, almost too vivid. I wonder what a green peacock would mean to Freud."

"I wonder."

R sounded only half-interested. He was not his usual self. His paleness was the same, but he lacked the familiar quiet fever in his voice, the passionate response. Apparently he had been listening to the boy's monologue with indifference. No, he hadn't been listening at all.

The foppishly high collar of R's student uniform was sprinkled lightly with dandruff. The dark light made his golden Cherry Blossom badge glow, and magnified his somewhat prominent nose. His nose was handsomely shaped if a bit too large; now it wore an unmistakable expression of anxiety. R's distress seemed to have become manifest in his nose.

On the desk were scattered old dust-covered proof sheets, rulers, red pencils lacking lead, bound volumes of the alumni magazine, manuscript paper on which someone had begun to write. The boy loved this literary confusion. R shuffled the ancient proof sheets as if forlornly putting things in their place, and got his slender white fingers dusty. The boy grinned. But R clicked his tongue in annoyance, slapped the dust from his hands, and said:

"The truth is, there was something I wanted to talk to you about today."

"What is it?"

"The truth is," R faltered, then spat the words out. "I'm suffering. Something unbearable has happened."

"Are you in love?" the boy inquired coolly.

"Yes."

R explained the circumstances. He was in love with someone else's young wife, had been discovered by his father, and forced to stop seeing her.

The boy's eyes opened wide, and he stared at R. "Here's someone in love.

For the first time I'm seeing love right in front of my eyes." It was not a very beautiful sight. In fact, it was rather unpleasant. R's usual vitality was gone; he was crestfallen. He looked morose. The boy had often seen this kind of expression on the faces of people who had lost something or missed a train.

Still, being taken into confidence by a senior did tickle the boy's vanity. He was not unhappy. He made a valiant effort to assume a look of melancholy. But the banality of the appearance of a person in love was a little hard to bear.

Finally he found some words of consolation.

"That's terrible. But I'm sure a good poem will come out of it all."

Limply, R replied: "This is no time for poetry."

"But isn't poetry salvation at a time like this?"

The happiness lent by a poem's creation flashed through the boy's mind. He thought any sorrow or agony could be struck away with the power of that happiness.

"It doesn't work like that. You don't understand yet."

The utterance wounded the boy's self-esteem. His heart chilled, and he plotted a revenge.

"But if you were a real poet, a genius, wouldn't poetry save you at such a time?"

"Goethe wrote *Werther*," R answered, "and saved himself from suicide. But he was able to write it only because, deep in his heart, Goethe knew that nothing, not poetry or anything else, could save him, and that the only thing left was suicide."

"Then why didn't Goethe commit suicide? If writing and suicide are the same thing, then why didn't he choose suicide? Because he was a coward? Or because he was a genius?"

"Because he was a genius."

"Then . . ."

The boy was going to press one more question, but he didn't understand it himself. The idea rose vaguely in his mind that what had saved Goethe from suicide was his egotism. He was seized with the desire to use this notion to defend himself.

R's utterance "You don't understand yet" had wounded him deeply. At his age, nothing was stronger than feelings of inferiority about age. Although he didn't come out and speak it, a logic most aptly derisive of R was born in the boy's mind: "He's no genius. Why, he falls in love."

R's love was certainly a true one. It was the kind of love a genius must never have. R took the love of Fujitsubo and Genji, the love of Pelléas and Mélisande, the love of Tristan and Isolde, the love of the Princesse de Clèves and the Duc de Nemours as illustrations of illicit love to ornament his distress.

As the boy listened, he was shocked that there wasn't one element in R's confession he didn't already know. All had been written, all had been anticipated, all had been rehearsed. The love written in books was more vital than this. The love sung in poems was more beautiful. He couldn't comprehend why R would go to reality for dreams more sublime. He didn't understand where this craving for the mediocre came from.

R seemed to have been soothed by his own words, and he now began an endless recounting of his girl's beauty. She must have been an extraordinary beauty, but the boy couldn't see a single image of her. "Next time I'll show you a picture," R said. Then, a little embarrassed, he wound up dramatically:

"She told me I have a really handsome forehead."

The boy looked at the forehead below R's combed-back hair. The skin on his prominent brow glimmered faintly in the dim light coming through the doorway; it looked as if two fistlike bumps were jutting out on his forehead.

What a beetle brow, the boy thought. He didn't have the slightest feeling it was handsome. Mine bulges too, he told himself. Having a beetle brow and being handsome are not the same thing.

It was then that the boy awoke to something. He had seen the ridiculous impurity that always works its way into an awareness of love or life, that ridiculous impurity without which we cannot survive in either: namely, the conviction that your beetle brow is handsome.

The boy felt that he too, if in a more intellectual way, might have been making his way through life on a similar kind of conviction. Something in the thought made him shudder. "What are you thinking about?" R asked in his usual gentle tone.

The boy bit his lip and smiled. It was slowly getting dark outside. He could hear shouts from where the Baseball Club was practicing. As a ball struck by a bat shot into the sky, there was a dry, lucid echo.

Someday maybe I'll stop writing poetry too, the boy thought for the first time in his life. But he was yet to learn that he had never been a poet.

TRANSLATED BY IAN H. LEVY

■KAWABATA YASUNARI

In 1968, during the celebrations of the Meiji Centennial, Kawabata Yasunari became the first Japanese Nobel laureate in literature. The citation says that he was given the award "for his narrative mastery, which with great sensibility expresses the essence of the Japanese mind." A man who prized solitude, who indeed had a solitary, faraway look even in the midst of throngs, Kawabata had long before commented on the emptiness of fame; yet he dutifully attended the innumerable ceremonies, parties, and functions which were held in his honor. After returning from Stockholm he made several more trips abroad, to lecture or to attend writers' conferences; in 1971 he campaigned actively for a friend who was running for Governor of Tokyo. He committed suicide alone in his studio near Kamakura in April, 1972, leaving no note or explanation.

Kawabata Yasunari was born in Osaka in 1899. He lost his parents while still an infant; his grandmother and only sister died shortly afterward; he was fourteen at the death of his grandfather, with whom he had lived alone since the age of seven. After that he lived in a middle-school dormitory, until he left Osaka to attend the elite First Higher School in Tokyo. His literary career was under way before he graduated from Tokyo Imperial University in 1924. Soon his reputation was established by the tiny vignettes to which he gave the name *tanagokoro no shōsetsu* ("palm-of-the-hand stories"), and by a wistful autobiographical tale, *The Izu Dancer* (*Izu no odoriko*, 1926, tr. 1955).

None of Kawabata's major novels was completed until after World War II. His long works took shape very slowly, one fragmentary episode being added to another from time to time, as if by a leisurely process of free association. Thus, *Snow Country* (*Yukiguni*, tr. 1956) began as a short story. The material stretched over into a second installment, published the same month (January, 1935) in a magazine with a later deadline. Further chapters were added—two more toward the end of the year, two in 1936, and so on—until after many extensions and revisions a presumably final version was completed in 1947. A more tenuous character study, *Thousand Cranes* (*Sembazuru*, tr. 1958), was published as a book in 1951, but further episodes continued to appear sporadically in succeeding years. Instead of analyzing his characters at length or showing them in sustained dramatic scenes, Kawabata prefers to hint at their inner lives by noting gestures, bits of startling dialogue, momentary feelings. The emphasis is on the immediate moment, with its memories and desires. Such moments, strung together with the vibrant irrational continuity of the traditional Japanese genre of linked verse (*renga*), the historical precursor of the haiku, follow one another in an impression-istic, meandering manner which conveys a keen awareness of emotional states and of the natural world.

Kawabata wrote well over a hundred very short stories—each only a few pages—and once said that these *tanagokoro no shōsetsu* were his favorite works. Most of them were written while he was in his twenties. They were his "youthful poetry." "Most literary men write poetry when they are young, but I wrote these vignettes instead." Later he found some of them repellent: "I can't help feeling antipathy toward the self I see in them." Still, he continued writing *tanagokoro no shōsetsu*, publishing some two dozen during his most productive postwar years. "The Pomegranate" (*Zakuro*) appeared in 1945, "The Camellia" (*Sazanka*) in 1946, "The Plum" (*Kōbai*) in 1948, "The Jay" (*Kakesu*) and "Summer and Winter" (*Natsu to fuyu*) in 1949, "The Bamboo Leaves" (*Sasabune*) in 1950, and "The Cereus" (*Gekka bijin*) in 1963, near the end of this creative period in his life. Within these brief tales may be found not only the familiar elements of Kawabata's wider fictional world—the drifting constellations of human rela-tionships, the recurrent beauties of nature—but also the somber themes of his late masterpiece *The Sound of the Mountain* (*Yama no oto*, 1954, tr. 1970): awareness of a new era, of change and loss, and a quiet, bittersweet resignation to solitude, old age, and approaching death.

❖ Seven Very Short Stories

THE POMEGRANATE

In the high wind that night the pomegranate tree was stripped of its leaves.

The leaves lay in a circle around the base.

Kimiko was startled to see it naked in the morning, and wondered at the flawlessness of the circle. She would have expected the wind to disturb it.

There was a pomegranate, a very fine one, left behind in the tree.

"Just come and look at it," she called to her mother.

"I had forgotten." Her mother glanced up at the tree and went back to the kitchen.

It made Kimiko think of their loneliness. The pomegranate over the veranda too seemed lonely and forgotten.

Two weeks or so before, her seven-year-old nephew had come visiting, and had noticed the pomegranates immediately. He had scrambled up into the tree. Kimiko had felt that she was in the presence of life.

"There is a big one up above," she called from the veranda.

"But if I pick it I can't get back down."

It was true. To climb down with pomegranates in both hands would not be easy. Kimiko smiled. He was a dear.

Until he had come the house had forgotten the pomegranate. And until now they had forgotten it again.

Then the fruit had been hidden in the leaves. Now it stood clear against the sky.

There was strength in the fruit and in the circle of leaves at the base. Kimiko went and knocked it down with a bamboo pole.

It was so ripe that the seeds seemed to force it open. They glistened in the sunlight when she laid it on the veranda, and the sun seemed to go on through them.

She felt somehow apologetic.

Upstairs with her sewing at about ten, she heard Keikichi's voice. Though the door was unlocked, he seemed to have come around to the garden. There was urgency in his voice.

"Kimiko, Kimiko!" her mother called. "Keikichi is here."

Kimiko had let her needle come unthreaded. She pushed it into the pin-cushion.

"Kimiko had been saying how she wanted to see you again before you leave." Keikichi was going to war. "But we could hardly go and see you without an invitation, and you didn't come and didn't come. It was good of you to come today."

She asked him to stay for lunch, but he was in a hurry.

"Well, do at least have a pomegranate. We grew it ourselves." She called up to Kimiko again.

He greeted her with his eyes, as if it were more than he could do to wait for her to come down. She stopped on the stairs.

Something warm seemed to come into his eyes, and the pomegranate fell from his hand.

They looked at each other and smiled.

When she realized that she was smiling she flushed. Keikichi got up from the veranda.

"Take care of yourself, Kimiko."

"And you."

He had already turned away and was saying good-by to her mother.

Kimiko looked on at the garden gate after he had left.

"He was in such a hurry," said her mother. "And it's such a fine pomegranate."

He had left it on the veranda.

Apparently he had dropped it as that warm something came into his eyes and he was beginning to open it. He had not broken it completely in two. It lay with the seeds up.

Her mother took it to the kitchen and washed it, and handed it to Kimiko.

Kimiko frowned and pulled back, and then, flushing once more, took it in some confusion.

Keikichi would seem to have taken a few seeds from the edge.

With her mother watching her, it would have been strange for Kimiko to refuse to eat. She bit nonchalantly into it. The sourness filled her mouth. She felt a kind of sad happiness, as if it were penetrating far down inside her.

Uninterested, her mother had stood up.

She went to a mirror and sat down. "Just look at my hair, will you. I said good-by to Keikichi with this wild mop of hair."

Kimiko could hear the comb.

"When your father died," her mother said softly, "I was afraid to comb my hair. When I combed my hair I would forget what I was doing. When I came to myself it would be as if your father were waiting for me to finish."

Kimiko remembered her mother's habit of eating what her father had left on his plate.

She felt something pull at her, a happiness that made her want to weep.

Her mother had probably given her the pomegranate because of a reluctance to throw it away. Only because of that. It had become a habit not to throw things away.

Alone with her private happiness, Kimiko felt shy before her mother.

She thought that it had been a better farewell than Keikichi could have been aware of, and that she could wait any length of time for him to come back.

She looked toward her mother. The sun was falling on the paper doors beyond which she sat at her mirror.

She was somehow afraid to bite into the pomegranate on her knee.

THE CAMELLIA

In this, the second autumn since the War, there have been four childbirths in my neighborhood of ten households.

The oldest of the mothers, also the most prolific, had twins. They were both girls, but one died two weeks later. The mother had so much milk that she gave some to the child in the house next door, which had its first girl, after two boys. I was asked to name the girl, and I chose the name Kazuko. Kazuko could conceivably be numbered among difficult and irregular readings for the character with which it is written, and I certainly did not want to complicate the girl's life; but I chose the name because that character is the one with which "peace" is written.

The twins were both girls and four of the five children born in the neighborhood were girls. People laughed and said that we were seeing the results of the new constitution, and in the joke too I felt peace.

Probably it was mere chance that four-fifths of the children were girls, and probably my neighborhood association was unusually prolific; but there was a good harvest of babies that autumn the country over. It was, of course, a gift of peace. The birth rate had fallen during the War, and now it soared, most naturally, since young husbands had come home from the War. Yet it was not only in the families of returned soldiers that babies were born. There were babies as well in houses whose fathers had stayed at home. There were rather astonishing births to middle-aged parents. The sense of security produced by the end of the War had in turn produced children.

Nothing showed peace in more concrete form. It was the most personal and instinctive of phenomena, quite indifferent to defeat and deprivation and population problems. It was like the bursting forth of an obstructed spring, like the sprouting of withered grass. We may rejoice if congratulations are in order for revival and liberation. There is also an element of the animal in it all, something to make us a little sorry for the race.

No doubt the babies helped their parents forget the weariness of war.

For me, now fifty, the end of the War did not bring children. An aging marriage had only become blander during the War years, and habits did not change with the return of peace.

I awoke from the War to find that the evening of life was approaching. I told myself that it should not be so, but the defeat brought physical and spiritual debilitation. It was as if our country and our time had withered, and as if, in quiet solitude, I were gazing from another world upon the glow of life.

The mother of the lone boy was the youngest of the four mothers. Though she looked sturdy enough, a delicate frame made the delivery a slow one. It was said that on the second day, incapable of urinating through a tube, she got up. It was her first child, though she had had a miscarriage.

My sixteen-year-old daughter was much interested in all these babies. She visited the families with whom she felt at home, and talked of them. When she would suddenly run out of the house it would be to go see a baby. A sudden urge seemed to take her.

"Mrs. Shimamura says the other baby has come back," she said one day, sitting down beside me. "Do you think it has?"

"No."

"Oh?"

She looked disappointed. Not so much disappointed, perhaps, as short of breath after the run home. I was uncertain. Perhaps I had been wrong in my quick denial.

"You've been to see the Shimamura baby again?" I asked quietly.

She nodded.

"Is it all that pretty?"

"It's too early to tell."

"Oh?"

"Mrs. Shimamura came in while I was with it. She said it was the other baby back again. She had another baby, you remember? I suppose that is what she was talking about."

"I wonder." My answer was vague, though again I leaned in the direction of denial. "I should imagine that a mother would feel that way. But I wonder. We don't even know whether the other was a boy or a girl."

"That's true." She nodded briefly.

Though I still felt uneasy, she did not seem to take the matter very seriously, and that was the end of it. Since the miscarriage had been in the sixth month, perhaps it had after all been possible to tell the sex of the baby; but I said no more.

Both the Shimamuras were saying the earlier baby had come back—or so I heard from someone in the neighborhood.

I had thought it a rather morbid notion, but changed my mind. Such beliefs had in the past been common and seemed healthy enough. Nor had they died out in our own day. Perhaps the Shimamuras felt a certainty none of the rest of us could have that the other baby had been reborn. There could be no doubt, even if it was no more than sentimentality, that it brought comfort and happiness.

The earlier baby had been the result of a three-days' leave when Shimamura's unit was being transferred. He had been away when the miscarriage occurred, and the second baby came upwards of a year after his return. There was sorrow and compensation.

My daughter had referred to "the other baby" as if it were a finished human being, but of course no one else treated it as such. Probably only the Shimamuras thought of it as if it had lived. I could not myself say whether or not it had. It was in the womb and that was all. It did not know sunlight and perhaps it had no soul. But there is little to choose among us, and perhaps it had the purest and happiest life of all. There was in any event something, some urge to live.

No one, of course, could argue that this child and the other had come from the same cells. Nor can we recognize with certainty a relationship between the miscarriage and the pregnancy. We have no way of knowing where it comes from, the urge to life. We would be hard put even to say whether earlier life and later stand in isolation, or whether all life is part of a flow. Reason tells us that the notion of the rebirth of the first child, the dead child, is unscientific, and that is all. It is as difficult to find evidence that there is not rebirth as that there is.

I felt somehow in sympathy with the Shimamuras, and somehow too in sympathy with the miscarried baby, until then nothing to me. I felt as if it had lived.

Being a sort who insisted on getting up the second day after delivery, Mrs. Shimamura would be someone who liked tidiness and pretty things. My daughter would go to her with problems about knitting and the crafts she was learning in school. Until relatives had taken refuge from the Tokyo bombings, Mrs. Shimamura had lived alone with her mother, and my daughter evidently felt comfortable with them. I was charged with fire prevention for the neighborhood association and I worried rather a lot about the old mother and the pregnant daughter whose husband was off at war.

I had been made fire marshal because I alone of the men in the neighborhood was at home in the daytime. Perhaps I was qualified too because, being of a timid nature, I did not make demands on people. I could read and write the night watch away, and it was my policy not to disturb people's sleep. I went my rounds and awakened no one, and fortunately in Kamakura that was enough.

One evening when the plums were in bloom a light seemed to be coming from the Shimamura kitchen. As I tried to look over the gate my walking stick fell inside. I meant to go for it the next day, but did not, thinking that an Occidental walking stick dropped in the night behind a house occupied only by women might seem suggestive.

Mrs. Shimamura brought it back the next afternoon. She called my daughter to the gate.

"Your father dropped it when he was doing the rounds last night."

"Really? Where?"

"Inside our back gate."

"Very careless of him."

"It must have been dark."

It was in a mountain valley behind Kamakura. When there was an air-raid alarm I would be the first to take refuge. When I had climbed to the cave that was our shelter, I would look down over the neighborhood.

There had been an attack of carrier planes from early in the morning. There was a great roaring overhead, and there was shooting.

"Be careful, Mrs. Shimamura," I called, going a few steps from the cave.

"The birds, the little birds. See how frightened they are."

There were two or three little birds in a large plum tree. They were trying to fly from branch to branch, but, in a confusion of wings, were making no progress. The wings were like little spasms in the narrow space enclosed by the branches. Even when the birds came to a branch they seemed unable to take hold, but beat their wings and seemed about to fall feet forward over the branch.

From the cave, Mrs. Shimamura looked on at the quivering of the birds. Her knees tight in her arms, she was looking up at them.

Something fell with a sharp report into the bamboo thicket beside us.

With my feelings of sympathy at the story of the reborn Shimamura child came the memory of the quivering birds. Mrs. Shimamura had been carrying the first child at the time.

The second child was safely delivered.

There were many miscarriages during the War, and few births. There were many female disorders. Now, this autumn, there were four births in ten houses.

As I walked with my daughter down the lane beside the Shimamura house, I saw that a camellia at the hedge was coming into bloom. I am fond of the autumn camellia, perhaps because of its season.

Suddenly sad for all the children who were denied sunlight because of the War, I was sad too for the life that had gone from me during the War. I wondered if it would be reborn into something somewhere.

THE PLUM

Sitting opposite each other and looking up at the two or three red blossoms on the old plum tree, the mother and father were having an argument.

For some decades now, the first blossoms had come out on that same lower branch. It had not changed a bit, said the father, since the mother had come to the house as a bride. She did not remember, said the mother. This evasion annoyed him. She had had no time for plums, she said. She had wasted her time, he said. The trouble seemed to be that she was disinclined to share his feeling for the brevity of human life compared to the life of the old plum.

The conversation moved on to New Year's sweets. He said that on the second of January he had brought sweets from the Fugetsudo. She said that she had no recollection of them.

"But I remember very well that I had the car stop at both the Meiji and the Fugetsudo, and I bought them at both places."

"I remember the Meiji. But you have not once bought anything at the Fugetsudo since I have been in this house."

"You do make sweeping statements."

"You have never brought me any."

"But you ate them. I know I brought them."

"You make me uncomfortable. You dreamed of them. You're talking about something you dreamed of."

"Oh?"

Out in the kitchen getting lunch, the daughter listened to the argument. She knew the truth, but felt no urge to reveal it. She stood smiling beside the kettle.

"You're sure you brought them home?" The mother seemed by way of recognizing at least that the father may have made the purchase.

"I had them—but did I maybe leave them in the car?" He was wavering.

"If you had left them in the car the driver would have brought them. He wouldn't just have gone off with them. It was a company car."

"That's true."

The daughter was a little uneasy.

It made her uneasy that her mother should have forgotten, and that her father should have let his confidence be shaken so easily.

He had taken a walk on the second of January and had the car follow, and he had bought a large box of sweet rice cakes at the Fugetsudo. Her mother had helped eat them.

There was silence, after which with great calm, the mother remembered.

"Oh, those! You did, didn't you."

"I did."

"We had too many."

"And I bought them."

"But did you buy such cheap things at the Fugetsudo?"

"I did."

"I remember. We gave them away to someone. All wrapped up. Who would it have been?"

"Yes. You gave them to someone." He spoke as if a stiffness in the neck had suddenly gone away. "To Fusae, maybe?"

"Fusae, maybe. Yes. I said we mustn't let the children see."

"It was Fusae."

With that the argument ended. The sense of accord seemed to please both of them.

But the facts were different. They had given the sweets not to Fusae, their former maid, but to the boy next door.

The daughter waited for her mother to remember that too. But only the sound of the tea kettle came from the breakfast room.

She brought lunch.

"Did you hear our argument, Yoshiko?" asked her father.

"Yes."

"Your mother is pretty far gone. The worse it gets the more she pretends nothing is wrong. You must help her remember things."

"I wonder which of us is farther gone. I lost this one, but I wonder."

The daughter thought of saying something about Fusae and the boy next door but did not.

Two years later her father died. He had had a slight stroke and seldom went to the office afterwards.

And still the first plum blossoms came out on that lower branch. Yoshiko often thought of the Fugetsudo matter. She never spoke of it to her mother. Very probably her mother had forgotten.

THE JAY

The jay was noisy from dawn.

It seemed to have flown from a lower branch of the pine tree as Yoshiko was opening the shutters and then come back again. They could hear its wings from the breakfast table.

"What a racket," said her brother, starting to get up.

"Leave it alone," said her grandmother. "I think the little one must have fallen from the nest yesterday. I could still hear the mother last night after dark. I suppose she couldn't find it. And isn't that nice, here she is back again this morning."

"Are you sure?" asked Yoshiko.

Save for a liver attack some ten years before, her grandmother had never been ill, but she had suffered from cataracts ever since she was very young. Now she could barely see, and with the left eye only. She had to be handed her food. She could grope her way around the house, but she never went out alone into the garden.

She would sometimes stand or sit at the glass door and gaze at her fingers, spread out in the sunlight. Her whole life seemed to be concentrated in the gaze.

Yoshiko would be afraid of her. She would want to call from behind, and then she would slip away.

Yoshiko was filled with admiration that her blind grandmother could talk about the jay as if she had seen it.

When she went out to do the breakfast dishes, the jay was calling from the roof next door.

There were a chestnut and several persimmons in the back yard. She could see against them that a gentle rain was falling, so gentle that she could not make it out except against the dark background.

The jay flew to the chestnut, skimmed the ground, and flew back again, calling out all the while.

Would the nestling still be near, that the mother was so reluctant to leave?

Yoshiko went to her room. She must be ready by noon.

Her mother and father would be bringing her fiancé's mother.

As she sat down before the mirror she glanced at the white dots on her fingernails. They were said to be a sign that someone would come with gifts, but she had read in a newspaper that they really showed a deficiency in vitamin C or something of the sort. She was pleased with her face when she had finished making herself up. She thought her eyebrows and lips rather charming. She liked the set of her kimono.

She had thought she would wait for her mother to help her, and then she was glad that she had dressed by herself.

Her father and mother, actually her stepmother, did not live with them.

Her father had divorced her mother when Yoshiko was four and her brother two. It was said that her mother had been gaudy and extravagant, but Yoshiko suspected that there had been deeper causes.

Her father had said nothing when her brother had found a picture of their mother and shown it to him. He had frowned and torn the picture to pieces.

When Yoshiko was thirteen her new mother came into the house. Later Yoshiko was to think it rather remarkable of her father to have waited almost ten years. Her new mother was a kind woman and they lived a quiet, happy life.

When her brother entered high school and went to live in a dormitory, it was plain to all of them that his attitude toward his stepmother was changing.

"I've seen Mother," he said to Yoshiko. "She is married and living in Azabu. She is very beautiful. She was glad to see me."

Yoshiko was too startled to answer. She was sure that she had turned white, and she was trembling.

Her stepmother came in from the next room.

"It's all right. There's nothing wrong at all with his seeing his own mother. It's only natural. I knew it would happen. It doesn't bother me at all."

Her stepmother seemed drained of strength, and so tiny that Yoshiko felt somehow protective.

Her brother got up and went out. Yoshiko wanted to slap him.

"You are not to say anything, Yoshiko," said her stepmother softly. "It would only make things worse."

Yoshiko was in tears.

Her father brought her brother home from the dormitory. She thought that would be the end of the matter; and then her father and stepmother moved away.

She was frightened. She felt that she had had the full force of—a man's anger, perhaps, or vengefulness? She wondered if she and her brother had something of the same thing in them. She had felt certain, as he had left the room, that her brother had inherited that terrible masculine something.

Yet she felt too that she knew her father's loneliness those ten years he had waited to take a new wife.

She was startled when her father came with talk of a prospective bride-groom.

"You have had a hard time of it, Yoshiko, and I am sorry. I have told his mother that I want you to have the girlhood you never had."

There were tears in Yoshiko's eyes.

With Yoshiko married, there would be no one to take care of her grand-mother and brother, and so it was decided that they would live with her father and stepmother. The decision was what touched Yoshiko most. Because of what her father had been through she had been frightened of marriage, but now that it was coming it did not seem so frightening after all.

She went to her grandmother when she had finished dressing.

"Can you see the red, Grandmother?"

"I can see that there is something red." She pulled Yoshiko to her and looked intently at her kimono and obi. "I have forgotten what you look like, Yoshiko. How nice if I could see you again."

Embarrassed, Yoshiko put her hand to her grandmother's head.

She went out into the garden. She wanted to run and meet her father and stepmother. She opened a hand, but the rain was scarcely enough to wet it. Lifting her skirts she looked through the shrubs and bamboo, and found the nestling jay in the grass under the *hagi*.

She stole up to it. Head pulled in, it was a tight little ball. It seemed without strength and she had no trouble taking it. She looked around but could not find the mother.

She ran to the house.

"I've found it, Grandmother. It seems very weak."

"Really? You must give it water."

Her grandmother was very calm.

She brought a cup of water and put its beak in, and it drank most prettily, swelling its small throat.

"Kikikikiki." It quickly revived.

Hearing, the mother jay called from a power line.

"Kikiki." The nestling struggled in Yoshiko's hand.

"How very nice," said her grandmother. "You must give it back."

Yoshiko went into the garden. The mother jay left the power line and sat watching Yoshiko from the cherry tree.

Raising her hand to show the nestling, Yoshiko put it on the ground.

She watched from inside the glass door. The nestling called forlornly up. The mother came nearer and then was at the lower branches of the pine tree just above. The nestling flapped its wings as if it were about to take flight, and fell forward, calling out to its mother.

Very cautious, the mother still did not alight.

Then, in a swoop, it was beside the nestling, whose joy was boundless. The head shook, the outstretched wings were trembling, it was like a spoiled child. The mother seemed to be feeding it.

Yoshiko wished that her father and stepmother would hurry. She wanted them to see.

SUMMER AND WINTER

The last day of the summer Bon Festival fell on a Sunday.

Kayoko's husband had gone in the morning to a baseball tournament in the middle-school grounds, come home for lunch, and gone back again.

It was time for Kayoko to start thinking about dinner. She remembered something. There was a mannequin in a shop window near her parents'. She had seen the kimono she was wearing today on the mannequin.

She had passed the shop with the mannequin in its window every day on her way to catch the streetcar for work. Though its dress was changed to match the seasons, the mannequin always struck the same pose. The shop had about it the inelegant look of the outskirts of town. Kayoko felt somehow depressed at a mannequin which must always be striking that same pose.

But as she passed day after day, it came to seem that the expression on the mannequin's face was always changing. Then she began to think that it matched her own feelings. A little longer and she began to guess her own feelings by the expression on the mannequin's face. She would look at the mannequin morning and evening as if it were a fortuneteller.

Upon her engagement she had bought the summer kimono the mannequin was wearing, as a sort of memento.

It seemed to her that the lights and shades in her life had been more extreme in those days.

When he came back in the evening twilight, the skirt of his kimono hitched up, her husband was red-faced under his straw hat.

"It's hot. I'm dizzy, it's so hot."

"You're pouring sweat. Go and have a bath."

"Maybe I should."

He did not seem enthusiastic, but went off to the public bath when Kayoko pressed soap and towel on him.

She felt that she had been rescued. She had eggplants on a wire grill, and it was his practice at this point to take off a lid and raise a cover and criticize her cooking. He did not seem to know how she disliked the practice.

When he came back from the bath he threw down the soap and towel and lay down on the parlor floor. He seemed even redder and shorter of breath than before. She brought a pillow, and saw that he was in genuine discomfort.

"Shall I bring a cold towel?"

"Yes."

She wrung out a towel and put it on his forehead. Then she opened a door to let the breeze through and fanned at him with a large kitchen fan.

"You needn't fan quite so hard."

He frowned and brought his hands to his forehead.

She put down the fan and ran to buy ice, which she put into an ice pack.

"It's too cold." But he submitted to her ministrations.

He went out to the veranda and vomited a white foamy liquid. Not looking at the cup of salt water Kayoko had brought, he lay back down again.

"Go ahead and eat," he said. "You must be hungry."

The flush had left him. He was pale.

"You'd better get a bucket and wash it away." He was breathing quietly and soon he was asleep.

After looking for a time at his sleeping face, she began a lonely dinner. She heard raindrops on the tin roof, the beginning of a quick summer shower.

"What about the laundry?"

The rain had awakened him. She hastily put down her chopsticks.

"Did you put the cork back on the sake bottle?" he asked when she had come back from taking in the laundry.

She had forgotten that too. He looked unhappy and sighed and closed his eyes.

A bad day is a bad day. There seemed to be a mosquito inside the mosquito net. Kayoko awoke itching. She turned on the light and waited for the mosquito to show itself, but it stayed hidden. She brought a fan and fanned at the corners of the net, but still she could not find it. Perhaps she would do better in the dark. She turned out the light. Soon the mosquito was on her forehead and she swatted it. She had been careful not to disturb her husband.

Unable to sleep, she went out to the veranda and opened a door.

There should have been a moon, but it was cloudy.

"Come back to bed," he almost shouted at her. "You won't be able to get up in the morning."

"Have you been crying?" he asked when she had come back under the net.

"Crying?"

"You should be."

"Why?"

He rolled over, facing away from her.

Kayoko was having stomach pains, apparently from bad oysters the evening before, but she was not in bed. She lay beside the brazier, facing her husband.

She wanted to hear about Michiko, and she was a little insistent with her questions. He spoke calmly and slowly.

"I first knew that she liked me when I said it was time we found a husband for her, and she must tell me what sort of man she liked. She was cooking an omelette for me, I think. She didn't answer. How was I to know if she wouldn't tell me, I said. 'Someone like you,' she said, very quietly. She didn't look at me. 'Like me? But I drink.' She said she wouldn't mind if he didn't drink any more than that. And she went upstairs."

Kayoko had heard the story before, but she was fond of it. Michiko was her husband's cousin.

It took her mind from the pain.

"And what did you think of her?"

"Nothing. After all she's my cousin."

"You're a very cold person, making a pretty girl say such a thing and then not caring."

"She was sickly and I wouldn't have wanted to marry her. What point would there have been in caring if I didn't want to marry her?"

"What happened to the omelette?"

"You would think of that. I imagine we ate it."

Perhaps Kayoko's husband had been telling Michiko how omelettes are cooked, and so she had gone upstairs, and he had eaten it by himself afterwards. Kayoko was amused.

"But if you have shopping to do you'd better be at it," he said. "It's already four."

Suddenly the winter wind seemed louder and the pain was worse.

She thought it rather awful of him to send her out in the cold, knowing that she was not well. Could he not see the difference between being strong enough to laugh at his story and strong enough to go out?

She was shivering. She pulled into the shelter of an alley.

This callousness, she thought, showed that he had rated her feelings at precisely nothing. Perhaps Michiko, who had that single time shown her feelings, artlessly and awkwardly, was the happier one. Perhaps he would one day feel that only Michiko had loved him. Something in his nature, perhaps, would make the day come.

He was at the bath when she came back.

She went into the kitchen. A chill ran down her spine like a dash of cold water. The pain was worse again. She went to bed, having done nothing about dinner.

"Is it worse?" he asked when he came back from the bath. "Do you have a hot-water bottle?"

She shook her head. He brought a hot-water bottle. She was worried about dinner.

"It doesn't matter," he said, closing the door after him.

She heard him making tea in the next room. She had everything out, and he was always giving her lessons; but apparently it was too much trouble to cook for himself. The tea had a very brisk and efficient sound to it.

To judge from Michiko's picture, thought Kayoko, she herself had had little except good health to recommend her as a bride. Tomorrow, no doubt, she would be up and about. But it was an unsure sort of thought, compared to the sturdy sureness with which she could hear him chewing on a pickle.

She thought that he was complaining a little less than last summer.

THE BAMBOO LEAVES

Putting the bucket down beside the hollyhocks, Akiko pulled several leaves from the dwarf bamboo under the plum tree and dropped them into the water.

"Boats. Do you like them?"

The boy gazed intently down into the bucket. Then he looked up at Akiko and smiled.

"Akiko made you the nice boats," said his mother, "because you're such a good boy. Akiko will play with you if you're good."

He was the brother of Akiko's fiancé. She had come out into the garden because she had sensed that the mother wanted to be alone with her father. The boy was being troublesome, and she had brought him with her. He was her fiancé's youngest brother.

He churned at the leaves. "They're having a fight." He was very pleased.

She wrung the kimono she had been washing and hung it out to dry.

The War was over, but her fiancé had not yet come back.

"Fight," said the boy, churning the water more violently. "Fight harder."

"You're splashing it all over yourself."

"But they won't move."

It was true that when he withdrew his hand they were quite still.

"We'll take them out to the river. That will keep them moving."

The boy gathered up the leaves. Akiko poured the water over the hollyhocks and took the bucket back to the kitchen.

She stood on a stone upriver and dropped the leaves in one by one.

He clapped with delight. "Mine is winning! Look, look!"

He ran downstream, not to lose track of the boat in the lead.

She threw the last ones in and started after him.

She must be careful that her left foot was full on the ground.

She had had infantile paralysis and her left heel did not touch the ground. It was narrow and tender and the arch was high. She had been unable to jump rope or to walk any distance. She had been resigned to not marrying, and then she had become engaged. Sure that determination could overcome physical defects, she tried more seriously than before to walk with her left heel on the ground. It blistered easily, but she persisted. Then came the defeat and she gave up. The scars from the blisters were still there, like very bad chilblains.

She was using her left heel for the first time in a very long while because the little boy was her fiancé's brother.

It was a narrow stream with weeds hanging over. Two or three of the boats caught in them.

Some ten paces ahead of her, the boy was looking after the boats, as if unaware of her approach. He paid no attention to her way of walking.

The hollow at the nape of his neck made her think of her fiancé. She wanted to take the boy in her arms.

The mother came out. She said good-by and led him off by the hand.

"Good-by," he said calmly.

Either her fiancé was dead or the engagement had been canceled. It had probably been wartime sentimentality that had made him want to marry a cripple in the first place.

She did not go inside. She went instead to look at the house being put up next door. It was much the largest house in the neighborhood and everyone was watching it. Construction had been stopped during the War and weeds had grown high around the lumber; and then suddenly it was moving ahead once more. There were two nervous pine trees at the gate.

To Akiko it looked like a hard, unyielding sort of house. But it had very great numbers of windows. The parlor seemed almost completely encased in glass.

There had been speculation as to the sort of people who would move in, but no one knew for sure.

THE CEREUS

For three summers now, Komiya had invited several of his wife's school friends to look at the night-blooming cereus.

"Beautiful," said Mrs. Murayama, the first to arrive, as she stepped into the parlor. "See how many there are. More than last year." She gazed at the cereus. "There were seven last year? How many are there tonight?"

It was an old-fashioned Western frame house with a large parlor. The table had been pushed aside and the cereus was at the center on a circular stand. The stand was slightly below knee level, but Mrs. Murayama was looking up at the blossoms.

"Like a white fantasy." She had said the same thing last year. Two years before when she had first seen the cereus, she had said the same thing, with rather more enthusiasm.

She went nearer and looked up at it for a few moments and then turned to thank Komiya.

"Good evening, Toshiko," she said to the girl beside him. "Thank you for letting me come. You're bigger and prettier. The cereus is blooming twice as well as last year and so are you."

The girl looked up at her but did not answer. She did not seem shy but she did not smile.

"You must have worked very hard on it," said Mrs. Murayama to Komiya, "to have it blooming so nicely."

"I think this will be the best evening this year." Hence the sudden invitation, he no doubt meant to say, though somehow his voice did not say it.

Mrs. Murayama lived nearby, at Kugenuma. He had called her and told her that this was the evening, and she had called her friends in Tokyo. She told him the results: two of the five women invited had other engagements and a third would have to wait for her husband to come home, and Mrs. Imasato and Mrs. Omori would definitely come.

"Mrs. Omori said that since there would only be three of us she wondered if she might ask Shimaki Sumiko to come along. She's not been here before. She's about the only one in the class left unmarried."

Toshiko got up and started out through the door beyond the cereus.

"Let's look at it together, Toshiko," said Mrs. Omori.

"I saw it bloom."

"You actually saw it come into bloom? With your father? You must tell me what it was like."

The girl went out without looking back.

Two years before, Mrs. Murayama remembered, Komiya had told her that it came into bloom like a lotus, waving as if in a gentle breeze.

"Does she dislike seeing her mother's friends? Is it that she doesn't want to hear about her mother? I wish Sachiko were with us. Though if she were here I suppose you wouldn't be troubling yourself."

Mrs. Murayama had first seen the cereus when she had come one summer evening two years before to tell him that his estranged wife wanted a reconciliation. She had come again with several friends and asked him to forgive his wife.

They heard an automobile, and Mrs. Imasato had arrived. It was nearly ten. The cereus opened in the evening and the blossoms faded at two or three in the morning. It was a flower of a single night. About twenty minutes later Mrs. Omori arrived with Shimaki Sumiko. Mrs. Murayama introduced Sumiko to Komiya.

"She's too young and pretty. That's why she's still single."

"It's because I've been ill so much." Sumiko's eyes were shining as she looked at the cereus. She was the only one who had not seen it before. She walked slowly around it and brought her face near.

The blossoms came from thick stems at the end of longish leaves. The great white flowers were swaying gently in the breeze through the window. It was a strange flower, the petals somehow different from those of a long-petaled chrysanthemum or a white dahlia. It was like a flower in a dream. A profusion of deep-green leaves stretched upward from the bamboo that supported the three stalks. There too were the most flowers. As with other varieties of cactus, the pistils were long and leaves grew from other leaves.

Sumiko did not notice that Komiya, struck by her intentness, had come up beside her.

"There are considerable numbers of them here and there in Japan, but it is unusual to have thirteen blossoms in one night. It blooms six or seven nights a year. Tonight seems likely to be the best."

He told her that what looked like a large lily bud would be blooming to-morrow. Of the little bean-like protuberances on the leaves some would be leaves and some would be buds. It would take a month for the smaller buds to bloom.

Sumiko was enveloped in the sweet perfume, sweeter than a lily but not as insistent.

Not taking her eyes from the cereus, Sumiko sat down. "A violin. Who is playing?"

"My daughter."

"What a pretty piece. What is it?"

"I'm afraid I don't know."

"A good accompaniment to the cereus," said Mrs. Omori.

After looking at the ceiling for a time, Sumiko went out on the lawn. The sea was immediately below.

She said when she came back inside: "She was on the balcony upstairs. She wasn't facing the sea but standing with her back to it. I wonder if that is better."

TRANSLATED BY EDWARD SEIDENSTICKER

■: KANEKO MITSUHARU

Kaneko Mitsuharu was born Ōga Yasukazu in 1895, the son of a sake dealer near Nagoya, but was adopted by the prosperous Kaneko family and brought up in Kyoto and Tokyo. He attended two universities and an art academy without completing any of his studies, and quickly dissipated his inheritance. By 1919, however, he had published a book of poems at his own expense; after a year in Europe he produced the glittering romantic poetry of *A Gold Beetle* (*Koganemushi*, 1923), a collection intended as his farewell to youth. He married, but did not settle down.

In 1928 Kaneko left Japan on his longest journey, only occasionally with his wife, from China to Southeast Asia, and from Singapore to Paris. This time he spent four years abroad, returning as a major poet whose rich symbolist technique veiled a bitterly critical view of colonialism, militarism, and ultranationalism. His silence during the war years was inevitable, as foreshadowed by the defiant assertion in the preface to his superbly caustic collection *Sharks* (*Same*, 1937): "I do not and will not write poetry unless something makes me angry, or makes me want to scorn or ridicule it." After the War he published his secret hoard of manuscripts and began to express his rebellious spirit more vigorously than ever. The next three decades saw Kaneko at his most prolific, a virtuoso poet and an unrelenting satirist of all that offended him in Japan, and in himself. He died in June, 1975, a few months before the publication of a fourteen-volume *Complete Works*. At the funeral, in accordance with Kaneko's request that it be "as lively as possible," his friend Nosaka Akiyuki sang a guitar-accompanied folk song instead of delivering the conventional eulogy.

"Song of Loneliness" (*Sabishisa no uta*) is from *Parachute* (*Rakkasan*, 1948); "The Sun" (*Taiyō*) and "The Receiver" (*Juwaki*) are from *Inhumanity* (*Hijō*, 1955).

❖ Three Poems

SONG OF LONELINESS

A state is called the coldest of all cold monsters.
Coldly lieth it also; and this lie creepeth from its mouth:
"I, the state, am the people."
—NIETZSCHE: *Thus Spake Zarathustra*

I

Where does it ooze from, this loneliness?
From the skin of that twilight-blooming woman?
Her face? The way she looks from behind?

From my frail filament of a heart
Or the fleeting scenes that tempt it?

Moonlight, dimmed by a paper screen?

A dead leaf skittering across frayed mats?

Loneliness creeps down our spines
Like dampness or mold, before we are aware of it,
Rots our hearts, seeps out through our pores.

The loneliness of women bought and sold,
Of orphans brought up hungry.
The loneliness of men who think "That's life!"
Hollow effigies dangling without a self.
Vessels of clay.

A few grains of rice offered on a plate,
A cracked plate
Discarded among dry weeds.

From these loneliness arises.
At the margin where life reverts to Nothingness,
In our suspicious hearts
Searching for one another.

From things yellowed with age, from faded things,
From the family code of a stern mother-in-law
Little by little
Loneliness spreads imperceptibly
Like rain leaking down
Walls and sliding doors,
Like tear stains.

The eye-stinging smoke of burning leaves.
A stealthily flowing stream.
The dreary round of the seasons, branches swaying,
Eloquent stones, grass going to seed. All that passes.

Trampling through the tall thicket
Of withered reeds
My loneliness sets out on a journey.
A cold sun sinks
In the mackerel sky.

Loneliness plods on
Seeking a night's lodging.

All night long I listen to the sound of the mountains
Alone, my head propped on my arm,
But suddenly as I shake an empty sake bottle
I hear the crying of the child I left at home.

II

I was born in the midst of the dense fog
Of this loneliness-enveloped land.

Fog scudding across the lake
Hiding mountain peaks and gorges
Seals off the path of my fifty years
And what lies ahead.

Boiling up forever with the murky vapors,
Here only loneliness remains fresh.

From loneliness we extract life's faint sweetness
And distill it into poetry.

At the edge of loneliness we gaze on bellflowers, asters,
Women still dewy, beginning to droop, ready to be plucked.
Blossoms in the shadowy border of despair.

A trace of bitterness in lipstick, haggardness under powder—in these I hear
The mournful prayer echoing out of a woman's darkening fate . . .
A lock of black hair wrapped in tissue—a thick rope of hair bound with its
     strands.
A Yoshiwara song set to this lonely tune.

A one-pounder inlaid with loneliness.

Enclosed east and west by oceans, not a crack to slip through, we Japanese
     shut ourselves in
Believing ours was the land of the rising sun.

Sadness spelled out in supple calligraphy, sensitivity sharpened toothpick-thin.
Famous landscapes as vivid as ever, washed a thousand times in loneliness.

Kisagata, the Sea of Nio.
The ripples of Shiga
Drawn with a feather brush.

The peaks of Chokai and Haguro
Piercing the clouds.

Miraculous hot springs welling up in the traces of a priest's staff.

Haze in the far hills, mountain cherries, mother-of-pearl autumn insects in
     lacquer.
The silk-print pattern of flowers in chaotic bloom.
Poets and novelists who see pathos in nature
Lamenting that beautiful things pass all too soon.
You're right, loneliness is the sorrowful way of Japan, its unique gift.

But after loneliness, poverty. From paddy fields, from the long tradition of a
     peasant's wretched life,
From ignorance and despair, loneliness spreads.

Ah, but my loneliness
Was to be born in such a land.
To grow up here, make friends,

Sit at a peeling lacquered table
For beanpaste soup and butterbur in the morning,
A salad of bamboo shoots at supper.

And finally, old, bequeathing to my children
The desolation inherited from my ancestors,
To go to sleep in the shade of the anise leaves.

After I die—five, ten, a hundred years,
To the very end of eternity—loneliness will persist,
Beneath the soil, around the seas, from tip to tip of the archipelago,
Clouds and mist layered tenfold, twentyfold.
A cold drizzle, a sudden clearing,
Through a rift in the restless clouds
Green hills and rivers reveal their pain
And I am undone. My strength ebbs.

Not that I have found loneliness only in Japan's ancient heritage.
I see it just the same in men wearing business suits, smoking cigarettes,
    mouthing Western ideas.
At gatherings, in coffee shops, talking to friends, dancing with bobbed-haired
    girls,
I see loneliness ooze damply from people's bodies, trail after them,
Trickling, widening, running deep, flowing on and on forever.

III

Once, much as I despised it, I grew secretly attached to loneliness.
Folk songs. The sad tunes of down-at-heel street musicians.
Noodleshop lanterns behind the brothel quarter, steamy bowls of *soba*.

A fight scene, fanatic slant-eyes of country actors.
The taste of green tea on rice we all return to, simple
    elegance. Faith in the gods.
People reeking of the Japanese toilet,
Like me.

Those who sit over coffee across my table
Are reading the same evening paper.
At school we learned the same characters. Being Japanese,
We were taught there is no greater blessing than to be Japanese.
(Well and good. But we were a bit naïve.)

Above us the same eternal line of Emperors.

How we resemble one another, in every boring detail!
The color of our skins, our eyes, our feelings, our fastidiousness,
The void of lives not our own—from all these a huge loneliness
 ascends, streaming up to the heavens.

IV

At last our guardian gods of loneliness brought us war.
It was not your fault, certainly not mine. It was caused
 by loneliness.

Loneliness made us shoulder rifles; lured by loneliness
We abandoned wives and mothers and pursued the waving banners.
Craftsmen, laundrymen, clerks, students—
Reeds bending before the wind.

No distinctions among us. All taught to die.

Hoodlums, cowards, nice fellows, blinded by the name of the Emperor,
 rushed out joyfully like boisterous children.

Now, men on the home front tremble,
Afraid of a call to arms in the morning mail,
Try to suppress their doubts and fears,
And decide to give up and spend the day
Getting drunk on someone else's liquor.
Egoism, shallow love.
Patient, silent, beggarlike women
Line up waiting for rations.
Never before have I seen such deep loneliness
As in these faces more sorrowful day by day
Confronting the doom of a people who have destroyed their land.
But, no matter. Such loneliness is nothing to me now.

My loneliness, what makes me really lonely,
Is that I can't feel by my side a single will to halt this drift to ruin,
To get to the root of loneliness, to join the rest of the world. That's all.

May 5, 1945: The Boys' Festival

TRANSLATED BY HOWARD HIBBETT

THE SUN

For more than twenty years, I haven't shown him my content face.
To me he looked like an old coin, so one day, while no one was watching, I
    kicked him into a manhole,
Turned up my collar and left.

Since then, no one has seen the sun. In the humid patch of fern
Wet spores like frog eggs, I gathered clammy snails.
With sticky tongues the stems licked my hands . . .
The dark tube and its inner wall breathing.

Only I know the whereabouts
Of the aged sun, rolling in the sewer.

Who could accuse me as an offender? Conscience!
Why do I feed loyal dogs biscuits?
Why is majority truth? Why not I?

I put an iron lid on irrationality, on the symbol of power.
If he escapes, I will be crucified; electrocuted!
With all my might I shall keep him captive.

THE RECEIVER

Bigger than an elephant's back
The sun that scorches Africa
Wearing dark glasses
Strides through Japan.

Listen, Sun,
I know I shouldn't have been born
But tangled in the world
Forever chaotic
I sit as usual
By a telephone.

In the shaky receiver
A woodpecker is nesting.
I occasionally hear
Drifters' talk.

What I wait for
—tell you the truth—
Is not such an important call.

I'm expecting word about a loan
To repay my debts.
Factions, freedom and peace
Are no longer my concerns.

You men who pull triggers
Like shooting at heaven
With blanks
To ejaculate so randomly,

Move me
If you are still able.
From the receiver
An empty shell

To a better spot
You may guide me
Even if it is a toilet
Where there is no phone

Or to a lousy mecca
Of the hairy men,
To the side of Christ
Worn and bleached by lascivious sweat
Under the egg-smeared sky.

TRANSLATED BY JAMES R. MORITA

▐▌ SEKINE HIROSHI

Sekine Hiroshi, who was born in 1920, grew up in the freewheeling entertainment district of Asakusa in downtown Tokyo. After completing elementary school he spent his youth doing manual work in various factories. During the War he was a reporter for industrial newspapers, and began publishing poetry, criticism, and fiction. He learned Russian in order to read Mayakovsky, and still believes that literature can play an important part in social revolution. (His favorite contemporary poet is Allen Ginsberg.) Most of his own poems are straightforward and quotidian, almost prosaic snatches of daily life.

Since the War, Sekine has been active both as a journalist and, always, as a poet. Until the "Red purge" of 1950 he worked for the labor movement. With Abe Kōbō and other friends he founded the left-wing poetry magazine *Archipelago* (*Rettō*, 1952–1955). He was expelled from the Communist Party in 1960 because of a disagreement on tactics against the renewal of the U.S.-Japan Mutual Security Treaty.

"Dream Island" (*Yume no shima*) is a poem from his first book, *Picture Homework* (*E no shukudai*, 1953). Long before the "garbage war" of the mid-sixties, the original plan for a "Dream Island" amusement park on reclaimed land in Tokyo harbor had given way to a plan for an industrial site, and then to its enduring role as the municipal dump.

Both "The Golden Pavilion" (*Kinkakuji*) and "Abe Sada" appeared in Sekine's fifth poetry collection, *Abe Sada* (1971). The former poem is a mock confession to the 1950 burning of the fourteenth-century Golden Pavilion in Kyoto by a temple acolyte, the subject of a rather different interpretation in Mishima's celebrated novel. The title poem is also based on an actual incident. Abe Sada is in fact a notorious murderess whose remarkably vivid confessional statement is echoed verbatim in much of the poem. She committed her private act of violence on May 18, 1936, a few months after the attempted coup by young Army officers on February 26 (The 2/26 Incident) that helped push Japan farther down the road to war. In 1974 Sekine visited the aging but still vivacious Abe Sada at her bar near the Sumida River in Tokyo. He finds it ironic that the

Americans released her along with many political prisoners after she had served only eight years in prison.

❖ Three Poems

ABE SADA

the conclusion of the 2/26 incident
was the war
but my incident, in the same year
is still not concluded
Ishii Teruo asked me to appear in his film
Scandalous Female Criminals of Modern Japan
and I answered all the questions
a man and a woman mutually in love
only once in a lifetime
Ishida Kichizo was it for me
he died in ecstasy
so I don't think what I did was wrong
he said "Strangle me . . .
tighter, tighter."
he never got angry, even when I bit and beat him
but he said "Don't kill me."
Ishida never wanted to die
but he wanted to die
no, he wanted to die
but he never wanted to die

after three long days apart
—or was it a hundred years?—
we were so happy to be back together
we couldn't sleep all night
we loved so hard we cried
I pulled out a butcher knife
the way I'd seen in a play
and pretended to cut him
"Hey Kichi . . ."
he really loved it
"That butcher knife's no good.
Get a big carving knife
and slice, don't just hack."

"I'll chop off your thing
so you can't use it on other women."
"Foolish girl!"

the next day I hid the butcher knife
behind the picture frame so the maid wouldn't see it
on the evening of the 13th
we called in a geisha
and sang and danced for over an hour
from dusk on the 15th till eleven
I went out to see Doctor Omiya
whom I'd known for a long time
and then again on the evening of the 16th
while Ishida was out at the barber's
but all the rest of the time
until the dawn of the 18th
—when I killed Ishida—
we spent sleeping naked together
and never left our burning bed
unlike our previous meetings
we hardly slept at all
and never even stopped to bathe

I met Doctor Omiya at five in the Ginza
we went straight to the Dream City Hotel
and did the usual
but all I could think about was Ishida
I didn't feel a thing
but I got fifty yen for it
the Doctor got out of the taxi first
and I rode back to our inn in Oku

Ishida had been sleeping
"Hey, what have you got against me?"
"As if I were seeing another man . . . !"
"Now it's my turn to use the carving knife."
he pinched me and tugged at my hair
then when I was in the bath he asked
if I was trying to wash my conscience
but I liked the way he teased me
I didn't hide the fifty yen
and Ishida knew it had to be from some man
he enjoyed pretending to be jealous . . .

it was around the 12th or 13th
I happened to wrap my sash cord around his neck
I pulled it tight and then a little tighter
later he told me what pleasure he felt
when I choked him "just at that instant"
it sounded like a good idea
but when he did it to me
I got no pleasure at all
Ishida felt sorry for me
so I got on top and began to choke him again

on the evening of the 16th
I got quite excited when Ishida took me in his arms
I lost control
and wanted to do it
and choke him as hard as I possibly could
so I mounted him
and rhythmically loosened and tightened
the cord around his neck

Ishida looked close to ecstasy
when I pulled tight, his tongue stuck way out
when I let go, it went back in again
then I choked him as he drank sake
"When I pull tight you shake down there.
It feels very nice."
"It hurts a lot, but I'll try to bear it
for your pleasure."

he got tired and began to blink
so I asked him if he wanted me to stop
"No! Do anything you want with my body."
I kept tightening and loosening for about two hours
then, early in the morning on the 17th
while I was playing with Ishida's body
I pulled the cord really tight
he groaned
and suddenly lost his strength
I let go in surprise
soon he was up again and hugged me hard
tears were running from his eyes
I stroked his chest, and finally he spoke
"What happened? My neck's on fire."

there was a bright red ring around his neck
so I washed it in the bath
he was exaggerating the pain
to liven things up
I touched his thing
and his strength came back in no time
I even had to slap it
when he saw the ugly ring around his neck
all he said was "You did a real job on me."

when we woke up later that morning
Ishida wanted to hide
he didn't even go down to wash
so I brought some water and bathed it gently
he ordered some boiled loaches and pickles
I had to drink the sake by myself
around eleven we felt it coming
and slipped back under the covers and went all out
we didn't get up until one
his neck was better but it still looked bad
he refused to go out looking like that
I offered to call a doctor
"The last time you called a doctor
he asked me if I was taking drugs.
This time if you have him look at me
it'll be at the police station."
I disagreed but let it go
I cooled and massaged it but it didn't improve
so I went out to a drugstore
"Some guests were fighting.
One of them was almost strangled
and his neck's all red."
"In that case the blood vessels are swollen.
There's nothing you can do to help,
just keep him in bed and restrict him to liquids.
It'll take a month or two."
I bought one box of eye medicine
for his bloodshot eyes
and a box of 30 Calmotin tranquilizers
to make him relax
on the way back I picked up a watermelon
I told him what the druggist had said
"Damn! I don't have enough money

to stay here forever. What shall I do?"
I felt so bad about his trouble
that I completely forgot about the butcher knife
and borrowed a carving knife from the maid
I sliced the watermelon
and gave it to Ishida
then I had some soup warmed
and put in three tablets of Calmotin
"Three tablets won't do anything to me."
"I'm sure you could swallow them all."
I put in five more tablets
we talked as we ate, with me half holding him up
so it was natural that my hand wandered
down to his thing
when my hand touched it . . . *that* happened
but he didn't have enough strength to make love

it was late at night
so I ordered a single portion of rice and vegetables
into which I put five more tablets of Calmotin
Ishida began to blink his eyes
but he didn't go to sleep
"I've got to go home," he said
"I can't afford this, I've got to go home."
"Don't go, please, for my sake!"
"And what if the maid sees me like this?
I've got to go home. If you feel uncomfortable
in the house in Shitaya, then find
someplace you like better and stay there."
"That wouldn't be any fun.
Stay here with me!"
"Well, all right . . . I'll charge the bill
and pay the maid when I come back in a couple of days."
"I don't like that either."
"You knew from the start I had children—
we can't be together all the time."
I knew Ishida was really planning to leave
I couldn't help crying
he had tears in his eyes too

the more gently he spoke the more upset I got
I had to think of some way to keep him
my ears wouldn't listen to what he was saying

". . . my wife is just a household decoration . . .
you don't need to be so jealous . . .
I've got to think about my business too, you know."
just then the maid brought
the chicken soup I'd ordered
I fed it to Ishida
around midnight we went to bed
he wasn't feeling strong
but he managed to get hard
he put me on top and did his best
to comfort me

"I'm going to take a nap.
Stay up and look after my neck, will you?"
I sat up
and rubbed him with my cheeks
finally he managed to sleep

we'd been apart from May 7th till the 10th
and I'd grown more and more bitter
about what was happening between us
finally I realized I'd have to kill him
then I got scared and stifled the thought
with all sorts of trivialities
but that night as we were talking
and later as I stared at his sleeping face
I began to imagine his wife
sitting over him at home
in exactly the same way . . .
I knew he wouldn't come back
for a month or maybe two
I couldn't stand it
I tried to force myself to be generous
but I just couldn't share him with her
so I asked him to commit suicide with me
or at least run away together
but all he offered
was to set me up in a teahouse
where he could drop in when he pleased
I wanted to have him forever
and there was just no other way
I had to kill him

once in a while Ishida would open his eyes
and stare at me, reassured
once, before dropping off again, he said
"You will choke me again
while I'm sleeping, won't you?"
"All right."
"But don't let go too soon
or it'll hurt a lot afterwards."
I wondered if he was asking me to kill him—
but he couldn't have meant it
it must have been a joke

he looked asleep so I reached with my right hand
for my pink pajama cord
with my left hand I pulled one end
twice around his neck
then I started to pull with both hands
Ishida's eyes popped open
and he tried to embrace me
I rubbed my face against his cheek
and asked him to forgive me
the next time I pulled as tight as I could
"Aaaah-ah"
HIS HANDS TREMBLED AS HE GROANED
soon his whole body was twitching

I was also shaking
and I gulped down a bottle of sake on the table
then I knotted the cord tight
around the middle of his throat
to make sure he wouldn't wake up
I wrapped the rest of the cord
around and around his neck
I hid the two ends of the cord
under his pillow and went downstairs
to look around
the clock in the office
showed just after two in the morning
it was a great relief to have done it
something heavy had been lifted off me
I took back a bottle of beer

and drank it in bed with Ishida
his mouth looked very dry
so I licked his tongue and wet it
I wiped off his face
and lay beside him till dawn
feeling closer to him
than when he had been alive
I played with his thing
and held it against mine
"Ishida's really dead!
I guess I'll have to die too."
as I played with his thing
I felt the desire to cut it off
and take it away with me
I pulled out the butcher knife
from behind the picture frame
and applied it at the base
but it wouldn't come off easily
I had to cut and cut a long time

it got pretty bloody
so I stuffed the wound with tissue paper
I got blood on my fingers
and on the sleeves and collar of my kimono
I wrote "Sada and Kichi, two alone" in blood
on his left thigh
and on the sheet too
then I carved my name "Sada"
on his left arm with the butcher knife
and I washed my hands
in the basin by the window sill
I took the jacket
off a hook by his pillow
and wrapped his penis and testicles in it
I took Ishida's six-foot loincloth
from the closet and wrapped it
around my waist and put the bundle in it
I put his underwear and shirt
on under my kimono
I cleaned the room completely
. . . a farewell kiss . . .
it was eight by the time I left
"I'm just going out for some pastry.

Please don't disturb him before noon."
I hired a car from the company
the teahouse guests always used
I went as far as Shinjuku
and then left it
I got a taxi at Shinjuku Station
at nine in Ueno I sold my clothes
at a pawnshop
I got a good price and used almost
half of it to buy a gray formal kimono
I changed in the back room
I asked a young clerk to go buy me
a cotton kerchief
in which I wrapped the butcher knife
and at a shoe store near the tracks
I bought a nice pair of clogs
then I called the teahouse maid
"I'll be back around noon
so be sure not to bother him."
she agreed and I felt much better
they couldn't have discovered him yet
then off to Kanda
to see the Doctor for a few minutes.

"Let's try the Green Grotto Inn."
in the taxi I couldn't help crying
"From now on, no matter what happens,
please remember that you only
bought me with money, nothing more."
he seemed to think I was apologizing
for having a lover
"Don't worry, I understand everything.
I've been looking for a new apartment recently
though I haven't been able to find a good one.
I finally quit my principal's job
so I'm in the best mood I've ever been in
since we met."
his ignorant kindness made me cry even more
as we got ready for bed . . .
I asked the maid to spread the bedding
secretly I took out Ishida's loincloth
and shirt and underwear
and hid the paper package under the quilt

while we were doing it he told me
"Sorry, but you smell funny."

I knew I had to kill Ishida
but until I actually did it
I never thought about what would happen to me
afterwards I realized I couldn't go on living
I'd have to die too
I really didn't mind dying
but I worried about Doctor Omiya
if only I hadn't asked the maid to deliver
my letter to him the day before
the Doctor needn't have been a part of it at all
as it was, the police would take him in
just because he got a letter from me
I felt very sorry
and wanted to apologize to him right there
I hadn't had enough money to pay the teahouse
and if Doctor Omiya could have given me some
I would have been able to take things easy
but he was out at a party
so the maid had them hold it for him
if only I hadn't sent that letter
I would have been free to hang myself
on the teahouse clothesline
or in our room on the second floor
the thought of poor Doctor Omiya
kept holding me back
I decided to go out instead
and got very lonely for Ishida
I put on his shirt
and pressed his thing against mine
but it really annoys me, you know
when people say I'm abnormal

I just couldn't feel anything
with Doctor Omiya it was pure obligation
I got dressed while he was in the bath
we left the Green Grotto at one
he got out of the taxi first
and asked me to meet him again on the 25th
I went as far as Shimbashi

after leaving the Doctor
I made up my mind to die, no matter what
but first I wanted to feel Ishida a little longer
to carry his treasure with me
around Tokyo for a while
and then to go to Osaka
where I'd jump off Mt. Ikoma
into the valley beneath
I'd also heard about Mt. Mihara
but I didn't know how to get there
I'd been to Mt. Ikoma, you know

I was cold in the summer silk kimono
I'd bought earlier, so I bought a wool one . . .
besides, I don't look my best in silk . . .
and a new sash and bustle in Shimbashi
my feet were so pinched in the clogs I'd bought
that I got some soft leather sandals
and put the silk kimono in the wrapping paper
then I got some glasses
so people wouldn't recognize me, naturally

around four I had some raw fish
I couldn't finish much and put the rest in the paper
I took my time and strolled around
and then got a taxi to the nearest park
I sat there on the bench thinking
if only I could fly like a dove . . .
then I had a cup of coffee
and read the evening paper
there was nothing unusual
so I was still safe
at ten I went to the inn in Asakusa
where I'd stayed before when
I wanted to be alone
I got a room on the second floor
under my quilt I opened the paper package
and sucked on it a little
and tried to put it in me
I kept thinking about so many things
I hardly slept the whole night

early the next morning
a newspaper at the front desk
with a picture of me when I was young
all about a scandal in Oku
I couldn't let them see it
so I hid the paper under my quilt
rain was falling
when I paid my bill at ten
so I borrowed clogs and an umbrella
rain . . .
there would be no style
in running off to Osaka so fast
I decided to take the night train
then I went to see a movie
Onatsu and Seijuro
about two lovers who commit suicide together
I was hungry, but I couldn't bear
to be caught while I was eating
I got a third-class ticket to Osaka
leaving at 6:19
I still had two hours
and five different newspapers to read on the train
I drank a bottle of sake on an empty stomach
and got really drunk
I also got very sleepy
so I went to a hotel and took a bath
had a beer
and called in a masseur

and the papers!
they had me down as another Takahashi Oden
and a lot more
I don't even like to remember
they said every station was crawling with detectives
I'd never make it out of Tokyo
much less to Osaka
too bad for the owner, I thought
but I'll have to die in this hotel
if I didn't it would only be
a matter of time till I was arrested
I wanted to die as swiftly as possible
but the ceiling beam was too low
so I couldn't hang myself . . .

well, I stayed up till one
waiting to be arrested

the police didn't come that night
the next morning I went in the other room
with a desk and wrote out my will
I went back to sleep
I had two bottles of beer
brought at midnight
I wanted to make another try at dying

I was made public
I don't know why everyone got so excited, though
it's not unusual
for a woman to love a man's thing
even if a woman doesn't like raw fish at first
if her husband likes it she learns to too
a woman will often sleep
holding a pillow while her man is gone
does a woman ever get sick smelling
the dirty clothes of the man she loves?
and she likes to drink
the hot water he leaves in his cup
eat chewed food
from her man's mouth

when a man buys a geisha's freedom
it's so he can monopolize her
there are a lot of women who dream about
doing the thing I did—love is love—
the only difference is that they don't do it
that's why the result of my love
is still unconcluded
it's only just begun
the incident was accidental
but now I'm caught between a sliding paper door
and the door of a concrete box apartment
no, I'm jammed

THE GOLDEN PAVILION

it was an almost perfectly expensive way
to enjoy a life beyond care
but compared to the grand style of instancing and gliding
     toward death
cultivated by the old Fujiwara clan
the Ashikagas were thieves and impostors
sweating nervously as they grasped after momentary pleasure

on July 2, 1950
I burned down the Golden Pavilion
in five years
it was rebuilt
and it was then that I realized
that the mere hundred thousand or so it took
to re-create Shogun Ashikaga Yoshimitsu's magnificent artifice
was not nearly enough
to build an ordinary middle-class apartment building

Supreme Commander Ashikaga Yoshimitsu
squeezed the Southern and Northern courts
and wrung out a single regime
by outflanking the power of the throne
if he had attacked frontally
all he could have expected were a few stale lines
and the title of Grand Minister of State
the nobles and the other warrior cliques
could have blocked him
from toppling the divinized Emperor himself
so Yoshimitsu devised two stratagems
one followed the precedent of Taira no Kiyomori
who had taken Buddhist vows
for Yoshimitsu scripture chanting was anything but a retirement
it was a much better role than the quotidian bit parts
played by the warriors and nobles
it was a kind of ultimate pronunciation
that bound them all to him
he took the name Heavenly Mountain Pilgrim
and provided himself with everything
from royal robes to imperial ritual texts
gratefully he obtained land in the Northern Hills

from the estate of the social-climbing Saionji clan
and built there his residence
including a three-story Golden Pavilion
to house Buddha's relics
patterned after the Hermit Cave Hall
where retired monk Emperors held cloistered courts
he directed his legal wife Hino Yasuko
to assume the title Imperial Mother
and his beloved son Yoshimochi
to be transformed into a prince of the blood
in short, he cast his family as the imperial family
the other stratagem was to cloak his dictatorship
behind the title King of Japan
in his dealings with the Mings in China

I never believed the war actually ended
or the distinction between democracy and disguised dictatorship
the beauty of the Golden Pavilion is not precarious
it is a triumphant blend of Zen and native Japanese style
with a monumentally firm foundation in kleptomania
what I burned was an imitation:
an imitation of
the imitation that still
continues to draw crowds

DREAM ISLAND

Here I am trying to cut through a rope
without cutting a thread!
is it just my imagination
or am I really locked up inside a box?
I've tried a lot of places
but I just can't get out of myself

I discovered Dream Island
as I went out walking one winter afternoon
I'd come to a small steel mill
where an engineer told me in a nasal voice
that there, out in Tokyo Bay, there was Dream Island!
I knew I'd heard the name somewhere—
a poster at the beach that summer . . .
or was I just remembering the future?

That was it

There'd been talk of building an incinerator
out on some sandy lapse of bay
I went to the opposite shore to get another view
I'm a believer in technology, but this was
the old dream of leading a camel through a needle's eye—
the only thing you can get through a needle's eye is thread
the thread stitching me and my sadness and my woman
to Dream Island
right now it's all I've got

TRANSLATED BY CHRISTOPHER DRAKE

■■TAMURA RYŪICHI

Tamura Ryūichi was born in Tokyo in 1923 and began writing self-consciously avant-garde poetry at the age of fourteen. After graduating from Meiji University in 1943, he served in the Imperial Navy; unlike most of his friends, he managed to survive the War on shore duty. Returning to a devastated Tokyo, he helped to found the influential poetry magazine appropriately called *The Waste Land* (*Arechi*, 1947–1948, revived as an annual from 1951 to 1958). Eliot and Auden are still his favorite poets.

    Tamura's own bleak postwar poems of autumn, "bandaged rain," and death set the tone of his first collection *Four Thousand Days and Nights* (*Yonsen no hi to yoru*, 1956), published more than ten years after Japan's defeat. In some half-dozen later volumes Tamura Ryūichi has gone beyond the unrelieved despair for which he became famous toward a new lyricism opening out, however tentatively, on a landscape suffused with music. Both "The Man with a Green Face" (*Midoriiro no kao no otoko*) and "Human House" (*Ningen no uchi*) appeared in *New Year's Letters* (*Shinnen no tegami*, 1973). The "Green Face" recalls the Andrew Marvell epigraph of his previous collection *Green Thoughts* (*Midori no shisō*, 1967): "Annihilating all that's made / To a green thought in a green shade."

❖ Two Poems

THE MAN WITH A GREEN FACE

it was a beautiful morning
shoulder to shoulder
we watched the squadron sail out of sight
a huge silence commands
the sea of freedom and necessity

and only illusions are real
we never stopped to question that

of course the squadron never returned
of course reality was an illusion
in all ports, in all fatherlands
shoulder to shoulder
we gazed at the horizon
but freedom and necessity
occurred only within history—
only the man with a green face
tries to leave history
we let go of each other's shoulders
and smashed the morning's beauty
with our dangling arms

we need something to kill our hunger
we need more imagination so we won't dream
we have to leave *we* behind
it won't help to look for the man with a green face
in a crowd or a group
and if you say that only evil exists
then history will whisper back:
all great things are evil

HUMAN HOUSE

I'll probably be back late
I said and left the house
my house is made of words
an iceberg's in my old chest
and my bathtub has horizons
unseen by any human eye
from my telephone: time, a whole desert
on my dining table sit bread, salt, and water
a woman lives in the water
hyacinths bloom from her eyeballs
of course she herself is a metaphor
women change as fast as words do
like cats, they're extremely fickle
I can't even find out her name

I'll probably be back late

no business to transact, no meeting
I ride a glacial streetcar
walk fluorescent underground passages
cut across a shaded square
and ride in a mollusk elevator
violet tongues and gray lips on the streetcar
rainbow throats and green lungs underground
and in the square, words like bubbles
lathering verbal information, informational information
adjectives, all the hollow adjectives
and adverbs, paltry begging adverbs
and nouns, a morass of boring nouns
but I can't find a verb anywhere
all I want are verbs
I'm fed up with a society created
only in the past and future tenses
I want a present tense

just because you open the door
doesn't mean there has to be a room
just because there's a window
doesn't mean there's an interior too
just because people live and die
doesn't mean there's space
so far I've opened a huge door
shut the door
and gone out
so I could come in by another door
what world is there outside the door?
what beauty? what exquisite sounds?
dripping water
birds
waves thudding on the rocks
the sound of men and beasts breathing

TRANSLATED BY CHRISTOPHER DRAKE

■■ YOSHIOKA MINORU

One of the more difficult, and rewarding, of contemporary Japanese poets, Yoshioka Minoru at first hoped to be a sculptor, but turned to writing poetry in the traditional haiku and tanka genres. He acknowledges his "strong desire to create shapes." But these shapes must embody "multiple time-circuits," Yoshioka adds. "The complexity that actively connects things while at the same time repeating unpredictable displacements creates a surface tension. So it's necessary for us to have compound eyes that see everything simultaneously—like the face of a woman in one of Picasso's paintings. A center is nothing but a dot, yes, but we must make many loci and, by moving multiple centers, we can effect proliferation and rotation in a poem. Hint by hint, beautiful shadows are cast by a blurred light source, and a small universe expands."

Yoshioka Minoru was born in Tokyo in 1919. He left school at fourteen to work for a medical publishing house, served in the army for four years on the Manchurian front, and has been on the staff of a leading publishing company since 1951. His earliest book of poetry to attract critical attention was *Still Life* (*Seibutsu*, 1955), issued in a private edition of 200 copies. The two "Still Life" poems here are among four of this title included in it. "Paul Klee's Dining Table" (*Pōru Kurē no shokutaku*) first appeared in 1968, in a book of collected poems. The prose poem "Nude Woman" (*Ratai*) is from *Spindle Form* (*Bōsuikei*, 1962).

❖ Four Poems

STILL LIFE

Within the hard surface of night's bowl
Intensifying their bright colors
The autumn fruits
Apples, pears, grapes, and so forth

Each as they pile
Upon another
Goes closer to sleep
To one theme
To spacious music
Each core, reaching its own heart
Reposes
Around it circles
The time of rich putrefaction
Now before the teeth of the dead
The fruits and their kind
Which unlike stones do not strike
Add to their weight
And in the deep bowl
Behind this semblance of night
On occasion
Hugely tilt

STILL LIFE

The night recedes the further to encircle them
The bones placed
Temporarily in the fish
Extricate themselves
From the sea where stars are
And secretly dissolve
On the plate
The light
Moves to another plate
Where life's hunger is inherited
In the hollow of the plate
First the shadows
Then the eggs are called in

PAUL KLEE'S DINING TABLE

Each of the things familiar to the solitary heart
Once unties the hard figure of light
Enters the dark uninhabited house
And in the shadow of a haughty metal
Forms a vivid image
Settles meekly
In the depth of this narrow room

Forks grow like feeble weeds
Glasses that have lost lips tilt in the air
And a sour drink flows
Sausage skins and fish of bones go under
In the city of water that can't be surveyed from above
Left behind, a precipice of cloth
A cap glances up
With the weight of dark rays held
An empty bottle stands
Inhabits the table top, alone
Standing around anyone becomes lonely
And grows to be a thin neck
Uninvited
From morning to night in a corner of the entrance
Folded, dripping, an umbrella
Around the table chairs come close
Plates and bowls gather
Among them there are plates with food messily eaten for no reason
More sad than these are unsoiled plates
Piling and piling on the shelves
As it is, night does not echo under the butter
The congenial banquet is about to end
With mother's swelling belly
A pot of salt, from which
Comes a voice
Getting no response it returns where it belongs
A table for which a busboy will never show up
Surrounding it from four sides
The white walls, as if they had just
Swallowed an ocean, hushed

NUDE WOMAN

I try to steal out of every idiot's world a reality to hide, an egg hung skillfully inside a fur. From then on I soil the first night of my creation. There, illuminated many times by the color of a geranium, the beautiful breasts, which may slowly upturn, depending upon the way they are touched. I'll reconcile. Aimlessly tracing the horizon and reigning toward the sand, the entirety of the flesh. There, extremely ripe strawberries have been placed. I negate them and leave. But, swirling up the shore devoid of perspective and blown out, the hair and the seaweed, their dark green glow. I'm dyed bright with that cold color. Liberated little by little as if sinking in the water, now rather than then, I won't be able to look through anyone. The thighs and the waist abruptly sink from the waterline where I stand,

and glow on the shellfish of the sea. Then the waves undulate harder. I am awakened to the characteristics of an iceberg which is cold even in summer, but the organism is powerful enough to change my contention. A mass that doesn't echo in the distance, that at once stops and drifts, that I can't weigh: its excess shade, its welcome reception. I'll surely be despised, because I am a painter, because I am no more than a technique-giver in tattered clothes who moves the substance elsewhere. I spread, or push out, a network of innumerable blood vessels, and create a woman with plural eyes and mouths. If the future can be foreseen: after a big enterprise of my sleep, the white statue of a woman boldly eats things.

TRANSLATED BY HIROAKI SATO

▌▌ KANAI MIEKO

Kanai Mieko was born in 1947 in Takasaki, a small city about sixty miles inland from Tokyo, and has continued to live there even after graduating in 1966 from the Takasaki Girls' High School. By the age of twenty she had begun winning literary awards for both poetry and fiction. Her first collection of short stories, *Love Life* (*Ai no seikatsu*), appeared in 1968—to her chagrin, several years earlier than her long-planned maiden volume of poetry. The title poem of *The House of Madam Juju* (*Madamu Juju no ie*, 1971) refers to the famous "Madam Juju" line of Japanese cosmetics, and to its widely advertised warning to women over twenty-five to preserve their skins by "rhythmical massage" with Madam Juju's creams. The poem also alludes to the Beatles' acid-euphoric song "Strawberry Fields Forever." Young girls are often called "strawberry" in colloquial Japanese.

❖ Poem

THE HOUSE OF MADAM JUJU

Turning, following the arrows through
the slimy passages of the city's intestines
to the house of Madam Juju
above the revolving dome of the sea.
A wind blows up out of the subways and underground
arcades smelling of rich soup
a wind with just a hint of late autumn
as you slide your cracked lips along
the burning naked body of Madam Juju.
How skillfully you suck
mulberry facets from deep in marble.
And young women drip liquid on

the strawberry fields above the revolving sea.
The young women pant and claw
in Madam Juju's soft embrace,
their blue-tinted eyes shut, moaning
they drop tears of ecstasy
and exchange saliva with the obscene Madam.
The red stain of crushed strawberries
is drying on the back of your shirt.
The sun and blissful clouds above the strawberry fields
brighten in the afterglow of thought
and will disappear over the flaccid horizon.

> But strawberry fields forever
> Strawberry fields, yes, forever

Madam Juju wipes up the young ladies' liquid
with her whip while the sun trembles down.
You disappear through the gate
of the whiplashing Madam Juju.
Tender screams!
Your hips twitch continually
under Madam Juju's stinging blows
in a recital of tireless, eternal convulsions
forever, spastically repeating words of love.
As she raises her whip Madam Juju
encourages you, gently, almost singing

> *Shoot every arrow!*
> *Take careful aim*
> *The violence of words of love*
> *That awful violence ah*
> *A single shaft of love*

The gland of night writhes like an acrobat
over the strawberry field horizon
to the house of Madam Juju.
The whipping party starts at dusk
as the rhythmical movements of the young women
lay waste to the strawberry fields.
It will go on forever.
You won't find satisfaction
even if you climb to the morning star.

TRANSLATED BY CHRISTOPHER DRAKE

■ ABE AKIRA

Abe Akira was born in 1934 in Hiroshima, where his father, a naval officer, was stationed, but has lived since childhood in the seaside town of Kugenuma, within commuting distance of Tokyo. After graduating from Tokyo University with a degree in French literature, he worked for a broadcasting company until 1971, when he left to devote his full time to writing. Meanwhile, his literary career had begun with the publication in 1962 of "The Children's Room" (*Kodomobeya*), a moving account of growing up with a mentally retarded older brother. Almost all of his many stories are based on incidents from his own life and the lives of members of his family, whether recent experiences or fading memories. Each has its own intrinsic interest, but each also reveals a new aspect of a familiar character.

Thus, Abe Akira has worked more completely within the I-novel tradition than perhaps any other writer in this volume. His autobiographical writings range from minor sketches—a fond recollection of a case of athlete's foot contracted in early college days, a piece on "horn-rimmed glasses" describing the uncanny experience of being mistaken successively, during a ten-minute stroll on the Ginza, for Furui Yoshikichi, Abe Kōbō, Kojima Nobuo, and Ōe Kenzaburō—to his major novel *Commander's Leave* (*Shirei no kyūka*, 1970), which ends long after the War with his father's death from cancer.

Yet Abe is not uncritical of his chosen genre: he goes far beyond most I-novelists in his concern for the fictional shaping of his materials. And "Peaches," a beautifully self-contained lyrical tale, shows us the autobiographical author questioning the most fundamental source of his art—his memory.

❖ Peaches

(*Momo,* 1972)

I know all too well that memory can be deceptive, and I have surely heard this said by others. But I am constantly being shocked anew at how outrageously deceptive memory is. Yes, it beguiles us at every turn. Not too long ago I was taken by surprise again.

Winter. Night. The moon.

I am a young boy and with my mother. We push a baby carriage filled with peaches.

The single road connecting our town with the town on the west runs through open farmland, then slopes gently downward beyond an elevated stretch of sand hills. It is a narrow, rock-strewn country road. On the slope, there are no houses, only thick pine woods lining either side.

My mother and I make our way slowly down the hill. Soon we will come to the river at the bottom. The river runs to the sea. Beyond the river's wooden bridge, rice paddies stretch out into the distance. The air throbs with the bull-frogs' heavy cries, the wet smacking of the mudsnails. We are almost home.

I doubt if there has been a year in the thirty or more that have gone by since then when I did not recall that night scene. The image in my mind is always the same—if not so fixed as a painting, then perhaps more like some frames of underexposed film flickering on the screen. Especially on cold winter nights when I walk alone through the darkness with my coat collar turned up has the fragmentary memory of that night on the road come back to me.

And each time, I have said to myself—Oh yes, I remember that, odd how well I do remember that night. The very words of this monologue, too, are the same, repeated year after year with all the intensity of a second-rate actor. And while I am busy congratulating myself on my stagecraft, the memory always slips away, its veracity untested.

But the scene needs more commentary.

My mother had taken me along to the neighboring town that night to lay in a stock of peaches at an orchard or some such place. She could get better ones than at the local grocer's, and they would be fresh-picked. It was probably worth making a special trip and buying enough to fill the carriage.

Peaches. Fruit like pure, sweet nectar—nothing else. Easily bruised, quick to spoil. And each heavy, almost unnervingly so. Filled with several dozen of these heavy peaches, the carriage must have been more difficult to push than if it had held a live baby. And like the downy skin of a newborn baby, each could be scuffed and bruised in an instant if my mother did not move the carriage slowly, carefully.

The darkness may have exaggerated the distance, long as it was. The night was cold and, up well past my bedtime, I must have been very sleepy. Partway down the hill, my mother stopped and wrapped her beige shawl around me.

More than the cold, it was my fear of the dark shapes arising one after another along the moonlit road that prompted her to do this. She probably had to cover my eyes with the shawl and walk holding me against her.

Perhaps she had been careless enough to tease me about foxes along the way, and this was what aroused my fears, dark shadows or no. For she had told me several stories of the foxes she had encountered as a little girl. My mother was born in Osaka at the turn of the century and she spent her childhood in the city, but on walks to the deserted countryside she would always hear the foxes crying, and people would say that they cast a spell on passers-by.

Her stories must have come back to me one after another, the shawl around my head powerless to calm my fears. Why did she have to start talking about foxes *here?* Let's get down this hill and near some houses!

But to walk any faster would have been out of the question. The carriage would have bounced along the rocky road, damaging the peaches. —I had been the baby in this carriage until not very long ago. Now it was only good for carting things. Most of the time, it stayed in the storage shed in the corner of the yard.

And so the young mother and her little boy, pressing close and sharing whispers, slowly pushed the old, little-used baby carriage down the hill of the deserted country road. Bathed in moonlight, the one added the clip-clop of her wooden sandals, the other the soft padding of his tennis shoes to the creak of the carriage's rusting wheels.

This, then, was the scene that had lived in the fondest part of my memory for so many years. In none of its details had I found anything to wonder at.

And then one day—in fact, just two or three days ago—as I was gazing blankly at the view from my window, it struck me with such force that, for a moment, I was unable to breathe. Peaches in the winter? Frogs and mudsnails in the winter? How could I have failed to notice *that* until now? And, stranger still, what had inspired me—possessed me—at this one moment to seize upon the vital clue? For it was this that lay bare the hoax that memory had played on me year after year. Now, for the first time, I saw the wildly impossible connection that memory had made: carting a load of peaches on a cold winter night! Nowadays, perhaps. But back then? Unthinkable.

One after another, doubts began to overtake me. I would have to think it through from beginning to end. All right, then, exactly when was it? Why, in fact, were my mother and I walking down that hill so late at night? Were those really peaches in the carriage? And if not, what were we bringing from the other town?

When it came to this, all I could be sure of was that one year, on one particular night, my mother and I had come down the hill on the road that linked our town with the next one. These unsubstantial facts were all that remained. Had it been peach season or shawl season? I did not know. I was far too young to have been alone—of that I was certain. But of that and nothing else.

We still had the baby carriage that night, which meant I could not have gone past the first few years of elementary school—or "People's School,"as it was called during the War. The one photograph that shows me in the carriage— wearing a little white robe, my face a white mask of baby powder—was taken a month before my second birthday. If we were using the carriage to cart things, it must have been falling apart, the hood broken, the waterproof cloth of the body peeling. Had I been so rough on it as all that? Had we thrown it in the storage shed because it was a wreck? And how about my age? It does seem that I walked both to and from the other town, a goodly distance for me even now. My mother didn't have to carry me. Surely I had left kindergarten by then and was going to school.

This was probably true, because I seemed to recall that when we got home late that evening, my brother, who was in middle school, was very put out with my mother and me. By then the War was on, and my father, a Navy man, was no longer at home. Even assuming there was a moon that night, the road should have been dark due to the blackout. Still, the War was in its early stages; the air raids had not really started. It was probably the summer or the winter of 1942: my brother, so annoyed with us then, had left home by the following year. That night, he was probably hard at work preparing for the Naval Academy entrance examination. He must have been angry at my mother for being so late with his dinner.

But even as I go on making one reasonable-sounding guess after another, I realize that my "evidence" has no more validity than any other tricks of memory. Not a thing I have mentioned here is certain. Indeed, I can refute every item without half trying.

First, there is the old baby carriage. How long did we actually have it around the house? When did we get rid of it? And how? By leaving it in a nearby field? Sending it to the junk dealer's? I have no definite answers. It could just as well have stayed in the storage shed during the War and even for a time thereafter. Then the hoax would have been so easy to play: I might simply have confused that night scene with a postwar episode of stocking up on something.

Far from my mother's leading me by the hand, it seems more likely that I was there to protect her, that the road was unsafe for a woman alone at night. By then I would have been in my sixth year of elementary school or my first year of middle school. And we were wheeling not a carriage-load of peaches, but of black-market rice or potatoes or sweet potatoes or—if I'm going to insist on a cold winter night—perhaps some New Year's rice cakes. Then again, fuel being as hard to come by as food, it might have been kindling or charcoal or scraps of coal with which to stoke our old-fashioned bathtub.

Under this kind of scrutiny, the lovely image of a mother and child slowly pushing a carriage downhill on a moonlit night is suddenly transformed into a suspicious-looking couple transporting black-market goods. We would then have had our reasons for moving about under cover of night.

But where does my scowling brother fit in? He should not have been there waiting for us. Following his demobilization after the War, he was almost never at home. And if it so happened that he was in the house on that particular day, he would have had no reason to be angry with us. If anything, he would have been grateful. And so it was not my brother, probably, but my father who was waiting for us. It was always my father who stayed at home. Or rather, as a former officer, waiting at home was the only job there was for him to do.

But no, this has to be wrong. Those were peaches, I'm sure of it. All I have to do to make the memory consistent is change the cold winter evening to a summer night. This casts doubt, of course, on my mother's wrapping her shawl around me and the feeling I have that she told me old tales of foxes as we walked along. But literary tradition aside, there is nothing wrong with the subject of foxes in summer. Only the shawl is out of place.

As far as literary hoaxes go, the most obvious one is the moonlight that comes flooding into my so-called memory. It would have been no trouble at all for me to have been led from an old story of the fox's cry on a cold winter night into yet another story that my mother probably told me around that same time.

It was a story about a distant relative of hers, a young girl, something that happened when my mother was herself a girl. Born a cripple, the girl was sent to a convent when the other girls her age were marrying. She was suspected of having stolen something from one of the other nuns, however, and the older nuns beat her cruelly. That day, or perhaps it was the next day, or a short time thereafter, the girl drowned herself in a pond. It happened on a moonlit winter night, my mother said, unfolding the bright scene of death before me.

Within the grounds of the convent—somewhere in Kyoto, or possibly Nara —there was a large pond, on the banks of which grew a giant plum tree. Its heavy, gnarled branches stretched out low over the water to the middle of the pond. It looked just like a bridge, my mother said, as though she had seen the tree herself. Dragging her crippled leg, the poor young nun crawled quietly along the branch in her white robes as the moonlight flooded down. Then she fell and disappeared beneath the surface. The thing she had supposedly stolen was found some days later among another nun's belongings.

I suspect my mother embroidered rather freely on the story of the young girl's suicide but, child that I was, it moved me very deeply. More than the horror of her fate itself, however, what struck me was the fact that such a dark drama of ill-fated life should be concealed somewhere out on the farthest branches of the blood that tied me to others. Its ancient stage settings, like something out of the Nara or Heian past; the indistinct backdrop, like the ones in the shadow plays: these were what left an impression on me.

Is the image in my mind, then, of the same tradition as my mother's eerie tale? Did I create it for myself, as one often hears is done, by unconsciously fusing two wholly distinct memories into a single night's occurrence? Was this one of those "beautiful recollections," a pack of lies put through a sentimental tinting job until it comes out "like a little story"? It might well have been.

The memory I have (or seem to have) of pushing the carriage down the hill with my mother is unique: it happened that once and never again. Her wrapping her shawl around me when we were out together was a common enough scene, however, and her storytelling was by no means confined to nighttime walks. It could and did happen anywhere—at the dinner table, in my room, and probably most often while she was sewing.

At that age—be it summer or winter—I would most often walk with my mother at night on the way back from my aunt's house, which lay in precisely the opposite direction from the hill, in the town to the east. There was a river in that direction as well, but it was a river we followed for a while rather than crossed. The water's dark surface used to frighten me badly, for my cousins had told me of a boy my own age who had fallen in when hunting crabs on the bank and had sunk into the mud and died. The story had an eerie epilogue, which the girls had eagerly supplied: on windy nights, you could hear the dead boy's sobbing from the riverbank.

I would hide my face in my mother's sleeve, trying not to see the faint glow of the river as we passed by in the dark. Here, too, there were few dwellings, and the road was lonely and hemmed in by pine woods, but once we left the river behind I felt safe. Sometimes my mother would stop to gather a few pine cones and put them in her basket. One night, she stopped walking quite unexpectedly and, instructing me to stay put, waded cautiously into the deep grass by the roadside. I watched until she squatted down, then waited, praying that no one would come from either direction.

Thus, while I was familiar with the road to the east from an early age, I passed the hill in the other direction late at night only that once. If I am right in recalling that those were peaches we carted, it could have been no later than shortly after the War broke out. While my father was away, my mother had part of the lawn dug up and four peach trees planted. They were mature trees and bore fruit the following year—in such numbers that my mother had to spend many evenings tearing up old copies of her ladies' magazines and pasting the pages together to make covers for the still-green peaches. Every summer through the War years and after, we had more peaches than we could eat, and she was kept busy giving them away to relatives and neighbors. We never had to buy any.

All of which leads me to believe that the night in question had to have been in 1942. The trip she made to buy that load of peaches may have given my mother the idea to plant her own trees. Or, possibly, having decided to raise peaches, she went to the orchard in the next town to see how it was done. But in fact, where these questions are concerned, my memory tells me nothing at all.

What I do remember, however, as inseparably associated with the peach trees, are the face and voice of a man. It was he who encouraged her to plant them, who actually brought the young trees and put them into the ground. And every year he would come with fertilizer, inspect and prune the trees, and have a long chat with my mother before he left. He was the son of a local landowner whose family had built and rented many houses here for several generations and who also farmed the land. He was "the son," but he was of my mother's generation and by then was head of the household. He had often visited us before the War, too. My father bought our land from his father. Apparently, it had once been their watermelon patch.

My mother never invited the man in, but whenever he would drop over to say hello, bringing a bundle of vegetables at the peak of the season, she would serve him tea on the open veranda outside the dining room and sit nearby to talk. She left the care of the peach trees entirely to him, and the time would come when she would ask him to dig a bomb shelter as well. He could be asked to scoop the nightsoil, do any job. A round, ruddy man, he wore a cloth cap and a workman's vest with a large pocket on the front. He had a loud, ringing laugh that he would suppress for no one.

The dining-room veranda was my "territory." On the cement floor underneath were kept bundles of firewood, bales of charcoal, dried tulip and hyacinth bulbs, cobwebbed flowerpots, and a watering can. It was a sunny spot, and cats from other houses would come to stretch out there. I once saw a sick-looking cat eating weeds that had sprouted from the cracks in the cement. They were long, slender plants with seed clusters like bon-bons. I used to lie on the veranda, looking at all these things through the spaces in the planks.

One day, as the afternoon sun was fading from the veranda, the man and my mother sat there engrossed in conversation. It was just then that I came home from school.

Their talk was more light banter than anything serious.

". . . I know *your* type. You've done it all. With all sorts of women . . ." I heard my mother saying.

"No, not me, no . . ."

To hide his embarrassment, he laughed his ringing laugh, but he did not look at my mother. His eyes stayed fixed on the peach trees he had planted.

I was having my afternoon snack close by, and all at once I found myself listening to their every word. The banter continued for a time, but then my mother caught her breath.

"What? She will? The woman?" I heard her say.

I knew nothing about sex at that age, of course, but I had some vague idea of what they were talking about, enough to know that it was a dangerous topic.

Not long afterwards, on a day when the smell of the peaches was stifling in the summer heat, I was in my room with my mother, listening to the broadcast announcing the end of the War. It was September before my father came back, and too late for him to be served peaches. But the fruit that lay rotting on the ground continued to fill the garden and the house with its heavy, sweet perfume, and my father must have been aware of it long before he reached the doorway.

Still, what had my mother been talking about with the man that day? As I thought about it, years later, their strangely forced repartee began to flare up, incandescent, a point of peculiar brilliance in my memory. Here was the landlord, a man with a reputation for debauchery, trying to laugh off indecencies that he had broached with reluctance, while on the other hand, there was my mother, increasingly serious to the point of catching her breath. Indeed it was she, a woman in her prime left alone to guard the chastity of her marriage bed, who sought to draw out this kind of talk. The sharp contrast between the two of them struck my heart again and again: the man grown weary of women; the woman separated from her husband by years of war. As far as I could tell, her life had undergone no change, and it was precisely because of this that I recalled the scene as though witnessing a dangerous tightrope act.

I had been a child then, but surely I had said to myself—my mother is a soldier's wife, not the kind of woman to enjoy such vulgar talk with another man. But my skin, no doubt, had been feeling something a little different. I still liked to sleep with my mother in those days. And in winter, especially, there were many opportunities to do so. At bedtime, of course, I would get into my own bed, but I would snuggle into hers after going to the toilet in the middle of the night. Too sleepy to chase me out, she would have to make room for me. Then, drifting on the edge of sleep, she would clasp me to her breast, entwine her naked legs with mine. Where her nightgown had slipped open, the flesh was hot, as if with fever.

Before long, this had become my nightly pleasure, until finally I myself no longer knew whether I was waking up because I actually had to go to the toilet, or going to the toilet was an excuse to be held by my mother. Surely, when she held me, the feeling that came through my skin was not just my own pleasure, but the jagged restlessness of my mother's flesh, and the sinful awareness that I had thrust myself into the void left by my father and was enjoying her greedily.

Yes, a third person not actually present could well have been part of that night scene on the hill. And was it not my father? Some unusual circumstance must have been responsible for my mother's being there at that strange time and having me with her.

They had quarreled, perhaps, and the repercussions had come to me. I do seem to remember something that happened between them just before the War.

My father was warming one hand over the charcoal brazier and commanding my mother, sitting opposite him, to "Go, I said! Go now!"

The ringing of the copper kettle made the silence that followed seem horribly long and suffocating.

"I'm telling you, go and settle it properly, once and for all," he said, his authority overwhelming. My mother hung her head in silence. He turned away.

"But it's so late . . ." she murmured in desperation.

"I don't give a damn. You go," he said and looked away again.

"Please, not tonight. I'll go in the morning. I swear I will."

"I said tonight and I meant it."

Their confrontation went on, and eventually my mother seemed to be crying.

"Oh, please forgive me," she sobbed. "Forgive your wife!"

She reached for the hand he held over the brazier, but he swept her hand away as if it were something vile, knocking the fire tongs into the ashes. As they fell, she crumpled before him, clinging to his knees.

Perhaps he had only been trying to avoid her touch, but his hand had struck hers, and this filled me with terror. Now it was my turn to burst into tears, I suspect, and my mother, resigned to what she must do, probably led me out into the night.

The failing for which my mother was being blamed that night may have amounted to nothing at all. Obstinate military man that he was, my father often tormented her this way, and she submitted meekly.

That scene, too, ends abruptly, and I have no idea where it leads, no way of knowing what came of it. But even now I can hear my mother in tears at my father's knee—"Oh, please forgive me. Forgive your wife!" Her cry rings through the darkness, caressing, seductive. I do not doubt that my father heard the almost unseemly erotic appeal in her voice, the soft, clinging tones of the Osaka woman. And he did not succumb to her sexual onslaught because I was there, watching.

Was not *this* my cold winter night? And if it was, then my mother had taken me to the neighboring town not to buy anything, but to accomplish something far more important—or at least, something far more painful. But the further I pursue this line of reasoning, the more confused I become, for another part of me clings stubbornly to the memory of pushing the old baby carriage down the hill with my mother through the winter moonlight, our breath white in the cold.

After wandering thus in endless circles, I feel as though I have been hurled once again onto the hill on the road that—today as then—links our town with the next.

I know that my mother and I passed that place wheeling a baby carriage— but does all certainty end there?

Having retreated fifty paces, let me fall back a hundred: perhaps I was merely *riding* in that carriage? Or, yielding another hundred paces: perhaps the dark hill —the one place that seemed more eerily unknown than any other to my boyhood imagination—perhaps this setting could be an image that stayed with me from a time when I passed there alone several years later. And through some weird manipulation of memory, I may have been arbitrarily throwing into this setting an image of myself in the carriage wrapped in my mother's shawl, or an image of myself on another road on another night that I passed asleep and only heard about later, or yet a wholly different scene of my mother and me pushing something in the carriage.

What emerges from this is the arcane spectacle of me as a boy, wheeling a baby carriage that holds my infant self.

TRANSLATED BY JAY RUBIN

◫ TANIZAKI JUNICHIRŌ

Tanizaki Junichirō was perhaps the greatest (as well as the most vigorous) of modern Japanese novelists. Only Natsume Sōseki, whose increasingly somber novels were produced in a single decade of feverish work, seems a convincing rival. For over half a century Tanizaki pursued a single grand theme—the eternal, elusive feminine—in a matchless variety of styles and techniques and always in superb prose. He was already famous in 1910 for an elegantly sadomasochistic fable "The Tattooer" (*Shisei*) that is still a favorite among anthologists; in 1930 the first of many Complete Editions of his works was issued; his reemergence after the War in the role of "old master" was as an active writer, and he remained active until his death, in 1965, after celebrating his seventy-ninth birthday.

Tanizaki was born in Tokyo in 1886, in the old downtown merchant quarter. His father, an adopted son, failed at one enterprise after another, but it was his strong-willed mother, a beauty who loved the Kabuki theater and who had been portrayed in woodcut prints, that haunted his imagination. He left Tokyo University without graduating, became a successful writer, and began a life of strenuous bohemianism which was not allowed to interfere with hard work. In the early 1920s he wrote scenarios for a newly established Yokohama film studio, but left in despair at its commercialism. After the great earthquake of 1923 he moved to the Kansai region and began to cultivate a taste for the traditional arts. *A Fool's Love* (*Chijin no ai*, 1925) summed up his infatuation with the Westernized atmosphere (and actresses) of Yokohama; *Some Prefer Nettles* (*Tade kuu mushi*, 1929, tr. 1955), an ambivalent study of a modern couple drifting toward divorce amid the attractions of an older way of life, foreshadowed his own notorious divorce, in a similarly amicable arrangement with his wife's lover. A brief second marriage was followed in 1935 by his enduring marriage to Nezu Matsuko of Osaka.

Most of Tanizaki's fiction of the 1930s has a serene classical tone; much of it, indeed, is set in the past, ranging as far back as medieval times. From 1935 to 1938 he devoted himself to translating into modern Japanese the classic *Tale of Genji*, with its spacious gallery of portraits of women. After the War he twice revised his translation, to fill in the gaps caused by prewar censorship and to simplify the language to suit the needs of younger readers. Wartime pressure delayed the publication of his own most ambitious novel, *The Makioka Sisters* (*Sasameyuki*, tr. 1957), a leisurely chronicle of upper-class Osaka life with its central character modeled on his wife Matsuko. In 1949, after its completion, he was given the Imperial Cultural Decoration, the highest official honor for a Japanese writer. In 1956, however, Tanizaki once again startled the literary world with *The Key* (*Kagi*, tr. 1961), a spare melodramatic tale told through the intermingled (and equally mendacious) diaries of a middle-aged man and his sexually demanding wife. *Diary of a Mad Old Man* (*Fūten rōjin nikki*, 1962, tr. 1965), his last novel, is a tragicomedy of death confronted—and transcended by erotic fantasies in old age.

The Bridge of Dreams is a short novel in the manner of the nostalgic memoir, another late work in which Tanizaki creates a luxuriant fantasy. This time he anchors his restless imagination in the remembered reality of a house and garden where he had lived in Kyoto a decade before. The confessional narrative of a young man who has grown up in the shadow of a guilt-laden obsession with the memory of his mother, and with the beauty of the girl who took her place, suggests the theme and atmosphere of the final chapters of *The Tale of Genji*, darkened by the influence of modern psychological fiction. The moving coda of *Genji* describes a young man's frustrated pursuit of a girl whom he identifies with the memory of her dead sister; and its last chapter is entitled "The Bridge of Dreams"—an image symbolizing the insubstantial beauty of life itself, which Prince Genji once called "a bridge linking dream to dream."

❖ The Bridge of Dreams

(*Yume no ukihashi,* 1959)

On reading the last chapter of The Tale of Genji:

> *Today when the summer thrush*
> *Came to sing at Heron's Nest*
> *I crossed the Bridge of Dreams.*

This poem was written by my mother. But I have had two mothers—the second was a stepmother—and although I am inclined to think my real mother wrote it, I cannot be sure. The reasons for this uncertainty will become clear later: one of them is that both women went by the name of Chinu. I remember hearing as a child that Mother was named after the Bay of Chinu, since she was born nearby at Hamadera, where her family, who were Kyoto people, had a seaside villa. She is listed as Chinu in the official city records. My second mother was also called Chinu from the time she came to our house. She never used her real name, Tsuneko, again. Even my father's letters to her were invariably addressed to "Chinu"; you can't tell by the name which of the two he meant. And the "Bridge of Dreams" poem is simply signed "Chinu."

Anyway, I know of no other poems by either woman. I happen to be acquainted with this one because the square slip of wave-patterned paper on which it is written was reverently mounted in a hanging scroll to be kept as a family heirloom. According to my old nurse, who is now in her sixties, this kind of handmade paper was decorated by the ancient "flowing ink" process (that is, by dipping it in water and letting it absorb a swirl of ink) and had to be ordered all the way from Echizen. My mother must have gone to a great deal of trouble to get it. For years I puzzled over the Konoe-style calligraphy of the poem, and the many unusual Chinese characters that even an adult—let alone a child— would find hard to read. No one uses such characters nowadays. I am reminded that we have a set of poem cards which seem to have been written by one of my mothers in that same esoteric style.

As for the quality of the hand, I am not really able to judge. "They tell me nobody else wrote such a beautiful Konoe style," my nurse used to say; and to my own amateur taste, for whatever that is worth, it appears to be the work of quite an accomplished calligrapher. But you would expect a woman to choose the slender, graceful style of the Kozei school. It seems odd that she preferred the thick, fleshy Konoe line, with its heavy sprinkling of Chinese characters. Probably that reveals something of her personality.

When it comes to poetry I am even less qualified to speak, but I hardly think this verse has any special merit. The line "I crossed the Bridge of Dreams" must mean "Today I read 'The Bridge of Dreams'—the last chapter of *The Tale of Genji.*" Since that is only a short chapter, one that would take very little time to read, no doubt she is saying that today she at last finished the whole of *Genji.* "Heron's Nest" is the name by which our house has been known ever since my grandfather's time, a name given to it because night herons often alighted in its garden. Even now, herons occasionally come swooping down. Although I have seldom actually seen them, I have often heard their long, strident cry.

Heron's Nest is on a lane running eastward through the woods below the Shimogamo Shrine in Kyoto. When you go into the woods a little way, with the main building of the shrine on your left, you come to a narrow stone bridge over a stream: our gate is just beyond it. People who live in the neighborhood say that the stream flowing under this bridge is the subject of the famous poem by Chomei:

> *The stony Shallow Stream—*
> *So pure that even the moon*
> *Seeks it out to dwell in it.*

But this seems doubtful. Yoshida Togo's gazetteer describes our "Shallow Stream" as "the brook that flows southward, east of the Shimogamo Shrine, into the Kamo River." Then it adds: "However, the 'Shallow Stream' mentioned in ancient topographical writings was the Kamo River itself, of which the brook in question is merely a tributary having its source in Matsugasaki." That is probably right, since Chomei is quoted elsewhere as saying that "Shallow Stream" is the old name of the Kamo River. The Kamo is also mentioned by that name in a poem by Jozan, which I will cite later, and the poet's prefatory note explains: "On refusing to cross the Kamo River into Kyoto." Of course our little stream is no longer especially pure and limpid, but until my childhood it was as clear as Chomei's poem might suggest. I remember that in mid-June, during the ceremony of purification, people bathed in its shallow waters.

The garden pond at Heron's Nest was linked to this stream by earthen drainage pipes to prevent it from overflowing. Once inside our main gate, with its two thick cedar pillars, you went down a flagstone walk to an inner gate. Dwarf bamboo were planted along both sides of the walk, and a pair of stone figures of Korean court officials (apparently of the Yi Dynasty) stood face to face on either side of it. The inner gate, which was always kept closed, had a roof thatched with cypress bark in an elegant rustic style. Each gate pillar bore a narrow bamboo tablet inscribed with one line of a Chinese couplet:

> *Deep in the grove the many birds are gay.*
> *Far from the dust the pine and bamboo are clean.*

But my father said he had no idea whose poem or whose calligraphy it was.

When you rang the doorbell (the button was beside one of the poem tablets) someone came out to open the gate for you. Then you went along under the shade of a large chestnut tree to the front door; in the main entrance hall, you saw mounted over the transom a piece of calligraphy from the brush of the scholar-poet Rai Sanyo:

> *The hawk soars, the fish dives.*

What gave Heron's Nest its value was its landscape garden of almost an acre; the house itself was low and rambling but not particularly large. There were only some eight rooms, including the maids' room and the smaller entrance hall; but the kitchen was a spacious one, big enough for an average restaurant, and there was an artesian well next to the sink. Originally my grandfather lived on Muromachi Street near the Bukko Temple, and used Heron's Nest as his villa. Later, though, he sold the Muromachi Street house and made this his home, adding a sizable storehouse at its northwest corner. Going back and forth to the storehouse for a scroll or vase was quite inconvenient, since you had to go through the kitchen.

Our household consisted of seven persons—my parents and me, my nurse

Okane, and three maids—and we found the house comfortable enough. Father liked a quiet life. He put in an appearance at his bank now and then, but spent most of his time at home, seldom inviting guests. It seems that my grandfather enjoyed the tea ceremony and led an active social life: he had a fine old teahouse brought in by the side of the pond, and built another small place for entertaining, which he called the Silk-Tree Pavilion, in the southeast corner of the garden. But after his death his prized teahouse and pavilion were no longer used, except as a place to take an afternoon nap or read or practice calligraphy.

All of my father's love was concentrated on my mother. With this house, this garden, and this wife, he seemed perfectly happy. Sometimes he would have her play the koto for him, and he would listen intently, but that was almost his only amusement at home. A garden of less than an acre seems a little cramped to be called a true landscape garden, but it had been laid out with the greatest care and gave the impression of being far deeper and more secluded than it actually was.

When you went through the sliding doors on the other side of the main entrance hall you found yourself in an average-sized room of eight mats, beyond which was a wide, twelve-mat chamber, the largest room in the house. The twelve-mat room was somewhat after the fashion of the Palace style, with a veranda along the eastern and southern sides, enclosed by a formal balustrade. On the south, in order to screen out the sun, the wide eaves were extended by latticework with a luxuriant growth of wild akebia vine hanging out over the pond; the water came lapping up under the vine leaves to the edge of the veranda. If you leaned on the rail and gazed across the pond you saw a waterfall plunging out of a densely wooded hill, its waters flowing under double globeflowers in the spring or begonias in autumn, emerging as a rippling stream for a little way, and then dropping into the pond. Just at the point where the stream entered the pond a bamboo device called a "water mortar" was set up: as soon as the water filled its bamboo tube, which was pivoted off-center, one end resting on a stone, the tube would tilt the other way, letting the water run out, and then drop back to its original position with a hollow clack. Since the tube was supposed to be of fresh green bamboo, with a cleanly cut open end, the gardener had to replace it often. This sort of device is mentioned in a fourteenth-century poem:

> *Has the water upstream*
> *Become a lazy current?*
> *The sound of the mortar is rarely heard.*

Even today, the sound of a water mortar echoes through the garden of the well-known Hall of Poets, the home of the early Edo poet Ishikawa Jozan in the northern suburbs of Kyoto. There, too, is displayed an explanatory text written in Chinese by Jozan. I suppose the reason why we had a water mortar is that my grandfather went there, read the description, and got the impulse to copy the device for his own house. It is said that Jozan's poem about not wishing to cross the Kamo River was written as a polite way of declining an invitation from the Emperor:

Alas, I am ashamed to cross it—
Though only a Shallow Stream
It would mirror my wrinkled age.

A rubbing of the poem hangs in an alcove in the Hall of Poets, and we had one at our house too.

When I was about three or four, I was enchanted by the clack, clack of our water mortar.

"Tadasu!" Mother would call. "Don't go over there or you'll fall in the pond!" But no matter how often she stopped me, I would run out into the garden and make my way through the tall bamboo grass of the artificial hill, trying to get to the edge of the stream.

"Wait! It's dangerous! You mustn't go there alone!" Mother or Okane would hurry after me in alarm and seize me by the back of my sash. Squirming forward while one of them held fast to me, I would peer down into the stream. As I watched, the green bamboo tube of the mortar slowly filled, tipped, spilling its water into the pond, and then dropped back into place with a sharp rap against the stone. After a few minutes it was full again, repeating the process. I suppose this clacking noise is my earliest memory of our house. Day and night it echoed in my ears, all the while that I was growing up.

Okane was always on her guard with me, hardly daring to let me out of her sight. Yet my mother often scolded her. "Do be careful, Okane!" she would say. There was an earth-covered footbridge over the pond, and whenever I tried to cross it Okane was sure to stop me. Sometimes Mother came running after me too. Most of the pond was shallow, but it was over six feet deep at one place, where a hole had been sunk so that the fish could survive if the rest of the water dried up. The hole was near the bridge, and Mother warned me about it time and again. "It would be dreadful if you fell in there," she used to say. "Even a grownup couldn't get out."

On the other side of the bridge was an arbor, and next to it the teahouse, my favorite playroom.

"Wait outside, Okane!" I would tell my nurse. "You mustn't come in after me." I was delighted with the low-roofed, narrow little building because it seemed exactly like a toy house for a child. I would play there for hours: sprawling out on its straw-matted floor, going through the tiny doorways, turning the water on and off in the pantry, untying the braided cords of the wooden boxes I found and taking out the tea objects, or putting on one of the wide rush hats the guests wore when coming to the tea ceremony in the rain.

Okane, who was standing outside, would begin to worry. "Tadasu!" she would call. "Don't stay any longer—your mother won't like it." Or again: "Look! There's a great big centipede here! It's terrible if a centipede bites you!" I actually did see large centipedes in the teahouse a few times, but I was never bitten.

I was far more afraid of the half-dozen stone figures of Buddhist saints which stood here and there on the hill and around the pond. These were only three or four feet high, considerably smaller than the Korean statues before the inner gate, but their ugly, grotesque faces seemed somehow very Japanese. Some of them had hideously distorted noses and seemed to be staring at you out of the corners of their eyes; others seemed on the verge of a sly, malicious laugh. I never went near them after sunset.

Now and then Mother called me over to the veranda when she fed crumbs to the fish.

"Here, little fish," she said, scattering crumbs out into the pond as the carp came swimming up from their hiding place in that deep hollow. Sometimes I sat close to her on the edge of the veranda, leaning against the low rail and tossing crumbs to them too; or else I sat on her lap, feeling the warm, resilient touch of her rather full thighs as she held me snugly in her embrace.

In the summer my parents and I used to have supper by the pond, and sit there to enjoy the cool of evening. Occasionally we ordered food from a restaurant or had a man come in from a caterer, bringing all the ingredients and cooking them in our huge kitchen. Father would put a bottle of beer under the spout of the bamboo mortar. Mother would sit at the edge of the pond and dangle her feet in the water, where they looked more beautiful than ever. She was a small, delicately built woman, with plump, white little dumpling-like feet which she held quite motionless as she soaked them in the water, letting the coolness seep through her body. Years later, after I was grown up, I came across this line of Chinese verse:

> *When she washes the inkstone,*
> *the fish come to swallow ink.*

Even as a young child I thought how pleasant it would be if the fish in our pond came gliding playfully around her beautiful feet, instead of coming only when we fed them.

I remember that on one of those summer evenings I noticed some long, thin, slippery-looking leaves in my soup, and asked Mother what they were.

"That's called *nenunawa*," she said.

"Oh? What's *that?*"

"A kind of water plant, like a lotus—they gather it at Mizoro Pond," she explained in her soft, well-bred voice.

Father laughed. "If you say it's *nenunawa* people won't know what you're talking about," he told her. "They call it *junsai* nowadays."

"But doesn't *nenunawa* sound long and slippery, just the way it is? That's the name for it in all the old poems, you know." And she began reciting one of them. From that time on it was always called *nenunawa* at our house, even by the maids and by the men who came to cook for us.

At nine o'clock I would be told that it was bedtime, and be taken away by my nurse. I don't know how late my parents stayed up; they slept in the room with the veranda around it, while Okane and I were in a small room of six mats on the north side, across the corridor from them. Sometimes I fretted and lay awake a long time, pleading: "Let me sleep with Mama!"

Then Mother would come to look in at me. "My, what a little baby I have tonight," she would say, taking me up in her arms and carrying me to her bedroom. Even though the bed had already been prepared for sleeping, Father would not be in it—perhaps he was still out in the pavilion. Mother herself had yet to dress for bed. She lay down beside me just as she was, not taking off her sash, and held me so that my head nestled under her chin. The light was on, but I buried my face inside the neck opening of her kimono and had a blurred impression of being swathed in darkness. The faint scent of her hair, which was done up in a chignon, wafted into my nostrils. Seeking out her nipples with my mouth, I played with them like an infant, took them between my lips, ran my tongue over them. She always let me do that as long as I wanted, without a word of reproach. I believe I used to suckle at her breasts until I was a fairly large child, perhaps because in those days people were not at all strict about weaning their children. When I used my tongue as hard as I could, licking her nipples and pressing around them, the milk flowed out nicely. The mingled scents of her hair and milk hovered there in her bosom, around my face. As dark as it was, I could still dimly see her white breasts.

"Go to sleep now," she would murmur; and as she comforted me, patting me on the head and stroking my back, she began to sing her usual lullaby:

> *Go to sleep, go to sleep.*
> *Don't cry, there's a good child, go to sleep.*
> *It's Mother cuddling you,*
> *Mother cradling you,*
> *Don't cry, there's a good child, go to sleep.*

She would sing it over and over while I drifted off into a peaceful sleep, still clutching her breasts and running my tongue around her nipples. Often my dreams were penetrated by the distant clack of the water mortar, far beyond my shuttered windows.

Okane also knew a number of lullabies, such as this one:

> *When I asked the pillow, "Is he asleep?"*
> *The honest pillow said, "He is!"*

She sang many others for me too, but I was never easily lulled asleep by her songs. (Nor, in the room I shared with her, could I hear the sound of the water mortar.) Mother's voice had a seductive rhythm all its own, a rhythm that filled my mind with pleasant fancies and quickly put me to sleep.

Although I have thus far written "mother" without specifying which of the two I meant, my intention has been to relate only memories of my true mother. Yet it occurs to me that these recollections seem a little too detailed for a child of three or four. Seeing her dangle her feet in the pond, or hearing her talk about *nenunawa*, for instance—would such things, if they had really happened when I was a child of that age, have left any impression whatever? Possibly impressions of the first mother were overlaid by those of the second, confusing my memory. For early one autumn, just as the chestnut tree at our doorway was beginning to shed its leaves, my twenty-two-year-old mother, who was with child, contracted an infection of the womb and died. I was five at the time. A few years later I had a stepmother.

I cannot recall my first mother's features distinctly. According to Okane, she was very beautiful, but all that I can summon to my mind's eye is the vague image of a full, round face. Since I often looked up at her as she held me in her arms, I could see her nostrils clearly. The lamplight gave a pink luminosity to her lovely nose: seen from that angle, it appeared to be all the more exquisitely proportioned —not in the least like Okane's nose, or anyone else's. But when I try to remember her other features—her eyes, her mouth—I can only visualize them in a very general way. Here too I am perhaps being misled by the superimposed image of my second mother. After my real mother's death Father used to read the sutras and say prayers for her every morning and evening before her memorial tablet, and I often sat beside him praying too. But as hard as I stared at her photograph, which stood beside the tablet on our Buddhist altar, I never had the sudden poignant feeling that this was my own mother—the woman who had suckled me at her breasts.

All I could tell from the picture was that she wore her hair in an old-fashioned style, and that she seemed even plumper than I had remembered. It was too faded to re-create in my mind the way she actually looked.

"Papa," I asked, "is that really Mama's picture?"

"Yes, of course it is," he said. "It was taken before we were married, when she was about sixteen."

"But it doesn't look like her, does it? Why don't you put up something better? Don't you have another one?"

"Your mother didn't like to be photographed, so this is the only one I could find of her by herself. After we were married we had some pictures taken together, but the man did such a bad job retouching them that she thought they spoiled her face. Now this one shows her when she was a very young girl, and she may seem different from the way you remember her. But that was how she really looked at the time."

I could see then that it did bear a certain resemblance to her, though by no means enough to bring the forgotten image of my mother back to life.

I would think of her wistfully as I leaned on the balustrade and watched the carp swimming in the pond, yearn for her as I listened to the clack of the bamboo mortar. But it was especially at night, when I was lying in bed in my nurse's arms, that I felt an indescribable longing for my dead mother. That sweet, dimly white dream world there in her warm bosom among the mingled scents of her hair and her milk—why had it disappeared? Was this what "death" meant? Where could she have gone? Okane tried to console me by singing Mother's lullabies, but that made my grief all the worse. "No, no!" I cried, thrashing about in bed. "I don't like you to sing for me! I want Mama!" Kicking off the covers, I howled and wept.

At last my father would come in to say: "Tadasu, you mustn't give Okane so much trouble. Now be a good boy and go to sleep." But I cried even harder.

"Your mother has died," he would tell me, his voice thickening and faltering. "It doesn't do any good to cry about it. I feel as much like crying as you do —maybe more—but I'm being brave. You try to be brave too."

Then Okane would say: "If you want to see your mama, you ought to pray as hard as you can. If you do, she'll come to you in a dream, and say: 'Tadasu, you're such a good little boy!' But if you cry she won't come!"

Sometimes Father would give up in despair at my incessant wailing and screaming, and say: "All right then, come sleep with me." Taking me along to his room, he would lie down with me in his arms. But I found his masculine smell so different from my mother's fragrance that I was inconsolable. Rather than sleep with him, I preferred to sleep with my nurse.

"Papa, you make me feel sick. I want to go back to Okane."

"Well, go sleep in the other room then."

But Okane would scold me for it when I got back into bed with her. "Even if your father *does* make you feel sick, why do you have to say such an awful thing?" She used to say I looked exactly like him, not like my mother. That made me unhappy too.

Father always spent an hour morning and evening reading aloud from the sutras before the memorial tablet. As soon as I thought he was going to stop I would steal up to the altar and sit beside him for the few remaining minutes, running my little string of prayer beads through my fingers. But sometimes he led me there by the hand, saying: "Come to pray for your mother"; and I had to sit still beside him for the whole hour.

The next spring, when I was six, I entered elementary school, and from that time on I seldom made a nuisance of myself at night. But I longed for Mother all the more. Even my unsociable father, who had never cared for any company except my mother's, seemed to feel lonely, and began going out occasionally for diversion. On Sundays he often took Okane and me along to dine at a riverside restaurant in Yamabana, or on an excursion to the hills west of the city.

One day he said to me: "When your mother was alive we often used to go out to Yamabana for dinner. Do you remember that, Tadasu?"

"I only remember once. Weren't some frogs croaking in the river behind us?"

"That's right. Do you remember hearing your mother sing a song there one evening?"

"I don't think so."

Then, as if it had suddenly occurred to him: "Tadasu, suppose there was someone just like your mother, and suppose she was willing to come and *be* your mother—how would you feel about that?"

"Do you really think there *is* such a person?" I asked dubiously. "Do you know anyone, Papa?"

"No," he replied hastily, "I only said 'suppose.' " He seemed anxious to drop the subject.

I am not sure exactly how old I was when Father and I had that conversation. Nor have I any way of knowing whether he already had someone in mind, or whether it was simply a chance remark. But when I was in the second grade— in the spring, when the double globeflowers at the mouth of the waterfall were in full bloom—I came home from school one day and was startled to hear the sound of a koto from the inner room. Who could be playing? My mother had been an accomplished musician of the Ikuta school, and I had often seen Father sitting beside her on the veranda, listening absorbedly as she played for him on her six-foot-long koto, which was decorated with a pine-tree pattern worked in gold lacquer. After her death, her beloved koto was wrapped in a cloth dyed with our family crest of paulownia leaves and flowers, placed in a black-lacquered box, and put away in the storehouse, where it had remained undisturbed ever since. Could that be her koto? I wondered, as I came in through the side entrance. Just then Okane appeared, and whispered into my ear. "Tadasu, be very quiet and peek in the other room. There's a pretty young lady here today!"

When I went through the eight-mat room to the other side, pushed open the sliding doors a little, and peered in, Father noticed me at once and beckoned. The strange lady was engrossed in her koto; even after I came up beside her she kept on playing without so much as turning her head. She sat where my mother used to sit, and in the very same pose, her instrument laid out at the same angle, her left hand stretched out in the same way as she pressed the strings. The koto was not Mother's—it was a plain one, completely unadorned. But Father's position and attitude as he sat there listening so attentively were exactly the same as in my mother's time. It was only after she finished and took off the ivory finger picks that the strange lady turned to smile at me.

"Are you Tadasu?" she inquired politely, in a well-bred Kyoto accent. "You look just like your father."

"Make a nice bow," Father said, putting his hand on my head.

"Did you just come home from school?" she asked. Then she slipped the picks back on her fingers and began to play again. I didn't recognize the piece, but it sounded extremely difficult. Meanwhile I sat obediently beside my father and watched her every movement, hardly daring to breathe. Even after she stopped playing for us, she made no attempt to shower me with compliments— all she did was smile when our eyes met. She talked to Father in a calm, relaxed way, and seemed to have an air of composure. Soon a ricksha came for her; she was gone before dusk. But she left her koto with us. We stood it up against the wall in the alcove of the eight-mat room.

I was sure that Father would ask me what I thought of her, whether I didn't agree that she looked like my mother. But he said nothing, nor did I try to find out how they happened to become acquainted. Somehow I hesitated to bring the matter up. To tell the truth, if I'd been asked whether or not she looked like my mother I would scarcely have known what to say. At least, my first glimpse of her had not given me the impression that here indeed was the reincarnation of my mother. And yet her soft, round face, her delicate body, her calm, unhurried speech, in particular her polite reserve and utter lack of flattery when we met, together with her indefinable attractiveness and charm—in all this she seemed to resemble my mother, and I felt friendly toward her.

"Who was that?" I asked Okane later.

"I really don't know," she said. Possibly she had been warned not to tell me.

"Is this the first time she's come here?"

"No, she was here about twice before. . . . It's the first time she's played the koto, though."

I saw the woman once more that summer, around the season when you begin to hear the song of the thrush. That time she seemed even more at ease, staying to feed crumbs to the fish with Father and me after playing the koto. But she left before supper. Again her koto was put in the alcove—maybe she came to the house more often than I knew.

One day in March, when I was eight years old, Father called me into the veranda room to talk to me. I think it was after supper, about eight o'clock in the evening, when no one else was around.

"I have something to discuss with you, Tadasu," he began, in an unusually solemn tone. "I don't know how you feel about the lady who's been coming to visit us, but for various reasons—reasons that concern you as well as me—I'm thinking of marrying her. You'll be in the third grade this year, so I want you to try to understand what I'm saying. As you know, I had the greatest love for your mother. If she were only alive today I wouldn't want anyone else. Her death was a terrible blow to me—I couldn't get over it. But then I happened to meet this lady. You say you don't remember your mother's face very clearly, but you'll soon find that this lady resembles her in all sorts of ways. Of course no two people are quite alike, unless they're twins. That isn't what I mean by resembling her. I mean the impression she makes, the way she talks, the way she carries herself, her quiet, easygoing personality, sweet and gentle, and yet deep—that's why I say she's like your mother. If I hadn't met her I'd never have wanted to marry again. It's only because there *is* such a person that I've come to feel this way. Maybe your mother saw to it that I happened to find this lady, for your sake as well as mine. If she'll come and stay with us, she'll be a wonderful help to you as you grow up. And now that the second anniversary of your mother's death has passed, this seems like a proper time for marrying her. What do you think, Tadasu? You understand what I've been telling you, don't you?"

Curiously enough, I had already given my consent long before he finished what he intended to say. Seeing my face light up, he added: "There's one thing more I'd like you to remember. When she comes you mustn't think of her as your second mother. Think that your mother has been away somewhere for a while and has just come home. Even if I didn't tell you so, you'd soon begin to look at it that way. Your two mothers will become one, with no distinction between them. Your first mother's name was Chinu, and your new mother's name is Chinu too. And in everything she says and does, your new mother will behave the way the first one did."

After that, Father stopped taking me in to sit beside him during his morning and evening worship at the memorial tablet. The time he spent reading the sutras gradually became shorter. Then one evening in April the wedding ceremony was held in the veranda room. Maybe there was a reception afterward, in some restaurant, but I have no remembrance of that. The ceremony itself was a very quiet affair: only a few close relatives attended on either side. From that day on Father called his bride "Chinu," and I, having been told to call her "Mama," found that the word came to my lips with surprising ease.

For the past two or three years I had been accustomed to sleeping in the room next to Father's, but from the night my new mother arrived I went back to sharing the little room across the corridor with Okane. Father seemed to be truly happy, and began living the same kind of tranquil domestic life he had enjoyed with my first mother. Even Okane and the maids, who had been with us for years and who might have been expected to gossip and criticize their new mistress, were won over completely by her. Probably it was because of her natural kindness and warmth—anyway, they served her as faithfully as they had her predecessor.

Our household returned to its old routine. Father would sit listening attentively while Mother played the koto, just as he used to when my real mother was alive; and he always had the gold-lacquered koto brought out for the occasion. In summer the three of us would have supper beside the pond. Father would take his beer to cool under the spout of the bamboo mortar. Mother would dangle her feet in the pond. As I looked at her feet through the water I found myself remembering my real mother's feet. I felt as if they were the same; or rather, to put it more accurately, whenever I caught a glimpse of my new mother's feet I recalled that those of my own mother, the memory of which had long ago faded, had had the same lovely shape.

My stepmother also called the water plant we had in soup *nenunawa,* and told me how it was gathered at Mizoro Pond.

"I imagine that sooner or later you'll hear at school about the Court anthologies," she remarked one day. "Well, there's a poem in the earliest one that goes like this." And she recited a poem which had a pun on the word *nenunawa*.

As I have said before, I suspect that these incidents occurred during my real mother's lifetime and were only being repeated. No doubt Father had instructed my present mother how to behave, and was trying his best to confuse me about what my two mothers had said or done, so that I would identify them in my mind.

One evening—I believe it was that autumn—Mother came into my room just as I was about to go to sleep with Okane.

"Tadasu," she asked, "do you remember how your mama used to nurse you till you were about four years old?"

"Yes," I said.

"And do you remember how she always sang lullabies to you?"

"I remember."

"Wouldn't you still like to have your mama do those things?"

"I suppose so . . ." I answered, flushing, aware that my heart had begun to pound.

"Then come and sleep with me tonight."

She took my hand and led me to the veranda room. The bed was ready for sleeping, but Father had not yet come in. Mother herself was still fully dressed, still wearing her usual sash. The light was shining overhead. I could hear the clack of the bamboo mortar. Everything was the way it used to be. Mother got into bed first, propped her head on the wooden pillow (her hair was done up in an old-fashioned chignon), and lifted the covers for me to crawl in after her. I was already too tall to bury myself easily under her chin, but being face to face with her made me feel so awkward that I shrank as far as I could under the covers. When I did, the neckline of her kimono was just at my nose.

Then I heard her whisper: "Tadasu, do you want some milk?" As she spoke, she bent her head down to look at me. Her cool hair brushed against my forehead.

"You must've been awfully lonely, with no one but Okane to sleep with for such a long time. If you wanted to sleep with Mama, why didn't you say so earlier? Were you feeling shy about it?"

I nodded.

"What a funny little boy you are! Now, hurry up and see if you can find the milk!"

I drew the top of her kimono open, pressed my face between her breasts, and played with her nipples with both hands. Because she was still looking down at me, a beam of light shone in over the edge of the bedclothes. I held one nipple and then the other in my mouth, sucking and using my tongue avidly to start the flow of milk. But as hard as I tried, it wouldn't come.

"Ooh, that tickles!" Mother exclaimed.

"I can't get a drop," I told her. "Maybe I've forgotten how."

"I'm sorry," she said. "Just be patient—I'll have a baby one of these days, and then there'll be lots of milk for you."

Even so, I wouldn't let go of her breasts, and kept sucking at them. I knew it was hopeless, but still I enjoyed the sensation of rolling around in my mouth those firm little buds at the tips of her soft, full breasts.

"I'm terribly sorry—and you've worked so hard at it! Do you want to go on trying anyway?"

Nodding my head, I kept on suckling. Once again, by some strange association, I seemed to drift among the mingled scents of hair oil and milk that had hovered in my mother's bosom so long ago. That warm, dimly white dream world —the world I thought had disappeared forever—had unexpectedly returned.

Then Mother began to sing the old lullaby, in the very rhythm that I knew so well:

> "Go to sleep, go to sleep,
> Don't cry, there's a good child, go to sleep . . ."

But in spite of her singing I was too excited to relax that night, and I went on sucking away greedily at her nipples.

Within half a year, though I hadn't forgotten my real mother, I could no longer distinguish sharply between her and the present one. When I tried to remember my real mother's face, my stepmother's appeared before me; when I tried to remember her voice, my stepmother's echoed in my ears. Gradually the two images merged: I found it hard to believe that I had ever had a different mother. Everything turned out just as Father had planned.

When I reached the age of twelve or thirteen, I began sleeping alone at night. But even then I would sometimes long to be held in my mother's bosom. "Mama, let me sleep with you!" I would beg. Drawing open her kimono, I would suck at her milkless breasts, and listen to her lullabies. And after drifting peacefully asleep I would awaken the next morning to find that in the meantime— I had no idea when—someone had carried me back and put me to bed alone in my own small room. Whenever I said: "Let me sleep with you!" Mother was glad to do as I wished, and Father made no objection.

For a long time I didn't know where this second mother was born, what her background was, or how she happened to marry my father; such subjects were never brought up in my presence. I knew I might have found some clue in the city records, but I obeyed my father's orders: "Think of her as your real mother. You mustn't take the attitude that she's a stepmother." Also, I had some qualms about what I might find. However, when I was about to enter higher school I had to get an abstract from the records, and at that time I learned that my stepmother's real name was not Chinu but Tsuneko.

The following year my nurse Okane, who was then fifty-seven, ended her long service with us and retired to her home town of Nagahama. One day in late October before she left I went along with her to visit the Shimogamo Shrine. She made an offering, prayed briefly before the main altar, and then said in a voice filled with emotion: "I don't know when I'll see this shrine again. . . ." After that she suggested we go for a little walk through the shrine forest, toward the Aoi Bridge.

As we were walking along she suddenly turned to me and said: "You know all about it, Tadasu, don't you?"

"Know about what?" I asked, surprised.

"If you haven't heard, I won't say any more . . ."

"What are you talking about?"

"I wonder if I ought to tell you," she said, hesitating. Then, still strangely evasive: "Tadasu, do you know much about your stepmother?"

"No," I answered. "I know that her real name is Tsuneko."

"How did you find that out?"

"I had to get an abstract from the city records last year."

"Is that really all you know?"

"That's all. Father said I shouldn't be too inquisitive about her, and you didn't tell me anything either, so I decided not to ask."

"As long as I was working at your house I didn't want to mention it, but once I go back to the country I can't say when I'll set eyes on you again. So I think maybe I ought to tell you after all. You mustn't let your father hear about it, though."

"Never mind then," I said, without really meaning it. "Don't tell me—I think I ought to do what Father says."

But she insisted. "Anyway, you're bound to find out sooner or later. It's something you ought to know."

I couldn't help being fascinated by her long, rambling story, told to me bit by bit as we walked along the shrine road.

"I've only heard this at second hand, so I can't be sure," Okane began, and went on to give me a full account of my stepmother's past.

It seems that she was born into a Kyoto family that owned a large stationery shop in the Nijo district, specializing in decorative papers and writing brushes. But when she was about nine years old the family went bankrupt; by the time of Okane's story their shop no longer existed. At eleven, she was taken in as an apprentice geisha at one of the houses in Gion; from twelve to fifteen she entertained at parties as a dancer. You could probably have discovered the professional name she used at that time, the name of the geisha house, and so on; but Okane didn't know. Then, at fifteen, she is supposed to have had her debts paid off by the son of a wholesale cotton merchant, and to have been taken into the family as his bride. Opinions differ as to whether or not she was his legal wife, some declaring that her name was never entered in the official records.

Anyhow, she enjoyed all the privileges of a wife, and for about three years lived comfortably as the young mistress of a prosperous household. But at eighteen, for one reason or another, she was divorced. Some say that family pressure drove her out; others that her dissipated husband simply tired of her. No doubt she received a considerable sum of money at the time, but she went back to her parents' drab little house in Rokujo, turned the upstairs room into a studio, and made her living by teaching flower arrangement and the tea ceremony to the young women of the neighborhood.

Apparently it was during those days that my father became acquainted with her. But no one knew how he happened to meet her, or where they were seeing each other before she came to Heron's Nest as his bride. Two and a half years passed from the time of my mother's death until Father's second marriage. As vividly as the girl may have reminded him of his lost wife, he could hardly have fallen in love with her less than a year after the death of the woman he had so much adored; probably he made his mind up only a few months before the wedding took place. His first wife had died at twenty-two; his second was twenty when she married him; Father himself was thirty-three, thirteen years her senior; and I, at eight, was almost that much younger.

Learning about my stepmother's background aroused strong curiosity in me, along with all sorts of other feelings. I had never dreamed that she was once a professional entertainer in Gion. Of course she was very different from the ordinary girl of that kind: she came from a respectable family, and had left the gay quarter after only a few years to take up the life of the young mistress of a well-to-do household, during which time she seems to have acquired a number of polite feminine accomplishments. Yet I had to admire her for preserving her unaffected charm and graciousness, in spite of having been a Gion dancer. But what of the evident refinement of her voice, that soft speech in the tradition of the old Kyoto merchant class? Even if she had only spent two or three years in Gion one would expect to find some trace of it in her speech. Did her first husband and his parents make a point of correcting her?

I suppose it was natural for my father, at a time when he was sad and lonely, to be attracted by such a woman. And it was natural, too, for him to come to believe that a woman like her would have all the fine qualities of his former wife and could help me forget the sorrow of having lost my mother. I began to realize how much thought he had given to this, not merely for his own sake but for mine. Even if my stepmother shared his wish to make me think of my two mothers as a single woman, it was his own extraordinary effort that enabled him to mold her in the image of my real mother. I could see that the love he lavished on my stepmother and me only strengthened his love for his first wife all the more. And so, while it might seem that exposing the secrets of my new mother's earlier life had frustrated all of Father's patient efforts, the result was to deepen my gratitude to him and my respect for my stepmother.

After Okane left we added another maid, so that there were four in all. And in January of the following year I learned that Mother was pregnant. It was in the eleventh year of her marriage to my father. Since she had never had a child before, even by her former husband, both Father and she seemed to be surprised that such a thing could happen, after all these years.

"I feel ashamed to be getting big like this, at my age," she used to say. Or again: "When you're past thirty it's hard to give birth for the first time, I hear." Both Mother and Father had concentrated all their parental love on me, and perhaps they worried about my reaction to this event. If they did, they needn't have: I cannot describe how pleased I was to think that, after all these years as an only child, I was about to have a little brother or sister. I suppose, too, that Father's heart was darkened now and then by the ominous memory of my first mother's death in pregnancy. But what struck me as odd was that neither Father nor Mother seemed to want to bring up the matter; I began to notice that they looked strangely gloomy whenever the subject was mentioned.

"Since I have Tadasu I don't need another child," she would say, half-jokingly. "I'm too old to have a baby." Knowing her as I did, I thought it unlikely that she said such a thing merely to hide her embarrassment at being pregnant.

"What are you talking about, Mother?" I would object. "You mustn't say foolish things like that!" But somehow Father seemed to agree with her.

The doctor who examined her said that Mother's heart was rather weak, but that it was not bad enough to be a cause for concern—on the whole, she had a strong constitution. And in May of that year she gave birth to a baby boy. Her delivery took place at our house: the little six-mat room that I had been using was given over to her. The baby was a healthy one, and in due time Father gave it the name Takeshi. But when I came home from school one day—I believe it was about two weeks later—I was startled to find that Takeshi wasn't there.

"Father, where is Takeshi?" I asked.

"We've sent him out to Shizuichino for adoption," he told me. "Someday I think you'll understand, but for the present, please don't ask too many questions. I didn't plan this by myself—from the time we knew the child was coming your mother and I discussed it together every night. She wanted to do it even more than I did. Maybe we shouldn't have gone ahead without a word to you, but I was afraid that talking to you about it might do more harm than good."

For a moment I looked at him incredulously. Mother, who had left her bed only the day before, seemed to have deliberately slipped off somewhere, to leave us alone. "Where's Mother?" I asked.

"I think she may have gone out to the garden," he said, as if he didn't know.

I went out to look for her at once. She was in the middle of the bridge, clapping her hands and calling the fish, and scattering food to them. When she saw me, she went over to the other side of the pond, sat down on a celadon porcelain drum beside one of those sinister-looking stone saints, and beckoned me to come and sit on the other drum, facing her.

"I was just talking to Father," I said. "What on earth is the meaning of this?"

"Were you surprised, Tadasu?" Her soft, round face dimpled in a smile. The expression in her eyes was far too serene for a mother struggling to hold back her grief at having just been robbed of her beloved newborn infant.

"Of course I was."

"But haven't I always said that Tadasu is the only child I need?" Her calm expression remained unchanged. "Your father and I both thought it was for the best. Let's talk about it another time."

That night the room I had given up to Mother and her baby was once again my bedroom. The more I thought about what had happened, the more puzzled I became. It was dawn before I fell asleep.

Here I should like to say a little about Shizuichino, the place to which Takeshi had been sent.

Shizuichino is the modern name for the Ichiharano district, where the legendary hero Raiko is supposed to have killed the two robber chiefs. Even now one of its villages is called Ichihara, and that is also the name of the local station on the electric-car line to Mount Kurama. However, it was only in recent years that the car line opened; before that, you had to make the six- or seven-mile trip from Kyoto to Shizuichino by ricksha, or go by carriage as far as Miyake-Hachiman and then walk about three and a half miles. For several generations we had had close ties with a family named Nose who were prosperous farmers in this district—I suppose one of my ancestors had been sent out to nurse at their house. Even in Father's time, the head of the Nose family and his wife would come to pay their respects to us at the Bon Festival and at New Year's, bringing with them a cartload of fresh vegetables. Their Kamo eggplants and green soybeans were unobtainable at the market; we were always delighted to see them coming with their little handcart. Since we often went to stay overnight with them in the fall, to go mushroom hunting, I had been familiar with that region since childhood.

The road from the Nose house to the mushroom hill led along the Kurama River, one of the sources of the Kamo. We were already well above Kyoto: as we climbed still higher we could see the city lying below us. They say that the great scholar Fujiwara Seika retired here, after declining the invitation of the Shogun Ieyasu to come to Edo. The mountain villa Seika lived in has long since disappeared, but its site was in a wide bend of the meandering Kurama River. Not far away were the places he chose as the "Eight Scenic Beauties," to which he gave such names as Pillow-Stream Grotto and Flying-Bird Pool.

Another nearby point of interest was the Fudaraku Temple, popularly known as the Komachi Temple, where Ono no Komachi and her tormented suitor are said to lie buried. According to the *Illustrated Guide to the Capital*, this is also the temple which the Emperor Go-Shirakawa visited during his journey to Ohara, as related in *The Tale of the Heike*. There is a passage in one of the No plays about Komachi to the effect that many years ago a man who happened to be passing Ichiharano heard a voice from a clump of tall *susuki* grass recite this poem:

> *When the autumn wind blows,*
> *Eyeless Komachi wails in pain.*

> *But where is her lovely face*
> *In this wilderness of susuki?*

Whereupon the priest who recalls the poem decides to go to Ichiharano and pray for the repose of Komachi's soul. I have seen an old painting which shows *susuki* growing out of the eye sockets of what is presumably Komachi's skull; and in the Komachi Temple there was a "wailing stone" on which was carved the poem I have quoted. In my childhood, that whole area was a lonely waste covered with a rank growth of *susuki* grass.

A few days after I learned the astonishing news about Takeshi I decided that I had to make a secret visit to the Nose family in Shizuichino. Not that I was determined to steal Takeshi away from them and bring him home again. I am not the sort of person to do a thing like that on my own initiative. It was simply that I felt an overpowering rush of pity for my poor little brother, taken from his mother's arms to a house far away in the country. At least I could make sure that he was well, I thought, and then go home and urge Father and Mother to reconsider. If they didn't listen to me at first, I meant to go on visiting Takeshi regularly, keeping our link with him intact. Sooner or later they would understand how I felt.

I set out early in the morning and reached the house a little before noon. Fortunately, Nose and his wife had just returned from the fields, but when I asked to see Takeshi they seemed embarrassed.

"Takeshi isn't here," they told me.

"He isn't? Then where is he?"

"Well, now . . ." they began, exchanging worried glances as if they were at a loss for an answer.

But after I repeated my question several times, Nose's wife broke down and said: "We left him with some people a little farther out." Then they explained that because there wasn't anyone in the house just then to nurse a baby, and because my parents wanted Takeshi farther away, they took him out to live with some old friends of theirs, people you could trust.

When I asked where "a little farther out" was, Nose seemed even more embarrassed. "Your parents know where it is," he said; "so please ask them. It wouldn't do for me to tell you myself."

His wife chimed in: "They said if you ever happened to ask us we shouldn't tell you!" But I was finally able to worm it out of them that the place in question was a village called Seriu.

There is a folk song with the line "Out beyond Kyoto, by Ohara and Seriu"; and the Kabuki play *The Village School* has a passage about "hiding their lord's child in the village of Seriu, nestled in the hills." But this Seriu is over the Ebumi Pass on the road from Shizuichino to Ohara, and now has a different name. The Seriu that Nose and his wife were talking about is a mountain village in Tamba, even more remote and isolated. To go there, you take the electric car to Kibune, the second stop after Shizuichino, and cross the Seriu Pass into Tamba. The pass is a difficult one, more than twice as high as the Ebumi Pass, and there is not a single house in the five miles from Kibune to Seriu.

Why would my parents have sent my little brother to such a place? Even the Seriu in the play—the village "nestled in the hills" where a lord's child was kept in hiding—wasn't that far from Kyoto. Why had Takeshi been hidden away deep in the mountains of Tamba? I felt that I should try to find him that very day, but since all I knew was the name of the village I would have had to look for him from house to house. Anyway, there was hardly time for me to go on to Kibune and cross that steep mountain pass. Giving up for the time being, I went back home, thoroughly dejected, along the same road I had come that morning.

For the next two or three days my relations with my parents were strained; even at supper we seldom talked. Whether or not they had heard from the Nose family, they never said a word about my trip to Shizuichino, nor did I mention having gone. Mother was bothered by the swelling of her breasts and often secluded herself in the teahouse to use a milking device to relieve the pressure, or call one of the maids to massage her. Around this time my father seemed to be in poor health, and began taking afternoon naps in the veranda room, his head on a Chinese pillow of crimson papier-mâché. He seemed feverish too; I often saw him with a thermometer in his mouth.

I intended to go to Seriu as soon as possible, and was trying to think of an excuse to be away from home overnight. But one afternoon—it must have been late spring, since the silk tree my grandfather had been so proud of was in blossom —I decided to spend a little time reading in the pavilion. Taking along a novel, I went through the garden, past the flowering tree, and up the pavilion steps. Suddenly I noticed that Mother was sitting there on a cushion before me, busily milking her breasts. That was something she did in the teahouse, I thought. I had never imagined I'd find her on the pavilion veranda in that state: leaning over in a languid pose, her kimono open so that her naked breasts were bared to my view. Startled, I turned to leave, but she called after me in her usual calm voice: "Don't go away, Tadasu."

"I'll come again later," I said. "I didn't mean to disturb you."

"It's stifling in the teahouse, so I thought I'd sit out here. Did you want to read?"

"I'll come later," I repeated, feeling very uncomfortable. But again she stopped me from leaving.

"You needn't go—I'll be done in a moment. Just stay where you are." And then: "Look! My breasts are so full they hurt!"

I said nothing, and she continued: "You must remember how you tried to nurse at them till you were twelve or thirteen. You used to fret because nothing would come out, no matter how hard you sucked."

Mother removed the milking device from her left nipple and placed it over the right one. Her breast swelled up inside the glass receptacle, almost filling it, and a number of tiny streams of milk spurted from her nipple. She emptied the milk into a drinking glass and held it up to show me.

"I told you I'd have a baby someday and there'd be lots of milk for you too, didn't I?" I had somewhat recovered from my initial shock and was watching her fixedly, though I hardly knew what to say.

"Do you remember how it tastes?" she asked. I lowered my gaze and shook my head.

"Then try a little," she said, holding the glass out to me. "Go on and try it!"

The next moment, before I realized what I was doing, my hand reached out for the glass, and I took a sip of the sweet white liquid.

"How is it? Does it remind you of how it used to taste? Your mother nursed you till you were four, I think." It was extraordinary for my stepmother to say "your mother" to me, distinguishing between herself and my father's first wife.

"I wonder if you remember how to nurse," she went on. "You can try, if you like." Mother held one of her breasts in her hand and offered me the nipple. "Just try it and see!"

I sat down before her so close that our knees were touching, bent my head toward her, and took one of her nipples between my lips. At first it was hard for me to get any milk, but as I kept on suckling, my tongue began to recover its old skill. I was several inches taller than she was, but I leaned down and buried my face in her bosom, greedily sucking up the milk that came gushing out. "Mama," I began murmuring instinctively, in a spoiled, childish voice.

I suppose Mother and I were in each other's embrace for about half an hour. At last she said: "That's enough for today, isn't it?" and drew her breast away from my mouth. I thrust her aside without a word, jumped down from the veranda, and ran off into the garden.

But what was the meaning of her behavior that afternoon? I knew she hadn't deliberately planned it, since we met in the pavilion by accident. Did our sudden encounter give her the impulse to embarrass and upset me? If our meeting was as much a surprise to her as it was to me, perhaps she merely yielded to a passing whim. Yet she had seemed far too cool to be playing such a mischievous trick: she had acted as if this were nothing out of the ordinary. Maybe she would have been just as calm even if someone had come upon us. Maybe, in spite of my having grown up, she still thought of me as a child. Mother's state of mind was a mystery to me, but my own actions had been equally abnormal. The moment I saw her breasts there before me, so unexpectedly revealed, I was back in the dream world that I had longed for, back in the power of the old memories that had haunted me for so many years. Then, because she lured me into it by having me drink her milk, I ended by doing the crazy thing I did. In an agony of shame, wondering how I could have harbored such insane feelings, I paced back and forth around the pond alone. But at the same time that I regretted my behavior, and tortured myself for it, I felt that I wanted to do it again—not once, but over and over. I knew that if I were placed in those circumstances again—if I were lured by her that way—I would not have the will power to resist.

After that I stayed away from the pavilion; and Mother, possibly aware of how I felt, seemed to be using only the teahouse. Somehow the desire that had occupied such a large place in my heart—the desire to go to Seriu to see Takeshi —was no longer quite so strong. First of all, I wanted to find out why my parents had disposed of him in that way. Was it Father's idea or Mother's? As far as I could judge, it seemed likely that my stepmother—out of deference to my own mother—had decided that she ought not to keep her child here with us. And perhaps Father shared her scruples. Undoubtedly his love for his former wife was still intense, and he may well have thought it wrong for him to have any other child than the one she left him. Perhaps that is why my stepmother gave up her baby. For her, such an act would have shown self-sacrificing devotion to my father —and wasn't she more attached to me than to her own son? I could only suppose that they had come to their decision for reasons of this sort. But why hadn't they confided in me, or at least given me some hint of their intentions? Why had they kept Takeshi's whereabouts such a dark secret?

I have mentioned that Father's health seemed to be failing, and it occurred to me that that might have influenced his decision. Since about the end of the last year he had begun to look pale, and had become noticeably thinner. Although he seldom coughed or cleared his throat, he seemed to have a low fever, which made me suspect that he was suffering from some kind of chest trouble. Our family doctor was a man named Kato, whose office was on Teramachi at Imadegawa. During the early stages of his illness Father never had him come to the house. "I'm going for a walk," he would say, and then take the streetcar to visit Dr. Kato. It was not until after the episode in the pavilion that I managed to find out where he was going.

"Father," I asked, "is anything wrong with you?"

"No, not in particular," he answered vaguely.

"But why do you have a prescription from Dr. Kato?"

"It isn't serious. I'm just having a little trouble passing water."

"Then it's inflammation of the bladder?"

"Yes," he said. "Something like that."

At last it became obvious to everyone that Father had to urinate frequently. You could see that he was always going to relieve himself. Also, his coloring was worse than ever, and he had lost his appetite completely. That summer, after the rainy season, he began to spend most of the day resting, as if he felt exhausted; in the evening he sometimes came out to have dinner with us beside the pond, but even then he was listless and seemed to be making the effort out of consideration for Mother and me.

I felt suspicious because he was so evasive about his illness, even concealing his regular visits to his doctor. One day I made a visit of my own to Dr. Kato's office and asked him about it.

"Father tells me he has inflammation of the bladder," I said. "I wonder if that's really all it is."

"It's true that he has an inflamed bladder," said Dr. Kato, who had known me all my life. "But hasn't he told you any more than that?" He looked a little surprised.

"You know how retiring and secretive Father is. He doesn't like to talk about his illness."

"That puts me in a difficult position," Dr. Kato said. "Of course I haven't been too blunt with your father about it, but I've let him know his condition is serious. So I suppose that he and your mother are pretty well prepared for the worst—I can't understand why they've kept it from you. Probably they want to spare you any unnecessary grief. To my own way of thinking, I'm not sure it's wise to hide the truth from you, since you're already so worried. I've known your family for a good many years—your grandfather was a patient of mine—and so I don't think there should be any objection if I take it on myself to inform you." He paused a moment, and went on: "I'm sorry to have to say this, but as you must have gathered by now your father's condition is not at all hopeful." Then he told me the whole story.

It was last autumn that Father noticed a change in the state of his health and went to be examined by Dr. Kato. He complained of various symptoms— fever, blood in his urine, pain after urinating, a sensation of pressure in his lower abdomen—and Dr. Kato found immediately, by touch, that both of his kidneys were swollen. He also discovered tuberculous bacilli in the urine. This is very serious, he thought; and he urged Father to go to the urology department at the university hospital for a special examination, with X-rays. Father seems to have been reluctant. However, he finally went, after Dr. Kato urged him repeatedly and gave him a letter of introduction to a friend of his at the hospital.

Two days later Dr. Kato learned the results of the examination from his friend: just as he had feared, both the cystoscope and the X-rays showed clearly that the disease was tuberculosis of the kidneys, and that Father's condition was fatal. If only one of his kidneys had been attacked he could probably have been saved by its removal. Even in such cases, the prognosis was bad: thirty or forty percent of the patients died. Unfortunately both of my father's kidneys were affected, so nothing could be done for him. Though he still didn't seem to be a very sick man, he would soon have to take to his bed—at the longest, he might live another year or two.

"This isn't the kind of thing you can afford to neglect," Dr. Kato had warned him at the time, in a roundabout way. "From now on I'll come to see you once or twice a week—you ought to stay at home and rest as much as possible." And he added: "I must ask you to refrain from sexual intercourse. There's no danger of respiratory contagion at present, so you needn't worry as far as the rest of the family is concerned. But your wife will have to be careful."

"Is it some kind of tuberculosis?"

"Well, yes. But it isn't tuberculosis of the lungs."

"Then what is it?"

"The bacilli have attacked the kidney. Since you have two kidneys, it's nothing to be so alarmed about."

Dr. Kato managed to gloss it over for the moment in that way, and Father quietly accepted his advice. "I understand," he said. "I'll do as you've told me. But I like going out for walks, and as long as I'm able to get around I'll come to your office."

Father continued to visit Dr. Kato as usual, apparently not wishing to have him call at our house. Most of the time he came alone, but now and then Mother accompanied him. Although Dr. Kato felt an obligation to inform her frankly of her husband's condition, he had not yet found an opportunity to do so.

Then one day Father surprised him by saying: "Doctor, how much longer do I have, the way things are going?"

"Why do you talk like that?" Dr. Kato asked him.

Father smiled faintly. "You needn't keep anything from me. I've had a premonition about it all along."

"But why?"

"I don't know . . . maybe you'd call it instinct. It's just a feeling I've had. How about it, Doctor? I know what to expect, so please tell me the truth."

Dr. Kato was well acquainted with Father's character and took him at his word. Father had always been an acutely perceptive man; possibly he had been able to guess the nature of his illness from the way the specialists at the university treated him. Sooner or later I'll have to tell him or tell someone in his family, Dr. Kato thought; if he's so well prepared for it maybe I'd better do it now and get it over with. Indirectly, but without trying to evade my father's questions any longer, he confirmed his fears.

This is what Dr. Kato reported to me. Then he warned me that, since the disease often ended by invading the lungs, all of us—not just my mother—had to be careful.

I come now to the part of my narrative that I find most difficult.

I have tentatively given this narrative the title of *The Bridge of Dreams*, and have written it, however amateurishly, in the form of a novel. But everything that I have set forth actually happened—there is not one falsehood in it. Still, if I were asked why I took it into my head to write at all, I should be unable to reply. I am not writing out of any desire to have others read this. At least, I don't intend to let anyone see it as long as I am alive. If someone happens across it after my death, there will be no harm in that; but even if it is lost in oblivion, if no one ever reads it, I shall have no regret. I write for the sake of writing, simply because I enjoy looking back at the events of the past and trying to remember them one by one. Of course, all that I record here is true: I do not allow myself the slightest falsehood or distortion. But there are limits even to telling the truth; there is a line one ought not to cross. And so, although I certainly never write anything untrue, neither do I write the whole of the truth. Perhaps I leave part of it unwritten out of consideration for my father, for my mother, for myself . . . If anyone says that not to tell the whole truth is in fact to lie, that is his own interpretation. I shall not venture to deny it.

What Dr. Kato revealed to me about my father's physical condition filled my mind with wild, nightmarish fancies. If it was last fall that Father became aware of his unhappy fate, he was then forty-three years old, Mother was thirty, and I was eighteen. At thirty, however, Mother looked four or five years younger —people took her for my sister. Suddenly I recalled the story of her earlier life, which Okane had told me as we walked through the shrine forest before she left us last year. "You mustn't let your father hear about it," she had said, but might she not have done so on his instructions? Perhaps he had reason to want to sever the connection between my real mother and my stepmother, who had become so closely linked in my mind.

Also, I thought of what had happened not long ago in the Silk-Tree Pavilion. Perhaps Father had had something to do with *that.* I hardly think Mother would have tried to tantalize me so shamelessly without his permission. The fact is, although I stayed away from the pavilion for several weeks after that incident, I went there to suckle at Mother's breast more than once. Sometimes Father was away, sometimes at home: it seems unlikely that he didn't realize what she was doing, or that she concealed it from him. Possibly, knowing he hadn't long to live, he was trying to create a deeper intimacy between Mother and me, so that she would think of me as taking his place—and she made no objection. That is all I can bring myself to say. However, such a theory would explain why they sent Takeshi to Seriu . . . It may seem that I have imagined the most preposterous things about my parents, but what Father told me on his deathbed, as I shall relate presently, appears to bear me out.

I don't know when Mother learned that Father's days were numbered; perhaps he told her as soon as he knew. But that afternoon in the pavilion when she used the phrase "your mother"—was it really by chance, as it seemed then, or had she intended to say that? Indeed, Father must have told her about his illness even before she gave birth to Takeshi in May. Once they anticipated what the future held in store for them they may have come to an understanding—even if they never discussed the matter openly—and sent Takeshi off for adoption.

What seemed strange was that, as far as I could tell, Mother showed no sign of gloom or depression at the impending separation from her husband. It would have been contrary to her nature to display her emotions plainly—but was there even a shadow of secret grief across that bland, lovely face? Was she forcibly suppressing her tears, thinking she must not let me see her lose control of herself? Whenever I looked at them, her eyes were dry and clear. Even now I cannot say that I really understand how she felt, the complex emotions that seem to have existed beneath her surface calm. Until Father was at his dying hour she never tried to talk to me about his death.

It was in August that Father lost the strength to get out of bed. By then his entire body was swollen. Dr. Kato came to see him almost every day. Father grew steadily weaker, losing even the will to sit up to eat. Mother hardly left his bedside.

"You ought to hire a nurse," Dr. Kato told her.

But Mother said: "I'll take care of him myself." She let no one else touch him. Evidently that was also my father's wish. All his meals—though he ate only a few bites—were carefully planned by her; she would order his favorite delicacies, such as sweetfish or sea eel, and serve them to him. As his urination became more and more frequent she had to be always ready to give him the bedpan. It was during the midsummer heat, and he suffered from bedsores, which she also cared for. Often, too, she had to wipe his body with a solution of alcohol. Mother never spared herself any pains at these tasks, all of which she did with her own hands. Father grumbled if anyone else tried to help him, but he never uttered a word of complaint about what she did. His nerves became so tense that the least sound seemed to bother him: even the bamboo mortar in the garden was too noisy, and he had us stop it. Toward the end he spoke only when he needed something, and then only to Mother. Occasionally friends or relatives came to visit him, but he didn't seem to want to see them. Mother was busy with him day and night; whenever she was too exhausted to go on, her place was taken by my old nurse, Okane, who had come back to help us. I was amazed to discover that Mother had so much stamina and perseverance.

It was one day in late September, the day after an unusually heavy rainstorm when the "Shallow Stream" overflowed its banks and backed up into our pond, clouding the water, that Mother and I were summoned to Father's bedside. He was lying on his back, but he had us turn him over on his side so that he could look into our faces more easily. Beckoning me to sit close to him, he said: "Come here, Tadasu. Your mother can listen from where she is." He kept his gaze fixed on me all the while he spoke, as if he were seeking something in the depths of my eyes.

"I haven't much longer," he said. "But this was meant to be, so I am resigned to it. When I go to the other world your mother will be waiting for me, and I'm happy at the thought of meeting her again after all these years. What worries me most is your poor stepmother. She still has a long life ahead of her, but once I'm gone she'll have only you to rely on. So please take good care of her—give her all your love. Everyone says you resemble me. I think so myself. As you get older you'll look even more like me. If she has you, she'll feel as if I am still alive. I want you to think of taking my place with her as your chief aim in life, as the only kind of happiness you need."

Never had he looked at me that way before, deep into my eyes. Though I felt I could not fully understand the meaning of his gaze, I nodded my consent; and he gave a sigh of relief. Then, after pausing a few minutes until he was breathing easily once more, he went on:

"In order to make her happy you'll have to marry, but instead of marrying for your own sake you must marry for your mother's, to have someone who will help you take care of her. I've been thinking of Kajikawa's daughter Sawako . . ."

Kajikawa was a gardener who had come to our house regularly for many years. (His father had been an apprentice of the man who laid out the garden at Heron's Nest.) We saw him frequently, since he and his helpers still worked in our garden several days a week. And we knew his daughter Sawako too: ever since she had been in Girls' High School she used to call on us once a year, on the day of the Aoi Festival.

Sawako had a fair complexion and a slender, oval face of the classic melon-seed shape, the kind of face you see in ukiyoe woodblock prints. I suppose some people would consider her beautiful. After graduating from high school, she began wearing extremely heavy makeup, and was even more striking. It had seemed to me that a girl with a lovely white skin needn't paint herself so; but the year before last she stopped by during the midsummer festival, after viewing the great bonfire in the Eastern Hills from the Kamo riverbank, and since she said she was hot we invited her to have a bath, which she did, reappearing later and passing so near me that I noticed a few freckles on her cheeks. That explains why she wears so much makeup, I thought. After that I didn't see her for a long time, but about ten days ago she and Kajikawa had come to pay a sick call. I found their visit rather disturbing. Father, who usually refused to see any visitors, asked that they be brought to his room and spent over twenty minutes talking with them. Realizing that something was up, I half expected what he had to say to me.

"I dare say you know a good deal about the girl," Father continued; and he gave me a brief description of how Sawako had been brought up and what she was like. But there was nothing particularly new to me, since I had been hearing about her for years. She was nineteen, my own age, having also been born in 1906; she was intelligent and talented, and had been graduated from Girls' High School three years ago with an excellent record; after graduation she had kept busy taking lessons of one kind or another, acquiring a range of accomplishments far beyond what one might have expected of a gardener's daughter. Thus she had all the qualifications to make a fine bride for any family—except that 1906 was the Year of the Fiery Horse, by the old calendar, and she was a victim of the superstition that women born in that year are shrews. As a result, she had not yet received an attractive offer of marriage.

All this was long since familiar to me, and Father concluded by asking me to take her as my wife. Then he added that both the girl and her parents would be delighted to accept such a proposal. "If you'll only agree to it, everything will be settled," he said. "But in that case there's one thing more I'd like to ask of you. If you have a child, send it elsewhere, just as your mother gave up her own child for your sake. There's no need to say anything to Sawako or her parents right away—you might as well keep this to yourself until the time comes when you have to tell them. The earlier you're married, the better. Have the ceremony as soon as the year of mourning is over. I can't think of a suitable go-between at the moment, but you and your mother can discuss that with Kajikawa and decide on someone."

After having talked for such a long time, Father closed his eyes and drew a deep breath. He seemed suddenly reassured that I would obey his wishes. Mother and I turned him on his back again.

The next day Father began to show symptoms of uremia. He could eat nothing whatever, his mind was hazy, and now and then he talked deliriously. He lived about three more days, until the beginning of October; but all that we could catch of his incoherent speech was my mother's name, "Chinu," and the broken phrase "the bridge . . . of dreams," a phrase he repeated over and over. Those were the last words I heard my father utter.

Okane had come back from the country in August to help us, and as soon as the Buddhist service of the Seventh Day was over she went home. Relatives we hadn't seen for years gathered at the house even for the services of the Thirty-fifth and Forty-ninth Days; but their number gradually dwindled until, on the Hundredth Day, only two or three people made an appearance.

The following spring I was graduated from higher school and entered the law department of the university. After the death of my unsociable father, the guests who called at Heron's Nest, never very many, became so rare that at last there was hardly anyone but Sawako and her parents, who came about once a week. Mother would spend the whole day indoors, worshipping before Father's memorial tablet or, if she needed diversion, taking out my first mother's koto and playing it for a while. Because our house seemed so lonely and quiet now, she decided to start the bamboo mortar up again after its long silence; and she had Kajikawa cut a piece of green bamboo for it. Once again I could hear the familiar clack, clack that I had always loved.

Mother had borne up well while she was nursing Father the year before; even throughout the long series of Buddhist services that followed his death she always received our guests with dignity and self-control, and looked as full-cheeked and glowing with health as ever. But lately she seemed to show signs of fatigue, and sometimes had one of the maids massage her. Sawako offered her services whenever she was there.

One day when the silk tree was beginning to blossom I went out to the pavilion, knowing that I would find Mother and Sawako. Mother was lying in her usual place, on two cushions, while Sawako was energetically rubbing her arms.

"Sawako's good at massaging, isn't she?" I said.

"She's really wonderful!" Mother replied. "I don't know anyone who can equal her. She makes me so drowsy I almost drop off to sleep—it's a delicious feeling!"

"She *does* seem to know how to use her hands. Sawako, did you ever take lessons at this?"

"No, no lessons," she answered; "but I'm used to massaging my parents every day."

"That's what I thought," Mother said. "No wonder she'd put even a professional to shame. Tadasu, let her try it on you."

"I don't need a massage. But maybe I'll be her pupil and learn how to do it."

"Why should you learn?" asked Mother.

"Then I can massage you too. I ought to be able to learn that much."

"But your hands are too rough—"

"They're not rough, for a man. Isn't that so, Sawako? Just feel them!"

"Let's see," Sawako said, clasping my fingers in her own, and then stroking my palms. "My, you really do have nice smooth hands! You'll be fine!"

"It's because I've never gone in much for sports."

"Once you get the knack of it you'll soon be an expert!"

For some weeks after that I had Sawako teach me the various massaging techniques, and practiced them on Mother. Sometimes she got so ticklish that she shrieked with laughter.

In July the three of us would sit by the pond together to enjoy the cool of evening. Like my father, I would take a few bottles of beer to put under the spout of the bamboo mortar. Mother drank too, several glasses if I urged her; but Sawako always refused.

Mother would dangle her bare feet in the water, saying: "Sawako, you ought to try this. It makes you delightfully cool!"

But Sawako would sit there primly in her rather formal summer dress, with a heavy silk sash bound tightly around her waist. "Your feet are so pretty!" she would say. "I couldn't possibly show ugly ones like mine beside them!"

It seemed to me that she was too reserved. She might have been a little freer and more intimate with someone who would eventually become her mother-in-law. But she seemed too solicitous, too eager to please; often her words had a tinge of insincerity. Even her attitude toward me was curiously old-fashioned, for a girl who had been graduated from high school. Perhaps marriage would change her, but at the moment I couldn't help feeling that our relations were those of master and servant. Of course, it may have been precisely that quality in her which appealed to my father, and no doubt Mother's strength and firmness made her seem retiring, by contrast. Yet she seemed inadequate, somehow, for a young girl who was to become the third member of our small family.

A month or two after the silk-tree and pomegranate blossoms had fallen, when the crape myrtle was beginning to bloom and the plantain ripening, I had become fairly skillful at massaging and often asked Mother to come out to the pavilion for a treatment.

"A few minutes then, if you like," she would reply.

Naturally I took Sawako's place whenever she wasn't there, but even when she was with us I would brush her aside and say: "Let me try it—you watch!" Unable to forget the days when Mother had given her breasts to me, I now found my sole pleasure in massaging her. It was around then that Sawako, who had always worn her hair in Western style, began having it done up in a traditional high-piled Shimada, a coiffure that set off beautifully her ukiyoe-like face. She appeared to be getting ready for the Buddhist service that would be held on the first anniversary of my father's death, a time which was drawing near. Mother herself ordered new clothes for the occasion: among them, a formal robe of dark purple figured satin with a hollyhock pattern on the skirt, and a broad sash of thick-woven white silk dyed with a pattern of the seven autumn flowers.

The anniversary service was held at a temple at Hyakumamben, and we had dinner served in the reception hall of its private quarters. Both Mother and I noticed how cold and distant my relatives were. Some of them left as soon as they had burned incense, without stopping to join us at dinner. Ever since Father had married a former entertainer my relatives had held an oddly hostile and disdainful attitude toward our family. And now, to make matters worse, I was engaged to marry the gardener's daughter: it was only to be expected that they would talk. Still, I hadn't thought they would treat us quite so brusquely. Mother carried it off with her usual aplomb; but Sawako, who had gone to great trouble to dress appropriately for the occasion, seemed so dejected that I had to feel sorry for her.

"I'm beginning to wonder how our wedding will turn out," I said to Mother. "Do you suppose those people will come?"

"Why should you worry? You're not getting married for *their* benefit—it's enough if you and I and Sawako are happy." Mother seemed unconcerned, but before long I discovered that the hostility of our relatives was even more bitter than I had imagined.

Okane, who had come from Nagahama for the service, stayed with us a few days before going home. On the morning of the day she left, she suggested we go for another walk through the shrine forest.

"Okane, do you have something to tell me?" I asked.

"Yes, I do."

"I think I know what it is. It's about my wedding, isn't it?"

"That's not the only thing."

"Then what is it?"

"Well . . . but you mustn't get angry, Tadasu."

"I won't. Go ahead and say it."

"Anyway, you're sure to hear about it from somebody, so I guess it ought to come from me." Then, little by little, she told me the following story.

Of course it was true that my relatives were opposed to my forthcoming marriage, but that wasn't the only reason why they disapproved of us. Mother and I were the objects of their criticism, more than the match with Kajikawa's daughter. To put it bluntly, they believed that we were committing incest. According to them, Okane said, Mother and I began carrying on that way while Father was still alive, and Father himself, once he knew he wouldn't recover, had tolerated it—even encouraged it. Some went so far as to ask whose baby had been smuggled out to Tamba, suggesting that Takeshi was my own child, not my father's.

I wondered how on earth these people, who had been avoiding us for years, could have heard anything that would make them spread such wild rumors. But Okane explained that everyone in our neighborhood had been gossiping this way about us for a long time. It seems they all knew that Mother and I spent many hours alone together in the Silk-Tree Pavilion, which is probably why the rumors began to circulate. My relatives thought that my dying father arranged for me to marry Sawako because only a girl with her disadvantages would accept such a match. Most scandalous of all, his reason for wanting me to keep up appearances by taking a wife was presumably to have me continue my immoral relationship with Mother. Kajikawa was well aware of these circumstances in giving his daughter, and Sawako was going to marry out of respect for her father's wishes —needless to say, they had their eyes on our property. And so my relatives were outraged first of all by my father's part in this, then by Mother's, by mine, by Kajikawa's, and by his daughter's, in that order.

"Tadasu, be careful!" Okane ended by warning me. "Everybody knows people will talk, but they can say terrible things!" And she gave me a strange look out of the corner of her eye.

"Let them say what they please," I answered. "Nasty rumors like that will soon be forgotten."

"Well, maybe they'll come to the wedding next month after all," she said doubtfully as we parted.

I have no interest in going into detail about later events. But perhaps I should summarize the important ones.

Our wedding ceremony was held on an auspicious day in November of that year. To please Mother, I wore a crested black silk kimono of Father's instead of a morning coat. Hardly any of my relatives appeared for the wedding; even the ones on Mother's side stayed away. Those who came were chiefly persons related to the Kajikawa family. Dr. Kato and his wife were kind enough to act as go-between. The doctor had been taking lessons in the No drama for many years, and he was more than happy to oblige by chanting the usual lines from *Takasago*. But as I listened to his sonorous voice my thoughts were far away.

After our marriage, Sawako's attitude toward Mother and me showed no particular change. We spent a few days in Nara and Ise for our honeymoon, but I was always careful to take precautions against having a child—that was one thing I never neglected. On the surface, Mother appeared to get along with her newly wed son and daughter-in-law in perfect harmony. After Father's death, she had continued to sleep in the twelve-mat veranda room, and she stayed there even after Sawako came; Sawako and I slept in my little six-mat room. That was as it should be, we felt, since I was still going to school and was still a dependent. For the same reason, Mother was in charge of all the household accounts.

As for Mother's life in those days, anyone would have taken it to be enviably carefree and leisurely. She amused herself by practicing Konoe-style calligraphy, reading classical Japanese literature, playing the koto, or strolling in the garden; and whenever she felt tired, day or night, she would have one of us give her a massage. During the day she had her massages in the pavilion, but at night she always called Sawako to her bedroom. Occasionally the three of us would go out to the theater, or on an excursion; but Mother was inclined to be frugal and paid close attention to even trivial sums of money, warning us to do our best to avoid needless expense. She was especially strict with Sawako and caused her a good deal of worry over the food bills. Mother was looking fresher and more youthful than ever, and so plump that she was beginning to get a double chin. Indeed, she was almost too plump—as if now that Father was dead her worries were over.

Our life went on in that way while I finished two more years at the university. Then about eleven o'clock one night in late June, shortly after I had gone to bed, I found myself being shaken by Sawako and told to get up.

"It's your mother!" she exclaimed, hurrying me off toward the other bedroom. "Something dreadful has happened!"

"Mother!" I called. "What's wrong?" There was no reply. She was lying there face down, moaning weakly and clutching her pillow with both hands.

"I'll show you what did it!" Sawako said, picking up a round fan from the floor near the head of the bed to reveal a large crushed centipede. Sawako explained that Mother had wanted a massage, and she had been giving her one for almost an hour. Mother was lying on her back asleep, breathing evenly, as Sawako rubbed her legs all the way down to her ankles. Suddenly she gave a scream of pain, and her feet arched convulsively. When Sawako looked up in alarm she saw a centipede crawling across Mother's breast, near the heart. Startled into action, she snatched up a nearby fan and brushed the insect away, luckily flicking it to the floor, where she covered it with the fan and then crushed it.

"If I'd only paid more attention . . ." Sawako said, looking deadly pale. "I was so busy massaging her . . ."

Dr. Kato came over immediately and took emergency measures, giving one injection after another; but Mother's suffering seemed to increase by the moment. All her symptoms—her color, breathing, pulse, and the rest—showed that her condition was more serious than we had thought. Dr. Kato stayed by her side, doing his best to save her; but around dawn she took a turn for the worse, and died soon afterward.

"It must have been shock," Dr. Kato told us.

Sawako was weeping aloud. "I'm to blame, I'm to blame," she kept repeating.

I have no intention of trying to describe the feelings of horror, grief, despair, dejection, which swept over me then; nor do I think it reflects credit on myself to be suspicious of anyone without a shred of evidence. Yet I cannot escape certain nagging doubts . . .

It was some forty years since my grandfather had built the house he called Heron's Nest, which was by then at its most beautiful, well seasoned, with the patina of age that suits a Japanese-style building of this kind. In Grandfather's day the wood must have been too new to have such character, and as it grows older it will doubtless lose its satiny luster. The one really old building at Heron's Nest was the teahouse that Grandfather had brought there; and during my childhood, as I have said, it was infested by centipedes. But after that centipedes began to be seen frequently both in the pavilion and in the main house. There was nothing strange about finding one of them in the veranda room, where Mother was sleeping. Probably she had often seen centipedes in her room before, and Sawako, who was always going in to massage her, must have had the same experience. And so I wonder if Mother's death was entirely accidental. Might not someone have had a scheme in mind for using a centipede, if one of them appeared? Perhaps it was only a rather nasty joke, with no thought that a mere insect bite could be fatal. But supposing that her weak heart had been taken into account, that the possibility had seemed attractive . . . Even if the scheme failed, no one could prove that the centipede had been deliberately caught and placed there.

Maybe the centipede did crawl onto her by accident. But Mother was a person who fell asleep very easily: whenever we massaged her she relaxed and dropped off into a sound sleep. She disliked a hard massage, preferring to have us stroke her so lightly and gently that her sleep was not disturbed. It would have been quite possible for someone to put a small object on her body without immediately awakening her. When I ran into her room, she was lying face down writhing with pain; but Sawako said that earlier she had been lying on her back. I found it hard to believe that Sawako, who was massaging her legs, saw the centipede on Mother's breast the moment she looked up. Mother wasn't lying there naked; she was wearing her night kimono. It was odd that Sawako happened to see the insect—surely it would have been crawling under the kimono, out of sight. Perhaps she knew it was there.

I wish to emphasize that this is purely my own assumption, nothing more. But because this notion has become so firmly lodged in my mind, has haunted me for so long, I have at last tried to set it down in writing. After all, I intend to keep this record secret as long as I live.

Three more years have passed since then.

When I finished school two years ago, I was given a job as a clerk at the bank of which Father had been a director; and last spring, for reasons of my own, I divorced Sawako. A number of difficult conditions were proposed by her family, and in the end I had to agree to their terms. The whole complicated affair was so unpleasant that I have no desire to write about it. At the same time that I took steps to be divorced I sold Heron's Nest, so full of memories for me, both happy and sad, and built a small house for myself near the Honen Temple. I had Takeshi come to live with me, insisting on bringing him back from Seriu in spite of his own reluctance as well as that of his foster parents. And I asked Okane, who was quietly living out her days at Nagahama, to come and look after him, at least for a few years. Fortunately, she is still in good health, at sixty-four, and still able to take care of children. "If that's what you want, I'll help out with the little boy," she said, and left her comfortable retirement to come and live with us. Takeshi is six. At first he refused to be won over by Okane and me, but now we have become very close. Next year he will begin going to school. What makes me happiest is that he looks exactly like Mother. Not only that, he seems to have inherited something of her calm, open, generous temperament. I have no wish to marry again: I simply want to go on living as long as possible with Takeshi, my one link with Mother. Because my real mother died when I was a child, and my father and stepmother when I was some years older, I want to live for Takeshi until he is grown. I want to spare him the loneliness I knew.

June 27, 1931 (the anniversary of Mother's death)

Otokuni Tadasu

TRANSLATED BY HOWARD HIBBETT

◼◼ NAGAI TATSUO

Nagai Tatsuo, born in Tokyo in 1904, was forced to quit school in his early teens because of ill health, but within a few years he became a published author. In 1927 he joined the staff of the Bungei Shunjū Company, a major publishing firm, after which he spent most of his time in editorial work. He continued to write for various literary magazines, however, and in 1934 produced a slender volume of short stories, *Picture Book* (*Ehon*), in an edition of 350 copies. For over two decades he concentrated on his role as editor and literary entrepreneur; his second collection of stories did not appear until 1949. Meanwhile, he became a director of the company and established its Manchurian branch, and was accordingly purged by the Occupation in 1947 from the management of a newspaper which he had helped to found. Since then he has again been active as a writer of stories and essays, many of them among the finest of his long career. Nagai has also written newspaper serials and biographical novels, but he is known above all as a master of the short story. In 1968 he was elected to the Japan Academy.

"Brief Encounter" is in Nagai's characteristic manner: a delicate blend of humor and pathos, delineating poignant moments in the lives of undistinguished people. Many of his stories depict survivors in the confusion of postwar Japan; but even "A Blue Rainy Season" (*Aotsuyu*, 1965), a story of family suicide drawing on his own fears of Japan's impending defeat, is not without touches of resigned humor.

❖ Brief Encounter

("Aibiki" kara, 1948)

I must ask you to read a part of my letter before you begin the story proper:

> I received your letter and the enclosed money order. Thank you very much.
>
> Thank you for the remarkable news that the ring I left with you has joined your engagement ring and been reborn as a tooth. I find myself less surprised and sorry than wanting to tell how much it helped with the fresh, new view of life I mentioned to you.
>
> As you have shown in your own person, the gold tooth artlessly in place somewhere behind an eyetooth is especially pleasing when glimpsed in the smile of a woman in her middle twenties. (Was yours perhaps one into which your husband himself put all his affection and skill? Forgive me. I will say no more about your false tooth. Even by way of sympathy.) I only hope this: that the two rings, the symbol of your gloom and the symbol of my new, fresh mood, will become admirable new teeth for the good of the people of Tokyo.
>
> It occurs to me, as I stop writing for a minute to light a cigarette, that letter-writing scenes are disappearing from the movies. To be sure, telephones and telegraphs are relieving the race of the troublesome chore; but I feel a certain nostalgia for the expression on her face for those few seconds when, having laid down the pen, she raises the envelope to her lips.
>
> What was I going to say? At first, not used to the work, I was exhausted; but now a month has gone by, and, sound and healthy again, I am in with the youngsters, having the experience of life in the mines . . .

I had quite cleaned out the room.

The medium-sized Boston bag that held my belongings lay in the middle of the alcove, and twenty or thirty books were stacked against the wall. There was a newspaper on the desk by the window. The bedding was folded neatly in front of the cupboard, with the pillow on top, as if to weigh it down.

I said good-by at the main house, and when I came back to my six-mat room, somehow cut off, amputated from the human world, the red kitten was curled by the pillow.

I felt myself smiling. "And what do you think *you're* doing here?" In my hat and coat, I knelt by the bedding and stroked the animal softly. Its eyes still closed, it rolled over on its back, and, in a most excellent mood, purred for me.

It had been in the main house for three months or so, and it would come to see me several times every day. Although nearly forty, I had never kept a cat or a dog. This was the first time I had ever lived near a cat.

I put my ear to its stomach and listened for a moment to the purring. Then, going out to the corridor that faced the garden and led to the main house, I put on my shoes. I had a raincoat over my arm. They had told me in the main house that the forecast was for rain.

Since they had agreed to store everything I did not immediately need, the disposition of my assets could not have been simpler.

I left the door open a little, for the kitten.

Several days earlier I had told my brother that I thought I might go to see a foreign movie—I would be off in the mines for a while, and would not have another chance. This morning a note had come by messenger.

"I was not able to get tickets for *The Best Years of Our Lives.* I enclose instead tickets for an English movie that is said to be very good, and with them an express ticket. The latter is for tomorrow. I will see you at the station."

The note was in my pocket when I got off at Shimbashi. I had come in from Hodogaya on the electric line, and I had been wondering all the way what to do. There were two tickets to *Brief Encounter,* with the Japanese title *Aibiki,* "Assignation." I had no idea what sort of movie it was, but that was the title. It seemed to tease me, to jeer at me, to prod me.

My brother was too serious a sort to be teasing me with the two tickets, that much was sure; but it was ironical all the same, sending two tickets to a bachelor in his late thirties. What was I to do with the other?

As I walked down the stairs at Shimbashi I decided to invite A, who worked in an office behind the Ginza.

I thought I would make a joke of it: "Someone gave me tickets to a movie called *Aibiki,* and I have them to get rid of. I know it's a little behind the times for two grown men to go to that sort of movie together, but I won't be seeing you again for a while. Come on along."

Unfortunately, A was out. Very well; I would give the ticket to someone in front of the theater. I crossed the bridge in the direction of the H Theater.

There were three or four people at the ticket window. I walked briskly up —and then changed my mind. There was a couple, and there were young girls. The expression "a man in his forties" had come into my mind, and the image of middle-age accosting youth. After it, derisively, came those other terms that seemed applicable: "ex-soldier," "broken-down soldier," and the rest.

I went into the theater. The girl showed me to my seat. The next seat of course was vacant. As if asking them to sit down, I gave it to my hat and raincoat.

There was no reason at all to invite someone else just because I had two tickets. This was much better—I could spread out. The trouble with me was that I was still a prisoner of inflexible concepts.

People came in, the theater filled. The bell rang. The news went dizzyingly in review.

Why was it, my brother had remarked the other day, that there was always something stale and musty about newsreels even when they had the latest scoops? The destruction after the storm was the same, whether the scene was Japan or America. The American woman, blown down the street, clung precariously to a telephone pole, and, frowning into the storm, she turned to the camera and smiled a childlike smile, as if to say that people *did* have interesting experiences.

The lights went on again when the newsreel was over. I felt somehow isolated from the crowd, but then the lights dimmed and the words "Brief Encounter" flashed against the rising curtain. I planted my elbow firmly on the arm of the vacant seat.

I had the aisle seat, and I felt a sort of pressure on my right. Someone, bent slightly forward, was standing there in the dark, waiting to be allowed past.

Automatically I looked back, but the only vacant seat was the one beside me. The ticket for it was in my pocket. I picked up my coat and hat nonetheless and put them on my knee.

The person bowed and slipped adroitly past. It was a woman in foreign dress, leaving a faint perfume behind her. I heard her open her handbag. She seemed to be taking out her glasses. I felt even after she had sat down that she was fairly tall for a woman.

Life was new and fresh, clearly it was—I reaffirmed the philosophy I had acquired during the preceding half year. But how to explain the mystery of the seat beside me?

The dull confession of a plain, tired wife, in an atmosphere of indescribable gloom. It began to pull at me. At first I resisted, but presently I was caught up in it.

There is no need here to recount the plot or to give my reactions, and indeed I am not qualified to. When I thought of it again some days later on the train, I suddenly thought too of *Earth,* that somber Japanese novel of peasant life, a cheap edition of which I had borrowed from a young comrade when I was stationed on the southern front. The movie was about a secret affair of a nameless woman in a small town, and the views of an ex-soldier are of no importance.

Yet I must mention something I would rather not: I thought again, for the first time in a great while, of my ex-wife, whom, a year before, I had let go without a shade of regret. Although no one could know that I had thought of her, I felt most ashamed of myself afterwards.

I was slightly dissatisfied with the last scene, in which the amiable husband forgave the wife. She had not committed the final error, it is true, but the affair had left her an empty shell. Perhaps that was what made me remember my wife. On that point, at least, I was superior to the husband of the movie.

Brief Encounter was over. I seem to have lost myself in thought, for the woman was asking to be let by. I stood up. I followed her, and we were the last to leave the theater.

The weather forecast had been accurate. The exit was screened by a white curtain, a May rain. There were some ten young people caught without umbrellas.

I stepped beyond them and lighted a cigarette. I was ready for the rain, but felt no need to hurry. The woman too took a cigarette from a silver case. There was a subtle quickness in her gestures, the movement from gesture to gesture. She had on a dark green suit, and she was indeed tall for a woman. I had glanced at her as she looked up into the sky, and been struck by the lashes of the slightly narrowed eyes. A woman's age is among the things I am incapable of judging, but she was not yet thirty, of that I was sure. Perhaps twenty-four or twenty-five, perhaps twenty-seven.

"It's not going to stop, either," she said suddenly. The black eyes moved toward me as she spoke.

"I'm afraid not." I looked at the rain hitting the pavement. Now and then a couple under a single umbrella stumbled through the spray.

"I thought it was so near, and I wouldn't need an umbrella. Stupid of me." A mischievous laugh came into the eyes. There was a trace of lipstick on her cigarette. I had not realized that it was possible to color the lips such a calm, tranquil color.

"It's near, is it?"

"Just over there." The eyes, still smiling, and a finger pointed to the left. "Next door to the curio shop."

I spread open my raincoat. "I have this. I'm going in that direction anyway —suppose I stop by and have someone come with an umbrella."

"Please don't bother. It's so near. I'll run on when I've made up my mind to get wet. Really." She spoke briskly, but with no suggestion of wanting to brush me aside.

"Suppose I do it this way." I pulled the coat over my head like a photographer, and smiled at her. The people who were waiting for a lull in the rain looked at us curiously.

Cocking her head a little to one side, she smiled back. I seemed to have put her at ease.

"Really? I shouldn't ask you to—but may I?" She came a step or two nearer. "The building next to the curio shop. A dentist named Suematsu. If you could ask the girl at the reception desk to come with a coat and an umbrella, I'd really be most grateful."

It pleased me to think that I was helping someone I would never see again. I ran through the rain. But I still did not understand about that seat.

There was a compact little building some two hundred yards away, around the corner from the curio shop. I had no trouble finding the dentist's office on the second floor. "Suematsu Shingo, Doctor of Dental Surgery; Suematsu Akira, Dentist," the sign said in horizontal characters. It also said that Sunday was a holiday, and that the office was open only until two on Saturdays. Today was a Saturday.

Just inside the door there was a little window over the reception desk, where a girl of eighteen or nineteen was sitting. I told her my business, and she answered quietly.

Feeling somewhat nostalgic at the antiseptic smell of the office, I closed the door behind me. As I started down I could hear the rain below.

"Excuse me." Someone was calling from the head of the stairs.

It was the reception girl. Two umbrellas and an oil-cloth coat in hand, she stood by the wall, waiting for me to come up again.

"If I leave there will be no one here. Would you mind waiting till I get back?"

"Not at all, not at all."

She seemed to think that I was a friend of the woman's. Such a simple girl —should she be so trusting? There was something heart-warming about her. I walked slowly up and down before the Suematsu door.

"What a rain, and no sign of letting up. When did it begin?" The bright voice of the woman came from the stairs. Then she saw me, and once more I looked closely into her eyes. "Well! What a bother for you! That's our Miss Tateno, as easygoing as ever. She had you watch the place, did she? Come on in, now that you've gone to so much trouble. For just a minute. It would be strange to let him go like this, wouldn't it, Miss Tateno?"

Turning from me to the receptionist, she pushed open the door without letting me answer.

"It's strange to think it would be strange."

She laughed, and opened another door, to a clean little waiting room that could accommodate perhaps three or four people.

"Have a seat. I'll be back in a minute." I took off my wet coat and sat on the sofa.

In the quiet I could hear water, and, faintly, the sound of a comb running through someone's hair.

"What about the coffee in the thermos bottle? Yes, let's have that. You have some too." She spoke to the girl in a voice so quiet that I wondered how it could come from the same person. "It was a gloomy, gloomy movie. I'm exhausted." I next heard someone opening a can. "I don't say it wasn't interesting, but I wonder how it would be for a young person."

Miss Tateno looked much brighter when she came in with coffee. She had changed from her office uniform. The place seemed more like a parlor.

"I shouldn't have asked you to wait. You must forgive me." She had on a blouse, I suppose you would call it—a clear, pale cerulean blue. (I know, having investigated these colors.) The sleeves were short, and the brooch was an ivory flower set in gold. I stood up.

"There was a terrible rainstorm in *Brief Encounter* too."

"Yes. I must look a little like the doctor."

"Maybe it feels good when you get as wet as that." The woman sat down lightly in the chair opposite me.

If one had praised the fairness of her complexion, she would probably have answered: "Oh? And I've never done a thing for it. You should praise my father and mother."

But since in her hair, for all the careful attention that had gone into dressing it, there was a faint touch of calculated disarray, as of a keystone pulled slightly loose, so that the hair set off the beauty of the throat—since there was this air about her whole person, one could not doubt that a considerable sum had been invested in the almost unpowdered whiteness of the skin.

"You're going shopping in the rain?" She cast a quiet glance over my shoulder. "You are? Well, don't worry about me. I'll sit here with this gentleman a little longer, and then close the office."

Miss Tateno said nothing, but I gathered that she was leaving. The woman got up and went toward her.

"I'm sorry I had to say such unpleasant things. You must forgive me."

"Please don't apologize."

"You're not to worry. Understand? I'm completely over it now. I'll be in early Monday morning, looking very cheerful." She laughed softly. "Bye-bye."

I sensed that she had taken the girl's hand by way of apology. The "Bye-bye" had a high, clear ring to it.

"Something unpleasant happened, and I ran out to the movie. I felt dreadful, it was such a dismal movie." She had sat down again, and her eyes were still on the silver case after she had offered me a cigarette and taken one herself.

I wondered what the unpleasantness might have been, but did not feel that I could ask. Instead I turned the conversation to the matter that puzzled me. "I had two tickets to the movie, and the second one was a problem. It made me feel very useless."

"You should have taken your wife."

"Well, you see, as a matter of fact—" It was not a subject I found easy to talk about.

"May I ask if you were in the service? In the Navy, perhaps?"

"Precisely."

"I had two cousins in the Navy. Up until a few years ago I was rather popular with the young officers." But I did not want to talk about the past.

"And what did you do with the other ticket?" she asked.

"I wanted to invite a friend—a man, of course—but he was out. I went by myself."

"What a pity. And for a *Brief Encounter,* too."

"But here I am drinking coffee with you. Why did you take that seat?"

"That seat?" Her eyes narrowed questioningly, and there was a pause. "Oh! I took the wrong seat. How stupid of me!" For the first time I felt a touch of coquetry.

"I thought it a great privilege."

"I was upset and a little excited, and there was no usher. I go there often, it's so close, and I thought my seat ought to be about there. And I'm a little nearsighted."

"I see." I saw everything. I saw too that a slight case of myopia could make a woman's eyes rather seductive.

"I think it's letting up. You said you had business on the Ginza?"

"Nothing of any importance." I too looked out the window.

"If you're in no hurry, stay as long as you like. I have nothing to do myself."

"I go away tomorrow."

"How I envy you. Where are you going?"

"I'll be in Kyushu for a while."

"Men have all the advantages. On business."

"No money in it, as they say. I'm going to work. In a coal mine."

"Oh?"

"I've done all sorts of things to keep myself alive since I came back. I've come to the conclusion that it's not too difficult if keeping yourself alive is all you want. But everything seems so strange, now that the military blinkers are off. Everything seems so fresh and new, so alive, from the time I get up in the morning till I go to bed at night."

"You were a commander?"

"A lieutenant-commander at the end of the war. I didn't do so well when it came to promotions." I spoke rapidly. I did not want to talk about the past. "There was a kitten that used to come and see me all the time. It was very interesting. I had never liked cats—so cold and willful. But then I would watch that kitten, and it seemed strange that such an animal could have been born. Everything was interesting to it, even its own tail. It was never bored. If that liveliness to new impressions could go on say four or five years, a cat would be a remarkable beast."

"Isn't it the truth. They get so fat and sluggish when they are older. I kept three cats once, but then it came to me that it was not very good form for a childless woman to be fond of cats, and I gave them away."

"I want to have all the experiences I can before I get fat and sluggish myself. I'm in a great hurry."

"And that's why you're going into a coal mine?"

"I want to do away with the ex-soldier."

"You'll join the Communist Party, then, and the labor movement?"

"Possibly. But the Party is too much like the service. It has no respect for you as an individual." I sensed that I was being asked leading questions. And so I made a leading remark: "To someone like me it's a fairy story, a well-matched husband and wife running a clean little office together."

"A fairy story—it was at first." She looked at me again with that slightly quizzical expression, and immediately lowered her eyes. Her manner changed abruptly. She evidently did not mean to be taken by my lead. "You're kept busy, that's all, repairing bad teeth day after day. Unless someone has to have a difficult bridge made, you can hardly breathe for the boredom. I'd like to use heaps of gold and platinum on something really good."

With that, I remembered my business on the Ginza. I hesitated a second, then took a little wad of paper from my pocket. I had found it in the desk drawer when I cleaned the room that morning. "It's a little sudden, but could you use this?"

The delicately manicured hand took up the paper, and from it came an engagement ring.

I explained in some confusion: "I found it this morning when I was cleaning up. I wondered if I might be able to sell it on the Ginza. I know it would be more dashing if I were to drop it into the river from Kachidoki Bridge or somewhere, but I've never been much for romantic things, and I thought I'd put it up for sale instead."

"I could take it for you. Shall I?"

"It's been no use for a year—no, for much longer than that. It's not a question of the money," I added, when I saw a cloud come over her face.

The curve of her neck, slightly arched against the back of the chair, turned toward the window. She fingered the ring languidly. "Three grams, maybe four? Well, let me take it for you. I think the rain has stopped."

I too had been looking uncomfortably at the faint yellowish sunlight coming through the window. It was time to leave.

As the hand with the ring dropped to her lap, she took a deep breath, and two points came to life on her blouse. Then her face, propped on her other hand, turned to me with a delicate quickness, as if to dismiss something. "Excuse me. Here I am brooding when I have company." She hunched over, and the smiling face came nearer. "When I'm busy I usually have lunch just up the street. I've left a supply of rice there. I thought of having something today before I go home, and if you have nothing else to do, suppose you come along." Without waiting for my answer, she took her handbag from the little table. "The price of gold changes every day, but let me give you a thousand yen anyway. Business is business. I'll send the rest to your mine when I know exactly how much it comes to."

The frankness of the smooth-flowing words helped a little.

I waited in the hall.

She came out, her lips alive, and the office door closed sharply.

In the evening sunlight after the May rain, we crossed the bridge toward the Ginza. It is pointless, at such times, to describe life as "new and fresh."

She exchanged quiet greetings with the waiters and sat down opposite me.

"They say beer doesn't go well with it, but—" We emptied our glasses.

"Your husband?" The talk of drink gave me courage to mention something that had puzzled me.

"Oh, don't worry about 'your husband.' " As she poured more beer for me —indeed, by pouring more beer—she fended off my question. "Were you on the southern front for a long time?"

"Here and there for two years."

"And you were separated from your wife a year after you came back?"

"I guessed everything immediately. It wasn't fun, but I wanted to be rid of the past, and I made a clean break with her. But that isn't a very pleasant subject."

"I'm sorry. That last scene of *Brief Encounter*—remember? Where the husband forgives the wife? It bothered me. It made me very sad to think how they would pass the years afterward. And so I brought it up. But no more."

True, that ending was no ending. Might we not better have left the matter to the critics, however?

"We got nothing at all from military life. Or one thing only. We islanders with our island minds can still remember Java or Luzon when we see a sunset like this. The sunrise some morning makes us all think of sunrises on the continent, while we plow our fields and row our boats. That is the one thing it gave us."

"Men have all the advantages." Her long eyelashes lowered, she watched the shining beads that rose from the bottom of the glass. It is dangerous to be too impressed by feminine poses at certain times. "Oh, yes. You mustn't forget to give me your Kyushu address."

I took out my card case. A long, narrow piece of paper came out with it.

She opened her handbag.

"I have a pen."

"Thank you." Idly, I turned over the piece of paper. It was the second theater ticket.

"Oh, good! Write on the back of that."

I looked at her and we laughed.

With a delicate fountain pen I wrote down the name of the mine and the dormitory.

"When I was in the south, the boys under me all had pictures of their girlfriends and their fiancées and their brides, and whenever they had a spare minute they would take out their pictures and look at them and show them off to the others. It was very strange, though—the habit would make them forget the real women."

She did not answer.

" 'Hey! What was my old woman's face like?' someone would say, and someone else would say, 'Now that you mention it, I can't remember my girl's face either. Be quiet a minute while I close my eyes and think.' It happened all the time."

"Interesting."

"How shall I describe it? The impulse to beautify women is always at work, and it builds up an image that moves away from the actual person. Even at my age."

"May I ask you to do the same with your image of me?" She tilted her head slightly and smiled.

"It may well happen."

Amused, I had my longest look into her eyes.

We parted at Tokyo Station, she to take the Central Line, I the Yokosuka Line. The next day I left for this mine.

A month later I had a registered letter from her:

First, our business.

The enclosed money order covers what I owe you for the item you left with me. I talked with a man we do business with, and bought it at the price he quoted.

It is becoming the cap for a young lady's second molar. She is a very pretty young lady and she is soon to be married. The lower bicuspid next to it will be capped with platinum, and for that I mean to use my own engagement ring.

The day I met you in that strange way was the day I decided on a divorce, after a great deal of unpleasantness. The reason is a most ordinary one, which I shall leave to your imagination.

I hesitated for a time about capping the teeth of a young girl soon to be married with two unlucky engagement rings, but then I came to think that they might be a sort of mascot for her in her new life.

I work hard, all day long. It is new and fresh, this not being anyone's wife.

I trust that you are taking care of yourself.

Have you noted any tendency to beautify my image?

The letter with which I began was my answer.

That is all there is to the story.

It would please me beyond measure if, among my readers, there should be some who felt like going back to reread the beginning.

TRANSLATED BY EDWARD SEIDENSTICKER

■ YOSHIYUKI JUNNOSUKE

Yoshiyuki Junnosuke was born in provincial Okayama in 1924, but grew up in Tokyo in a household of irreproachable modernity. His mother was famous as the first Western-style beautician in Japan; his father, Eisuke, had a brief career as an avant-garde writer, then turned stockbroker and threw out his entire library except for the three books he himself had written. Exempted from military service because of asthma, Junnosuke studied English literature at Tokyo University, joined various literary groups (one of which issued a little magazine near the end of the War, as a testimony to its antimilitarism), and left school in 1947 to work as a full-time staff member of a scandal magazine called *Modern Japan* (*Modan Nihon*). His six years in the lower reaches of journalism, years in which he had hardly any time for reading, were as rewarding artistically as his later, better-paid journalistic activity was distracting. In spite of poverty, overwork, and illness he managed to keep up his conscientious pursuit of both writing and dissipation. In 1954, while hospitalized with tuberculosis, he was awarded the Akutagawa Prize for "Sudden Shower" (*Shūu*, tr. 1972), a sensitive, bittersweet story about a young man who finds himself falling in love with a prostitute and being annoyed at his jealousy over her.

Yoshiyuki's first novel, *Street of Primary Colors* (*Genshoku no machi*, 1956), is also about prostitutes and their clients, and set in the garish neon-lit night world of postwar Tokyo. "In Akiko's Room" (*Shōfu no heya:* literally, "A Prostitute's Room") is yet another, more concentrated version of the time-honored tale of the Yoshiwara, and of other, less familiar geisha or brothel quarters. Like Nagai Kafū, the leading modern master of this demanding genre, Yoshiyuki writes of the world of outcast women both as a refuge from the hypocrisies of ordinary society and as an irresistibly alluring setting for romantic self-degradation. Yoshiyuki's fiction has been classed with the confessional I-novel, which so frequently confesses nothing more shocking than the purchase of a willing lady for an evening. He points out, however, that his artistic aim is "entirely different from that of the I-novelists, whose desire is to write 'sincerely,' 'as it is,' and 'with a warm, true-hearted sentiment.' " Yoshiyuki prefers to keep a discreet distance from his characters. "I believe only in clarity," he says, and quotes *Tonio Kröger:* "If you attach too much importance to what you have to say, if it means too much to you emotionally, then you may be certain that your work will be a complete fiasco." The cool, polished surface of his fiction faithfully reflects a world of mingled frivolity and futility.

Few of Yoshiyuki's many novels and stories were deemed worthy of inclusion in his modestly limited eight-volume *Collected Works* of 1971–1972; one regrets the absence of some of his more ephemeral fiction, which has an attenuated charm of its own. Although Yoshiyuki has made his reputation as a writer of erotic fiction, even his oppressively claustrophobic novel *The Dark Room* (*Anshitsu,* 1969, tr. 1975), a nihilistic account of a man's attempt to escape depression through sex, has a fastidious delicacy recalling the elegant "soft literature" of the later Edo period. The urbane refinement of his astringent prose style is much admired.

❖ In Akiko's Room
(*Shōfu no heya,* 1958)

That day I took my dusty college uniform out of the closet and put it on for the first time in a year. I was no longer a student. I was supporting myself as a reporter on a scandal magazine. While I had been working there part-time, the editor told me to make up my mind whether I wanted a regular job or not. Without hesitation I decided to drop out of school. I didn't withdraw formally, though, so I suppose I was still on the college rolls.

But I felt awkward in my old uniform. Sure enough, I could see in the mirror that it didn't fit very well. Now that I had gone out into "society" to work, now that I had become a full-fledged adult, I seemed to bulge out of it. I straightened my back, set my mouth in a firm line, and tried to look as innocent as my school uniform. Then I left the rooming house.

I had an assignment to interview the wife of a cabinet minister who was said to be involved in corruption. I was to see her instead of her husband because she was the more colorful of the two, a strong-minded woman who had stirred up her own share of gossip. Her dislike of reporters was well known, and I had every reason to fear that I wouldn't get beyond the door. I had to devise a stratagem. Collecting every scrap of information I could find, I had sketched a mental portrait of her. I decided to wear my school uniform, since it was from a prestigious college. Also, I kept in mind that she was a passionate devotee of physiognomy.

What with other business, it was evening by the time I stood at the minister's massive, tight-shut door. Meeting strangers was always painful for me. Steeling my nerves, I made a stab at the doorbell. A faint chime echoed somewhere within the large mansion.

A maid appeared. I gave her my calling card and asked to see her mistress. She withdrew, and the minister's wife came to the door holding my card with her fingertips.

"I wonder if I might speak to you for a moment," I said in my best student's manner. The minister's wife looked me over from head to toe, scrutinized the insignia on my collar emblems and jacket buttons, and then led me into a parlor.

"Is it true that you belong to the Tokyu School of physiognomy, Madam?" I inquired, launching immediately into her favorite subject. During the War, I had studied that method of physiognomy myself. In those days I made it a practice not to believe anything people said, but to concentrate on their expression at the moment they spoke. Perhaps I was trying to show them that I didn't believe in words.

My question did the trick. Gradually warming to the subject, the minister's wife chattered on so enthusiastically that I couldn't get a word in. Froth gathered at the corners of her mouth as she began delving into the history of physiognomy.

"Then the Abbot Takuan would glare into the other man's eyes—" She froze, staring straight at me, just as she was gesturing to emphasize her point. Then she took my card from the table and carefully examined it. The card didn't identify me as a reporter, but the name of the magazine was printed in small type in its left-hand corner. The next moment, she was in a rage.

"So you're a reporter! I thought you were a student, going on about physiognomy that way. What are you here for? I loathe reporters! Always spying on people to find out what they had for lunch, and all that. Now get out. Fast!"

She rose and came toward me menacingly. I stood up, resigned to the fact that the interview was over. As I was putting on my shoes in the entryway she kept after me.

"Get out!"

As I opened the door I heard the click of a switch. She had turned off the porch light.

"That's the way it goes," I muttered to myself, forcing a smile. I tried to look at it from her point of view. But I still felt humiliated.

I went on downtown and stopped for a drink near the station.

Before long I began to feel like myself again. When I left the bar my steps took me toward the quarter where the streets were lined with brothels.

I caught sight of Akiko standing in front of her house. She was waiting for one of the men going by to notice her and stop.

I went straight up to her, nodded hello, and followed her into the house. When we were face to face in her room she murmured something that took me by surprise.

"You look like a beaten dog."

"I do?"

"Yes."

"What a thing to say."

"You're always like that when you come to my room. By the time you leave you're a little more human. But you're pretty hard on me in between. Do you only come here when something's wrong?"

I didn't answer. Her words set me thinking. I had meant to dispel all traces of my humiliation, not to be a taunted man hurrying for solace to the quarter of taunted women. I had thought of myself as sauntering tipsily into the quarter enticed by a desire for pleasure. And now that pose was shattered. Suddenly I could see myself as I looked in her eyes. Hunched over, I would come slinking along toward her as she stood there in front of her house. I would go into her room like a beaten dog, and then turn brutal and devour her body.

I had no intention of using brute force with Akiko. Yet I couldn't help thinking she was right. Maybe I had gone to her to confirm that I was alive. Or maybe I was releasing my suppressed anger against her.

That day I gently nestled close to Akiko. What was there to fear in two hurt animals huddling together for warmth, licking each other's wounds? I said nothing, but carried on a long, intricate conversation with her body. And her body conveyed all sorts of meanings that had been lost to me when I was merely forcing myself on her.

From that day on I felt a haunting loneliness whenever I was away from her. It seemed absurd not to have her by my side. Every part of her body had its own eloquent expression for me. I could see in my mind's eye the sinuously curving valley between her breasts, the slight hollow at her collarbone when she turned her neck. Then I would get up and head for the brothel-lined streets.

As soon as I set foot in the quarter I felt a sense of kinship with all the women who stood in the doorways of those tasteless, garishly painted houses. I was at home with them. There was nothing surreptitious or guilty about me as I made my way toward Akiko's room. And the women were kind to me. Apparently it pleased them to know that I had a steady girl.

Sometimes one of them would call out: "How about trying me, for a change?"

As I walked down these streets mingled voices would pursue me. Once I heard a woman say: "Take a turn around the block and then come back again, won't you?" I smiled wryly, remembering something that had happened earlier that afternoon. I had gone on assignment to see a certain personage. When the maid appeared she stood in the door as if to block my way.

"The master is resting," she announced. "Please take a walk around the block and then come back again."

An experience like that would be forgotten the moment I reached the quarter. I would go into Akiko's room, not as a beaten dog but as a human being. I had found a place of refuge and I was willing to enjoy it. In Akiko's room I could recover my emotional equilibrium. But that didn't last.

It was Akiko herself who threw me off balance.

One day when I arrived she turned to me with a vague smile and said: "I'm sorry—I didn't think you'd be coming."

I had been with her the day before.

"Is your time all taken up?"

"It's not that."

I couldn't imagine what was bothering her. When I asked, she only smiled that vague smile. But when I touched her I realized that she was physically exhausted. Her body was mute. Usually her eyes would mist over with pleasure, but that day they were lifeless glass balls.

"If I'd known you were coming I wouldn't have let myself get so tired."

I understood.

"Was Kuroda here?"

She had told me that a middle-aged man named Kuroda had become her best customer. Akiko hesitated. "No, it was a stranger, a man I never saw before."

"A stranger?"

Somehow that irritated me. I thought I had protected myself by visiting a woman who could be bought for money, a woman I realized I would have to share with many men. I had known the pain of loving a woman and wasn't ready to expose myself to that again. Foolishly, I had thought that in Akiko's room I was safe.

My irritation came from jealousy.

In my student days I had been in love with a girl who had a fiancé. When I called at her house one afternoon I saw a pair of brown leather shoes lying in the entryway. Evidently the man they belonged to had arrived just ahead of me. The shoes had been kicked off casually; there they lay on the concrete floor, toes pointed toward the inner rooms, looking very much at home. I had never set eyes on the girl's fiancé, but I knew instinctively that his feet had been encased in those brown shoes until a moment ago. The way the shoes had been discarded showed that he was on intimate terms with her family. I felt a bitter jealousy toward those brown shoes.

But because Akiko was a prostitute a different kind of jealousy attacked me.

Shaking her limp shoulders I started to question her.

"What kind of a man? A big man? A sailor? Somebody built like a wrestler?"

"Just an ordinary man."

"Do you get that tired with me?"

Akiko only smiled.

I left Akiko's room. As usual, the narrow streets of the quarter were crowded. I stood on a corner and let my gaze wander over the scene.

All those bodies moving along the streets were men. The bodies waiting in the dark rectangles of open doorways were women. That was ordinary enough here in the brothel quarter, but I found the notion strangely oppressive. If a man chose to stop before one of those waiting women, she would lead him to a secret room. Then, her body under his, she would willingly spread her legs.

In the outside world all sorts of complicated formalities had to be observed before two bodies meeting for the first time would arrive at this state. Such complications were the subject of innumerable stories; my own past jealousies grew from minor incidents of that kind. But now as I stood on a street corner gazing at the scene before me I began to feel a new jealousy gnawing at me. I was possessed by the fantasy that the stranger who had exhausted Akiko was pressing deeper and deeper into her. The inmost recesses of her flesh were being invaded. I knew my own body, and I thought I knew Akiko's body almost as well. Yet perhaps a minute part of her was still unknown to me, a small dark part that I imagined beginning to expand. I felt violent jealousy toward that dark, moist part.

After that, in Akiko's room, I was often aware of using brute force against her. Akiko's room was no longer a place of refuge. Sometimes when I noticed that she was lying there exhausted I would bend down to kiss the dark, sperm-scented part of her body, as if to verify that it was I myself, and not another man, who had tired her.

Still, I walked into the quarter as confidently as ever. And the prostitutes were kind to me.

Summer passed, and autumn was near its end. The first night of the Tori-no-ichi Fair I was in Akiko's room. Suddenly Akiko said to me: "I think I may give it up."

"Give what up?"

"This business."

"But what would you do?"

"Go to work in an office. Mr. Kuroda says he can arrange it."

"You mean you're going to be Kuroda's mistress?"

"I guess you could call it that. He wants to get me out of here."

I changed my line of questioning.

"Does this Kuroda tire you?"

"Mr. Kuroda is a kind, generous person. He's considerate. He's always trying to help me."

Akiko had graduated from a large city high school in Kansai. She could type in English and had a beautiful calligraphic hand. But I doubted that she could put up with regular office work, though I wasn't sure myself why I had such strong misgivings. Then Akiko said: "Come along to the Tori-no-ichi Fair. I want to buy a good-luck rake."

"But that's for raking in more business next year, you know. Isn't it a bit odd to buy one just when you're planning to leave?"

"Well, you never know. They say you have to get a bigger one every year."

I could see in my mind's eye a full-size bamboo rake festooned with good-luck charms: a treasure chest, a painted mask of a jolly fat woman, and the like. And I winced at the thought of pushing my way through the crowds side by side with Akiko, carrying that big, gaudy rake over my shoulder. But how big was the rake that Akiko bought last year? She must have it somewhere. I glanced around her room.

"Where's last year's rake?"

"Over there."

She pointed to a lintel beam behind me. A tiny undecorated rake no larger than the palm of my hand was wedged in by the handle.

"That's really a midget. How long have you been in the quarter?"

"Three years. Last year was the first time I bought a rake."

Akiko and I left the house. On the fringe of the brothel quarter a young hoodlum in sandals stood talking to a woman whose dress seemed molded to the curves of her body. Everything about her—the bare flesh of her shoulders, even the turn of her ankle above her black high-heeled shoes—emphasized her sexual function. It occurred to me that the lover of such a woman would have to transform himself into a gigantic penis. Physical deterioration for a woman like that would no doubt be slow. Perhaps the very fact of being here in the quarter would enable her to go on indefinitely radiating a fresh, youthful sensuality.

I glanced at Akiko beside me. It was over a year since I had first met her. To me, she was beautiful. I didn't think she had deteriorated during the year. Still, I knew that I was in no position to make a cool judgment on any change in Akiko. Once again I looked at her in profile. Her skin seemed vulnerable to the grime of the quarter—perhaps there was already a layer of grime deposited beneath it. Her heart seemed vulnerable too. I recalled a touch of slackness in her breasts.

The bustling scene of the fair was just ahead of us. I stopped for a moment and said: "You'd better not buy a rake this year. You ought to take Kuroda more seriously."

"I do take him seriously," she replied, turning to wait for me. "But I can't help feeling uneasy."

Akiko disappeared from the quarter.

She sent me the phone number of her office, but somehow I didn't want to call her. It bothered me to imagine her in a business office where every movement was supposed to be aimed at getting work done. Akiko's manner seemed proper enough, except when she was in bed; to look at her, you would think she was just an ordinary girl. In an office, though, some slight gesture of hers might stir a ripple of strangeness. If I telephoned her there, and she answered, wouldn't the people around her begin whispering together and exchanging glances? That would be painful for both of us.

I didn't call Akiko, but I kept on visiting the quarter she had left. One after another I went up to the rooms of the women I had come to know by sight. I never went to the same room more than once or twice. Still, all the women were kind to me. At the time I could hardly understand why.

Occasionally I had the disturbing experience of seeing one of these prostitutes outside the quarter. I remember a strikingly beautiful woman who used to stand in the red-and-blue neon-tinted street full of confidence, her breasts held high, as she looked contemptuously at the men passing by. One summer day I saw her while I was walking down a sloping road to a train station. The pavement reflected the midsummer sunlight, and dust glittered in the air. Bent over and trudging listlessly up the road, she had a baby strapped insecurely to her back, held by a black muslin band criss-crossed over her Western-style dress. As we passed I saw beads of sweat gathered on her forehead, and I thought I could hear her panting. The woman looked up at me. Her eyes were a yellowish, muddy color, with dark circles around them that made her look old. For an instant those lusterless eyes met mine, but there was no sign that she recognized me.

One day Akiko telephoned my office and said she'd like to meet me at noon Sunday. Hearing her voice for the first time in half a year, I had a premonition that her career as an office worker was nearing its end. Already Akiko seemed to be emerging from the atmosphere of the office, beginning to escape from that stifling room.

However, I didn't think she wanted to see me just to ask my advice about quitting her job. We met Sunday and had lunch together at a little restaurant downtown. Afterward I suggested we go to a hotel. Akiko hesitated, and then nodded.

"How's Kuroda?" I inquired as we walked along.

"I've never been unfaithful to him before," she whispered, drawing a little closer to me. "Not since I left the quarter."

She seemed to regret our meeting. But once we were in the hotel room I could hardly contain the violence of her body.

At midafternoon the hotel was almost empty. There was only the sound of a maid flailing away with her duster in the corridor outside our room, and the creaking of our crude wooden bed. Even after I was lying still the bed kept on creaking.

Finally Akiko lay exhausted beside me. She seemed embarrassed when she saw me looking at her.

"Will you go on working at the office?" I asked for the first time. Akiko smiled, and said nothing. That convinced me she would soon return to her old quarter, to the quarter I was still haunting.

About half a month later I found Akiko standing in the doorway of one of the houses, a different one from before. Just as I used to do, I nodded and followed her inside.

"When did you get back?" I asked, once we were in her room.

"Yesterday." Akiko put her arms around me and smiled. "If I'd met you yesterday—" She faltered, searching for the right phrase. "I'd have eaten you alive." So today her hunger was not all that acute, and yesterday there *was* a man she ate alive. Probably he was only a passing stranger. But even imagining her in the arms of that nameless man no longer gave me a twinge of jealousy.

I looked into Akiko's eyes. Just then it seemed to me that the two of us— Akiko, a woman shaped by the life of this quarter, a woman drawn back to it after once escaping, and myself, a man unable to give it up even after she had left— were exchanging the look of accomplices.

For the next year I roamed the quarter like a thoroughly dissolute pleasure-seeker. I could close my eyes and visualize a detailed map of the quarter. Nothing was missing, not the least alleyway or dust bin along the street. I was twenty-five and enjoyed posing as a libertine. I even felt a degree of passion. So there was bitterness in it, but there was also freshness.

Sometimes I went back to Akiko's room. Her body was far too familiar to give me any new stimulation; and yet for that very reason, even when I got so drunk as to be impotent with the other girls, in Akiko's room I would recover my virility. Once again her room became my refuge. Akiko was always kind and indulgent. When my money ran out I would spend the night with her, leaving my raincoat or my watch as security. There was a time when all my small personal possessions had ended up there. And the next morning she put breakfast money in my hand.

Akiko continued to indulge me. But one day I learned that her interest in me had cooled. She told me she had fallen in love.

"Oh?"

"He's young. Younger than you."

"What about Kuroda?"

"Mr. Kuroda is a kind, sympathetic man, he's always trying to help. He wants to get me out of the quarter again. I was a flop as an office girl, so this time he's found me a place in a bar. He's rented an apartment for me too."

"Then all you have to do is leave."

"That's right. Come to see me at the bar, won't you? I'll call you from there."

It was a full year since Akiko's return to the quarter, and now she was leaving again.

Akiko telephoned to let me know the bar's address. To my surprise, it was tucked away just off a prosperous shopping street downtown.

I went to visit the bar, and found Akiko sitting in a corner, bored. As soon as she saw me she hurried over with a look of relief on her face.

I sat down at the bar and began drinking steadily. Akiko sat beside me. We said nothing, though the other customers and their hostesses were joking and flirting in the usual lively, innocuous way. It occurred to me that Akiko's conversations with her customers in the quarter had been of a rather different kind. No doubt since coming to this bar she had merely sat beside her customers smiling that vague smile of hers.

Finally I asked how things were going.

"It's not so easy here."

I was silent.

"Mr. Kuroda gets mad and says I'm always complaining. He knows a school for fashion models—he keeps telling me I ought to try it."

The instant I heard that I felt a chill come over me, and I saw Akiko exactly as she was. If Kuroda had suggested it a few years ago, before she came to the quarter, it wouldn't have seemed so incongruous. But now it was downright cruel. Could she be aware of that? Probably not. The thought gave me a dark, wretched feeling, a feeling of bitter disappointment. I had the impression that the grime of the quarter was beginning to show through Akiko's skin. She alone in the bar seemed to be under a curious shadow.

But did Kuroda himself realize the cruelty of what he had said? Having once tried to rescue her and failed, and on the verge of failing again, how did he feel toward Akiko? Could he be so blindly in love with her?

The second time I visited the bar Akiko was already gone. I hadn't asked for the address of her apartment, and she didn't telephone me. She had disappeared without a trace.

As usual, I went on roaming the brothel quarter that Akiko had deserted a second time.

Three years had passed since my first visit to Akiko's room. There were always new faces among the women in front of the houses, and fewer and fewer women I had known for a long time. And there was a change in me as well.

In the old days I would slink in like a beaten dog, nestling up to a sad, sympathetic whore so that we could lick each other's wounds. I felt no difference between myself and the quarter. Later I strode around the quarter in the pose of a libertine. Straining every nerve to maintain that pose, I would scrupulously eye the women with as much passion as I could muster.

And now my attitude had changed. My wretchedness and disappointment in Akiko at the bar had darkened my vision of the quarter. This wretchedness was different from the kind I had nestled close to. I stood on a safe, slightly higher ground looking down on it. I was no longer at home in the brothel quarter. The neon-tinted streets had begun to fade before my eyes.

My change of feeling toward Akiko had become a change of attitude toward the quarter. I never believed that my feeling toward any one woman would go on indefinitely in the same way, with the same intensity. So perhaps the ordinary passage of time had brought that change. Yet it may also have reflected a change in my life. The company where I worked was becoming prosperous. As one of its staff members, I was treated more respectfully by the people I had to deal with, and so there were fewer humiliations. I couldn't simply call it my own good fortune. Perhaps this also had something to do with my changed attitude toward the quarter.

Out of habit, I kept on haunting the brothel quarter that was fading before my eyes. I had the casual hope that, among the many women waiting there, I might find one whose body would bring me unexpected delight.

But the women began to grow cold toward me. Not that they realized I had changed. Even a woman I never met before would treat me with the typical cold spitefulness of a whore. I often tasted the bitterness of the quarter.

I thought that if I could be more passionate in my search for a body to delight me I might escape with fewer such unpleasant encounters. But that hope was just as elusive.

I would follow a woman into her room. Already my lust would begin to cool. I would think of Akiko, and remember that while she was here I could keep my lust alive. Then my strength would ebb away completely.

One night, a little drunk, I was walking through the quarter. I approached a woman and followed her inside. As I stood in the doorway to her room I recalled that I had visited her before. I had been impotent. Hesitating, I muttered: "Tonight may be no good either."

The woman heard me, and peered into my face. She remembered. Suddenly she threw off her meek, gentle manner and shrilled out: "Why did you come here? Go on home!"

She shoved me back along the hall to the top of the stairs, and then gave another push with all her strength. Half-stumbling, I went careening down the stairs. A handful of salt came pelting after me as I struggled into my shoes to escape. The white crystals were sprinkled all over my head and shoulders.

As I was passing Akiko's old house, the only woman I still knew there called out to me.

"Akiko's back!"

"Where?"

She named a house that had the same owner. "Akiko's the madam." So Akiko was running it.

I walked over to the other house, repeating to myself "Akiko's the madam." Turning in at a narrow lane, I went around to the back door. Through a lattice window I could see Akiko inside bent over an abacus. She was wearing red-rimmed glasses.

When I tapped on the windowpane, Akiko turned and saw me. She smiled, took off her glasses, and let me in through the back door.

"Here I am again," she said, still smiling.

"What happened to your lover?" I asked, thinking of her young man.

"That's all over. He gave me a terrible time. I'm not so young myself anymore, I can't go on forever standing out in the street." Akiko glanced around the room that seemed to be her office. I couldn't find anything to say.

Akiko broke the silence. "Now he tells me I ought to try opening a tobacco shop."

"Who tells you?"

"Mr. Kuroda."

"Oh? Does Kuroda know about your young man?"

"Somehow it leaked out."

"You ought to let him set you up with a shop."

"I suppose so. Once I'm out of here I've got to get myself fixed up. Something's wrong with my uterus."

"You should take care of yourself."

I left Akiko and walked through the brothel quarter toward the streets beyond it. I was thinking about Kuroda. He never changed. And I? The quarter no longer needed me, and I no longer needed the quarter. Filled with self-loathing, I hurried away.

TRANSLATED BY HOWARD HIBBETT

∷ŌE KENZABURŌ

Ōe Kenzaburō was born in a mountain village on the island of Shikoku in 1935. After high school and a year's hiatus as a *rōnin* ("masterless samurai," a would-be student seeking a new school tie) he entered the Department of French Literature at Tokyo University. In 1958, a year before graduating, he published a book of short stories—and won the Akutagawa Prize for one of them, "The Catch" (*Shiiku*, tr. 1959), a story about a small Japanese boy and his betrayal by a black American pilot who is being held captive in his village. That year Ōe also completed his first novel, *Nip the Buds, Gun the Kids* (*Me-mushiri ko-uchi*), a bitter account of the brutal mistreatment of a group of reform-school boys who were evacuated during the War to a farm village.

Ōe's spectacular literary debut has been followed by a career remarkable even in Japan for productivity and for dedication to political causes. An uncompromising spokesman for the New Left, he has published many essays on social, political, and literary topics as well as novels and stories. Among his major works of fiction are *A Personal Matter* (*Kojinteki na taiken*, 1964, tr. 1968) and *The Silent Cry* (*Man'en gannen no futtobōru*, 1967, tr. 1974), both of which richly illustrate the theme described by John Nathan as "modern man's unreasoning will to survive in the face of imminent cataclysm and chaos: in the face of modern times."

"Aghwee the Sky Monster" is the story in which Ōe introduces the figures that have come to dominate his symbolic world: a father and his monstrously abnormal son. In *A Personal Matter*, a young man called Bird becomes the father of an infant afflicted at birth with a "brain hernia" which makes him appear to have two heads and dooms him, if he should live, to a vegetable existence. Bird conspires with a hospital doctor to destroy the baby by substituting sugar water for milk—and then staggers through four nightmarish guilt-ridden days, waiting for the baby to die. In *The Silent Cry*, the baby seems to have receded into the background; the father has placed him in an institution for retarded children. But this does not signify the father's freedom; it is only a temporary escape. And the threat to existence the baby represents still dictates the course of the father's life.

His response to that threat is to flee into his past in search of what he calls his roots. In fact he is looking for a basis for identity which precedes, and, as he hopes, will be free of, the baby. Inevitably, he does not find what he seeks; for the baby, no less than the age in which he lives, is inherent in him. At the end of the novel, after an elaborate and unsuccessful attempt to identify with ancestral heroes, the father contemplates leaving Japan for Africa, where he hopes to have better luck in discovering himself.

"Aghwee the Sky Monster" appeared early in the same year as *A Personal Matter,* and obviously represents the novel's alternative, unwritten ending, with punishment built into the fantasy. But the story can stand by itself, a vivid example of the imaginative vision that has made Ōe Kenzaburō one of the most original and exciting of postwar Japanese writers.

❖ Aghwee the Sky Monster

(*Sora no kaibutsu aguī,* 1964)

Alone in my room, I wear a piratical black patch over my right eye. The eye may look all right, but the truth is I have scarcely any sight in it. Scarcely, I say; it isn't totally blind. The consequence is that when I look at this world with both eyes I see two worlds perfectly superimposed, a vague and shadowy world on top of one that's bright and vivid. I can be walking down a paved street when a sense of peril and unbalance will stop me, like a rat just scurried out of a sewer, dead in my tracks. Or I'll discover a film of unhappiness and fatigue on the face of a cheerful friend and clog the flow of an easy chat with my sluggish stutter. I suppose I'll get used to this eventually. If I don't I intend to wear my patch not only in my room when I'm alone but on the street and with my friends. Strangers may pass with condescending smiles—what an old-fashioned joke!—but I'm old enough not to be annoyed by every little thing.

The story I intend to tell is about my first experience earning money; I began with my right eye because the memory of that experience ten years ago revived in me abruptly and quite out of context when violence was done to my eye last spring. Remembering, I should add, I was freed from the hatred uncoiling in my heart and beginning to fetter me. At the very end I'll talk about the accident itself.

Ten years ago I had twenty-twenty vision. Now one of my eyes is ruined. *Time* shifted, launched itself from the springboard of an eyeball squashed by a stone. When I first met that sentimental madman I had only a child's understanding of *time.* I was yet to have the cruel awareness of *time* drilling its eyes into my back and *time* lying in wait ahead.

Ten years ago I was eighteen years old and weighed one hundred and ten pounds, had just entered college and was looking for a part-time job. Although I still had trouble reading French, I wanted to buy a clothbound edition in two volumes of *L'Âme Enchanté*. It was a Moscow edition I wanted, with not only a foreword but footnotes and even the colophon in Russian, and wispy lines like bits of thread connecting the letters of the French text. It was a curious edition all right, but far sturdier and more elegant than the French, and much cheaper. At the time I discovered it in a bookstore specializing in East European publications I had no interest in Romain Rolland, yet I went immediately into action to make the volumes mine. In those days I often succumbed to some curious passion and it never bothered me, I had the feeling there was nothing to worry about so long as I was sufficiently obsessed.

As I had just entered college and wasn't registered at the employment center, I looked for work by making the rounds of people I knew. Finally my uncle introduced me to a banker who came up with an offer. "Did you happen to see a movie called *Harvey?*" he asked. I said yes, and tried for a smile of moderate but unmistakable dedication, appropriate for someone about to be employed for the first time. *Harvey* was that Jimmy Stewart film about a man living with an imaginary rabbit as big as a bear; it had made me laugh so hard I thought I would die. The banker didn't return my smile. "Recently, my son has been having the same sort of delusions about living with a monster. He's stopped working and stays in his room. I'd like him to get out from time to time, but of course he'd need a—chaperon. Would you be interested?"

I knew quite a bit about the banker's son. He was a young composer whose avant-garde music had won prizes in France and Italy and who was generally included in the photo roundups in the weekly magazines, the kind of article they always called "Japan's Artists of Tomorrow." I had never heard his major works, but I had seen several films for which he had done the music. There was one about the adventures of a juvenile delinquent that had a short, lyrical theme played on the harmonica. It was beautiful. Watching the picture, I remember feeling vaguely troubled by the idea of an adult nearly thirty years old (in fact, the composer was twenty-eight when he hired me, my present age) working out a theme for the harmonica. Because my own harmonica had become my little brother's property when I had entered elementary school. And possibly because I knew more about the composer, whose name was D, than just public facts; I knew he had created a scandal. Generally, I have nothing but contempt for scandals, but I knew that the composer's infant child had died, that he had gotten divorced as a result, and that he was rumored to be involved with a certain movie actress. I hadn't known that he was in the grips of something like the rabbit in Jimmy Stewart's movie, or that he had stopped working and secluded himself in his room. How serious was his condition, I wondered, was it a case of nervous breakdown, or was he clearly schizophrenic?

"I'm not certain I know just what you mean by chaperon," I said, reeling in my smile. "Naturally, I'd like to be of service if I can." This time, concealing my curiosity and apprehension, I tried to lend my voice and expression as much sympathy as possible without seeming forward. It was only a part-time job, but it was the first chance of employment I had had and I was determined to do my accommodating best.

"When my son decides he wants to go somewhere in Tokyo, you go along —just that. There's a nurse at the house and she has no trouble handling him, so you don't have to worry about violence." The banker made me feel like a soldier whose cowardice has been discovered. I blushed and said, trying to recover lost ground: "I'm fond of music, and I respect composers more than anyone, so I look forward to accompanying D and talking with him."

"All he thinks about these days is this thing in his head, and apparently that's all he talks about!" The banker's brusqueness made my face even redder. "You can go out to see him tomorrow," he said.

"At—your house?"

"That's right, did you think he was in an asylum?" From the banker's tone of voice I could only suppose that he was at bottom a nasty man.

"If I should get the job," I said with my eyes on the floor, "I'll drop by again to thank you." I could easily have cried.

"No, he'll be hiring you" (All right then, I resolved defiantly, I'll call D my employer!), "so that won't be necessary. All I care about is that he doesn't get into any trouble outside that might develop into a scandal. There's his career to think about. Naturally, what he does reflects on me—"

So that was it! I thought, so I was to be a moral sentinel guarding the banker's family against a second contamination by the poisons of scandal. Of course I didn't say a thing, I only nodded dependably, anxious to warm the banker's chilly heart with the heat of reliance on me. I didn't even ask the most pressing question, something truly difficult to ask, namely: This monster haunting your son, sir, is it a rabbit like Harvey, nearly six feet tall? A creature covered in bristly hair like an Abominable Snowman? What kind of a monster is it? In the end I remained silent and consoled myself with the thought that I might be able to pry the secret out of the nurse if I made friends with her.

Then I left the executive's office, and as I walked along the corridor grinding my teeth in humiliation as if I were Julien Sorel after a meeting with someone important, I became self-conscious to the tips of my fingers and tried assessing my attitude and its effectiveness. When I got out of college I chose not to seek nine-to-five employment, and I do believe the memory of my dialogue with that disagreeable banker played a large part in my decision.

Even so, when classes were over the next day, I took a train out to the residential suburb where the composer lived. As I passed through the gate of that castle of a house, I remember a roaring of terrific beasts, as at a zoo in the middle of the night. I was dismayed, I cowered, what if those were the screams of my employer? A good thing it didn't occur to me then that those savage screams might have been coming from the monster haunting D like Jimmy Stewart's rabbit. Whatever they were, it was so clear that the screaming had rattled me that the maid showing me the way was indiscreet enough to break into a laugh. Then I discovered someone else laughing, voicelessly, in the dimness beyond a window in an annex in the garden. It was the man who was supposed to employ me; he was laughing like a face in a movie without a sound track. And boiling all around him was that howling of wild beasts. I listened closely and realized that several of the same animals were shrieking in concert. And in voices too shrill to be of this world. Abandoned by the maid at the entrance to the annex, I decided the screaming must be part of the composer's tape collection, regained my courage, straightened up, and opened the door.

Inside, the annex reminded me of a kindergarten. There were no partitions in the large room, but two pianos, an electric organ, several tape recorders, a record-player, something we had called a "mixer" when I was in the high-school radio club—there was hardly room to thread your way through. What looked like a dog asleep on the floor, for example, turned out to be a tuba of reddish brass. It was just as I had imagined a composer's studio; I even had the illusion I had seen the place before. D had stopped working and secluded himself in his room —could his father have been mistaken about all that?

The composer was just bending to switch off the tape recorder. Enveloped in a chaos that was not without its own order, he moved his hands swiftly and in an instant those beastly screams were sucked into a dark hole of silence. Then he straightened and turned to me with a truly tranquil smile.

Having glanced around the room and seen that the nurse was not present, I was a little wary, but the composer gave me no reason in the world to expect that he was about to get violent.

"My father told me about you. Come in, there's room over there," he said in a low resonant voice.

I took off my shoes and stepped up onto the rug without putting on slippers. Then I looked around for a place to sit, but except for round stools in front of the pianos and the organ, there wasn't a bit of furniture in the room, not even a cushion. So I brought my feet together between a pair of bongo drums and some empty tape boxes and stood there uncomfortably. The composer was standing too, arms hanging at his sides. I wondered if he ever sat down. He didn't ask me to be seated either, just stood there silent and smiling.

"Could those have been monkey voices?" I said, trying to crack a silence that threatened to set more quickly than any cement.

"Rhinoceros—they sounded that way because I speeded the machine up. And I had the volume way up, too. At least I think they're rhinoceros—rhino is what I asked for when I had this tape made—of course I can't really be sure. But now that you're here, I'll be able to go to the zoo myself."

"I may take that to mean that I'm employed?"

"Of course! I didn't have you come out here to test you. How can a madman test a normal person?" The man who was to be my employer said this objectively and almost as if he were embarrassed. Which made me feel disgusted with the obsequiousness of what I had said—I may take that to mean that I'm employed? —I had sounded like a shopkeeper! The composer was different from his business-man father and I should have been more direct with him.

"I wish you wouldn't call yourself a madman. It's awkward for me." Trying to be frank was one thing, but what a brainless remark! But the composer met me halfway. "All right, if that's how you feel. I suppose that would make work easier."

Work is a vague word, but, at least during those few months when I was visiting him once a week, the composer didn't get even as close to work as going to the zoo to record a genuine rhino for himself. He merely wandered around Tokyo in various conveyances or on foot and visited a variety of places. When he mentioned work, he must therefore have had me in mind. And I worked quite a lot; I even went on a mission for him, all the way to Kyoto.

"Then when should I begin?" I said.

"Right away if it suits you. Now."

"That suits me fine."

"I'll have to get ready—would you wait outside?"

Head lowered cautiously, as though he were walking in a swamp, my em-ployer picked his way to the back of the room past musical instruments and sound equipment and piles of manuscripts to a black wooden door which he opened and then closed behind him. I got a quick look at a woman in a nurse's uniform, a woman in her early forties with a longish face and heavy shadows on her cheeks that might have been wrinkles or maybe scars. She seemed to encircle the composer with her right arm as she ushered him inside, while with her left hand she closed the door. If this was part of the routine, I would never have a chance to talk with the nurse before I went out with my employer. Standing in front of the closed door, in the darkest part of that dim room, I shuffled into my shoes and felt my anxiety about this job of mine increase. The composer had smiled the whole time and when I had prompted him he had replied. But he hadn't volunteered much. Should I have been more reserved? I wondered. Since "out-side" might have meant two things, and since I was determined that everything should be perfect on my first job, I decided to wait just inside the main gate, from where I could see the annex in the garden.

D was a small, thin man, but with a head that seemed larger than most. To make the bony cliff of his forehead seem a little less forbidding, he combed his pale, well-washed, and fluffy hair down over his brow. His mouth and jaw were small, and his teeth were horribly irregular. And yet, probably due to the color of his deeply recessed eyes, there was a static correctness about his face that went well with a tranquil smile. As for the overall impression, there was something canine about the man. He wore flannel trousers and a sweater with stripes like rows of fleas. His shoulders were a little stooped, his arms outlandishly long.

When he came out of the back door of the annex, my employer was wearing a blue wool cardigan over his other sweater and a pair of white tennis shoes. He reminded me of a grade-school music teacher. In one hand he held a black scarf, and as if he were puzzling whether to wrap it around his neck, there was perplexity in his grin to me as I waited at the gate. For as long as I knew D, except at the very end when he was lying in a hospital bed, that was how he dressed. I remember his outfit so well because I was always struck by something comical about an adult man wearing a cardigan around his shoulders, as if he were a woman in disguise. Its shapelessness and nondescript color made that sweater perfect for him. As the composer pigeon-toed toward me past the shrubbery, he absently lifted the hand that held the scarf and signaled me with it. Then he wrapped the scarf resolutely around his neck. It was already four in the afternoon and fairly cold out of doors.

D went through the gate, and as I was following him (our relationship was already that of employer and employee), I had the feeling I was being watched and turned around: behind the same window through which I had discovered my employer, that forty-year-old nurse with the scarred—or were they wrinkled?—cheeks was watching us the way a soldier remaining behind might see a deserter off, her lips clamped shut like a turtle. I resolved to get her alone as soon as I could to question her about D's condition. What was wrong with the woman, anyway? Here she was taking care of a young man with a nervous condition, maybe a madman, yet when her charge went out she had nothing to say to the chaperon accompanying him. Wasn't that professional negligence? Wasn't she at least obliged to fill in the new man on the job? Or was my employer a patient so gentle and harmless that nothing had to be said?

When he got to the sidewalk D shuttered open his tired-looking eyes in their deep sockets and glanced swiftly up and down the deserted residential street. I didn't know whether it was an indication of madness or what—sudden action without any continuity seemed to be a habit of his. The composer looked up at the clear, end-of-autumn sky, blinking rapidly. Though they were sunken, there was something remarkably expressive about his deep brown eyes. Then he stopped blinking and his eyes seemed to focus, as though he were searching the sky. I stood obliquely behind him, watching, and what impressed me most vividly was the movement of his Adam's apple, which was large as any fist. I wondered if he had been destined to become a large man; perhaps something had impeded his growth in infancy and now only his head from the neck up bespoke the giant he was meant to be.

Lowering his gaze from the sky, my employer found and held my puzzled eyes with his own and said casually, but with a gravity that made objection impossible: "On a clear day you can see things floating up there very well. I see him up there with them, and frequently he comes down to me when I go outdoors."

Instantly I felt threatened. Looking away from my employer, I wondered how to survive this first ordeal that had confronted me so quickly. Should I pretend to believe in what this man called "him," or would that be a mistake? Was I dealing with a raving madman, or was the composer just a poker-faced humorist trying to have some fun with me? As I stood there in distress, he extended me a helping hand: "I know you can't see the figures floating in the sky, and I know you wouldn't be aware of him even if he were right here at my side. All I ask is that you don't act amazed when he comes down to earth, even if I talk to him. Because you'd upset him if you were to break out laughing all of a sudden or were to try to shut me up. And if you happen to notice when we're talking that I want some support from you, I'd appreciate it if you'd chime right in and say something, you know, affirmative. You see, I'm explaining Tokyo to him as if it were a paradise. It might seem a lunatic paradise to you, but maybe you could think of it as satire and be affirmative anyway, at least when he's down here with me."

I listened carefully and thought I could make out at least the contours of what my employer expected of me. Then was "he" a rabbit as big as a man after all, nesting in the sky? But that wasn't what I asked; I restrained myself to asking only: "How will I know when he's down here with you?"

"Just by watching me; he only comes down when I'm outside."

"What about when you're in a car?"

"In a car or train, as long as I'm next to an open window he's likely to show up. There have been times when he's appeared when I was in the house, just standing next to an open window."

"And . . . right now?" I asked uncomfortably. I must have sounded like the class dunce who simply cannot grasp the multiplication principle.

"Right now it's just you and me," my employer said graciously. "Why don't we ride in to Shinjuku today? I haven't been on a train in a long time."

We walked to the station, and all the way I kept an eye peeled for a sign that something had appeared at my employer's side. But before I knew it we were on the train and, so far as I could tell, nothing had materialized. One thing I did notice: the composer ignored the people who passed us on the street even when they greeted him. As if he himself did not exist, as if the people who approached with hellos and how-are-yous were registering an illusion which they mistook for him, my employer utterly ignored all overtures to contact.

The same thing happened at the ticket window; D unilaterally declined to relate to other people. Handing me one thousand yen, he told me to buy tickets and then refused to take his own even when I held it out to him. I had to stop at the gate and have both our tickets punched while D swept through the turnstile onto the platform with the freedom of the invisible man. Even on the train, he behaved as if the other passengers were no more aware of him than of the atmosphere; huddling in a seat in the farthest corner of the car, he rode in silence with his eyes closed. I stood in front of him and watched in growing apprehension for whatever it was to float in through the open window and settle at his side. Naturally, I didn't believe in the monster's existence. It was just that I was determined not to miss the instant when D's delusions took hold of him; I felt I owed him that much in return for the money he was paying me. But, as it happened, he sat like some small animal playing dead all the way to Shinjuku Station, so I could only surmise that he hadn't had a visit from the sky. Of course, supposition was all it was: as long as other people were around us, my employer remained a sullen oyster of silence. But I learned quickly enough that my guess had been correct. Because when the moment came, it was more than apparent (from D's reaction, I mean) that something was visiting him.

We had left the station and were walking down the street. It was that time of day a little before evening when not many people are out; we ran across a small crowd gathered on a corner. We stopped to look; surrounded by the crowd, an old man was turning around and around in the street without so much as a glance at anyone. A dignified-looking old man, he was spinning in a frenzy, clutching a briefcase and an umbrella to his breast, mussing his gray, pomaded hair a little as he stamped his feet and shouted like a seal. The faces in the watching crowd were lusterless and dry in the evening chill that was stealing into the air; the old man's face alone was flushed, and sweating, and seemed about to steam.

Suddenly I noticed that D, who should have been standing at my side, had taken a few steps back and thrown one arm around the shoulders of an invisible something roughly his own height. Now he was peering affectionately into the space slightly above the empty circle of his arm. The crowd was too intent on the old man to be concerned with D's performance, but I was terrified. Slowly the composer turned to me, as if he wanted to introduce me to a friend. I didn't know how to respond; all I could do was panic and blush. It was like forgetting your silly lines in the junior-high-school play. The composer continued to stare at me, and now there was annoyance in his eyes. He was seeking an explanation for that intent old man turning singlemindedly in the street, for the benefit of his visitor from the sky. A paradisiacal explanation! But all I could do was wonder stupidly whether the old man might have been afflicted with Saint Vitus's dance.

When I sadly shook my head in silence, the light of inquiry went out of my employer's eyes. As if he were taking leave of a friend, he dropped his arm. Then he slowly shifted his gaze skyward until his head was all the way back and his large Adam's apple stood out in bold relief. The phantom had soared back into the sky and I was ashamed; I hadn't been equal to my job. As I stood there with my head hanging, the composer stepped up to me and indicated that my first day of work was at an end: "We can go home now. He's come down once today already, and you must be pretty tired." I did feel exhausted after all that tension.

We rode back in a taxi with the windows rolled up, and as soon as I'd been paid for the day, I left. But I didn't go straight to the station; I waited behind a telephone pole diagonally across from the house. Dusk deepened, the sky turned the color of a rose, and just as the promise of night was becoming fact, the nurse, in a short-skirted, one-piece dress of a color indistinct in the dimness, appeared through the main gate pushing a brand-new bicycle in front of her. Before she could get on the bicycle, I ran over to her. Without her nurse's uniform she was just an ordinary little woman in her early forties; vanished from her face was the mystery I had discovered through the annex window. And my appearance had unsettled her. She couldn't climb on the bike and pedal away, but neither would she stand still; she had begun to walk the bike along when I demanded that she explain our mutual employer's condition. She resisted, peevishly, but I had a good grip on the bicycle seat and so in the end she gave in. When she began to talk, her formidable lower jaw snapped shut at each break in the sentence; she was absolutely a talking turtle.

"He says it's a fat baby in a white cotton nightgown. Big as a kangaroo, he says. It's supposed to be afraid of dogs and policemen and it comes down out of the sky. He says its name is Aghwee! Let me tell you something, if you happen to be around when that spook gets hold of him, you'd better just play dumb, you can't afford to get involved—don't forget you're dealing with a loony! And another thing, don't you take him anyplace funny, even if he wants to go. On top of everything else, a little gonorrhea is all we need around here!"

I blushed and let go of the bicycle seat. The nurse, jangling her bell, pedaled away into the darkness as fast as she could go with legs as tubular as handlebars. Ah, a fat baby in a white cotton nightgown, big as a kangaroo!

When I showed up at the house the following week, the composer fixed me with those clear brown eyes of his and rattled me by saying, though not especially in reproof: "I hear you waited for the nurse and asked her about my visitor from the sky. You really take your work seriously."

That afternoon we took the same train in the opposite direction, into the country for half an hour to an amusement park on the banks of the Tama River. We tried all kinds of rides and, luckily for me, the baby as big as a kangaroo dropped out of the sky to visit D when he was up by himself in the Sky Sloop, wooden boxes shaped like boats that were hoisted slowly into the air on the blades of a kind of windmill. From a bench on the ground, I watched the composer talking with an imaginary passenger at his side. And until his visitor had climbed back into the sky, D refused to come down; again and again a signal from him sent me running to buy him another ticket.

Another incident that made an impression on me that day occurred as we were crossing the amusement park toward the exit, when D accidentally stepped in some wet cement. When he saw that his foot had left an imprint he became abnormally irritated, and until I had negotiated with the workmen, paid them something for their pains and had the footprint troweled away, he stubbornly refused to move from the spot. This was the only time the composer ever revealed to me the least violence in his nature. On the way home on the train, I suppose because he regretted having barked at me, he excused himself in this way: "I'm not living in present time anymore, at least not consciously. Do you know the rule that governs trips into the past in a time machine? For example, a man who travels back ten thousand years in time doesn't dare do anything in that world that might remain behind him. Because he doesn't exist in time ten thousand years ago, and if he left anything behind him there the result would be a warp, infinitely slight maybe but still a warp, in all of history from then until now, ten thousand years of it. That's the way the rule goes, and since I'm not living in present time, I mustn't do anything here in this world that might remain or leave an imprint."

"But why have you stopped living in present time?" I asked, and my employer sealed himself up like a golf ball and ignored me. I regretted my loose tongue; I had finally exceeded the limits permitted me, because I was too concerned with D's problem. Maybe the nurse was right; playing dumb was the only way, and I couldn't afford to get involved. I resolved not to.

We walked around Tokyo occasionally after that, and my new policy was a success. But the day came when the composer's problems began to involve me whether I liked it or not. One afternoon we got into a cab together and, for the first time since I had taken the job, D mentioned a specific destination, a swank apartment house in Daikan Yama laid out like a hotel. When we arrived, D waited in the coffee shop in the basement while I went up in the elevator alone to pick up something that was waiting for me. I was to receive it from D's former wife, who was now living alone in the apartment.

I knocked on a door that made me think of the cell blocks at Sing Sing (I was always going to the movies in those days; I have the feeling that about 95 percent of what I knew came directly from the movies) and it was opened by a short woman with a pudgy, red face on top of a neck that was just as pudgy, as round as a cylinder. She ordered me to take my shoes off and step inside, and pointed to a sofa near the window where I was to sit. This must be the way high society receives a stranger, I remember thinking at the time. For me, the son of a poor farmer, refusing her invitation and asking for delivery at the door would have taken the courage to defy Japanese high society, the courage of that butcher who threatened Louis XIV. I did as I was told, and stepped for the first time in my life into an American-style studio apartment.

The composer's former wife poured me some beer. She seemed somewhat older than D, and although she gestured grandly and intoned when she spoke, she was too round and overweight to achieve dignity. She was wearing a dress of some heavy cloth with the hem of the skirt unraveled in the manner of a squaw costume, and her necklace of diamonds set in gold looked like the work of an Inca craftsman (now that I think about them, these observations, too, smell distinctly of the movies). Her window overlooked the streets of Shibuya, but the light pouring through it into the room seemed to bother her terrifically; she was continually shifting in her chair, showing me legs as round and bloodshot as her neck, while she questioned me in the voice of a cross-examiner. I suppose I was her only source of information about her former husband. Sipping my black, bitter beer as if it were hot coffee, I answered her as best I could, but my knowledge of D was scant and inaccurate and I couldn't satisfy her. Then she started asking about D's actress girlfriend, whether she came to see him and things like that, and there was nothing I could say. Annoyed, I thought to myself, what business was it of hers, didn't she have any feminine pride?

"Does D still see that phantom?" she said at last.

"Yes, it's a baby the size of a kangaroo in a white cotton nightgown and he says its name is Aghwee; the nurse was telling me about it," I said enthusiastically, glad to encounter a question I could do justice to. "It's usually floating in the sky, but sometimes it flies down to D's side."

"Aghwee, you say? Then it must be the ghost of our dead baby. You know why he calls it Aghwee? Because our baby spoke only once while it was alive and that was what it said—Aghwee. That's a pretty mushy way to name the ghost that's haunting you, don't you think?" The woman spoke derisively; an ugly, corrosive odor reached me from her mouth. "Our baby was born with a lump on the back of its head that made it look as if it had two heads. The doctor diagnosed it as a brain hernia. When D heard the news he decided to protect himself and me from a catastrophe, so he got together with the doctor, and they killed the baby—I think they only gave it sugar water instead of milk no matter how loud it screamed. My husband killed the baby because he didn't want us to be saddled with a child who could only function as a vegetable, which is what the doctor had predicted! So he was acting out of fantastic egotism more than anything else. But then there was an autopsy and the lump turned out to be a benign tumor. That's when D began seeing ghosts; you see, he'd lost the courage he needed to sustain his egotism, so he declined to live his own life, just as he had declined to let the baby go on living. Not that he committed suicide, he just fled from reality into a world of phantoms. But once your hands are all bloody with a baby's murder, you can't get them clean again just by running from reality, anybody knows that. So here he is, hands as filthy as ever and carrying on about Aghwee."

The cruelty of her criticism was hard to bear, for my employer's sake. So I turned to her, redder in the face than ever with the excitement of her loquacity, and struck a blow for D. "Where were you while all this was going on? You were the mother, weren't you?"

"I had a Caesarean, and for a week afterwards I was in a coma with a high fever. It was all over when I woke up," said D's former wife, leaving my gauntlet on the floor. Then she stood up and moved toward the kitchen. "I guess you'll have some more beer?"

"No, thank you, I've had enough. Would you please give me whatever I'm supposed to take to D?"

"Of course, just let me gargle. I have to gargle every ten minutes, for pyorrhea—you must have noticed the smell?"

D's former wife put a brass key into a business envelope and handed it to me. Standing behind me while I tied my shoes, she asked what school I went to and then, mentioning a certain newspaper, added proudly: "I hear there's not even one subscriber in the dormitories there. You may be interested to know that my father will own that paper soon."

I let silence speak for my contempt.

I was about to get into the elevator when doubt knifed through me as though my chest were made of butter. I had to think. I let the elevator go and decided to use the stairs. If his former wife had described D's state of mind correctly, how could I be sure he wouldn't commit suicide with a pinch of cyanide or something taken from a box this key unlocked? All the way down the stairs I wondered what to do, and then I was standing in front of D's table and still hadn't arrived at a conclusion. The composer sat there with his eyes tightly shut, his tea untouched on the table. I suppose it wouldn't do for him to be seen drinking substances of this time, now that he had stopped living in it and had become a traveler from another.

"I saw her," I began, resolved all of a sudden to lie, "and we were talking all this time but she wouldn't give me anything."

My employer looked up at me placidly and said nothing, though doubt clouded his puppy eyes in their deep sockets. All the way back in the cab I sat in silence at his side, secretly perturbed. I wasn't sure whether he had seen through my lie. In my shirt pocket the key was heavy.

But I only kept it a week. For one thing, the idea of D's suicide began to seem silly; for another, I was worried he might ask his wife about the key. So I put it in a different envelope and mailed it to him special delivery. The next day I went out to the house a little worried and found my employer in the open space in front of the annex, burning a pile of music manuscripts. They must have been his own compositions: that key had unlocked the composer's music.

We didn't go out that day. Instead I helped D incinerate his whole opus. We had burned everything and had dug a hole and I was burying the ashes when suddenly D began to whisper. The phantom had dropped out of the sky. And until it left I continued working, slowly burying those ashes. That afternoon the sky monster called Aghwee (and there was no denying it was a mushy name) remained at my employer's side for fully twenty minutes.

From that day on, since I either stepped to one side or dropped behind whenever the phantom baby appeared, the composer must have realized that I was complying with only the first of his original instructions, not to act amazed, while his request that I back him up with something affirmative was consistently ignored. Yet he seemed satisfied, and so my job was made easier. I couldn't believe D was the kind of person to create a disturbance in the street; in fact his father's word of warning began to seem ridiculous, our tours of Tokyo together continued so uneventfully. I had already purchased the Moscow edition of L'Âme Enchanté I wanted, but I no longer had any intention of giving up such a marvelous job. My employer and I went everywhere together. D wanted to visit all the concert halls where works of his had been performed and all the schools he had ever been to. We would make special trips to places where he used to amuse himself—bars, movie theaters, indoor swimming pools—and then we would turn back without going inside. And the composer had a passion for all of Tokyo's many forms of public transportation; I'm sure we rode the entire metropolitan subway system. Since the monster baby couldn't descend from the sky while we were underground, I could enjoy the subway in peace of mind. Naturally, I tensed whenever we encountered dogs or officers of the law, remembering what the nurse had told me, but those encounters never coincided with an appearance by Aghwee. I discovered that I was loving my job. Not loving my employer or his phantom baby the size of a kangaroo. Simply loving my job.

One day the composer approached me about making a trip for him. He would pay traveling expenses, and my daily wage would be doubled; since I would have to stay overnight in a hotel and wouldn't be back until the second day, I would actually be earning four times what I usually made. Not only that, the purpose of the trip was to meet D's former girlfriend the movie actress, in D's place. I accepted eagerly, I was delighted. And so began that comic and pathetic journey.

D gave me the name of the hotel the actress had mentioned in a recent letter and the date she was expecting him to arrive. Then he had me learn a message to the girl: my employer was no longer living in present time; he was like a traveler who had arrived here in a time machine from a world ten thousand years in the future. Accordingly, he couldn't permit himself to create a new existence with his own signature on it through such acts as writing letters.

I memorized the message, and then it was late at night and I was sitting opposite a movie actress in the basement bar of a hotel in Kyoto, with a chance first to explain why D hadn't come himself, next to persuade his mistress of his conception of time, and finally to deliver his message. I concluded: "D would like you to be careful not to confuse his recent divorce with another divorce he once promised you he would get and since he isn't living in present time anymore, he says it's only natural that he won't be seeing you again." I felt my face color; for the first time I had the sensation that I had a truly difficult job.

"Is that what D-boy says? And what do you say? How do you feel about all this, that you'd run an errand all the way to Kyoto?"

"Frankly, I think D is being mushy."

"That's the way he is—I'd say he's being pretty mushy with you, too, asking this kind of favor!"

"I'm employed; I get paid by the day for what I do."

"What are you drinking there? Have some brandy."

I had some. Until then I'd been drinking the same dark beer D's former wife had given me, with an egg in it to thin it down. By some queer carom of a psychological billiard ball, I'd been influenced by a memory from D's former wife's apartment while waiting to meet his mistress. The actress had been drinking brandy from the start. It was the first imported brandy I'd ever had.

"And what's all this about D-boy seeing a ghost, a baby as big as a kangaroo? What did you call it, Raghbee?"

"Aghwee! The baby only spoke once before it died and that was what it said."

"And D thought it was telling him its name? Isn't that darling! If that baby had been normal, it was all decided that D was going to get a divorce and marry me. The day the baby was born we were in bed together in a hotel room and there was a phone call and then we knew something awful had happened. D jumped out of bed and went straight to the hospital. Not a word from him since—" The actress gulped her brandy down, filled her glass to the brim from the bottle of Hennessy on the table as if she were pouring fruit juice, and drained her glass again.

Our table was hidden from the bar by a display case full of cigarettes. Hanging on the wall above my shoulder was a large color poster with the actress's picture on it, a beer advertisement. The face in the poster glittered like gold, no less than the beer. The girl sitting opposite me was not quite so dazzling, there was even a depression in her forehead, just below the hairline, that looked deep enough to contain an adult thumb. But it was precisely the fault that made her more appealing than her picture.

She couldn't get the baby off her mind.

"Look, wouldn't it be terrifying to die without memories or experiences because you'd never done anything human while you were alive? That's how it would be if you died as an infant—wouldn't that be terrifying?"

"Not to the baby, I don't imagine," I said deferentially.

"But think about the world after death!" The actress's logic was full of leaps.

"The world after death?"

"If there is such a thing, the souls of the dead must live there with their memories for all eternity. But what about the soul of a baby who never knew anything and never had any experiences? I mean, what memories can it have?"

At a loss, I drank my brandy in silence.

"I'm terribly afraid of death, so I'm always thinking about it—you don't have to be disgusted with yourself because you don't have a quick answer for me. But you know what I think? The minute that baby died, I think D-boy decided not to create any new memories for himself, as if he had died, too, and that's why he stopped living, you know, positively, in present time. And I bet he calls that ghost baby down to earth all over Tokyo so he can create new memories for it!"

At the time I thought she must be right. This tipsy movie actress with a dent in her forehead big enough for a thumb is quite an original psychologist, I thought to myself. And much more D's type, I thought, than the pudgy, tomato-faced daughter of a newspaper baron. All of a sudden I realized that, even here in Kyoto with hundreds of miles between us, I, the model of a faithful employee, was thinking exclusively about D. No, there was something else, too, there was D's phantom. I realized that the baby whose appearance I waited for nervously every time my employer and I went out together hadn't been off my mind for a minute.

It was time for the bar to close and I didn't have a room. I'd managed to get as old as I was without ever staying in a hotel and I knew nothing about reservations. Luckily, the actress was known at the hotel, and a word from her got me a room. We went up in the elevator together, and I started to get off at my floor when she suggested we have one last drink and invited me to her room. From that point on I have only muddled comic and pathetic memories. When she had seated me in a chair, the actress returned to the door and looked up and down the hall, then went through a whole series of nervous motions, flounced on the bed as if to test the springs, turned lights on and switched them off, ran a little water in the tub. Then she poured me the brandy she had promised and, sipping a Coca Cola, she told me about another man chasing her during her affair with D, and finally going to bed with him, and D slapping her so hard the teeth rattled in her mouth. Then she asked if I thought today's college students went in for "heavy petting"? It depended on the student, I said—suddenly the actress had become a mother scolding a child for staying up too late and was telling me to find my own room and go to sleep. I said good night, went downstairs, and fell asleep immediately. I woke up at dawn with a fire in my throat.

The most comic and pathetic part was still to come. I understood the minute I opened my eyes that the actress had invited me to her room intending to seduce a college student who was wild for heavy petting. And with that understanding came rage and abject desire. I hadn't slept with a woman yet, but this humiliation demanded that I retaliate. I was drunk on what must have been my first Hennessy VSOP, and I was out of my head with the kind of poisonous desire that goes with being eighteen. It was only five o'clock in the morning and there was no sign of life in the halls. Like a panther wild with rage I sped to her door on padded feet. It was ajar. I stepped inside and found her seated at the dresser mirror with her back to me. Creeping up directly behind her (to this day I wonder what I was trying to do), I lunged at her neck with both hands. The actress whirled around with a broad smile on her face, rising as she turned, and then she had my hands in her own and was pumping them happily up and down as if she were welcoming a guest and singsonging: "Good morning! Good morning! Good morning!" Before I knew it I had been seated in a chair and we were sharing her toast and morning coffee and reading the newspaper together. After a while the movie actress said in a tone of voice she might have used to discuss the weather: "You were trying to rape me just now, weren't you." She went back to her makeup and I got out of there, fled downstairs to my own room and burrowed back into bed, trembling as though I had malaria. I was afraid that a report of this incident might reach D, but the subject of the movie actress never came up again. I continued to enjoy my job.

Winter had come. Our plan that afternoon was to bicycle through D's residential neighborhood and the surrounding fields. I was on a rusty old bike and my employer had borrowed the nurse's shiny new one. Gradually we expanded the radius of a circle around D's house, riding into a new housing development and coasting down hills in the direction of the fields. We were sweating, relishing the sensation of liberation, more and more exhilarated. I say "we" and include D because that afternoon it was evident that he was in high spirits, too. He was even whistling a theme from a Bach sonata for flute and harpsichord called *Siciliana*. I happened to know that because when I was in high school, I had played flute. I never learned to play well, but I did develop a habit of thrusting out my upper lip the way a tapir does. Naturally, I had friends who insisted my buck teeth were to blame. But the fact is, flutists frequently look like tapirs.

As we pedaled down the street, I picked up the tune and began to whistle along with D. Siciliana is a sustained and elegant theme, but I was out of breath from pedaling and my whistle kept lapsing into airy sibilance. Yet D's phrasing was perfect, absolutely legato. I stopped whistling then, ashamed to go on, and the composer glanced over at me with his lips still pursed in a whistle like a carp puckering up to breathe and smiled his tranquil smile. Granted there was a difference in the bikes, it was still unnatural and pathetic that an eighteen-year-old student, skinny maybe, but tall, should begin to tire and run short of breath before a twenty-eight-year-old composer who was a little man and sick besides. Unjust is what it was, and infuriating. My mood clouded instantly and I felt disgusted with the whole job. So I stood up on the pedals all of a sudden and sped away as furiously as a bicycle racer. I even turned, purposely, down a narrow gravel path between two vegetable fields. When I looked back a minute later, my employer was hunched over the handle bars, his large, round head nodding above his narrow shoulders, churning the gravel beneath his wheels in hot pursuit of me. I coasted to a stop, propped a foot on the barbed wire fence that bordered the field, and waited for D to catch up. I was already ashamed of my childishness.

His head still bobbing, my employer was approaching fast, and then I knew the phantom was with him. D was racing his bike down the extreme left of the gravel path, his face twisted to the right so that he was almost looking over his right shoulder, and the reason his head appeared to bob was that he was whispering encouragement to something running, or maybe flying, alongside the bicycle. Like a marathon coach pacing one of his runners. Ah, I thought, he's doing that on the premise that Aghwee is neck and neck with his speeding bike. The monster as large as a kangaroo, the fat, funny baby in a white cotton nightgown was bounding—like a kangaroo!—down that gravel path. I shuddered, then I kicked the barbed wire fence and slowly pedaled away, waiting for my employer and the monster in his imagination to catch up.

Don't think I'd let myself begin to believe in Aghwee's existence. I had taken the nurse's advice, sworn not to lose the anchor on my common sense, not to give way to lunacy as in those slightly solemn slapstick comedies where, say, the keeper of the madhouse goes mad; and, consciously derisive, I was thinking to myself that the neurotic composer was putting on a show with his bicycle just to follow up a lie he had told me once, and what a lot of trouble to go to! In other words, I was keeping a clinical distance between myself and D's phantom monster. Even so, there occurred a strange alteration in my state of mind.

It began this way: D had finally caught up and was biking along a few feet behind me when, as unexpectedly as a cloudburst and quite inescapably, we were enveloped by the belling of a pack of hounds. I looked up and saw them racing toward me down the gravel path, young adult Dobermans that stood two feet high, more than ten of them. Running breathlessly behind the pack, the thin black leather leashes grasped in one hand, was a man in overalls, chasing the dogs perhaps, or maybe they were dragging him along. Jet-black Dobermans, sleek as wet seals, with just a dusting of dry chocolate on their chests and jowls and pumping haunches. And down on us they howled, filling the gravel path, keening for the attack at such a forward tilt they looked about to topple on their foaming snouts. There was a meadow on the other side of the field; the man in overalls must have been training the beasts there and now he was on his way home with them.

Trembling with fear, I got off my bike and helplessly surveyed the field on the other side of the fence. The barbed wire came up to my chest. I might have had a chance myself but I would never have been able to boost the little composer to safety on the other side. The poisons of terror were beginning to numb my head, but for one lucid instant I could see the catastrophe that was bound to occur in a few seconds. As the Dobermans neared, D would sense that Aghwee was being attacked by a pack of the animals it most feared. He would probably hear the baby's frightened crying. And certainly he would meet the dogs head on, in defense of his baby. Then the Dobermans would rip him to pieces. Or he would try to escape with the baby and make a reckless leap to clear the fence and be just as cruelly torn. I was rocked by the pity of what I knew must happen. And while I stood there dumbly without a plan, those giant black-and-chocolate devils were closing in on us, snapping the air with awful jaws, so close by now that I could hear their alabaster claws clicking on the gravel. Suddenly I knew I could do nothing for D and his baby, and with that knowledge I went limp, unresisting as a pervert when he is seized in the subway, and was swallowed whole in the darkness of my fear. I backed off the gravel path until the barbed wire was a fire in my back, pulled my bike in front of me as if it were a wall, and shut my eyes tight. Then an animal stench battered me, together with the howling of the dogs and the pounding of their feet, and I could feel tears seeping past my eyelids. I abandoned myself to a wave of fear and it swept me away . . .

On my shoulder was a hand gentle as the essence of all gentleness; it felt like Aghwee touching me. But I knew it was my employer; he had let those fiendish dogs pass and no catastrophe of fear had befallen him. I continued crying anyway, with my eyes closed and my shoulders heaving. I was too old to cry in front of other people. I suppose the shock of fright had induced some kind of infantile regression in me. When I stopped crying, we walked our bikes past that barbed wire fence like prisoners in a concentration camp, in silence, our heads hanging, to the meadow beyond the field where strangers were playing ball and exercising dogs (D wasn't occupied with Aghwee anymore; the baby must have left while I was crying). We laid our bikes down and then sprawled on the grass ourselves. My tears had flooded away my pretensions and my rebelliousness and the perverse suspicion in my heart. And D was no longer wary of me. I lay back on the grass and clasped my hands beneath my head, curiously light and dry after all that crying. Then I closed my eyes and listened quietly while D peered down at me with his chin in his hand and spoke to me of Aghwee's world.

"Do you know a poem called 'Shame' by Nakahara Chuya? Listen to the second verse:

> The mournful sky
> high where branches tangle
> teems with dead baby souls;
> I blinked and saw
> above the distant fields
> fleece knit into a dream
> of mastodons.

"That's one aspect of the world of the dead baby I see. There are some Blake engravings, too, especially one called 'Christ Refusing the Banquet Offered by Satan'—have you ever seen it? And there's another, 'The Morning Stars Singing Together.' In both there are figures in the sky who have the same reality about them as the people on the ground, and whenever I look at them I'm sure Blake was hinting at an aspect of this other world. I once saw a Dali painting that was close, too, full of opaque beings floating in the sky about a hundred yards above the ground and glowing with an ivory-white light. Now that's exactly the world I see. And you know what those glowing things are that fill the sky? Beings we've lost from our lives down here on earth, and now they float up there in the sky about a hundred yards above the ground, quietly glowing like amoebas under a microscope. And sometimes they descend the way our Aghwee does." (My employer said it and I didn't protest, which doesn't mean I acquiesced.) "But it takes a sacrifice worthy of them to acquire the eyes to see them floating there and the ears to detect them when they descend to earth, and yet there are moments when suddenly we're endowed with that ability without any sacrifice or even effort on our part. I think that's what happened to you a few minutes ago."

Without any sacrifice or even effort on my part, just a few tears of expiation, my employer seemed to have wanted to say. The truth was I had shed tears out of fear and helplessness and a kind of vague terror about my future (my first job, an experiment in a kind of microcosm of life, was guarding this mad composer, and since I had failed to do that adequately, it was predictable that situations which left me stupefied because I couldn't cope with them would recur as one of the patterns of my life), but instead of interrupting with a protest, I continued to listen docilely.

"You're still young; probably you haven't lost anything in this world that you can never forget, that's so dear to you that you're aware of its absence all the time. Probably the sky a hundred yards or so above your head is still nothing more than sky to you. But all that means is that the storehouse happens to be empty at the moment. Or have you lost something that was really important to you?"

The composer paused for my answer, and I found myself remembering his former mistress, that movie actress with a dent in her forehead as big as an adult thumb. Naturally, no crucial loss of mine could have had anything to do with her; all that crying had eroded my head and a sentimental honey was seeping into the crevices.

"Well, have you?" For the first time since we had met, my employer was insistent. "Have you lost anything that was important to you?"

Suddenly I had to say something silly to cover my embarrassment.

"I lost a cat," I tried.

"A Siamese or what?"

"Just an ordinary cat with orange stripes; he disappeared about a week ago."

"If it's only been a week he might come back. Isn't it the season for them to wander?"

"That's what I thought, too, but now I know he won't be back."

"Why?"

"He was a tough tom with his own territory staked out. This morning I saw a weak-looking cat walking up and down his block and it wasn't even on its guard —my cat won't be coming back." When I'd stopped talking I realized I'd told a story intended for laughs in a voice that was hoarse with sadness.

"Then there's a cat floating in your sky," my employer said solemnly.

Through closed eyes I pictured an opaque cat as large as an ad balloon, glowing with an ivory-white light as it floated through the sky. It was a comical flight all right, but it also made me wistful.

"The figures floating in your sky begin to increase at an accelerating rate. That's why I haven't been living in present time ever since that incident with the baby, so I could stop that spreading. Since I'm not living in our time, I can't discover anything new, but I don't lose anything, either—the state of my sky never changes." There was profound relief in the composer's voice.

But was my own sky really empty except for one bloated cat with orange stripes? I opened my eyes and started to look up at the clear, now almost evening sky, when dread made me close my eyes again. Dread of myself, for what if I had seen a glowing herd of numberless beings we had lost from time down here on earth?

We lay on the grass in that meadow for quite a while, ringed by the passive affinity two people have for one another when the same gloom is gripping them.

And gradually I began to get my perspective back. I reproached myself: how unlike the eighteen-year-old pragmatist I really was to have let myself be influenced by a mad composer! I'm not suggesting my equilibrium was perfectly restored. The day I succumbed to that strange panic, I drew closer than ever to the sentiments of my employer and to that glowing herd in the sky one hundred yards above the ground. To an extent, what you might call the aftereffects remained with me.

And then the final day came. It was Christmas Eve. I'm certain about the date because D gave me a wristwatch with a little apology about being a day early. And I remember that a powdery snow fell for about an hour just after lunch. We went down to the Ginza together but it was already getting crowded, so we decided to walk out to Tokyo harbor. D wanted to see a Chilean freighter that was supposed to have docked that day. I was eager to go, too; I pictured a ship with snow blanketing her decks. We had left the Ginza crowds and were just passing the Kabuki Theater when D looked up at the dark and still snowy sky. Then Aghwee descended to his side. As usual, I walked a few steps behind the composer and his phantom. We came to a wide intersection. D and the baby had just stepped off the curb when the light changed. D stopped, and a fleet of trucks as bulky as elephants heaved into motion with their Christmas freight. That was when it happened. Suddenly D cried out and thrust both arms in front of him as if he were trying to rescue something; then he leaped in among those trucks and was struck to the ground. I watched stupidly from the curb.

"That was suicide; he just killed himself!" said a shaky voice at my side.

But I had no time to wonder whether it might have been suicide. In a minute that intersection had become backstage at a circus, jammed with milling trucks like elephants, and I was kneeling at D's side, holding his bloody body in my arms and trembling like a dog. I didn't know what to do; a policeman had dashed up and then disappeared on the run again.

D wasn't dead, it was more awful than that. He was dying, lying there in the filthy wet that had been a light snow, oozing blood and something like tree sap. The dark and snowy pattern of the sky ripped open and the stately light of a Spanish pietà made my employer's blood glisten like stupid grease. By that time a crowd had gathered, snatches of "Jingle Bells" wheeled above our heads like panic-stricken pigeons, and I knelt at D's side listening hard for nothing in particular and hearing screaming in the distance. But the crowd just stood there silently in the cold, as if indifferent to the screams. I have never listened so hard on a street corner again, nor again heard screams like that.

An ambulance finally arrived and my employer was lifted inside unconscious. He was caked with blood and mud, and shock seemed to have withered his body. In his white tennis shoes, he looked like an injured blind man. I climbed into the ambulance with a doctor and an orderly and a young man about my age who seemed haughty and aloof. He turned out to be the driver of the long-distance truck that had hit D. The congestion was getting worse all the time as the ambulance cut across the Ginza (according to some statistics I saw recently, there were record crowds that Christmas Eve). Those who heard the siren and stopped to watch us pass, nearly all of them, shared a look of circumspectly solemn concern. In one corner of my dazed head I reflected that the so-called inscrutable Japanese smile, while it seemed likely to exist, did not. Meanwhile D lay unconscious on that wobbly stretcher, bleeding his life away.

When we arrived at the hospital, orderlies rushed D away to some recess of the building. The same policeman as before appeared again out of nowhere and calmly asked me a lot of questions. Then I was permitted to go to D. The young truckdriver had already found the room and was sitting on a bench in the corridor next to the door. I sat down beside him and we waited for a long time. At first he only muttered about all the deliveries he still had to make, but after two hours or so he began to complain of being hungry in a surprisingly childish voice, and my hostility toward him dwindled. We waited some more, then the banker arrived with his wife and three daughters, who were all dressed up to go to a party. Ignoring us, they went inside. All four of the women had fat, squat bodies and red faces; they reminded me of D's former wife. I continued to wait. It had been hours by then, and the whole time I had been tormented by suspicion: hadn't my employer intended to kill himself from the beginning? Before taking his life he had settled things with his ex-wife and former mistress, burned his manuscripts, toured the city saying good-by to places he would miss —hadn't he hired me because he needed some good-natured help with those chores? Kept me from seeing through his plan by inventing a monster baby floating in the sky? In other words, wasn't it the case that my only real function had been to help D commit suicide? The young truckdriver had fallen asleep with his head on my shoulder and every minute or two he would be convulsed as though in pain. He must have been having a nightmare about running over a man with his truck.

It was pitch black outside when the banker appeared in the door and called me. I eased my shoulder from under the driver's head and stood up. The banker paid me my salary for the day and then let me into the room. D lay on his back with rubber tubes in his nostrils, as if for a joke. His face gave me pause; it was black as smoked meat. But I couldn't help voicing the doubt that had me so afraid. I called out to my dying employer: "Did you hire me just so you could commit suicide? Was all that about Aghwee just a cover-up?" Then my throat was clogged with tears and I was surprised to hear myself shouting: "I was about to believe in Aghwee!"

At that moment, as my tear-filled eyes began to dim, I saw a smile appear on D's darkened, shriveled face. It might have been a mocking smile or it might have been a smile of friendly mischief. The banker led me out of the room. The young man from the truck was stretched out on the bench asleep. On my way out, I slipped the thousand yen I had earned into his jacket pocket. I read in the evening paper the next day that the composer was dead.

And then it was this spring and I was walking down the street when a group of frightened children suddenly started throwing stones. It was so sudden and unprovoked, I don't know what I had done to threaten them. Whatever it was, fear had turned those children into killers, and one of them hit me in the right eye with a rock as big as a fist. I went down on one knee, pressed my hand to my eye and felt a lump of broken flesh. With my good eye I watched my dripping blood suck in the dirt in the street as though magnetically. It was then that I sensed a being I knew and missed leave the ground behind me—a being the size of a kangaroo—and soar into the teary blue of a sky that retained its winter brittleness. Good-by, Aghwee, I heard myself whispering in my heart. And then I knew that my hatred of those frightened children had melted away and that time had filled my sky during those ten years with figures that glowed with an ivory-white light, I suppose not all of them purely innocent. When I was wounded by those children and sacrificed my sight in one eye, so clearly a gratuitous sacrifice, I had been endowed, if for only an instant, with the power to perceive a creature that had descended from the heights of my sky.

TRANSLATED BY JOHN NATHAN

◧NOSAKA AKIYUKI

Nosaka Akiyuki has developed into something of an embarrassment for the literary establishment, to which he refuses to confine his remarkable energies. Although he has received various literary awards, he himself declares that much of his writing is meant purely for entertainment; indeed, much of it appears in magazines that serious critics seldom deign to read. As erstwhile editor of an off-color humor magazine, he reprinted an elegant little erotic tale attributed to Nagai Kafū, and promptly became embroiled in a sensational pornography trial. Several eminent men of letters spoke out in court on behalf of freedom of artistic expression, but the case has dragged on since 1973 without noticeable effect on Japan's surprisingly puritanical obscenity laws. (In April, 1976, a guilty verdict was handed down in the Tokyo District Court, but Nosaka, appalled both by the decision and by the "terrible" literary style of the judges' lengthy opinion, promptly announced his intention "to show a few new steps in the defendant's dance.")

Meanwhile, Nosaka has won a considerable following as a popular singer (wearing a white silk suit to complement his usual dark glasses), has run unsuccessfully for the office of Tokyo representative to the National Diet, has become a sought-after commentator on the issues of ecology and freedom of expression that he raised in his campaign, and has established a collective farm as a refuge from Tokyo. In one particularly outrageous novel based on the student riots of 1969—*The Rioters* (*Sōdōshitachi*, 1971)—he showed what he thought of Japan's oppressive educational system, with its entrance exams that begin at kindergarten, by reducing the pinnacle of that structure, Tokyo University, to a pile of rubble that quickly became the city's most exciting playground. It is not only in his essays that Nosaka reveals himself to be a penetrating social critic. Beneath his most frivolous-seeming undertakings there can often be detected a serious purpose.

Nosaka Akiyuki was born in 1930 in Kamakura, but, after his mother's early death, was brought up by his aunt and uncle in Kobe, the western port city where much of his fiction is set. Among the events that marked his youth were the discovery that he was an adopted child, the death of his uncle and crippling of his aunt during the fire-bombing of Kobe, the death of a young adopted sister from malnutrition a week after the end of the War, a brief stay in reform school in 1947, his return to family life with his own father and stepmother, and his matriculation in 1950 at Waseda University, where he nominally majored in French literature but dropped out in his senior year. Lured away from a subsequent period of Zen meditation to campaign for his father, a provincial politician, Nosaka returned to Tokyo in 1955 and was involved in television writing until his debut as a novelist in the early sixties.

Like many writers of his generation, Nosaka often finds his material in his teen-age experiences of the War. (Nosaka has said that his work belongs to the "Burnt-out-Ruins, Black-Market School.") Yet even in fiction as close to fact as his story "Firefly Grave" (*Hotaru no haka*, 1968), which is based on his sister's death, he has resisted the temptation to produce a simple chronicle of horrors. Nosaka is at his best when writing in the exuberant comic vein of the seventeenth-century master Saikaku. Still, for bedeviled characters like Subuyan of *The Pornographers* (*Erogotoshitachi*, 1966, tr. 1968) and Toshio of "American Hijiki," the long-past War remains an inescapable part of the present.

It should be noted that *hijiki*—scientifically classified as *Hizikia fusiforme*, and lacking any better English designation than "a kind of brown algae"—is one of several types of seaweed eaten by the Japanese, although this particular plant is better known for its cheapness than its gustatory appeal.

❖ American *Hijiki*
(*Amerika hijiki,* 1967)

A white spot out of nowhere in the burning sky—and look!—it puffs out round and in the middle of the round a kernel swinging slightly like a pendulum aimed straight at me. It has to be a parachute, but in the sky no sight no sound no nothing of a plane and before there's time to think how weird this is the chute glides down into the yard's crazy glut of loquat, birch, persimmon, beech, myrtle, hydrangea, never catching on a branch, never tearing off a leaf. "Hello, how are you?" grins this skinny foreigner—wait a minute, he looks just like General Percival. The white chute falls around his shoulders like a cape, slips down and covers the yard in a blanket of snow. All right, the man said hello, you've got to answer him. "I am very glad to see you"? No, that would be funny for an unexpected guest—if that's what this foreigner is. "Who are you?" would sound like I was grilling him. "Look, you son of a bitch, who are you? Who are you? Who are you?" Three times and if he doesn't answer, bang! let him have it. Wait, don't get carried away, first you've got to talk to him. "How . . . how . . . how . . ." comes crawling up from my belly to get hopelessly stuck in my mouth. This has happened to me before, this desperate, cornered feeling. When could it have been now, let me see . . .

And searching for the answer, Toshio woke from his dream pressed flat against the wall by the buttocks of his wife, Kyoko, curled up, shrimplike, beside him. A mean push sent her back to her side of the bed and knocked something to the floor.

Aha, the English conversation book Kyoko was mumbling over before they fell asleep. That explained to Toshio where his weird dream had come from.

An old American couple that Toshio had never met were coming tonight to stay with them. A month ago Kyoko, all excited and waving a red-white-and-blue-bordered air-mail envelope, had said to him, "Papa, the Higginses are coming to Japan! Let's have them stay here." She had met Mr. and Mrs. Higgins that spring in Hawaii.

It was a small operation, true enough, but Toshio ran a studio that produced TV commercials, and hoping to make up for the irregular hours he kept, meeting sponsors and overseeing film sessions, he had sent Kyoko and their three-year-old son, Keiichi, to Hawaii—not without a twinge of conscience at this unwonted luxury, but he had been able to get a break on the tickets through a connection with an airline and had hit on the small businessman's happy expedient of charging it to the company. Kyoko, who might well have been nervous about traveling alone with a child (What good will my junior-college English do me now?), if anything, took advantage of being a woman and boldly spread her wings, making many friends over there, Higgins among them. Retired from the State Department and living on a pension, he had married off his three daughters and —whatever his former rank might have been—he and his wife were now pursuing the enviable task of traveling around the world on a second honeymoon.

"Americans are so cold-blooded. Once the children get married, their parents are as good as strangers," said Kyoko, conveniently forgetting the way she treated her own parents. "It wouldn't hurt to be nice to them, I decided, and I did them a few little favors. You wouldn't believe how happy it made them. They said they liked me better than their very own daughters." And they treated her to meals in fancy hotels that she could never have afforded on her $500 budget, took her island-hopping in a chartered plane, and sent chocolates for Keiichi's birthday that July, in return for which she mailed them a mat of woven straw. Then letters went flying back and forth across the Pacific at least once a week, culminating in the announcement that the Higginses were coming to Japan.

"They're really lovely people. You'll be going to America someday, too, Papa. Think of the confidence it will give you to have someone there that you know. And Mr. Higgins says he's going to get Keiichi into an American college."

A good bit of Kyoko's interest in the Higginses sounded like self-interest, he was tempted to say. Supposing three-year-old Keiichi went to college at all, it would be fifteen years from now. What made her think a retired official could last that long? But Kyoko's calculations, after all, were merely a way to justify all the money they would have to spend if they were going to entertain Mr. and Mrs. Higgins. And she was carried away with the honor of having an American houseguest.

"They always said they wanted to see where I live. And they want to meet you." She had assumed his consent before Toshio could say a word. "Grandma and Grandpa Higgins are coming to see us, Keiichi. You remember them, don't you? Grandpa always used to say 'Hello' to you, and you'd wave to him and answer, 'Ba-ha-hye,' " she twittered.

So now it's Hello-Ba-ha-hye Japan-American amity, is it? Twenty-two years ago it was Q-Q Japan-American amity.

"America is a country of gentlemen. They all respect ladies. 'Ladies first' is the motto. And they're all polite. Well, you fellows won't have to think about 'Ladies first' for a while, but politeness is another thing. What worries me·is you're going to be rude and make the Americans think Japan is full of barbarians." All of a sudden the War was over and after four years of persistent, ratlike picking on the students to console himself for having to teach an enemy language, the English teacher (he was such a coward he used to sit quivering in the air-raid shelter chanting sutras) walked into his first class and started in on us like this. Then he wrote "THANK YOU" and "EXCUSE ME" across the blackboard, surveyed us all with a look of contempt, and said: "Anyone know how to pronounce these? No, of course not. This one is 'San-Q,' and this one is 'Ekusu-Q-zu-mee.' Got that? The accent is on the Q." He underlined the Q with a forceful stroke that snapped the chalk and sent it flying. Grim smiles filled the classroom. ("Here we go again." Until two months ago, the Chinese classics teacher had stopped teaching and spent all his time lecturing on the War. "In the final battle for Japan, Heaven shall be with us." And whenever he'd write the characters for "American and English Devil-Brutes" on the board, he would be so overcome with loathing that the chalk would always screech and crack in two.)

"All you have to do is smile and say 'Q' and America-san will understand. Got that?"

The class ended with this "Q-Q" and we went out to fill in the bomb shelter that had been dug around the edge of the schoolyard. If you hit someone with a rock, it was "Q." When you asked someone to take the other end of a beam, it was "Q." Soon we were using it for everything.

It's no wonder we don't know English. After three years of middle school, the only words I could spell were "Black" and "Love." About the only thing I learned to say that seemed like real English was "Umbrerra." And nobody understood the difference between "I," "my," and "me." The first thing I learned when I got into middle school in 1943 was how to read Japanese written in Roman letters. At home I found a butter container that said "Hokkaido Kono Kosha" and I realized it was the name of the dairy. That was the first time I had ever deciphered the "horizontal writing." Before I had a chance to perfect "Dis izu a pen," though, military drill took the place of English classes, and all we got from the English teacher on rainy days were hymns to the glory of college boys who went to the front.

"American college students do nothing but enjoy themselves, going to dance parties on weekends, that kind of thing. Compared to them, Japanese college students . . . etc., etc." "The only English you kids have to know is 'Yes or no?' When we took Singapore, General Yamashita said to the enemy general, Percival" —*and here he pounded on the desk, his cheek distorted in a nervous spasm, his eyeballs bulging*—*" 'Yes or no!' What valor."*

We had an exam, all right, but on the translation problem you could get full credit for "She's house."

The great villain was Percival. "The foreign dogs may be tall," shouted the judo instructor, "but they're weak from the waist down. This comes from sitting in chairs. Squatting on floor mats gives us Japanese strong legs and hips." A plaque reading "Reflect on That Which Lies Under Foot" hung above him. He stood there with the Union Jack and a white flag of surrender bearing down heavily on one shoulder, his skinny shanks protruding from his short pants. "So all you've got to do with a foreigner is get your leg around to his rear end and flip him over backwards. Trip him from the inside, trip him from the outside, just work on his legs and he'll go down easy. Right? Now, everybody up!" During the free-for-all, everyone would imagine he was fighting Percival, throw the poor old guy down, jump on his back, and get him in a headlock. "Yes or no! Yes or no!"

In the second year of middle school, we went out to the farming villages to do labor service. After the fall of Saipan, this meant what they called "decongestion of dwellings." The floor mats, the sliding doors and windows, the storm shutters of a house would all be loaded into a big wagon and taken to the nearest wartime "people's" elementary school. When the house was just a shell, the firemen would throw a rope around the central pillar and yank it down. You could see signs of how the people had rushed to get out: the bathtub full of water, old diapers hanging under the toilet eaves, a Hotei scroll, a three-pronged spear from feudal times, an empty coin bank (this was "booty" we hid in the hedge and took home afterwards), and a big, thick book filled with nothing but English. "Maybe they were spies." "It could be some kind of code." We flipped through it as if in a treasure hunt, everyone straining to find a word he knew. Finally, the head of the class found "silk hat" and said, "It means a hat made of silk." In that instant, the bare floorboards, the old calendar, the pillar with the mark of a torn-off amulet all disappeared to be replaced by the scene of a ball and men in silk hats. We had always known the words shiruku hatto, *but the class-head's translation came as a revelation. "That's amazing," said one boy, "I never knew 'shiruku hatto' meant 'silk hat.' " And even now, when I hear the words* shiruku hatto, *as a matter of reflex I think, "A hat made of silk."*

When he saw the first letter from Higgins displayed conspicuously on the dinner table like a flower straight from Kyoko's heart, the air-mail envelope's garish border caused an unpleasant commotion in Toshio's chest. Not that he was worried about looking bad if Kyoko asked him to read it to her: it was the simple shock of getting a letter from an American. But Kyoko, overjoyed, had managed to read it and told him what Higgins had to say.

"I'll have to answer him. Can somebody at the company translate a letter for me?"

"Well, sure, I suppose so."

"Here, I've got it all written."

Toshio found the letter a schoolgirlish string of pretty clichés. For the moment, he was willing to give it to one of the young men at the office who were hard at work on English in the unshakable belief that a trip to America had been ordained for the future. But on careful rereading, the sentence, "My husband joins me in expressing our sincerest gratitude for your many kindnesses," didn't set well with him and he tore this part out before submitting it to the translator. Higgins' second letter, however, came hard on the heels of the first with the assurance that Kyoko could send her "delightful" letters in Japanese because Higgins had a Japanese neighbor to read them to him. Moved by this show of consideration, Kyoko wrote a long letter on the fancy stationery that Toshio had brought her from Kyoto. Toshio did not ask what was in the letter, but she had apparently sent an open-hearted—and somewhat ostentatious—account of just about everything concerning the family.

"Mr. Higgins says making TV films is the most promising profession in America, too. He says you must be very busy, so be careful not to overtax yourself. Papa, are you listening? This is for you."

Some TV film companies were the kind that Hollywood studios bought, and then there were those like Toshio's that produced a lot of five- or at best fifteen-second commercials at low profit. True, if you looked in the phone book, they would both be under the same heading, but Toshio was not in the mood to start explaining the difference between them to Kyoko, who was becoming annoyed at his inattention.

"Papa, you ought to go to America, too. It would enhance your image."

"No, it's too late for me. Anyhow, the way everybody and his brother is going overseas these days, people who've never gone once may have a certain scarcity value. We're the only ones uncontaminated by superficial exposure to foreign countries."

"That's just sour grapes. And as far as the language goes, you manage one way or another when you get there."

Once it had been decided that Kyoko would be going to Hawaii, she had bought some English conversation records and practiced phrases she would need for going through customs, words for shopping and such, as a result of which she discovered that "They don't say 'Papa' and 'Mama' in America, it says. They use 'Daddy' and 'Mommie.' A 'Mama' is supposed to be a vulgar woman." She proceeded to teach the new words to Keiichi. Toshio had allowed himself to be called "Papa" now that "*Otochan*" was too old-fashioned, but "Daddy" was more than he could stomach, and after a spirited argument, he maintained with a finality rare for him, "I don't care what you do in Hawaii, but in Japan I am to be called 'Papa.' "

Until we lost the War, any English we managed to learn was written English. Afterwards, it was spoken English, as symbolized by new lyrics like "Comu, comu, eburybody" for traditional children's songs. The English-Speaking Society got started when I was in my fourth year of middle school, attracting the student elite. "Oowat-tsumara-izyoo?" one of them, an older boy, said to me in the sunny place outside the wrestling (formerly judo) gym. I thought, maybe "tsumara" means "tomorrow" and he's asking me what I plan to do. Before I could make sense of it, though, he jeered at me and said: "They won't understand you if you say it the old way, 'Howatto izu matah ooizu yoo?' You've got to say, 'Oowat-tsumara-izyoo?' Anyhow, habagoot-taimu." He went off laughing with his friends.

I quit school after the fourth year. My father was killed in the War, my mother was an invalid, and my little sister (in her second year at girls' school) ran the house. To feed the three of us I went from a stocking factory to a battery factory to being an ad-taker for the Kyoto-Osaka Daily.

I don't know if it was my appearance that won her confidence—steady-looking for that time, with the bottom two of my seven-button cadet jacket smashed, and for pants, cotton jodhpurs narrow at the shanks—but one day when I had cut work and was walking around Naka-no-shima Park, a girl came over to me and said: "Are you a schoolboy? If you are, there's something I want you to do." She wanted to get to know an American soldier and asked me to introduce her. Sure enough, where she was looking there stood a soldier staring idly at the boats on the river. "I'll pay you. Just meet me here tomorrow."

I knew well enough that "How ah you" was the right thing to say, but I had never tried using it on one of them. The soldier, maybe sensing what was going on, came over to us. "Sukueezu," I thought he said, holding out a thick hand to me. For a second, I didn't understand, then remembered the English teacher, who doubled as manager of the baseball team, explaining to a dumbfounded player: "Sukueezu means wring, press, tighten—squeeze. Don't you remember? You learned if you sukueezu snow, you get a snowball."

When I timidly grasped the soldier's hand, he looked at me as if to say "Is that the best you can do?" and squeezed me back as easily as crumpling up a scrap of paper. I almost jumped with the pain. Maybe he just wanted to look good in front of the girl, but she started laughing when she saw me wince, and the soldier immediately started talking to her. She panicked and looked to me for help, but while I could catch a few fragments—"name," "friend"—I had no idea what he was saying.

Real classwork had only started for me in the fourth year, but there were not enough English teachers and I had this old guy who worked part-time and specialized in onomatopoeic words. "In Japan, we say that streetcar bells ring 'chin-chin,' but in America they say 'ding-dong.' " Nyao was "meow," kokekok-ko was "cockadoodle-doo." Some kids, deadly serious, would make vocabulary cards that said "chin-chin" on the front and "ding-dong" on the back. The next thing you knew, the teacher would come up with a sentence like "He cannot be cornered" that you felt couldn't possibly be real English even if you didn't know what it meant. After learning English from guys like this, what the soldier said to me could have been a Chinaman talking in his sleep.

I knew I had to say something, started pointing back and forth between the soldier and the girl, when this totally unexpected shout of "Daburu, daburu" came out of me. "OK, OK," he said, looking satisfied and putting his arm around the girl. "Taxi," he ordered. True, there were these humped-over-looking cabs running past now and then, but the problem for me was getting one to stop. When he saw me looking baffled, the soldier ripped out a sheet of paper and wrote "TAXI" in great big letters with a ball-point pen, then shoved it under my nose, whining and urging me to get a cab. Probably realizing it was hopeless, the girl signaled for him to follow and started walking. I looked at the word "TAXI" written in genuine English, then put it in my breast pocket, handling it as carefully as if it had been a movie star's autograph, and murmuring the word to myself in imitation of the soldier's pronunciation. The next day, expecting nothing, I went back to the same place and there she was, holding a half-pound can of MJB coffee and a can of Hershey's cocoa. She looked almost proud of herself. "Know somebody that'll buy this stuff?" I told her about a coffeehouse in Naka-no-shima Park, a hangout for GI whores, where this Korean handled the coffee, chocolate, cheese, and cigarettes that the soldiers used for money. "You take care of it," she pleaded. "I'll give you a cut." When I went to the coffeehouse (they had junky pastries for ten yen, coffee for five), the Korean was out, but the minute she saw what I had, this fat lady who also looked like a dealer said, "I'll take them off your hands." She pulled a roll of bills out of a big, black purse like the ones the bus conductors use and gave me four hundred yen without batting an eyelash. "You got cigarettes? Twelve hundred yen a carton." Another woman in the place, obviously a GI whore, was singing "Only five minutes more, give me five minutes more" in a surprisingly pretty voice.

When it came to songs in English, I knew my share. It seems as though debates, strikes, band, and baseball were the whole of our middle-school education. The biggest loudmouth would represent the class in the debates. "Student Uniforms: Pro and Con" was one, but of the pros and cons both, not half could afford the luxury of a uniform. The girls, though, all had nice sailor dresses. I guess it was around December the year after the War ended, I stood staring open-mouthed at five or six Otemae girls who came almost dancing out of nowhere, pleated skirts fluttering before my eyes, along the moat of bombed-out Osaka Castle. Of course, my little sister was still wearing wartime farm trousers then. In the new middle schools (the ones upgraded from higher elementary schools) it was normal for all the students, girls included, to dress as they had during the War. Band was something that the rich kids with uniforms had asked for, and for their first recital they played—without sheet music but with a decent collection of instruments—

"You Are My Sunshine," "There's a Lamp Shinin' Bright in a Cabin," "Moonlight on the River Colorado," and the big showpiece, "La Comparsita." A fifth-year student (a local landowner's son who, it was rumored, had already bought women in the Hashimoto red-light district) was master of ceremonies, and when he announced the tango as "Rodriguez's 'La Comparsita,' " the weighty ring of that "Rodriguez's" just bowled us over. Even the Crown Prince used to sing "Twinkle Twinkle Little Star," according to the newspapers.

The souvenir photographer in Naka-no-shima was a part-time student at the Foreign Language School and good at spoken English, so I used to go to his place when he was free and get English lessons in exchange for cigarette butts. I needed English for my pimping—if you can call getting one or two women a day for soldiers pimping. The girls were all pale, bony-shouldered aspiring whores who had gotten word that they could meet America-san and get chocolate if they came here, the soldiers all sad-faced boys who stood watching what was then the swift, clear flow of the Dojima River, maybe thinking of home, but not over here in Naka-no-shima because it was supposed to be girl-hunting territory. Amateurs, the girls had no idea how to turn their nicely bagged spoils into cash. My daily cut from selling the stuff to the Korean came to a hundred yen anyhow, which was a lot more profitable than the door-to-door selling of photo magazines and newspaper delivery boxes I did when not taking ads. I gave this job everything I had and started entertaining the soldiers with "I hohpu you hahbu a good-doh taimu" or, leering, "Watto kind ob pojishon do you rike?"—whether or not I understood exactly what I was saying. Kyoko is right, I managed the language one way or another. I guess one school friend who happened by was less shocked at my miserable clothing than the sight of me trading English with the soldiers, because word got around that I was an interpreter ("You should hear that guy's English!") and a lot of the kids I hadn't seen since I quit school started showing up to watch me work.

Once it was certain that Higgins would be coming to Japan, Kyoko got excited about English conversation again, even teaching some to Keiichi. "Goom-mohneen. When you wake up, you say, 'Goom-mohneen.' Go ahead, try it." And: "How about you, Papa? You ought to practice a little. You'll have to show them around—to Kabuki, Tokyo Tower. They were so nice to me in Hawaii."

"It's out of the question. I'm much too busy."

"I'm sure you can manage two or three days. Husband and wife are a single unit in America. People in Hawaii used to ask me where you were. I covered up by saying you'd be coming later."

What the hell are you talking about? The only reason you got to go to Hawaii was because I stayed home and worked! But what really gets me down is the thought of having to show them around Tokyo. The building on the right is the tallest in Japan. Rooku atto za righto beerudingu, zatto izu za highesto. Why should I have to start playing the Naka-no-shima pimp all over again? It amazes me to see anybody grinning and talking to Americans without the slightest hesitation. Walking along the Ginza, I see these young guys happily chattering away to Americans, the really bald-faced ones strolling down the avenue arm-in-arm with American girls like it was the most normal thing in the world. Sure, there were some in our day who talked to them, too, I remember. Once, on a crowded streetcar, a tense college student got up the nerve to ask some soldiers: "Ho-what-toh do you sheenku ob Japahn?" One of them shrugged, the other fixed him with a stare and said: "Half good, half bad." The student nodded gravely as though he had just had some profound philosophy explained to him. He took the stick of gum held out to him by the one who shrugged, rolled it like a cigarette, and popped it into his mouth, much to the envy of the other passengers. Why was it?—a soldier just had to look at you in those days and he was ready to give you chewing gum, cigarettes. Were they frightened to be in a place that had only just ceased being enemy soil? Did our hunger make them pity us?

But you can't get full on chewing gum. In the summer of 1946 we were living in Omiyamachi on the outskirts of Osaka, near a farm—which may have been why our food rations were often late or never came at all. More or less appointing herself to the duty, my sister would go several times a day to look at the blackboard outside the rice store and come back crushed when she found nothing posted. Once, we turned the house upside-down but found only rock salt and baking powder. We were so desperate we dissolved them in water and drank it, but this tastes bad, no matter how hungry you are. Just then the barber's wife, her big, bovine breasts hanging out, came to tell us, "There's been a delivery. Seven days' rations!" This was it! I grabbed the bean-paste strainer and started out. The strainer wasn't going to be big enough for seven days' worth, though. We'd need the sack. The strainer had become a habit because we had only been getting two or three days' provisions at a time, just a fistful for a household of three, which made a big sack embarrassing. We ran out to the rice store, where a couple of housewives were standing near the stacks of olive-drab U.S. Army cartons. "My old man hasn't been able to do it to me since he got back from Manchuria." "Ain't you the lucky one! Mine comes at me every time I've had a bath and finally got cooled off. Then I'm hot and sweaty all over again." And they laughed obscenely while they waited for their share. I understood what they were talking about and told my sister to go wait for me at home. Her navel always stuck out a little and once a sharp-eyed housewife who used to be a nurse saw her walking around without a top because she had nothing to wear. "Oh, what a cute little outie! But it's going to be kind of embarrassing when you get undressed for your husband," she said right to her face.

What would it be this time? Cheese? Apricots? I was used to these olive-drab cartons and knew we weren't getting rice but American provisions. The sugar-cured apricots had nothing to them, but you felt you were getting some nourishment from the cheese, which tasted pretty good in bean-paste soup. We all watched as the rice man split open a carton with a big kitchen knife and came out with these little packets wrapped in dazzling red-and-green paper. As if to keep our curiosity in check, he said: "A substitute rice ration—a seven-day supply of chewing gum.

That's what these cartons are." He pulled out something like a jewel case. This was a three-days' supply.

I carried off nine of these little boxes, each containing fifty five-stick packs, a week's rations for the three of us. It was a good, heavy load that had the feel of luxury. "What is it? What is it?" My sister came flying at me and screeching for joy when she heard it was gum. My mother placed a box on the crude, little altar of plain wood. The local carpenter had made it in exchange for the fancy kimono my mother had taken with her when we evacuated the city. She dedicated the gum to my father's spirit with a ding of the prayer bell, and our joyful little evening repast was under way, each of us peeling his gum wrappers and chewing in silence. At twenty-five sticks each per meal, it would have been exhausting to chew them one at a time. We would throw in a new stick whenever the sweetness began to fade. Anyone who saw our mouths working would swear they were stuffed with doughy pastry. Then my sister, holding a brown lump of chewed gum in her fingertips, said: "I guess we have to spit this out when we're through." The second I answered "Sure," I realized we had to live for seven days on this gum, this stuff that made not the slightest dent in our hunger. Anything is better than nothing, they say, but this anything was our own saliva, and when the hunger pangs attacked again, my eyes filled with tears of anger and self-pity. In the end, I sold it on the black market—which was on the verge of being closed down—and bought some corn flour to keep us from starving. So I have no reason to be bitter. One thing is sure, though: you can't get full on chewing gum.

Gibu me shigaretto, chocoreto, san-Q. No one who's had the experience of begging from a soldier could carry on a free-and-easy conversation with an American, I know it. Look at those guys with their monkey faces, and the Americans with their high-bridged noses and deep-set eyes. And now all of a sudden you hear people saying the Japanese have interesting faces, beautiful skin—can they be serious? Often in a beer hall I'll see a sailor at a nearby table, or some foreigner who seems shabby if you just look at his clothes, but his face is all civilization and I catch myself staring at his three-dimensional features. Compared to the Japanese all around him, he's a shining star. Look at those muscular arms, the massive chest. How can you not feel ashamed next to him?

"Mr. Higgins' ancestors come from England, he says. He has a white beard, just like some famous stage actor." Yes, Toshio knew well enough what Higgins looked like from those color snapshots of him in a bathing suit against Black Sand Beach or Diamond Head, the chest muscles sagging, of course, but the belly good and firm, and Mrs. Higgins standing by in a bikinilike thing despite her age. "He's so white he gets sunburned immediately. And he's hairy, but the texture of the hair is different from ours—soft, with a golden glow, very handsome." Probably it was the food, and for a while after they got back, she fed Keiichi nothing but meat. That hadn't lasted long, of course, but she had started in again recently. "Americans are very fond of steak, you know. Japanese beef is so good, I'm sure

I can make something they'll like." For practice, she started keeping big, American-style chunks of beef in the refrigerator, making steaks every night and serving them with lectures on "rare" and "medium" like some overzealous hotel waiter.

Kyoko put a pink terrycloth cover on the toilet seat, no doubt thinking it a point of etiquette because she saw it done in Hawaii. Their Japanese-style bath worried her: could the Higginses manage to wash and rinse *before* they got in to soak? She took special pains in killing cockroaches. She bought a mattress for herself and Toshio, deciding that the Higginses would sleep in their bedroom. Vinyl flowers in the living room were bad enough, but she enlarged and framed their wedding photo and a snapshot of herself and Keiichi in Hawaii—this, he was pretty sure, was something she had gotten from an American TV show. He complained at first, but it was easier to let Kyoko handle everything her own way. He decided to be above it all and observe the progress of the changing cheap décor from the sidelines.

Once, while I was an imitation pimp in Naka-no-shima, one of my old classmates, a Shinsaibashi butcher's son, asked me to bring an American to their house for dinner. What for? I asked him. The way he told it, his old man had made so much money selling beef it scared him to have the cash around. He had built a new house with doors that opened and closed electrically, but he still didn't know what to do with his money. He liked to have a good time and gave a lot of parties and now he wanted to have an America-san over "to thank him for the trouble we've caused him, making him take a special trip all the way to Japan." I agreed to find somebody, figuring there might be a good chunk of beef in it for me, and brought along a twenty-one-year-old Texan soldier named Kenneth after doing my best to explain to him what this was all about. They sat him crosslegged on a tiger skin before the ceremonial alcove of their luxurious villa and put two miniature lacquered tables in front of him, serving one tiny dish after another of the purest Japanese-style catered cuisine. Kenneth didn't know what to do with his long legs, there was no hope of his liking the carp boiled in bean soup or the raw slices of sea bream, and all he did was drink glass after glass of beer. Finally, the kids started to do this terrible dancing and miming of a Japanese folk song. I was climbing the walls with embarrassment, but the butcher looked enormously satisfied with all this, kept puffing on his long, skinny pipe and repeating the only English he knew, "Japahn pye-pu, Japahn pye-pu."

They could never have a repeat performance of that fiasco, but *if* Higgins made a face and refused Kyoko's cooking, and *if* Kyoko encouraged Keiichi, who had been happily imitating those awful singers on TV, "Sing for Grandpa Higgins now, Keiichi, rettsu shingu" . . . Just imagining the scene, Toshio felt the blood rush to his head.

"Do you think this will fit him?" Kyoko tore off the department-store wrapping and showed him a maroon bathrobe. "I bought the largest size they had. Here, try it on, Papa." She had him into it before Toshio could say a word. His five-foot-nine-inch frame was big for a Japanese and the robe fit him perfectly.

"Let's see, he must be about this much taller than you." She stretched out a hand to indicate the difference between Higgins and himself. "I suppose we'll have to ask him to make do with this. Mrs. Higgins can wear a yukata."

"Look at the Americans. Their average height is five feet, ten inches. For us, it's only five feet three. This difference of seven inches figures in everything, and I believe that's why we lost the War. A basic difference in physical strength is invariably manifested in national strength," said the social studies (formerly just "history") teacher. This fellow might be talking off the top of his head or spouting sheer nonsense, but he was so good at it, you never knew how seriously to take him. Maybe this was just his way of covering up the embarrassment he felt at suddenly having to preach Democratic Japan after Holy Japan from textbooks filled with the censors' black blottings, but at the time of America's first postwar atomic bomb test on Eniwetok Atoll, he scared us with prophetic pronouncements like "If the chain reaction is infinite, the earth will be blown to bits," and "Do you know why the Americans are making us hand over the lead pipes that are found in the burnt-out ruins? So they can send them home as material to block radiation! The Third World War is at hand. America and Russia are bound to fight it out." But he didn't have to tell me about a difference in physical strength making for a difference in national strength. I knew it all too well from experience.

September 25, 1945, was a fantastically clear day. It seems as if there was never a cloud in the burning sky from summer into autumn that year—which is not true, of course. I have heart-withering memories as well of an early typhoon and the rice plants in the paddies falling in swirls, the very footprints of the wind. This tied in perfectly with expectations of a bad crop. But on September 25, in any case (as had been true of August 15, the day the War ended), we had what would have been a "Japanese beauty" of a day if it had not been the day everyone said the American Army was finally coming. We were let out of school—not that we had any classes to speak of, since most of our time was spent cleaning up the fire-bombed ruins. For no very good reason, I had always thought the Americans would be coming in planes or boats, but when I walked toward the ocean from the shelter we were living in there in the ruins of Kobe's Shinzaike, a motorcycle with a sidecar came roaring down the highway carrying a tense-looking policeman who wore a hat with a chin-strap, and following a hundred yards or so behind him was a winding column of jeeps and canvas-hooded troop trucks that I later realized had raced past my eyes in what, compared with the motorcycle, could only have been called a majestic silence.

Six years earlier, I had watched the same sort of truck detachment going down the highway, except then it had been at night and the soldiers were Japanese. The troops had put up with families near Kobe Harbor, waiting nearly three full weeks for their ship to come. Two men stayed at our house, which was great fun for me. When their orders came all of a sudden, it was close to nine at night. I went with my mother to see the soldiers piling silently into truck after truck on the highway, heard orders ringing like the cries of some strange bird, but we looked in vain for the two men who had stayed with us, swallowed up now in the darkness. It seems to me that eventually a victory song welled up, but this must be a trick of the memory. I do remember that the tears were pouring out of me. The trucks moved off down the highway, heading west, and searchlights sent two unwavering beams aloft, picking clouds out of the night sky.

The Americans also went from east to west down the highway. At first I chased them with my eyes like counting cars in a freight train, but there was no end to them. "Look, they brought along fishing poles," shouted a boy with an egg-shaped head. He was one of the few bare-headed people in the crowd that quickly formed along the road, most still wearing gaiters and army caps. He was right: all the jeeps had long, flexible things like fishing poles that swayed with each bump. "The Chinks went to war with umbrellas, the Americans take fishing rods. They are different," said an old man. I don't know what was supposed to be so "different," but it did seem odd to think of American soldiers fishing just like us for the same fish from the same beaches. But then a young fellow who looked like an already-demobilized soldier answered: "That's an antenna, a radio antenna." In all innocence, I had to admire them: so the Americans took radios along when they went to war!

All at once, without an order or a shout of any kind, the column came to a halt and the soldiers, who until then had looked like part of the machinery with their uniforms the same color as the trucks, sprang out—almost as if they had been shot out—holding rifles. Once on the ground, they leaned casually against the vehicles, looking at us, their cheeks as red as devils'. "Who says they're white? They're red devils!" said one frightened boy of my age as if my thoughts had been his own. A couple of hundred yards east down the wall of people, a cry arose that could have been a cheer or a scream. I looked over to see two American soldiers who stood a head—no, a head and shoulders—above the crowd that surrounded them. As I was about to step into the road to see what was happening, three big men came up before I knew it and, standing six feet from me, their mouths working constantly, started opening packs of gum and throwing the sticks in our direction. They were so offhand about it, we were all too startled to move. The soldiers started gesturing for us to pick up the gum, and I suspect the first one to take a stick did so less out of a willingness to accept charity than a fear of being punished if he refused. This was a man in a crepe undershirt and knee-length drawers, brown shoes, and garters to hold up his socks, who timidly stretched out his hand and showed not the least pleasure at having received a stick of chewing gum. The rest were like pigeons flocking for beans.

I had never thought much about it until then, but the second I saw the American soldiers I remembered the judo teacher's spirited lecture on how easy it would be to knock down the hairy beasts if you got them below the waist, where they were weak. Half seriously, I looked them over—and my illusions died on the spot. Maybe General Percival was an exception, because the soldiers I was looking at now had arms like roof beams and hips like millstones, and underneath pants *that glowed with a sheen our civilian uniforms never had, you could see their big, powerful buttocks. I had been granted beginner's status in the Martial Arts Society and I knew how to trip up the biggest lugs in school, but I could never do a thing to these American soldiers. What magnificent builds! No wonder Japan lost the War. Why were we fighting these giants to begin with? If you went after these guys with the wooden rifles we used in bayonet drill, they'd snap in two. Feeding us like pigeons began to bore them after a while, I suppose, and the soldiers climbed back into their trucks. A few people ran after them, as though sorry to see them go, but a soldier grabbed up his rifle and scared the daylights out of them. The soldier laughed, and jeering laughter rose in the crowd as well.*

Next day, there was labor service at the customs house. We had to throw all the papers in the building out of the windows. Everything was to be burned, supposedly as part of a "major clean-up," but whatever they didn't want the Occupation Army to find had certainly been taken care of long ago. This was sheer madness inspired by an overdose of fear, because the most these papers had on them was lines. If they're going to burn these, I might as well take them, I decided, because all I had for notepaper then was the backs of old cash memos from the stationer's. I stuffed some in my shirt, but this was not the customs house for nothing. My smuggling was uncovered in no time and the papers burned to ashes.

Just three months earlier, we had gathered in front of the customs house and walked to the beach at Onohama, weaving in and out of the Mitsui and Mitsubishi warehouses crammed into the area, to build a protective wall for Japan's latest piece of weaponry, a 125-mm. anti-aircraft gun they said could pierce steel plating at an altitude of 50,000 feet. "Equipped with radar and gearing, this gun is capable of firing at planes that are approaching, overhead, and going—all three," explained the platoon leader. Kobe was thus protected by a veritable wall of iron, he said, but there were only six of these guns. He also let us look through his binoculars. You could see Jupiter perfectly even though it was broad daylight.

The B-29s that made a straight line across Osaka Bay and attacked the city on June 1 met with a savage barrage of fire from these 125-mm. guns that failed to down a single plane. I tried to be encouraging. "What fantastic guns! They really spit fire!" But the soldiers, unfazed, answered matter-of-factly: "That is why they're called spitfires."

Then, I had been helping the Army shoot back at the Americans. Three months later, I was cleaning up to receive them as guests. The only difference was that work on the gun emplacement got me a loaf of bread, while for labor service after we lost I always got money—one yen fifty sen a day. Once, during the lunch break at the customs house, I went down to the beach. Both the anti-aircraft gun and the radar antenna (it looked like a fish grill) had disappeared without a trace. The only things on the beach were a few dozen concrete pipes, and in the water a line of small warships, American minesweepers cleaning up the mines the Americans themselves had planted.

"How old is Mr. Higgins?" it suddenly occurred to Toshio to ask.

"I'm not sure. Sixty-two? Sixty-three? Why?"

"Did he ever say he fought in the War?"

"No, of course not. Who'd go to Hawaii for a vacation and talk about such awful things?" Then Kyoko added, "Except you." She hurriedly went on: *"Please don't start talking about the War, even if he did fight in it. It won't make him feel very good to hear that your father was killed."*

Whenever Toshio brought a friend his own age home for a drink, the liquor at its height would call forth war songs, stories of experiences in the war effort, and Kyoko, feeling left out, would grumble, "It's so stupid, the same old stories over and over," which was probably why she had included this warning in Higgins's case. She need not have feared, however: Toshio did not know enough English to share war stories with an American.

"You just have to forget these terrible things. Every summer they come out with new war stories, more memoirs—well, I just hate it. I mean, *I* remember my mother carrying me piggyback into the air-raid shelter, *I* ate those starchy wartime foods, but I hate the way they dig up the War and bring back memories of August 15 year after year after year. It's as though they're proud of having suffered so much."

In the face of Kyoko's increasingly earnest appeal, Toshio could only remain silent. At the company, whenever he would let slip a remark or two on the air raids or the black market, the younger men would smile faintly as if to say "Here we go again." The fear would suddenly overtake him that the others were seeing through a tale that grew more exaggerated with each telling, and he would cut himself short with a pang of emotion. This coming August 15 would be the twenty-second anniversary, after all: why shouldn't his stories be taken as an old man's senile prattling?

On August 15, I had my mother and sister with me in our shelter in the Shinzaike ruins. It might sound funny to say that they were with me, a fourteen-year-old boy, but fourteen-year-olds were the only ones left in Japan by then who could be called upon to do a man's work. I was the only one who could bail out the shelter when it rained or go to the well when the pipes failed. My mother was practically an invalid with her asthma and neuralgia. I can't be sure now whether it was the day before or that morning, but the word was passed that some important news was coming. I probably heard it from one of our neighbors. (We had lots of neighbors living in shacks of galvanized sheeting put up where a wall had been left standing, or in air-raid shelters with three-foot-high roofs.) I went to join the group of thirty or so in the neighborhood council who had to gather in front of the still intact Young Men's Association because the neighborhood council building had been destroyed. "I'm telling you, they're going to declare martial law." "Maybe His Majesty himself is going to take command of the Army?" There had been a major air raid on Osaka on the fourteenth, and Kobe itself had been strafed by carrier planes; none of us had the slightest idea that the War would end the next day. We heard the strangely disembodied voice saying ". . . and thus am torn asunder . . . to bear the unbearable, endure the unendurable . . ." but we were more mystified than anything else. The announcer solemnly reread the Emperor's proclamation, and the broadcast was over. Everyone probably realized in a vague sort of way that the War had ended, but nobody wanted to risk being the first to let it slip out. "Harmony has been restored, that's what it means," said the head of the neighborhood council, the white hairs conspicuous on his long-unshaven head. His choice of words brought to mind the "restoration of harmony" between Ieyasu and Hideyori after the Summer Siege (or was it the Winter Siege?) of Osaka Castle over three hundred years ago, but it conveyed no immediate sense of our having lost the War. I suppose I was in a state of excitement, because for a while I didn't notice the streams of sweat that had come from standing under the burning sky, but then I walked straight back to the shelter. "It looks like there's no more war, Mama." My little sister, combing the lice from her hair, was the first to answer. "You mean Father's coming home?" My mother went on silently rubbing her skinny knees with talcum powder, and after a while said only, "We'll have to be careful."

"Look! The B-29s are dropping something," my sister shouted. At the time, I was trying to get what little coolness was available in the hot, steamy shelter by blowing into my shirt. "Get back in here, stupid!" They might have been more bombs. "It's all right, they're just parachutes." When I timidly stuck my head out, the sun was on its way down, casting its red glow on Mt. Rokko, and the three-plane formation of B-29s had already flown so far that they were beginning to blend into the contrasting deep blue of the sky above the ocean. In a long band that started directly overhead, countless numbers of billowing, overlapping parachutes were streaming westward at a slight incline, almost as if they had a will of their own. My sister clung to me, afraid, and I held her close, ducking down again just in case. "What could they have dropped?" My voice quavered. The new bomb they dropped on Hiroshima was an atomic bomb, and that was supposed to have had a parachute, but certainly they would never drop so many—and not here, where there was nothing but burnt-out ruins as far as you could see. The parachutes fell more slowly as they neared the ground, then glided in and collapsed sideways when they hit. It was the hour of the evening calm and absolutely windless. The parachutes never moved.

An old man holding his shovel like a rifle and an old woman wearing a scarf on her head in spite of the sweltering heat kept going in and out of their shack and pointing at the parachutes. Amid the strange silence, the first one to start running was a shirtless boy of about first-year middle-school age. I started walking, too, frightened and fascinated to see what the things could be. The first one I came to was in a tennis-court-turned-potato-field. The white cloth of the chute was draped over its cargo—a bomb or something—but nobody wanted to go near it. "Stay away! Move! Get away!" a policeman shouted through a megaphone, walking over with his bicycle. I climbed a tree that had escaped burning, to get a better view. All along the highway to the west were white clumps that looked just like the puddles that formed in bomb craters. "Waah! There's hundreds of them!" I immediately announced my discovery. Some of the white clumps were surrounded by crowds, while others between the highway and the ocean had still not been noticed. An old woman appeared, looking for help. "One of them fell right next to my shelter." "Did you see what it was?" Everyone had watched the parachutes sailing down to the ground, but nobody had gotten a clear look at what they carried. "I don't know, I think it's some kind of big barrel. I have some eggs in my shelter —do you think it's safe to go get them?" The fear of duds and time-bombs was too deeply ingrained. No one was willing to offer his assurances. We just stood there looking fearfully at the white ghost that would suddenly come alive now and then when the almost imperceptible breeze filled the chute.

Their boots crunching on the earth, some soldiers came running in our direction. At last! The dud squad! But no, there were only ten shirtless, unarmed men. They set to work on the chute without order or hesitation. The crowd pressed forward, tightening the circle. When the chute was stripped off, an olive-drab metal drum emerged. I had seen plenty of old, scorched gasoline drums, but this one had the gloss of newness, and there were small English script and numbers on it. Three soldiers pushed it over and started rolling it, oblivious of the thick growth of potato leaves in their furrows. "What is it?" someone finally dared to ask. "Isn't it a bomb?" "They dropped stuff for the prisoners. The Americans take good care of their men."

There was a prisoner-of-war camp at Wakihama, and the prisoners often used to carry freight on the pier, but could these things really be for them? "Well, we're the prisoners as of today," one man said good-humoredly and produced a pack of cigarettes. "These are good smokes, from Roosevelt—no, Truman." He gave one to a civil corpsman. "They've got everything in these barrels!" When they finally got the barrel to the roadside, they kicked it along, then rolled it up into a wagon. As soon as they went rattling off with it, the crowd dispersed in all directions. I ran for those white clumps I had seen on the beach side of the highway. Hell, if they were going to give these treasure cans that had "everything" in them to the POWs, I'd take one for myself, I thought, driven more by hunger than hatred for the enemy. The sun was down, the burnt-out ruins on the verge of darkness. Just as I had run around looking for a shelter in the June 5 air raid, the black smoke enveloping me and turning the afternoon into evening, I made for the white chutes, now searching for what had fallen from the sky instead of fleeing from it, as we had until yesterday.

Every one of the drums was an anthill crawling with grown-ups in a sweat to get the things open with hammers and crowbars. I got yelled at for just looking at them from a distance. On the way back to the shelter, I heard the voice of the old woman who had been worrying about her eggs, now screeching through the darkness: "No! No! This thing fell on our land, so it's ours! I don't care what you say, I'm not giving it up! Get out of here! Get out!"

The Army took charge of the situation. There was too much stuff to give it all to the POWs, so each neighborhood council would take the responsibility of dividing it up evenly—and quickly, because there was no telling when the American Army might show up. If there were something in a drum besides food, this had to be reported immediately, and if someone were found to have taken possession of any such thing, he might be immediately executed. Sending along sufficient threats, they allotted two drums to each block, though of course anyone who had taken anything from the drums got to keep it. The contents of the drums were ready to be parceled out next afternoon in front of the Young Men's Association, but everything was wrapped in green and it was impossible to tell what was what. "Can anybody here read English?" the head of the neighborhood council asked, trying to smile, but intellectuals like that had been smart enough to evacuate long ago. It was the people who belonged to the place that stayed behind—the tinsmith, the carpenter, the tailor, the tobacconist, the grocer, the Golden Light priest, the grade-school teacher. I was an air-raid drillmaster and plenty used to looking smart in front of grown-ups, but not when it came to English. "How about opening all the packages so everything gets distributed fairly?" Each barrel had contained a single item—nothing but shoes, say, or all cigarettes, and these the neighborhood councils had divided up evenly. Now the first thing we opened were some long, narrow boxes. They were packed full like a kid's lunch box with cheese, canned beans, green toilet paper, three cigarettes, chewing gum, chocolate candy, a hard biscuit, soap, matches, jam, marmalade, and three white pills. These were distributed two boxes per household. Then we opened some round cans that were stuffed full of cheese or bacon, ham, beans, sugar. I felt like taking everything for myself, even if it meant killing everybody there, and I suppose everybody else felt the same. Sighs went up when the sugar can was spilled into a cardboard carton. "Luxury Is the Enemy." "We Desire Nothing—Until Victory Is Won." Whenever I had seen these slogans, it had seemed to me they were talking about sugar. Luxury is sugar; when victory is won, we can eat as much as we like. So on the day we lost, what came falling out of the sky but sugar, along with a bunch of other treasures, including some wrinkled, black stuff like little pieces of thread. This was distributed loose, each family getting what could be scooped up in both hands. It was the only thing we didn't recognize, but nobody had time to worry about that. Anything that came out of the green cartons, even if it had been sand, you would have carefully stowed away, checking your share against what everyone else got. There was even some absorbent cotton, and when a middle-aged lady in glasses asked that it be distributed to the women, the civil corpsman turned her down flat. "No favors for anybody!" he shouted, red with anger. I had a vague idea what the women wanted cotton for. A little after we were burned out, my mother went to the drugstore for advice. "My period is awfully late this time." "So's mine," said another customer about her age. The pharmacist joined in and an embarrassing conversation ensued, ending with: "Still, it's a lot less trouble this way as long as you can't get cotton." Apparently a lot of women stopped having their periods after the bombing started.

"We don't know when the Americans are going to come here. This is a special ration we stole from the prisoners, so get rid of it as soon as you can. Let's not take any chances," the head of the neighborhood council warned us, and the first thing I did when I got back to the shelter was repeat this emphatically. We had gotten into the habit of stretching everything to the limit, so if my mother had said to me, "Let's just have the beans today," I would have looked long and hard at our portion and then cried like a little kid watching his mother put away his favorite cookies "for later." The only reason I hadn't started eating the sugar on the way was my excitement: all I wanted to do was hurry back and show off the food as if I had gotten it through some daring exploit.

My mother did as I said and offered a biscuit and cigarettes before my father's picture in a corner of our shelter. It only occurred to me after I had sampled most of this special ration from America, but if my father's spirit was alive somewhere, what would he have thought of all this? It was so strange—helping yourself to something that belonged to the "American and English Devil-Brutes" who had killed your father and then offering it up before his spirit!

"What is this?" I asked, once the initial excitement had ended. The stringy, black stuff was the only thing that seemed to need cooking, but neither the taste nor the smell helped us to figure out what it was. "I'll go ask somebody," I said, aware of nothing but an overwhelming desire to eat. I ran out and asked the laundry woman. "I don't know," she said, as puzzled as the rest of us, "I guess you have to soak it for a while until it's soft, then boil it. It looks a lot like hijiki." Could that be it? Hijiki was supposedly something they used to cook together with fried bean curd. I had heard that the dish was a favorite of the Osaka merchants' apprentices. Our cracked earthenware brazier was held together by wire, but I immediately got a fire going and set a pot on it that we had saved from the bombing. When I started boiling the stuff as the laundry woman had suggested, the water turned an increasingly dark, rusty brown color. "Is hijiki supposed to be like this?" I asked my mother. She came over to look, dragging her bad leg. "The bitterness is coming out. American hijiki has a lot of bitter stuff, doesn't it!" I tried draining it and changing the water, but still couldn't get rid of the rusty brown. The fourth change of water stayed clear, so I flavored it with rock salt and took a taste after it had boiled down. It turned out to be this sticky, absolutely tasteless stuff like the black ersatz noodles they made from seaweed—only worse. Chewing did no good. It just seemed to stick to the inside of my mouth. And swallowing it was an impossibility. "That's funny, maybe I boiled it too long." My mother and sister both made faces when they tried it. "The Americans eat some pretty awful things, too," my mother grumbled, but we certainly couldn't throw it out. Having been boiled, it would probably keep for a while. We left it in the pot and refreshed our mouths with chewing gum. Nobody ever did figure out how to cook this American hijiki. The head of the neighborhood council asked a soldier about it three days later and told us: "He says it was something called 'burakku teh,' the *tea leaves they use in America." But by then, there was not a speck of it left in any of the shelters.*

The narrow streets between the burnt-out houses were filled with discarded silver chewing-gum wrappers. One of the first men to grab a drum for himself had found it filled with chewing gum. No matter how much he chewed, of course, he was unable to get rid of it all. It would be dangerous for him if the Americans showed up and, besides, his jaw was getting tired, so he handed it all out to the kids, who chewed it like cinnamon and threw it away as soon as the flavor was gone. At first, everybody smoothed the wrinkles out of the silver papers and saved them for origami, but there were so many they ceased to have any value and soon the streets were covered with silver paper snow, glittering in the summer sun. This was like hiding your head and leaving your tail exposed. If the Americans saw it, they would realize immediately that the drums had been stolen. But nobody worried about that. The special ration was gone soon enough, except the sugar, which we kept nibbling at, but even after we had gone back to the old boiled miscellanies and starchy soups, the silver chewing-gum wrappers, like the colorful trash spread around a shrine after a festival, kept the special ration of dreams from America alive in the yellow-brown landscape.

"America" for Toshio meant American *hijiki,* summer snow in the burnt-out ruins, big hips under glossy gabardine, a thick hand held out for him to *sukueezu,* seven days' rice rations of chewing gum, habagoot-taimu, MacArthur with the Emperor just up to his shoulders, Q-Q and Japan-American amity, half-pound cans of MJB coffee, DDT doused on him in the station by a black soldier, a lone bulldozer smoothing over the burnt-out ruins, jeeps with fishing poles, and a Christmas tree in an American civilian's house, its only decorations electric lights blinking silently on and off.

In response to Kyoko's entreaties, Toshio agreed to have the company car take them to meet the Higginses at Haneda Airport. "You'll be coming, too, won't you, Papa?" she pressed, in answer to which a busy schedule would have been too obvious an excuse. But worse, he hated the thought of being seen through ("What are you afraid of?") if he refused. And so, on to the chaos of the airport and Kyoko flaunting her one-time experience of foreign travel, gliding into International Arrivals with "Oh, look, Keiichi, remember we got on the plane over there? And customs is way over there."

"I'll be in the bar."

There was still time until the plane arrived. Toshio took the escalator upstairs. "Straight whiskey, double." He gulped it down like an alcoholic. "I will *not* speak to him in English" had been his first firm resolve on waking this morning, not that he could have done so had he wanted to, but the fragments of conversation he had used back then in Naka-no-shima might suddenly come to life again and start pouring out under pressure to use English. "No, right from the start I'll give him the old standard '*Yaa, irasshai*' or '*Konnichi wa,*' and if he doesn't understand me, to hell with him. You come to Japan, speak Japanese. I won't even say 'goon-nighto' to him." As he drank, the fluttering in the chest that had been with him since lunch gradually subsided and he began to sense the thrill of striking back at the enemy.

The crowd came pouring through the gate: a bearded American student wearing cotton pants and rubber thong sandals and looking as though he was on a trip to the nearest town, a horrifyingly tall couple, a middle-aged man who walked with the quick, high-strung steps of the successful businessman in familiar territory, beaming Japanese travelers who really did have slanted eyes and muddy-looking skin when you saw them like this mixed in with foreigners, Hawaiian Nisei all round-faced with thick heads of hair. "Hi, Higgins-san!" screeched Kyoko, and there he was in blue blazer, gray pants, leather necktie, and the white beard that Toshio knew so well, and with him a little old lady wearing bright red lipstick and looking smaller than she had in the snapshots. Shaking his head "Yes, yes," Higgins walked over to them, hugged Kyoko, and patted Keiichi on the head. Even Kyoko seemed at a loss to produce English right away, flagging after "How ah you" and trying to overcome her awkwardness by gesturing towards Toshio with "My husband." Toshio threw out his chest, extended his hand, and said, *"Yaa, irasshai"* somewhat hoarsely, to which Higgins responded in faltering but correct Japanese, *"Konnichi wa, hajimemashite."* So utterly unprepared for this was Toshio that whatever composure he had mustered up gave way to a hurried scraping together of vocabulary fragments that would enable him to answer in English, which he felt he must by all means do. "Werucome, berry good-do." Higgins received these disconnected bits with a smile and said in his shaky Japanese: "We could come Japan, I am very glad." Toshio could think of nothing for this but a few polite groans. Meanwhile, Kyoko and Mrs. Higgins were managing to communicate with English and sign language. To Toshio, Mrs. Higgins said the usual "How are you," and he answered by echoing the phrase, his firm resolve by now having disappeared somewhere.

Using "Ladies first" as an excuse, Toshio got Kyoko into the back seat with Mr. and Mrs. Higgins and sat next to the driver with Keiichi.

"You're just terrible, Mr. Higgins. You didn't tell me in Hawaii that you knew Japanese."

"Yes, then I was without confidence. But when we decided to come Japan, I tried hard to remember." During the War, he said, he had studied conversational Japanese at the University of Michigan's Japanese language school and then come to Japan for six months in 1946 with the Occupation forces. Toshio recalled the rumor going around back then that there were Americans walking the streets pretending not to know Japanese, and when they heard someone criticizing America they would send him off to Okinawa to do hard labor. Higgins said he had been doing newspaper work in Japan. If it was 1946, everything had still been a pile of rubble. Speeding along the expressway from the airport, Toshio thought several times of asking with pride: "Japan has changed quite a lot, don't you think?" Higgins should have been the one to show surprise, but he kept silent while his wife chimed in with "Wonderful, wonderful" each time Kyoko pointed out Tokyo Tower strung with lights or the panorama of high-rise buildings.

"Do you like to drink, Mr. Higgins?"

"Yes, I do," he nodded happily and handed a cigar to Toshio, who had turned to face him.

"San-Q," said Toshio, no longer hesitant about speaking English. But the cigar was another matter: weren't you supposed to snip one end off before you smoked it? American officers used to bite the end off and spit it out. All right, then . . . but it was more than he could manage. When he looked up, Higgins was carefully running his big tongue all over his cigar, which seemed to be absorbing his full attention. He looked like some kind of animal. When he started feeling for a match, Toshio quickly proffered his lighter.

They left the expressway, heading for home in Yotsuya, and as they approached the famous Ginza Yonchome intersection, Toshio, unable to resist the role of guide any longer, said: "This is the Ginza." Higgins would have to be surprised at the glut of neon here. It was supposed to be more spectacular than that of New York or Hollywood.

"The Ginza, I know. The PX was here."

They passed the building where the PX had been, before there was time to point it out.

"If you like, we can have dinner here instead of going straight home," Toshio suggested. Kyoko had made preparations for dinner, but she went along with him, and Higgins, apparently willing to leave everything up to Toshio, stepped gleefully from the car.

Toshio could not decide whether to take them to a restaurant with a foreign chef, or to one serving sukiyaki and tempura. But Higgins asked: "Is sushi here?"

"You eat sushi, Mr. Higgins? It has raw fish, you know."

"Yes, there are sushi restaurants in America. Kame-zushi, Kiyo-zushi, very good."

Mrs. Higgins, apparently startled at the tidal wave of people, kept pressing her husband for information.

"My lovely wife is asking me this a festival?" he said to Toshio, smiling.

Toshio wanted to follow Higgins' reasonably workable Japanese with something clever in English, but the best he could do was, "Oar-ways rush-shu, *ne,*" an explanation for Mrs. Higgins in strict GI-whore style. It seemed to have gotten through to her, though, because she nodded and started yammering at him in incomprehensible English. He nodded back and gave her the famous Japahnese sumairu.

Holding their chopsticks in what should have been an unusable position, Mr. and Mrs. Higgins deftly picked up the bits of raw fish and vinegared rice balls plopped before them by the sushi chef. "In America, too, the different kinds of sushi they call *toro, kohada, kappa-maki,*" said Higgins, drinking green tea and looking as if he and his wife had been in Japan for years.

"Mr. Higgins and I are going to have a drink together, Kyoko, so you take Mrs. Higgins home. —Right, Mr. Higgins?"

"Fi-ine," Higgins nodded, smiling.

"But they must be so tired," Kyoko objected. "And it's not very nice for Mrs. Higgins."

But Mrs. Higgins seemed satisfied with her husband's explanation, to which Toshio added the wholly unnecessary "Stag-gu pahtee."

"Well, all right, maybe we can do a little shopping," Kyoko said, then awkwardly repeated this in English for Mrs. Higgins.

"Don't come home too late," she reminded Toshio as usual, and started off with Mrs. Higgins and Keiichi.

"Your son is up until late. Is it all right?" Higgins volunteered a sort of admonition.

True, the children usually stayed home when the husband and wife went out in America, Toshio recalled with some embarrassment. He was pretty sure he had seen that in "Blondie."

They went to a nightclub where Toshio often entertained important sponsors.

"What's this? Are you doing business with foreigners now?"

"No, no," Toshio hurried to explain. "He's been to Japan before and his Japanese is *very* good." He was taking no chances on Higgins' catching some rude remark. But the manager had his wits about him and quickly got two English-speaking bar hostesses for Toshio and his foreign guest. Toshio felt a little awkward with the unfamiliar girls, but Higgins seemed relieved at having been liberated from Japanese and started chattering away, turning to Toshio now and then with a bit of flattery. "Young ladies speak wonderful English." Soon he was hugging them and holding hands.

Aha, this old dog likes the girls, I see, thought Toshio, convinced that he would be providing inadequate service if he failed to find Higgins a woman. Perhaps a call girl tomorrow night? He thought of an agent in that particular line of goods with whom he had had some dealings in connection with work.

"Mr. Higgins, do you have anything planned for tomorrow?"

Higgins produced a memo book, which he showed to Toshio. "Three o'clock, Press Club. Five o'clock, I see a friend at CBS, have dinner. Why?"

Toshio, almost annoyed that Higgins should have so many acquaintances in Japan, said: "That's all right, the evening will be just as good. I was thinking of introducing you to a nice gahru."

"Thank you." Higgins did not seem especially pleased.

"How about after you have dinner with your CBS friend?"

"What time?"

"Eight o'clock should be all right."

"OK."

Toshio left the table abruptly with the look of a man who had important business to carry forward. He telephoned the call girl agent.

"He's a foreigner, now, an old guy. I think he'd probably like a really young girl." It would be fifty percent extra for foreigners, the agent said, but the girl would be absolutely stacked. Toshio ordered a girl for himself and they arranged to meet in a hotel in Sugamo.

Higgins was having the girls fill old-fashioned glasses half full of straight whiskey for him and drinking them down in a single gulp. He was not the least bit drunk, however, and from the one bag he refused to part with when the company car took the luggage home, he produced a cardboard-lined envelope. "Nude photos, I took them," he said, and displayed a series of explicit spread-leg standing poses among the hors d'oeuvres and fruit on the table, obviously enjoying the commotion raised by the shrieking hostesses. "My camera work, pretty good, isn't it? I took lots the time I in Japan, too."

For a second, Toshio was ready to pick a fight—I suppose you gave young girls chewing gum, chocolate, stockings, and forced them to get undressed for your camera?—but the feeling quickly passed as he began to get interested in the near-obscene photographs of blonde girls. Suddenly a little blob of something went shooting past him and he looked up to find Higgins pulling a narrow rubber band through the spaces between his teeth. He was flicking whatever food was lodged there in any direction it happened to fly, along with trailing bits of stuff that could have been saliva or tartar but was in any case disturbing to the hostesses, who wiped themselves but did not object openly to Higgins' bad manners.

They went to two more places after that, Higgins totally unaffected by the alcohol he kept gulping down, the two of them harmonizing on "You Are My Sunshine" in the cab and arriving home at three a.m. Toshio showed Higgins upstairs, then crawled in next to Kyoko and Keiichi, who were sleeping amidst a jumble of what must have been presents from the Higginses—chewing gum, cookies, perfume, brandy, and the kind of cheap muumuu the Hawaiian natives wear.

He woke with a terrible hangover, called to say he would be late for work, and was still munching pain-killers when he said good morning to the Higginses, who had been up for some time. Higgins, showing not the slightest trace of last night's drunk, stood looking out at the lawn and said: "It needs a little mowing." Kyoko had done a thorough job on the inside of the house but had not gotten to the yard and, yes, it *was* an overgrown jungle, punctuated here and there with a touch of dried dog shit. Toshio thought it rather considerate of them to serve Higgins iced coffee, but this he curtly refused, asking instead for green tea. He ate only a single slice of bread, never touching the salad or the fried eggs, then asked: "Do they sell English-language newspapers around here?" They ought to have them at the local distributor's, Toshio answered, still in too deep a fog to go out and buy one for his guest.

"I'm taking Mrs. Higgins to the Kabuki theater today," said Kyoko. "She says her husband is going to be busy. We'll be eating out, so what will you do?"

Toshio could hardly say he was going to buy a couple of women with Higgins, and Higgins, who could certainly overhear this conversation, was busy licking another cigar and never said a word. "That's all right, I'll find something to do," said Toshio.

Mrs. Higgins had gotten hold of Keiichi and was trying to make him learn English pronunciation. "Good morning, how are you?" He kept responding with sheer nonsense, obviously wanting to be left alone, but she would not give up.

"Why don't you leave Keiichi with your mother?" Toshio suggested quietly in the kitchen.

"She's not feeling well. Why?"

"You're sure to be coming home late tonight, and spending all that time with grown-ups will just tire him out. Besides, he'll get into the habit of staying up late."

"Don't worry, he gets along beautifully with Mrs. Higgins, and he can learn a little English from her, too." Kyoko may have thought Toshio was finding fault with her for leaving the house like that with Mrs. Higgins, and she added sulkily: "Here's a better idea. Why don't you come home early and baby-sit? I don't see why you're so worried about him developing new habits. He never goes to bed until you get home, no matter how late. He says he's 'waiting up for Papa.'" With this unfavorable shift in wind direction, Toshio left the kitchen. Keiichi's happy twittering attracted his attention to the yard, where Higgins, cigar in mouth, was slowly pushing the lawnmower they had bought when the lawn was first planted and left thereafter in the storage shed. His form was a perfect replica of the advertising posters.

"Oh, please, Mr. Higgins," shouted Kyoko, "please don't do that." And to Toshio: "I *asked* you to mow the lawn, didn't I? That thing is too heavy for me. I'm so embarrassed."

The ladies were going to the beauty parlor and then on to Kabuki, they said, departing with Keiichi after lunch. Toshio's hangover had passed, but he could not leave Higgins at home alone and, for something to do, suggested a beer after Higgins had finished mowing and had rinsed himself off in the bath. "Have you got whiskey?" Toshio found himself keeping Higgins company in an authentic drinking bout with the sun still on high and pouring himself whiskey-and-water even after Higgins had left for his three o'clock appointment, when it was too late to go to work. Having nothing better to do, he peeked into the second-floor bedroom and found it littered with Mrs. Higgins' clothing. Inspection of a suitcase revealed a dozen or more gaudily colored panties that he could not conceive of as belonging to that little old lady.

Toshio was good and drunk by the time they met at Hotel N at eight o'clock.

"What do you say?" he started in playfully on Higgins, "You can take both girls and I'll keep out of your way. You've got a numbah one gahru tonight, old boy. Caviar. Yoo noh? Caviar inside." Higgins did not understand. "In a word, cunt. Yoo noh? Eets rike caviar inside." Higgins, it appeared, had fooled around quite a bit in his day, because he recognized this and laughed aloud when he heard "octopus trap." "I know 'string purse,'" he volunteered.

They found the agent alone in the Sugamo hotel, his attitude wholly changed from what it had been last night when he was so quick to make promises. "There's just a limited number of girls who are willing to take foreigners. And you didn't give me enough time. I did manage something, but she's not so young. I absolutely guarantee her technique, though." She was thirty-two, he said, and used to work the American base at Tachikawa.

"How about mine?"

"For you, I've got a real nice one. Practically untouched."

"Look, wouldn't she take him if I doubled her fee? This guy is an important customer." What if Higgins decided he didn't like the thirty-two-year-old? Toshio couldn't give him inferior goods after his promise of a numbah one. He was getting frantic.

"I'm afraid I can't force the girl," the agent said almost loftily, "but I will talk to her and see."

"Please try. Money is no object."

He went to the room where Higgins was waiting. He was sitting in the ceremonial alcove to avoid the bedding spread all over the matted floor, and fiddling with his camera.

"Is it all right to take pictures, the young lady?" he asked.

Face shots would be no problem, but if they were going to be obscene photos like last night's, Toshio could not be sure. "OK, I'll try negotiating," he said, now the compleat pimp.

Twenty minutes later the two girls arrived. The agent motioned Toshio aside. "I got it all worked out. It looks OK for a double fee."

"How about photos?"

"By which you mean . . . ?"

"Nudes. There's nothing to worry about. He's going straight back to America."

"Well, the girl will have to decide that for herself. You'd better talk to her," he said, as if he expected her to refuse.

The young one was a slender beauty who could pass for a fashion model, the graduate GI whore—sitting slouchy and sullen—was a tough-looking woman with a square jaw. The two seemed not to know each other. Higgins stayed quiet in his alcove seat. This called for a little pimping.

"What's your name, honey?"

"Miyuki," said the younger one.

"Meet mistah Higgins-san," he said, figuring there was no need to use a pseudonym. "Your room is over here." He showed them the way, letting Higgins into the room first and explaining to the girl, "This American likes cameras and he wants to take your picture. He'll be going straight home, and you'll just be in his album to represent Japanese womanhood. Of course there'll be some money—"

"Not me, mister. No deal." She glared at him as if he had been the one with the camera.

Dragging himself back to his room, he found the graduate in a black slip, and though his heart wasn't in it, he gave himself up to his drunkenness and took his clothes off. He had no idea what it was supposed to mean, but the minute he lay down she purred "Baby, I'm a widow," and stretched out on top of him, whining. Her famous "technique" was strictly for her own satisfaction. Maybe this was what she had learned to do for foreigners. She started kissing him all over and digging her nails in, while Toshio struggled like mad to keep the brand of infidelity from being impressed on his skin. His only stimulus the exact opposite kind of scene that he vividly imagined must be taking place in the next room between Higgins and Miyuki, who could justly be called a beautiful little girl, Toshio eventually climaxed and went to take a bath, there to discover himself splotched with sickening red hickeys on the side, the upper arm, close to a nipple —and suddenly he was sober.

He sent the graduate away and started drinking beer from the refrigerator, but still there was no sign of Higgins. Lying down, he dozed off for a while and woke with a start just as the two of them were coming into the room, Miyuki clinging to Higgins without a trace of her former venom.

"Oh, Higgins-san, your Japanese is so good!" Now she was paying him compliments.

"Thank you very much," said Higgins, rewinding the film in his camera. So he had managed to get his pictures, too.

The agent called to ask how everything had gone. "All right," said Toshio.

"What I'm really calling about is this first-class shiro-kuro couple I'm handling. How do you think your foreign friend would like them? I doubt if you can see a show like this anywhere else." It would be thirty thousand yen, complete with a blue film, he said. The man had been a big hit in the Asakusa entertainment district, had stopped performing for a while, and now was making a comeback. His thing was truly magnificent and well worth a look.

"Higgins-san, yoo noh what they call shiro-kuro?"

"No, I don't."

"Eh, obsheen show, ne. Fahcking show."

"I understand," he grinned.

"Fine," he said to the agent, "make it tomorrow, six o'clock." And to Higgins: "They'll do it here, toomohrow, Japahnese numbah one penis."

Higgins nodded.

Again they went from one Ginza bar to another, Higgins in no way hesitant about being treated. Of course, if he *had* taken out his wallet, Toshio would have indignantly stopped him. Kyoko was still up when they got home after one last stop in Roppongi for sushi.

"I wish you had told me you were going to be with Mr. Higgins," she said resentfully. "I started worrying when you were so late. Mrs. Higgins told me you were out together drinking again. I was awfully embarrassed." Was it all right for him to stay out every night? Didn't he have to go to work? There had been several calls from the company, she said pointedly.

"What's the difference whether it's all right or not? He's *your* guest, isn't he? I'm providing all this service, so what are you complaining about?"

"Service doesn't have to mean drinking every night until three and four in the morning. He can't take that kind of pace. He's an old man."

Who's an old man? he wanted to say, but that was out of the question.

"And that old lady could learn some manners, too, the way she goes poking into everything. She was inspecting the refrigerator!" Was the mother-in-law impulse something they had in America, too? she wondered. Unable to pick a fight with Toshio over the guests she had inflicted on herself, Kyoko snuggled up to him. But if this was going to lead to love-making, Toshio had the evening's event to worry about. It would be too strange for him to stay in his underwear in this hot weather, but if he got undressed, she'd see the hickeys.

"I'll take a bath." He pressed her back nonchalantly.

"You can't," she snapped. "Mrs. Higgins washed herself *inside* the tub and drained the dirty water." It would have been so much trouble to clean the tub, fill it again, and wait for the water to heat up that she and Keiichi had gone without bathing. "And *you* can stand it, too!" She turned angrily away, and he lay down again, relieved.

Aware of the fatigue that follows a binge, that sensation of being dragged into darkness, Toshio was still wide awake in another part of his mind.

What is it that makes me perform such service for this old man? When I'm around him, what makes me feel that I have to give everything I've got to make him happy? He comes from the country that killed my father, but I don't resent him at all. Far from it, I feel nostalgically close to him. What am I doing when I buy him drinks and women? Trying to cancel out a fourteen-year-old's terror at the sight of those huge Occupation soldiers? Paying him back for the food they sent when we were so hungry we couldn't stand it—the parachuted special rations, the allotments of soy-bean residue that was nothing but animal feed to the Americans? Maybe it's true they were just getting rid of their agricultural surplus on us, but how many thousands and thousands of people would have starved to death if the Americans hadn't sent corn when they did? Still, this doesn't explain why I feel so close to Higgins. Maybe he feels that same nostalgia, recalling the days when he was here with the Occupation. Considering his age, the time he spent in Japan might have been the fullest period of his life, something he had been missing and reverted to the minute he came back here. That might explain his almost insulting behavior, his serene willingness to let me go on buying him drinks. That's not hard to understand. But the question is, why should I go along with it? Why should I be so happy to play the pimp the way the grown-ups did back then? Nothing holy rubs off on me for drinking booze with some lousy Yankee. Could it be that I'm feeling nostalgic for those days, too? No, that shouldn't be. Those were miserable times, when you were so hungry you learned to chew your cud like a cow, bringing the food back for a second, a third taste. Swimming out from the beach at Koroen and being chased by an American boat and almost drowning; getting beaten up in Naka-no-shima by an angry American soldier whose girl had run out on him: no, any way you looked at it, there were no happy memories. It was the bombing, after all, that ruined my mother's health and finally killed her; it was America, you could say, that put my sister's life in my hands and caused us so much suffering. Why, then, should the sight of Higgins make me want to do such service? Is this like the virgin who can never forget the repulsive man who raped her?

The new day brought back Kyoko's good spirits. They would be taking a bus tour of Tokyo, something Mrs. Higgins wanted very much to do. "If it weren't for an opportunity like this, I'd never take Keiichi to see the Sengakuji Temple," she said, Kyoko herself far from lacking in enthusiasm. "What are you going to do today? With Mr. Higgins again?"

"Um."

"Come home early tonight. I'm making dinner for them."

Higgins had gotten up early and gone out for a stroll, undaunted by his ignorance of the neighborhood. "There is a nice church," he said with satisfaction, drinking a whiskey. Toshio, usually confident of his capacity, was unable to join him. He could not ignore work completely, and he invited Higgins to leave with him. But Higgins answered simply, "I will relax a little more. Feel free." There was nothing Toshio could do but hand over the key and ask him to lock the door when he went out. Higgins assented as easily as if he had been sponging on them for years.

When Toshio explained to his staff somewhat apologetically that he had a guest from America, the total absence of any hint from him heretofore of contact with foreigners made their unanimous surprise that much greater. "Are we going to move in on the U.S. market? Japanese animation techniques have a good reputation over there." Toshio did not feel like explaining how far off the mark that was. "If you need an interpreter, I'd be glad to offer my services," said another young man, his eyes sparkling.

"No, he's just a rich American here for a visit."

"Wow, that's terrific. An old friend of yours?"

"Uh-huh, from the Occupation." This almost had the feel of truth for Toshio himself. To him, all Americans were Occupation soldiers, and an American child was just a small Occupation soldier. This was something his young staff could never understand. For them, America was a place you had to visit once, like a famous temple, a place where something holy rubbed off on you, a place that enhanced your image, a traveler's paradise where you could get by for next to nothing if you used your connections cleverly.

They went to the Sugamo hotel again as arranged, Toshio asking on the way how things had gone yesterday. Higgins winked. "She had a very lovely body. But my models in America are more stacked," he said, boasting of the obvious. All right, brother, hold your hat, now you're going to see the *shiro-kuro* show and numbah one penis, the pride of Japan. Let not their magnificence astound you. Toshio was eager to get started. Soon the agent appeared with the couple, the man on the small side, about Toshio's age, the woman in her mid-twenties. They bowed with exaggerated formality and withdrew to change their clothes.

"This is his first performance for a Foreigner-san, he tells me. Anyhow, he's got an amazing thing there. I get a complex just looking at it, it's so huge," the agent expressed his earlier opinion. Eventually, the couple appeared in light robes and lay on the floor mattress. Unable to get a good view, Higgins pointed towards the head of the mattress and signaled that he would like to change his seat. "Please, by all means, get as close as you like. Take a good look at Japan's Forty-Eight Holds."

"Fohty-eighto pojishon," Toshio explained, eliciting a nod from Higgins.

The man started by plastering the girl with passionate kisses on the lips, the neck, down to the breasts, and then she was panting, her robe opening bit by bit, revealing more and more flesh, when suddenly there was a loud "Thump!" and Toshio saw that Higgins, engrossed in the spectacle, had fallen over sideways from his low pile of floor cushions near the couple's pillow. He reseated himself calmly, without embarrassment. That'll teach you, thought Toshio, and suddenly he realized:

The reason I'm doing all this service for Higgins is that somehow, one way or another, I want to bring him to his knees. I don't care if it's by drinking him unconscious or driving him crazy over a woman, I want to turn this grinning, maddeningly self-possessed son of a bitch on to something—anything—Japanese and make him knuckle under. That's what I'm after!

Soon the woman was completely naked and obviously no longer acting in response to the seemingly endless foreplay. She was truly dying for the man, who now spread her legs and, poised before her on his knees, opened the front of his robe. Indeed, his was equipment worthy of a veteran, for even now it had yet to attain its full heroic stature but rose, ever dark and coiling, in defiance of the coming storm. The man spat into his palm and began to massage himself slowly. Higgins stretched his neck forward, staring intently. The woman by now was frantic, wrapping her legs around the man and pulling him closer. He continued with his prayerlike manipulation, which did result in some additional upthrust, but he was far from ready to come to grips with anything. He went on like this with his right hand, caressing the woman's body with his left, and after he had taken several steps that were familiar to Toshio from occasions when performance failed to match desire after heavy drinking, he simply lay on top of her. The woman moaned, but clearly union had not taken place. Was this part of the act? But no, the man wore a look of exasperation. He returned to his knees and started massaging himself again, having shrunk in the meantime to something far short of numbah one. Aware at last of what was happening, the woman got on top and used her mouth, but there was no sign of recovery.

Toshio glanced at the agent, who wore a twisted smile and looked very puzzled. The man now had his face down near Higgins' feet and, bathed in sweat, he knit his brows and closed his eyes as if in intense meditation. Every now and then he would spread his legs wide like a woman and stretch them out, while the woman ran her fingers over his chest, his thighs, the desperate valor of her efforts clear to all. Before he knew it, Toshio was straining as if he himself had been struck impotent.

What the hell are you doing? You're numbah one, aren't you? Come on, show this American. That huge thing of yours is the pride of Japan. Knock him out with it! Scare the shit out of him!

It was a matter of pecker nationalism: his thing *had* to stand, or it would mean dishonor to the race. Toshio almost wanted to take the man's place, his own thing now taut and ready. Noticing this, he glanced at Higgins' crotch, but nothing was happening there.

"Yot-chan, what's wrong?" the agent cried out, unable to contain himself after nearly half an hour's struggle.

Lying on his back, too exhausted even to sit up, the man answered hoarsely: "I'm sorry, this has never happened before. I don't know what to say."

The woman, too, was at a loss. "Maybe he's tired. This never happens."

"Well, take a break, have a beer," said Toshio, less discomfited before Higgins than sorry for this man who had drained all his energy trying to achieve erection.

Refusing the beer, the man said with extreme formality: "This has been terribly embarrassing. I will return your money, and I hope to have an opportunity to perform for you as a complimentary service."

"No, not at all, don't let it worry you. This happens to men all the time. Come on, have a drink," Toshio tried to comfort him, but the man fled from the room. Higgins was silently licking another cigar.

"This was a totally unheard-of occurrence. To think that Yot-chan could have failed!" said the agent, recounting tales of the prowess of that magnificent organ. "I'm sure this didn't happen just because a Foreigner-san was here!" he concluded, turning to Higgins with a laugh.

This man they call Yot-chan must be in his mid-thirties, and if so, Higgins might well have been the cause of his sudden impotence. If Yot-chan had the same sort of experience that I did in the Occupation—and he must have, whatever the differences between Tokyo and Osaka-Kobe—if he has memories of "Gibu me chewingamu," if he can recall being frightened by the soldiers' huge builds, then it's no wonder he shriveled up like that. Yot-chan might have been in a state of perfect professional detachment, but when Higgins sat down over him like a ton of bricks, inside his head the jeeps started rolling, the strains of "Comu, comu, eburybody" began to echo again, and he recalled, as clearly as if it were yesterday, the hopeless feeling when there was no more fleet, no more Zero fighters, recalled the emptiness of the blinding, burning sky above the burnt-out ruins, and in that instant the impotence overtook him. Higgins could never understand that. No Japanese can understand it, probably, if he's not my age. No Japanese who can have an ordinary conversation with an American, who can go to America and have Americans all around him without going crazy, who can see an American enter his field of vision and feel no need to brace himself, who can speak English without embarrassment, who condemns Americans, who applauds Americans, no Japanese like this can understand the America inside Yot-chan—inside me.

Exhausted, Toshio said to Higgins, "We ought to go home now. Kyoko's making a sukiyaki party."

"I must excuse myself. Am going to see a friend at the Embassy." And after a "Thank you very much" to the agent that sounded like pure sarcasm, he walked away with a brisk at-homeness unthinkable after a twenty-year absence from the country.

Toshio found Kyoko in a rage. "The nerve of the woman! She knew I was making dinner for them. All of a sudden she says she's going to stay with friends in Yokohama tonight!" On the table stood a large platter of the finest Matsuzaka beef and enormous quantities of all the other sukiyaki ingredients in anticipation of large American appetites. "Anyhow, the three of us will eat it. And you'd better have a lot!" Then Kyoko started in on Mrs. Higgins. "I couldn't do enough for that old lady, but she never noticed. I was explaining everything on the tour bus, but she just kept reading her English guidebook. And she's so stingy! I saw the things she picked out when we went shopping—all cheap. The toys she bought for Keiichi are like what the sidewalk vendors sell. That doesn't stop her from opening her big mouth, though. I can be standing right there when she gets mad at Keiichi and she'll scold him without a nod to me, his mother. I've never seen such rudeness. They come in here and expect us to do everything for them. All right, they were nice to me in Hawaii, so to show my appreciation I invited them to stay with us, but how long do they think they're going to stay? Toshio? Toshio, are you listening to me? How long do they think they can stay here?"

"Who knows? A month?"

"Never! I won't have it! I'll tell them outright they have to leave!"

Higgins will go back sooner or later, I suppose. But it won't make any difference. As long as I live, there will be an American sitting inside me like a ton of bricks, and every now and then this American inside me, my American, will drag me around by the nose and make me scream "Gibu me chewingamu, Q-Q," because what I have is an incurable disease, the Great American Allergy.

"Toshio, what are you going to do tomorrow? Just let them take care of themselves."

I suppose I'll get him a geisha next time, for variety. Japahnese geisha gahru, courtesy of Toshio the pimp.

And from a mound that never diminished, however quickly he moved his chopsticks, Toshio went on stuffing his already full stomach with the prized cuts of beef, eating and eating in joyless abandonment as if it had been American *hijiki.*

TRANSLATED BY JAY RUBIN

A NOTE ON THE TYPE

This book was set, via computer-driven cathode ray tube, in
Avanta, an adaptation of Electra, a type face designed by W. A.
Dwiggins. The Electra face is a simple and readable type suitable
for printing books by present-day processes. It is not based on any
historical model, and hence does not echo any particular time or
fashion.

Composed, printed and bound by The Haddon Craftsmen, Inc.,
Scranton, Pennsylvania.

The book was designed by Earl Tidwell.